全球大宗商品市場：
從現貨到期貨

Global commodities market:
From spot to futures

香港交易所首席中國經濟學家
巴曙松教授　主編

Edited by Prof. BA Shusong,
HKEX Chief China Economist

商務印書館

全球大宗商品市場：從現貨到期貨

主　　　編：巴曙松
副 主 編：蔡秀清
編　　　委：張天赫　董　峰　馬諾文　朱　曉　巴　晴　羅得恩
責任編輯：甄梓祺
出　　　版：商務印書館（香港）有限公司
　　　　　　香港筲箕灣耀興道 3 號東滙廣場 8 樓
　　　　　　http://www.commercialpress.com.hk
發　　　行：香港聯合書刊物流有限公司
　　　　　　香港新界荃灣德士古道 220-248 號荃灣工業中心 16 樓
印　　　刷：美雅印刷製本有限公司
　　　　　　九龍觀塘榮業街 6 號海濱工業大廈 4 樓 A 室
版　　　次：2024 年 6 月第 1 版第 3 次印刷
　　　　　　© 2020 香港交易及結算所有限公司

　　　　　　ISBN 978 962 07 6640 4
　　　　　　Printed in Hong Kong

Global commodities market: From spot to futures

Chief editor: BA Shusong

Deputy chief editor: Essie TSOI

Editors: Dennis ZHANG   DONG Feng   Robin MARTIN
Jennifer ZHU   BA Qing   Daniel LAW

Executive editor: Kelvin YAN

Publisher: The Commercial Press (H.K) Ltd.,
8/F, Eastern Central Plaza, 3 Yiu Hing Road,
Shau Kei Wan, Hong Kong

Distributor: The SUP Publishing Logistics (H.K.) Ltd.,
16/F, Tsuen Wan Industrial Centre,
220-248 Texaco Road, Tsuen Wan, Hong Kong

Printer: Elegance Printing and Book Binding Co. Ltd.
Block A, 4th Floor, Hoi Bun Building
6 Wing Yip Street, Kwun Tong, Kowloon, Hong Kong

© 2020 Hong Kong Exchanges and Clearing Limited
First edition, Third printing, June 2024

ISBN: 978 962 07 6640 4
Printed in Hong Kong

目錄

Contents

風險與免責聲明

買賣證券的風險

證券買賣涉及風險。證券價格有時可能會非常波動。證券價格可升可跌，甚至變成毫無價值。買賣證券未必一定能夠賺取利潤，反而可能會招致損失。

買賣期貨及期權的風險

期貨及期權涉及高風險，買賣期貨及期權所招致的損失有可能超過開倉時繳付的按金，令投資者或須在短時間內繳付額外按金。若未能繳付，投資者的持倉或須平倉，任何虧損概要自行承擔。因此，投資者務須清楚明白買賣期貨及期權的風險，並衡量是否適合自己。投資者進行交易前，宜根據本身財務狀況及投資目標，向經紀或財務顧問查詢是否適合買賣期貨及期權合約。

免責聲明

本書所載資料及分析只屬資訊性質，概不構成要約、招攬、邀請或推薦買賣任何證券、期貨合約或其他產品，亦不構成提供任何形式的建議或服務。書中表達的意見不一定代表香港交易及結算所有限公司（「香港交易所」）或本書其他作者所屬的機構（「有關機構」）的立場。書中內容概不構成亦不得被視為投資或專業建議。儘管本書所載資料均取自認為是可靠的來源或按當中內容編備而成，但本書各作者、香港交易所和有關機構及其各自的附屬公司、董事及僱員概不就有關資料（就任何特定目的而言）的準確性、適時性或完整性作任何保證。本書各作者、香港交易所和有關機構及其各自的附屬公司、董事及僱員對使用或依賴本書所載的任何資料而引致任何損失或損害概不負責。

Risk statements and disclaimer

Risks of securities trading

Trading in securities carries risks. The prices of securities fluctuate, sometimes dramatically. The price of a security may move up or down, and may become valueless. It is as likely that losses will be incurred rather than profit made as a result of buying and selling securities.

Risks of trading futures and options

Futures and options involve a high degree of risk. Losses from futures and options trading can exceed initial margin funds and investors may be required to pay additional margin funds on short notice. Failure to do so may result in the position being liquidated and the investor being liable for any resulting deficit. Investors must therefore understand the risks of trading in futures and options and should assess whether they are suitable for them. Investors are encouraged to consult a broker or financial adviser on their suitability for futures and options trading in light of their financial position and investment objectives before trading.

Disclaimer

All information and views contained in this book are for informational purposes only and do not constitute an offer, solicitation, invitation or recommendation to buy or sell any securities, futures contracts or other products or to provide any advice or service of any kind. The views expressed in this book do not necessarily represent the position of Hong Kong Exchanges and Clearing Limited ("HKEX") or the other institutions to which the authors of this book belong ("Relevant Institutions"). Nothing in this book constitutes or should be regarded as investment or professional advice. While information contained in this book is obtained or compiled from sources believed to be reliable, the authors of this book, HKEX, the Relevant Institutions or any of HKEX's or the Relevant Institutions' subsidiaries, directors or employees will neither guarantee its accuracy, timeliness or completeness for any particular purpose, nor be responsible for any loss or damage arising from the use of, or reliance upon, any information contained in this book.

序 言

動盪的商品市場更需要專業的思考

　　大宗商品市場在全球經濟活動中的地位與影響牽一髮而動全身，相互的關係越來越密切。比如 2010 年後，全球主要經濟體發展增速逐步變緩，以銅、鐵礦石為首的工業金屬價格回落，曾經一度盛行的貿易融資也大幅收縮。不同國家間的軍事與貿易摩擦，給農產品、貴金屬市場帶來了巨大的價格波動。同時，新能源、新材料開啟了行業升級，以鈷、鋰為代表的新能源動力材料，也經歷了波瀾壯闊的大發展週期。聚焦近期，2019 年引人關注的新型冠狀病毒對社會、經濟帶來巨大衝擊。眾多國家為保護人民健康安全，被迫採取嚴格的隔離防護政策。短暫的經濟停擺造成相關大宗商品短期的供需失衡，市場隨之劇烈波動。顯然，要把握金融市場發展趨勢，越來越要重視、研究大宗商品市場。

　　在過去二十年，國際金融市場、科技領域的發展熱潮也間接促進了大宗商品相關交易所的發展。以洲際交易所（Intercontinental Exchange，ICE）為例，這間 2000 年才於美國亞特蘭大成立的小型交易所，在十多年間，通過上市融資和一系列併購，迅速崛起。倫敦國際石油交易所 IPE、紐約期貨交易所 NYBOT、新加坡商品期貨交易所 SMX、倫敦國際金融期貨交易所 LIFFE，紛紛成為它的囊中之物。ICE 也在 20 年內，迅速把業務擴展到能源、農產品和金融期貨等領域，與同樣經歷眾多併購的 CME 集團在各個大宗商品領域分庭抗禮。交易所之間的併購，一方面使收購方在短時間內能迅速擴張；另一方面，被購方也將受益於業務板塊多元化、管理經營多樣化和市場差異互補化等積極效應。更重要的是相關行業也可以更好地參與其中，使得更多大宗商品交易從場外市場轉至交易所的場內市場進行。一方面透過中央結算降低交易對手方風險，另一方面利用交易所的電子交易系統減低交易成本。

　　同時在過去二十年，中國也逐漸發展為當今世界第二大經濟體，無論是從供給側還是需求側，對全球大宗商品市場的影響都舉足輕重。相關企業的「價格發現」和「風險管理」需求巨大，也有力推動了內地相關期貨和衍生品市場的發展。從趨勢看，中國市場在大宗商品和其衍生品市場的影響力和話語權都持續提升，國際化和對外開放程度也穩步提高。「上海金」、「滬銅」、「連鐵」等內地品種的價格已經和國際價格聯動，也被國際投資者廣泛關注。中國內地的大宗商品交易所現在已有眾多主要的大宗商品品種上市，也在近年逐步允許合格的境外參與者參與買賣。例如，2018 年上海國際能源交易中心掛牌了人民幣計價的原油期貨，同年在大連商品交易所已上市的鐵礦石期貨也正式引入境外交易者業務。這是中國內地大宗商品期貨市場國際化邁出的重要一步。

　　在如此大背景下，香港交易所作為大宗商品市場的後發者，任重而道遠。我們認清趨勢，於 2012 年成功收購了倫敦金屬交易所（London Metal Exchange，LME）。LME 的歷史最遠可以追溯到 1571 年成立的倫敦皇家交易所（The Royal Exchange），它也被認為可能是世界上最早的商品交易所。這次收購，不僅為香港交易所的大宗商品市場發展開啟了新篇章，也改寫了倫敦大宗商品市場的歷史，同時在促進中國與全球市場之間的互動提供了新的平台，是我們參與國際大宗商品市場建設的第一步。

　　但是大宗商品市場的發展最具特色的，是其特殊的現貨到期貨市場的演變。標準化的期貨合約，有着嚴格規定的商品規格和數量，明確的時間週期和指定的交收地點。它是通過在現貨商品屬性的基礎上，建立並發展遠期金融屬性。這兩種屬性虛實轉換、遠近結合、此消彼長，微妙而靈活地把商品現貨市場和期貨市場結合在一起。常年耕耘大宗商品市場的人都有共識，「價格發現」和「風險管理」是大宗商品市場最重要的發展初衷。然而在這條發展的道路上，挑戰重重。比如與大宗商品相關的期貨與現貨市場，眾所周知，現貨市場生機勃勃，運作環節眾多。期貨市場金融化程度高、流動性好。但是「現貨市場雖然龐大，但卻非常分散」、「現貨市場金融化低，金融市場缺乏現貨錨定」等等都是明顯的問題。如果不參與期貨市場，現貨市場在下行週期中會面臨諸多經營挑戰。同樣如果缺乏成熟發達的現貨市場做保障，期貨市場的價格發現功能就會偏離，甚至在極端市場條件下出現嚴重扭曲。

比如 2020 年以來由於新型冠狀病毒疫情導致經濟活動停滯，傳統旺季需求降低。各國的封關政策也形成局部供需和儲運中斷，這都造成並加劇了全球大宗商品期貨和現貨市場的割裂。以黃金為例，CME 交易所旗下的黃金期貨相比倫敦黃金現貨市場的期現價差 (EFP) 居高不下，超過 2008 年全球金融危機雷曼崩盤時的水平。交易所甚至需要臨時新設合約和增加交割品種來緩解期現市場的割裂。由此市場熱議多頭參與者可能提不到貨，空頭參與者看到溢價的期貨價格又難以運輸交貨履約。同時相對便宜的現貨價格又設置有准入門檻，中小機構難以參與。居間的實體黃金交易商面臨巨大的價格波動和運輸交割風險，紛紛離場觀望。整體黃金市場有價無市，買賣價差變寬，期貨市場多空雙方均面臨很大風險，實體企業也只能耐心等待疫情好轉、供需恢復。

同期，由於新冠疫情帶來的世界經濟放緩以及石油輸出國組織和其他主要原油生產國的能源政策導致原油價格急劇下跌。按照 CME 旗下 WTI 原油合約規則，交割通過奧克拉荷馬州庫欣的管道或儲油設備進行。金融市場有大量的非交割金融產品掛鉤該合約價格，在期貨市場形成巨大的多頭頭寸。在新冠病毒疫情衝擊下，原油需求大幅度萎縮、庫存增加、庫容減少，但是可供交割的原油依舊源源不斷的流入管道。終於在 2020 年 5 月期貨合約臨近交割時，大量該合約的非交割頭寸被迫平倉。恐慌情緒甚至將 WTI 合約價格首次推至負價格，大量國際投資機構蒙受「負價格」帶來的巨額損失。

這些例子都說明了如果沒有合理縝密的期貨交割規則和強大的現貨交割體系，大宗商品市場的發展或許終將面臨定價失調的窘境。這些事件也帶給金融市場深遠的討論，比如大量的「紙黃金」、「紙原油」掛鉤實物交割的合約，在出現極端事件時，投資者到底是更希望拿到現貨還是更希望僅追蹤價格？香港交易所一直在思考未來商品市場應該怎麼解決這些問題。從歷史發展進程看，大宗商品市場發展的路徑是歐洲 — 美國 — 中國，我們所擁有的後發優勢是越來越標準化、金融化；後發市場也更傾向頂端金融產品、忽略實物屬性。但是極端情況下也會導致價格偏離實體的趨勢越來越嚴重，業界怎麼解決這個問題？其實就是要解決期貨市場不能偏離現貨市場，期現市場如何良性互通、形成合理暢順的價格傳導機制、形成合理的定價生態的問題。這也是我們收購 LME，在中國內地建立前海聯合交易中心（Qianhai Mercantile Exchange，QME）的初衷和戰略考量。

　　當前，要把握全球大宗商品市場的發展趨勢，需要從歷史發展的脈絡中去梳理，也需要從全球大格局中去定位，還需要從中國與全球市場的互動中去創新。立足香港，把海外市場與內地市場放在一個迅速發展的市場體系中觀察，從而以開放的思維來積極發展香港的大宗商品市場，不僅有利於完善香港的金融市場版圖，也有利於把香港連接中國與全球市場的獨特功能延伸到大宗商品領域，這也正是我們的期待和努力的方向。

李小加

香港交易及結算所有限公司　集團行政總裁

2020 年 5 月

Preface

Volatile commodities market demands deeper critical thinking

The commodities market is now so closely linked to the global economy that a small change in the former will trigger the butterfly effect on the latter. For example, after 2010, the growth rate of the world's major economies gradually slowed down and the prices of industrial metals such as copper and iron ore kept falling with trade finance, which was once popular, shrinking sharply. Enormous price fluctuations are seen in the agricultural products and precious metals markets due to military and trade frictions between countries. At the same time, as alternative energy and new material industries quickly develop, power metals like cobalt and lithium have seen their cycle of booms and busts too. And more recently, the new coronavirus pandemic has dealt a heavy blow to societies and economies worldwide, with strict lockdown and protective health and safety measures enforced. The temporary economic shutdown caused short-term imbalance in supply and demand for the underlying commodities, triggering tremendous market fluctuations. In light of these developments, it is increasingly important for us to focus on and study the commodities market in order to better understand the trend of the financial market.

In the last two decades, the fast growth in financial markets and the advancement of technology in the world have indirectly driven the development of commodity exchanges. Taking the Intercontinental Exchange (ICE) as an example, it has taken just slightly more than a decade for this small exchange established in Atlanta, the United States in 2000 to rise to its current position, through public listing and financing and a series of mergers and acquisitions (M&A) that included International Petroleum Exchange (IPE) in London, New York Board of Trade (NYBOT), Singapore Mercantile Exchange (SMX) and London International Financial Futures and Options Exchange (LIFFE). In 20 years, ICE rapidly expanded into energy, agricultural products and financial futures, achieving an equal footing with the CME Group which has also undergone many M&A activities in various commodities sectors. Such acquisitions between exchanges benefited both the acquirers and acquirees in that they enabled the acquirers to scale up quickly while allowing the acquirees to achieve portfolio diversification, management improvement and market differentiation. More importantly, these development significantly benefited the industry as more over-the-counter commodity transactions migrate to exchanges for execution, resulting in reduced counterparty risk through central clearing and settlement and lower transaction costs with the support of electronic trading infrastructure.

In the meantime, Mainland China has steadily risen to become the world's second largest economy over the last two decades, with significant impacts on both the supply and demand sides of the global commodities markets. Chinese companies' demands for price discovery and risk management have given a huge impetus to the growth of the commodity derivatives markets in the Mainland. We also see a trend of continuous growth of Mainland China's influence in physical and derivatives markets as the economy opens up progressively. The prices of Mainland commodity derivatives, such as gold on SGE (Shanghai Gold Exchange), copper on SHFE (Shanghai Futures Exchange) and Iron Ore on DCE (Dalian Commodity Exchange), have been widely followed by international investors given their correlation with international markets. Also in recent years, multiple key products listed on these commodity exchanges became accessible to qualified foreign investors. For example, Shanghai International Energy Exchange (INE) introduced the RMB-denominated crude oil futures in 2018. In that same year, DCE's iron ore futures contract was officially made available to foreign investors. These events mark a milestone in Mainland China's internationalisation of its commodity futures markets.

Against this background, HKEX, as a latecomer to the commodities market, has a crucial role to play and a long way to go. With a long-term goal in mind, we successfully acquired the London Metal Exchange (LME) in 2012. The history of the LME can be traced back to the Royal Exchange established in 1571, which is considered as possibly the earliest commodity exchange in the world. The acquisition not only opened a new chapter for HKEX's business development but also rewrote the history of the London commodities market. As our first step into commodities, it provides a new platform for promoting the interaction between Mainland China and the global market.

Yet the most distinctive feature of commodities market development lies in the unique evolution from the spot (physical) market to the futures market. A standard commodity futures contract stipulates strict specifications such as quality and quantity, as well as location and time of delivery. Its financial attributes as a forward contract are built on its physical basis. These two attributes are closely related, acting upon each other to establish the close link between physical and futures markets. People in the market know very well the main purposes of commodity futures — price discovery and risk management. However, the journey to such goals has been bumpy. For example, the physical market is vibrant but fragmented, whereas the futures market is highly liquid but can lose its price anchor. Without the support of the futures market, the physical market faces many operational challenges as it moves through business cycles. Similarly, without the support of a mature and robust physical market, the futures market's price discovery function will be deflected, or even severely distorted under extreme market conditions.

For instance, since the beginning of 2020, due to the coronavirus epidemic, economic activities have come to a halt and demand fell during what used to be a peak season for many commodities. The lockdown imposed in various countries causes interruptions to supply and demand as well as storage and transportation, resulting in disconnection between commodity futures and physical markets. Taking gold as an example, the price spread in the exchange of futures for physical (EFP) between CME's gold futures and London spot gold remained elevated in this period, even exceeding the level seen at Lehman's collapse during the 2008 Global Financial Crisis. This prompted CME to offer new contracts with increased delivery varieties as emergency measures to alleviate the situation. There were heated discussions in the market that participants with long positions may not be able to take delivery while those with short positions might fail to deliver despite high prices. Despite the relatively low spot prices, small and medium-sized institutions were constrained from participating in the market due to entry thresholds. Many gold traders had no choice but walk away in the face of the wild price fluctuations and logistics risk, leaving the market with poor liquidity and much widened bid-ask spread, and exposing market participants to enormous risks which can only be dissipated until epidemic goes away and business fundamentals goes back to normal.

Also in this period, as the world economy slackened, the crude oil market fell sharply due to impact of the pandemic and subsequent energy policy of the Organization of the Petroleum Exporting Countries (OPEC) and other major oil producer countries. As the flagship North America crude oil contract, WTI crude oil futures on CME sees a large number of non-deliverable (cash-settled) financial products linked to its contract price, with considerable long positions built as oil price fell since the start of the year. By design, WTI's delivery takes place through pipelines and oil storage facilities in Cushing, Oklahoma. Stricken by the coronavirus pandemic, the demand for crude oil shrank dramatically, resulting in quick build-up of inventories and loss of storage capacity. As May contract delivery date approached, many non-deliverable financial positions were forced to liquidate. Panic in the market sent WTI for May contract to negative price territory for the first time in history, incurring massive losses for many international investors.

These examples show that without rigorous futures delivery system and a robust physical market, the development of the commodities market may eventually be thwarted for its price discovery functions. These events also induce discussions on issues like whether the myriad of financial products linked to the commodities prices should be designed to only track the underlying price or also to enable physical delivery at time of extreme price actions. HKEX has been studying how to solve these problems. As seen from the history, commodities markets were first developed in Europe, followed by the United States and now Mainland China. As a latecomer, we benefit from the market being more standardised and financialised. But such a market is prone to focusing on the financial attributes of commodities while ignoring the physical ones. In extreme cases, it may cause profound deviation of futures prices from the physical market. How can the industry solve this problem? It boils down to the point that the futures and physical markets should go hand in hand and develop smooth price transmission mechanism and rational market pricing eco-system. This is exactly our original intention and strategic consideration when acquiring the LME and establishing Qianhai Mercantile Exchange (QME) in Mainland China.

Now, if we are to project the future trend of the global commodities market, it is necessary to sort out the key elements from a historical perspective, position ourselves in the global setting and provide innovative solutions for the interaction between the markets in China and the world. With its foothold in Hong Kong, we can observe closely the development of both the overseas and burgeoning Mainland market, and adopt an open mind for the development of Hong Kong's commodities market. This will not only broaden the spectrum of Hong Kong's financial market, but also give full play to Hong Kong's unique function in connecting China with the global market. This has always been our dream and aspiration.

Charles LI

Chief Executive,
Hong Kong Exchanges and Clearing Limited
May 2020

第一篇

全球大宗商品市場的格局

第1章

貨通天下，海納百川
—— 為中國架起連接全球大宗商品市場的橋樑

李小加

香港交易所集團行政總裁

摘 要

如何為中國架起一座接連全球大宗商品市場的橋樑，實現「貨通天下，海納百川」這一願景？

多年來，這個問題一直在我腦海中縈繞不去，時常讓我陷入長久的沉思。我相信，不少業內人士也在為同樣的問題去思考，去論證，去摸索，甚至去嘗試，去實踐，孜孜不倦，期望能尋覓出一個最佳的答案，或找到一種最切實有效的方法。

在本章節中，我將同大家一起，來大致梳理並概括一下內地大宗商品市場的特點，發展的新趨勢和未來的成長空間，並以回顧收購倫敦金屬交易所前後的一些經歷和前海聯合交易中心的設立過程為背景。希望在這樣的整理與回顧中，我們能從中找出一些隱約的脈絡和聯繫。

中國經濟將繼續高速的增長和發展，金融市場會趨於更加開放。隨着這股浪潮，內地商品市場國際化的呼聲會越來越高，也顯得更加迫切。

在撰寫和編輯本文的過程中，我們也更加強烈地意識到香港與內地之間那份緊密相連的紐帶關係的重要性，更清晰地看到香港在這一過程中所能發揮的作用，所能做的積極努力和給予的支持。

希望大家眾志成城，朝着這個目標繼續努力，讓夢想實現的一天早日到來！

1 引言

　　讓我們來看一張時間跨度長約半個世紀的倫敦金屬交易所（LME）銅價格[1]歷史走勢圖。乍看之下，這五十年間，金屬市場跌宕起伏、變幻莫測，但細心的投資者不難發現，它每一次的高低回轉都好像與中國社會經濟發展的進程如影隨形。

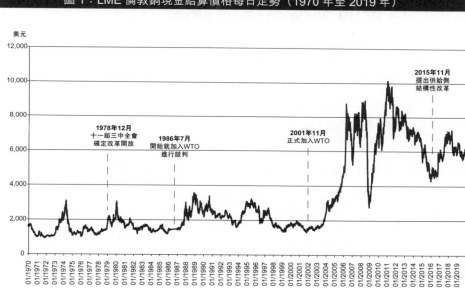

圖 1：LME 倫敦銅現金結算價格每日走勢（1970 年至 2019 年）

美元

2015年11月
提出供給側
結構性改革

1978年12月
十一屆三中全會
確定改革開放

1986年7月
開始就加入WTO
進行談判

2001年11月
正式加入WTO

註：WTO 是指世界貿易組織（World Trade Organisation）。
資料來源：LME。

　　然而，這並非是一種巧合。

　　隨着中國 2001 年加入世貿組織，全球經濟一體化加速，中國經濟亦飛速發展，並取得了舉世矚目的成就。2018 年，中國國內生產總值（GDP）高達 919,281 億元人民幣[2]，遠超日本和歐洲發達國家，已穩居世界第二大經濟體、第一大工業

1　這是指 LME 的銅現金結算價格，由 LME 於 2020 年 1 月 23 日提供。
2　資料來源：中國國家統計局。

國。我們相信，中國的 GDP 突破 100 萬億元人民幣亦指日可待。

不難發現，這一組驕人的數字背後折射出的一個事實：過去數十年來，中國一直保持着對來自全球的能源、金屬和農產品等一系列大宗商品的強勁需求。

2 中國內地商品市場的特點、新趨勢和巨大的未來發展新空間

中國目前已是全球大宗商品的消費大國，但在國際市場中還是價格接受者。伴隨中國經濟的崛起，客觀上我們需要一個發達、高效、開放的商品市場幫助中國提升國際影響力，成為價格制定者。結合中國內地的現實需求與國際市場的發展趨勢，我們認為可以從以下幾個方面去努力：

(1) 突破內地商品價格的區域局限，擴大內地商品價格的國際影響力

目前來看，中國內地的商品市場具有極強的區域屬性，指引着本區域內自產和舶來商品的價格，並形成了一個內生的完整生態圈。

這些「本地」價格的跨區域指引性和國際影響力在不斷提升，跟與其遙相呼應的國際市場商品價格的互動也在增強。按中國經濟發展的現實需求，乘商品市場的不斷發展之勢，中國內地的商品價格有條件通過多種方式，逐步融入到全球商品貿易的計價和結算機制體系當中。

(2) 擴大產業鏈的覆蓋面，促進實體經濟與商品市場的密切互動

作為人口大國，中國在工業、農業和能源領域的資源相對較為稀缺，不少重要基本物資，都長期依賴大量的進口。

全球經濟一體化的形成，為世界帶來了清晰的產業分工格局。中國在過去的幾十年中，已發展成為「世界的工廠」，一直扮演着資源生產國和成品消費國之間的來料加工者的角色。在內地的商品市場中，很難找到靠近產業鏈最兩端的眾多

企業的身影。

從供應鏈上來看，現有的交割體系還沒有覆蓋到商品的貿易環節和主要流通節點，例如：覆蓋到主要的淨消費國或淨生產國，以及主要的貿易樞紐國。在實物交割方面，更多原產自其他國家的商品品牌，在內地市場中還有待得到認可。

(3) 吸引更廣泛的市場主體參與，促進商品市場從業機構業務的多元化和國際化

一個發達的商品市場，需要發達的從業機構體系來支持。內地的期貨公司都是中介經紀機構，作為市場參與主體的一個重要組成部份，為客戶提供進入市場的渠道，是連接交易所與其他市場參與者的橋樑。據中國期貨協會統計，截至2018 年，內地共有 149 家期貨公司，其分支營業機構遍佈各大城市和主要省份。

相較而言，成熟市場上國外同行能開展的大宗商品相關業務則更加豐富，服務內容通常涵蓋：併購諮詢、經紀服務、貿易和結構性融資、基建運營、現貨和期貨自營交易等。這樣的業務佈局，除了使業務整體達到規模經濟效應，突顯垂直整合的優勢，也體現了其對整個行業的深刻理解和深入行業價值鏈條、全方位服務產業和各參與機構的意願。隨着科技的進步，即便是以非機構為客戶主體的經紀商，也大多會選擇通過互聯網和資訊傳播技術的應用，把自己打造成數字化的線上經紀商。

從趨勢看，內地期貨公司以及中資金融機構業務國際化和多元化的進程在不斷加快。內地同行本身具有熟悉中國內地市場的優勢，如果能從國際化角度取得新的突破，就可以打造一個更有競爭力的從業機構羣體，從而支持內地期貨市場的新發展。

內地的大宗商品現貨交易市場，還是以當日的現貨價結算為主，而較少採用與期貨市場相結合的方式，實現遠期或更多靈活的定價模式。這種把遠期靈活定價機制引入到現貨交易中的做法在國際市場上則比較普遍。因此，內地期貨市場的參與者構成中機構所佔的比例還不高，實物的交割量與其成交量和貿易量相比，佔比還很小。

以上幾點，説明中國內地商品市場仍有巨大的發展潛力，需要通過各方的共同努力，推動中國內地商品市場業務的規範化、多元化和國際化。

3 香港可以在連接內地商品市場 與國際市場中發揮甚麼獨特作用？

香港處於連接中國內地市場與全球市場的獨特樞紐地位，在內地商品市場發展的進程中，我們冀望能有條件探索出符合其現況、發揮其優勢且滿足國家所需的獨特的大宗商品發展之路。

因此，香港交易所開始探索一個「兩條腿並行」的大宗商品發展戰略：「走出去買、走進去建」，與內地交易所「互聯互通，互掛互惠」。

「走出去買」即海外兼併收購。2012 年，我們成功收購了具有 140 多年歷史的倫敦金屬交易所（London Metal Exchange，簡稱 LME），走出了併購國際金融基礎設施的第一步。

「走進去建」就是回到祖國腹地，與內地監管部門和相關機構深度合作，發揮我們的獨特優勢去搭建一個紮根內地、服務實體、守法合規的大宗商品現貨交易平台，希望它能打通金融與實體經濟聯繫的渠道，補足市場空缺。因此，設立前海聯合交易中心成為了我們大宗商品發展戰略中重要的另一步。

「走出去」和「走進去」戰略的最終目標是利用香港得天獨厚的亞太優勢，將「走出去」收購的平台與「走進去」建設的兩個不同平台有效地互聯互通，利用自己的國際金融基礎設施，加快中國大宗商品市場國際化的進程，真正實現國際大宗商品定價的東移。這對於中國發起的「一帶一路」倡議有着重要意義，「一帶一路」沿線涉及 60 多個國家，預計未來十年中國與沿線國家的貿易額將達 2.5 萬億美元[3]，其中相當比例將是大宗商品資源，發展潛力巨大。對內地而言，如何應對和有效管理商品價格波動所帶來的風險也將直接影響到「一帶一路」倡議下的許多具體專案的順利推進。「一帶一路」沿線有香港和倫敦兩個國際金融中心，如果我們的「兩條腿並行」的戰略順利實施，那麼，我們就可以把倫敦和香港的國際經驗與中國的實體經濟需求以前海為節點進行對接。

3　資料來源：滙豐銀行〈亞洲崛起：全球經濟新面貌〉，刊登於《信報》，2017 年 5 月 5 日。

3.1　LME 的收購

我們一直都不避諱地承認，坐擁世界三大良港之一，且商貿往來繁忙的香港，歷來都不是大宗商品交易和結算的中心地。雖享有亞洲金融中心的盛譽，在我們的市場裏，卻難以尋覓到這類資產的身影。

每當談論起這個話題，面對如此尷尬的事實，在人們的臉上，總會不經意地掠過一絲無奈和遺憾的表情。雖也曾有過多次嘗試和改變的努力，但仍舊是一籌莫展。

時過境遷，我們終於等到了一個千載難逢，能幫助我們破局的機會。

2012 年，香港交易所集團對倫敦金屬交易所（LME）發出了正式的收購邀約。參與談判的雙方代表，顯得既自信又彷徨，因為每個人的內心都在不斷翻騰，他們或許不曾想過：有一天，全球期貨市場的歷史和格局有可能在自己的手中被改寫。

LME 是一家經營超過百年的老店，其市場地位和重要性，好比英女皇皇冠上的明珠。同時，它也是一間私人公司，董事會由持有 LME 股權的各家會員機構的代表組成。朝着董事會成員名單望去，是一長串浸淫全球資本市場的顯赫名字，而關於收購意向的投票權，就在這些機構的代表手中。

幾經波折，我們最終在多家競標者參與的激烈競爭中脫穎而出，達成心願。

在收購意向達成當天的聯合聲明中，有幾處特別引人注意的地方：（一）保留 LME 現有的商業模式；（二）致力為 LME 拓展亞洲和中國市場；（三）尋求與 LME 會員和市場參與者的長期共同發展。

回首這段往事，我們不免感慨，世事無常，精明的 LME 股東們，不僅把手中的一票投給了我們，也投給了香港，更重要是，他們把自己的信任與期望投給了崛起的中國。

如何為 LME 找到重新定位？如何把它打造成一家更順應時代變化、科技變革和市場潮流的現代化新型交易所？如何讓它更好地繼續發揮其獨特功能和作用，為亞洲乃至全球市場提供更加優質的服務？這一連串的問題，成了擺在我們面前的當務之急。

為此，我們分不同階段做了如下所述的一些工作。

(1)　第一階段：全力拓展亞洲業務

2013 年，LME 認證中國台灣的高雄港為指定交割點。這是繼分佈於新加坡、馬來西亞、韓國及日本的其他交割點之後，在亞洲新增的第九個交割點。

2014 年，我們首度與 LME 共同推出「會籍互惠安排計劃」(Reciprocal Membership Agreement，RMA)，在此計劃下，若干 LME 會員通過獲得香港交易所旗下香港期貨交易所的會員資格，進入香港市場，使其能同時服務兩個市場，讓達成雙邊交易變得更為簡便。

2019 年我們亦決定繼續推行該計劃，有關此計劃詳情將在後續章節中詳細說明。

(2)　第二階段：籌建 LME 結算所（LME Clear），為未來的發展打下堅實基礎

經過兩年多的籌備，LME 自建的交易結算機構 LME Clear 終於在 2014 年問世。

對我們而言，LME Clear 的成立，不僅為 LME 收回了交易結算的自主權，大大提高了營收。它也為未來的新產品研發和上線，提供了高效的便利。中央結算的運行機制，也是現代交易所應該具備的必要元素之一。

(3)　第三階段：為摸索出大宗商品業務在香港市場的發展道路，提供借鑒和幫助

這個階段的工作包括建立跨地域產品相互上市、授權的安排，以及與主要市場參與者和機構建立戰略夥伴關係。我們憑藉 LME 帶來的啟發，從基礎金屬着手開始嘗試，並進一步延伸至其他的大宗商品類別。

因此，我們在香港市場推出了一系列金屬期貨產品，分別覆蓋有色、黑色和貴金屬等領域。

3.2　前海聯合交易中心（QME）的設立

對 LME 的成功收購，讓我們有機會去近距離地深入瞭解它。

是甚麼力量幫助 LME 經受住了時間的考驗，在兩次世界大戰、國際錫業協會解散等重大歷史事件面前不畏紛擾，依然能保持頑強的生命力，得以不斷發展和壯大？

答案不言而喻：LME 能擁有今天這般舉足輕重的市場地位，或許源自它溶入血脈當中的「現貨基因」，和與金屬貿易市場長期保持着的一種無法分割的聯繫。受此影響，不難發現，這間交易所在歷次重大演變和轉折中所作的每一項關鍵抉擇，都有其必然性。

帶着這樣的啟示，當得知有機會獲准籌建一間以中國內地為市場核心的大宗商品交易機構時，我們的團隊，勢必把從 LME 所獲的理念和市場運行方式植入其中，寄望它能落地生根、服務經濟、回饋社會。

終於，這顆希望的種子，落地深圳前海，故命名「前海聯合交易中心」(QME)，它將是一個大宗商品的現貨交易平台。

如果深圳被譽為改革開放的前沿城市，那麼前海就好比是這個城市甚至整個珠三角區域的一個未來中心、下一個孕育現代服務業和創新行業的「曼哈頓」。如此說來，QME 能成長於這樣的一片土壤和氛圍中，也是順應時代發展背景下的產物。

懷着這份感悟，秉持一份傳承，我們對籌建中的 QME 有了一些初步構想。作為我們對大宗商品行業深刻理解的具體體現，QME 將具備三個必要元素：(1) 實現每日交收；(2) 服務產業鏈條；(3) 設定倉儲體系。

(1)　元素一：實現每日交收

綜觀全球各大期貨交易所，它們大多沿襲或採用了按月報價和交割的交易形式。能在期貨市場實現每日結算，並交收實物的交易所，可謂鳳毛麟角。毫無疑問，只有每天結算和交收的機制，才能使商品的流通性得以提升，為買賣雙方大大節省等待交割、交收貨物的時間。

日常生活當中，這是再普通不過的物品買賣與交換模式，好像完全不值得「小題大作」。例如，在樓下的便利店，你可以拿着選購好的貨品，去收銀台支付，立刻做到錢貨兩清。

但是，在一個採用中央對手方，集中結算的交易市場裏面，要做到每日交收，需要擁有強大的結算能力和保證金管理能力作為支援，這並非易事，可謂「知易行難」！

LME 能實現在滾動的三個月時間內，做到每日結算與交割。正是這樣的緣故，在今天看來，它才能獨樹一幟，堅守着創立之初的一份執念，發揮着特有的市場作用。

這一反映現貨市場運行的必要元素，一開始，就被我們為 QME 的設立而吸納，正所謂「前事不忘，後事之師」。

(2)　元素二：服務產業鏈條

同樣可以追溯的是，當今世界主要的期貨交易所大多發源於 19 世紀，它們往往創立於商品貿易的中心集散城市，為農產品種植者或金屬生產商，解決生產交付週期中價格波動所帶來的煩惱。

由此可見，商品現貨市場是期貨市場存在的基石，後者依附於一條自上而下，由生產商、加工商、貿易商、消費商和回收商所組成的完整產業鏈條之上。這些商戶們，因生而受困於商品的價格波動，又需要尋找一個避險之處。故此，兩者之間形成了一條長期的相生相伴的關係紐帶。

源自於這樣的感悟和認識，未來的 QME，將緊緊地吸附於大宗商品的產業鏈條，將與現貨交易商們逐步建立起一種難以分割的自然聯繫。

(3)　元素三：設立倉儲體系

鹽，尋常人家裏的一種普通調味品，卻有着五千年的悠久歷史，它曾是歷朝歷代佔據政府主要財政收入的一種重要商品。西元十三世紀，意大利商人馬可孛羅東遊時有所記載，對古代中國鹽業的發達為之震撼。

為了保證販鹽過程的順利，那時還曾出現了鏢局這個行業，這算是今天押運行業的鼻祖吧。可見，在商品貿易環節中，貨物和財物的安全是多麼至關重要。

人們驚歎於 LME 覆蓋全球的交割倉儲網路體系時，卻往往會忽略這樣一個事實：這個體系其實是一個由多家獨立運營的倉儲機構所組成的聯合體。它們之中，有些與 LME 誕生於同一個時代，在長達一個半世紀的時間裏，與之攜手相伴，風雨同舟。

以史為鑒，在孕育 QME 的構想之初，倉儲體系的打造，成為了不可或缺的一環。

這是否讓人在 QME 的雛形身上依稀看到了些許 LME 的影子？或許有一天，

前海的這顆小幼苗能長成參天大樹，能與之情同手足的 LME 遙相呼應，相得益彰。這一天的到來，恰是我們這個構想中的最後一步。

「不積跬步，無以至千里；不積小流，無以至江海」，為了這個構想，我們的團隊將日以繼夜，一點一滴，用行動去實踐它，讓時間去證明它。

4 香港積極支援內地商品市場的國際化進程

金融是經濟的血液。今天的中國內地金融市場正加速開放，金融行業正成為中國建設現代化經濟及全面開放的主力軍。期貨市場是金融市場中的一個重要組成部份，在新的市場環境下同樣被賦予了國際化的歷史使命。

現階段，中國內地期貨市場的國際化可沿着四種路徑去推進，不同的發展路徑有不同的優勢與挑戰。而在不同的國際化模式中，香港都有條件積極參與，提供各種專業支援與合作。

4.1　路徑一：直接佈局，穩步推進的海外拓展之路

近年來，內地商品市場「走出去」的嘗試和舉措頻繁。

其中既有選擇在海外市場設立辦事處，致力於通過這一海外前哨，擴大國際影響力，吸引全球的投資者，也有的冀望通過獲得在香港證券及期貨事務監察委員會條例下的自動化交易服務（ATS）的註冊許可，在香港開展自動化交易服務。

直接進行海外佈局的優點是整個過程可以完全由內地機構把控，挑戰則是更加深入和艱巨的基礎設施搭建工作，例如：境外交割庫網路的擴張，全球交割點的增加，國際會員的招募和管理等。尤其是在制定和對接國際通行的法律監管制度和行業規範方面，是很多內地機構在開啟國際化進程之前很少涉足的領域。而香港作為內地和全球之間的制度翻譯機和轉換器，可以在以上領域，為內地機構提供多方面的協助。

4.2　路徑二：「引進來」—— 吸引海外投資者融入內地市場

為推動內地期貨市場的國際化，從國務院到中國證券監督管理委員會、國家外匯管理局，到最高人民法院等，都分別為特定品種期貨交易就交易管理、外匯、合同法和期貨糾紛等方面制定了一系列的暫行辦法和指導性的通知。在這樣特別的安排下，境外交易者一是可以通過境內期貨公司直接參與交易，二是可以通過境外經紀機構委託內地期貨公司參與交易。此類交易可允許保稅交割，以人民幣為計價和結算貨幣的同時，允許美元作保證金，還可以通過專用結算賬戶實現資金收付，匯兌及劃轉。

這一安排成績斐然，目前已經成功吸引到多家經紀機構完成委託業務備案；境外投資機構持續增長。

從下一步的發展看，如何繼續降低境外投資者和境外經紀機構的准入門檻，境外經紀機構與內地期貨公司的關係如何從單純的單向委託關係，擴大到全面參與交易和資金監管等核心的工作當中；如何完善相關的監管法律法規體系，都還需要付出不少努力。在內地市場完全開放之前，香港市場同樣可以提供多方面的支援。

4.3　路徑三：「有限的聯通」—— 中國價格的出海

長久以來，市場一直有這樣的期待：有一天，在香港或其他海外市場，會掛牌上市追蹤中國某個商品或一籃子商品指數的交易所買賣基金（ETF）產品，該類產品能為境外投資者在海外市場提供接觸中國價格的機會，使得國際投資者能在不改變投資市場範圍授權和原有的運營條件下「借道」於此，間接參與中國期貨市場。為境外投資者提供極大便利的同時，這也為中國價格在國際市場上提供了展示的機會和平台，逐漸提升它在國際市場上的覆蓋面和影響力。

ETF 的發行商，基於對沖風險的要求，將按規定進入內地期貨市場買賣相應數量的資產標的物。如果該 ETF 被廣為接受和青睞，獲得大量的認購，這將為內地交易所引入來自境外的相關投資需求，在一定程度上增添了海外投資者的參與度，為內地市場注入新的活力。

中國價格的出海，可以在未來通過香港以及香港交易所集團旗下的 LME 實現。

4.4　路徑四：「商品通」—— 全面的商品互聯互通

如何助力內地期貨交易所加快國際化的進程？

香港交易所和內地兩家證券交易所 —— 上海證券交易所和深圳證券交易所分別於 2014 年和 2016 年合作推出「滬港通」和「深港通」（合稱「滬深港通」）。滬深港通自開通以來一直平穩運行，為世界開創了全新的資本市場雙向開放模式。繼此，2017 年香港交易所與中國外滙交易中心合作推出與中國銀行間債券市場聯通的「債券通」，深受海外投資者歡迎。

「互聯互通」這一概念的實踐，創立了共贏的合作模式，並在證券和債券市場上獲得了成功。這既體現了國際投資者對於香港作為立足亞洲的國際金融中心地位的肯定，也反映了境外機構對進入內地資本市場並持有相關金融資產的濃厚興趣。這一合作模式，成功連通了內地和香港兩個不同制度體系下的資本市場，在加快內地資本市場開放與國際化的同時，也體現了「一國兩制」為香港帶來的優勢。

以金屬期貨為例，LME 聚集了全球的從礦山、冶煉、貿易、加工到回收整個行業鏈條的參與者，並在此基礎上匯聚了來自實業或金融背景的不同機構客戶羣體。而內地相關的期貨交易所則擁有龐大的以個人為主體的客戶羣體。這兩個市場，到目前為止，宛如兩條沒有直接交滙的河流。試想一下，如果這兩條大河能有機會連通在一起，那將是多麼激動人心的景象？

「互聯互通」的實踐，如果能推行到商品期貨領域，我們將有望見到一幅跨越「內地—香港—倫敦」的世界級大宗商品市場藍圖。這一構想立足於全球商品市場的發展現狀與內地商品市場發展的客觀需要，對支援內地商品市場的新發展與國際化，對鞏固香港國際金融中心的地位等方面都將產生巨大推動力並帶來深遠的影響。

因此，我衷心希望香港交易所集團旗下的期貨交易所及商品交易平台能與內地機構有機會實現融合。在為雙方創造共贏的基礎上，讓這樣的融合，為定價、為行業、為市場、為國家發揮應有的貢獻。

第2章

全球金屬市場
—— 中國市場的崛起和現狀

劉小磊

上海有色網信息科技股份有限公司
分析師

摘 要

　　中國金屬市場不斷擴大，鋼、鋁等金屬產品產量均超過全球總供給的一半以上，中國金屬市場成為全球不可忽視的一部份。中國金屬相關從業者對期貨等金融工具的依賴度提升，越來越多的金屬品種加入期貨市場，未來包括氧化鋁、鎂、鈦、錳等金屬或將進入期貨交易，相關企業在期貨市場中的交易規模和交易頻率不斷提升。

　　金屬相關企業在中國內地市場以及與國際市場交流的過程中，產生了具有中國特色的期現套利、內外套利等交易模式，成為全球大宗商品交易中不可忽視的力量。

　　具有中國特色的政策，包括「供給側改革」、「環保政策」等，已然成為供需因素之外影響內地金屬市場的重要因素。

　　在中國市場崛起的過程中，機遇與挑戰並存，但我們更應看到未來中國市場的活力。從發展角度看，中國市場的轉型過程中，也將產生更加豐富的金融交易手段。

(續)

反傾銷	案件類型	日期
南非對埃及鋁製餐具反傾銷案	貿易夥伴間案件	27/10/1995
阿根廷對美國氮化鋁反傾銷案	貿易夥伴間案件	23/05/1996
歐盟對泰國大功率鋁電解電容器反傾銷案	貿易夥伴間案件	29/11/1997
歐盟對美國大功率鋁電解電容器反傾銷案	貿易夥伴間案件	29/11/1997
歐盟對中國鋁箔反傾銷案	出口應訴	18/02/2000
歐盟對俄羅斯鋁箔反傾銷案	貿易夥伴間案件	18/02/2000
阿根廷對中國磷化鋁殺蟲劑反傾銷案	出口應訴	22/08/2001
南非對印度架空鋁芯電纜反傾銷案	貿易夥伴間案件	10/10/2003
美國對南非鋁板反傾銷案	貿易夥伴間案件	12/11/2003
阿根廷對印度固態磷化鋁反傾銷案	貿易夥伴間案件	15/04/2005
墨西哥對委內瑞拉鋁製軟管容器反傾銷案	貿易夥伴間案件	25/11/2005
巴西對中國 PS 版（鋁製預塗感光平版）反傾銷案	出口應訴	18/04/2006
巴西對美國 PS 版（鋁製預塗感光平版）反傾銷案	貿易夥伴間案件	18/04/2006
南非對中國擠壓鋁型材反傾銷案	出口應訴	10/08/2007
土耳其對中國鋁製版模具反傾銷案	出口應訴	20/03/2008
歐盟對中國鋁箔反傾銷案	出口應訴	12/07/2008
歐盟對亞美尼亞鋁箔反傾銷案	貿易夥伴間案件	12/07/2008
歐盟對巴西鋁箔反傾銷案	貿易夥伴間案件	12/07/2008
加拿大對中國鋁型材反傾銷案	出口應訴	18/08/2008
加拿大對中國鋁型材反補貼案	出口應訴	18/08/2008
印度對中國鋁板及鋁箔特別保障措施案	出口應訴	27/01/2009
印度對進口未鍛軋鋁、鋁廢碎料保障措施案	出口應訴	22/05/2009
澳大利亞對中國鋁型材反傾銷案	出口應訴	24/06/2009
澳大利亞對中國鋁型材反補貼案	出口應訴	24/06/2009
歐盟對中國鋁合金輪轂反傾銷案	出口應訴	13/08/2009
印尼對進口鋁箔製食品容器保障措施案	出口應訴	19/01/2010
美國對中國鋁型材反傾銷案	出口應訴	27/04/2010
美國對中國鋁型材反補貼案	出口應訴	27/04/2010
泰國對中國熱浸鍍鋅冷軋鋼、熱浸板或塗鋁鋅合金冷軋鋼反傾銷案	出口應訴	08/07/2011
泰國對中國鋁鋅合金鍍層板反傾銷案	出口應訴	08/07/2011
哥倫比亞對中國鋁層壓板反傾銷案	出口應訴	03/08/2011
歐盟對中國鋁散熱器反傾銷案	出口應訴	12/08/2011
澳大利亞對中國鋁製車輪反傾銷案	出口應訴	07/11/2011

(續)

反傾銷	案件類型	日期
澳大利亞對中國鋁製車輪反補貼案	出口應訴	07/11/2011
澳大利亞對中國鋁製車輪反傾銷案	出口應訴	07/11/2011
澳大利亞對中國鋁製車輪反補貼案	出口應訴	07/11/2011
歐盟對中國成卷鋁箔反傾銷案	出口應訴	20/12/2011
歐盟對中國成卷鋁箔反傾銷案	出口應訴	20/12/2011
加拿大對中國鋁製單元式幕牆反傾銷案	出口應訴	16/07/2012
加拿大對中國鋁製單元式幕牆反補貼案	出口應訴	16/07/2012
加拿大對中國鋁製單元式幕牆反傾銷案	出口應訴	16/07/2012
加拿大對中國鋁製單元式幕牆反補貼案	出口應訴	16/07/2012
澳大利亞對中國台灣鍍鋁鋅板反傾銷案	貿易夥伴間案件	05/09/2012
澳大利亞對中國鍍鋁鋅板反傾銷案	出口應訴	05/09/2012
澳大利亞對韓國鍍鋁鋅板反傾銷案	貿易夥伴間案件	05/09/2012
澳大利亞對中國台灣鍍鋁鋅板反傾銷案	貿易夥伴間案件	05/09/2012
澳大利亞對中國鍍鋁鋅板反傾銷案	出口應訴	05/09/2012
澳大利亞對韓國鍍鋁鋅板反傾銷案	貿易夥伴間案件	05/09/2012
澳大利亞對中國鍍鋁鋅板反補貼案	出口應訴	26/11/2012
澳大利亞對中國鍍鋁鋅板反補貼案	出口應訴	26/11/2012
印度對中國鑄造鋁合金車輪或合金車輪反傾銷案	出口應訴	10/12/2012
印度對泰國鑄造鋁合金車輪或合金車輪反傾銷案	貿易夥伴間案件	10/12/2012
印度對韓國鑄造鋁合金車輪或合金車輪反傾銷案	貿易夥伴間案件	10/12/2012
印度對韓國鑄造鋁合金車輪或合金車輪反傾銷案	貿易夥伴間案件	10/12/2012
哥倫比亞對中國鋁擠壓件反傾銷案	出口應訴	27/02/2013
加拿大對中國鋁製單元式幕牆反傾銷案	出口應訴	04/03/2013
加拿大對中國鋁製單元式幕牆反補貼案	出口應訴	04/03/2013
土耳其對中國鋁箔反傾銷案	出口應訴	21/12/2013
巴西對中國鋁製預塗感光平板反傾銷案	出口應訴	25/02/2014
巴西對中國鋁製預塗感光平板反傾銷案	出口應訴	25/02/2014
巴西對中國香港鋁製預塗感光平板反傾銷案	貿易夥伴間案件	25/02/2014
巴西對台灣地區鋁製預塗感光平板反傾銷案	貿易夥伴間案件	25/02/2014
巴西對歐盟鋁製預塗感光平板反傾銷案	貿易夥伴間案件	25/02/2014
巴西對美國鋁製預塗感光平板反傾銷案	貿易夥伴間案件	25/02/2014
印度對進口非合金未鍛軋鋁錠保障措施案	出口應訴	07/04/2014
印度對進口非合金未鍛軋鋁錠保障措施案	出口應訴	07/04/2014

(續)

反傾銷	案件類型	日期
千里達和多巴哥對中國鋁擠壓材反傾銷案	出口應訴	22/08/2014
千里達和多巴哥對中國鋁擠壓材反傾銷案	出口應訴	22/08/2014
歐盟對俄羅斯鋁箔反傾銷案	貿易夥伴間案件	08/10/2014
歐盟對俄羅斯鋁箔反傾銷案	貿易夥伴間案件	08/10/2014
歐盟對中國鋁箔反傾銷案	出口應訴	12/12/2014
歐盟對中國鋁箔反傾銷案	出口應訴	12/12/2014
墨西哥對中國鋁製炊具反傾銷案	出口應訴	15/04/2015
墨西哥對中國鋁製炊具反傾銷案	出口應訴	15/04/2015
印度對中國鋁箔反傾銷案	出口應訴	15/12/2015
印度對中國鋁箔反傾銷案	出口應訴	15/12/2015
印度對中國鋁散熱器及其元件和散熱器芯反傾銷案	出口應訴	01/01/2016
印度對中國鋁散熱器及其元件和散熱器芯反傾銷案	出口應訴	01/01/2016
印度對進口未鍛壓鋁保障措施案	出口應訴	19/04/2016
印度對進口未鍛壓鋁保障措施案	出口應訴	19/04/2016
阿根廷對中國鋁合金輪轂反傾銷案	出口應訴	07/07/2016
阿根廷對中國鋁合金輪轂反傾銷案	出口應訴	07/07/2016
約旦對進口鋁條、鋁杆和鋁型材保障措施案	出口應訴	24/07/2016
澳大利亞對越南鋁型材反傾銷案	貿易夥伴間案件	16/08/2016
澳大利亞對越南鋁型材反補貼案	貿易夥伴間案件	16/08/2016
澳大利亞對馬來西亞鋁型材反傾銷案	貿易夥伴間案件	16/08/2016
澳大利亞對馬來西亞鋁型材反補貼案	貿易夥伴間案件	16/08/2016
韓國對中國鋁製預塗感光板反傾銷案	出口應訴	08/09/2016
巴拉圭對中國鋁擠壓材產品反傾銷案	出口應訴	28/09/2016
中國原鋁補貼措施世貿爭端案	世貿爭端	12/01/2017
美國對中國鋁箔反傾銷案	出口應訴	28/03/2017
美國對中國鋁箔反補貼案	出口應訴	28/03/2017
墨西哥對中國鋁膜氣球反傾銷案	出口應訴	26/06/2017
澳大利亞對中國鋁型材反傾銷案	出口應訴	19/10/2017
澳大利亞對泰國鋁型材反傾銷案	貿易夥伴間案件	19/10/2017
美國對中國鋁合金薄板反傾銷案	出口應訴	28/11/2017
美國對中國鋁合金薄板反補貼案	出口應訴	28/11/2017
歐亞經濟委員會（原俄白哈關稅同盟）對中國鋁輪轂反傾銷案	出口應訴	26/02/2018
歐亞經濟委員會（原俄白哈關稅同盟）對中國鑄鋁轉盤反傾銷案	出口應訴	02/03/2018

(續)

反傾銷	案件類型	日期
美國對華鋼鐵和鋁產品的措施世貿爭端案	世貿爭端	05/04/2018
黎巴嫩對中國特殊型鋁材反傾銷案	出口應訴	11/05/2018
黎巴嫩對埃及特殊型鋁材反傾銷案	貿易夥伴間案件	11/05/2018
黎巴嫩對沙烏地阿拉伯特殊型鋁材反傾銷案	貿易夥伴間案件	11/05/2018
黎巴嫩對阿聯酋特殊型鋁材反傾銷案	貿易夥伴間案件	11/05/2018
印度訴美國鋼鋁產品徵稅和配額世貿爭端案	世貿爭端	18/05/2018
歐盟訴美國對鋼鋁產品的關稅措施世貿爭端案	世貿爭端	01/06/2018
日本訴美國鋼鋁產品的關稅措施世貿爭端案	世貿爭端	05/06/2018
加拿大訴美國鋼鋁產品的關稅措施世貿爭端案	世貿爭端	06/06/2018
挪威訴美國鋼鋁產品的關稅措施世貿爭端案	世貿爭端	14/06/2018
阿根廷對中國家用鋁製散熱器反傾銷案	出口應訴	28/06/2018
阿根廷對意大利家用鋁製散熱器反傾銷案	貿易夥伴間案件	28/06/2018
阿根廷對西班牙家用鋁製散熱器反傾銷案	貿易夥伴間案件	28/06/2018
瑞士訴美國鋼鋁產品的關稅措施世貿爭端案	世貿爭端	09/07/2018
俄羅斯訴美國鋼鋁產品的關稅措施世貿爭端案	世貿爭端	27/07/2018
土耳其訴美國對鋼鋁產品的關稅措施世貿爭端案	世貿爭端	20/08/2018
墨西哥對中國鋁箔卷反傾銷案	出口應訴	28/08/2018
印尼對進口鋁箔卷保障措施案	出口應訴	09/10/2018
美國對中國鋁製電線電纜反傾銷案	出口應訴	12/10/2018
美國對中國鋁製電線電纜反補貼案	出口應訴	12/10/2018
巴基斯坦對土耳其鋁製飲料瓶反傾銷案	貿易夥伴間案件	01/11/2018
巴基斯坦對斯里蘭卡鋁製飲料瓶反傾銷案	貿易夥伴間案件	01/11/2018
巴基斯坦對約旦鋁製飲料瓶反傾銷案	貿易夥伴間案件	01/11/2018
巴基斯坦對阿聯酋鋁製飲料瓶反傾銷案	貿易夥伴間案件	01/11/2018
墨西哥對中國鋁製高壓鍋反傾銷案	出口應訴	20/12/2018
越南對中國鋁型材反傾銷案	出口應訴	11/01/2019
阿根廷對中國鋁板反傾銷案	出口應訴	25/02/2019
阿根廷對中國鋁箔反傾銷案	出口應訴	08/03/2019
印度對中國鍍鋁鋅合金扁軋鋼產品反傾銷案	出口應訴	02/04/2019
印度對越南鍍鋁鋅合金扁軋鋼產品反傾銷案	貿易夥伴間案件	02/04/2019
印度對韓國鍍鋁鋅合金扁軋鋼產品反傾銷案	貿易夥伴間案件	02/04/2019
歐亞經濟委員會（原俄白哈關稅同盟）對中國鋁帶反傾銷案	出口應訴	07/05/2019
歐亞經濟委員會（原俄白哈關稅同盟）對阿塞拜疆鋁帶反傾銷案	貿易夥伴間案件	07/05/2019

3 中國內地的金屬現貨與期貨市場

3.1　市場現狀

改革開放 40 年以來，中國金屬行業蓬勃發展，從供給和需求兩方面，一方面中國經濟發展過程中，需要龐大的原材料作為補充，另一方面，中國企業在供給方面抓住龐大市場擴張的時機，不斷加大投資擴大供給。這個過程中逐漸形成期貨和現貨兩個市場，這兩個市場的運作主要受上期所和 LME 等交易所中可交割的品牌所限制，其他非場內交易的金屬品種需要進行場外交易。除此之外，即使是場內可交易的品種，仍有非常多的品牌不能併入交割流程。與交易所期貨品種相比，場外的現貨交易市場仍然非常龐大，這也給未來與金屬相關的期貨市場的發展帶來非常廣闊的空間。

3.2　套期保值及期現套利實例

在現貨套期保值方面，以電解鋁生產企業為例，3 月某電解鋁生產企業電解鋁生產成本為每公噸 13,000 元人民幣（下同），3 月電解鋁現貨售價為每公噸 14,000 元，遠期 5 月期貨價格為每公噸 14,300 元，現貨企業如果考慮鎖定 5 月現貨利潤，可以考慮在 5 月賣出相應期貨合約進行套期保值，待時間進入 5 月以後，若鋁期貨價格上漲至每公噸 14,500 元，現貨價格上漲至每公噸 14,200 元，則電解鋁企業在期貨上每公噸虧損 200 元，而現貨端獲利 200 元，其利潤繼續保持穩定為每公噸 1,000 元；若進入 5 月以後，期貨價格下跌 300 元至每公噸 14,000 元，現貨價格下跌至每公噸 13,700 元，則電解鋁企業在期貨端每公噸獲利 300 元，在現貨端虧損 300 元，整體期貨和現貨維持對沖，即電解鋁企業的利潤繼續保持穩定在每公噸 1,000 元。電解鋁企業即通過期貨端的套期保值行為來規避鋁價在未來的波動風險。

在期現套利方面，由於金屬期貨和現貨市場的價格形成機制不同，令現貨和期貨市場產生一定的套利空間。首先，現貨市場價格是參考如上海有色網等第三方機構現貨日度報價為主，國內冶煉企業、礦山企業、加工企業、貿易企業等為參與主體，其結算基準參考第三方機構報價。其次，第三方報價的標的多為非可交割金屬產品，報價基礎是完全依賴現貨市場當日的買賣成交情況，這與當日庫存，買賣強度等因素相關。第三，期貨價格產生於期貨市場交易者，包括冶煉企業、貿易商企業、下游加工企業為主，以可交割的標準倉單為標的物。

以電解鋁為例，現貨市場中參考 SMM A00 現貨鋁錠每日報價為基準，SMM A00 現貨鋁錠與上期所相關期貨當月合約之間每日會有固定升貼水，這個固定升貼水的產生來自每日現貨市場中買賣集中的時間和總量基礎上（見圖6）。當 SMM A00 現貨鋁錠價格低於期貨價格時，及當日現貨對期貨呈現貼水格局時，參與貿易的企業可以選擇買入現貨同時在期貨上賣空，待持有時間臨近交割日期，SMM A00 現貨鋁錠價格對期貨當月合約貼水收窄，貿易商可以選擇在此時賣出現貨並買入期貨合約上平倉，從而獲得無風險套利空間。

圖6：SMM A00 鋁現貨與期貨價差（升貼水）的走勢
（2010 年 1 月 4 日至 2020 年 2 月 21 日）

資料來源：SMM。

除鋁錠的期現套利機會外，銅、鋅、鎳、錫、鉛等金屬品種也可以在期貨市場中運用這種價差結構進行套利交易。

3.3　內地金屬市場生產週期中不同階段對金融衍生品的不同需求

處於產業鏈不同位置的市場參與者對期貨市場的需求也不完全相同。相對來說，由於對應的期貨品種數量有限，仍然有非常多的金屬品種沒有期貨交易，也就沒有相應的對沖價格波動風險的工具，如金屬矽、金屬鎂、金屬鈦等。

除了品種間的差異外，單一品種中的產業鏈上中下游的產品，由於其定價方式不同，也缺乏相應的價格波動風險對沖工具，如鋁產業鏈中上游的鋁土礦、氧化鋁等產品。鋁產業鏈中的原材料成本（電解鋁）可以通過原鋁的期貨品種進行對沖價格風險，但對下游中的加工產品而言，其價格風險目前並沒有相應的期貨產品進行對沖（見圖 7）。

總的來說，產業鏈中不同階段的產品都有對其價格波動風險的厭惡情緒，故亦有非常強的避險需求。

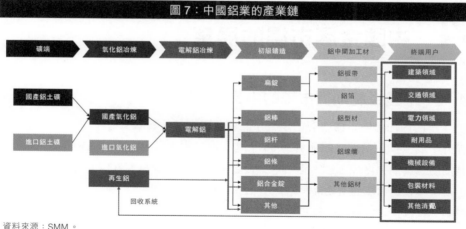

圖 7：中國鋁業的產業鏈

資料來源：SMM。

綜合來看，與原鋁有原材料關係的下游企業使用期貨作為保值工具明顯強於上游的礦和氧化鋁。同理我們可以看到鋼鐵行業裏上游的鐵礦可以作為單一期貨品種，另外亦有當前上期所正在籌備的獨立的氧化鋁期貨品種。可以預期，隨着中國金屬商品市場的發展，未來將有越來越多的金屬品種有望成為期貨交易品種，而期貨也將為相關企業提供這些產品的價格風險對沖工具。

此外，不同生產階段的產品定價模式相差巨大，因此其對期貨的需求也有不同。

對於原材料生產方面如電解鋁企業，其對期貨的依賴主要是以其作為產品定價基礎和用於套期保值交易；而下游的消費企業，對期貨的依賴主要源自期貨的定價和套期保值功能。電解鋁消費企業和電解鋁生產企業使用期貨的買賣保值出現差異，在於生產企業主要是期貨的賣方保值，而消費企業主要是期貨的買方保值為主。與此同時，隨着現貨市場逐漸擴大，作為中間商的貿易企業加入，造成套期保值的需求增加，而中間商的套期保值需求也出現分化。從事電解鋁貿易的企業，在期貨上既可以賣出保值，也可以買入保值，主要根據現貨和期貨的價差結構，即現貨對期貨的升貼水而定。

4 中國金屬市場的展望

4.1 中國金屬期貨市場的中長期展望

中國內地金屬市場中有色金屬和黑色金屬交易品種的交易額和交易量均不斷提升。以上期所為例，該所於 2000 年只有銅、鋁兩個金屬交易品種，到 2010 年其交易金屬品種增加至銅、鋁、鋅、黃金、螺紋鋼、線材等 6 個品種，至 2019 年上期所與金屬相關的交易品種增加至 12 個，包括銅、鋁、鉛、鋅、錫、鎳、黃金、白銀、螺紋鋼、線材、熱軋板卷以及不銹鋼。

上期所金屬相關期貨的交易額增長至 2019 年的 81.15 萬億元，2000 至 2019 年間的複合年均增長率為 6.4%，金屬相關交易量增長至 2019 年的 103,712 萬手，2000 至 2019 年間的複合年均增長率為 7.7%（見圖 8 及圖 9）。

　　與貿易流相一致的全球農產品主要消費區域有三個地區：（1）以中國為核心的人口聚集的亞洲地區；（2）以美國為核心的人均農產品資源消耗巨大的北美地區；（3）人口聚集和經濟發達的歐洲地區。

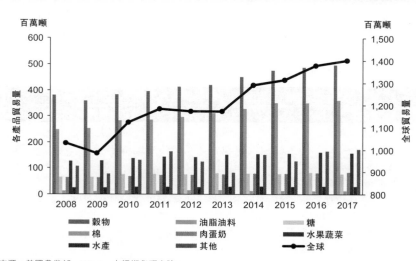

圖 3：全球農產品貿易量（2008 年至 2017 年）

資料來源：美國農業部、Wind、中糧期貨研究院。

　　穀物和油籽是全球貿易量最大的農產品，北美、南美則是全球最重要的國際糧油輸出地，北美以美國為主要的糧油輸出地，南美以巴西和阿根廷為主要糧油輸出地，目前世界糧油貿易主要以原產品形式進行，即產品生產和加工環節相隔離，產品加工環節主要在消費國，但油籽貿易中阿根廷則以輸出油籽壓制產品為主，主要是充分利用本國的農產品加工比較優勢，獲取更多的農產品加工鏈利潤。

1.1.2　國際農產品期貨市場的概況

　　農產品期貨市場是農產品市場的重要衍生和組成部份。自 1848 年芝加哥期貨交易所（Chicago Board of Trade，簡稱 CBOT）成立以來，國際農產品期貨市場立足於龐大的農產品現貨市場取得了長足的發展，時至今日，各主要農業國家和地區均設立了農產品期貨交易所，覆蓋了主要類別的農產品期貨，具體明細見下

表 1。在主要農產品期貨交易所中，以 CME 集團旗下的 CBOT 和美國洲際交易所（ICE）最有影響力，目前國際市場糧、油、糖、棉的貿易均以 CBOT 和 ICE 相關商品期貨價格為定價基準。

　　CBOT 上市的農產品期貨主要分為穀物類和油籽類，其中穀物類期貨品種包括玉米、小麥、燕麥和稻穀，油籽類期貨包括大豆、豆粕和豆油；ICE 上市的農產品期貨主要為軟商品期貨，包括棉花、糖、可可和咖啡。CBOT 和 ICE 上市農產品期貨品種持倉量呈現緩慢上升趨勢，且成交量遠超現貨產量，市場流動性十分充裕。

表1：全球主要農產品期貨交易所			
交易所	所在國家	上市農產品種類	期貨品種數目
CBOT	美國	穀物、油脂油料	7
ICE	美國	軟商品、果汁	5
芝加哥商品交易所 Chicago Mercantile Exchange (CME)	美國	畜產品、林產品	4
大連商品交易所	中國	穀物、油脂油料、雞蛋	9
鄭州商品交易所	中國	穀物、油脂油料、軟商品	13
馬來西亞期貨交易所 Bursa Malaysia Derivatives Exchange (BMD)	馬來西亞	棕櫚油	1

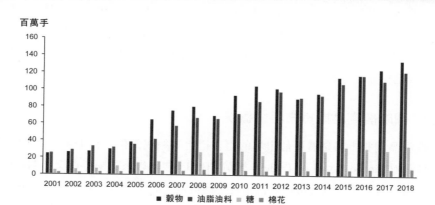

圖 4：CBOT 與 ICE 的期貨成交量（2001 年至 2018 年）

資料來源：彭博、Wind、中糧期貨研究院。

圖 5：CBOT 穀物及油脂油料期貨月底持倉量（2009 年 12 月至 2019 年 11 月）

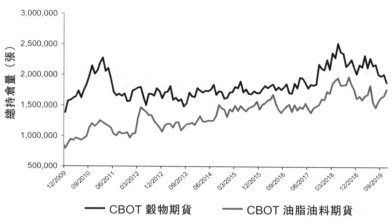

資料來源：美國農業部、Wind、中糧期貨研究院。

圖 6：ICE 棉花及白糖期貨月底持倉量（2009 年 12 月至 2019 年 11 月）

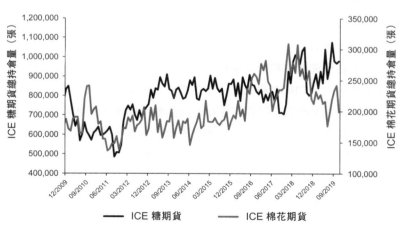

資料來源：美國農業部、Wind、中糧期貨研究院。

2 內地中國農產品期貨市場的發展

2.1 內地農產品期貨市場發展的四個階段

中國內地期貨市場自 1988 年起步探索，經過三十多年的發展，期貨市場取得了巨大成就，不僅為實體企業發揮規避市場價格風險的功能，也逐步成為內地當代新興資本市場的重要構成，成為投資者實現資產配置的重要工具市場。回顧內地期貨市場的發展歷程，可為四個階段：起步探索、清理整頓、規範發展、全面發展。

表 2：內地期貨市場發展的四個階段		
階段	時間	重大標識事件
起步探索	1988 - 1994	1990 年 10 月鄭州糧食批發市場引入期貨交易，成為首個商品期貨市場
		1992 年 10 月第一家期貨經紀公司成立
清理整頓	1994 - 2000	1993、1998 年兩輪整頓，至 1999 年內地期貨交易所精簡為三家
		1999 年《期貨交易管理條例》等系列法律法規相繼頒佈
		2000 年 12 月中國期貨業協會成立，行業自律組織誕生
規範發展	2000 - 2010	2006 年 5 月中國期貨保證金監控中心成立
		2007 年 3 月國務院頒佈《期貨交易管理條例》
全面發展	2010 至今	2010 年 4 月滬深 300 股指期貨上市
		2017 年 3 月首個商品期權上市
		2018 年 3 月首個國際化品種原油期貨上市
		2019 年 10 月前內地衍生品品種達到 70 個

資料來源：中糧期貨研究院。

在內地期貨市場三十多年的發展歷程中，農產品期貨市場也同樣歷經四個階段，農產品期貨市場從無到有，從新興發展到規範創新，不斷地進步完善[8]。

(1) 起步探索階段（1988 年至 1994 年）

1988 年 6 月，國務院開始選取期貨市場品種試點，1990 年底鄭州糧食批發市場獲批引入期貨交易試點，成立內地首個商品期貨市場。1993 年 6 月鄭州糧食批

---

8 見常清〈中國期貨史上的關鍵抉擇〉，載於《金融業發展》，2016 年 6 月 8 日。

發市場標準化的期貨合約的推出，標誌着向期貨市場過渡正式完成。鄭商所試點後，多家交易所開始出現，同時經營農產品期貨業務，截至 1993 年底，內地運行的期貨交易所總共達到了 38 個。這一階段，內地期貨市場發展過於快速，各類投機事件、炒作、以及逼倉的事件較多。例如內地基本不產咖啡，且居民消費量和貿易額也極低，但某些交易所竟然上市了咖啡期貨。另外，各個交易所為吸引客戶資源，相互競爭激烈，上市的糧油期貨品種存在交叉重疊問題。1993 年 5 月上海糧油商品交易所上市粳米期貨品種，到了 8 月內地出現災情，糧食價格不斷上漲，多頭佔據上風，給當時的居民生活帶來了一定困難。至此，國務院於 1993 年 10 月 12 日頒佈《國務院關於有效化解期貨市場盲目發展的通知》，該通知的出台有效抑制了內地期貨市場的氾濫發展。

(2)　清理整頓階段（1994 年至 2000 年）

前期期貨市場的氾濫發展，衍生出一系列負面突發事件，如 1994 年粳米和咖啡的「9609 期貨合約」事件、1995 年的 C513 玉米期貨價格暴漲事件、1996 年天津紅小豆期貨事件。1994 年 3 月內地暫停於海外市場進行的衍生品交易，同時國務院對粳米、菜籽油、食糖進行了暫停期貨交易處理。1995 年「327 國債期貨」事件，進一步促成國務院於 1996 年對期貨市場進行第二次整頓，該時期整頓的效果非常顯著，這也是農產品期貨品種數量、交易量和交易額大幅下滑的主要原因。至 1999 年內地期貨交易所精簡為三家 —— 上海期貨交易所（簡稱「上期所」）、鄭州商品交易所（簡稱「鄭商所」）和大連商品交易所（簡稱「大商所」）。2000 年 11 月中國期貨業協會成立，它的出現影響了整個期貨行業監管體系。

(3)　規範發展階段（2000 年至 2010 年）

2001 年，鄭商所交易的農產品只有綠豆和小麥，大商所僅有豆粕和大豆兩個品種，全國的農產品期貨品種一共四個。隨着市場秩序平穩發展，農產品期貨品種每年都在增加。規範發展的十年時間，農產品期貨市場無論是在交易規模還是在交易金額上均在迅速上漲。1992 年，中國證券監督管理委員會（簡稱「中國證監會」）成立，內地期貨市場也實現三級監管制度。2006 年 6 月 24 日，中國期貨保證金監控中心批准設立，在保障資金安全維護投資主體利益方面的意義深遠。

(4) 全面發展階段（2010 年至今）

隨着內地期貨交易市場的體系逐漸形成之後，內地期貨市場推出的期貨品種逐漸多樣化、結構也更加合理。2010 年以來，內地農產品期貨的上市品種也日益增多，截至 2019 年底，共有 22 個農產品期貨品種，其中鄭商所 13 個，大商所 9 個。此外，2017 年證監會批准鄭商所和大商所開展白糖、豆粕期權交易 —— 內地首個場內農產品期權正式落地，內地衍生品市場正式開啟期權時代。2019 年 1 月玉米和棉花期權上市。

在期貨品種的基礎上，進一步發展農產品期權交易，能夠更好地滿足農業企業精細化、多樣化的風險管理需求，對完善農產品價格形成機制、提高農業產業化水平、加快轉變內地農業發展方式無疑具有積極的作用。上市品種的推陳出新，為管理應對期貨風險發展內地市場、掌握農產品的國際定價權打下了堅實的基礎[9]。期貨市場的規範化和法制化程度也逐年提升，各種監管體系以及法律體系進一步完善。2014 年 5 月國務院頒佈新的「國九條」文件[10]，此次頒佈的文件作為內地深化金融市場改革的綱領性文件有着深遠的意義。2016 年中國證監會頒佈了《證券期貨投資者適當性管理辦法》，這是內地出台的首部證券期貨方面保護投資者利益的文件。

表 3：內地農產品期貨品種的變動（2001 年至 2019 年）				
年份	鄭商所新增農產品期貨品種	大商所新增農產品期貨品種	品種總數	註釋
2001	普麥、綠豆	大豆、豆粕	4	原期貨
2002		黃大豆一號	4	更改名稱
2003	強麥		5	
2004	棉花	黃大豆二號、玉米	8	
2006	白糖	豆油	10	
2007	菜籽油	棕櫚油	12	
2009	早秈稻		12	綠豆自鄭商所退市
2012	菜籽油、油菜籽		14	
2013	粳稻	雞蛋	16	

9　見常清〈創新期貨交易方式　精準服務實體產業〉，載於《中國證券報》，2016 年 8 月 8 日。

10　〈國務院關於進一步促進資本市場健康發展的若干意見〉，2014 年 5 月 8 日。

(續)

表 3：內地農產品期貨品種的變動（2001 年至 2019 年）			
年份	鄭商所新增農產品期貨品種	大商所新增農產品期貨品種	品種總數	註釋
2014	晚秈稻	玉米澱粉	18	
2017	棉紗、蘋果		20	
2019	紅棗	粳米	22	

資料來源：中糧期貨研究院。

2.2　內地農產品期貨市場的脫虛向實

　　內地期貨市場自 2001 年恢復發展以來，期貨交易所和期貨經紀公司都在不斷的探索如何更好地發揮期貨市場的功能、服務實體經濟。內地期貨市場已經在套期保值功能的基礎上，結合實際考慮，向新的結構性產品方面邁進 [11]：

　　第一，在期貨市場成立初期，利用其價格發現的功能，來解決價格雙軌制問題，實現大宗商品價格統一由市場形成的目標，完成了商品價格改革的歷史任務。

　　第二，隨着期貨市場功能的完善和實體企業對期貨工具的深入應用，市場參與者日益成熟、市場制度日益完善，期貨市場避險的功能和作用也得到進一步發揮，多種創新模式有了施展的空間。

　　第三，在實體企業取得保值效果後，期貨業內就如何更好地服務實體經濟的問題展開新的探索和研究，例如期貨點價方式在油脂油料、棉花、玉米行業的應用和發展。此外「期貨＋保險」在農產品領域大放異彩，2016-2019 年「中央一號文件」[12] 中均有明確提出穩步擴大「期貨＋保險」試點；在 2019 年多部委聯合下發的《關於金融服務鄉村振興的指導意見》中也提出：穩步擴大「保險＋期貨」試點，探索「訂單農業＋保險＋期貨（權）」試點。2016-2018 年，期貨市場累計開展「期貨＋保險」試點項目 249 個，其中上期所 53 個、鄭商所 66 個、大商所 130 個，涉及玉米、大豆、棉花、白糖、蘋果和天然橡膠 6 個期貨品種，承保現貨數量 395 萬噸，涉及面積 1072 萬畝，為 39 萬農戶提供了價格和收入保障 [13]。

11　見申盼盼、胡一波與李彥蓉（2019）〈我國農產品期貨市場現狀及發展路徑〉，載於《農業工程》，2019 年第 9(8) 期，150-152 頁。

12　2016-2019 年中央一號文件：《關於落實發展新理念加快農業現代化實現全面小康目標的若干意見》、《關於深入推進農業供給側結構性改革加快培育農業農村發展新動能的若干意見》、《關於實施鄉村振興戰略的意見》、《關於堅持農業農村優先發展做好「三農」工作的若干意見》。

13　資料來源：中國期貨業協會。

第四，期權結合期貨套保可以優化資金效率，含權貿易針對各種交易風險而採取不同應對策略可以優化貿易模式，將場外期權以貿易條款的方式體現。把期權嵌套進普通的貿易形成「含權貿易」形成了豆粕基差點價的新模式、新熱點。越來越多的風險管理公司將期現業務和場外期權業務結合，尋找業務突破點，目前應用得比較廣泛的有保底價、封頂價以及二次點價等。

2.3　內地農產品期貨市場的國際化路徑

內地期貨市場國際化歷程是不斷「引進來」加「走出去」的進程。探索起步階段，內地期貨公司和投資者「走出去」開展外盤交易，以境外代理業務為主的期貨交易日漸活躍，但因境外代理鏈冗長、成本高企，導致衝突和風險事件不斷發生。1994 年 3 月國務院發文明令禁止境外期貨代理業務。清理整頓階段，內地期貨市場國際化進程基本發展滯緩。隨着中國加入世界貿易組織（WTO），內地期貨市場國際化的進程重啟，境內投資者再次「走出去」獲得境外套期保值業務參與許可權，期貨公司也加大「走出去」步伐，在香港和海外設立分支代理機構，同時期貨交易所也邁開國際化步伐、謀求突破。

期貨品種的國際化是整個期貨市場國際化的核心，2018 年是中國內地期貨市場品種國際化的元年，當年原油期貨上市並同時引入境外投資者、鐵礦石和 PTA 期貨亦引入境外投資者，標誌着內地期貨市場品種國際化邁出第一步。2019 年天然橡膠「20 號膠」上市，成為內地第四個國際化品種。不過，在農產品市場領域，仍需進一步提速對境外開放的步伐 [14]。

為適應中國在世界日益重要的經濟地位轉變，內地的農產品期貨市場應從單純地建設內地大宗商品定價中心轉向成為具有國際定價權的國際化期貨市場，讓「中國價格」也成為世界農產品市場定價的重要組成部份。市場的發展應結合內地資本對外開放的新形勢，以積極對外推出在國際貿易市場佔有巨大份額的農產品的期貨為突破口，探索對外開放的思路和策略；同時應不斷完善對外開放的相關政策與法規，減少境外投資者入場交易的不必要限制，積極引入境外投資者。

此外，內地農產品期貨市場的開放亦應加快，擴大合格境外機構投資者範圍，

14　見胡俞越（2016）〈我國期貨市場國際化的路徑選擇〉，載於《期貨日報》，2016 年 9 月 9 日。

使更多的境外投資者參與到內地農產品期貨市場交易之中，加強內地與境外期貨市場投資主體的流通性；另外須增加市場投資主體的數量並豐富市場主體的類型，同時可以加強內地與境外投資主體交流合作，促進內地市場投資主體的發展。

3 全球農產品市場及其衍生品的發展前景

3.1 農產品市場全球一體化的變局

農產品市場的全球一體化使得農業生產要素和資本產生了巨大的流動。隨着貿易規模的不斷加大，國家間的依存度越來越高，但是隨着近年中美貿易爭端的出現，全球農業一體化格局必然會出現變化。

農產品貿易是基礎性貿易，不同農產品貿易競爭手段主要通過價格高低、地理優勢和附加值等來實現。同時，農產品還具有產品和地理的可替代性，農業貿易競爭隨之而來，市場化調節和政府行政干預之間存在長期博弈，農業貿易壁壘也隨之而產生。

近年中美貿易爭端的發生有助於打破舊有的全球農業貿易的阻礙，促使各國政府再次審視國家糧食安全，主動減少農業貿易壁壘，減少國際農業貿易的單邊依賴，構建多元化的農業貿易通道和方式。

多元化農業貿易通道和方式的搭建會導致國家間農業發展政策和導向的改變，老牌國際糧商的產業佈局和產業鏈優勢也可能因此被削弱，新的競爭性企業可能因此獲得發展或者拓展機遇。它們可能會借助某些環節或領域的比較優勢加入到國際農產品貿易的隊伍之中，而這也正是以 ABCD 為代表的老牌國際糧商的發展之路，老牌的國際糧商在上百年的發展歷程中，均經歷了數次的時代變革和戰爭的衝擊，但它們每次都將變革和衝擊當成發展機遇，或是縱深產業佈局，或是開闢貿易路線，不斷增強自身的生存和競爭力。中美貿易爭端對全球農產業一體化的擾動對分佈於農業產業鏈不同環節的企業來說，既是挑戰也是機遇。

3.2　中國農產品市場的機遇與挑戰

目前內地農產品期貨市場的發展在全球市場中的地位越來越重要，但品種數量少、缺乏定價權。在內地經濟新常態發展的背景下，農產品市場化加快、價格波動頻繁，而且自 2018 年以來的中美經貿摩擦進一步加劇了內地農產品期貨的波動和風險，農產品期貨的價格發現和套期保值功能仍有待提升。三十多年的發展，內地的鄭商所和大商所的國際競爭力不斷提高，但是仍然未能取得像歐美發達市場如 CME 與 ICE 的期貨定價影響力，在核心競爭力方面仍然有許多需要改善的空間 [15]。

面對百年未有之大變局，在新常態、新時代的發展背景下，內地期貨行業都亟待變革，農產品期貨市場迎來了前所未有的機遇和挑戰。

第一，擴展農產品期貨新品種。內地的農產品交易品種單一，交易結構也不盡合理。建議內地將合規的農產品期貨合約儘快發展上市，例如生豬、大蒜期貨等新品種的上市開發。

第二，改進品種結構、退出及修改機制。內地上市的農產品期貨品種，只有豆粕、棉花、白糖、豆油、棕櫚油、玉米等品種的持倉比例較高，其他品種所佔份額較小，存在結構不合理、失衡的現象。部份品種上市後因為合約設計，資金流向，標的物市場認知度，交割制度設計等原因導致參與者少，甚至成為「僵屍品種」，這些品種不論成交量還是成交金額都非常小，很難起到價格發現、套期保值、資源配置功能，大部份價格與現貨價格相關度也不高，很難對相關產業起到價格指引作用。

第三，完善立法工作，建全監管體系。要保證期貨市場交易秩序平穩，就需要健全的法律法規體系保駕護航，來真正實現「公開、公平、公正」的交易原則。建議儘快推出《期貨法》，法律規範才是期貨市場健康穩定發展的基石，建立和健全法律法規體系以及監管體制機制。

第四，探索完善期權、指數工具創新。至 2019 年底內地場內期權僅有 4 個農產品品種，應該加快探索其他農產品期權的上市，探索活躍場內期權市場，為投

15　見張國勝與王文舉（2019）〈中國期貨業發展的階段性特徵及未來展望〉，載於《經濟管理研究》，2019 年第 40(11) 期，41-55 頁。

資者提供更多價格對沖工具、為實體企業套保需求。農產品指數期貨能夠反映整個農產品市場的價格走勢情況，是農產品現貨市場的晴雨錶，具有許多單一農產品期貨所不具備的優點，不僅能夠滿足套期保值者需求，也能為投資者提供了一種新的投資工具。

　　第五，加快「走出去」步伐，加強內地與香港機構的合作。在「一帶一路」倡議及「粵港澳大灣區」發展策略下，內地期貨公司應加快「走出去」步伐，推動國際化業務、謀求突破。內地與香港機構應加強合作，積極推動內地期貨公司在香港設立國際期貨業務平台，促進內地期貨市場的國際化轉型，為內地與國際投資者提供多元化投資渠道。

第4章

實踐中的大宗商品交易與套期保值

袁恩賜博士

花旗環球金融亞洲有限公司董事總經理
花旗研究部大宗商品亞太主管

Edward L. MORSE, Ph.D.

花旗環球金融有限公司董事總經理
花旗研究部大宗商品全球主管

廖忱

花旗環球金融亞洲有限公司
花旗亞太研究部大宗商品分析師、副總裁

蘇筱琳

花旗環球金融亞洲有限公司
花旗亞太研究部大宗商品助理副總裁

摘 要

　　本章就以下各議題展開討論：（1）大宗商品定價；（2）大宗商品生產者與消費者的套期保值行為；（3）金融市場參與者的大宗商品投資和交易行為；（4）銀行和貿易公司等促進大宗商品交易的行為。在綜合討論後，文章重點指出選擇正確的基準價格的重要性、分析基準價格得以成功的內在原因，以及其在中國的應用。

1　大宗商品的實用性及定價

1.1　基本概念

　　大宗商品的供應和需求通常具有季節性且波動較大，這些特性對大宗商品的消費模式有一定影響。鑒於供應和需求在時間上的不吻合，商品需要被儲存起來以供未來的消費。這種時間上的不吻合可以是常規性及季節性，這在農產品和能源產品中尤其突出。幾千年以來，人們認識到商品的儲存有其價值亦涉及成本。當市場預期某種商品於未來的使用價值較現在為高時，會激勵人們對於倉儲的投資。在現代社會，期貨合約中的遠期價格可以顯示儲存某種商品的淨現值（net present value）於何時大於即期消費的淨現值，例如在期貨的「正向市場」（contango）中，遠期價格可能會高於購買原材料的費用與倉儲成本的總和。當某種商品（例如石油）的儲存空間所剩無幾時，投資者會基於對該商品倉儲的淨現值（即倉儲行為的價值）的評估來抬高遠期價格，並從中獲利。

　　大宗商品一般亦高度政治化。全世界超過一半的大宗商品屬於農產品和能源類別，即通俗意義上的食品和燃料。一方面民眾認為自己有權利購買廉價的商品，另一方面生產者期待高價出售，且希望把提價的「重任」交給第三方機構，例如石油輸出國組織（OPEC）。在這樣一個「零和世界」中，該類組織被建立以承擔價格調整的責任。

1.2　大宗商品的定價

　　短期來看，**供應、需求和庫存**三個要素最為重要。顯然，其中一個要素相對於其他要素的強弱會決定價格下跌還是上漲。但是，季節性因素也很可能直接影響平衡。庫存是重要的，它可以在絕對量上增加或減少，然而它亦會反映出遠期需求價值的變化。因此，僅僅因為供應表面上大於需求，並不一定意味着市場疲軟。重要的是隨着庫存絕對量的變化而可以覆蓋未來需求的能力（即可以提供多少天的消費）是增加還是減少。如果需求快速增長，儘管庫存的絕對水平已然上升，但能夠滿足需求的天數可能會減少，這就會使市場看漲而非看跌。當需求增量達到某一水平，使在當前價格下所能向市場提供的最便宜的石油或其他商品都已經被抽空的時候，額外的需求增量就會促使商品價格上漲。比如多一噸銅的增量需求，就可能需要更昂貴地開採銅，從而觸發銅的價格全面上漲。

長期來看，**大宗商品的投資週期**也會影響其定價。每種大宗商品都一樣會受到週期性趨勢的影響，導致公司前赴後繼調動資本響應高價，結果對新供應投資過度。這會促使價格猛然下跌而又致使公司在一段時間內不願投資新產能，導致了下一段時期的投資不足。農產品的投資週期較短，當前的價格信號可能會誘使農民為此一週期裏表現好的產品增加明年產出的播種面積，並減少此一週期表現不佳的農作物的播種面積。從一年到下一年，播種面積的這種變化會相當大地影響產量。乾散貨（bulk commodities）的週期比農產品要長，而基本金屬和貴金屬（特別是能源產品）的週期會更長。

超級週期是有機會出現的，但在很大程度上卻不可預測。當成本處於很長的穩定期時，價格會向平均價靠攏（均值回歸），遠期曲線也會較穩定。當然也有成本通脹和通縮的時期。一般來說，科技和技術變革會降低商品生產的長期成本。縱使如此，不同商品的週期很少會重疊。當然商品生產通常都是高耗能的，因此能源價格的變動會使不同商品的週期產生聯動性。

多年來，市場有過不少努力，擬通過競投與發展可交易大宗商品的交易所來**把大宗商品金融化**，但是總體來說，這些都是只包括少部份大宗商品生產者和消費者的小市場。

金融衍生品和其他金融工具，不管是於交易所場內交易或於場外交易，均有利於投資者買賣大宗商品。這些金融工具為大宗商品投資提供便利，使投資者不必擔心收貨過程中的倉儲成本和風險，這些風險包括農產品的疾病侵染、害蟲和鼠患、液體品質的下降、金屬生銹或其他問題。市場提供了使生產者和消費者可以套期保值的工具，促進了市場參與者在期貨曲線的中長端進行套期保值，短期性的套期保值亦可行。在 2003 年至 2007 年期間，對新金融工具的投資剛好在所謂「商品超級週期」中快速增長[1]。若我們看看這些市場中的主要參與者，會發現受託管的資金如退休基金通常會持長倉（即主要是商品買入方），形成大宗商品資產

1　2003-2007 年的「商品超級週期」指的是商品價格不斷上漲。對能源和金屬的需求（尤其是來自中國的需求）攀升，
　　而供應則因產出未能配合而緊張，導致供需基本面緊張以致價格上漲。

管理的基礎。這些（投資）一般都會在期貨曲線的近端。除此之外，大宗商品市場也有一些「快錢」（例如對沖基金）進行短期投機。這部份的投資主要集中於期貨曲線的前端或短期合約。在大宗商品期貨市場短端投資的還有商品交易顧問（CTA）和程式交易者。

2　大宗商品生產者和消費者的套期保值行為

生產者進行套期保值以確保未來產出所享有的收入，而消費者進行套期保值以鎖定未來商品消費的成本，這些都是通用的風險管理策略。本節討論國家石油公司、勘探和生產公司、其他能源消費者、金屬生產商與消費者、以及農業生產商如何進行套期保值。

大宗商品消費者和生產者進行**價格保障**的主要目的是規避可能危害現金流並影響長期資本計劃的市場風險。通常在以下幾種情況會有這樣的需要來保障產出的收入：（i）生產者通過發債對新的產出進行融資，而該債務需要在未來某確定時間償還；（ii）產出的收入已指定用於特殊項目；（iii）總體生產水平受到威脅，特別是在價格下跌的情況下；（iv）需要保證多年期資本計劃。對於生產者來說，在可以量化風險防範成本的基礎上，通常適合進行下行價格風險管理的套期保值（即對沖）計劃，從而最大程度地減少價格波動的影響。大宗商品消費者則適合做上行價格風險管理。但是，有時一些市場參與者可能會放棄戰略性的套期保值。一方面，由於現貨價格和遠期價格的上漲，一些生產商會停止對沖，認為沒有必要。另一方面，一些消費者會因價格下跌而停止對沖，他們認為價格可能會長期保持低位。可是價格長期上漲或價格長期下跌卻不可能同時發生的。此外，有些被採用的策略不一定是最合適的，例如零成本期權[2]，由於其價格上限，並不一定總是最

2　零成本期權是一種保護性期權策略，可以抵銷認沽期權和認購期權中的溢價。投資者/交易員買入價外的認沽期權，同時賣出具有相同到期日和相同溢價的價外認購期權，使認購期權和認沽期權的頭寸彼此抵銷。這種策略可以通過購買對利潤和虧損設置上限和下限的認購和認沽期權來對沖相關資產的價格波動。

好的選擇，對於生產商來說，其在價格波動或上漲的環境中涉及的成本會很高。「認沽期權保障」[3] 有時可能是更好的對沖機制。買入認沽期權進行風險管理和價格保障最簡單不過，而且可以通過不同的方式來完成。例如通過結算期為一年的年度掉期，也可以通過月度結算來尋求價格保障，當然也有更複雜的操作方式。但是，套期保值也可能會受企業內部政治因素影響，因為有人可能會對套期保值所產生的損失表達不滿。

一些國有企業和石油生產國的政府機構還會進行**戰略對沖**。例如有一產油國的財政部進入市場以保障現金流免受石油銷售的影響。國家會執行年度計劃，購買認沽期權，為其石油銷售價格提供保底。2020 年是特別的一年，提供了一個很好的例子。這年許多其他產油國在油價暴跌後遭受嚴重的收入損失，而墨西哥連續多年進行的年度對沖計劃卻保障了其現金流和政府收入。

在美國，獨立勘探和生產的公司進行**生產者套期保值**也廣為人知。美國商品期貨交易委員會發佈每週倉位的數據記錄，並在掉期數據存儲庫（Swap Data Repository）中進行報告，數據反映出該等套期保值的交易量。舉例，2016 年 11 月 29 日至 2016 年 12 月 6 日當週，ICE 布蘭特原油商業空頭增加，週度增加了 11.9 萬手（1.19 億桶），是該類別商品自 2011 年有記錄以來的第二大單週增幅[4]。這主要因為當時預計 OPEC 的產量協議會導致 2016 年末石油生產增加，同時美國以外的其他主要石油生產國也在增產。

除了絕對價格的水平，**期貨曲線的形狀**也會吸引生產者或消費者進行套期保值。一方面，對於消費者而言，隨着期限結構的加強（即期貨曲線上近期價格上漲幅度高於遠期價格），甚至當期貨曲線出現倒掛（即近期價格高於遠期價格），將遠期價格鎖定在低於近期價格的位置（即使不考慮倉儲成本對價差的影響）都具有吸引力。另一方面，對於生產者來說，若遠期價格高於近期價格，特別是如果價差看起來可能進一步擴大，而價格又高於生產成本的話，就會吸引生產者對沖。如上一節所述，倉儲成本是期貨曲線形狀和對沖活動的關鍵。

中國大宗商品市場參與者也越來越多地使用金融產品來降低價格風險。例如，

3　「認沽」期權是一種金融工具，允許期權持有人以預定價格和預定時間出售標的金融資產。當相關金融資產的價格低於預定價格時，行使該期權是有利可圖的。

4　資料來源：美國商品期貨交易委員會。

中國一家主要的銅生產商於 1992 年開始使用期貨市場進行套期保值,並且建立其下屬的期貨經紀公司為其作內部買賣。它的套期保值策略成功地幫助該公司渡過了 2008 年銅價暴跌時的艱難時期。中國金融市場(包括期貨市場)這些年來進一步發展擴大了可用的金融工具,並提高了中國公司對風險管理重要性的認識。例如從 2016 年 12 月到 2017 年 4 月 26 日,中國有 20 多家有色金屬公司披露了其 2017 年大宗商品期貨對沖計劃[5]。套期保值的大宗商品種類包括金,鋁,銅,鋅,錫和鎳。

　　農產品市場方面,生產者的套期保值也會受到月差(time spreads)和倉儲成本的影響。如同其他大宗商品進行套期保值一樣,農產品供應商需要在考慮庫存基礎上來管理和確保其現金流量。但是播種、收穫、裝載和交付都存在時滯,故生產者需要於整個過程中管理其成本和倉儲需求。例如,假設期貨曲線的前端(即近期價格)受到投資者頭寸變動和投機性交易活動的壓制,致使期現價差比倉儲成本大(近期價格遠低於遠期價格)。在這種情況下,生產者應在期貨曲線的遠端賣出合約以鎖定利潤。農業生產者還需考慮套期保值的時限,因為農產品保存不易,容易變質。

3　金融市場參與者的投資和交易活動

　　大宗商品的實物生產者和消費者的倉位大小與時限通常不會完全吻合,這就會引起風險溢價,為金融參與者提供成為交易對手的機會。就某些合約而言,生產者較消費者更常進行套期保值。這種「錯配」不僅顯現於(不匹配的)長倉 / 短倉合約的總數,也會顯現於期貨曲線的不同位置和單個合約中。例如,生產者主要用(賣出)短期和長期合約來對沖,而消費者則主要利用(買入)短期合約來對沖,很少用長期合約來對沖。因此,金融投資者除了可以從基本面角度的因素去做買

5　資料來源:新聞報導。

賣的決定，還可以利用這些錯配的機會來獲益。當庫存容量幾乎抽空或滿額時，利用倉儲套利的空間就會變得有限，從而引發「凸性」（convexity）可以被跨期阿爾法策略投資者（alpha investors）[6] 獲取。許多大宗商品也在需求（例如能源產品）或供應（例如農產品）方面表現出強烈的季節性特徵，使得避險需求和風險溢價體現出季節性。

以下分節討論通常按基本面觀點而為的主動管理，以及利用各種風險溢價套利的被動管理。

3.1　主動管理

主動管理（又稱積極管理）的經典案例是對價格做出單邊趨勢的判斷。如果交易者對某一商品的基本面分析指出其價格很大機會進一步上漲，他們可以買入該商品（持長倉），反之則持空倉。

由於地點、時間和商品質不同，同一商品的價格在不同地區及時間等會有所不同，從而帶來套利機會。交易者可以利用這些套利機會來獲益，同時提高市場效率。一些投資者可能較商品生產者和消費者更能獲取完備的資訊，從而可以預見到一些生產項目或市場發展的進程時間，而讓這些投資者較其他人對於商品的期現價差和區域價差有更好的把握。例如在美國的石油和天然氣行業中，一些投資者可以通過關注勘探和生產、中游、煉油和公用事業等多個環節，更好地了解生產進度和新管道上線的日期；通過整合這些資料和建立模型，深入分析行業內和跨行業的大量資訊，某些投資者會比市場其他參與者更有優勢。

美國的瓦哈天然氣（Waha Natural Gas）就是一個例子。2018 年初的前幾年，位於美國石油資源豐富的二疊紀盆地（Permian Basin）的瓦哈天然氣，與美國基準價格的亨利港天然氣（Henry Hub）價格的期貨基差跟歷史瓦哈現貨基差沒有太大差異。二疊紀盆地的個別勘探和生產公司即使非常了解自己公司的預期產量，但並不了解其他生產者的預期產量。假設投資者可以預測出石油和相關天然氣產量

6　「跨期阿爾法策略」利用期貨曲線的形狀和合同價格從某一個月度合約轉倉至另一月度合約（例如從第二個月轉倉至當月的合約）的價格轉變趨勢來套取利益。例如，當期貨曲線向後傾斜或處於逆向時，投資者將獲得正的轉倉收益。當臨近的合約到期時，由於期貨曲線逆向傾斜，因此投資者以較高的價格賣出，並以較低的價格購買了較遠期的合約。若曲線形狀得以持續且市場狀況得以維持，則該遠期合約在成為近期合約的過程中，價格將上漲，因此產生正向的轉倉收益。

大幅增長（通過各種分析和市場信息），同時可以看到天然氣管道容量不足以將所有天然氣帶出該地區，就可能會預測出瓦哈天然氣價格將可能會暴跌，甚至可能跌至負價。投資者可以根據這種觀點進行交易。這個例子說明，生產者和消費者即使對其本身的商品市場有充分認識，亦未必能對能源行業中的多個細分環節有足夠廣泛及 / 或深入的了解。在這情況之下，投資者可以憑藉出色的資訊和對行業的了解而跑贏大市。

3.2　被動投資

由於研究交文獻指出投資大宗商品可以提高經風險調整的收益率（risk-adjusted returns），一些相對被動的投資者可能單純將大宗商品作為一資產類別納入其資產配置之中。彭博商品指數（BCOM）和標準普爾商品指數（GSCI）等長倉指數是被動投資者對大宗商品作風險投資常用的工具，這些指數涵蓋能源，金屬和農產品。然而，由於簡單的長倉策略在大宗商品超級週期（牛市行情）結束後變得不再具有吸引力，因此投資者已轉向採納可以獲得市場平均收益甚至超額收益的策略，例如基於月間價差或季節性溢價的策略。

（1）大宗商品滾動策略的總收益

除了 BCOM 和 GSCI 等長倉指數之外，一些增強型被動大宗商品指數（enhanced passive commodity indices）還試圖通過投資最近月的期貨合約並以固定期限滾動（即轉倉）來模擬大宗商品的理論收益。例如當期貨曲線向上傾斜或處於升水時，投資者可能會獲得負的滾動收益。當臨近的合約「t」到期時，由於期貨曲線是向上傾斜的，因此投資者以較低的價格賣出此近期合約，並以較高的價格購買較遠期的「t+1」合約。若曲線形狀得以維持（即類似地向上傾斜）並且類似的市場狀況亦得以維持，則該遠期合約（即將成為近期合約）的價格應會下跌，因此產生負滾動收益。投資者可以通過做空這種負的滾動收益來從中獲利，反之亦然。

圖 1：總收益的構成 —— 即期收益和滾動收益

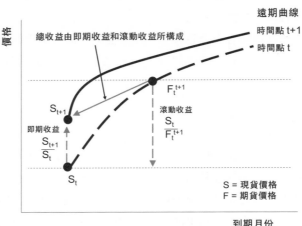

（2）風險溢價的季節性

　　季節性波動是大宗商品市場中風險溢價的主要來源之一。與許多金融市場不同，大宗商品期貨市場會帶有現貨市場具有的強烈季節性特徵與供需平衡之關係，例如各種能源商品的需求會表現出強烈的季節性變化。較冷的冬季天氣會刺激對採暖燃料的需求；煉油廠的定期檢修和重啟會導致其對原油的需求在一年中有週期性的上升與下降；而夏季則因空調和冰箱的使用通常會看到用電量的高峰。同樣，由於農作物週期不同，農產品的供應會出現季節性變化，北半球在秋季的收割季節通常會使穀物和其他農作物等軟性商品（soft commodities）的供應達致高峰。

　　此外，需求和供應的極端風險也可能在一年中的特定期間達到頂峰，例如異常寒冷的冬天可能會令對天然氣的需求極速增加。其他風險包括美國墨西哥灣沿岸的年度颶風季節，或乾旱的夏季會影響美國玉米收穫。由於這些季節性因素帶來的風險變化，對沖需求自然會集中在一年中的特定月份或期貨曲線的特定交割日期附近，故風險溢價（不論正或負）亦然。

　　投資者想要獲取季節性帶來的額外收益，就必須關注風險溢價的季節性，而這與現貨價格的季節性不同，區分這兩者很重要。風險溢價定義為期貨價格與預期的未來現貨價格之間的差額。若期貨價格低於預期的未來現貨價格，溢價風險會是正數。在這種情況下，投資者購買該期貨合約並等到到期日就可能獲得額外的回報。但若期貨價格高於預期的未來現貨價格，風險溢價則為負數。在這種情況下，買入期貨合約的投資者預期會虧損。若現貨價格的季節性已經在期貨曲線中體現出來，那麼就再沒有季節性的風險溢價可以攫取，投資者也就無法獲得額外收益。然而，量化季節性風險溢價是具有挑戰性的，因為很難直接觀察到預期的未來現貨價格，故亦無法知道風險溢價。縱使如此，從被動投資的角度來看，生產者和消費者的持續對沖行為可以使投資者捕捉到這樣的季節性風險溢價。從更主動的投資角度來看，投資者可以通過對供求基本面及其對價格的影響進行深入了解，從而額外攫取這些季節性風險溢價。

圖 2：現貨價格季節性高位時的負風險溢價

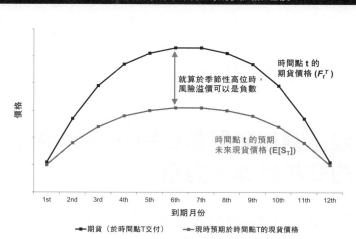

（3）通脹對沖

投資者經常利用大宗商品和其他實際資產來減少在預期之外的通貨膨脹對投資組合的實際回報所產生的負面影響，其效果卻會因所涉的資產類別和投資期間而異。當通貨膨脹在控制範圍內時，一般消費者（同樣也是投資者）不會過多注意其購買力的問題。但若通貨膨脹較高或投資期間延續多年時，投資者所持股票和債券等名義資產的購買力可能會嚴重受損，而大宗商品（主要是能源和食品）直接或間接構成美國市民大眾接近一半的「購物籃」，故會牽動通貨膨脹。

然而，區分預期內的通貨膨脹和預期外的通貨膨脹很重要。預期內的通貨膨脹通常已經反映在資產價格中，而預期外的通貨膨脹則沒有。有關通貨膨脹預期水平的調查和一些粗糙的衡量標準通常是短視和回顧性的[7]。但若有既知的固定的投資期間和風險承受能力水平，便能幫助拼湊一個最佳對沖通脹的投資組合。

構建合適的通脹對沖是一個複雜的過程，需要全面了解投資組合與通脹之間的關係。關鍵步驟如下：

- 評估個別的投資目標及其對非預期通脹的容忍度；
- 決定是轉而持有防禦通脹的股票／債券倉位，還是直接進行通脹對沖；
- 確定有潛力用作通脹對沖的資產類別，例如國債通脹保護證券（TIPS）、房地產投資信託基金（REITS）或大宗商品；
- 確定投資者在直接通脹對沖中的投資期間和風險承受能力；和
- 根據投資期間內每個潛在通脹對沖的各種風險和通脹對沖特徵而優化投資組合。

4 包括銀行和貿易公司在內的中介機構的交易促進者角色

由於商品生產者和消費者通常位於不同的地方，並具有不同的套期保值期限，因此中介機構可以在考慮運輸和貨運成本的基礎上幫助匹配大宗商品生產者和消費者，以達到交易的最佳組合。銀行和貿易公司在風險管理方面扮演類似的角色，例如為客戶進行套期保值，有時是貿易融資。然而，銀行傳統上在票據交易、衍生品和定制金融產品方面比較活躍；而貿易公司則更主要涉及實物商品的買賣交付，因為它們擁有更廣泛的物流網路以及上下游設施。

7　參見，例如，Axelrod 與 Sandor 等（2018）「美國家庭對通貨膨脹的認識和期望」（"Perceptions and expectations of inflation by U.S. households"），《金融與經濟討論叢刊》（*Finance and Economics Discussion Series*）2018-073，美國聯邦儲備系統理事會。

銀行作為做市商為市場提供流動性，有效促進價格形成，提供風險管理解決方案，以及從事項目融資和貿易融資。作為做市商，銀行將買賣雙方聚集在市場中，並承擔一定的價格風險。一些銀行也參與實體（現貨）大宗商品市場，但通常只限於幫助生產者和消費者做套期保值。由於大宗商品的運輸佔用了公司相當部份的營運資金，銀行也會提供營運資金解決方案。可是因為監管愈趨嚴格，尤其是 2008 年全球金融危機之後，使銀行對實物資產的持有和在實體市場的參與均受到更大的限制。當銀行業成為現代全球金融中不可或缺的組成部份、並且成為金融與實體經濟之間的橋樑時，制定法規的目標之一是減少銀行可以承擔的不必要風險。銀行不僅從事貿易融資，而且還參與項目融資，通過信貸擴張來幫助基礎設施項目融資。

舉一個實例說明銀行作為中介的作用。例如，中國的一家空調生產商可能希望在未來一年內出於預算目的對沖銅價風險，而智利的一家銅礦開採者可能也希望對沖銅價，但其為資本投資作對沖的期間為五年。這裏消費者和生產者所需產品（製成的銅產品與銅礦）在不同時間、期限和地理位置的錯配，就催生了對市場中介的需求。這種情況下其他的市場參與者，例如具有長期對沖意願的企業消費者和看好銅價的投資者，都可以利用中介完成匹配。在這一過程中，銀行可幫助促成不同市場參與者的交易活動。

銀行密切參與貿易融資和商品交易，皆因商品從賣方 A 到買方 B 的運輸通常涉及許多其他參與運輸和倉儲的交易對手。例如，進口商（即買方）的銀行會向出口商（即賣方）的銀行簽發信用證（Letter of Credit），這是對買方在滿足出口商協議條款後的商品付款能力的確認；而出口商則需要出示通常稱為提貨單（Bill of Lading）的單據，以證明已經將商品裝運。

銀行還提供其他各類型的融資服務。這些包括在美國頁岩油氣項目中常見的基於儲備的借貸（reserve-based lending）、建築融資、債務融資（例如銀行定期貸款和債券市場私募）、夾層融資（夾層債務和租賃）、集合融資（倒置租賃和資產證券化），以及有限合夥制（master limited partnership）等。融資交易還可能包括衍生品套期保值（利率、外匯、商品、電力），以鎖定商品生產的現金流或消費成本。例如，在 Y 國的一個可再生能源項目有一來自 X 國的外國投資者，這投資者可能既希望通過債務融資來提供為購買該項目所需的資金，又希望可以進行衍生品對沖來確保未來的現金流。由於這是一次跨境購買，未來的收入可能會從 Y 國匯回 X 國，因此衍生品對沖的類型可能包括融資債務的利率、項目未來現金流的外匯、可再生能源項目的電價，甚至可能使用天然氣作為 X 國長期電力價格的替代對沖。

除了以上討論的交易類型外，所涉及的交易有時也可能產生於投資銀行業務部門的併購業務或商業銀行部的借貸業務。例如，幫助 A 公司購買 B 公司的銀行可以向 A 公司貸款或協助其發行證券融資。但是為了保障其貸款，銀行可能會要求 A 公司對 B 公司的國內外生產進行對沖，以確保現金流，這可能涉及對沖利率、外匯和商品生產。

由於在 2008 年全球金融危機之後的監管要求越發趨嚴，銀行通常不再從事自營交易業務（自營業務涉及使用公司自身的資產負債表和資本進行交易），而是主要協助客戶進行交易。對於面對監管環境較為為寬鬆的貿易公司而言，自營交易則為其主要業務（見以下的討論）。

與在商品金融方面較活躍的銀行不同，商品貿易公司通常在現貨商品世界中更為活躍，充當中介人的角色，將生產者（賣方）和消費者（買方）聯繫起來。這涉及配對不同地點、不同時區（或期限長短）和不同產品需求（買賣雙方的需求錯配）的交易。對於貿易公司而言，規模對其運營業務很重要，因為這使得它們可以更好地尋找交易對手、收集市場情報，以及隨着利潤率下降而須增加收入。在每日大約 1 億桶規模的全球原油市場中，一些最大的商品交易商每天可單獨交易 500 至 1,000 萬桶原油和石油產品，像殼牌和英國石油公司在內的一些大型能源公司自己的貿易部門也像貿易公司一樣運作。貿易公司交易量的增長也與市場的增長緊密相關。貿易公司也在不斷探索新的貿易機會。例如，隨着原油業務利潤的收窄，液化天然氣由於其在不同地區之間的價格差異較大，其貿易自 2018 年以來一直在迅速擴張。實體貿易公司的強項在於他們可以通過自身的資源和網路了解長期分散的區域天然氣市場的供求基本面。他們在全球範圍內有能力調動油輪及運輸其他商品的船隻，可以容易地應用於液化天然氣的海上運輸上。

在現貨商品市場中，貿易公司還可以根據不同地點、時間跨度和產品質量來匹配市場供求。貿易公司還可以通過與原材料生產商的直接關係和承購協議來提供採購服務。它也具有儲存能力（例如在運輸前將鐵礦石儲存六個月，以配合鋼廠所需的時間）。它可以提供混礦服務（例如將不同種類的巴西礦加以混合以滿足買方的品位要求）和物流網路（例如使用鐵路車、卡車、駁船和就乾散貨船將鐵礦石從貿易公司的倉庫運往客戶）。與銀行相比，對於貿易公司的監管要求是寬鬆得多，因此利用現貨市場交易活動和信息操作的自營交易往往是其核心業務。

　　以下是一例子説明貿易公司如何促使生產者與消費者之間的交易。中國的一家鋼廠可能希望在八個月後生產達到峰值時購買特定品位的鐵礦石用於其鋼鐵生產，而巴西的一家鐵礦石生產商則希望現在將其開採的礦石出售給市場。中國的鐵礦石消費者和巴西的生產者不一定彼此認識，亦位於不同國家，其購買／銷售的時間段略有不同，並且對礦石品位的需求也不同。作為市場中介的貿易公司往往可以位處整個供應鏈以連接買方和賣方，並將所需的產品交付給買方。在此示例中，他們需要將商品（鐵礦石）從巴西運到中國（地點匹配），通過將鐵礦石存放在自有倉庫中來保證交貨時間（時間匹配），並通過混礦來滿足中國鋼鐵廠的需求。

　　舉另一個例子：如果汽車製造商在六個月後需要鋁，並且願意為將來的接貨支付溢價，那麼具有實物交易能力的市場參與者（即貿易商）可以通過使用現貨和期貨價差來獲利。市場參與者可以以今天的價格（例如每噸 1,500 美元）購買鋁，而在期貨市場上以溢價（例如汽車製造商同意以每噸 1,600 美元）出售，到期日為六個月後。在六個月這期間內，中介商（在本例中為貿易公司）可以以相對較低的成本在自己的倉庫中儲存鋁（假設每噸倉儲成本為 50 美元），從而獲利。

5　選擇正確的價格基準

5.1　價格基準賴以成功的條件

　　價格是將金融和現貨市場中所有市場參與者聯繫在一起的關鍵，因此選擇和使用正確的價格基準至關重要。價格基準得以成功需要一些特定的條件。

　　許多亞洲國家對所謂的大宗商品價格中的「亞洲溢價」，特別是能源價格方面的溢價表示不滿。在原油市場裏，一些政府和市場參與者認為，建立本地或區域性商品合約可以消除所謂的「亞洲溢價」，並且可以促進更加透明的價格發現，特別是當亞洲地區的大宗商品消費佔全球總需求的巨大份額時。這些政府和市場參與者認為現在沒有可用的合約來反映亞洲的市場基本面。能源價格現在主要由北美和歐洲的交易所主導，儘管亞洲的需求和交易活動激增，但是卻沒有能反映亞洲基本面的價格指數。在一些市場參與者看來，就連中東的阿曼和迪拜原油也不是很好的價格基準，因為中東出口商採用複雜的價格計算方程式，似乎在公平的市場價格上添加溢價。

然而，重要的是要分清下列兩種概念：擁有定價權和使價格更準確地反映區域基本面。擁有期貨交易所和能源合約（最理想的是它們具有很高的流動性），並不意味着該交易所的主體國家會對能源價格有更大的決定權，因為價格應該反映市場供求關係。具有良好流動性的期貨合約應更準確地反映區域基本面，但這不會給東道國帶來對基準價格的額外定價能力。

事實上，價格基準得以成功被採納為全球基準，至少在其初期都擁有下述特徵。總體而言，要將一大宗商品（例如石油）合約融入到全球市場中，該合約必須證明其價值並體現出比其他品種（例如迪拜作為中等含硫原油的基準）更優勝。就石油而言，以下特徵就能讓一期貨合約確保其標的物原油的流動性、一致性和競爭力，從而使市場參與者對所交付的產品抱有信心，以及確保價格不會受到操縱：

- **高交易量：** 有足夠的數量進行交易，並且已經有大量的買賣雙方可以支持現貨銷售和非正式的遠期市場。
- **產品質量一致：** 買家需要確定他們可以使用和定價這種油，而產品的質量經年累月都保持一致。如果質量發生變化，則煉出的成品油的成份會有不同，相對應原有油品的價值也不同。「啞鈴化」的混合原油也不甚可取，因為平均原油質量可能看起來相同，但其成品油產出會有所不同，例如原本的原油可以產生更多的中間餾份的成品油，但混合方式的原油則會煉出更多輕質和重質的成品油。
- **供應安全：** 市場希望石油供應能得到保證，會有充足的石油持續供應。
- **市場參與者的多樣性：** 原油的定價必須有競爭力，確保沒有參與者（包括活躍的買賣雙方在內）擁有過大的市場力量來扭曲價格。
- **獲廣泛接受：** 市場參與者必須對原油能夠廣泛交易抱有信心，以及對其廣被接納為可代表其所擁有的等級和來源地的原油亦抱有信心。

- **合同的不可侵犯性及法治：**歸根結底，對於市場參與者而言，重要的是要能夠回本，不會受到市場不公平的對待。畢竟，市場參與者在市場上是為了賺錢，不是為了賠錢。

- **對清算機制的信心：**易於交易以及對交易過程的信心對於吸引參與者進入市場十分重要。整個過程還包括處理交易清算的能力，收集和維持保證金的能力、資金的安全性，以及順暢與可信賴的儲存和交付過程。

- **貨幣的完全可自由兌換：**這與上述一脈相通，若市場有資本管制或貨幣不可完全自由兌換會降低市場參與者進入市場的意願，因為這可導致最終無法將獲利匯回。

　　在原油市場上，布蘭特原油於 1980 年代初表現出上述所有這些特質。但當其交易量開始下降時，其他原油品種就加入市場。最初有質量相似的兩種產品，即 Forties 和 Oseberg，建成了 Brent-Forties-Oseberg（BFO）的組合以增強整體交易量。後來又添加了 Ekofisk 等級，從而形成了 Brent-Forties-Oseberg-Ekofisk（BFOE）的組合。當 Forties 首次與來自 Buzzard 油田的原油混合時，混合後的原油變得更酸，使得 Forties 變成四個原油組成部份（Brent、Forties、Oseberg、Ekofisk）中價格最低的等級。

　　西德克薩斯洲中等質量石油（WTI）也具有上述價格基準的一些特質，但由於其內陸性和最初無法出口，尤其是存在於 2012 年開始的頁岩油熱潮所引發的生產過剩和基礎設施等問題，從表面上看，它應不能成為一個好的全球價格基準。然而，其相應期貨交易量支持其巨大的流動性克服了這些挑戰。紐約商品交易所（NYMEX）選擇 WTI 作為其期貨合約的主要交付原油，主要是出於運營原因。廣泛的管道網路確保了國內的供應分佈夠廣，而巨大的交易量和流動性使價格能夠迅速反映基本面的變化，從而提高價格透明度。可是自頁岩油快速發展以來，儘管 WTI 價格在全球已然舉足輕重，但由於管道和出口的限制，WTI 價格仍會不時與其他全球原油價格相差甚遠 —— 由於這些限制，布蘭特 /WTI 價差於 2012 年末擴大至每桶近 30 美元 [8]，之後對出口限制的放寬極大地幫助消除了這些價差錯位。然而，即使美國出口大幅增長，WTI 也很難像布蘭特原油那樣成為全球價格基準。

8　資料來源：彭博。

5.2 亞洲的案例

出於各種原因，亞洲還沒有一個較佳的價格基準。在石油貿易中，布蘭特、WTI 和迪拜均位於生產區附近，因此生產商和消費者都可以對沖，但迪拜的交易仍比布蘭特和 WTI 少得多。如今，迪拜原油主要以布蘭特和迪拜的差價方式用於低含硫原油與高含硫原油的價差交易。在亞洲市場裏，馬來西亞的 Tapis 和印尼的 Minas 由於生產量和現貨銷售量較少，並且只有幾家公司控制生產（所以不具高度競爭性），限制了兩者成為有效的價格基準。雖然可以以某一消費國的合約作為價格基準，例如一些成熟的商品交易所如倫敦金屬交易所（LME）就位處交易活躍的消費國，然而在石油交易中這是否可行是存在疑問的。

在亞洲，一個有趣的案例是大連鐵礦石合約；它在全球最大的進口和消費國（中國）市場上推出。自 2013 年推出以來，吸引了大量國內資金，尤其是在 2016 年上半年，當時該合約成為全球交易量最高的十大商品期貨合約之一[9]。與上海石油合約中的混合原油情況類似，大連商品交易所（簡稱「大商所」）的鐵礦石合約允許以廣泛的鐵礦石品種作交付，從 65% 的卡拉加斯礦粉到 61% 的羅伊山礦粉，都可用來交付，大部份可交付的產品會有相應的溢價或折扣。大商所已將鐵礦石合約的交易開放給境外參與者。

但大商所鐵礦石合約的一些特徵值得注意。它吸引了大量的散戶投機資金，而且現貨合約在結算時的價格與活躍交易的合約價格之間存在差異。由於大量的投機買賣與高頻交易，大商所鐵礦石的每日交易量一直高於未平倉合約量，這現象與中國許多其他工業金屬期貨合約的情況相似，但就有別於其他全球交易的金屬合約。

大商所鐵礦石合約的活躍交易是否有助中國在鐵礦石現貨市場上獲得定價權尚有爭議。一方面，在過去幾年中，大商所合約在價格發現方面一直領先於其離岸對手，即新加坡交易所（簡稱「新交所」）的鐵礦石掉期合約。大商所提供的夜間交易，亦有助其在白天交易時段之後也可以繼續進行價格發現。另一方面，我們認為中國鐵礦石定價能力的提高主要歸因於中國在現貨市場中的主導地位 —— 中國是全球最大的消費國，佔全球鐵礦海上進口量的 70%[10]。就算沒有大商所合約，

9　資料來源：彭博。

10　資料來源：基於全球貿易資訊服務（GTIS）提供各國進出口數據所得。

中國於鐵礦的定價能力也會提高。但是大商所鐵礦石合約的確也得益於全球其他地區缺乏有力的合約。鐵礦石市場中的參與者很廣泛，有比較均衡的套期保值資金量來增加市場流動性，即使這種套期保值交易量與投機流量相比仍然很小。鐵礦石的主要做市商包括大型鋼鐵廠和實物交易公司。鐵礦石市場的現貨流動性也相當大，通常有大量礦石位於中國港口，其中相當一部份有資格交付大商所合約。最後，鐵礦石合約從一樣有活躍交易的鋼和焦煤合約中將流動性吸引過來，特別是投機流量，這使市場參與者能夠進行「相對價值」策略的交易，包括與鋼廠利潤相關的交易。

　　全球投資者和現貨參與者的參與對於期貨合約的成功至關重要。可靠的價格基準不應與全球其他價格基準大幅偏離，除非受到基本面供需的約束 —— 例如布蘭特 /WTI 的價差就由於管道運輸的問題擴大至每桶近 30 美元（參見上文第 5.1 節）。同時值得注意的是僅僅有大量國內投機者進行合約交易並不一定會使此合約成為成功反映市場基本面、可作基準的可行合約。事實上，國內投機者既可大量增加流動性，也可破壞其流動性。

　　交易者和套期保值者通常會選擇買賣最具流動性的合約。例如，NYMEX 擁有布蘭特合約，但交易量很少，因為布蘭特原油交易主要集中於美國洲際交易所（ICE）。回顧過去，即使在逐步淘汰了含鉛汽油之後，貿易商也主要使用含鉛普通汽油合約（始於 1980 年代，用於交易和對沖汽油）。儘管有無鉛汽油合約可用，但在交易所停止了含鉛汽油合約的交易之前其流動性仍然很低。

　　對於中國內地的交易所而言，適當的流動性和市場參與度有助推進其發展。一些內地交易所的交易量非常高，但主要來自本地乃至與實體現貨市場沒有多少聯繫的日間交易者（投機者）。實體現貨市場中真實的買賣雙方需要通過本地交易所進行套期保值的交易以助其風險管理，其所需交易的商品種類會是市場中最普遍供應和消費的類別（如石油）。這突顯了價格基準條件裏的「品質一致性」、「供應安全」和「獲廣泛接受」的重要性。由於中國是大宗商品主要進口國，國際供應商就需要參與進來進行套期保值。在這層面上，市場參與者的多樣性、合約的不可侵犯性、法治、對清算機制的信心，以及貨幣的完全可兌換性則顯得重要。參與當地市場交易的大宗商品消費者通常是本地商業機構，但許多生產者（賣家）卻分佈於全球，這就需要賣家對跨境交易、接收收益和當地法律體系的公平性感到

非常有信心，才會參與當地市場。因此，在這些方面實施強而有力的政策支持會
幫助促進國際參與者（至少會考慮）於內地市場進行交易。在某些情況下，這些基
礎和機制無可避免地會受到考驗和壓力，如何處理這些問題是證明內地交易所的
健全性和吸引力的關鍵。

6 結論

　　大宗商品從古至今都是經濟活動的基礎，生產者製造以供消費者之用。儘管
從理論上來說，實物商品的生產者和消費者應是彼此的自然交易對手，但它們的
套期保值時間、計劃期、地點、生產或消費的商品的質量與數量等方面都會有所
差異，這就讓銀行和貿易公司等中介機構，以及投資者有機會參與其中，將雙方
連接在一起，整合成完整的市場。倉儲本身可以用來彌補供需的錯配，但大多數
生產者和消費者很難自發配對，在適當的地點和適當的時間形成適當的交易組合。
例如，生產商的主要業務是生產某種商品，他們可能更願意進行長期套期保值；
而對大宗商品消費者而言，商品成本可能僅構成其總運營成本的一部份，所以他
們可能只對短期套期保值感興趣。這些時間、地點、商品質量等級和數量上的不
匹配為投資者和中介機構提供了套利的空間。貿易公司通常提供服務以彌合現貨
市場方面的差異，而銀行通常彌合金融方面的差異，同時幫助金融投資者攫取由
生產者或消費者的套期保值所產生的風險溢價。

　　對所有市場參與者來說，為相關的大宗商品使用正確的價格基準對於價格發
現、交易和套期保值至關重要，而大宗商品交易所可以促進這些交易。於交易所
市場上較成功的價格基準，至少在初期階段均有某些相同的特徵，才能成為全球
性的價格基準。這些特徵包括：交易量大、商品質量穩定、供應安全、市場參與
者多樣化、獲廣泛接受、合約的不可侵犯性、法治，對清算機制的信心，以及貨
幣的完全可自由兌換。這些條件也是確保中國內地交易所邁向成功的基礎。

第5章

全球大宗商品衍生產品市場概覽

香港交易及結算所有限公司
首席中國經濟學家辦公室

摘 要

　　大宗商品是指可供公眾買賣而供應相當同質化的實物資產，主要種類包括貴金屬、基本金屬（即非貴金屬）、農產品及能源產品。大宗商品的交易是指於實物（現貨）市場買賣大宗商品，同時亦包括買賣大宗商品衍生產品，當中既有交易所場內的標準化期貨及期權產品，也有場外的非標準化產品（例如掉期產品）。

　　過去十年，場內大宗商品衍生產品的交易呈現上升趨勢，伴隨的是亞洲區交易所的市場份額不斷增加。原因包括：（1）全球經濟增長，大宗商品貿易對沖的需求增加；（2）於組合投資中使用大宗商品衍生產品來對沖投資於股本證券及債券等金融產品的風險或單純用作投資用途的趨勢有所增加；及（3）內地經濟的崛起進一步推動全球商品貿易的增長及相關的對沖需求，而內地大宗商品交易所的交易活動於全球市場愈益舉足輕重。

　　全球超過一半的衍生產品交易所都有提供大宗商品的衍生產品，多數為期貨。大宗商品以產品數目計，領先的是歐美成熟市場，而成交量方面則是內地大宗商品衍生產品交易所佔優。大宗商品的四大類別中有三類（貴金屬、非貴金屬及農產品）按2019年成交量的交易所排名，三家內地交易所中至少有一家位列全球三甲。內地交易所僅於能源產品方面較為遜色，而能源產品卻佔據了全球大宗商品衍生產品的大部份成交量（主要來自原油期貨）。況且海外參與者參與內地大宗商品衍生產品市場仍有很大限制，只有少量指定產品開放給海外參與者。換句話說，內地交易所的高成交量基本上都是來自境內參與者。與西方成熟市場相比，內地交易所的大宗商品合約單位通常較小，成交周轉率亦相對較高。

　　隨着內地交易所進一步開放發展，全球大宗商品衍生產品市場的格局自當會不斷演變。

1　甚麼是大宗商品？甚麼是大宗商品衍生產品？

大宗商品的一個基本經濟定義，就是來自天然資源的實物商品，可供公眾買賣及其供應是相當同質化[1]。大宗商品包含許多不同的資產類別，涵蓋不同的產業，包括貴金屬、工業用或基本金屬、能源、禽畜及穀物以及其他農產品（通常稱為「軟商品」，即生產方式為養殖或種植（而非天然提取或開採）的大宗商品）。

大宗商品為實物資產，與股本證券及債券等金融資產不同。金融資產是按資產預期現金流的折現值進行估值，而大宗商品是按實物資產未來可能形成的價格（按實物資產供求等因素計算）的折現預測進行估值[2]。

衍生產品是一種證券，其價值衍生自所掛鈎的資產或一組資產（基準）。衍生產品的形式通常包括期貨、遠期、期權及掉期[3]。大宗商品衍生產品指的是以大宗商品或大宗商品基準為掛鈎資產的衍生產品，通常被商品生產商及消費者用以對沖掛鈎商品的未來價格變動。另外會有利用掛鈎大宗商品價格變動進行投機的投機者，以及利用市場失效的因素（例如市場之間的價格效率有缺失）來謀取利益的套戥者，亦會買賣大宗商品衍生產品。

大宗商品的交易是指於實物（現貨）市場買賣大宗商品，同時亦包括於場內或場外買賣大宗商品衍生產品。在衍生產品交易所買賣的是標準化的大宗商品期貨及期權合約，而非標準化的遠期、期權及掉期產品則於場外進行交易。大宗商品投資者亦可選擇投資於證券交易所提供的大宗商品結構性產品，包括「交易所買賣大宗商品」（ETC），即追蹤掛鈎商品指數（以單一或一組大宗商品為基礎）表現的交易所買賣基金（ETF）；以及反映掛鈎商品或商品指數價格變動的大宗商品差價合約（CFD）。

1　資料來源：特許金融分析師協會（CFA）網站（https://www.cfainstitute.org）。

2　資料來源：同上。

3　期貨合約是交易雙方為以協定的價格在未來某個日期購買及交收某項資產而訂立的協議。期貨合約於交易所進行買賣，條款標準化。遠期合約與期貨合約類似，但合約條款為買賣雙方磋商而定的條款，並於場外（而非於交易所）進行買賣。期權合約是雙方之間的協議，以特定的價格在未來某個日期買賣資產，但到該未來日期當天，期權買方不一定要行使其購買或出售資產的權利。掉期合約是用一種現金流交換另一種現金流的協議。大宗商品掉期亦是掉期產品的一種，其現金流取決於掛鈎商品的價格。掉期產品的交易通常於場外進行。

大宗商品衍生產品的場外交易以往相當活躍。然而，自 2008 年年中爆發全球金融危機，揭露了場外衍生產品市場不受監管及不透明的嚴重問題後，大宗商品衍生產品的場外交易便大幅減少，這有別於大宗商品衍生產品場內交易的穩定增長。下文將探討全球大宗商品衍生產品的交易趨勢。

1.1　場外大宗商品衍生產品的交易

圖 1 及圖 2 顯示 1998 年 6 月底至 2019 年 6 月底的 21 年間未平倉的場外大宗商品衍生產品的合計名義金額及合計總市值 [4]（根據國際清算銀行 (BIS) 的半年度場外衍生產品統計數據）。場外大宗商品衍生產品的名義金額及總市值於 2004 年年底之後急升，至 2008 年 6 月達到高峰，然後於 2008 年出現的全球金融危機之後的數年間大幅回落。

圖 1：場外大宗商品衍生產品的合計名義金額（1998 年 6 月至 2019 年 6 月）

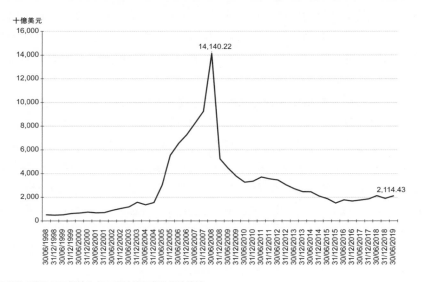

資料來源：載於 BIS 網站的 BIS 場外衍生產品統計數據。

4　根據 BIS 統計數據的定義，未平倉合約的總市值（gross market value）所反映的，是萬一市場參與者所有對手方均未有支付合約付款而要按報告日期的市價取替合約時，對市場參與者所可能招致的最大損失。

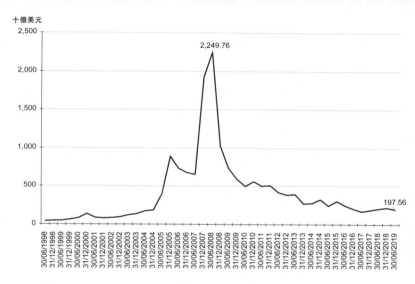

圖 2：場外大宗商品衍生產品的合計總市值（1998 年 6 月至 2019 年 6 月）

資料來源：載於 BIS 網站的 BIS 場外衍生產品統計數據。

　　場外大宗商品衍生產品交易之前的急升，是伴隨着 2007 年美國爆發次貸危機、房地產泡沫爆破後的大宗商品價格（例如油價）飆升。究其原因，可能是房地產及其他投資的投機性資金流入大宗商品，及/或全球急速發展使市場憂慮原材料短缺，令相關市場紛紛出現長倉。然而，2008 年的全球金融危機暴露了場外市場缺乏透明度的問題，市場在金融危機後進行一系列的監管改革之後，場外大宗商品衍生產品市場進一步作出標準化，並更傾向對場外大宗商品合約進行中央結算[5]。

　　根據國際掉期與衍生工具協會（ISDA）的資料，場外大宗商品衍生產品市場的標準化程度已相當高。幾乎所有場外大宗商品衍生產品的交易均按標準法律條款進行，這些標準法律條款一般為雙方協定的 ISDA 主協議中所載的條款或（就部份情況而言）有關國家的同等條款。絕大部份合約均透過「確認對盤平台」以電子

5　資料來源：《場外大宗商品衍生產品交易程序生命周期事紀》（*OTC Commodity Derivatives Trade Processing Lifecycle Events*），國際掉期與衍生工具協會（ISDA）白皮書，2012 年 4 月。該白皮書亦是本節所載的場外大宗商品衍生產品市場的資料來源。

方式確認。透過產品模板化及於大部份非經濟界別採用市場慣例標準，交易其實非常標準化。行業框架現已使交易在條款定制化的同時仍可享有標準化基礎設施帶來的好處。

場外大宗商品衍生產品市場的交易流程已採用極高水平的直通式處理模式，包括使用電子交易記錄系統、透過確認對盤平台確認交易，以至採用中央交易對手方（CCP）結算。非中央結算的交易亦廣泛採用雙邊抵押品安排。大宗商品期貨、期權及遠期產品交易中有很高比例於交易所進行，並透過 CCP 進行結算。不少交易所均為場外交易提供 CCP 服務。交易所旗下為大宗商品衍生產品交易提供有關場外結算服務的結算所包括：ICE Clear（油氣產品、原油、煤、排放物等）、CME ClearPort（天然氣、基本金屬、貴金屬、油品、原油、農產品等）及 LCH.Clearnet（基本金屬、貴金屬、塑膠產品、貨運、鐵礦石等）。另外，透過經紀、報價機構、電子交易平台或確認服務以及結算所等各式市場機構，交易前及交易後的透明度都相當高。

1.2　場內大宗商品衍生產品的交易

大宗商品以衍生產品的形式（一般為期貨及期權）於全球交易所進行買賣。根據美國期貨業協會（FIA）的分類，場內期貨及期權的掛鈎大宗商品資產分為四大類——貴金屬、非貴金屬（即基本金屬）、農產品及能源產品。這些衍生產品以實物商品為掛鈎資產，不同於金融衍生產品的掛鈎資產類別（包括股本證券（指數及個股）、利率及貨幣）。

圖 3 及圖 4 顯示 2009 年至 2019 年間全球各資產類別的場內衍生產品年度成交量及年末未平倉合約量的增長趨勢。按成交量及未平倉合約量計，股本證券衍生產品均貢獻最大，但大宗商品衍生產品的佔比亦見上升，於成交量的佔比由 2009 年的 12% 升至 2019 年的 18%，同期於未平倉合約量的佔比則由 8% 升至 11%（見圖 5）。值得注意的是，因其於成交量及未平倉合約量佔比的差距，大宗商品衍生產品的周轉率（於一段期間內的成交量相對於期末未平倉合約量的比率）較金融衍生產品的周轉率為高，並由 2009 年的 38% 攀升至 2019 年的 66%（見圖 6）。

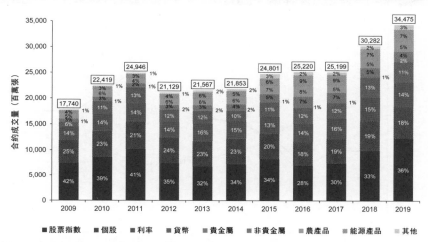

圖 3：全球交易所所有衍生產品的年度成交量（按資產類別劃分）（2009 年至 2019 年）

■股票指數　■個股　■利率　■貨幣　■貴金屬　■非貴金屬　■農產品　■能源產品　■其他

資料來源：FIA 月度統計數據（各年的 12 月份報告）。

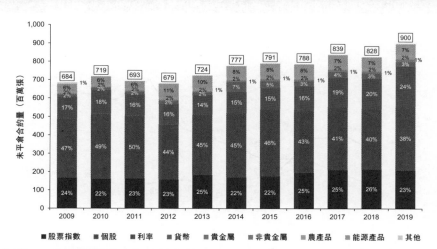

圖 4：全球交易所所有衍生產品的年末未平倉合約量（按資產類別劃分）
（2009 年至 2019 年）

■股票指數　■個股　■利率　■貨幣　■貴金屬　■非貴金屬　■農產品　■能源產品　■其他

資料來源：FIA 月度統計數據（各年的 12 月份報告）。

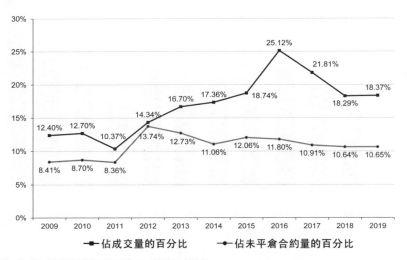

圖 5：大宗商品衍生產品於全球衍生產品成交量及未平倉合約量的佔比
（2009 年至 2019 年）

資料來源：按 FIA 月度統計數據（各年的 12 月份報告）計算。

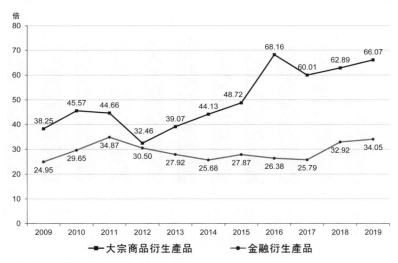

圖 6：大宗商品衍生產品與金融衍生產品的周轉率（2009 年至 2019 年）

資料來源：按 FIA 月度統計數據（各年的 12 月份報告）計算。

在大宗商品衍生產品所佔比率及周轉率逐步增長的同時，亞洲交易所在全球衍生產品的成交量及未平倉合約量的佔比亦不斷增加 —— 於成交量的佔比由 2009 年的 35% 升至 2019 年的 42%，於未平倉合約量的佔比由 2009 年的 4% 升至 2019 年的 9%（見圖 7 及圖 8）。

圖 7：全球交易所所有衍生產品的年度成交量（按地區劃分）（2009 年至 2019 年）

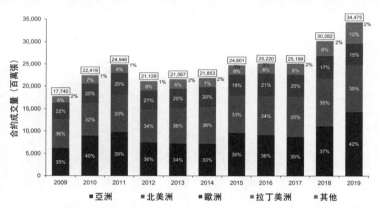

資料來源：FIA 月度統計數據（各年的 12 月份報告）。

圖 8：全球交易所所有衍生產品的年末未平倉合約量（按地區劃分）（2009 年至 2019 年）

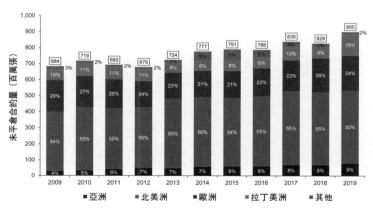

資料來源：FIA 月度統計數據（各年的 12 月份報告）。

　　將數據進一步分析，更可見到 2009 年至 2019 年間，亞洲交易所在全球大宗商品衍生產品成交量中的佔比於 55% 左右的水平上落（最高為 2016 年的 61%），但其於未平倉合約量中的佔比卻由 9% 大幅增加至 20%（見圖 9 及圖 10）。期內亞洲區交易所的大宗商品衍生產品成交量及未平倉合約量的複合年均增長率分別達 111% 及 114%，超越美洲的交易所並與歐洲的交易所相若[6]。

圖 9：全球交易所大宗商品衍生產品的年度成交量（按地區劃分）（2009 年至 2019 年）

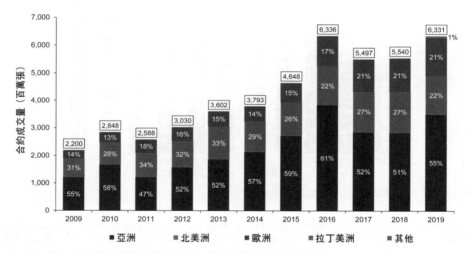

註：不包括 FIA 統計數據中歸類為「其他」的產品（涉及的資產類別包括大宗商品及非大宗商品）。
資料來源：FIA 月度統計數據（各年的 12 月份報告）。

6　期內各地區交易所的成交量及未平倉合約量的複合年均增長率如下：北美洲為 108% 及 101%，拉丁美洲為 104% 及 103%，歐洲為 116% 及 115%。資料來源：按 FIA 統計數據計算。

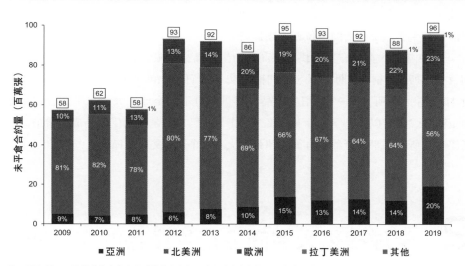

圖 10：全球交易所大宗商品衍生產品的年末未平倉合約量（按地區劃分）
（2009 年至 2019 年）

註：不包括 FIA 統計數據中歸類為「其他」的產品（涉及的資產類別包括大宗商品及非大宗商品）。

資料來源：FIA 月度統計數據（各年的 12 月份報告）。

　　大宗商品衍生產品交易活動及亞洲區交易所所佔比率同見增長，主要原因有三：

　　（1）全球經濟增長 —— 全球經濟的增長自然刺激大宗商品的生產、消費使用及貿易增長，令大宗商品生產商及消費者利用大宗商品衍生產品對沖其實物商品倉盤的需要越來越大。對沖活動增多，大宗商品衍生產品交易自然增加。

　　（2）組合投資使用大宗商品衍生產品的趨勢上升[7] —— 全球投資者可利用大宗商品衍生產品對沖其股本證券或債券投資的風險，或在低息環境下尋求較高回報。此外，大宗商品投資工具（例如大宗商品期貨指數基金）的供應不斷增加，投資者隨時可以將這些產品加入其全球性投資組合，增加其投資資產的類別。

　　（3）內地經濟及內地大宗商品交易所的崛起 —— 中國內地已是全球經濟增長

7　見 Parantap Basu 與 William T. Gavin（2011）〈大宗商品衍生產品增長的原因為何？〉（"What explains the growth in commodity derivatives?"），《聖路易斯聯邦儲備銀行評論》（*Federal Reserve Bank of St. Louis Review*），2011 年 1 月／2 月。

的主要動力。截至 2018 年止的十年間，內地的國內生產總值年均實際增長率達
12.7%，大幅高於全球經濟的 3.5%[8]，2010 年已超越日本成為全球第二大經濟體[9]。
其間，除經濟增長外，為應對內地大宗商品行業日益增長的對沖需求，內地的大
宗商品衍生產品交易所的地位亦不斷提高。

2009 年時，內地三家提供大宗商品衍生產品交易服務的期貨交易所 —— 上海
期貨交易所（簡稱「上期所」）、鄭州商品交易所（簡稱「鄭商所」）及大連商品交易
所（簡稱「大商所」）—— 的衍生產品成交量都打不入全球十大，未平倉合約量方
面更落在二十名以外[10]。十年後，該三家交易所已成為全球衍生產品成交量最高的
三家交易所，未平倉合約量方面亦位列十大。（詳見下文第 3 節。）

2 全球提供大宗商品衍生產品的交易所

截至 2019 年年底，全球有 83 家交易所向 FIA 匯報衍生產品數據，當中涉及
大宗商品衍生產品的佔 45 家，合共提供 1,463 隻大宗商品衍生產品[11]（見表 1），其
中大部份為期貨（1,162 隻，佔總數 79%），少數是期權。在大宗商品資產四大類
別中，能源產品佔數最多，共 876 隻，佔總數 60%（佔期貨 63%，佔期權 46%）；
其次為農產品，共 308 隻，佔總數 21%（佔期貨 18%，佔期權 34%）。提供大宗商
品期貨的交易所數目（44 家）較提供大宗商品期權的交易所數目（28 家）為多。非
貴金屬產品的數量最少（24 隻期貨及期權），有提供這類產品的交易所亦佔數最少
（17 家）。

8　資料來源：Wind。

9　資料來源：〈中國取代日本成為全球第二大經濟體〉（"China overtakes Japan as world's second-biggest
　　economy"），BBC 網站的《BBC 新聞》（*BBC News*），2011 年 2 月 14 日。

10　資料來源：有關排名是根據 FIA 月度統計數據（2009 年 12 月份報告）所得。

11　本文有關 2019 年大宗商品產品及交投活動的詳盡分析中，除另有指明外，是將 FIA 數據內歸類為「其他」的產品
　　按相關資產重新分類為大宗商品產品及非大宗商品產品。歸入大宗商品產品類者，在分析中列作「其他」大宗商品
　　類別，其相關資產包括化學產品及大宗商品指數。

表 1：全球交易所提供的大宗商品產品（2019 年年底）				
產品類型	資產類別	提供產品的交易所數目	產品數目	佔該類資產 產品數目的比重
期貨	貴金屬	22	106	9.1%
	非貴金屬	16	85	7.3%
	農產品	33	206	17.7%
	能源產品	27	737	63.4%
	其他	6	28	2.4%
總計		44	1,162	100%
期權	貴金屬	11	28	9.3%
	非貴金屬	8	29	9.6%
	農產品	19	102	33.9%
	能源產品	11	139	46.2%
	其他	2	3	1.0%
總計		28	301	100%
期貨及/或期權	貴金屬	24	134	9.2%
	非貴金屬	17	114	7.8%
	農產品	34	308	21.1%
	能源產品	28	876	59.9%
	其他	6	31	2.1%
總計		45	1,463	100%

註：由於四捨五入之誤差，百分比的總和未必相等於 100%。

資料來源：FIA 月度統計數據（2019 年 12 月份報告）。

（2019 年年底提供大宗商品衍生產品的交易所完整名單載於附錄。）

多家交易所當中，美國的紐約商品期貨交易所（NYMEX）提供最多數量的大宗商品產品（576 隻，佔 2019 年年底全球總數的 39%），當中絕大部份都是能源產品（561 隻，佔全球能源產品總數的 64%）。同樣位於美國的 Nasdaq NFX 緊隨其後，但其所提供的大宗商品產品數目（118 隻，佔全球總數的 8%）遠低於 NYMEX。事實上，按大宗商品的產品數量計，十大交易所中有六家都位於美國。若期貨和期權分開計算，2019 年年底期貨及期權產品數目最多的十大交易所中有五家都是位於美國。以大宗商品期權產品數目計算，美國的交易所佔了頭四位。（見圖 11）

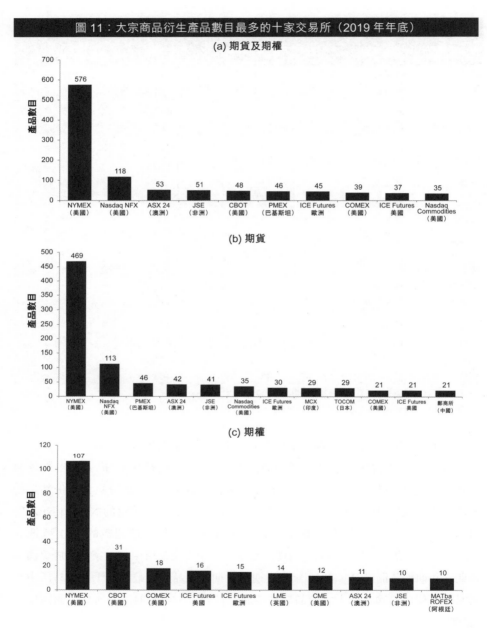

圖 11：大宗商品衍生產品數目最多的十家交易所（2019 年年底）

(a) 期貨及期權

(b) 期貨

(c) 期權

資料來源：FIA 月度統計數據（2019 年 12 月份報告）。

　　圖 12 顯示 2019 年年底各大宗商品資產類別產品數目最多的五家交易所。最多貴金屬產品的是巴基斯坦商品交易所（PMEX）；最多非貴金屬產品的是倫敦金屬交易所（LME）；農產品最多的是芝加哥期貨交易所（CBOT）；而能源產品最多的是 NYMEX。

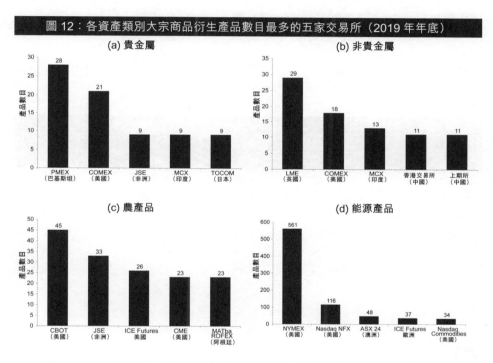

圖 12：各資產類別大宗商品衍生產品數目最多的五家交易所（2019 年年底）

資料來源：FIA 月度統計數據（2019 年 12 月份報告）。

　　就成交量而言，2019 年期貨產品佔各大宗商品資產類別的總成交量逾九成，期權產品只佔少數（見表 2）。同年年底大宗商品衍生產品的未平倉合約量中，亦以期貨產品佔多數，只是比率不及其佔成交量的比率高（見表 3）。這反映了商品期貨作為大宗商品行業對沖工具首選的真正特性。（有關交易活動的進一步詳細分析見第 3 節。）

表 2：全球大宗商品衍生產品按種類於場內的成交量（2019 年）

資產類別	成交量（百萬張合約）		佔比	
	期貨	期權	期貨	期權
貴金屬	562.53	19.77	96.60%	3.40%
非貴金屬	1,423.91	15.85	98.90%	1.10%
農產品	1,650.58	117.14	93.37%	6.63%
能源產品	2,403.36	138.23	94.56%	5.44%
其他	886.48	0.39	99.96%	0.04%
整體	6,926.87	291.38	95.96%	4.04%

資料來源：FIA 月度統計數據（2019 年 12 月份報告）。

表 3：全球大宗商品衍生產品按種類於場內的未平倉合約量（2019 年年底）

資產類別	未平倉合約量（百萬張合約）		佔比	
	期貨	期權	期貨	期權
貴金屬	3.44	1.46	70.16%	29.84%
非貴金屬	7.50	1.22	86.03%	13.97%
農產品	17.04	5.36	76.08%	23.92%
能源產品	45.39	14.43	75.88%	24.12%
其他	3.53	0.08	97.85%	2.15%
整體	76.89	22.54	77.33%	22.67%

資料來源：FIA 月度統計數據（2019 年 12 月份報告）。

3 全球場內大宗商品衍生產品的交易活動

3.1 大宗商品衍生產品交易的增長趨勢

在過去十年，全球交易所的大宗商品衍生產品交易激增 —— 成交量及未平倉合約量的整體複合年均增長率分別高達 111% 及 105%，各資產類別的兩者複合年均增長率亦全部超過 100%。能源產品自 2016 年起超越農產品，連續四年成為最高交易量的資產類別；2009 年至 2019 年間，能源產品的未平倉合約量一直佔市場總數超過一半。（見圖 13 及圖 14）

圖 13：大宗商品衍生產品的年度成交量（按資產類別劃分）（2009 年至 2019 年）

圖 13：大宗商品衍生產品的年度成交量（按資產類別劃分）（2009 年至 2019 年）

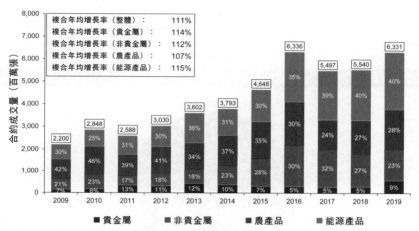

註：不包括 FIA 統計數據中歸類為「其他」的產品（涉及的資產類別包括大宗商品及非大宗商品）。

資料來源：FIA 每月統計數據（各年的 12 月份報告）。

圖 14：大宗商品衍生產品的年底未平倉合約量（按資產類別劃分）（2009 年至 2019 年）

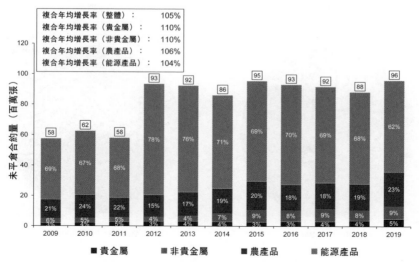

註：不包括 FIA 統計數據中歸類為「其他」的產品（涉及的資產類別包括大宗商品及非大宗商品）。

資料來源：FIA 每月統計數據（各年的 12 月份報告）。

　　仔細觀察 2019 年場內大宗商品活動的構成，能源產品佔期貨成交量的 35%，
佔期權成交量的 47%，農產品則分別佔 24% 及 40%。由於期貨佔大宗商品衍生產
品總成交量的 96%（其餘 4% 為期權），因此能源產品亦佔全球交易所大宗商品衍
生產品總成交量的 35%，其次是農產品（24%）。（見圖 15）

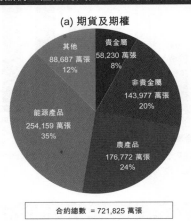
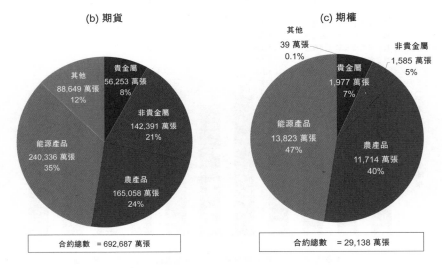

圖 15：全球大宗商品衍生產品的成交量（按資產類別劃分）（2019 年）

(a) 期貨及期權

其他
88,687 萬張
12%

貴金屬
58,230 萬張
8%

非貴金屬
143,977 萬張
20%

能源產品
254,159 萬張
35%

農產品
176,772 萬張
24%

合約總數 = 721,825 萬張

(b) 期貨

其他
88,649 萬張
12%

貴金屬
56,253 萬張
8%

非貴金屬
142,391 萬張
21%

能源產品
240,336 萬張
35%

農產品
165,058 萬張
24%

合約總數 = 692,687 萬張

(c) 期權

其他
39 萬張
0.1%

非貴金屬
1,585 萬張
5%

貴金屬
1,977 萬張
7%

能源產品
13,823 萬張
47%

農產品
11,714 萬張
40%

合約總數 = 29,138 萬張

註：由於四捨五入之誤差，百分比的總和未必相等於 100%。

資料來源：FIA 每月統計數據（2019 年 12 月份報告）。

　　大宗商品交易活動的地域分佈方面，大宗商品期貨的交易大多數在亞太區的交易所進行（佔 2019 年成交量的 63%），而大宗商品期權的交易則大多數在北美的交易所進行（佔 2019 年成交量的 64%）。由於商品期貨交易量佔據大宗商品衍生產品交易量的大部份，因此 2019 年亞太區交易所佔全球大宗商品衍生產品總成交量的大部份（61%）。（見圖 16）

圖 16：全球大宗商品衍生產品的成交量（按地區劃分）（2019 年）

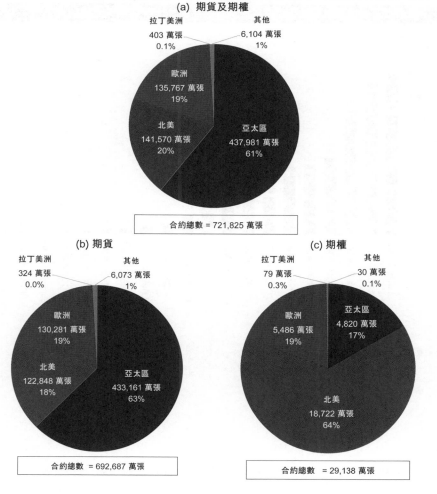

註：由於四捨五入之誤差，百分比的總和未必相等於 100%。

資料來源：FIA 每月統計數據（2019 年 12 月份報告）。

3.2　主要大宗商品交易所

　　圖 17 及圖 18 顯示 2019 年大宗商品衍生產品按成交量及年底未平倉合約量排名最高的二十家交易所。三家內地交易所（上期所、大商所及鄭商所）的成交量位列三甲，但按未平倉合約量的排名則低於歐美的交易所。要注意的是，有別於容許自由入市的西方成熟市場，內地衍生產品市場目前嚴格限制外資參與[12]。換句說，內地交易所的高成交量基本上完全來自境內參與者。

圖 17：大宗商品衍生產品成交量最高的二十家交易所（2019 年）

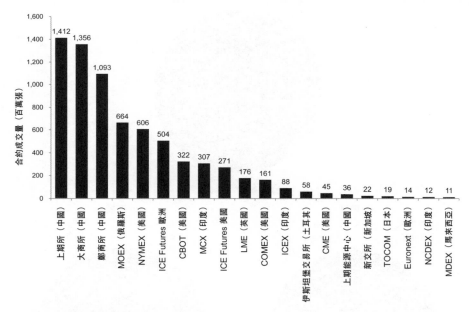

資料來源：FIA 每月統計數據（2019 年 12 月份報告）。

12　外國參與者只可買賣數隻指定產品（見陸家嘴論壇網站上所載中國證券監督管理委員會主席於 2019 年 6 月 13 日在第十一屆陸家嘴論壇上的演講）。

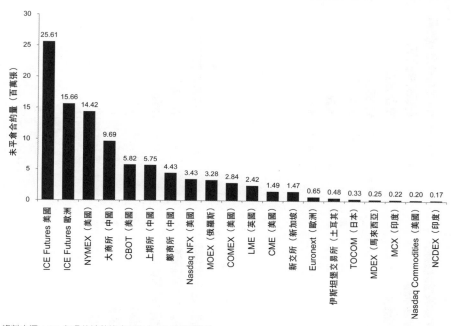

圖 18：大宗商品衍生產品未平倉合約量最高的二十家交易所（2019 年年底）

資料來源：FIA 每月統計數據（2019 年 12 月份報告）。

　　按資產類別計，2019 年上期所於貴金屬和非貴金屬成交量的排名中居首，貴金屬成交量排名第二及第三分別是美國的 COMEX 和印度商品交易所（ICEX），非貴金屬成交量排名第二及第三則分別是大商所和 LME；大商所在全球交易所的農產品成交量中排名最高，其次是鄭商所和 CBOT；俄羅斯的莫斯科交易所（MOEX）的能源產品交易量領先其他交易所，緊隨其後的是 NYMEX 和 ICE Futures 歐洲。（見圖 19）

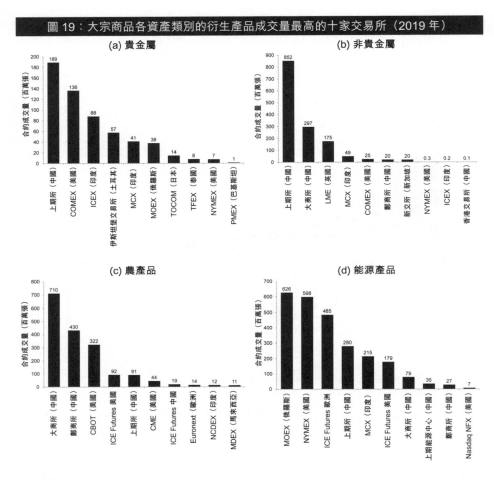

圖 19：大宗商品各資產類別的衍生產品成交量最高的十家交易所（2019 年）

(a) 貴金屬

(b) 非貴金屬

(c) 農產品

(d) 能源產品

資料來源：FIA 每月統計數據（2019 年 12 月份報告）。

　　未平倉合約量方面，2019 年年底貴金屬未平倉合約量中居首的是 COMEX，其次是上期所和土耳其的伊斯坦堡交易所；非貴金屬類未平倉合約量排名第一的也是上期所，第二及第三分別是 LME 和新加坡交易所（簡稱「新交所」）；大商所在農產品方面領先其他交易所，緊隨其後的是 CBOT 和 ICE Futures 美國；能源產品方面，ICE Futures 美國位列榜首，其次是 ICE Futures 歐洲和 NYMEX。（見圖 20）

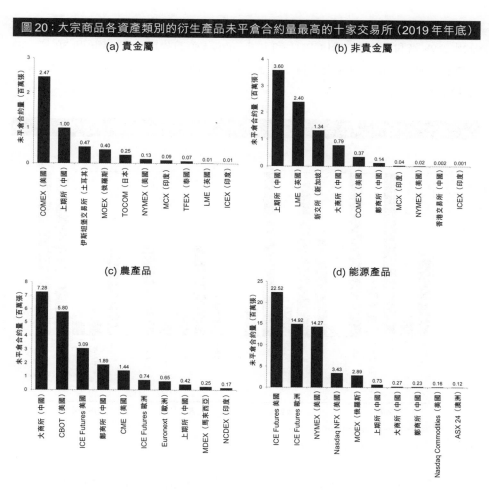

圖 20：大宗商品各資產類別的衍生產品未平倉合約量最高的十家交易所（2019 年年底）

資料來源：FIA 每月統計數據（2019 年 12 月份報告）。

　　值得注意的是，2019 年各種資產類別成交量最高的五家交易所當中，亞洲區交易所的大宗商品衍生產品成交周轉率遠遠高於歐美的交易所（見圖 21）。最極端的例子是印度的交易所：貴金屬成交周轉率逾 17,000 倍（ICEX）和 400 倍（印度多種商品交易所，MCX），非貴金屬成交周轉率逾 1,000 倍（MCX），能源產品逾 2,000 倍（MCX）。至於其他交易所，在貴金屬成交周轉率方面，內地交易所達 190 倍（上期所），COMEX 只有 55 倍；非貴金屬方面，上期所及大商所分別是

237 倍和 374 倍，而 LME 僅為 73 倍；農產品方面，大商所及鄭商所的成交周轉率
分別為 98 倍和 227 倍，而 CBOT 和 ICE Futures 美國分別只有 55 倍和 30 倍；能
源產品方面，上期所的成交周轉率達 382 倍，NYMEX 和 ICE Futures 歐洲分別只
有 42 倍和 33 倍。

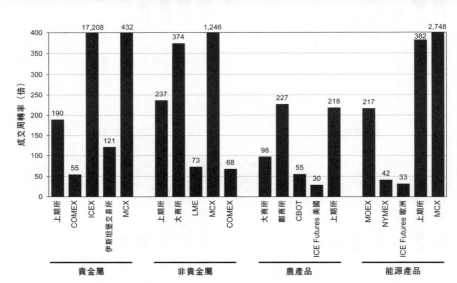

圖 21：大宗商品衍生產品成交量最高的五家交易所的成交周轉率（2019 年）

註：成交周轉率超過 300 倍的棒柱未作完整顯示。
資料來源：FIA 每月統計數據（2019 年 12 月份報告）。

綜上所述，內地期貨交易所於四大主要大宗商品衍生產品資產類別中的三類
（貴金屬、非貴金屬和農產品）的成交量均是全球領先交易所之一，獨能源產品方
面表現相對較遜。亞洲區交易所（包括內地交易所）的大宗商品衍生產品成交周轉
率一般遠高於歐美同業。

3.3　主要產品

3.3.1　貴金屬

　　場內交投最暢旺的貴金屬產品是白銀和黃金。2019 年貴金屬成交量最高的交

易所——上期所——僅提供白銀期貨和黃金期貨及期權，而排名第二的 COMEX
提供 21 種貴金屬期貨及期權，但當中成交量只集中於數隻黃金與白銀產品——
黃金期貨佔貴金屬總成交量的 64％，白銀期貨佔 18％，黃金期權佔 11％。與
COMEX 的相應產品相比，上期所的合約單位較小。排名第三的 ICEX 提供鑽石期
貨。（見表 4）

表 4：成交量最高的三家交易所的三大產品（2019 年）—— 貴金屬					
交易所	交易所佔該資產類別全球成交量的百分比	產品	合約單位	2019 年成交量（合約張數）	佔該所全部貴金屬產品的百分比 [1]	佔全球成交量的累計百分比 [2]
上期所	32.5%	白銀期貨	15 千克	142,823,743	75.5%	32.5%
		黃金期貨	1 千克	46,208,567	24.4%	
		黃金期貨的期權	1 千克	40,926	0.0%	
COMEX	23.4%	黃金期貨	100 盎司（約 3.11 千克）	86,508,741	63.6%	21.6%
		白銀期貨	5,000 盎司（約 155.68 千克）	24,149,148	17.7%	
		黃金期權	100 盎司（約 3.11 千克）	15,043,949	11.1%	
ICEX	15.1%	鑽石 1 卡期貨	1 卡	86,164,857	98.2%	15.1%
		鑽石 0.5 卡期貨	0.5 卡	1,544,910	1.8%	
		鑽石 0.3 卡期貨	0.3 卡	463	0.0%	

註：
（1）產品成交量佔該所全部貴金屬產品成交量的百分比。
（2）三大產品總成交量佔所有貴金屬產品全球成交量的百分比。
資料來源：FIA 每月統計數據（2019 年 12 月份報告）。

3.3.2　非貴金屬

2019 年非貴金屬產品成交量最高的是上期所，其該類產品成交量最高的三
隻產品分別是螺紋鋼期貨、鎳期貨和鋅期貨。排名第二的大商所僅提供鐵礦石產
品，但單此金屬產品的成交量已經佔全球所有非貴金屬成交量的 21％。位列第三

的 LME 則以鋁、銅和鋅產品的成交量最高。上期所的鋅期貨合約單位同樣遠小於
LME 的相應產品。（見表 5）

表 5：成交量最高的三家交易所的三大產品（2019 年）—— 非貴金屬						
交易所	交易所佔該資產類別全球成交量的百分比	產品	合約單位	2019 年成交量（合約張數）	佔該所全部非貴金屬產品的百分比[(1)]	佔全球成交量的累計百分比[(2)]
上期所	59.2%	螺紋鋼期貨	10 噸	465,171,782	54.6%	48.4%
		鎳期貨	1 噸	160,444,120	18.8%	
		鋅期貨	5 噸	71,066,468	8.3%	
大商所	20.6%	鐵礦石期貨	100 公噸	296,538,011	99.9%	20.6%
		鐵礦石期貨的期權	100 公噸	363,865	0.1%	
LME	12.2%	鋁期貨	25 公噸	66,046,920	37.6%	9.2%
		倫敦銅期貨（A 級銅）	25 公噸	37,047,230	21.1%	
		倫敦鋅期貨（特種高級鋅）	25 公噸	29,648,051	16.9%	

註：
（1）產品成交量佔該所全部非貴金屬產品成交量的百分比。
（2）三大產品總成交量佔所有非貴金屬產品全球成交量的百分比。

資料來源：FIA 每月統計數據（2019 年 12 月份報告）。

3.3.3　農產品

於全球交易所買賣的農產品種類繁多。主要產品包括大商所的豆粕期貨、
棕櫚油期貨和玉米期貨；另有鄭商所的菜籽粕期貨、白糖期貨和棉花期貨；也有
CBOT 的玉米期貨、大豆期貨和小麥期貨。（見表 6）

表 6：成交量最高的三家交易所的三大產品（2019 年）—— 農產品						
交易所	交易所佔該資產類別全球成交量的百分比	產品	合約單位	2019 年成交量（合約張數）	佔該所全部農產品的百分比 (1)	佔全球成交量的累計百分比 (2)
大商所	40.2%	豆粕期貨	10 公噸	272,869,691	38.4%	28.7%
		棕櫚油期貨	10 公噸	135,504,196	19.1%	
		玉米期貨	10 公噸	99,119,054	14.0%	
鄭商所	24.3%	菜籽粕期貨	10 公噸	138,085,360	32.1%	18.2%
		白糖期貨	10 公噸	119,288,327	27.8%	
		綿花 1 號期貨	5 公噸	63,971,129	14.9%	
CBOT	18.2%	玉米期貨	5,000 蒲式耳（約 136 公噸）	134,508,582	41.8%	13.5%
		大豆期貨	5,000 蒲式耳（約 136 公噸）	66,841,024	20.8%	
		芝加哥軟紅冬小麥期貨	5,000 蒲式耳（約 136 公噸）	37,753,766	11.7%	

註：
(1) 產品成交量佔該所全部農產品成交量的百分比。
(2) 三大產品總成交量佔所有農產品全球成交量的百分比。
資料來源：FIA 每月統計數據（2019 年 12 月份報告）。

3.3.4 能源

各個資產類別中，能源類的場內產品數量最多（見上文第 2 節）。2019 年年底全球 876 隻能源產品中，單是 NYMEX 就提供了其中的 561 隻（64%）。但 NYMEX 成交量最高的十大能源產品已佔該所能源產品總成交量的 96%[13]。

能源產品以原油產品為主。2019 年按成交量排最高的三家交易所（俄羅斯 MOEX、美國 NYMEX 和 ICE Futures 歐洲）成交量最高的能源產品都是原油（見表 7）。

---

13 資料來源：FIA 每月統計數據（2019 年 12 月份報告）。

交易所	交易所佔該資產類別全球成交量的百分比	產品	合約單位	2019 年成交量（合約張數）	佔該所全部能源產品的百分比[1]	佔全球成交量的累計百分比[2]
表 7：成交量最高的三家交易所的三大產品（2019 年）—— 能源產品						
MOEX	24.6%	布蘭特原油期貨	10 桶	625,284,893	99.9%	24.6%
		輕原油期貨	10 桶	769,032	0.1%	
NYMEX	23.5%	西德州中級輕原油期貨	1,000 桶	291,465,320	48.7%	17.5%
		亨利港天然氣期貨	10,000 百萬英熱單位（MMBtu）	103,394,504	17.3%	
		美國無鉛汽油期貨	42,000 加侖	49,851,807	8.3%	
ICE Futures 歐洲	19.1%	布蘭特原油期貨	1,000 桶	246,921,939	50.9%	15.1%
		低硫汽油期貨	100 公噸	80,210,173	16.5%	
		西德州中級輕原油期貨	1,000 桶	57,292,213	11.8%	

註：
(1) 產品成交量佔該所全部能源產品成交量的百分比。
(2) 三大產品總成交量佔所有能源產品全球成交量的百分比。
資料來源：FIA 每月統計數據（2019 年 12 月份報告）。

4 總結

　　大宗商品的衍生產品交易向來場內場外皆有。場外市場的交易於 2008 年全球金融危機後已然減退，而場內大宗商品衍生產品（主要為期貨）的交易有上升趨勢，同時亞洲區交易所的市場份額亦不斷增加。這可歸因於全球經濟增長、於組合投資中使用大宗商品的趨勢有所增加，以及內地經濟及內地大宗商品交易所於全球市場中崛起。

　　雖然歐美成熟市場於大宗商品的產品數目方面領先，但成交量方面則是內地大宗商品衍生產品交易所佔優。大宗商品的四大類別中有三類（貴金屬、非貴金屬及農產品）按 2019 年成交量的交易所排名，三家內地交易所中至少有一家位列全球三甲。內地交易所僅於能源產品方面較為遜色，而能源產品卻佔據了全球大宗商品衍生產品的大部份成交量（主要來自原油期貨）。

　　與西方成熟市場相比，內地交易所的大宗商品合約單位通常較小，成交周轉率相對較高。與海外同業相比，內地大宗商品衍生產品交易所現時對外資的參與仍然有很大限制。隨着內地交易所進一步開放發展，全球大宗商品衍生產品市場的格局自當會不斷演變。

世界各地交易所簡稱

註：括弧內表示國家 / 地區名稱。

ASX 24	澳洲證券交易所 Trade24（澳洲）
CBOT	芝加哥期貨交易所（美國）
CME	芝加哥商品交易所（美國）
Euronext	泛歐交易所集團（歐洲）
ICEX	印度商品交易所（印度）
JSE	約翰內斯堡證券交易所（南非）
LME	倫敦金屬交易所（英國）
MDEX	馬來西亞衍生產品交易所（馬來西亞）
MOEX	莫斯科交易所（俄羅斯）
MCX	印度多種商品交易所（印度）
Nasdaq Commodities	納斯達克大宗商品平台（美國）
Nasdaq NFX	納斯達克期貨平台（美國）
NCDEX	全國商品及衍生產品交易所（印度）
NYMEX	紐約商品期貨交易所（美國）
PMEX	巴基斯坦商品交易所（巴基斯坦）
TFEX	泰國期貨交易所（泰國）
TOCOM	東京商品交易所（日本）
大商所	大連商品交易所（中國）
上期所	上海期貨交易所（中國）
上期能源中心	上海國際能源交易中心（中國）
香港交易所	香港交易及結算所有限公司（中國）
新交所	新加坡交易所（新加坡）
鄭商所	鄭州商品交易所（中國）

附錄

有提供大宗商品衍生產品的交易所名單
（2019 年年底）

編號	交易所名稱	大宗商品衍生產品數目
1	新加坡亞太交易所	5
2	澳洲證券交易所 Trade24	53
3	巴西證券交易所（B3）	17
4	伊斯坦堡證券交易所	5
5	意大利交易所 — IDEM	1
6	布達佩斯證券交易所	1
7	芝加哥期貨交易所	48
8	芝加哥商品交易所	28
9	COMEX	39
10	大連商品交易所	22
11	迪拜黃金及商品交易所	11
12	迪拜商品交易所	3
13	歐洲期貨交易所	12
14	泛歐交易所集團衍生產品市場	7
15	香港交易及結算所	13
16	ICE Futures 加拿大	3
17	ICE Futures 歐洲	45
18	ICE Futures 新加坡	3
19	ICE Futures 美國	37
20	印度國際交易所	3
21	印度商品交易所	12
22	印尼商品及衍生產品交易所	6
23	約翰內斯堡證券交易所	51
24	韓國交易所	2
25	倫敦金屬交易所	31
26	馬來西亞衍生產品交易所	4
27	阿根廷布宜諾斯艾利斯及羅薩里歐期貨交易所	27
28	明尼阿波利斯穀物交易所	2

編號	交易所名稱	大宗商品衍生產品數目
29	莫斯科交易所	16
30	印度多種商品交易所	34
31	納斯達克大宗商品平台	35
32	納斯達克期貨平台	118
33	印度全國商品及衍生產品交易所	22
34	紐約商品期貨交易所	576
35	新西蘭期貨交易所	8
36	北美衍生產品交易所	7
37	大阪堂島商品交易所	10
38	巴基斯坦商品交易所	46
39	上海期貨交易所	19
40	上海國際能源交易中心	2
41	新加坡交易所	16
42	台灣期貨交易所	4
43	泰國期貨交易所	5
44	東京商品交易所	29
45	鄭州商品交易所	25
衍生產品總數		1,463

註：交易所名稱為資料來源的譯名／本名（按英文名稱的字母順序排列）。

資料來源：FIA 月度統計數據（2019 年 12 月份報告）。

第6章

倫敦金屬交易所
—— 全球工業金屬交易及定價中心

倫敦金屬交易所

摘　要

本文概述倫敦金屬交易所的簡史並綜覽其市場架構、買賣合約、運作及服務。

倫敦金屬交易所簡介

倫敦金屬交易所（簡稱 LME）是全球工業金屬價格發現、保值和交易的中心。實物金屬行業（進行金屬開採、生產及加工的企業，以及買賣金屬的金融市場參與者）會通過 LME 交易並對沖價格風險。

LME 是香港交易所集團旗下的全資子公司，為金屬及金融市場參與者提供交易平台，構建出穩健的受監管市場並提供全天候交易渠道，每天 24 小時都可找到買賣對手和獲取價格，無論是想交易、保值還是對沖價格風險，都可以在這裏完成交易。

LME 絕大部份有色金屬（又稱「基本金屬」）的期貨買賣業務均於以下三個交易場地進行：LMEselect（電子平台）、交易圈（公開喊價市場）及 24 小時電話交易市場。2019 年，LME 的交易額達 1.76 億手，涉及 13.5 萬億美元及 39 億噸金屬。

市場參與者可在 LME 買賣各種不同的合約，包括期貨、期權和現金結算期貨，以及平均價格及溢價合約。現時可供交易的金屬包括氧化鋁、鋁、鋁合金、鈷、銅、黃金、北美特種鋁合金合約、鉛、鉬、鎳、白銀、鋼材、錫及鋅。

LME 之所以重要，除了是期貨交投極其活躍之外，還在於其與金屬業界的緊密聯繫。全球性的 LME 認可倉庫網絡所提供的實物交收服務及龐大的流通量，使 LME 成為業內理想的交易場所做套期保值，並提供可信而穩妥的參考價格。於 LME 平台「發現」的價格會成為全球參考價格及實物交易的基準價格，並會用於投資組合、商品指數及金屬 ETF（交易所買賣基金）的定價。

LME 自 1877 年正式成立以來，一直在尋求如何在繼承傳統的同時實現創新。今天的 LME 各類合約繼續為實物金屬行業所日常使用，與傳統客戶羣體關係密切。隨着近年推出現金結算合約組合、擴大 LME 黑色金屬產品線、推出黃金和白銀期貨、與新能源電池及電動汽車行業從業者探討合作，並致力於開發透明的鋰價格訂價方案，越來越多參與者將有機會受惠於 LME 的風險管理工具及其流動性。

LME 自設清算所 LME Clear，以減低金屬市場的對手方風險。LME 合約通過交易圈、電子市場及電話進行的交易均由 LME Clear 結算。

LME 屬於「認可投資交易所」，由英國金融市場行為監管局（簡稱 FCA）直接監管。FCA 亦負責監管進行投資業務的 LME 會員。作為認可投資交易所，LME 維持其合約在市場進行有序的交易，並為投資者提供妥善的保障。LME Clear 由英國央行監管。

1 LME 的歷史

LME 的起源可追溯至 1571 年伊莉莎白一世統治時期倫敦開設皇家交易所之時，當時金屬及許多其他大宗商品的買家賣家開始定期聚集。

下表為 LME 歷年大事記。

表 1：LME 歷年大事記	
日期	事件
1800 年代初	倫敦城康希爾街內的 Jerusalem Coffee House 成為金屬業界中人最熱門的聚腳地，交易圈傳統就此誕生。
1869 年	蘇彝士運河開通後，由馬來亞運送錫的時間減至三個月，與由智利運送銅的時間一致，造就了 LME 三個月以下的遠期合約可每日交割，並沿用至今。
1877 年	交易人士組成 London Metals and Mining Company，並遷到倫敦城朗伯德街一家帽子店樓上，作為其首個辦事處。交易所成立，提供銅及錫標準期貨合約。
1881 年	會員數目急升，突破 300 後於倫敦城 Whittington 大道正式建立交易所，往後在此營運了 98 年。
1903 年	鉛標準期貨合約上市並開始交易。
1914 年	第一次世界大戰導致停市數個月。
1915 年	鋅標準期貨合約上市並交易。
1939 年	第二次世界大戰爆發，交易幾近癱瘓。
1963 年	鹿特丹一家倉庫成為 LME 首家於歐洲的認可倉庫。
1978 年	該年 12 月推出原鋁產品，自此有關合約成為 LME 流通量最高（即交易量最大）的合約。
1979 年	鎳標準期貨合約上市並交易。
1987 年	LME 成為中央結算及受監管的交易所。
1987 年	新加坡一家倉庫成為 LME 首家非歐洲地區的認可倉庫。
1988 年	LME 成為「認可投資交易所」。

(續)

表 1：LME 歷年大事記	
日期	事件
1989 年	LME 推出首個電子價格傳送系統 Vendor Feed System（VFS）。同年，LME 認可其首家日本倉庫。
1991 年	巴爾的摩一家倉庫成為 LME 首家於美國的認可倉庫。
1992 年	鋁合金標準期貨合約上市並開始交易。
1994 年	於芬卓奇街（Fenchurch Street）Plantation House 營運 14 年後，LME 遷至倫敦城利德賀街（Leadenhall Street）。
2000 年	LME 轉行股份制。
2006 年	LME 推出每月現金結算的銅、鋁及鋅小型期貨合約。
2008 年	LME 進軍黑色金屬，推出兩隻地區性鋼坯合約。2010 年 7 月，兩者合併為單一全球性合約。
2010 年	LME 推出兩隻小金屬期貨合約（鈷及鉬）。
2012 年	香港交易及結算所有限公司（簡稱「香港交易所」）收購 LME。
2014 年	LME 針對金屬行業的需要，自設全新清算所 LME Clear。
2015 年	LME 推出 LME 廢鋼及 LME 螺紋鋼合約，連同一系列實物交收的鋁溢價合約。
2015 年	LME 遷至現址（Finsbury Square）。
2017 年	LME 貴金屬服務（LMEprecious）推出，為貴金屬市場提供 LME 黃金及白銀合約。
2019 年	LME 對旗下註冊金屬品牌實行負責任採購要求。香港交易所衍生產品市場推出倫敦鋁、銅、鉛、鎳、錫及鋅小型合約，並推出七隻新的現金結算合約，相關產品為氧化鋁、鋁溢價、鈷、鉬及熱軋卷鋼。

2 誰是 LME 市場的參與者？

　　LME 連繫着實物現貨市場與金融市場的參與者，建立全球流動性。這些參與者為了投資或對沖價格風險而買賣 LME 期貨及期權產品，在這過程中實現了金屬價格的發現。

　　LME 參與者包括：

- 金屬生產商，如採礦商、冶煉商及精煉商；
- 金屬消費者，如工業製造商；
- 貿易商及現貨交易人士；

- 銀行、財務基金及大宗商品交易顧問；
- 自營交易商、程式／高頻交易商；及
- 經紀與結算機構。

2.1 現貨市場參與者

自 1877 年以來，LME 的角色都是協助金屬生產商及消費者管理。價格風險管理的具體途徑如下：

- **保值** —— 生產商及消費者透過 LME 對沖價格風險。現貨合約訂立與其結算之間可能相距數日、數星期、數個月以至數年，其間金屬價格可能出現許多變動。現貨市場想設法減低的就是這類風險。保值的好處包括：
  - 提供有關價格變動的保障；
  - 可鎖定利潤，為客戶提供長期固定價格；
  - 有助制定更佳的財務預算；
  - 有機會將存貨套現或用作融資抵押；
  - 保障實物存貨不受價格下跌影響；及
  - 在生產出現困難時對沖實物購買量。
- **價格發現** —— LME 每天為全球市場提供透明及真實的參考價格。價格發現所涉及的都是風險資本，真實反映全球供需情況。對沖能力高下便是視乎這些價格。
- **價格趨同** —— LME 的實物結算合約都是透過旗下分佈全球的倉庫網絡進行實物結算。這一點非常重要，因為這表示在 LME 市場上發現的期貨價格與實物金屬價格接軌，即反映實物價格。
- **實物結算** —— 只有 LME 註冊品牌才獲接納作實物交割。LME 並且不斷根據測試結果及參考一系列全球標準來調整其註冊品牌，務求令其上市合約切合市場所需。
- **交割日架構** —— 不論在交割時間的選擇上，又或是切合業內現實需要及作相應對沖的靈活度上，現時還沒有哪個市場能及得上 LME。
- **定價參考** —— 在 LME 交易平台發現的價格是國際現貨市場合約作估值及結算的參考價格。

3　現貨市場

當出現供應極度短缺或過度供應的情況，LME 亦可為生產商及消費者發揮儼如最後一個現貨市場的作用，這會透過 LME 的全球倉庫網絡來實現。

所有憑倉單存放於 LME 核准倉庫的金屬均為 LME 認可生產商出產的 LME 註冊品牌金屬，這確保了有關金屬均符合 LME 有關大宗商品等級、質素及形狀的嚴格規定。LME 的倉庫網絡對現貨市場發揮着輔助作用。在有全球倉儲設施及一系列 LME 上市品牌的配套支持下，進行實物交割可達到價格趨同，確保有關價格與現貨市場一致。

LME 同時具備現貨期貨價格接軌、全球超過 550 個 LME 倉儲設施及近 500 個上市金屬品牌等優勢，再加上現實中現貨市場都是使用 LME 價格磋商交易、LME 市場高流通量等特點，等同為全球市場提供堪可信賴的參考價格。

3.1　交割日架構

LME 的主要特色之一，就是其現貨合約獨有的交割日架構及着眼於現貨市場。LME 合約的交割日架構反映現貨市場所需的交貨日期與性質。作為買賣雙方的市場參與者經磋商而制定金屬交易合約後，可利用 LME 合約對沖未來長短期的金屬價格風險或作風險投資：三個月內的合約可每個營業日交割；三個月以上至六個月的合約可每週交割；七個月至 123 個月的合約（視乎相關金屬而定）可每月交割。亦即是說可以對沖長達十年的價格風險。下圖展示現貨至 123 個月內的交割日架構。

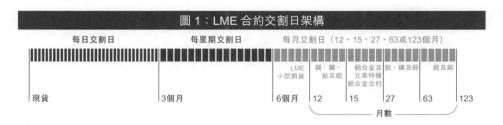

圖 1：LME 合約交割日架構

每日交割日	每星期交割日	每月交割日（12、15、27、63或123個月）			
		LME 小型期貨	錫、鋼、鈷及鉬	鋁合金及北美特種鋁合金合約	鉛、鎳及鋅
					鋁及銅
現貨	3個月	6個月	12	15	27	63	123

月數

現貨 (Cash) 結算日是最接近的交割日期，為合約交易日後兩個工作天。在任何交易日，一般均以三個月交割的 LME 合約 (即可每日交割的最長期合約) 的交易量為最高，亦是 LME 電子平台 LMEselect 上最常買賣的合約。

「第三個星期三」合約是一種每月交割的期貨，LME 所有主要合約均有提供。這些是月度期貨合約，只會在每個月的第三個星期三到期。LME 期權亦使用「第三個星期三」期貨合約作為其相關資產。多達 65% 的未平倉合約量落在 LME「第三個星期三」合約的到期日。

三個月期的合約會與「第三個星期三」月度合約互動，作為 LME 交割日架構下流通量集中的支點。

3.2 跨期買賣

跨期買賣 (或稱「調期交易」) 是指買入特定交割日的合約，又同時售出另一不同交割日的合約。這樣，市場參與者可調整日期並轉移即將到期的倉盤。這亦是為實物存貨對沖或作融資的方法。金融交易商則可於 LME 這個流動性高的市場進行跨期買賣，從遠期曲線形態的變動中賺取利潤。

4 交易場地及定價

4.1 LME 交易場地

4.1.1 交易圈

交易時段：倫敦時間 11:40 — 17:00

公開叫價交易大堂：流動性集中於稱為「Rings (交易圈)」的短暫交易時段。LME 每隻金屬有多達 200 個可供交易的到期日，而公開叫價是買賣多個到期日的最有效率的交易方法。LME 官方現貨結算價 (LME Official Price)、LME 非正式牌價 (LME Unofficial Price)，以及 LME 收市價 (LME Closing Price) 全部或部份均來自交易圈的交易活動。

- 業內人士訂立現貨合約時會使用 LME 官方現貨結算價。
- LME 非官方牌價是交易圈第三節中產生的最後買賣報價，是下午交易的良好指標，便於不同時區的客戶使用作為參考價。
- LME Clear 及 LME 會員使用 LME 收市價（又稱最後收盤價）計算保證金及按市價計值。

4.1.2　LMEselect

交易時段：倫敦時間 01:00 — 19:00

電子交易平台：為所有 LME 合約交易提供一系列先進的功能，所有功能均專為 LME 獨有的交割日架構而設。LME 貴金屬於 LMEselect 的交易時段為 01:00 — 20:00。

本書付印之時，LME 正着手開發新的電子交易平台取代 LMEselect。現有的 LMEsource 數據平台亦會優化，以包括 LME 所有交易渠道（LMEselect、場外的辦公室電話市場及交易圈）的數據。新的交易平台會有全新的結構，利用香港交易所的技術，帶來更高的表現效率及更高的穩定性，亦將會比現有平台更靈活，有助促進未來發展。

4.1.3　場外的辦公室電話市場

交易時段：24 小時

會員的指示性報價通過供應商網絡發佈，可透過電話執行。

實時買賣價每天 24 小時由 LMElive（LME 的市場數據服務）及認可數據供應商提供。LMElive 以數碼方式提供價格資訊，可助使用者對期貨及期權交易有較全面的觀察。LME 亦會根據交易日中較高流動性的時段整合並發佈一系列的參考價格。

5 LME 合約

LME 是金屬期貨及期權買賣雙方的交匯點。期貨合約長倉持有人有義務在到期日買入相關金屬，而期貨合約短倉持有人則有義務於到期日交付相關金屬，除非有關倉位於該日期前已平倉。

期權買方（持有人）有權利但並無義務在將來指定日期或之前以指定價格買入或賣出相關金屬。

LME 向世界各地金屬生產商及消費者提供管理金屬價格波動風險的途徑。

金屬生產商出售自身採煉的金屬，擔心的是價格下跌；而金屬消費者採購金屬用以生產其他製品，擔心的是價格上漲。利用 LME 期貨及期權合約對沖這些價格波動，金屬業界得以專注其核心業務。

嚴格而言，LME 基本金屬合約都是遠期合約，意思是說，合約的盈虧是在到期之時（而不是之前）兌現，這點與標準期貨不同。

所有 LME 合約按既定的買賣單位進行交易，而各合約的買賣單位會有所不同，視乎合約類型以及相關金屬而定。

廣義上，LME 合約有兩大類 —— 實物結算和現金結算。

下表為 2020 年 2 月的 LME 合約列表，顯示合約的結算方式、每種金屬提供的合約類型，以及交割日等。（合約類型見下文第 5.1 節。）

表 2：LME 合約（2020 年 5 月）					
合約名稱	結算類型	買賣單位	合約類型	交割日	推出買賣年份
LME 氧化鋁（CRU/Fastmarkets MB）	現金	50 公噸	期貨	合約期 15 個月內：每月交割	2019
LME 鋁	實物	25 公噸	• 期貨 • 月平均價期貨 • LME 小型期貨合約 • 香港交易所倫敦小型期貨合約 • 交易期權 • 交易平均價期權	• 合約期 25 日內：每日交割 • 合約期 3 至 6 個月：每週交割 • 合約期 7 至 123 個月（交易期權及交易平均價期權最長為 63 個月）：每月交割	1978

(續)

表 2：LME 合約（2020 年 5 月）					
合約名稱	結算類型	買賣單位	合約類型	交割日	推出買賣年份
LME 鋁合金	實物	20 公噸	• 期貨 • 月平均價期貨 • 交易期權 • 交易平均價期權	• 合約期 3 個月內：每日交割 • 合約期 3 至 6 個月：每週交割 • 合約期 7 至 27 個月：每月交割	1992
LME 鋁溢價 美國溢價 / 西歐溢價 / 東亞溢價 / 東南亞溢價	實物	25 公噸	期貨	每個到期月份的第三個星期三，另受交易規例規管	2017
LME 鋁溢價 已完稅美國中西部溢價（普氏）/ 未完稅歐洲溢價（Fastmarkets MB）	現金	25 公噸	期貨	合約期 15 個月內：每月交割	2019
LME 鈷	實物	1 公噸	期貨	• 合約期 3 個月內：每日交割 • 合約期 3 至 6 個月：每週交割 • 合約期 7 至 15 個月：每月交割	2010
LME 鈷 （Fastmarkets MB）	現金	1 公噸	期貨	合約期 15 個月內：每月交割	2019
LME 銅	實物	25 公噸	• 期貨 • 月平均價期貨 • LME 小型期貨合約 • 香港交易所倫敦小型期貨合約 • 交易期權 • 交易平均價期權	• 合約期 25 日內：每日交割 • 合約期 3 至 6 個月：每週交割 • 合約期 7 至 123 個月（交易期權及交易平均價期權最長為63個月）：每月交割	1877
LME 黃金	實物	100 金衡盎司	期貨	• 合約期 25 日內：每日交割 • 合約期 24 個月內：每月交割 • 合約期 5 年內：每季交割	2017

(續)

表 2：LME 合約（2020 年 5 月）					
合約名稱	結算類型	買賣單位	合約類型	交割日	推出買賣年份
LME 鉛	實物	25 公噸	• 期貨 • 月平均價期貨 • LME 小型期貨合約 • 香港交易所倫敦小型期貨合約 • 交易期權 • 交易平均價期權	• 合約期 25 日內：每日交割 • 合約期 3 至 6 個月：每週交割 • 合約期 7 至 63 個月：每月交割	1920
LME 鉬（普氏）	現金	2,205 磅	期貨	合約期 15 個月內：每月交割	2019
LME 北美特種鋁合金	實物	20 公噸	• 期貨 • 月平均價期貨 • 交易期權 • 交易平均價期權	• 合約期 3 個月內：每日交割 • 合約期 3 至 6 個月：每週交割 • 合約期 7 至 27 個月：每月交割	2002
LME 鎳	實物	6 公噸	• 期貨 • 月平均價期貨 • LME 小型期貨合約 • 香港交易所倫敦小型期貨合約 • 交易期權 • 交易平均價期權	• 合約期 3 個月內：每日交割 • 合約期 3 至 6 個月：每週交割 • 合約期 7 至 63 個月：每月交割	1979
LME 白銀	實物	5,000 金衡盎司	期貨	• 合約期 25 日內：每日交割 • 合約期 24 個月內：每月交割 • 合約期 5 年內：每季交割	2017
LME 熱軋鋼捲中國離岸價（Argus）	現金	10 公噸	期貨	每月交割，最長 15 個月	2019
LME 熱軋鋼捲北美（普氏）	現金	10 短噸	期貨	每月交割，最長 15 個月	2019
LME 螺紋鋼	現金	10 公噸	期貨	每月交割，最長 15 個月	2015
LME 廢鋼	現金	10 公噸	期貨	每月交割，最長 15 個月	2015
LME 鋅	實物	25 公噸	• 期貨 • 月平均價期貨 • LME 小型期貨合約 • 香港交易所倫敦小型期貨合約 • 交易期權 • 交易平均價期權	• 合約期 3 個月內：每日交割 • 合約期 3 至 6 個月：每週交割 • 合約期 7 至 63 個月：每月交割	1920

5.1　合約類型

(1)　實物結算合約

　　LME 實物結算的期貨合約設計特別，以對應現貨市場的交易。到期前未平倉（即未作反向的買/賣）的期貨合約均以實物結算。LME 期貨於交割日結算，合約期間會收取初始保證金和追收變動保證金。LME 合約可使用存於 LME 核准倉庫的實物存貨作結算。因為大多數參與者都是利用 LME 合約來抵銷價格波動的風險又或從中獲利，會實際交付金屬的交易不到 1%。絕大部份 LME 合約在結算前已經「平倉」。

　　LME 期權合約較期貨合約更為靈活，是金屬及金融業界降低價格風險（透過對沖交易）又或作價格風險投資（根據預期價格波動）的另一渠道。LME 期權合約期可長達 63 個月（視乎金屬種類），於合約到期當日或之前任何時間均可行使（為美式期權）。期權的相關資產是對應的 LME 以實物結算的「第三個星期三」期貨合約。LME 期權現時適用於八種金屬。

(2)　現金結算合約

　　除實物結算的期貨合約外，LME 還提供一系列現金結算的期貨合約。這些合約並非與相關金屬實物綁定，而是按平均價格結算。結算價最常見是由報價機構提供，報價機構的角色在調查市場（根據買賣報價及成交再加上市場資訊）來評估公平值，由此得出相關資產的估價。LME 再用該估價計算其現金結算合約的最終結算價。

(3)　交易平均價期權

　　透過交易平均價期權（TAPO），金屬行業能夠以靈活的方式對沖其業務合約的平均金屬價格風險。這類合約的用處在於實物合約大都是按一段時間的平均價議定合約條款。TAPO 為現金結算的亞洲期權，合約回報取決於合約月份的每月平均結算價。鋁、鋁合金、北美特種鋁合金、銅、鉛、鎳、錫及鋅都提供 TAPO 買賣。

(4) 月平均價期貨

月平均價期貨特別為需要對沖每月平均價格的金屬業界而設。這是世界首個場內買賣的同類產品，所有 LME 有色金屬都有提供月平均價期貨。

(5) LME 小型期貨合約

LME 小型期貨合約是以 5 公噸為買賣單位的現金結算月度期貨合約，按相應的 LME「母」合約的官方結算價結算。此產品適用於銅、鋁及鋅。

(6) 香港交易所倫敦小型期貨合約

香港交易所倫敦小型期貨合約旨在切合亞洲參與者的需求，便利他們使用離岸人民幣或美元計值的期貨來緩衝金屬價格風險或作價格風險投資。這類合約在香港交易所旗下的衍生產品平台買賣，涵蓋鋁、鋅、銅、鎳、錫及鉛六種基本金屬。有如 LME 小型期貨合約，香港交易所倫敦小型期貨合約按相應的 LME「母」合約的官方結算價以現金結算。

5.2 LMEprecious（LME 貴金屬）

LMEprecious 是 LME、世界黃金協會以及多家主要行業參與者創設的舉措，旨在引進本地倫敦貴金屬產品作場內交易。LME 黃金及 LME 白銀期貨為該等金屬的交易、價格發現及風險管理提供新的機遇，從而為貴金屬業打造更佳的市場架構。

LMEprecious 是為回應市場需求、透過與貴金屬市場的主要持份者作密切諮詢而設。LMEprecious 提供黃金及白銀的每日及月度合約，為市場參與者提供更多選擇，實現黃金及白銀市場現代化，以更好地反映貴金屬市場中全球參與者的需求。

LME 現時與「倫敦鉑金及鈀金市場」（London Platinum and Palladium Market）合作，以管理及發佈倫敦金銀市場協會（LBMA）的鉑金及鈀金價格。此舉透過 LME 定制的電子拍賣平台 —— LMEbullion —— 實現。

5.3　電動汽車電池材料

　　LME 正為電池材料及電動車行業開發新型風險管理工具，目前正與全球市場相關產業鏈各個環節的參與者共同探討，辨識這些行業最新的風險管理需要，務求提供對應的產品服務。部份主要電池金屬如鎳、鉛、銅、鈷以及鋁在 LME 已有成熟發展。LME 希望開發新的期貨合約，提供進一步對沖及買賣電池材料的機會；打頭陣的是 2019 年推出的現金結算 LME 鈷（Fastmarkets MB）合約，現時亦繼續與 Fastmarkets MB 研究就鋰金屬制定穩健而具透明度的定價方案。

6　LME 倉儲

　　LME 倉庫用於儲存 LME 註冊的金屬品牌，亦即 LME 實物交割合約的相關資產。因應實物交割需要，LME 批准並授權相關倉儲牌照，建立分佈全球各地的倉庫網絡及儲存設施。目前歐美及亞洲多處共有逾 550 個 LME 核准的儲存設施。

　　由於可透過 LME 核准的全球倉庫網絡進行實物交收，LME 合約成為業內理想的對沖渠道。LME 交收系統的背後，依賴的是保證用戶會收到指定質量和數量的金屬。為確保質量一致，所有送入 LME 核准儲存設施的金屬必須是 LME 註冊的品牌，並符合質量、形狀及重量方面的規格。製造商若擬將產品註冊為 LME 合約的交付商品，必須符合每個品牌的若干標準，方有機會取得 LME 批准。

　　LME 並沒有擁有或營運倉庫，對倉庫內的物料亦無所有權。LME 只是授權倉庫公司及其所營運的倉庫，代倉單持有人儲存那些 LME 註冊的金屬品牌，並透過倫敦代理人為其送進 LME 核准倉庫的物料發出 LME 倉單（即賦予對倉庫內金屬的所有權的文件）。倉單通過 LME 安全性高的電子倉單轉移系統 LMEsword 從金屬賣方轉移至金屬買方。LMEsword 方便倉單所有權的轉移及庫存報告等流程。倉單均在中央存管處持有，格式統一，含獨立編碼。倉單的持有人亦可使用 LMEsword 轉移倉單上金屬的所有權，為庫存融資和其他商業安排提供便利。LME 市場數據供應商每日編制和發佈詳細的庫存量報告。LMEsword 亦編制每日庫存報告，是保持市場公開有序運作的重要一環。

LME 倉庫公司必須符合嚴格標準，才會獲准儲存金屬。這些公司一般位處相關物料的高消耗地區或便於物料裝運的物流交易中心。

倉單上所有存放於 LME 核准儲存設施的金屬，均是來自 LME 核准製造商的 LME 註冊品牌，以確保符合 LME 對商品等級、質量及外形的嚴格規定。

LME 對其全球實體倉庫網絡所需的改革不時作出評估，以確保當中所採用的都是實物市場基建儲存及物流的最佳方案。

6.1　地點溢價及折讓

若買入的 LME 合約是實物交收合約，買家可收到任何一個的 LME 核准倉庫地點的金屬倉單，相關金屬可以是任何經註冊的 LME 品牌或外形。倉單透過 LMEsword 由賣方隨機分配予買方。

在 LME 買賣的金屬價格是全球通用的價格。不過，由於部份地區的供求比例較其他地區緊絀，而地區之間的運輸亦涉及成本，個別指定交割地點的金屬價格可能會較 LME 價格出現溢價或折讓。另外，若買方要求指定金屬品牌，亦會有相同情況。

此外，若買方想取消金屬倉單而從庫中取貨，價格需加入額外溢價，以反映從庫中出貨的成本，以及相關 LME 地點有否出現出貨輪候隊伍。

6.2　LME 的負責任採購要求

LME 於 2019 年 10 月 25 日公佈對 LME 註冊品牌的負責任採購要求，參照經濟合作與發展組織（OECD）的《受衝突影響或高風險地區礦產的負責任供應鏈盡職調查指南》（*Due Diligence Guidance for Responsible Supply Chains of Minerals from Conflict-Affected and High-Risk Areas*）。

7　LME Clear

LME Clear 是專為 LME 用戶而設的結算所。LME Clear 於 2014 年成立，是經過諮詢市場意見而設立，旨在向市場提供具成本效益並符合歐洲市場基礎設施監管規則（EMIR）的清算服務，為所有在 LME 進行的交易提供創新的清算及交收服務。

LME Clear 是所有 LME 結算會員及其交易活動的中央對手方，向每份交易合約提供財務擔保，擔當「每一買方的賣方及每一賣方的買方」。若結算會員有違約失責情況，LME Clear 會介入，迅速有效地處理違約結算會員尚未完成的風險倉盤。

LME Clear 的結算系統稱為 LMEmercury，會員透過此系統可實時監察和評估其所承擔的風險，意味着其對持倉組合管理、期權到期處理和申報等主要業務活動掌握更多控制權。

LME Clear 會不時因應客戶所需而推出新服務。最近新增的服務包括倉單轉移服務、優化的水平價差初始保證金計演算法（inter-prompt spread methodology）、頭寸壓縮、接受倉單及離岸人民幣為抵押品、新的均價交易解決方案，以及新的非淨額持倉綜合帳戶（gross aggregated account）。

7.1　倉單作為抵押品

LME 倉單屬不記名文件，持有倉單等同擁有存放於 LME 核准倉庫內的金屬的所有權。換言之，LME 倉單是一份證明持有人持有一批存放於 LME 核准倉庫內的金屬的不記名文件。作為於 LME 交易的金屬的終端市場，於 LME 倉庫內具有倉單的金屬數量通常會被視為相關金屬的真正全球供求狀況指標。

現時 LME Clear 的抵押品服務已進一步擴大抵押品的範圍，除現金及高質的政府債券之外，亦接受會員以 LME 金屬倉單作為保證金要求的抵押品。

每類金屬的合約只接受同類金屬的倉單作為抵押品，例如鋁倉單只能用作鋁合約倉盤的抵押品。現時可接受相應金屬倉單作為抵押品的金屬合約有銅、鋁、鋅、鎳、鉛及錫六種。

7.2 在值風險保證金方法

LME 現正自主設計一個基於 Value at Risk（在值風險，簡稱 VaR）的初始保證金演算法模型，作為其科技發展宏圖的一部份，以期待通過此模型為結算會員及其客戶提供最適合及高效的 LME 市場初始保證金計算方法。VaR 是被廣泛採用的風險估值方法，許多資產類別的中央對手方及其他金融機構均有使用。計算 VaR 有多種不同數學模型。一般而言，VaR 是按持倉組合計算，按所應用的一系列模擬結果，估計有關組合的潛在虧損水平。

VaR 的主要優點是其着眼於為整個組合做市場風險評估、反映當前市場狀況，並考慮到組合風險的各個組成部份。LME 新的 VaR 演算法亦會特別針對 LME 市場而設計。

相比之下，LME 現時採納的方法着眼於個別倉位的不同合計結果，以及每一合計結果（而非持倉組合）的潛在損失，這方法效率可能較低，尤其對於有許多跨期水平價差交易的組合而言。

8 總結

LME 百多年來一直為金屬及金融業界提供交易和管理金屬價格風險的途徑。時刻緊貼市場、開發創新產品及服務，令 LME 始終走在國際大宗商品市場的前沿。展望未來，LME 會繼續推出各項新舉措，像重大的技術開發及優化措施、負責任採購金屬的要求，以及環境考慮因素等，協助塑造金屬市場的未來。LME 與香港交易所集團一直都緊密合作，為於中國內地的市場開發產品及制定計劃。進一步詳情見本書第 12 章。

附錄

LME 產品及服務的詞彙

LME Clear	LME 所有交易的結算所
LMEbullion	LME 為管理倫敦金銀市場協會（LBMA）鉑金及鈀金價格而定制的電子拍賣平台
LMElive	LME 的市場數據應用程式，向客戶提供與在 LME 買賣的金屬有關的 LME 定價、資訊和工具。
LMEmercury	LME Clear 的核心結算系統，進行交易的會員公司可從中實時監察風險
LMEminis	鋁、銅及鋅三種金屬以現金結算的 5 公噸合約，以相應的「母」合約的 LME 官方結算價進行結算
LMEprecious	為市場提供場內交易的本地倫敦貴金屬風險管理產品（包括 LME 黃金及白銀）的計劃
LMEselect	LME 的電子交易平台
LMEsource	LME 的實時多點傳送的市場數據發佈平台
LMEsword	便利轉移 LME 倉單所有權及庫存報告的 LME 系統
交易圈（Ring）	LME 的公開喊價交易場地，第 1 類會員公司的代表在此面對面進行主要工業用金屬的交易

第二篇

內地與香港
大宗商品市場的演變

第 7 章

中國內地大宗商品現貨市場的
歷史沿革、現狀及其與期貨市場的關聯

深圳前海聯合交易中心有限公司

摘 要

　　本文簡要梳理了中國內地大宗商品的定義、分類,以及其商品交易所的發展歷程與現狀,縱觀國際大宗商品現貨與期貨市場發展的經驗,並提出了建設多層次市場體系、打造國際大宗商品交易中心的建議。

1　內地大宗商品的概念與特徵

根據《大宗商品電子交易規範》(GB/T 18769-2003) 的界定，大宗商品是指可進入流通領域，但非零售環節，具有商品屬性，用於工農業生產與消費使用的大批量買賣的物質商品。

大宗商品關乎國計民生。石油輸出國組織 (OPEC) 減產導致的原油價格上漲會直接影響上班族的出行方式，乾旱造成的大豆減產也會改變餐桌上下一頓飯菜的搭配。

2019 年，受「豬週期」下行、非洲豬瘟疫情衝擊、中美貿易戰等因素疊加影響，中國內地的豬肉價格出現大幅度上漲。豬肉是重要的大宗農副產品，也是日常消費的主要肉類。2018 年，中國內地居民人均豬肉消費量為 22.83 千克 [1]，按總人口 13.95 億 [2] 計算，年度總消費量高達 3,185 萬噸。

2019 年第一季度與中國內地豬價同步起飛的，還有美國生豬期貨市場。芝加哥商品交易所 (Chicago Mercantile Exchange，簡稱 CME) 的美國瘦肉豬期貨 (Lean Hogs Futures) 多個品種續漲至合約高點，活躍合約的期貨結算價一度接近 100 美分／磅。此後在貿易摩擦加劇、資金面及供需驅動等多因素共同作用下，現貨與期貨價格呈現「剪刀差」走勢 (見圖 1)。

1　資料來源：中國國家統計局。
2　資料來源：中國國家統計局。

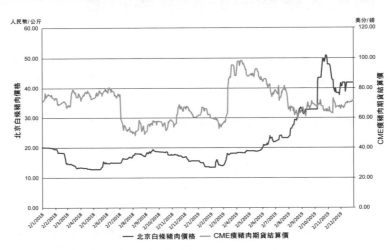

資料來源：Wind（源自中國農業資訊網、CME）。

　　毋庸置疑，大宗商品是工農業生產的重要原料及產成品，是實體經濟的基石。
而長遠來看，大宗商品也是使資產組合多樣化的重要投資標的。有報道[3]指出，
美國主要農產品期貨品種中，非商業多頭持倉佔市場合計多頭持倉的比例保持在
25%-35%的區間內，包括商品指數基金在內的各類資產管理產品是商品期貨市場
重要的參與者。

　　數量多、價格波動大、金融屬性強，大宗商品已成為影響實體經濟和金融市
場運行的重要因素。

3　〈機構「敲門」大宗商品資產配置價值凸顯〉，載於《中國證券報·中證網》，2019年8月28日。

2　內地大宗商品的分類

　　按照交易屬性劃分，大宗商品可分為商品類與權益類兩類。按照是否在期貨交易所上市交易又可以分成商品期貨品種和現貨品種。

表 1：大宗商品分類		
分類	子分類	品類
商品類	能源	原油、汽油、天然氣、動力煤等
	基礎原材料	鐵、銅、鋁、鉛、鋅、鎳、鎢、橡膠、鐵礦石等
	貴金屬	黃金、鉑金、白銀等
	農副產品	玉米、大豆、小麥、稻穀、燕麥、大麥、黑麥、豬腩、活豬、活牛、小牛、大豆粉、大豆油、可可、咖啡、棉花、羊毛、糖、橙汁、菜籽油等
權益類	航運權、林權、碳排放權等	

2.1　商品類大宗商品

　　傳統大宗商品範疇僅包含商品類，交易品種遍佈各類型期貨、現貨交易所。表 2 列出內地商品類期貨的主要品種。

表 2：商品期貨品種					
品種名	2017 年		2018 年		2019 年	
	交易量（萬手）	交易額（億元人民幣）	交易量（萬手）	交易額（億元人民幣）	交易量（萬手）	交易額（億元人民幣）
黃大豆 1 號	2,632	10,246	2,211	8,079	1,845	6,422
線型低密度聚乙烯（LLDPE）	6,142	29,148	3,674	17,105	6,344	24,492
豆粕	16,288	45,854	23,816	73,500	27,287	76,030
豆油	5,716	35,473	5,414	31,020	8,754	52,512
黃大豆 2 號	4	14	2,448	8,337	1,779	5,499
玉米	12,732	21,071	6,681	12,323	9,912	18,841
玉米澱粉	5,043	9,927	2,261	5,103	1,656	3,808
棕櫚油	6,805	37,804	4,434	21,635	13,550	71,298
聚氯乙烯	3,900	12,783	3,636	12,192	3,379	11,246

(續)

品種名	表 2：商品期貨品種					
	2017 年		2018 年		2019 年	
	交易量（萬手）	交易額（億元人民幣）	交易量（萬手）	交易額（億元人民幣）	交易量（萬手）	交易額（億元人民幣）
焦煤	4,219	31,144	4,647	35,478	2,287	17,763
焦炭	4,012	77,295	6,907	149,675	5,568	111,372
鐵礦石	32,874	170,795	23,649	115,281	29,654	198,731
雞蛋	3,726	14,228	1,992	7,847	3,713	15,673
膠合板	0	1	0	0	0	0
聚丙烯	5,669	24,264	4,935	23,009	9,371	38,902
纖維板	—		3	13	117	235
粳米	—	—	—	—	41	150
苯乙烯	—	—	—	—	396	1,442
鋁	6,542	49,265	4,662	33,557	3,276	22,746
燃料油	0	3	3,927	12,048	17,672	42,710
天然橡膠	8,934	137,511	6,185	73,625	5,385	64,483
銅	5,410	133,874	5,125	129,768	3,652	87,251
鋅	9,145	107,026	9,235	104,117	7,107	72,001
螺紋鋼	70,202	242,706	53,098	201,710	46,517	169,470
線材	0	0	16	58	17	68
黃金	1,948	54,193	1,612	44,248	4,621	149,962
白銀	5,311	32,028	4,225	23,232	14,282	89,385
鉛	1,251	11,555	1,020	9,605	771	6,359
錫	208	3,014	274	4,044	325	4,541
鎳	7,415	65,030	11,482	119,696	16,044	183,879
石油瀝青	9,744	25,327	6,980	21,964	10,291	32,733
熱軋卷板	10,313	37,779	8,682	33,056	7,041	25,440
原油	—	—	2,651	127,383	3,464	154,760
20 號膠	—	—	—	—	94	997
苯二甲酸 (PTA)	14,039	36,964	17,085	55,862	31,247	88,820
白糖	6,106	39,561	6,397	33,194	11,250	59,494
菜籽油	2,599	17,374	3,508	23,262	3,779	26,958
棉花	2,606	20,124	5,847	49,272	6,381	43,616
強麥	38	218	11	55	1	6
早秈稻	0	1	4	20	0	1
晚秈稻	0	0	54	308	2	10

(續)

表 2：商品期貨品種						
品種名	2017 年		2018 年		2019 年	
	交易量（萬手）	交易額（億元人民幣）	交易量（萬手）	交易額（億元人民幣）	交易量（萬手）	交易額（億元人民幣）
玻璃	4,109	11,072	2,514	7,069	3,092	8,830
甲醇	13,701	36,574	16,390	46,842	26,509	61,002
油菜籽	0	1	0	1	6	25
菜籽粕	7,974	18,510	10,436	25,419	13,809	32,013
普麥	0	0	0	0	0	0
動力煤	3,071	18,353	4,887	30,198	2,749	15,957
粳稻	0	0	1	8	0	2
錳矽	2,492	8,513	1,885	7,537	1,117	3,941
矽鐵	1,628	5,604	2,156	7,094	931	2,768
蘋果	79	637	9,996	94,013	3,746	33,655
尿素	—	—	—	—	469	1,630

資料來源：中國期貨業協會、Wind。

2.2　權益類大宗商品

權益類大宗商品涵蓋範圍廣泛，包括航權、航運、礦權、林權、碳排放權等。權益類商品截至 2019 年末在內地仍未有對應的期貨品種。這裏重點介紹航運與碳排放權交易。

2.2.1　航運交易

航運交易業務包括船舶買賣和租賃交易、郵輪遊艇交易、航運金融和航運保險等。

1996 年 11 月，上海航運交易所獲中國國務院批准設立，是中國內地唯一一家國家級航運交易所。重慶、廣州、武漢、寧波、廈門航運交易所隨後相繼成立。然而由於航運和船舶交易標的個體差異性極大，以致每筆交易的可能參與者都相當有限。

表 3：上海航運交易所部份船舶交易成交情況						
成交日期	船型	載重噸	建造日期	船籍港	航區	成交價格（萬元人民幣）
2019-12-24	乾散貨船	626	2009-06-18	湖州	內河	62
2019-12-24	乾散貨船	430	2006-04-29	湖州	內河	29.58
2019-12-23	其他	3,490	2016-05-25	益陽	內河	300
2019-12-23	乾散貨船	3,000	2005-04-22	蕪湖	內河	180
2019-12-23	多用途船	1,825	2012-11-07	貴港	內河	206.8
2019-12-23	成品油輪	980	2012-08-16	常德	內河	26

資料來源：上海航運交易所。

2.2.2　碳排放權

碳排放權交易是《京都議定書》為促進全球減少溫室氣體排放採用市場機制建立的以《聯合國氣候變化框架公約》(United Nations Framework Convention on Climate Change，簡稱 UNFCCC) 作為依據的溫室氣體排放權（減排量）交易，碳排放權交易允許企業在總量不突破的前提下，交易碳排放量配額。其經濟學原理在於：不同企業由於所處國家、行業或是技術、管理方式上存在着的差異，實現溫室氣體減排的成本是不同的。碳排放權交易市場的運行就是鼓勵減排成本低的企業超額減排，將其所獲得的剩餘碳配額或溫室氣體減排量通過交易的方式出售給減排成本高的企業，從而幫助減排成本高的企業實現設定的減排目標，並有效降低實現目標的減排成本。

2011 年 10 月，中國國家發展和改革委員會印發《關於開展碳排放權交易試點工作的通知》，批准在北京、天津、上海、重慶、深圳、湖北省、廣東省共兩省五市開展碳排放權的交易試點。截至 2019 年末，中國已有 8 家主要的碳排放交易所在全國不同地區：

- 廣東：廣州碳排放權交易所
- 深圳：深圳排放權交易所
- 北京：北京環境交易所
- 上海：上海環境能源交易所
- 湖北：湖北碳排放權交易所
- 天津：天津排放權交易所

- 重慶：重慶碳排放權交易中心
- 福建：海峽股權交易中心

其中深圳排放權交易所在 2013 年 6 月 18 日率先啟動了交易。截至 2019 年年底，8 家碳排放交易所累計交易量達 2.73 億噸，累計交易額 57.6 億元人民幣。

圖 2：內地主要碳排放權交易場所累計交易量的分佈	圖 3：內地主要碳排放權交易場所的累計交易額

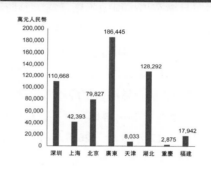

註：各場所開業至 2019 年 12 月 31 日的交易量。　　　　　　註：各場所開業至 2019 年 12 月 31 日的交易額。

資料來源：深圳排放權交易所、上海環境能源交易所、北京環境交易所、廣州碳排放權交易所、天津排放權交易所、湖北碳排放權交易中心、重慶碳排放權交易中心、海峽股權交易中心。

3　內地商品現貨市場歷史沿革及現狀

3.1　內地商品現貨市場歷史沿革

中國內地的大宗商品現貨市場即除全國性期貨交易所之外的交易大宗商品的市場，起源於 20 世紀 80 年代，在當時中國內地的計劃經濟體制下，資源配置完全採用行政手段完成，大宗商品生產及流通的數量、價格、方式均由政府部門指導確定。

1985 年，重慶提出建設工業和農產品貿易中心，大宗商品交易進入批發市場的發展階段，逐步由行政手段分配轉向自由貿易模式。1989 年，中國商務部決定建設批發市場，並推行中遠期訂貨這一類似期貨的交易方式。隨着電腦及網路技術的快速發展，1997 年中國內地推出了通過網路搭建的電子商務平台，並在平台上開展即期現貨交易與中遠期訂貨交易。自此，大宗商品市場進入了快速發展階段，由政府、大中型企業及行業協會等發起的各類大宗商品交易平台紛紛成立，交易品種與方式也日漸豐富。

然而大宗商品市場快速發展的同時，由於監管缺位，交易平台上的違法違規問題日漸突出，風險不斷暴露。為防範金融風險、規範市場秩序，中國國務院先後發文《國務院關於清理整頓各類交易場所、切實防範金融風險的決定》（國發〔2011〕38 號）、《國務院辦公廳關於清理整頓各類交易場所的實施意見》（國辦發〔2012〕37 號）等文件，並建立由中國證券監督管理委員會牽頭、有關部門參與的「清理整頓各類交易場所部際聯席會議」（即「部際聯席會議」）制度。

以「總量控制、審慎審批、合理佈局」為基本原則，部際聯席會議先後於 2012 年 2 月、2012 年 7 月、2017 年 1 月、2019 年 7 月召開四次會議並通報各類交易場所清理整頓工作進展情況。根據聯席會議當時的統計數據，中國內地 36 個省、直轄市、自治區及特別行政區現共設有商品類交易場所 596 家，其中開展貴金屬交易的有 89 家，開展原油交易的有 59 家（23 家同時開展貴金屬和原油交易）；文化藝術品類交易場所共有 113 家，其中開展郵幣卡交易的有 37 家。這近 600 家商品類交易場所中有超過三分之一因違法違規交易被叫停，尚未上線新交易品種或探索出合規盈利模式，仍處於等待觀望狀態，成為「殭屍」交易場所。

商品類交易所具有規模效應，不在數量多，而在品質、品牌與影響力，各大交易所應充分結合本地資源稟賦、產業需求，合理開設交易品種、服務實體經濟，共同促使行業健康發展。

3.2　內地商品現貨市場現狀

相較於期貨交易所而言，大宗商品現貨市場具有分散、靈活、個性化的特徵，能夠針對有一定投資需求或某種特定避險要求的投資者提供專業化的工具產品。其存在有效地填補了商品期貨市場地域與客戶覆蓋度的不足，有助於解決高度標準化期貨市場個性化不足的問題，可以極大便利具有避險和投資需求的投資者參與商品市場。

　　在交易方式上，內地大宗商品現貨市場主要以實物商品為交易標的。在交易制度上，現貨交易較期貨交易而言更加靈活，成本也更低。在交易品種上，現貨市場涉及農副產品、金屬、能源、化工等多個領域，基本覆蓋了國內各類活躍的商品交易品種。

表 4：國內主要地方大宗商品現貨交易所介紹		
成立年份	交易所名稱	相關介紹以及主營商品
2002	上海黃金交易所	提供黃金、白銀、鉑等貴金屬交易的場所、設施及相關服務，實行價格優先、時間優先撮合成交。非標準品種通過詢價等方式進行，實行自主報價、協商成交。會員可自行選擇通過現場或遠程方式進行交易。
2008	天津貴金屬交易所	天津貴金屬交易所是經天津市政府批准，由天津產權交易中心發起設立的公司制交易所。交易所上市交易的品種有現貨鉑金、現貨鈀金、現貨鎳、現貨白銀、現貨銅和現貨鋁六種貴金屬。由中國中信集團控股，天津產權交易中心，中國黃金集團公司等企業參股。交易所營業範圍為「貴金屬（含黃金、白銀）、有色金屬現貨批發、零售、延期交收，並為其提供電子平台；前述相關諮詢服務及許可的其他業務」。
2011	浙江舟山大宗商品交易所	浙江舟山大宗商品交易所經舟山市人民政府發起，由市政府設立的中國（舟山）大宗商品交易中心管理委員會直接監管，交易商品主要為浙商油、鎢精礦，第三方託管銀行為建設銀行和工商銀行。
2012	海南大宗商品交易中心	由海南省農墾集團控股 51%，聯合上海大新華易物流網絡有限公司、海南潤德投資有限公司、新湖控股有限公司、海南神農大豐種業科技股份有限公司等四家股東共同發起設立，註冊資本金 1 億元人民幣。主要交易品種為檳榔、鉑金、鈀金、白銀。
2013	南寧商品交易所	南寧商品交易所又稱中國—東盟商品交易所，主要提供化工產品、農產品、林產品、鋼鐵產品、有色金屬、成品油等大宗商品現貨品種的交易。
2013	渤海商品交易所	按照天津市人民政府對渤海商品交易所的定位和要求，渤海商品交易所在石油及化工商品、金屬商品、煤炭等能源商品、農林商品等專業領域，根據不同需求，不斷推出符合需求標準的現貨交易品種。
2014	福建金雅商品交易中心	隸屬華兆投資（北京）股份有限公司，公司主要為現貨交易市場提供 B2B（Business-to-Business，企業對企業）、B2C（Business-to-Consumer，企業對客戶）等多種模式的電子交易服務，交易商品有白銀、瀝青、銅、鎳。
2014	廣東國際商品交易中心	廣東國際商品交易中心是經廣東省人民政府審批同意，由廣東省商業企業集團主導，廣州祥能投資集團有限公司參與組建。註冊資金 1 億元人民幣，是內地首家以國際化、專業化為主導的商品交易平台。交易商品以燃料油、粵銀、粵銅為主。

資料來源：各交易所官網、新聞資料整理。

目前中國內地大宗商品現貨市場以大宗商品電子交易市場為代表，在合約品種、市場主體、運行機制、風險管控等方面與國際成熟的大宗商品場外現貨市場都存在較大差距，在其完善期貨市場功能、優化資源配置等方面的作用也受到限制。

4 大宗商品現貨市場與期貨市場的關聯

4.1 國際大宗商品市場的發展歷程

國際大宗商品交易市場先後經歷了三個階段：首先是傳統的現貨交易，其次是場外衍生品市場，最後才是當前的場內期貨市場。所以其大宗商品交易體系十分成熟完善，市場功能也可以得到充分的體現與發揮。

上世紀 70 年代後，國際大宗商品交易市場高速發展，在此背景下各國激烈地爭奪全球商品定價權。很多國際性交易所均構建了健全的動態交易系統、完善的現貨交割體系，以及各具特色的金融及物流服務。

目前，國際上比較具有影響力的大宗商品交易市場主要有倫敦金屬交易所（London Metal Exchange，簡稱 LME）、新加坡商品交易所（Singapore Commodity Exchange Limited，簡稱 SICOM）、洲際交易所集團（Intercontinental Exchange，簡稱 ICE）、CME 等。這些大宗商品交易市場一般於經濟較為發達的地區形成，背靠強大的商業及金融體系。

表 5：國際部份主要大宗商品交易市場		
地區	成立年份	名稱
歐洲	1877	倫敦金屬交易所
	1988	歐洲期貨交易所
北美	1856	美國堪薩斯商品交易所
	1874	芝加哥商品交易所
	1874	加拿大蒙特利爾交易所
	1998	美國洲際交易所

(續)

表 5：國際部份主要大宗商品交易市場		
地區	成立年份	名稱
亞洲	1951	東京工業品交易所
	1952	東京穀物交易所
	1990	鄭州商品交易所
	1990	上海期貨交易所
	1993	大連商品交易所
	2007	迪拜商品交易所
	2010	新加坡商品交易所

對上述國際主要大宗商品交易所發展模式進行梳理後，我們發現大宗商品交易場所發展可以分為「先發」和「後發」兩大類。

「先發模式」是指根據大宗商品交易市場在現貨貿易逐步向期貨合約交易發展歷史過程中，逐漸成為地區性乃至國際性的大宗商品交易場所，如芝加哥商業交易所。現代意義上的期貨交易實際產生於19世紀中期的芝加哥，芝加哥作為美國重要的糧食集散地，通過採用標準化遠期合約逐步發展成為大宗商品期貨交易中心。倫敦金屬交易所也是在倫敦成為國際性金融中心的發展過程中逐步建成的。

基於此種模式下大宗商品交易市場體系呈現「現貨 —— 中遠期 —— 期貨 —— 場外」市場發展路徑，在市場發展初期，基礎現貨市場較為活躍，總體表現出即期性、分散化等特點。隨着現貨市場的發展，市場參與者逐步產生了風險規避需求，因而逐步形成了大宗商品中遠期交易，合約中對價格、品種、期限、保證金、數量等參數進行約定。隨着中遠期市場的進一步發展，參與商對履約風險控制、遠期合約流動性等提出了更高要求，並結合技術的進步和金融信用體系的發展，逐漸提高期貨合約的標準化水平，推進期貨的場內市場發展。但是標準化的合約難以完全滿足交易商定制化的需求，隨着金融衍生品市場的發展，大宗商品的場外市場不斷壯大。

「後發模式」是指政府根據金融市場發展和區域性金融中心建設的需要，利用自身特點和地緣優勢，主動差異化發展建成國際性大宗商品交易場所。中國內地的期貨交易所就是此類模式的典型案例。定位明確、政策保障，此類交易所發展往往極其迅速，但因不是從現貨一步步演進而來，商品市場配套支持不夠完善。

4.2　內地大宗商品現貨市場與期貨市場的關聯

　　大宗商品市場的交易通常可以分為三個層面：第一層是實體經濟參與者，包括生產商、消費者及現貨物流企業；第二層是服務實體經濟參與者的貿易及金融服務的提供商或中介機構；第三層則是純金融投資者。

　　對比內地與境外商品市場，能夠發現境外商品市場的參與客戶為典型的正金字塔，三個層面的參與者均有覆蓋，但主要參與者是第一層與第二層。而內地商品市場卻像個倒金字塔：第一層的實體經濟參與者與第二層的貿易、金融服務提供者及中介機構所參與的現貨市場還不太發達和規範，倉儲認證增信環節薄弱，流通領域融資困難，整個現貨生態系統效率低下、成本高企、風險叢生；但是第三層的期貨市場交易卻異常活躍，投資羣體以散戶為主，實物交割有限。也正因此，內地商品期貨市場與現貨市場的關聯度還不夠高，大宗商品市場的金融服務遠遠不能滿足實體經濟需求。

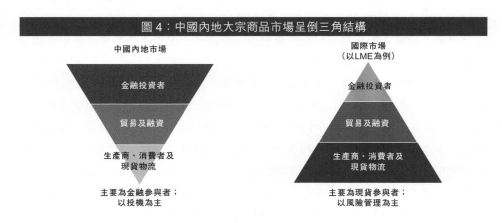

圖 4：中國內地大宗商品市場呈倒三角結構

4.3　規範內地大宗商品現貨市場的建議

4.3.1　建設多層次市場體系

　　發展多層次大宗商品市場能有效對接市場經濟中多元參與主體，滿足實體經濟多樣化的商品流轉和風險管理需求。

　　首先，要建立期貨、現貨聯動的市場交易機制，在全國期貨市場與地方現貨
市場之間設計一整套包含大宗商品及其衍生品的完整市場體系，充分發揮全國性
商品交易所、地方期貨中介機構以及地方性商品交易平台的積極作用，為市場參
與者提供多元化、個性化的大宗商品交易和風險管理服務。

　　其次，要利用好現有市場形態、功能和機制，尤其是健全期貨市場的集中定
價與清算職能，充分建立全國性期貨市場與地方性大宗商品現貨市場的連接，使
大宗商品市場能更好地服務於實體經濟。

4.3.2　打造國際大宗商品交易中心

　　國際大宗商品交易中心，是世界各地大宗商品貿易的關鍵節點，代表着一個
地區參與全球貨物貿易競爭的水平。

　　現階段，中國作為最大的大宗商品生產國、進口國及消費國，其商品貿易規
模不斷擴大，但尚未形成具有世界影響力的大宗商品交易中心，在一定程度上制
約了中國在世界貿易中的競爭力。

　　未來，通過創新交易、交割與結算模式，依託現貨產業鏈、貿易鏈，打造高
品質的大宗商品國際化交易市場將會是當下內地商品交易所的必經之路。

5　結語

　　大宗商品與人類生產生活息息相關，近年來已成為資產管理的重要投資標的。
隨着中國經濟的快速發展與加速開放，其大宗商品市場的國際化程度進一步加深，
但作為多種大宗商品最大進口國與消費國，中國內地大宗商品市場仍然存在起步
晚、開放程度不高、定價話語權有待繼續提升的問題，在市場建設中發展不均衡、
業務重疊、監管缺位等現象也普遍存在。

　　通過梳理國際上具有影響力的大宗商品交易市場發展歷程，我們發現中國內
地的期貨交易所為典型後發模式：定位明確、政策充分支持、發展極為迅速，但

商品市場配套支持也因此不夠完善，商品期貨交易所與現貨市場的相關度不夠高，金融服務也遠遠無法滿足實體經濟需求。為規範中國內地大宗商品現貨市場，我們建議監管單位應充分支持現貨市場發展、引領打造多層次市場體系，並建設國際大宗商品交易中心、提升世界貿易中的競爭力。

第 8 章

中國內地大宗商品市場的
國際地位與對外開放

深圳前海聯合交易中心有限公司

摘 要

　　本文梳理並分析了中國內地大宗商品市場的國際地位，發現內地大宗商品市場的需求與產業鏈定價權不匹配，提出了加強內地交易所的協同效應、推進金融監管體制的改革及合理利用香港金融中心的優勢等商品市場對外開放的政策建議。

1 內地大宗商品市場的國際地位

1.1　消費大國

　　中國是僅次於美國的全球第二大經濟體，現已成為鐵礦石、銅、鎳、煤炭、棉花等主要大宗商品的最大消費國，進口了全球近 70% 的鐵礦石[1]和 40% 的銅精礦[2]。在世界經濟增長放緩、國際環境更加嚴峻複雜、國內經濟下行壓力持續加大的大環境下，中國內地的大部份大宗商品進口量依然保持較高速增長，油品進口增速尤其明顯：2018 年中國內地的原油進口量高達 4.62 億噸，成品油進口量 3,348 萬噸，分別較 2017 年增長 10.09% 及 12.96%。2018 年中國內地原油進口量佔當年石油出口國組織（OPEC）全球總出口量的 37.61%，已超越美國（佔 18.60%），成為全球最大的原油進口國[3]。

表 1：部份大宗商品進口情況				
品類	2018 年進口金額		2018 年進口數量	
	（億美元）	對比 2017 年的變化	（萬噸）	對比 2017 年的變化
大豆	380.87	-3.91%	8,804	-7.84%
煤	247.61	9.39%	28,189	4.06%
原油	2,403.80	48.08%	46,189	10.09%
鋼材	164.35	8.34%	1,317	-0.98%

資料來源：中國國家統計局。

1.2　定價權缺失

　　從國際大宗商品市場供需結構來看，中國內地無疑是諸多品種的最大需求方。

[1]　國際鋼鐵協會資料顯示，2017 年全球鐵礦石進口量為 15.77 億噸，其中中國進口量為 10.75 億噸，佔比 68%。（資料來源：Wind。）
[2]　資料來源：Observatory of Economic Complexity (OEC) 網站（https://oec.world/en/profile/hs92/260300/），於 2020 年 1 月 17 日閱覽。
[3]　資料來源：中國國家統計局、中國海關總署、石油輸出國組織（OPEC），經計算得出。

然而在世界大宗商品市場中，中國需求的日益增加卻成了影響大宗商品漲價的重要因素。中國內地的原油對外依存度超過 70%，原油進口價格從 2017 年的平均 386.89 美元 / 噸漲至 520.43 美元 / 噸，漲幅高達 34.51%[4]。由於缺乏國際定價權，中國儼然已成為全球大宗商品價格波動的最大受害者。

　　中國內地參與大宗商品市場的貿易商數量多且分散，沒有形成一個統一有效的行業聯盟，而且重點企業對於產業鏈上下游整體的控制力弱，因此出現了這樣一種奇怪現象：在國際大宗商品現貨交易中，中國內地商品進口往往順從國際價格，而出口企業卻競相壓價。作為世界上最重要的大宗商品貿易國，中國的需求優勢尚未充分轉換形成產業鏈定價優勢，對於主要大宗商品的價格影響力十分有限，面臨着僅僅作為國際市場價格被動接受者的現實困境。

2　內地大宗商品市場的對外開放情況

2.1　境外投資者的准入

　　引入境外投資者是現階段中國內地大宗商品市場對外開放的重要手段。通過政策吸引全球投資者廣泛參與境內大宗商品交易，有助於促使中國商品市場價格得到國際市場的廣泛關注和使用，充分發揮期貨市場避險和套期保值作用。交易品種准入門檻的降低、參與主體准入的對外開放也可以促進中國內地與周邊其他國家和地區在商品、資本、交通、資訊等方面的自由流通，這對於積極發展與沿線國家的經濟合作夥伴關係，促進「一帶一路」建設，實現經濟社會發展水平的共同提升，進而共同打造政治互信、經濟融合、文化包容的利益共同體有深遠意義。

　　當下，境外投資者的准入政策主要如表 2 所示。

4　資料來源：中國國家統計局、中國海關總署、OPEC，經計算得出。

發佈年份	政策條例名稱	發佈機構	相關介紹
2015	《境外交易者和境外經紀機構從事境內特定品種期貨交易管理暫行辦法》	中國證券監督管理委員會	規定境外交易者可以根據自身情況和業務需要，選擇通過境內期貨公司或者境外經紀機構從事境內特定品種期貨交易；符合條件的境外交易者也可直接在期貨交易所從事境內特定品種期貨交易。境外經紀機構可根據情況，在接受境外交易者委託後，委託境內期貨公司進行境內特定品種期貨交易。該辦法為境外投資者直接進入期貨交易所進行期貨交易預留了空間，有利於提高中國內地期貨交易的國際化程度，解決了境外貿易機構在境內從事原油期貨等特定品種的交易問題。
2017	《期貨交易管理條例（2017 年修訂）》	中華人民共和國國務院	該條例第八條指出期貨交易所會員應當是在中華人民共和國境內登記註冊的企業法人或者其他經濟組織。該條例第十七條明確期貨公司業務實行許可制度，由國務院期貨監督管理機構按照其商品期貨、金融期貨業務種類頒發許可證。期貨公司除申請經營境內期貨經紀業務外，還可以申請經營境外期貨經紀、期貨投資諮詢以及國務院期貨監督管理機構規定的其他期貨業務。該次修訂大大擴展了境外大宗商品場內交易機構在中國內地可從事的業務範圍，有利於增強內地大宗商品市場對境外機構的吸引力，使得境外機構能夠在更加公平的條件下參與內地大宗商品市場的競爭，推進內地大宗商品市場與國際市場的互聯互通。
2017	《外商投資期貨公司管理辦法》	中國證券監督管理委員會	根據銀行、證券、保險等金融行業對外開放的經驗，引進境外戰略投資者有利於學習成熟理念、優化股權結構和體制機制，為境內期貨公司注入品牌和核心技術，同時便於打通境外市場以充分利用國際客戶資源，提高公司的全球市場知名度，完成從本土到國際化的轉變。

表 2：內地商品市場針對境外投資者准入門檻的相關政策條例

資料來源：根據新聞報導整理。

　　2005 年以來先後有摩根大通、高盛、蘇格蘭皇家銀行、法國興業銀行、瑞銀等國際投資銀行參股境內期貨公司嘗試國際化運作。但根據中國內地當時的監管規定，外資不能控股內地期貨公司、境外資本不能參與境內期貨交易所的設立，內地商品市場的開放尚有相當的路要走。為解決以上問題，進一步深化對外開放水平，2019 年 10 月 23 日中國國務院發佈了《關於進一步做好利用外資工作的意見》，提出將在 2020 年取消證券公司、證券投資基金管理公司、期貨公司、壽險公司外資持股比例不超過 51% 的限制，加快金融業的開放進程，這或將加速中國內地商品市場的對外開放。

表 3：部份參與內地期貨交易的外資金融機構

名稱	參股外資金融機構	參股比例	經營情況
銀河期貨	蘇格蘭皇家銀行	16.68%	為中國內地第一家合資期貨公司，在 2019 年期貨行業協會的排名中位於第四，評級為 AA
摩根大通期貨	摩根大通	49%	2019 年期貨行業協會排名為第 30 名，評級為 A
中信新際期貨	新際集團	42%	於 2014 年被中信期貨吸收合併，外資退出

資料來源：根據新聞報導整理。

2.2　內地商品交易所及品種的開放情況

2.2.1　商品期貨交易所的對外開放

　　上海、大連和鄭州三家商品期貨交易所商品期貨與期權成交總量約佔全球大宗商品成交量的近六成[5]，期貨期權品種已達到 70 個，基本涵蓋國民經濟發展的各大領域。在境內交易專業化、規範化的過程中，三家期貨交易所也在探索國際化道路。2018 年 5 月 4 日，鐵礦石期貨作為內地首個已上市品種，成功試點引入境外交易者。隨後上海期貨交易所子公司上海國際能源交易中心（簡稱 INE）也先後上線原油及 20 號膠期貨，全面引入境外交易者參與交易。

表 4：內地商品期貨交易所的開放情況

交易所名稱	國際化品種及相關介紹
大連商品交易所	2018 年 5 月 4 日，大連商品交易所允許境外交易者參與其鐵礦石期貨的交易。經過一年多的穩定運行，鐵礦石期貨國際化已基本起步。境外交易者參與積極，市場結構持續優化。2018 年，中國鐵礦石期貨成交量是世界第二大鐵礦石衍生品市場 — 新交所（SGX）— 的鐵礦石掉期和期貨的 22 倍，繼續保持全球最大鐵礦石衍生品市場的地位，為企業套保提供了充足的流動性。近年來以鐵礦石期貨價格為基準的基差貿易也逐步開展，2017 年鐵礦石現貨基差貿易量不足 500 萬噸，2018 年攀升到 1,000 萬噸，2019 年上半年已與 2018 年全年的量持平。
鄭州商品交易所	2018 年 11 月 30 日，苯二甲酸（PTA）期貨正式引入境外交易者入場交易。以 PTA 期貨為試點引入境外交易者，將進一步推動中國成為全球聚酯產品的定價中心。
上海期貨交易所及其子公司 INE	2019 年 3 月 26 日，內地首個國際化期貨品種 —— 原油期貨在 INE 掛牌交易，開啟原油期貨市場的國際化進程。原油期貨運行情況良好，於 2018 年年末日成交量已達到單邊 15 萬手的水平，成為全球第三大原油交易市場，價格已逐步得到市場的認可。2019 年 8 月 12 日，20 號膠期貨正式在上海期貨交易所掛牌上市，是繼原油期貨後，內地推出的第二隻「國際平台、人民幣計價」模式的期貨交易品種，將全面引入境外交易者參與。

資料來源：根據新聞報導整理。

5　資料來源：〈我國大宗商品期貨成交量已連續 7 年位居世界第一〉，載於《央視網》網站 2017 年 6 月 18 日。

中國內地已有原油、鐵礦石、PTA、20 號膠四個期貨品種引入境外交易者，走向國際市場。截至 2019 年年末，INE 原油期貨累計成交量 1.22 億手，累計成交額 56.4 萬億元[6]，境外開戶數量較上市初期增長數倍。隨着更多期貨品種的國際化，更多的境外投資者會參與到中國內地的期貨市場中來，自然也會有更多的外資機構進入內地期貨行業，這也有助於促進內地期貨行業機構專業服務能力的提升。

表 5：部份內地國際化期貨交易品種的交易現狀			
品種	2019 年日均成交量	境外交易者情況	境外交易者的交易佔比
鐵礦石期貨	~243.1 萬手	截至 2019 年 10 月底，已有來自 15 個國家和地區的 170 多個境外客戶開戶，其中新加坡地區客戶佔境外客戶總數的 20%。	截至 2019 年 4 月境外交易者的鐵礦石交易量佔比達到 19%。
PTA 期貨	~256.1 萬手	截至 2019 年 9 月底，共有 115 個境外客戶開戶，29 家境外仲介機構完成了備案。境外客戶持倉量突破 1 萬手，市場運行良好。	截至 2019 年末境外交易者 PTA 交易量佔比 7.6%。
原油期貨	~28.4 萬手	截至 2019 年 10 月底，境外客戶開戶數已經超過 100 家，來自包括英國、澳洲、新加坡等 9 個國家，以及中國香港、台灣和澳門地區。另外還完成了來自中國香港以及新加坡、英國、韓國、日本、荷蘭 53 家境外仲介機構的備案。	截至 2019 年 10 月，境外交易者的交易量佔比達到 17.5%，日均持倉量佔比為 23.7%。

資料來源：根據新聞報導及 Wind 資料整理。

從鐵礦石、PTA，再到原油和 20 號膠，內地期貨市場穩步擴大對外開放品種範圍。讓中國內地較為成熟、具有中國內地特色的商品率先走出去、吸引境外投資者入場交易，對於提升內地商品價格的國際影響力、為中國內地企業跨境經營提供價格參考和風險管理工具具有重大意義。

2.2.2　商品現貨交易所的對外開放

中國內地商品現貨交易所的對外開放起步相對較晚，做了先期探索工作的主要有上海黃金交易所及渤海大宗商品交易所。

6　資料來源：Wind（上海期貨交易所資料）。

表 6：內地商品現貨交易所的開放情況	
交易所名稱	國際化品種及相關介紹
上海黃金交易所	上海黃金交易所國際板是上海首個面向國際的交易平台，允許境外投資者在內地黃金市場進行投資，產品被稱為「上海金」。2019 年 7 月 31 日，上海黃金交易所國際板指定倉庫落地深圳。
渤海大宗商品交易所	天津渤海大宗商品交易所現有生活消費品、大宗農林、石油化工、礦產資源、有色金屬等七大板塊 80 餘種產品種類。渤海大宗商品交易所創新推出了 "BEST" 現貨交易制度[7]，依託交易所與電商平台融合，覆蓋全球資金結算、市場服務、資訊宣傳、倉儲物流等功能。2013 年 4 月在中國人民銀行的批准下，該交易所成為國內首個跨境交易人民幣結算平台試點。

資料來源：根據新聞報導整理。

3 內地商品市場對外開放的建議

推動內地大宗商品市場對外開放對於加速國際資本和商品流通，進而形成國際大宗商品交易信息網路，對於幫助中國內地的貿易商獲取買方議價權，以及獲取全球大宗商品市場上的人民幣定價權等均具有重要戰略意義。

第一，各內地大宗商品交易所宜充分利用地域優勢，加強交易協同效應、防止惡性競爭，實現互利共贏合作，豐富、明確各家交易所在大宗商品市場的成長路徑。

第二，可以考慮從制度層面深入推進金融監管體制改革，構建並完善宏觀審慎與微觀監管相結合的監管體系，促進中國內地大宗商品市場有序、健康地逐步實現對外開放。

第三，可充分利用香港的地域優勢和市場優勢，合理引入相關成熟配套制度設計，全面提升內地商品市場的開放水平。

---

7 具體包括延期交收補償制度、中間倉補收以及現貨即期交易等制度。

第9章

香港的大宗商品市場

香港交易及結算所有限公司
大宗商品發展部

摘 要

香港作為國際金融中心，在金融業界多個範疇均有出色成就，然而其大宗商品市場的發展則相對薄弱，與紐約及倫敦等其他大宗商品交易中心比起來顯得落後於人。要成為成功的大宗商品交易中心，關鍵元素之一是相關大宗商品交易所的市場容易進出、價格發現及對沖方面均可提供許多不同的解決方案。

現時香港唯一受自律監管的大宗商品現貨市場由金銀業貿易場營運，金銀業貿易場為其會員提供金銀貿易的平台、設施及相關服務。另一方面，香港唯一受監管的大宗商品衍生產品市場是由香港期貨交易所（簡稱「期交所」）營運；期交所近年積極拓展產品種類，支持及促進香港的大宗商品市場發展。

2014 年至 2019 年間，期交所推出了貴金屬、基本金屬及黑色金屬期貨合約，以促進亞洲時區的大宗商品對沖及套戥活動。期交所貴金屬方面，黃金期貨流通量逐漸上升，2019 年 6 月又推出六隻以美元及離岸人民幣計價的黃金期貨指數，為未來推出更多貴金屬衍生產品奠定基礎。

期交所基本金屬產品方面，2019 年 8 月推出了六隻以美元計價的倫敦金屬期貨小型合約，分別為鋁、銅、鉛、鎳、錫及鋅，簡化了倫敦金屬交易所（LME）傳統基本金屬合約的交易機制。與此同時，香港交易所與 LME 正就多項共同推行「倫港通」的協作計劃進行建設性討論。

香港交易所亦開始涉足黑色金屬。期交所以現金結算的 TSI CFR 中國鐵礦石 62% 鐵粉期貨合約（鐵礦石期貨）於 2017 年 11 月開始買賣，到 2019 年產品的交投已相當不俗。

香港交易所推出有關大宗商品的發展策略後，市場參與者就未來發展提出了許多意見及寶貴建議，包括在香港設立倉儲服務，以便進行基本金屬實物交收、調低現時黃金期貨的合約單位、認可由合資格本地精煉廠製造的金條等，都是需要多方面協調配合的工作。相信金銀業貿易場、期交所以及大宗商品場外交易市場之間仍有很多合作空間，以提升香港作為全球大宗商品貿易中心的國際地位。

1 香港大宗商品市場
—— 根基尚淺但潛力高

香港向有國際金融中心的美譽，備受全球尊崇，在金融業多個方面均有出色表現，包括：全亞洲保險公司最多、保險密度最高的地區[1]；擁有全球最大的離岸人民幣資金池[2]；近十年來新股集資額每年都躋身全球五大交易所之列[3]等。然而，一直以來側重發展股本證券產品，卻令定息產品及大宗商品等其他方面的發展相形見絀。須知拓展市場上資產類別的寬度和深度非常重要，可減輕香港金融市場對個別金融工具（即個別市場板塊）的依賴，令整體金融行業更具韌性，亦不會因個別市場板塊表現失色而受到拖累。

若與定息板塊相比，大宗商品板塊可能更為薄弱。大宗商品交易的經濟模式自成一格，有不少特有風險需要好好管理，還須用上特別技巧方可處理得當。所以，許多公司都專設獨立部門處理其大宗商品交易活動，凝聚了一眾擅長交易、營銷、物流和風險管理等技能的精英；而這些人才匯聚的盛況，通常都可在大宗商品交易樞紐得見。

環顧全球，稱得上大宗商品交易樞紐的有好幾個，例如芝加哥是主要的農產品中心、倫敦是金屬中心、休士頓是能源交易中心等；亞洲方面，位處區內商品貿易路線中心點的新加坡是橡膠、鐵礦石及貴金屬等商品的交易樞紐。這些樞紐大都是已有數十年歷史的大宗商品集散地，它們之所以成為世界數一數二的大宗商品交易中心、兼且「各有所長」，背後往往離不開其接近商品運輸的貨運路線和基建配套。

要成為成功的大宗商品貿易中心，關鍵元素之一是相關大宗商品交易所的市場容易進出、價格釐定及對沖方面可提供許多不同的解決方案，例如芝加哥期貨交易所（CBOT）的大豆期貨、洲際交易所集團（ICE）的西德克薩斯中間基原油（輕

1　2019 年營運中的認可公司有 162 家，2018 年的人均保費為 8,863 美元。資料來源：〈財智匯港〉，香港金融發展局單張，2019 年 9 月。

2　2019 年 6 月的總存款達人民幣 6,278 億元。資料來源：〈財智匯港〉，香港金融發展局單張，2019 年 9 月。

3　參照國際證券交易所聯會網站的市場數據。

質原油）期貨、新加坡商品交易所的橡膠期貨等。

現時香港唯一受規管的現貨商品市場是由金銀業貿易場營運，而香港期貨交易所（簡稱「期交所」，為香港交易及結算所有限公司（簡稱「香港交易所」）的全資附屬公司）則營運香港唯一受規管的大宗商品衍生產品市場。顧名思義，金銀業貿易場只提供黃金和白銀的現貨買賣。另一方面，有見香港的大宗商品市場一直是相對較弱的環節，期交所近年積極拓展產品種類，擴大旗下大宗商品的衍生產品選擇。下圖 1 介紹香港的黃金交易概況，而以下分節則簡述金銀業貿易場和期交所的相關業務。

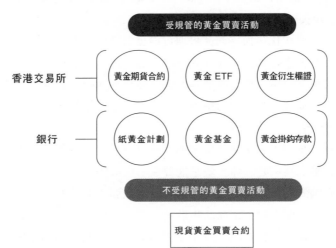

圖 1：香港的黃金交易

受規管的黃金買賣活動

香港交易所 — 黃金期貨合約　黃金 ETF　黃金衍生權證

銀行 — 紙黃金計劃　黃金基金　黃金掛鈎存款

不受規管的黃金買賣活動

現貨黃金買賣合約

資料來源：投資者及理財教育委員會網站。

1.1　金銀業貿易場 [4]

金銀業貿易場於 1910 年創立，是個自律監管的業界組織，職能包括提供買賣貴金屬的平台、設施及相關服務，並制定及實施業務規則，規範業界的交易行為。

4　資料來源：載於投資者及理財教育委員會網站上的〈認識買賣黃金及其相關產品的保障〉（2018 年 2 月 14 日），
　　於 2019 年 12 月 16 日瀏覽。

金銀業貿易場採用「行員制」，行員必須以公司名義登記。行員可以使用該場的交易平台進行貴金屬買賣活動。就倫敦金買賣而言，金銀業貿易場設有一個電子交易平台，讓其認可的電子交易行員處理客戶的交易（行員可以選擇將客戶的交易在該電子交易平台與其他行員交易或與客戶直接交易後再向金銀業貿易場申報），經電子交易平台處理的交易，會有一個交易編碼，讓投資者查閱交易內容。

不過，法例上並無規定黃金交易商須加入金銀業貿易場成為行員才可做黃金現貨買賣，這意味着並非只有金銀業貿易場的行員才可以從事現貨金買賣，因此香港黃金市場會有未受規管的場外交易。

1.2　香港期貨交易所（期交所）

期交所是受香港證券及期貨事務監察委員會（簡稱「證監會」）規管的期貨交易所。期交所於 1976 年成立，2000 年與香港聯合交易所（簡稱「聯交所」）及各自聯屬的結算所合併，成為香港交易所旗下全資附屬公司。期交所提供多種期權及期貨產品，掛鈎的資產包括股票市場指數、股票、短期利率、外匯及大宗商品。對應香港由金銀業貿易場營運的實體黃金市場，期交所現時涉及大宗商品的產品組合亦包括黃金期貨合約。（有關期交所場內大宗商品市場的更多詳情見第 2 節。）

期交所作為提供標準衍生產品合約的可信中央交易平台，在許多方面都可以大展拳腳，以支援和推動香港大宗商品市場的發展。

2　現有的場內大宗商品衍生產品市場

香港位處中國南大門，向以其優越的港口地理位置而聞名，再加上奉行自由市場和傳統轉口貿易港地位，這個金融中心也是全球主要金銀市場之一，現貨金交易相當活躍。此外，香港是全球最大的離岸人民幣中心，其獨特地位有助中國推動人民幣國際化的計劃。憑藉這些固有優勢，香港交易所銳意建立一個亞洲時區大宗商品平台，在香港提供具有國際競爭力的產品，更好的服務大宗商品市場。

香港交易所早在其《戰略規劃 2016-2018》中已經提及其目標包括在定息及貨幣產品和大宗商品領域，培育新的價格發現能力、樹立基準價格並開發多種風險管理工具。為了實現這一目標，香港交易所於 2017 年下半年推出了以美元和香港離岸人民幣計價並且可在香港實物交收的黃金期貨合約 **（美元黃金期貨及人民幣（香港）黃金期貨）**，以及美元計價和現金結算的 TSI CFR 中國鐵礦石 62% 鐵粉期貨 **（鐵礦石期貨）**。

及至《戰略規劃 2019-2021》，香港交易所就持續擴展大宗商品的產品組合、大宗商品的定價和商品「通」等方面的發展定出進一步的願景。按此，香港交易所於 2019 年下半年推出了以美元計價及現金結算的倫敦金屬期貨小型合約 **（美元倫敦金屬期貨小型合約）**，與 2014 年 12 月和 2015 年 12 月先後分兩批推出的以香港離岸人民幣計價的倫敦金屬期貨小型合約 **（人民幣（香港）倫敦金屬期貨小型合約）** 形成更全面的產品組合。

這樣的一個場內市場能夠提供貴金屬、基本金屬和黑色金屬的期貨合約（見下文各節），有助亞洲時區的投資者進行大宗商品對沖及套戥活動。事實上，香港的場內大宗商品平台凝聚了具中國內地背景的期交所參與者，又有來自世界各地的金融市場參與者的資金，儼然成為一個將中國的大宗商品貿易與世界聯繫起來的互動網絡。

2.1　貴金屬衍生產品

美元黃金期貨及人民幣（香港）黃金期貨的主要特徵之一是實物交收，這可使期貨價格與現貨價在透明且受監管的交易平台上接軌。

香港要發展一個「新的大宗商品市場」無疑有不少挑戰，但其黃金期貨市場的流動性已漸上軌道：產品的平均每日交易量已從 2019 年初大約 1,300 張合約增長至 2019 年底超過 2,000 張合約，增幅逾 50%（見圖 2）；未平倉合約的數字更於 2019 年 12 月 27 日錄得破紀錄的 1,272 張。為使期交所向流通量提供者和自營交易商提供的優惠更加集中、提高效率，2019 年流通量提供者及自營交易商的總數分別從約 30 名減少至 20 名。另外，美元黃金期貨的買賣差價於 2019 年內四至六成的交易時間中亦收窄到一至兩個價位 [5]。

5　資料來源：所有相關市場數據及資料來自香港交易所。

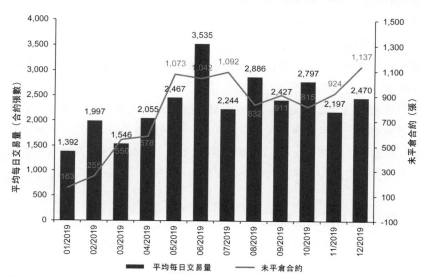

圖 2：香港黃金期貨每月的平均每日交易量及月底未平倉合約數量（2019）

資料來源：香港交易所。

2.2　基本金屬衍生產品

　　香港交易所於 2014 年 12 月 1 日推出人民幣（香港）倫敦鋁／鋅／銅期貨小型合約，是香港首批以人民幣交易的商品合約。合約的設計旨在切合中國現貨市場參與者的對沖需要，助其管理以人民幣定價的商品交易的風險、幫助持有人民幣的交易商減少保證金融資需要，以及在亞洲時區內建立金屬的人民幣定價。一年之後，香港交易所於 2015 年 12 月 14 日再推出第二批同類產品，分別是以人民幣計價的人民幣（香港）倫敦鎳／錫／鉛期貨小型合約。鎳、錫、鉛與鋁、鋅、銅均是香港交易所的全資附屬公司倫敦金屬交易所（LME）市場上成交最活躍的期貨合約。由於這六種金屬在獨特性、使用及供求因素方面各有特色，香港交易所的人民幣（香港）倫敦金屬期貨小型合約可以滿足基本金屬消費者、生產商和投資者的不同需要，特別是在亞洲交易時段內需要買賣期貨合約的客戶。

　　除人民幣產品外，香港交易所還於 2019 年 8 月 5 日推出了美元倫敦金屬期貨小型合約，包括與相應人民幣產品相同的六種基本金屬的期貨合約，為亞洲時區內涉足相關美元計價基本金屬買賣的用戶提供更多交易機會，同時亦為想涉足標的金屬投資的個人及機構投資者提供新的投資工具，讓其受惠於該等合約的每月現金結算且規模相對較小的好處。這個系列合約的推出簡化了在 LME 買賣傳統基本金屬合約的機制。合約的最後結算價是根據 LME 的正式結算價（第二輪特定商品交易收盤時釐定）而確定[6]。

倫敦金屬期貨小型合約標誌着香港交易所朝着香港與倫敦之間建立全面聯通平台（「倫港通」）[7] 的目標邁出了第一步。由於相關商品是在 LME 上買賣的相應基本金屬，香港的大宗商品交易平台大可聯同 LME 一起發展，將商品市場中的實物交易人士與金融交易人士都帶到同一個交易平台上來。

2.3　黑色金屬衍生產品

香港交易所於 2017 年 11 月 13 日推出其首隻黑色金屬產品——現金結算的 TSI CFR 中國鐵礦石 62% 鐵粉期貨（簡稱「鐵礦石期貨」）。新產品旨在提供極高的價格透明度，並讓所有市場參與者公平進出市場。有關產品提升鐵礦石衍生品市場的價格發現，亦有助降低交易成本。合約的最終結算價是在該合約月份公佈的所有 TSI CFR 中國鐵礦石 62% 鐵粉指數的算術平均值，而最後交易日是每個曆月非新加坡公眾假期的最後一個香港營業日。產品同時提供月度合約及季度合約，令合約覆蓋範圍更廣。

對於鐵礦石期貨而言，2019 年是生機煥發的一年。經推出優惠計劃再加上市場營銷努力，產品的市場參與度有所提升。每日交易量和未平倉合約張數均在這一年創出新高（見圖 3）。

6　在 LME，交易活動分多輪指定環節進行，每環節五分鐘（稱為「一輪」）；在交易期間，交易員和場內經紀在六米環形交易圈中進行公開喊價交易。不同產品有不同的交易時間。LME 的第二輪交易時間為中午 12 時 30 分至下午 1 時 15 分。LME 產品的正式價格在第二輪交易期間確定，是實物合約的參考價格。LME 的正式價格是第二輪交易時間的最後買賣報價，而 LME 的正式結算價是最後的現貨賣價。

7　詳見本書第 17 章：〈香港交易所大宗商品市場——連接內地與全球的互聯互通平台〉。

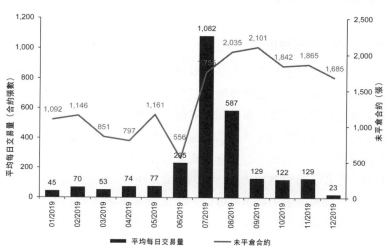

圖 3：鐵礦石期貨每月的平均每日交易量及月底未平倉合約數量（2019）

資料來源：香港交易所。

2.4　市場運作

要在期交所買賣大宗商品相當容易。

(1)　開立期貨戶口

投資者要先找期貨經紀開戶，此經紀須是期交所的參與者，可處理期交所產品的交易。期貨經紀將根據投資者的經驗、收入和淨資產，確定其允許投資者承擔多少風險（即向其收取多少保證金並設定持倉上限）。至於投資者透過經紀買賣期貨合約的渠道，不同經紀或有不同做法，有些提供網上交易系統，有些可能是期貨交易熱線。

(2)　存入初始保證金

落盤之前，投資者必須將足夠的資金存入戶口以支付初始保證金，金額相等於合約價值的一小部份。期交所根據市場波動風險釐定期貨保證金比率。視乎合約類型的價格波動性，經紀可能要求在此最低要求之外另再支付額外的初始保證金。初始保證金一般因產品而異，並會不時改動。

(3) 投資者資格及相關風險

由於可以透過存放抵押品而為交易取得融資，買賣大宗商品期貨的損失風險可以很大。投資者所蒙受的虧蝕可能會超過存放於期貨經紀作為抵押品的初始保證金、現金及任何其他資產，而且如果錯估合約價格升跌走向，投資者可能會在短時間內被要求存入額外的保證金款額或繳付利息。假如未能在指定的時間內支付所需的保證金款額或利息，有關合約或抵押品可能會在未經客戶同意下就出售套現。此外，投資者將要為期貨戶口內因此而出現的任何短欠數額及需繳付的利息負責。因此，投資者應根據本身的財政狀況及投資目標，仔細考慮這類交易是否適合自己。投資者還須留意幾個風險因素，包括地緣政治風險、投機風險、交付風險和企業管治風險。

(4) 向期貨經紀落盤

投資者向期貨經紀落盤時，應說明以下資料：

- 交易方向 —— 買／賣；
- 數量 —— 合約數量；
- 合約資料 —— 哪隻產品及哪個到期日；
- 買賣盤類型 —— 給指示經紀人該如何處理買／賣盤（常見類型為「市價盤」[8]、「限價盤」[9] 和「止蝕盤」[10]）
- 價格 —— 執行買／賣盤的價格；
- 有效時間 —— 買／賣盤的有效期（常見的包括「即日」[11] 和「取消前有效」[12]）
- 賬號 —— 投資者在經紀的追蹤系統中的戶口識別號碼。

買賣盤會被傳送至經紀所控制並連接到期交所的買賣盤管理系統。買賣盤提

---

8 市價盤：以當時市價買／賣合約。
9 限價盤：以指定或更佳的價格買／賣合約。
10 止蝕盤：以高於指定價位的價格買入或以低於指定價位的價格賣出合約。
11 即日盤：有效時間是直至輸入買／賣盤的交易日結束時 —— 有關交易日結束時，系統會自動把買／賣盤清除。
12 取消前有效的買賣盤：有效時間是直至買／賣盤被取消之時，不會被系統自動取消。這類買賣盤如果沒有成交，交易員必須主動取消方可將其從系統中刪除。

交期交所之前，經紀會先進行交易前風險檢查，以確保買賣盤符合批准的數量監控限制。成功通過檢查的買賣盤將發送到期交所的交易系統，未能通過的將不獲買賣盤管理系統受理。

(5)　交易過程

HKATS 為香港交易所旗下衍生產品市場的電子交易系統，系統中的買賣盤會即時按價格及時間的優先次序進行配對。這是指買賣盤會以最佳價格進行配對；若價格相同，則較先掛入公開掛盤冊的會比較後掛入的先作對盤交易，意即在每個價格實行「先進先出」。落盤都放在中央掛盤冊。一旦成交，交易的資料即透過買賣盤管理系統通知期交所參與者，另一邊亦同時傳送到香港期貨結算有限公司（簡稱「期貨結算公司」）作登記及結算。

(6)　按市值計價

按市值計價是結算所每天執行的程式，用以確定每張期貨合約所涉及資產的價值，然後在長短倉之間進行損益結算。結算所收取按金，是其用以減輕日後面對結算對手的信貸風險的主要手段。具體的按金要求，是透過評估個別期貨或期權合約又或期貨期權合約組合在 16 個不同的模擬情況下的單日最高潛在虧損，再加上所設定置信水平計算所得。結算所每日監察按金水平，確保有足夠按金。

期貨結算公司的組合風險按金系統（PRiME）是衍生產品結算及交收系統（DCASS）用以計算期貨及期權產品按金要求的按金計算方法。期交所參與者可使用香港交易所發佈的結算所風險系數檔案計算結算所按金。如果保證金戶口中的資金降至所要求的水平以下，經紀即會要求投資者補充資金至初始保證金水平。此過程稱為「保證金追收」。

(7)　持倉限額

期交所參與者為本身或為客戶持有的持倉若超出指定的申報水平，須於開設或累積該等持倉後的下一個營業日中午 12 時或之前向期交所遞交報告（「大額未平倉合約報告」），並須於持倉超出申報水平期間繼續遞交該等報告。證監會的《持倉限額及大額未平倉合約的申報規定指引》說明了對合計不同人士所持有或控制的持倉和分別在多間公司所持有或控制的持倉所設的規定，以及綜合賬戶的申報規定。

(8) 期貨合約的現金結算

如合約以現金結算，結算將於合約到期時按合約價值以貸記或借記形式進行。期交所以現金結算的大宗商品產品包括美元及人民幣（香港）倫敦金屬期貨小型合約，以及月度及季度美元 TSI 鐵礦石期貨。這些期貨合約的買賣雙方，如持倉直至最後結算時間，而初始價與最終結算價之間的現金差額顯示錄得利潤，利潤將以現金存入其戶口；如錄得虧損，相關金額將以現金從其戶口扣賬。結算所和經紀將確保各個交易者的賬戶按此存入或扣除相應款項，並且及時準確地進行現金結算。

(9) 期貨合約的實物交收

期交所的美元及人民幣（香港）黃金期貨合約在結算時以實物交收，交收時賣方將金條交予買方，買方則支付全額款項。計劃實物交收黃金期貨合約的經紀須於期貨結算公司所指定的所有核准交收倉庫設有賬戶作實物黃金交收之用，或與另一名於所有核准交收倉庫設有賬戶的期貨結算所參與者（稱為「實物交收參與者」）訂立黃金期貨合約實物交收安排。在最後結算的時候，進行交收的黃金將在最後交易日之後的營業日被標記，並將在最後結算日當天，從賣方的期貨結算所參與者的倉庫戶口劃轉至買方的期貨結算所參與者的倉庫戶口內。關於最後結算的詳細安排，請參考期交所的相關市場運作文件——《衍生產品交收服務》、《認可交收倉庫、認可精煉廠、認可運輸公司及認可檢測機構名單》及《提供實物交收服務的期交所參與者名錄》。

(10) 風險管理程式

期貨結算公司擁有若干權力以助其執行風險管理程式，並確保交收及交付順暢。如有需要，期貨結算公司可要求其參與者存入額外款額或補充已用資金；期貨結算公司可要求參與者提供證據，證明其持有履行其結算責任可能需要的相關商品或工具。期貨結算公司亦有權不時要求「非實物交收期貨結算所參與者」於期貨結算公司不時指定的時間內將任何未平倉合約平倉及 / 或轉移。風險管理程式受《期貨結算所規則及程序》規管。

(11) 流通量提供者 / 自營交易商制度

期交所商品期貨設有莊家制度。註冊莊家會按請求以連續報價的方式提供報價，為市場提供流通量，故亦稱為流通量提供者。自營交易商是以其公司戶口進行買賣的交易所參與者，也可以是由交易所參與者作其代表、透過其個人客戶戶口進行合資格產品買賣的客戶，該客戶須承諾滿足交易所指定合資格產品的每月最低交易結算合約張數的要求。期交所的大宗商品類產品都設有「流通量提供者 / 自營交易商計劃」，那是由期交所委任流通量提供者為新產品提供流通量的商業安排，涉及的要求及獎勵可以較具彈性，而不一定是交易所規則及程序內所載者。大宗商品衍生產品的流通量提供者 / 自營交易商若滿足若干相關的莊家責任並提供市場流動性，會獲得財務和非財務利益。

3 為推進未來發展可行的多方面統合工作

香港投資者極少參與大宗商品交易、相關金融產品發展貧乏，一般都被認為是香港商品交易基建不足所致。香港欠缺物流和倉儲安排等可便利大宗商品實物交易的相應配套。事實上，香港的大宗商品期貨合約原是為協助相關實物資產使用者對沖價格波動而設的。

以基本金屬為例，香港的經紀表示內地金屬用戶都要求實物交收，因為他們要用金屬作生產用途。市場參與者亦曾提及香港需要倉儲設施方可提供實物交

收 [13]。換言之，在香港買賣的金屬衍生產品需要有相關實物交收機制配合，方可吸引中國內地用戶在香港交易。然而，提供實物交收意味着要設立金屬貨倉，而那並非易事。在某意義上，大宗商品直通車計劃可能有所幫助，但要達到殊不容易。捨難取易，可以研究與內地交易所訂立授權協議，安排內地大宗商品產品在香港上市，又或與內地交易所攜手開發新產品，可在香港售予國際市場參與者及獲認可的內地實體。另外，香港交易所亦可計劃安排，讓期交所市場與 LME 市場加深融合，並且進一步利用 LME 平台與內地商品交易所協作，以及開發不可或缺的物流和倉儲基建，便利大宗商品的實物交易。

至於香港的黃金市場，由於中國內地從歐洲及其他地方入口的黃金大都取道香港，香港是全球最活躍的實物黃金交易市場之一 [14]。而作為中國這個全球最大黃金進口國的門戶，香港在這方面便顯出其戰略重要性。國際儲金銀行（bullion banks）、煉鑄商、金庫和運輸供應商在香港都有營運業務，再加上其黃金貿易轉口港的角色，香港在本質上有潛力成為亞洲區的黃金定價者，與西方成熟市場如紐約和倫敦看齊，有助中國以至亞洲突破只能做承價者的界限。金銀業貿易場、期交所與場外黃金市場之間大可探討進一步合作的空間，好好利用香港既有的貴金屬網絡。

有些參與者亦表示歡迎期交所的黃金期貨提供實物交收，只是現時最低交收單位為 1 公斤的水平，對個人客戶來說未免太高。他們建議期交所考慮調低合約金額和最低交收單位。

金銀業貿易場設有「認可煉鑄商名單」，列明其各種可交收黃金合約的認可香港煉鑄商，當中大都是港資公司，可生產 999.9 千足黃金。金銀業貿易場亦全資擁有和營運「香港貴金屬驗證中心」。過去亦有交易所參與者和金銀業貿易場行員向期交所建議，指其可考慮認可由這些本地煉鑄商製造的金條，接受其作為期交所黃金期貨合約的交收金條，並認可「香港貴金屬驗證中心」為其檢測機構，協助本地大宗商品公司衝出國際，繼而招徠區內大宗商品同業。這對場內市場而言意味着場內黃金合約的流通量會增加，黃金買賣的參與者也會更多元化。而對實物市場的參與者而言，有較佳的風險對沖工具等同交易成本可以降低，供應也更加穩

---

13 〈香港「尚未準備好成為商品交易中心」〉（"Hong Kong 'not ready to be a commodities trading centre'"），《南華早報》，2013 年 6 月 26 日。

14 2018 年，香港的人均消費者需求為 7.0 克，屬全球最高。資料來源：世界黃金協會〈黃金需求走向（2019 年第三季的統計數據）〉（"Gold Demand Trends Q3 2019 Statistics"），2019 年 11 月 5 日。

定。這個雙贏的局面會令市場每一方都可以受惠。

　　黃金市場就如匯市一樣，都是全天候進行買賣。市場每有重要政治事件或其他突發新聞（例如美國加息），金價都會即時反映。期交所大可研究延長黃金期貨的交易時間，始終最常聽到市場參與者說的，便是指中國內地和國際投資者都可能需要 24 小時服務。期交所亦可考慮擴大現有金屬產品的組合，進一步開發和加入一些以區內及內地定價為根據又別具特色的產品，逐步建立一個提供更全面產品的大宗商品平台。

　　事實上，亞洲佔全球大宗商品生產和消耗的比重不斷上升，在亞洲時區進行買賣的商品愈來愈多[15]。區內主要金融中心如新加坡和上海等紛紛進行戰略檢討，為保競爭力和領先地位而想出各式各樣的舉措。香港既有世界級營商基建、健全的監管環境，又有其獨一無二的互聯互通平台，將中國內地與世界聯通起來，理應可充分利用這些優勢、把握市場機遇，發展成為亞洲的大宗商品交易中心。香港務必要對大宗商品市場的發展定下全盤策略，才有望維持其作為全球最重要國際金融中心之一的地位。

　　要實現上述願景、盡握箇中市場機遇，政府、業界、監管當局和社會都必須通力合作，為香港的長遠利益努力。政府與政府之間相信亦要加大工作力度。

4　總結

　　香港不論在集資、離岸人民幣定價或風險管理方面都是世界公認的領先金融中心，但若論大宗商品，香港相較其他全球金融市場仍處於弱勢。

　　為將香港打造成全球大宗商品交易中心，香港交易所作為本地唯一期貨交易所 —— 期交所 —— 的母公司，積極採取了許多不同舉措。近十年來，香港交易所

15　2018 年，亞洲國家消費者對黃金的需求為 2,176.3 噸（2010 年：1,942.9 噸），佔全球總需求逾 65%（2010 年：少於 60%）。資料來源：世界黃金協會〈黃金需求走向（2019 年第三季的統計數據）〉（"Gold Demand Trends Q3 2019 Statistics"），2019 年 11 月 5 日。

先後推出了 16 隻場內大宗商品期貨合約，涉及貴金屬、黑色金屬及基本金屬等領域，以及六個非供交易的黃金指數，此外還收購了 LME 及成立了前海聯合交易中心。在這基礎之上，香港的大宗商品衍生產品市場已漸呈穩定升勢，只是潛力尚未完全發揮。究其原因，香港大宗商品業界主要面對兩大挑戰：按區域性定價及中國定價分別提供高度區分的不同產品，以及建立高效的配對交易機制。

鑒於香港的實物交收能力相對較弱，因此未來研發新產品時，大可着力於與內地交易所建立跨境產品上市及發牌等相關安排，然後再建立交易機制，將香港與內地市場互聯互通的範疇擴大至包括大宗商品在內，讓兩邊市場參與者可跨境進行大宗商品交易。這樣的措施需要香港交易所與香港及內地兩邊監管機構密切協作，一同在新政策的執行及合規方面探究可行方案，並廣泛諮詢市場參與者，釐定推出哪些能帶來高流通量的合適產品及交易路徑。

期交所參與者的意見亦反映市場期望現有產品可進一步優化，包括收窄黃金合約的價位及在產品合約年期上提供更多選擇。同樣地，交易機制改革（例如延長交易時段、加快實物交收流程以及認可本地精煉廠及檢測機構等）亦可提升香港作為大宗商品衍生產品市場的吸引力及競爭力。香港交易所亦會繼續積極研究新的掛鈎產品及合約種類，以應對瞬息萬變的工業發展及香港市場不斷增長的需求。

香港的大宗商品市場無論在流通量或產品及服務覆蓋面上均相對遜色於其他全球交易中心，但其背靠中國內地這個全球數一數二的大宗商品消費國，憑藉這樣的特殊地位，香港可說仍具備成為亞洲大宗商品定價中心的條件。若能着意在產品發展及市場基礎設施方面進一步優化，不僅有助香港轉型為真正提供多種資產類別的全方位金融中心，更可為投資者接通中國以至全球市場的流動性。

附錄

香港交易所衍生產品市場各大宗商品期貨合約的細則

(a)　美元黃金期貨

特性	詳情
合約標的	金含量不小於 99.99% 的、帶有認可精煉廠標籤及其序列號的 1 公斤黃金
交易代號	GDU
合約單位	1 千克
交易貨幣	美元
合約月份	現貨月及後續 11 個月
最低波幅	每克 0.01 美元
最後交易日	合約月份的第三個星期一 如該日並非香港營業日，則以緊接的下一個香港營業日作為最後交易日
交易時間 [1] （香港時間） （最後交易日除外）	日間交易時段：上午 8 時 30 分至下午 4 時 30 分 收市後期貨交易時段：下午 5 時 15 分至翌日凌晨 3 時
最後交易日的交易時間 [2] （香港時間）	上午 8 時 30 分至下午 4 時 30 分
最後結算日	最後交易日後第二個香港營業日
結算方式	實物交收
結算貨幣	美元
最終結算價	於最後交易日最後 30 分鐘交易時間所有到期合約月份交易的成交量加權平均成交價 [3]
交收地點	核准交收倉庫
最低交收單位	1 千克
假期	與期交所假期表相同
交易費 [4] （每邊每張合約計算）	1.00 美元
結算費 [4] （每邊每張合約計算）	2.00 美元
證監會徵費 [5] （每邊每張合約計算）	0.07 美元
佣金	可商議

註：
(1) 聖誕前夕、新年前夕及農曆新年前夕的交易時段將不會超過正午 12 時 30 分。該三天的交易時間為上午 8 時 30 分至正午 12 時 30 分。英國、美國及中華人民共和國的銀行假期當天不設收市後期貨交易時段。
(2) 聖誕前夕、新年前夕及農曆新年前夕的交易時段將不會超過正午 12 時 30 分。該三天的交易時間為上午 8 時 30 分至正午 12 時 30 分。
(3) 於最後交易日最後 30 分鐘交易時間成交、並由 (i) 個別市場系列的兩個買賣盤；或 (ii) 標準組合買賣盤與個別市場系列買賣盤在 HKATS 配對而產生的所有到期合約月份交易（大手交易除外）。
(4) 所示金額期交所可不時作更改。
(5) 金額為每張合約收取港幣 0.54 元的美元等值，按期交所釐定的匯率換算。

(b) 人民幣（香港）黃金期貨

合約項目	詳情
合約標的	金含量不小於 99.99% 的、帶有認可精煉廠標籤及其序列號的 1 公斤黃金
交易代號	GDR
合約單位	1 千克
交易貨幣	人民幣
合約月份	現貨月及後續 11 個月
最低波幅	每克人民幣 0.05 元
最後交易日	合約月份的第三個星期一 如該日並非香港營業日，則以緊接的下一個香港營業日作為最後交易日
交易時間 [(1)]（香港時間）（最後交易日除外）	日間交易時段：上午 8 時 30 分至下午 4 時 30 分 收市後期貨交易時段：下午 5 時 15 分至翌日凌晨 3 時
最後交易日的交易時間 [(2)]（香港時間）	上午 8 時 30 分至下午 4 時 30 分
最後結算日	最後交易日後第二個香港營業日
結算方式	實物交收
結算貨幣	人民幣
最終結算價	於最後交易日最後 30 分鐘交易時間所有到期合約月份交易的成交量加權平均成交價 [(3)]
交收地點	核准交收倉庫
最低交收單位	1 千克
假期	與期交所假期表相同
交易費 [(4)]（以每邊每張合約計算）	人民幣 6.00 元
結算費 [(4)]（以每邊每張合約計算）	人民幣 12.00 元
證監會徵費 [(5)]（以每邊每張合約計算）	人民幣 0.50 元

（續）

合約項目	詳情
佣金	可商議

註：

(1) 聖誕前夕、新年前夕及農曆新年前夕的交易時段將不會超過正午 12 時 30 分。該三天的交易時間為上午 8 時 30 分至正午 12 時 30 分。英國、美國及中華人民共和國銀行的假期當天不設收市後期貨交易時段。

(2) 聖誕前夕、新年前夕及農曆新年前夕的交易時段將不會超過正午 12 時 30 分。該三天的交易時間為上午 8 時 30 分至正午 12 時 30 分。

(3) 於最後交易日最後 30 分鐘交易時間成交、並由 (i) 個別市場系列的兩個買賣盤；或 (ii) 標準組合買賣盤與個別市場系列買賣盤在 HKATS 配對而產生的所有到期合約月份交易（大手交易除外）。

(4) 所示金額期交所可不時作更改。

(5) 金額為每張合約收取港幣 0.54 元的人民幣等值，按期交所釐定的匯率換算。

(c)　美元倫敦鋁 / 鋅 / 銅 / 鉛 / 鎳 / 錫期貨小型合約

合約項目	詳情					
	美元倫敦鋁期貨小型合約	美元倫敦鋅期貨小型合約	美元倫敦銅期貨小型合約	美元倫敦鉛期貨小型合約	美元倫敦鎳期貨小型合約	美元倫敦錫期貨小型合約
標的商品	電解鋁（定義按 LME 規則及規例不時界定）	電解鋅（定義按 LME 規則及規例不時界定）	電解銅（定義按 LME 規則及規例不時界定）	標準鉛（定義按 LME 規則及規例不時界定）	原鎳（定義按 LME 規則及規例不時界定）	錫（定義按 LME 規則及規例不時界定）
交易代碼	LUA	LUZ	LUC	LUP	LUN	LUS
合約單位	每張合約 5 噸			每張合約 1 噸		
交易貨幣	美元					
結算貨幣	美元					
合約月份	即月及後續 11 個曆月					
交易費 (1)	每邊每張合約 0.50 美元					
結算費 (1)	每手 0.20 美元					
證監會徵費 (2)	每邊每張合約 0.07 美元					
最後交易日	LME 就鋁 / 鋅 / 銅 / 鉛 / 鎳 / 錫期貨合約釐定的最後交易日（為即月第三個星期三的前兩個營業日）。如該日並非香港營業日，則以緊貼的前一個香港營業日作為最後交易日。					
交易時間（香港時間）（最後交易日除外）	日間交易時段：上午 9 時至下午 4 時 30 分 收市後期貨交易時段：下午 5 時 15 分至翌日凌晨 3 時 聖誕前夕、新年前夕及農曆新年前夕的交易時段至正午 12 時 30 分止。該三天的交易時間為上午 9 時至正午 12 時 30 分。 英國、美國及中華人民共和國的銀行假期當天不設收市後期貨交易時段。					

(續)

合約項目	詳情					
	美元倫敦鋁期貨小型合約	美元倫敦鋅期貨小型合約	美元倫敦銅期貨小型合約	美元倫敦鉛期貨小型合約	美元倫敦鎳期貨小型合約	美元倫敦錫期貨小型合約
最後交易日的交易時間	日間交易時段：上午9時至下午4時30分；收市後期貨交易時段：下午5時15分至晚上8時（英國夏令時間）/晚上9時（非英國夏令時間）	日間交易時段：上午9時至下午4時30分；收市後期貨交易時段：下午5時15分至晚上7時55分（英國夏令時間）/晚上8時55分（非英國夏令時間）	日間交易時段：上午9時至下午4時30分；收市後期貨交易時段：下午5時15分至晚上7時35分（英國夏令時間）/晚上8時35分（非英國夏令時間）	日間交易時段：上午9時至下午4時30分；收市後期貨交易時段：下午5時15分至晚上7時50分（英國夏令時間）/晚上8時50分（非英國夏令時間）	日間交易時段：上午9時至下午4時30分；收市後期貨交易時段：下午5時15分至晚上8時05分（英國夏令時間）/晚上9時05分（非英國夏令時間）	日間交易時段：上午9時至下午4時30分；收市後期貨交易時段：下午5時15分至晚上7時45分（英國夏令時間）/晚上8時45分（非英國夏令時間）
最低波幅	每噸 0.5 美元				每噸 1 美元	
最終結算日	最後交易日後的第二個香港營業日					
最終結算價	由結算所釐定，應為 LME 在即月第三個星期三的前兩個倫敦營業日所釐定及公佈的正式結算價					
結算方式	現金結算					
假期	與期交所假期表相同					
合共持倉限額（美元及人民幣（香港）合約張數）	25,000	25,000	50,000	25,000	50,000	15,000

註：
(1) 所示金額期交所可不時作更改。
(2) 金額為每張合約收取港幣 0.54 元的美元等值，按期交所釐定的匯率換算。

(d) 人民幣（香港）倫敦鋁／鋅／銅／鉛／鎳／錫期貨小型合約

合約項目	詳情					
	人民幣（香港）倫敦鋁期貨小型合約	人民幣（香港）倫敦鋅期貨小型合約	人民幣（香港）倫敦銅期貨小型合約	人民幣（香港）倫敦鉛期貨小型合約	人民幣（香港）倫敦鎳期貨小型合約	人民幣（香港）倫敦錫期貨小型合約
標的商品	電解鋁（定義按 LME 規則及規例不時界定）	電解鋅（定義按 LME 規則及規例不時界定）	電解銅（定義按 LME 規則及規例不時界定）	標準鉛（定義按 LME 規則及規例不時界定）	原鎳（定義按 LME 規則及規例不時界定）	錫（定義按 LME 規則及規例不時界定）
交易代碼	LRA	LRZ	LRC	LRP	LRN	LRS
合約單位	每張合約 5 噸			每張合約 1 噸		
交易貨幣	人民幣					
結算貨幣	人民幣					
合約月份	即月及後續 11 個曆月					
交易費 [1]	每邊每張合約人民幣 3.00 元					
結算費 [1]	每手人民幣 1.20 元					
證監會徵費 [2]	每邊每張合約人民幣 0.44 元					
最後交易日	LME 就鋁／鋅／銅／鉛／鎳／錫期貨合約釐定的最後交易日（為即月第三個星期三的前兩個營業日）。如該日並非香港營業日，則以緊貼的前一個香港營業日作為最後交易日。					
交易時間（香港時間）（最後交易日除外）	日間交易時段：上午 9 時至下午 4 時 30 分 收市後期貨交易時段：下午 5 時 15 分至翌日凌晨 3 時 聖誕前夕、新年前夕及農曆新年前夕的交易時段至正午 12 時 30 分止。該三天的交易時間為上午 9 時至正午 12 時 30 分。 英國、美國及中華人民共和國銀行的假期當天不設收市後期貨交易時段。					
最後交易日的交易時間	日間交易時段：上午 9 時至下午 4 時 30 分；收市後期貨交易時段：下午 5 時 15 分至晚上 8 時（英國夏令時間）／晚上 9 時（非英國夏令時間）	日間交易時段：上午 9 時至下午 4 時 30 分；收市後期貨交易時段：下午 5 時 15 分至晚上 7 時 55 分（英國夏令時間）／晚上 8 時 55 分（非英國夏令時間）	日間交易時段：上午 9 時至下午 4 時 30 分；收市後期貨交易時段：下午 5 時 15 分至晚上 7 時 35 分（英國夏令時間）／晚上 8 時 35 分（非英國夏令時間）	日間交易時段：上午 9 時至下午 4 時 30 分；收市後期貨交易時段：下午 5 時 15 分至晚上 7 時 50 分（英國夏令時間）／晚上 8 時 50 分（非英國夏令時間）	日間交易時段：上午 9 時至下午 4 時 30 分；收市後期貨交易時段：下午 5 時 15 分至晚上 8 時 05 分（英國夏令時間）／晚上 9 時 05 分（非英國夏令時間）	日間交易時段：上午 9 時至下午 4 時 30 分；收市後期貨交易時段：下午 5 時 15 分至晚上 7 時 45 分（英國夏令時間）／晚上 8 時 45 分（非英國夏令時間）

(續)

合約項目	詳情					
	人民幣（香港）倫敦鋁期貨小型合約	人民幣（香港）倫敦鋅期貨小型合約	人民幣（香港）倫敦銅期貨小型合約	人民幣（香港）倫敦鉛期貨小型合約	人民幣（香港）倫敦鎳期貨小型合約	人民幣（香港）倫敦錫期貨小型合約
最低波幅	每噸人民幣 5 元		每噸人民幣 10 元	每噸人民幣 5 元	每噸人民幣 10 元	
最終結算日	最後交易日後的第二個香港營業日					
最終結算價	由結算所釐定的整數，以 LME 就鋁／鋅／銅／鉛／鎳／錫期貨合約釐定及公佈的正式結算價，按香港財資市場公會在最後交易日上午 11 時 30 分左右（香港時間）公佈的美元兌人民幣（香港）即期匯率換算為人民幣等價金額，並按金額第一個小數位四捨五入為整數。					
結算方式	現金結算					
假期	與期交所假期表相同					
合共持倉限額（美元及人民幣（香港）合約張數）	25,000	25,000	50,000	25,000	50,000	15,000

註：
(1) 所示金額期交所可不時作更改。
(2) 金額為每張合約收取港幣 0.54 元的人民幣等值，按期交所釐定的匯率換算。

(e) 鐵礦石月度期貨合約

特性	詳情
交易代碼	FEM
標的	TSI CFR 中國鐵礦石 62% 鐵粉指數
合約單位	100 噸
交易貨幣	美元
報價	每噸美元及美仙
合約月份	現貨月及後續 23 個曆月
最低波幅	每噸 0.01 美元
最高波幅	無
最後交易日	每個曆月非新加坡公眾假期的最後一個香港營業日
交易時間[1]（香港時間）（最後交易日除外）	日間交易時段：上午 9 時至下午 4 時 30 分 收市後期貨交易時段：下午 5 時 15 分至翌日凌晨 3 時
最後交易日的交易時間[2]（香港時間）	日間交易時段：上午 9 時至下午 4 時 30 分 收市後期貨交易時段：下午 5 時 15 分至下午 6 時 30 分

(續)

特性	詳情
最後結算日	最後交易日後第二個香港營業日。除非：(i) 最後交易日為新年或農曆新年前最後一個香港營業日，(ii) 現貨月合約及現貨季合約的交易時間於下午 12 時 30 分結束，及 (iii) 其他合約月份的日間交易時段於下午 4 時 30 分結束，則最後結算日為最後交易日後首個香港營業日
最後結算價	該合約月份公佈的所有 TSI CFR 中國鐵礦石 62% 鐵粉指數的算術平均值，並四捨五入至小數後兩位數字
結算方式	現金結算
假期	與期交所假期表相同
交易費 (3) (以每邊每張合約計算)	1.00 美元
結算費 (3) (以每邊每張合約計算)	1.00 美元
證監會徵費 (4) (以每邊每張合約計算)	0.07 美元
佣金	可商議

註：
(1) 聖誕前夕、新年前夕及農曆新年前夕的交易時段將不會超過下午 12 時 30 分。該三天的交易時間為上午 9 時正至下午 12 時 30 分。
(2) 如最後交易日為新年或農曆新年前最後一個香港營業日，並為新年或農曆新年前 TSI CFR 中國鐵礦石 62% 鐵粉指數最後一次公佈的日子，該日交易時段將不會超過下午 12 時 30 分。該兩天的交易時間為上午 9 時至下午 12 時 30 分。
(3) 所示金額期交所可不時作更改。
(4) 金額為每張合約收取港幣 0.54 元的美元等值，按期交所釐定的匯率換算。

(f)　鐵礦石季度期貨合約

特性	詳情
交易代碼	FEQ
標的	TSI CFR 中國鐵礦石 62% 鐵粉指數
合約單位	100 噸
交易貨幣	美元
報價	每噸美元及美仙
合約月份	現貨季及後續 7 個曆季（曆季指 1 月至 3 月、4 月至 6 月、7 月至 9 月及 10 月至 12 月）
最低波幅	每噸 0.01 美元
最高波幅	無
最後交易日	每個曆季中最後一個月度合約的最後交易日

(續)

特性	詳情
交易時間 (1) (香港時間) (最後交易日除外)	日間交易時段：上午 9 時至下午 4 時 30 分 收市後期貨交易時段：下午 5 時 15 分至翌日凌晨 3 時
最後交易日的交易時間 (2) (香港時間)	日間交易時段：上午 9 時至下午 4 時 30 分 收市後期貨交易時段：下午 5 時 15 分至下午 6 時 30 分
最後結算日	最後交易日後第二個香港營業日。除非：(i) 最後交易日為新年或農曆新年前最後一個香港營業日，(ii) 現貨月合約及現貨季合約的交易時間於下午 12 時 30 分結束，及 (iii) 其他合約月份的日間交易時段於下午 4 時 30 分結束，則最後結算日為最後交易日後首個香港營業日
最後結算價	該合約季度相應的三個月度合約的最後結算價的算術平均值，並四捨五入至小數後兩位數字
結算方式	現金結算
假期	與期交所假期表相同
交易費 (3) (以每邊每張合約計算)	1.00 美元
結算費 (3) (以每邊每張合約計算)	1.00 美元
證監會徵費 (4) (以每邊每張合約計算)	0.07 美元
佣金	可商議

註：
(1) 聖誕前夕、新年前夕及農曆新年前夕交易時段將不會超過下午 12 時 30 分。該三天的交易時間為上午 9 時正至下午 12 時 30 分。
(2) 如最後交易日為新年或農曆新年前最後一個香港營業日，並為新年或農曆新年前 TSI CFR 中國鐵礦石 62% 鐵粉指數最後一次公佈的日子，該日交易時段將不會超過下午 12 時 30 分。該兩天的交易時間為上午 9 時至下午 12 時 30 分。
(3) 所示金額期交所可不時作更改。
(4) 金額為每張合約收取港幣 0.54 元的美元等值，按期交所釐定的匯率換算。

大宗商品現貨與
期貨市場的互聯互通

第10章

大宗商品期貨服務實體經濟
的國際經驗

香港交易及結算所有限公司
首席中國經濟學家辦公室

摘 要

　　大宗商品期貨合約是一種在交易所買賣的標準化協議，合約持有人有權按特定價格於未來特定日期買入或賣出預定數量的大宗商品。全球大宗商品期貨市場與現貨市場有着密切的關係。早期在美國及英國，主要的生產商及消費者會集結進行現貨交易，但實物交收的價格及時間存在不確定性，期貨市場便應運而生。因此，大宗商品期貨的價格就成為大宗商品現貨交易的基準價格。大宗商品期貨價格理論上受現貨市場許多元素所影響，包括現貨價格、利率、倉儲成本、合約年期以至使用存貨進行生產的潛在利益等。實證顯示，全球大宗商品期貨與現貨市場息息相關，而箇中關係體現在經濟基本因素及市場架構。

　　大宗商品期貨市場可滿足對沖者及金融投資者的不同需要。套期保值者是全球大宗商品期貨市場的主要參與者，當中包括大宗商品生產商、消費者及貿易公司，他們會利用大宗商品期貨套期保值，來對沖現貨價格的不利變動。而透過全球倉庫網絡進行商品期貨實物結算，可節省取得大宗商品作商業用途的成本，是現貨市場與期貨市場之間關係密切的關鍵。金融投資者把商品期貨視為被動型投資或主動型回報的資產類別。實證顯示，大宗商品期貨或可提供較高回報及較低波動性，能使投資組合更多元化。

　　與全球其他成熟市場相比，中國內地大宗商品期貨市場服務實體經濟的效益未如理想。中國內地的大宗商品現貨市場較分散，不同地區的交易價格往往不同，相應的商品期貨價格起不到參考作用。內地大宗商品期貨市場方面，由於投機交易活動的影響，價格波動或會較大，以致影響到對沖的成效。此外，內地可用於進行大宗商品期貨實物交收的倉庫選擇亦相對有限，和倉儲、運輸及進口關稅相關的成本或因此而上升，且產品類別及交易貨幣種類範圍也較窄，可能無法滿足內地不同的業務需要。這些因素都影響到內地大宗商品現貨與期貨市場之間的有效連接。雖然中國是全球第二大經濟體，亦是全球不少主要大宗商品的最大生產國及消費國之一，但是內地大宗商品期貨市場與全球市場的互動不多，在岸及離岸套期保值者對價格的看法無法充分反映於全球及內地大宗商品期貨市場上，造成兩邊市場的價格不同。

　　內地大宗商品期貨市場若要提升服務實體經濟的能力，必須加強內地現貨與期貨市場之間的聯繫，亦要提升內地期貨市場對全球市場價格的影響。這可以從多方面入手。首先，內地可整合現貨市場的交易、提升交易透明度，推動大宗商品現貨市場使用期貨價格作為基準價格。其次，內地市場可着力加強市場監管、拓展倉庫網絡，以減低因過度投機和運輸成本而造成期貨價格偏離經濟基本因素的程度。另外，期貨市場可增加產品類別及交易貨幣種類，切合不同行業的業務需要。再者，香港市場作為位處中國開放門戶的國際金融中心，大可擔當大宗商品市場「超級連繫人」的角色，以進一步增加內地大宗商品期貨市場與全球市場的互動，協助增強內地大宗商品期貨市場進一步服務實體經濟的能力。

1 大宗商品期貨與實體經濟的聯繫

　　大宗商品期貨合約是一種在交易所買賣的標準化協議，合約持有人有權按特定價格於未來特定日期買入或賣出預定數量的大宗商品。涉及的大宗商品可以是基本金屬、貴金屬、農產品、能源產品、化學品或其他種類商品。期貨合約可以實物結算（由賣方向買方交付相關的實物資產）或現金結算（買方與賣方之間交付現金結算價值）。

　　進行大宗商品期貨交易的人士包括生產商、消費者、貿易公司及金融投資者，與實體經濟商品現貨市場的參與者重疊。因此，商品期貨的價格通常就是相關大宗商品的基準價格。按交易金額計，美國及歐洲的交易所佔了全球大宗商品期貨交易的大部份比重（見圖 1），這在若干程度上反映了這些交易所於全球大宗商品市場，尤其是在定價權方面，扮演着關鍵角色。不過，按名義交易金額計，內地商品期貨交易所於 2019 年亦在全球名列前茅。

圖 1：首 10 家商品期貨名義交易金額最高的交易所（2019 年）

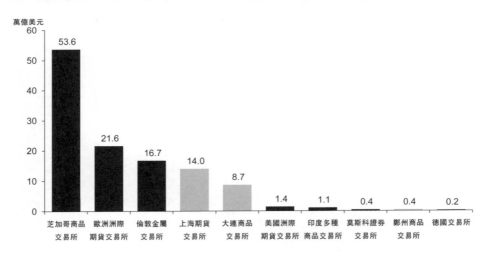

萬億美元

芝加哥商品交易所	53.6
歐洲洲際期貨交易所	21.6
倫敦金屬交易所	16.7
上海期貨交易所	14.0
大連商品交易所	8.7
美國洲際期貨交易所	1.4
印度多種商品交易所	1.1
莫斯科證券交易所	0.4
鄭州商品交易所	0.4
德國交易所	0.2

註：歐洲洲際期貨交易所和美國洲際期貨交易所的數據分別計至 2019 年 10 月和 2019 年 8 月。

資料來源：國際證券交易所聯會（WFE）網站上公佈的統計數據。

　　國際及內地的大宗商品市場架構不盡相同，因此兩邊的商品期貨交易所的發展歷程亦有別。全球市場的經驗展示了大宗商品現貨與期貨市場之間的緊密聯繫，這種聯繫對大宗商品的價格發現非常重要。這對中國商品期貨交易所的未來發展亦有一定啟示。

1.1　國際大宗商品期貨市場簡史

　　國際大宗商品期貨市場的歷史展示了其服務實體經濟的功用。在美國及英國，大宗商品現貨市場經過長期發展，匯集了足夠大量的大宗商品用家，其後商品期貨交易所才應運而生，將市場買賣中央化，應對市場需要較佳的價格發現及風險管理的需求。

　　在美國[1]，芝加哥在 19 世紀初完成運河及鐵路的基礎建設後，成為地區性農產品貿易中心，促使大宗商品現貨交易集中進行，解決了美國農產品生產商及消費者面對價格無序波動，無法預計供應量等問題。全球第一家期貨交易所芝加哥期貨交易所（Chicago Board of Trade，簡稱 CBOT）於 1848 年成立，成立初期為農產品生產商與消費者提供糧食現貨交易平台。CBOT 於 1851 年開創「遠期」合約[2] 交易的先河。之後，CBOT 於 1865 年推出全球首隻糧食交易商品期貨，合約是標準化協議，涉及實物交收及清算程序，並對買賣雙方制定「按金」（或稱「供貨保證金」）要求。之後紐約商品交易所（New York Mercantile Exchange，簡稱 NYMEX）及芝加哥商品交易所（Chicago Mercantile Exchange，簡稱 CME）先後於 1872 年和 1919 年成立，初期提供其他農產品的現貨交易服務，其後推出大宗商品期貨。自 20 世紀 60 年代後期開始，這些大宗商品交易所將產品範圍拓展至非農產品，包括金屬、貨幣、原油、利率及金融指數等。1994 年，NYMEX 與 Commodity Exchange（簡稱 COMEX）合併，後於 2008 年由 CME 集團收購（CME 集團是由 CME 與 CBOT 於 2007 年合併而成）。此後，CME 便是世界領先的農產品及原油定價中心。

1　資料來源：〈中西部的糧食交易：期貨交易所的歷史〉（"Midwest Grain Trade: History of Futures Exchanges"），載於 CME 集團網站，於 2019 年 11 月 8 日閱覽；〈美國六大期貨交易所 —— CBOT、CME、NYMEX……〉，載於 *kknews.cc*，2017 年 8 月 8 日。

2　遠期合約與期貨合約不同，其合約細則（例如合約金額及結算日期）並非標準化，而且通常是在場外而非場內進行交易。

英國[3]在用來生產青銅和合金的銅和錫的交易方面歷史悠久。最初，英國的金屬交易只局限於國內市場。直至數百年前，英國成為主要的金屬出口國後，倫敦便成為歐洲的實物金屬交易中心。倫敦金屬交易所（London Metal Exchange，簡稱 LME）於 1877 年成立，為大宗商品交易者、船隻承租人及融資人促成金屬交易的商業活動，而這些金屬交易都在「交易圈」內進行（是早期的公開叫價交易）。在 19 世紀初，英國當時一直在銅和錫可自給自足，有關報價亦長期固定。在工業革命後，金屬買賣商拓展交易範圍，因而面對從智利及馬來西亞等偏遠地區進口金屬礦石及精礦所帶來的到貨日期不穩定的問題。隨着電報面世，科技迅速發展，使到貨日期更容易預計，實物交易隨之亦可設定交收日期。此外，在蘇伊士運河開通後，運送銅和錫到倫敦的時間縮短至三個月。這些因素造就了 LME 的獨特系統，可按日交割遠至三個月，並沿用至今。及後其實物交易範圍更進一步拓展至包括銅、錫、鉛、鋅、鋁、鎳、以至黑色金屬、貴金屬及其他金屬等廣泛金屬種類。現時，LME 已是首屈一指的金屬定價中心，佔 2016 年全球交易所金屬交易總額的 70% 以上[4]。

從美國及歐洲大宗商品市場的發展歷程可見，對大宗商品的需求主要來自大宗商品用家，包括生產商、消費者、現貨物流企業及貿易公司，他們支撐着上游產業（生產鏈中的原材料供應商）及下游產業（原材料客戶及製成品生產商），以及實體經濟的商業活動。隨着現貨市場的發展，大宗商品種類增多，大宗商品用家亦須面對價格及實物交收的不確定性，大宗商品期貨市場也因此應運而生，以滿足大宗商品用家的不同需要。

1.2 市場中的價格發現何以需要大宗商品期貨市場？

現貨市場是實體經濟的重要一環，主導着大宗商品市場的交易。以 2001 年初的數字為例，傳統現貨市場（在貨品交付前才商定售價）便佔美國農業大宗商品約

3　資料來源：〈歷史〉（"History"），載於倫敦金屬交易所的網站，於 2019 年 11 月 8 日閱覽；〈期貨基礎知識六：期貨市場的發展過程〉，載於 *xueqiu.com*，於 2019 年 11 月 7 日閱覽。

4　資料來源：〈LME 暫停對基金的激勵計劃來安撫傳統會員〉（"LME pauses fund charm offensive to calm traditional members"），《路透》，2016 年 11 月 1 日。

60%[5]。在大宗商品現貨市場，交易的價格可經下列定價機制釐定[6]：

- **雙邊合約：** 這是現貨市場交易機制中最主要的交易形式。雙邊合約由買賣雙方自訂商品的規格、價格、數量、實物交付的時間和地點。

- **轉讓價：** 轉讓價是綜向整合企業中兩個實體之間（例如上游附屬公司與下游附屬公司）為內部交易而設定的價格。由於有關買賣只會在這些公司的財務報表中顯示，所以透明度偏低。就跨境轉讓交易而言，入口價通常會刻意被壓低，以減低關稅負擔。

- **標價：** 指政府為防止各方逃避關稅而制定的價格，可按生產成本或獨立方之間的最新交易價訂立。

- **生產商支配價：** 指由市場勢力極度集中的數家最大生產商所定的價格。

- **消費者主導價：** 指由市場勢力極度集中的數名最大消費者所定的價格。

- **私人拍賣：** 透過一般拍賣（最高出價成交）或減價拍賣（最低賣價成交）定價。私人拍賣可處理市場上買賣雙方數量眾多的情況，但商品規格並不統一，而且不是持續進行。

　　現貨市場可說是百貨百價，上述機制定出來的價格可以差距甚大。大宗商品用家選擇定價機制時要視乎許多因素，例如關稅、政府政策、大宗商品規格、交易時間以至生產商與消費者的相對市場勢力等。雖說有部份大宗商品用家可利用自訂合約取得優惠價，但這些交易價未必可當作所有市場交易的參考指標。以雙邊合約為例，主要生產商的合約價可以是部份大宗商品的參考價，但價格資訊並不透明，市場未必知曉。除此之外，這樣的參考價亦未必可靠。就金屬及能源產品而言，一項研究[7]指最大那四至五家鋁、鎳及原油生產商佔全球產量的份額在 1955 至 1990 年間大幅下降，這些生產商的交易價已不如往日具代表性。另外，由於雙邊合約的條款都是自訂，不同合約的大宗商品規格或合約期未必都能互作比

5　資料來源：MacDonald, J. M. 等 (2004)〈合約、市場及價格：梳理農業大宗商品的生產及使用〉("Contracts, markets, and prices: Organising the production and use of agricultural commodities")，載於美國農業部網站登載的《農業經濟報告》，第 837 號 (*Agricultural Economic Report No. 837*)。

6　見 Radetzki, M. (2013)〈大宗商品交易所鍥而不捨　確立主要大宗商品價格〉("The relentless progress of commodity exchanges in the establishment of primary commodity prices")，載於《資源政策》(*Resources Policy*)，第 38 冊，266-277 頁。

7　同上。

較。因此，對某些大宗商品來說，現貨市場交易的實際價格可與當前的最新參考價有不同程度的偏差，而沒有規律。

由此可見，大宗商品的期貨市場對現貨市場的價格發現有補足作用。大宗商品期貨在商品的規格、合約金額及交收日期方面非常統一。在大宗商品期貨交易所的交易，買賣雙方之間的競價活動可以持續，也沒有入市門檻。還有，期貨市場的價格資訊遠比現貨市場透明，對大宗商品市場中的價格發現也大有幫助。再者，由大宗商品期貨交易所擔當中央對手方的角色，可以減低對手方風險、便利交易的清算及交收。事實上，全球大宗商品市場中的金屬、農產品及能源產品的期貨交易量與日俱增，可證市場對商品期貨的龐大需求（見圖2）。期貨市場交投活躍，使期貨價格作為相關大宗商品的參考價更為可靠。

圖2：全球市場大宗商品期貨的每年成交量（按大宗商品類別劃分）（2009年至2019年）

註：不同交易所的商品期貨合約單位各異，不同產品的產品成交量相同並不代表其名義交易金額相同。

資料來源：美國期貨業協會。

1.3　大宗商品期貨作為現貨市場價格發現的關鍵的實證

全球市場的大宗商品期貨通常都以實物交收，涉及倉儲、保險等庫存成本。

另外，大宗商品用戶可選擇視之為消耗品以即時耗用或持有大宗商品的實物存貨，而非作為金融資產。所以，商品期貨的定價與金融期貨並不相同，金融期貨只計算預期價值的利率。

關於大宗商品期貨的定價，我們可視大宗商品用家有兩個方法在將來某個時間取得大宗商品。一是現在就用息率「r」借貸，以現貨價「S」買入商品，再付出存倉成本「k」持有貨品，便會獲得持有實物存貨的好處，在未來「T」年後可享便利收益率[8]「↓」；二是買入大宗商品期貨合約，確定在「T」年後按行使價「F」買入商品，然後將等同「F」的貼現價值金額投資於無風險資產，確保日後行使期貨買入大宗商品時有所涉款項的資金。在有效率的市場中，這兩種方法涉及的現金流及成本應該一樣。否則，投資者可選擇兩者中較便宜的方式取得大宗商品，然後經另一方法以較高價賣出，在無風險的情況下套戥獲利。由此可見，整個邏輯關係是，商品期貨價格「F」與現貨價「S」、利率「r」、存倉成本「k」及合約期「T」成正比，而與便利收益率「↓」成反比[9]。

除此之外，面對實體經濟中不同的大宗商品供求情況，存貨水平的高低也可影響到期貨價格。一項研究[10]分析在 LME 買賣的基本金屬的現貨價、期貨價及存貨量於 1997 年 7 月至 2009 年 6 月期間的數據，探討在低水[11]及高水[12]情況下價格及存貨怎樣調整。研究發現：

- 在低水的期貨市場，存貨水平很可能過低，不足以應付實體經濟的需求，使存貨對大宗商品用家而言更為寶貴（例如，用來確保生產過程不受影響、繼續運作），令便利收益率上升（見圖 3）。這也會推高現貨價，而將期貨價拖低至低於現貨價水平[13]。

- 在高水的期貨市場，存貨水平很可能非常充足，應付實體經濟需求綽綽有餘，令便利收益率下降，推使現貨價低於期貨價。

8　「便利收益率」適用於可儲存的大宗商品，其需求可從現有產能或存貨中滿足。潛在裨益包括能夠從暫時短缺中獲利以及生產程序能夠持續運作。

9　見 Pindyck, R. (2001)〈大宗商品現貨及期貨市場的互動：入門〉("The dynamics of commodity spot and futures markets: A primer")，載於《能源期刊》(Energy Journal)，第 22 期，1-29 頁。

10　Roache, S. 與 N. Erbil. (2010)〈大宗商品價格曲線及存貨如何受短期缺貨沖擊影響〉("How commodities price curves and inventories react to a short-run scarcity shock")，《國際貨幣基金工作報告 WP/10/222》。

11　「低水」指相關資產的期貨價低於現貨價。

12　「高水」指相關資產的期貨價高於現貨價。

13　這是「極其低水」市場的情況。若現貨價僅高於期貨價的貼現值，則是「略為低水」。

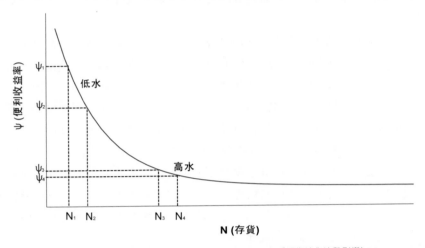

圖 3：便利收益率與存貨關係圖

資料來源：Roache, S. 與 N. Erbil. (2010)〈大宗商品價格曲線及存貨如何受短期缺貨沖擊影響〉(How commodities price curves and inventories react to a short-run scarcity shock)，《國際貨幣基金工作報告 WP/10/222》。

多項研究都提供實證，顯示大宗商品期貨市場與實體經濟的關係：

- 實證顯示大宗商品期貨的價格及未平倉合約與實體經濟有密切關聯。一項研究 [14] 以 1959 年 7 月至 2004 年 3 月期間美國商品研究局 (CRB) 的數據及 LME 的數據，以同等權重構建了一條涵蓋所有大宗商品期貨的指數，檢視這期間大宗商品期貨的價格表現。研究發現大宗商品期貨的價格回報與實際通脹、意料之外的通脹及通脹預期的變化成正比。另一項研究 [15] 則發現，美國的大宗商品期貨未平倉合約於 1964 年 12 月至 2008 年 12 月期間極其順應周期變化，與宏觀經濟活動同步升跌。該研究發現，大宗商品期貨的未平倉合約對大宗商品回報、債券回報及短期利率都有預測作用，這可能是期貨市場中大宗商品生產商與消費者的對沖活動的結果（見第 2.1 節）。

---

14 Gorton, G. 與 K. G. Rouwenhorst (2006)〈大宗商品期貨的事實與憧憬〉("Facts and fantasies about commodity futures")，載於《金融分析師期刊》(Financial Analysts Journal)，第 62 期，47-68 頁。

15 Hong, H. 與 M. Yogo (2012)〈期貨市場息率怎樣助我們了解宏觀經濟和資產價格？〉("What does futures market interest tell us about the macroeconomy and asset prices?")，載於《金融經濟期刊》(Journal of Financial Economics)，第 105 期，473-490 頁。

- 大宗商品期貨價格之間的聯繫反映出實體經濟中不同行業的聯繫。大宗商品期貨種類繁多，不同商品期貨市場的定價效率各異[16]。這與上游產業貨品價格的反應通常比下游產業快的事實一致。若原材料價格變動持續，下游產品的價格會作調整但稍慢。以日本汽車業的鈀、天然橡膠和汽油（佔全球逾半用量）的商品期貨的經濟聯繫為例[17]，若鈀期貨的波動性（或成交量）受到衝擊，天然橡膠和汽油期貨的成交量（或波動）都會受到影響。

- 大宗商品期貨價格也是物流業定價的參考指標。一項調查[18]研究了波羅的海交易所的乾貨大量付運的遠期協議、歐美市場的期貨及已付運大宗商品的場外衍生產品於 2006 年 5 月至 2009 年 10 月期間的每日價格數據。研究發現，價格回報及波幅的衝擊會先見於商品期貨，其後才蔓延至貨運衍生產品。

- 主要大宗商品市場的經濟基本因素和結構差別都是左右大宗商品期貨價格發現的因素。以大豆為例，美國和巴西是全球最大的大豆出口國（2016 年至 2017 年間佔總出口約 83%[19]）。CME 與巴西證券交易所的合資格投資者可直接買賣對方市場的期貨（或傳遞期貨買賣盤）的安排先後於 2008 年 9 月開通 CME 市場及於 2009 年 2 月開通巴西證券交易所市場。一項研究[20]發現，在兩個交易所重疊部份的交易時間內，合資格投資者增進兩個市場之間的信息傳遞，幫助大豆期貨的價格發現。

- 各大宗商品期貨市場與現貨市場的關聯在結構上的差別，會令不同期貨市場的價格不一。以銅期貨為例，CME 銅期貨價格於 2014 年至 2017 年

---

16 見 Kristoufek, I. 與 M. Vosvrda (2014)〈大宗商品期貨與市場效率〉("Commodity futures and market efficiency")，載於《能源經濟》(Energy Economics)，第 42 期，50-57 頁。

17 見 Chng, M. T. (2009)〈大宗商品期貨的經濟聯繫：對沖與交易涵義〉("Economic linkages across commodity futures: Hedging and trading implications")，載於《銀行與金融期刊》(Journal of Banking and Finance)，第 33 期，958-970 頁。

18 Kavussanos, M. G.、I. D. Visvikis 與 D. N. Dimitrakopoulos (2014)〈相關衍生產品市場之間的經濟外流：大宗商品及貨運市場〉("Economic spillovers between related derivatives markets: The case of commodity and freight markets")，載於《運輸調查 E 部》(Transportation Research Part E)，第 68 冊，79-102 頁。

19 資料來源：Gale, F.、C. Valdes 與 M. Ash〈中、美、巴西三國在大豆交易議題上唇齒相依〉("Interdependence of China, United States, and Brazil in soybean trade")，載於美國農業部經濟研究局的網站，2019 年 6 月。

20 Plato, G. 與 L. Hoffman (2011)〈美國與外國大宗商品期貨市場的價格發現：巴西大豆示例〉("Price Discovery in U.S. and Foreign Commodity Futures Markets: The Brazilian Soybean Example")，載於《有關應用大宗商品價格分析、預測及風險管理的 NCCC-134 會議程序》(Proceedings of the NCCC-134 Conference on Applied Commodity Price Analysis, Forecasting, and Risk Management)，密蘇里州聖路易斯。

3 月期間便高於 LME 的合約價格，原因是兩所的倉庫網絡覆蓋有別（LME 全球有 34 處有倉庫，但 CME 只在美國有倉庫），以及預期美國會實施關稅[21]。

- 另一項研究[22]發現，在大豆和銅的價格發現方面，美國期貨市場的推動力較中國市場大。美國市場的資訊流向對中國市場所產生的影響亦比反過來的影響大。這反映了在全球大宗商品期貨市場上定價話語權的差別。

在大宗商品的價格發現上，全球大宗商品期貨交易所擔當着非常重要的角色。大宗商品的現貨與期貨市場之間是否有密切聯繫、以服務大宗商品用戶的不同需要，是左右定價話語權強弱的一個因素。

2 大宗商品期貨須切合實體經濟用戶的需要

2.1 實體經濟中不同用家的需要

國際大宗商品期貨市場的主要參與者包括套期保值者及金融投資者。套期保值者包括商品生產商、消費者或貿易公司，都是因為承受大宗商品價格風險，所以買賣期貨合約，從而抵銷有關價格風險；金融投資者則是本來並無價格風險，參與買賣期貨合約後而承擔了有關價格風險。兩者在實體經濟的角色有別，大宗商品期貨市場的產品及服務以不同形式切合其需要。

21　見〈LME 與 CME 銅套戲：全球與地區價格相交接〉("LME and CME copper arbitrage: When global and regional prices meet")，載於 *LME Insight*，2017 年 3 月。

22　見 Liu, Q. 與 Y. An (2011)〈資訊聯通市場的訊息傳遞：美國及中國大宗商品期貨市場的實證〉("Information transmission in informationally linked markets: Evidence from US and Chinese commodity futures markets")，載於《國際貨幣與金融期刊》(*Journal of International Money and Finance*)，第 30 期，778-795 頁。

(1)　生產商

上游行業的生產商生產諸如原材料一類的大宗商品，用以進一步加工。除非因供應的政策指引或惡劣的天氣狀況而生產中斷，生產作業通常全年無休，否則要重啟生產設施花費不菲亦十分耗時（如煉鋼熔爐），因此生產過程中途難以隨便調整商品數量。換言之，生產商的產出供給都有固定的生產計劃，產出價格驟降就會造成虧損。

大宗商品生產商為了對沖產出價格下降的風險，方法之一是訂立實物交收的期貨短倉又或買入認沽期權，以確定在產出日期可按預定的價格出售既定數量的大宗商品。以 LME 市場為例，金屬合約制訂的實物交割期可長達 123 個月，能切合不同生產時間表的需要，包括可在三個月內每個交易日均可交割的合約，在三個月至六個月期間可每週週三交割的合約，以及在七個月至 123 個月內可每月第三個星期三交割的合約。由於生產商通常都希望其產出的銷售可以全年分佈平均，而且售價相對穩定，能將價格平均化的 LME 合約正好切合所需。生產商亦可透過期權策略來對沖，提高回報[23]。若干生產商可能持有超過其業務所需的長倉或短倉，以從價格波動中賺取潛在額外利潤（稱為「選擇性對沖」）。這些生產商傾向於在大宗商品期貨中選擇相對較多回報分佈傾向正數的長倉，又或較多回報分佈傾向負數的短倉。

由於對沖的大宗商品與對沖工具之間可能存在價差（例如大宗商品期貨合約訂明的特性及數量有所不同），故生產商在對沖後仍可能會承擔基準風險。儘管如此，大宗商品期貨的價格通常是現貨市場近似商品的參考價。例如有研究報告[24]指出，LME 各類合約的價格已經成為多種工業金屬雙邊交易的參考價。

由於大宗商品期貨能滿足生產商的對沖需要，國際大宗商品期貨市場的主要參與者通常都是生產商。儘管生產商及消費者主要依賴現貨市場買賣大宗商品，大宗商品期貨交易透過倉庫實物交割實現高效結算，亦對作為商業用途的大宗商品的交易有很大幫助，能增強大宗商品現貨與期貨市場之間的聯繫。因此，期貨

---

23 見 Taušer, J. 與 R. Čajka (2014)〈大宗商品風險管理中的套期保值技術〉("Hedging techniques in commodity risk management")，載於《農業經濟雜誌》(*Agricultural Economics*)，第 60 期，第 174 至 182 頁。

24 Valiante, D.〈大宗商品市場的價格形成：金融化及其他方面〉("Price formation in commodity markets: Financialisation and beyond")，載於歐洲政策研究中心（CEPS）的網站，2013 年 7 月。

價格在國際市場上可反映大宗商品市場價格，而套期保值者可利用期貨價格作為大宗商品現貨交易的基準價格。例如，LME 匯聚了基本金屬市場的主要生產商來進行價格發現 —— 全球最大的基本金屬套期保值者都聚於 LME 的交易圈（公開叫價場地）內進行交易，輔以其他交易機制。為便利買賣，LME 在全球 33 個地區擁有超過 550 個核准倉庫[25] 提供實物交割服務，將運輸成本減至最低。

(2) 消費者

大宗商品消費者包括下游產業中使用大宗商品作為原材料的二級生產商，或者大宗商品產品的終端用戶。他們購買大宗商品作為其生產投入的成本之一。為免因投入不足導致生產或消費受阻，他們或會保持一定存貨。因為最後作消費品出售的終端產品通常沒有中央化的二級市場，其價格變動一般不那麼頻繁。所以，萬一投入價格突然上漲，會對這些消費者的成本造成壓力，影響利潤。

大宗商品消費者為避免投入品價格上揚的風險，方法之一是訂立實物交收的期貨長倉或認購期權，確保可在預定日期購買特定數量的大宗商品作其生產的投入品。像大宗商品生產商一樣，消費者亦可能進行選擇性對沖，也會因為期貨合約的特性及數量未必完全切合所需而承擔對沖的基準風險。與大宗商品生產商相反的是，大宗商品的使用或消費的計劃通常有別於大宗商品的生產計劃。在這方面，主要的大宗商品期貨市場通常會為期貨合約提供平均定價（例如 LME 的每月平均價格期貨以及平均價格期權），以解決時間錯配的問題。除此之外，生產商及消費者的所在地區也許亦不相同。在這方面，主要的大宗商品期貨交易所有其本身的核准全球倉庫網絡，為其大宗商品期貨結算時進行實物交割。另外，倉庫存貨的妥善管理亦有助益。例如 LME 於 2013 至 2016 年間多番改革其倉庫管理，其中包括入庫和出庫量掛鈎的提存規則以及每個倉庫輪候時間的報告[26]，有效減少消費者需要長時間輪候方可從某些倉庫取出商品的情況。

---

25 LME 不擁有或經營倉庫，亦不擁有庫中所存放的物料。LME 只是核准有關的倉庫公司及其經營的倉庫來儲存 LME 註冊的金屬品牌。見香港交易所新聞稿〈香港交易所集團營運總裁冼博能於傳媒工作坊講解倫敦金屬交易所最新情況之發言稿（只供英文版）〉（2016 年 6 月 7 日）。

26 見《2013-2016 年倉庫改革》網頁，載於 LME 網站，於 2020 年 1 月 30 日閱覽。

(3)　貿易公司

大宗商品貿易公司是大宗商品生產商與消費者之間的中介，其角色在利用大宗商品期貨市場上的產品及服務來化解兩邊不配合的問題。全球商品交易市場有數家主要的貿易公司，最大的四家貿易公司於 2018 年的收入各自超過 1,000 億美元（而第五大貿易公司的收入僅為 300 至 400 億美元），這些公司業務涵蓋許多不同類型的大宗商品（如金屬、能源產品、農產品及二氧化碳排放）[27]。大宗商品貿易公司或會擁有本身的上游或下游業務。除此之外，大宗商品生產商及消費者要管理其持有的大宗商品或參與大宗商品交易所面對的價格波動風險時，都可能會尋求這些公司的幫助。要兼顧生產商及消費者的不同需要，貿易公司會集合一系列訂有不同到期日的大宗商品期貨長短倉盤的買賣指示。

大宗商品貿易公司也扮演為大宗商品貿易提供資金的角色[28]。大型的國際大宗商品貿易公司通常擁有本身的中游設施（如倉庫及航運碼頭），通過持有存貨來緩衝供需波動，並把握短期套利機會。這些貿易公司非常依賴銀行為其短期套利活動提供資金，一般每宗交易都付足 100% 抵押品，並定期（例如每週一次）按市值計價。它們亦為客戶提供不同形式的融資服務，包括傳統的貿易信貸（於貿易公司的資產負債表中列作應收款項），以及通過生產商、貿易公司及銀行之間的「承購協議」進行結構性交易，從而獲得預付款項去進行合約銷售。有分析[29]顯示大宗商品價格與銀行借貸及實體經濟的關係——中國的銀行借貸意外增加一個百分點，部份基本金屬（包括銅）的價格就會上升 10% 至 12%，而工業生產總值出現一個百分比的變動，鋁、銅及原油的價格會有 7% 至 9% 波動。這樣的大宗商品融資活動需要可信的紀錄以及妥善的倉存管理。

(4)　金融投資者

金融投資者包括買賣指數的公司以及資金管理人（如對沖基金），他們將大宗

27　資料來源：〈主要經濟體競爭的另一個戰場：商品價值供應鏈〉("Another battlefield of competition between major economies: Value chain of commodities)，載於 *Huexiu.com*，2019 年 9 月 25 日。

28　同上。

29　Roache, S. 與 M. Rousset (2015)〈中國：信貸、抵押品及商品價格〉("China: Credit, collateral and commodity prices")，《香港貨幣及金融研究中心工作報告》，2015 年 27 號。

商品期貨視為一種資產類別，買賣策略可以是主動（如期貨長短倉策略）或被動（例如透過指數期貨或交易所買賣基金（ETF）追蹤大宗商品期貨指數），從套利機會或投機活動中賺取交易利潤，或增加股票投資組合的多樣性[30]。一項研究作了分析，發現於 2008 年全球金融危機前後期間，在股票投資組合中加入大宗商品期貨指數或黃金期貨，能夠提高該段期間牛熊市的年化回報及經風險調整後的回報（即「夏普比率」）（見圖 4）。由於金融投資者更關注短期回報，他們更喜歡高度標準化、流動性高的期貨合約，又或現金結算合約，避免實物結算。

圖 4：包含商品期貨的投資組合與股票組合的年度化回報及夏普比率的比較

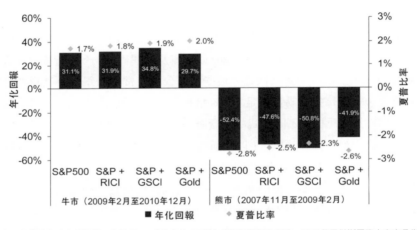

註：GSCI 是標普高盛商品指數，追踪於 CME 上市的 24 種大宗商品期貨的表現；RICI 是羅傑斯國際大宗商品指數，
　　追踪於四個國家九家交易所上市的 38 個大宗商品期貨的表現。
　　標準普爾 500 — 標準普爾 500 指數
　　S&P + RICI — 85％標準普爾 500 指數和 15％RICI 的投資組合
　　S&P + GSCI — 85％標準普爾 500 指數和 15％GSCI 的投資組合
　　S&P + Gold — 85％標準普爾 500 指數和 15％美國現貨金價格的投資組合

資料來源：Batavia, B., N. Parameswar 與 C. Wague (2012)〈極端環境下的投資組合多元化：加入商品期貨指數是否
　　有助益？〉（"Portfolio diversification in extreme environments: Are there benefits from adding commodity
　　futures indices?"），載於《歐洲研究》(European Research Studies)，第 15 期，33-48 頁。

　　金融投資者是國際商品期貨市場流動性的一個很重要的來源。他們的投資策

30　見 Mayer, J. (2009)《金融市場與商品市場逐漸相互依存》，聯合國貿易和發展會議（UNCTAD）的討論文件第 195
　　號。

略採用大宗商品期貨、期權或掉期等不同形式的組合。1994 年 1 月 2 日至 2014 年 11 月 1 日期間美國 26 隻商品期貨的實證數據[31] 顯示，短期的倉位變化主要受金融投資者（即投機者）所帶動，而長期的倉位變動則主要受套期保值者的對沖需求所驅動[32]。換言之，金融投資者的交易要比套期保值者更頻繁，懷疑投機交易增加了價格波動。不過，有研究[33] 發現，投機者的長短倉策略反而降低了美國五個農產品大宗商品期貨於 2006 至 2017 年間的市場波動。

然而，金融機構始終是國際大宗商品市場的少數參與羣體。舉例，LME 參與者大部份為生產商、消費者及貿易公司，三者已佔去 2016 年全球有色金屬成交額約 75%[34]，這亦解釋了何以 2019 年 LME 的市場交易周轉率（全年成交額除以年末持倉量的比率）僅約 73 倍，而內地一家大宗商品期貨交易所則超過 200 倍（見 3.2 節）。

2.2　實物交割：環球商品期貨市場服務實體經濟的潛在挑戰

為滿足實體經濟主要參與者的不同需要，大宗商品期貨市場的價格發現必須很高效率，令結算日當天現貨與期貨的價格趨同。若大宗商品的期貨價格大幅偏離結算時的現價，可能意味着（1）與不作對沖的情況相比，生產商收入較低，或消費者成本較高；以及（2）金融投資者的投資回報更加不確定。期貨合約結算時商品實物交割的效率高低，或會是現貨與期貨價格趨同的主要因素。

一項研究發現，美國若干主要農產品期貨（如玉米、大豆和小麥）在 2005 至 2010 年間的價格一直高於各自結算時的相關現價[35]。該研究審視了商品現

31　Kang, W.、K. G. Rouwenhorst 與 K. Tang (2020)〈兩種溢價的故事：套期保值者與投機者在大宗商品期貨市場的角色〉("A tale of two premiums: The role of hedgers and speculators in commodity futures markets")，載於《金融期刊》(Journal of Finance), Vol. 75, pp.377-417.

32　套期保值者是指商業交易者，包括生產商、加工商、製造商或處理有關商品或其產品或副產品的商人，而投機者是指非商業交易者。「商業交易者」和「非商業交易者」是於美國商品期貨交易委員會（CFTC）的交易商承約（COT）數據集內所作的分類。

33　Bohl, M.T. 與 C. Sulewski (2019)〈「長短倉」投機者對農產品期貨價格波動的影響〉("The impact of long-short speculators on the volatility of agricultural commodity futures prices")，載於《商品市場雜誌》(Journal of Commodity Markets)，第 16 期，1-30 頁。

34　資料來源：香港交易所市場發展聯席主管李剛於媒體工作坊介紹內地大宗商品市場概況之發言稿〈媒體工作坊──中國大宗商品市場概況之前世今生〉，載於香港交易所網站的新聞稿，2017 年 6 月 7 日。

35　Adjemian, M. K. 等 (2013)〈國內商品期貨市場的不接軌：前因後果與補救措施〉，("Non-convergence in domestic commodity futures markets: Causes, consequences, and remedies"，載於美國農業部經濟研究局的《經濟信息通報》(the USDA ERS's Economic Information Bulletin)，第 115 號。

貨與期貨價格不接軌的背後成因。雖然不少人認為這是金融投資者過度投機所致（見 2.1 節），但實證數據顯示，期貨合約結算時實物交割商品所涉的費用才是主要原因。其中一個關鍵因素是現貨與期貨市場儲存成本的差異 [36]——2008 年，在美國 CBOT 實物交割的小麥期貨的儲存費用，較現貨市場儲存費每月每單位低 4.5 美仙（2004 年至 2008 年間增加了 2.6 美仙）。在這方面，生產模式及運輸物流的變化會影響到期貨合約結算時實物交割商品的費用。例如，芝加哥穀物市場的生產和營銷渠道已經移離五大湖地區（CBOT 於 19 世紀中葉成立之時最先使用的交割市場便在五大湖地區，如今其商業重要性已經不如前），但 CBOT 玉米和大豆的交割點，直至 2000 年才有所改變，而小麥的交割點則直至 2009 年才改變。這些都導致於上述有關期間獲取商品進行套利活動的成本高昂，影響到期貨市場的價格發現。

　　商品期貨市場服務實體經濟的效率高低，主要視乎基礎設施是否便利期貨合約結算時的商品實物交割，尤其是倉庫網絡。美國 CME 的產品類型雖然廣泛，其倉庫網絡卻未必能滿足全球商品用戶的需求。例如 CME 的銅期貨合約僅可透過美國倉庫作實物交割，而 LME 的期貨合約則可在美國、歐洲、中東及亞洲等 24 個地方交割 [37]。商品用戶距離倉庫網絡近一點，運輸成本自然也低一點，也就便利其庫存的套利活動，進而促進商品的價格發現。

3　內地商品市場與世界商品市場的比較

　　內地大宗商品期貨市場服務實體經濟的成效被認為未如理想 [38]。基於國際其他大宗商品期貨市場的經驗，其主要原因有兩個：第一，內地大宗商品現貨與期貨

36　CME 集團的實物交收商品期貨在結算時，會向長倉持有人發出倉庫收據，該等持有人可以選擇將商品存放在交易所核准的倉庫，而交易所將收取相關的儲存費用。

37　有關 CME 銅期貨的資料為 2020 年 3 月 26 日數據（資料來源：〈基本金屬倉庫統計〉("Metal warehouse stocks statistics")，載於 CME 集團的網站，2020 年 3 月 30 日閱覽），LME 銅期貨的資料為 2020 年 3 月 30 日數字（資料來源：LME 網站上 "Stocks breakdown" 網頁上的每日數據）。

38　見胡俞越與張慧 (2017)〈中國商品期貨市場服務實體經濟評估〉，載於《期貨與金融衍生品》，第 98 期，16-29 頁。

市場之間的聯繫相對薄弱，期貨價格未必能作為現貨價格的參考價；第二，內地大宗商品期市的定價無法對全球大宗商品期貨價格產生足夠影響。儘管中國已成為主要大宗商品的最大生產國和消費國 [39]（見圖 5），內地的大宗商品用家（生產商和消費者）往往只能跟從國際大宗商品期貨的價格。

圖 5：中國在全球商品消耗量中所佔的份額（1997及2017）

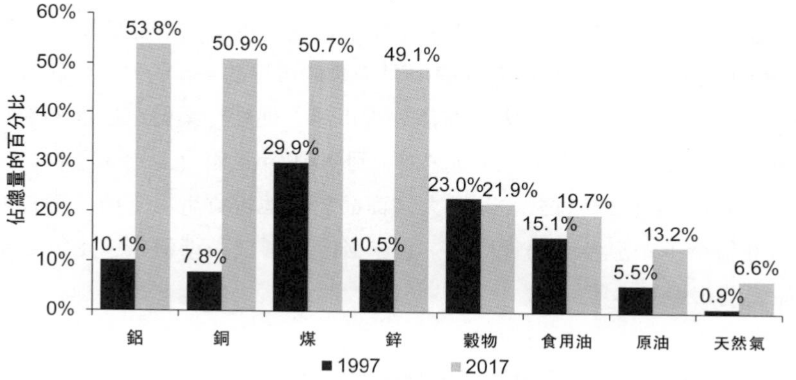

資料來源：〈關稅對大宗商品市場的影響〉("The implications of tariff for commodity markets")，刊於《大宗商品市場前景》(Commodity Markets Outlook)，載於世界銀行的網站，2018 年 10 月號。

　　以下分節嘗試探討內地大宗商品市場在服務實體經濟上相對全球其他發達國家不足的原因。

3.1　大宗商品現貨市場零散

　　環顧全球各種大宗商品市場，主導市場的大型生產商 [40] 都會在世界各地發展成熟的大宗商品期貨市場上積極進行套期保值，由此產生的商品期貨價格通常就會作為現貨交易的基準價格。

39　資料來源：〈圖表顯示中國四類主要商品消耗量激增〉("Charts show China's explosive consumption of four critical commodities")，載於 cnbc.com，2019 年 9 月 24 日。

40　數宗大生產商主導着包括鋁、可可和咖啡等多種商品的全球現貨交易。資料來源：Cinquegrana, P.〈商品和商品衍生品市場需要透明度〉("The need for transparency in commodity and commodity derivatives markets")，載於歐洲政策研究中心 (Centre for European Policy Studies (CEPS)) 的網站，2018 年 12 月 15 日。

然而，這種定價機制在內地卻很薄弱。舉例說，2017 年在美國和日本的鋼材生產量約有八成來自其鋼材業的四大巨頭，而在中國內地，這數字僅約兩成[41]。內地現貨商品市場嚴重依賴大量本地化商品貿易公司作為中介來進行商品交易，包括代理貿易和自營貿易[42]。傳統上，現貨價格都是基於生產區域的平均加工成本再加上溢價作為利潤而訂定。此外，現貨交易中的商品規格可以極其參差，同類商品可以出現眾多現貨價格。這些現貨交易可以通過地方政府、國有企業或市場參與者經營的電子交易平台進行[43]。主要參與者包括證券公司、期貨公司與其風險管理子公司，以及私募基金。這些電子交易平台還提供大宗商品的場外衍生產品的買賣，但未必有很健全的風險管理框架[44]。鑑於市場的不當行為，中國國務院於 2011 年發佈了政策文件[45] 整頓大宗商品現貨市場，促進行業健康發展。現貨交易平台的數目一度增至 2017 年的 3,000 多個，到 2019 年已整合至約 30 個[46]。

基於上述的現貨交易方式，某一大宗商品於內地現貨市場上的價格會因地區而異。這些價格不一定參考期貨價格，也未必歸一形成基準價格，定價也未必能及時反映當前市場基本情況。

3.2　投機活動於商品期貨市場佔主要比重

目前，中國內地有三家提供大宗商品期貨合約的期貨交易所 —— 上海期貨交易所（簡稱「上期所」）、鄭州商品交易所（簡稱「鄭商所」）和大連商品交易所（簡稱「大商所」）。三家交易所的商品期貨交易量在全球數一數二。全球各主要類別大宗商品的衍生產品（包括期貨和期權）於 2019 年的交易量排名（按合約張數計）的首五家交易所，都至少見到一家內地交易所的身影（見圖 6）。

41　資料來源：興業研究〈鋼鐵產業鏈及其背後的大國變遷 —— 螺紋鋼系列（一）〉，2019 年 2 月 27 日。

42　見〈2017 中國大宗商品貿易行業研究報告〉，載於聯合信用評級的網站，2017 年。

43　見〈大宗商品現貨平台交易模式分析與法律風險防範〉，載於 *zhihu.com*，2017 年 12 月 7 日。

44　相關例子見〈讓多家期貨公司集體穿倉的 PTA 場外期權爆倉事件是怎麼發生的？〉，載於 *yocajr.com*，2019 年 7 月 31 日。

45　《國務院關於清理整頓各類交易場所切實防範金融風險的決定》，國務院發佈，2011 年 11 月 24 日。

46　資料來源：〈2019 年現貨貿易良心測評〉，載於 *yaobang-metal.com*，2019 年 10 月 20 日。

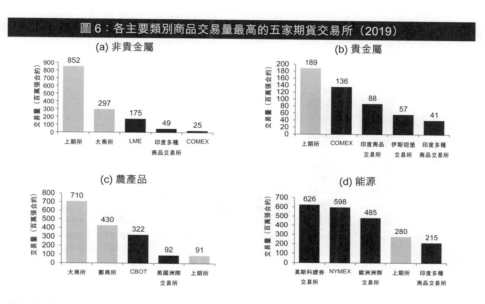

圖 6：各主要類別商品交易量最高的五家期貨交易所（2019）

(a) 非貴金屬

(b) 貴金屬

(c) 農產品

(d) 能源

註：不同市場的合約單位差異很大。例如，金屬合約的合約單位從 10 公噸到 100 噸不等，農產品合約由 10 公噸到 127 公噸不等，原油合約由 10 桶到 1,000 桶不等。

資料來源：美國期貨業協會月度統計數據（2019 年 12 月）。

　　伴隨內地大宗商品期貨交易所這樣高的成交量，還有很高的成交周轉率（即全年成交量除以年末未平倉合約數量）。2019 年，上期所、鄭商所和大商所的成交周轉率分別為 249 倍、247 倍和 140 倍，相對於 LME 和 CME 集團的分別 73 倍和 46 倍[47]（見圖 7）。這些數字可以理解為內地商品的持倉時間極短，意味着交易屬高度投機性質。據估計，上期所於 2016 年的螺紋鋼期貨及大商所的鐵礦石期貨（2016 年前者的成交周轉率約為 440 倍，後者約為 290 倍[48]）的平均持倉時間僅為 4 小時，遠低於 CME 的銅期貨和天然氣期貨的約 40 小時和 70 小時[49]。與此相關的是，內地商品交易所的期貨合約單位一般較小 —— 例如上期所的銅期貨合約單位為 5 噸，而 LME 的則為 25 噸[50]。

47　根據美國期貨業協會月度統計數據中全年截至 12 月的數字計算（2019 年 12 月）。

48　根據美國期貨業協會月度統計數據中全年截至 12 月的數字計算（2016 年 12 月）。

49　資料來源：〈持倉不足 4 小時足見中國商品市場狂熱〉("A life expectancy under 4 hours shows China commodity frenzy")，載於《彭博》，2016 年 4 月 26 日。

50　見上期所和 LME 的網站上所載的合約細則，2019 年 12 月 16 日閱覽。

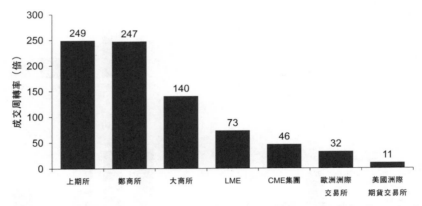

註：上期所的數字包含上海國際能源交易中心（簡稱「上期能源」）的產品；CME 集團的數字涵蓋 CBOT、CME、COMEX 和 NYMEX 的產品。

資料來源：美國期貨業協會月度統計數據（2019 年 12 月）。

　　這些投機活動很可能是與個人投資者的高參與度有關。一項研究[51]指出，內地個人投資者賬戶持有的未平倉合約於 2016 年的佔比超過 86%，美國的相應數字則只是 15%；同一項研究認為，個人投資者所得的信息很可能較少，易出現羊羣效應，會引致高度投機的交易模式。

　　投機活動和散戶買賣的佔比相對偏高，會令大宗商品期貨價格更加波動，並打擊進行套期保值的意欲。不過，近年已有跡象顯示內地期貨市場上套期保值者的參與正在增加，有助對沖散戶投機交易的主要佔比。以大商所為例，機構投資者佔市場未平倉合約總數的比重已從 2016 年 10 月底的 44% 升至 2018 年 7 月底的 54%[52]。

51　Fan, J. H 與 T. Zhang (2020)〈中國商品期貨不為人知的故事〉("The untold story of commodity futures in China")，載於《期貨市場雜誌》(*Journal of Futures Markets*)，第 40 期，671-706 頁。

52　資料來源：〈期貨市場投資者結構悄然變化〉("The gradual change of investor composition in the futures market")，載於 *jrj.com.cn*，2018 年 9 月 9 日。

3.3　倉庫網絡相對狹窄

國際上發展成熟的大宗商品期貨市場都有廣泛的倉庫網絡分佈世界各地（見上文第 2.1 及 2.2 節），相比之下，內地大宗商品期貨交易所用作實物交收的倉庫網絡相對狹窄。

首先，內地市場的倉庫網絡可能未有覆蓋全國。例如，上期所的銅期貨只透過位於上海、江蘇、江西及廣東的 17 個倉庫提供實物交收[53]，而英國 LME 的銅期貨則可利用全球 24 個地點的倉庫作實物交收[54]。其次，大宗商品期貨只可透過內地倉庫進行實物交收。從事大宗商品跨境進出口和對外投資支持「一帶一路」倡議項目的內地公司，不能因應業務需要而在離岸進行商品實物交收。第三，內地當局至今沒有批准任何一家外地大宗商品期貨交易所在內地設置倉庫，為在其市場上交易並在內地有業務需求的公司提供大宗商品實物交收。在岸套期保值者雖然可以在出現價差時，透過附屬公司在離岸市場買賣大宗商品期貨，但只可透過離岸倉庫交收再輸入內地，因此需付額外的倉儲及運輸成本（見第 2.2 節）以及跨境交易稅項（例如關稅及進口增值稅[55]）。

內地大宗商品期貨市場的倉庫網絡覆蓋範圍狹窄，不足以迎合不同地點的套期保值者業務所需，使用起來亦成本高昂，會減低市場用家透過內地商品期貨進行對沖的意欲。

3.4　產品類別和交易貨幣種類不多

全球大宗商品期貨市場涉及的大宗商品主要涵蓋金屬、能源、化學品及農產品。於 2020 年 1 月，CME 及洲際交易所集團（ICE）分別有超過 160 隻及逾 1,660 隻大宗商品衍生產品，涵蓋多種類型的大宗商品（見表 1）。全球大宗商品衍生產品種類繁多，會滿足到不同大宗商品用戶的各種需要（包括對沖及組合投資）。相比之下，內地大宗商品期貨交易所的產品選擇相對較少，只有 70 多隻大宗商品衍生產品，大部份是商品期貨（2020 年 1 月底數字為 60 隻），還有小量商品期權

53　見銅期貨的合約細則，載於上期所網站，2020 年 1 月 30 日閱覽。

54　〈2020 年 1 月倉庫公司存貨及輪候隊伍數據〉（"Warehouse company stocks and queue date January 2020"），載於 LME 的網站，2020 年 2 月 20 日閱覽。

55　見《國務院關稅稅則委員會公告 2018 年第 5 號》，財政部發佈，2018 年 7 月 24 日。

（2020 年 1 月底數字為 11 隻）（見表 1），這樣的選擇恐怕未能滿足內地不同行業
的需要。

表 1：部份交易所的大宗商品期貨及期權數目（按大宗商品類別劃分）（2020 年）						
大宗商品類別	ICE	CME	內地交易所			
			上期所（包括上期能源）	鄭商所	大商所	全部
農產品	46	46	—	16	13	29
能源	1,546	80	3	—	2	5
金屬	15	40	14	2	2	18
其他	58	—	6	8	5	19
總計	1,665	166	23	26	22	71

註：2020 年 1 月 22 日的數據。

資料來源：ICE、CME、上期所、大商所及鄭商所的網站。

　　內地交易所的大宗商品期貨只以人民幣定價。雖然這能滿足在岸的套期保值
者在中國內地的業務需要，但未必能配合離岸業務的用途（例如「一帶一路」項
目）。據報不少「一帶一路」相關項目都以美元融資[56]。由於內地的大宗商品期貨沒
有外幣計值，內地套期保值者很可能要轉向於國際其他大宗商品期貨市場進行對
沖。另外，在岸的金融投資者在大宗商品投資上的幣種選擇不多，未能滿足投資
組合多樣化的需求。

3.5　市場開放及與全球市場互動不足

　　國際主要的大宗商品期貨市場都是向國際投資者自由開放，但內地市場對外
國投資者仍有不少准入限制，對內地用戶參與海外大宗商品期貨市場亦嚴加管制：

- 就外資參與內地市場而言，只有指定的大宗商品期貨才直接向外國投資
  者開放。2020 年 2 月底，指定的期貨產品計有上期所附屬公司上海國際
  能源交易中心（簡稱「上期能源」）的原油及橡膠、鄭商所的精對苯二甲酸

56　見〈美元的制約可能令中國「一帶一路」計劃有更多多邊方案〉("Dollar constraints may lead to more multilateral approach for China's Belt and Road")，載於 *chathamhouse.org*，2018 年 10 月 23 日。

（PTA）及大商所的鐵礦石，其他的都只限在岸參與者（可包括若干中外合資公司）買賣。

- 內地用戶參與海外市場方面，只有少數國有企業得到官方批准，可在全球大宗商品期貨市場進行跨境對沖活動[57]。除此之外，在岸大宗商品用家也可透過離岸附屬公司在國際市場進行對沖，但離岸對沖交收商品後再進口須繳交稅項，就算以現金結算的離岸商品期貨的現金流亦備受限制。

因此，國際和內地的套期保值者與金融投資者都不能隨意參與對方市場，國際與內地的大宗商品期貨市場始終分割，價格互動並不充分。

由於內地農產品期貨現時未開放予外資參與，從美國與內地市場的農產品期貨未平倉合約數量的巨大差異就能看出投資者參與程度的不同。儘管內地經濟對全球經濟愈來愈舉足輕重，但美國市場的農產品期貨未平倉合約數量卻遠遠高於內地市場（見表 2）。圖 8 可顯示以大豆為例，中美大宗商品市場上的期貨價格並沒有趨同——2008 年至 2019 年間美國的大豆期貨價格一直低於內地的期貨價格。

表 2：中美農產品透過期貨的持倉量（2018）			
大宗商品類別	美國（百萬噸）（A）	中國（百萬噸）（B）	（A）/（B）比例（倍）
小麥	114.78	0.02	5,001
豆粕	41.26	18.42	2
玉米	252.98	9.08	28
大豆	116.40	1.63	71
大豆油	13.34	4.91	3
穀物	0.73	0.00	—
棉花	6.17	1.05	6
糖	46.13	3.37	14
總計	591.80	38.69	15

註：2018 年 3 月 13 日的數據。由於四捨五入的誤差，持倉量的個別數字相加未必等於總和。

資料來源：謝小卉 (2018)〈從歷史看大宗商品定價中心的形成及建議〉，載於《中國期貨》，第 65 號（2018 年第 5 期），51-56 頁。

57　2016 年有 31 家國企獲准進行跨境對沖活動。資料來源：〈觀韜解讀：國資委取消央企境外商品衍生業務核准事項〉，載於 *guantao.com*，2016 年 8 月 30 日。

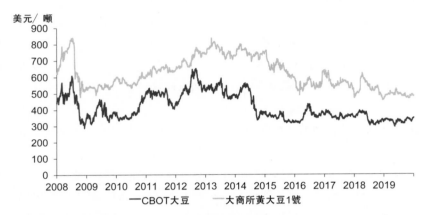

圖 8：CBOT 與大商所的大豆期貨每日價格（2008 年至 2019 年）

註：大商所黃大豆 1 號期貨的價格按彭博的美元兑人民幣每日匯價換算為美元。

資料來源：彭博。

4 內地大宗商品期貨市場如何能更好地服務實體經濟？

內地大宗商品期貨市場若要更好地服務實體經濟，就如環球大宗商品期貨市場般，首先必須加強內地大宗商品現貨與期貨市場之間的聯繫。這會有助大宗商品在期貨市場的價格發現，從而使期貨價格能成為現貨交易的基準價格，而大宗商品期貨亦能有效促進對沖活動。第二，中國現在既已是全球大宗商品的消費及生產大國，內地大宗商品期貨市場與全球市場理應有更多的互動，冀能逐漸提升中國在全球大宗商品方面的定價話語權，使內地的商品生產商及消費者也有機會參與全球大宗商品的價格制定，而不僅是價格接受者。以下是一些可望達到這兩項目標的途徑：

(1)　整合現貨市場的交易和提升交易透明度

整合現貨交易平台會有助形成基準現貨價格，這或可透過政策推動。這能促使更多在不同地方的套期保值者及其他市場用家於整合了的平台進行自訂的大宗商品交易。同時，交易透明度亦應有所提升，讓市場用家看得到大宗商品現貨市場的價格動態，包括與中央化的大宗商品期貨市場價格的差距。這會鼓勵套期保值者使用大宗商品期貨價格作為現貨交易的基準價格。

(2)　加強監管以打擊過度投機行為

過度投機會造成價格過於大幅波動，使期貨價格偏離相關資產的基礎因素，削弱期貨作為對沖工具的有效性。要抑制過度投機行為，美國在實行監管措施方面的經驗[58]顯示禁止期貨市場的高頻交易是一可行方法。另外，在波動性較高的市場中，限制買賣盤大小並對降低持倉限額及／或提高保證金要求及時作出調整，亦有助打擊過度投機行為。

(3)　拓展並加強實物交收的倉庫網絡

內地大宗商品期貨交易所的倉庫網絡的地理分佈可以拓展，以減少交收在岸大宗商品的時間及運輸成本。為了切合業務需要，倉庫存貨的管理效率和效能都應提高（例如採用高效的入庫及出庫程序），使物流時間更容易預計。另外，為支持跨境交易的對沖，當局可批准更多「保稅區」的倉庫為內地及國際大宗商品期貨的結算進行大宗商品的實物交收，以利用免稅跨境交收的優勢[59]。

(4)　擴闊產品類別及貨幣種類的範圍

要更好地滿足不同行業套期保值者及金融投資者的不同需要，大宗商品期貨市場應多方面拓展衍生產品的範圍，包括產品種類（例如期權或掉期）、相關大宗商品類別（例如在規格上有更多不同選擇）及定價的貨幣種類。

58　Berg, A. (2011)〈第 10 章：大宗商品的投機活動上升──由受討厭到受推崇〉("Chapter 10. The rise of commodity speculation: from villainous to venerable")，刊於《在全球市場波動下保衛食物安全》(*Safeguarding Food Security in Volatile Global Markets*)，聯合國糧食及農業組織 (FAO)。

59　見〈什麼是「保稅區」？〉("What's the bonded zone?")，載於 *ftz-shanghai.com*，於 2019 年 12 月 17 日閱覽。

(5) 進一步開放內地大宗商品期貨市場

當局可考慮拓展市場雙向的互聯互通範圍，增加與全球市場的互動。若有更多外資參與內地市場，將有助內地的大宗商品期貨納入全球用家的看法而定價。可行的方式包括允許海外用家直接參與更多不同的指定產品的交易、讓內地產品於離岸市場跨境上市、將合格投資者範圍拓展至合格境外機構投資者 (QFII)、人民幣合格境外機構投資者 (RQFII)[60] 和其他海外用家。同樣地，若讓內地用家更多地參與海外市場，亦將有助提升內地用家在全球市場的定價影響力。可行的方式包括擴大合資格於離岸市場進行跨境對沖的內地用家的範圍，以及允許離岸產品於內地市場進行跨境上市。此外，當局亦可設立像「滬深港通」及「債券通」一樣的大宗商品互聯互通平台，作為開放市場及便利市場互聯互通的有效渠道。

就上文討論的產品多樣性及市場開放而言，內地大宗商品市場可利用香港市場的相對優勢。香港市場能方便亞洲時區的用家買賣 LME 的金屬產品，對內地大宗商品期貨市場發揮着補足作用。作為內地及全球企業的「一帶一路」融資中心，香港市場可匯集大宗商品用家及投資者。事實上，不少內地及全球大宗商品貿易公司已於香港設立辦事處。內地與香港市場的「互聯互通」機制亦可拓展至大宗商品領域，促進海外及內地用家互相參與對方的市場。這一切都有助於香港市場形成一個匯聚內地及國際大宗商品用家的生態系統，支持大宗商品期貨市場發展，以及內地市場的進一步開放。

---

60 有關 QFII 及 RQFII 獲准進入內地商品期貨及期權市場的建議規則修訂已於 2019 年 1 月發佈。見《關於〈合格境外機構投資者及人民幣合格境外機構投資者境內證券期貨投資管理辦法（徵求意見稿）〉及其配套規則的說明》，中國證券監督管理委員會發佈，2019 年 1 月 31 日。

5　總結

　　根據國際商品期貨交易所的發展經驗，大宗商品現貨與期貨市場之間的緊密聯繫非常重要，因為大宗商品期貨須為現貨市場提供基準價格，從而讓實體經濟的生產商、消費者及中介機構可利用其作為有效的對沖工具。透過全球性的倉庫網絡，大宗商品期貨市場有助減低在實物交收時間上的不確定性以及令其更具成本效益，與現貨市場相輔相成。

　　反觀內地的商品期貨市場，則尚未能完全如上所述有效地服務實體經濟。於內地較為分散的現貨市場所作的定價，未必能為同一類別的大宗商品產生單一標準價，定價亦不常以大宗商品的期貨價格作為參考價。內地大宗商品期貨價格還未能成為現貨價格的參考價，原因也許是投機交易活動造成的大幅價格波動、倉庫網絡相對狹小導致實物交收的運輸成本高昂，以及產品類別和定價的貨幣種類選擇不多等的因素所造成。這些因素亦可能會削弱市場參與者通過內地的大宗商品期貨進行對沖的意欲。此外，市場開放不足亦造成內地與國際大宗商品市場之間的期貨價格差異。香港市場是位處中國大門的國際金融市場，大可擔當大宗商品市場「超級聯繫人」的角色，以進一步增加內地商品期貨市場與全球市場的互動，幫助內地大宗商品期貨市場茁壯成長及更好地服務實體經濟。

註：本章參考了就大宗商品市場發展向內地及香港期貨公司諮詢所獲取的意見及反饋。

第11章

前海聯合交易中心在中國內地大宗商品市場扮演的獨特角色

深圳前海聯合交易中心有限公司

摘 要

目前，國際上的大宗商品市場全球化特徵明顯。對中國內地而言，與實體產業密切相關的大宗原材料和工業製成品很多屬於大進大出，也迫切需要真正市場化、國際化的商品交易平台。前海聯合交易中心將有計劃、有步驟地建設一個規範透明的全國性大宗商品現貨交易所，促進現貨市場有序發展；創新探索融資新業態，解決大宗商品實體企業融資難問題；聯通境內外，分階段逐步建設全球商品的人民幣定價中心。

1　前海聯合交易中心的設立背景

中國是全球大宗商品最主要的貿易和消費國，但長期以來在全球市場上缺少定價權和話語權。其中重要的原因是內地商品市場的發展一直聚焦於商品期貨等帶有投機屬性的商品衍生品，而真正服務實體產業的商品現貨市場發展嚴重滯後，短板突出。本應由交易所扮演重要角色的現貨交易、交割和實物結算、供應鏈金融等與實體經濟密切相關的市場功能長期缺失，導致中國內地的基礎產業和消費優勢無從發揮，主要商品定價權仍然基本集中在倫敦、紐約和芝加哥等西方傳統交易中心。同時由於缺少具備公信力的全國性商品現貨交易所，無法提供滿足金融風控要求的基礎設施服務和行業標準規範，實體製造業和現貨流通市場融資及物流成本居高不下，導致大量企業特別是中小企業和貿易商始終面臨無法獲得有效金融支援的難題。無論從爭奪定價權還是服務實體的角度，中國內地現階段都迫切需要加快建設規範透明的全國性商品現貨交易市場，為產業鏈上、中、下游和機構參與者提供反映實體供需基本面的價格基準，從而與期貨市場和其他衍生品市場共同形成一個完整、多層次和成熟的現代商品市場體系。

目前，國際上的大宗商品市場全球化特徵明顯。對中國內地而言，與實體產業密切相關的大宗原材料和工業製成品很多屬於大進大出，也迫切需要有中國內地自己的、同時又是真正市場化、國際化的商品交易平台。香港交易及結算所（簡稱「香港交易所」）集團自 2012 年全資收購倫敦金屬交易所（LME）之後，於 2016 年 4 月在深圳前海合作區開始了前海聯合交易中心專案的前期籌建工作，作為其全球商品市場佈局的重要組成部份，並以切合國內市場和實體產業對於全國性商品現貨平台的現實需求。2016 年 10 月 11 日，深圳市人民政府金融發展服務辦公室向項目發起的主要股東香港交易所集團（以 HKEX Investment (China) Limited 作為投資主體）及代表深圳市政府出資的前海金融控股有限公司（簡稱「前海金控」）下發了《關於批准深圳前海聯合交易中心有限公司籌建的函》，同意兩家公司共同發起設立前海聯合交易中心（Qianhai Mercantile Exchange，簡稱 QME）。

經過逾四年的探索佈局，QME 已確立了由大宗商品現貨起步、實踐服務實體經濟的發展方向，將堅定立足前海自貿區的「先行先試」，通過交易所業態的創新探索，補齊內地商品現貨市場的短板，為實體產業鏈企業提供打通境內外的商品倉儲、交割、結算等現代供應鏈基礎設施和公共服務，利用物聯網、智慧識別和區塊鏈等前沿科技打造連接金融與實體的標準化資產體系，並與同為香港交易所集團旗下、長期作為全球大宗商品重要的美元定價中心的 LME 形成東西呼應，分階段將 QME 建成為全球大宗商品重要的人民幣定價中心，有力助推人民幣國際化和製造業強國建設的國家戰略。

2 QME 的定位與目標

2.1 重構內地商品市場格局，形成現貨價格基準

由於現貨市場發展嚴重滯後於期貨市場，目前中國內地大宗商品市場與實體產業鏈相關的現貨定價大都被迫需要從期貨價格進行倒算。然而期貨市場的價格生成機制與現貨市場不同，內地商品期貨市場往往受到場內投機資金的主導，加之眾多散戶跟風，導致價格波動經常偏離市場的基本面，不能真實反映實體經濟的供求平衡點，也無法滿足產業鏈上、中、下游企業在實際生產經營過程中對於商品現貨定價的需求。因此，當前迫切需要基於真實現貨交易的基準價格形成機制，通過現貨市場的價格發現切實起到調節實體上下游供需的作用，同時也是為商品期貨、期權等衍生品市場提供基於實體基本面的錨定價格。從這個邏輯出發，QME 作為面向實體企業和機構客戶的商品現貨交易所，將由服務產業起步，按照商品市場的發展規律，首先形成基於實體經濟活動和真實貿易背景的現貨基準價格，從而真正有效地服務產業鏈企業，滿足實體企業對於公開透明的市場交易價格的需求，並為內地在特定行業（如有色金屬、鋼鐵、煤炭等）的供給側改革提供更加高效和更加市場化的管理調控工具。

2.2　打造標準化資產體系，破解實體企業融資難題

內地市場長期面臨金融與實體脫節的難題，一方面大量實體企業特別是中小企業融資難、融資成本高，另一方面銀行和金融機構找不到優質安全的資金投放標的，「資產荒」現象嚴重。內地的實體產業基礎決定了市場上有大量底層現貨資產流轉，本來是開展基於動產和貨權的貿易融資與供應鏈金融的有利條件，但一直未能真正開展起來。其主要原因之一是缺少商品現貨的價格基準，使銀行等金融機構在開展貿易融資和供應鏈金融業務的過程中無法有效評估資產價值；二是商品現貨資產缺乏真實性、安全性和流動性保障，底層資產大多以場外非標準規格的形式存在，在交易、倉儲、交收等流轉環節中無法達到銀行和金融機構對於風險控制的要求，類似「青島港」[1]和「鋼貿危機」[2]事件時有發生。

QME 除了協助形成基於實際成交的商品現貨價格基準，還將着力打造創新的倉儲科技體系，把物聯網、智慧識別及區塊鏈等最新技術應用於交易交收以及倉儲物流等實體貿易的各個環節，通過科技賦能和系統對接實現商品現貨全生命週期的透明化及可追溯，發揮要素平台功能，以真正市場化的方式為實體行業提供建設標準化資產體系急缺的基礎設施和公共服務。現貨交易所在市場上的重要優勢便是能夠作為各方均能接受的中立方，協同廠商，牽頭生產、加工、貿易和終端消費企業以及倉庫、物流企業、保險公司和銀行金融機構等共同構建科技應用體系，通過統一的管理標準及技術標準打造以「區塊鏈倉單」為載體的可信性高的資產體系，將傳統的商品流通現貨轉化為優質安全、可直接穿透至底層並且具備良好流動性的短期資產。這樣一方面可推動銀行和金融機構打通在可靠風控條件下支援實體的重要途徑，協助企業特別是在傳統信貸邏輯下很難獲得融資的中小企業和貿易商解決資金鏈的後顧之憂，使企業能夠專注於技術研發與產品升級，有助於提升中國內地實體製造業的競爭力；另一方面，實體企業將能夠借助有公

1　2014 年 6 月初，青島港地區被揭發大宗商品融資詐騙案件，該地企業德誠礦業涉嫌利用同一批金屬庫存重複騙取融資貸款而遭到調查，多家銀行牽涉其中。資料來源：〈青島港融資詐騙案〉，百度百科（https://baike.baidu.com），於 2020 年 2 月 9 日閱覽。

2　2012 年以來，華東地區鋼貿業的資金鏈突然斷裂，鋼貿企業出現大面積的信貸違約和貿易違約情形，鋼貿商經營不善、甚至破產跑路的現象非常普遍，很多鋼貿企業被連帶追訴，整個鋼貿行業受到震盪和衝擊，此次事件被業內稱為「鋼貿危機」。資料來源：〈最高法官：從鋼貿危機看擔保品管理的漏洞〉，載於財新網站（http://opinion.caixin.com/2015-06-15/100819271.html），2015 年 6 月 15 日。

信力的現貨交易所生成和背書的倉單體系大幅提升生產周轉和資金運營效率，並向銀行等金融機構源源不絕輸送基於實體經濟活動和真實貿易背景的可證券化底層資產，在當前金融去槓桿和資管新規的背景下具有格外重要的意義。

2.3　聯通境內外，建設全球商品人民幣定價中心

就大宗商品領域而言，內地市場的最大優勢是實體產業基礎帶來的現貨貿易和消費體量，而非發展時間較短且過度投機化的商品期貨市場。要爭奪全球大宗商品的定價權，最好的策略一定是揚長避短，通過在國際市場有公信力的現貨交易所形成的、實質基於內地實體產業鏈上下游真實交易形成的現貨基準價格的輸出，真正體現中國內地在全球商品市場和戰略資源的定價權與話語權，並為內地企業在境外獲取關鍵領域上游現貨原材料帶來議價優勢和實實在在的利益。

作為香港交易所集團旗下在中國內地唯一運營的交易所法人主體和大宗商品現貨交易平台，QME 在聯通境內外商品市場方面具備成熟的條件和不可替代的特有優勢，將充分吸收集團內 LME 長期形成的制度規則體系和成功運作經驗，並結合香港作為國際金融中心的優勢，汲取粵港澳大灣區（簡稱「大灣區」）特別是深圳的科技創新活力，向內輻射中國內地的實體產業腹地，對外連接「一帶一路」沿線的資源市場，分階段逐步建設全球商品的人民幣定價中心，真正發揮出與 LME 形成的東西配合效應（見圖 1）。

圖 1：LME 與 QME 聯通

全方位聯通：
倉儲、交易、金融

（1）倉儲聯通

基於 QME 倉單體系，打造與 LME 互認的倉儲交割體系，在倉庫、品牌認證及倉儲管理系統等方面進行對接，以解決長期以來 LME 交割倉庫無法進入中國內地的難題，有效滿足企業需求。

（2）交易聯通

基於倉單互認體系，便利客戶開展跨市場交易、交割，降低內地實體企業的套期保值成本和市場對沖風險，提升人民幣作為國際結算貨幣的地位。

（3）金融聯通

發揮交易所場內平台優勢，在閉環、限額的前提下打通雙向資金流，探索資本項目有限度開放，便利金融機構在跨境貿易中提供全流程綜合金融支援。

在跨境要素市場流通的基礎上，QME 將充分依託香港交易所集團在境外市場擁有的完備金融牌照體系和產業與機構客戶資源，打造內地市場對外開放的新高地，積極探索將內地形成的、基於內地企業實體供需和真實交易產生的、以人民幣計價和結算的商品現貨基準價格向境外輸出，爭取成為香港、倫敦等成熟衍生品市場相關交易品種的實際結算價格基準，通過現貨交易所的價格傳遞真正加速實現全球大宗商品市場的人民幣定價權。

3 QME 業務發展情況

3.1　交易業務情況

3.1.1　現貨掛牌交易

QME 於 2018 年 10 月 19 日開業，推出的交易模式為現貨掛牌交易。現貨掛牌交易業務是指參與商根據 QME 相關業務規則，發佈擬交易的商品種類、規格、質量、數量、價格等供求信息，並與接受其掛牌信息和條件的參與商達成交易的交易模式。一旦達成交易，則生成交收合同，進入交收流程。現貨掛牌業務按照買賣方向的不同，分為銷售掛牌和採購掛牌；按照履約擔保方式的不同，分為倉單掛牌和擔保金掛牌；按照履約擔保金是否可以變動，分為固定擔保金掛牌和浮動擔保金掛牌。

現貨掛牌交易是完全的現貨交易。其特點是：參與商自主發佈銷售或採購信息，參與商自主選擇對手進行成交，不存在集中匹配成交的情況；其次，每筆成交均進行實物交收並開具發票，未進行實物交收或開具發票將構成交收違約；最後，參與現貨掛牌的參與商僅限實體企業，沒有自然人。

3.1.2　交易的倉單和商品

現貨掛牌交易的對象包括標準倉單商品和無倉單商品。

標準倉單是指由指定交收機構按照 QME 規定的程序簽發、且所載商品質量符合 QME 規定的倉單。標準倉單在倉單管理系統中以電子形式存在，不存在紙質形式的倉單。指定交收機構通過 QME 倉單管理系統簽發的電子倉單為提取其載明商品唯一合法的提貨權憑證。根據倉單簽發主體的不同，標準倉單分為倉庫標準倉單和廠庫標準倉單。倉庫標準倉單是指由指定交收倉庫按照 QME 規定的要求和程序簽發的提貨憑證。廠庫標準倉單是指由指定交收廠庫按照 QME 規定的要求和程序簽發的提貨憑證。

無倉單商品是指上述標準倉單以外的其他商品，未在 QME 指定交收機構生成電子倉單的商品。

3.1.3　結算與交收

結算是指參與商達成交易合同後，貨款的劃轉以及相關票據的流轉。具體可分為線上結算方式和線下結算方式。採用線上結算方式的，交收貨款的收付通過參與商結算賬戶劃轉辦理。結算時，買方須保證其對應市場內結算賬戶內具有相應的資金。未能於結算時存入足額資金，視為交收違約，按照交收違約進行處理。採用線下結算方式的，參與商通過各自開戶銀行，使用各類結算工具辦理交收貨款劃轉，並在線下完成符合合同約定的合法發票流轉。採用線下結算方式時，買方應在 QME 規定時間內通過 QME 系統上傳支付憑證影像，賣方應在 QME 規定時間內通過 QME 系統上傳符合合同約定的合法發票影像，QME 保留向相關機構查詢交易雙方的某項結算活動的權利。

商品交收，分為線上交收方式和線下交收方式。線上交收是指交易雙方於規定的時間或期限內，通過 QME 系統轉讓標準倉單，完成貨權轉讓的模式。線下交收指交易雙方於規定的時間或期限內，自行安排無倉單商品的交付，完成貨權轉讓的模式。

現貨掛牌業務達成交易後，買賣雙方進入結算與交收環節。買賣雙方應在規定的期限內完成提交倉單或發貨、支付貨款、交付倉單或商品、驗收倉單或商品、開票、驗票等結算及交收義務，否則構成交收違約。

3.2　倉儲科技

3.2.1　認證倉庫佈局

QME 努力佈局全國範圍內的認證倉庫，從產業實際需求出發，通過標準化認證倉庫為產業提供更加標準的服務，促進倉庫物流效率提升。截至 2019 年 12 月，QME 全國範圍內認證倉庫數量達到 13 個，覆蓋氧化鋁、鋁錠、鋁棒、銅杆、電解銅等多個產業鏈，為產業客戶提供全方位的倉庫與交易服務。

3.2.2　數位化倉庫改造

倉儲機構是商品存儲確權的載體，在倉庫部署物聯網感測器設備，可以為貨物真實性與貨權唯一性提供保障。物聯網感測器設備，需要納入部署在雲的統一管理平台管理，保證設備身份認證信息可靠、設備心跳數據正常、採集的數據不被篡改，建立可信的感測器網路。具可信性的物聯網方案使用技術對於商品貨物進行持續監控，降低人為監控產生的不穩定因素，為倉庫信用提供更強力的背書。

使用安全工業網關連接倉儲機構感測器與雲端物聯網管理平台，確保數據鏈路的保密性與可靠性，底層加密機制確保互聯網上傳輸感測器數據的安全性，有效降低倉儲機構部署感測器的成本及門檻，保障系統穩定運行。

物聯網管理平台使用組裝式設備註冊方式，設備第一次註冊使用其指紋信息便會被記錄，後續停止監控、替換、更新等操作會被記錄下來，確保可信的設備接入。同時，物聯網平台提供成熟的用戶管理及訪問權限管理，不同批次商品對應不同感測器，僅允許利益相關方訪問相關感測器數據，並提供更加完善的數據分析演算法，確保感測器對於商品持續監控的有效性和可信性。

管理平台會根據利益相關方要求，存儲歷史感測器數據，或轉發即時視頻服務機構的內部管理需要。物聯網平台保證系統性能和容量，及以較低成本讓眾多的設備共享到網路中。管理平台允許客戶自定感測器報警閾值和風險控制標準，使用機器執行監控規則，降低人為干預比重，降低人工操作風險並增強倉儲生態的可信性。

3.2.3　倉單 2.0 開放生態體系

QME 推動打造倉單 2.0 開放生態，通過科技對倉儲物流領域進行升級，並與銀行、保險實現系統打通，為業務閉環提供基礎。借助區塊鏈技術可以解決兩個問題，一是 QME 自身數據被認可的問題；二是物聯網設備信息有效性及其自身安全性的問題。同時，可以在建設一個共同的平台進行多方數據的交叉驗證。

倉庫智慧物聯網的建設，主要目的是為了加強信息準確性、貨物真實性及貨物安全性的保障，從而逐步通過科技賦能的方式降低對於倉庫主體信用作個別認定的需要。區塊鏈倉單平台的建設，可推動倉單資產生成與流轉、及生產要素流轉的資訊透明化，降低要素流通環節的壁壘與成本。此外，QME 實施倉單保險作為技術手段的補充，進一步加強了信息準確性、貨物真實性及貨物安全性的保障，對於金融機構等風險要求較高的參與商而言，可以很好地覆蓋尾端風險。

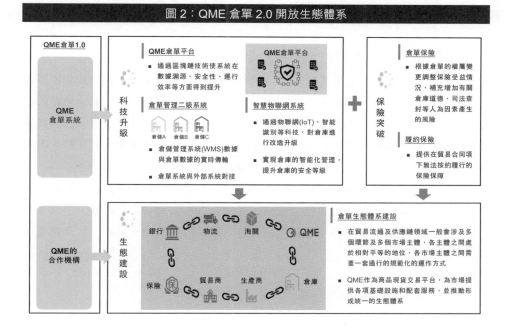

圖 2：QME 倉單 2.0 開放生態體系

　　物聯網和區塊鏈技術為平台建設提供堅實基礎，面向數以十萬計的實體企業節點與貿易企業節點提供技術支撐。物聯網平台需要開放包容、兼容各種感測器網路，形成結構性數據輸出結果，並提供高效的視頻等感測器數據及高容量的存儲系統。區塊鏈平台支撐大容量的節點覆蓋，確保數位資產的安全性及隱私保護等。

　　倉單 2.0 的開放生態體系將改革傳統要素流通方式，推動數位化平台經濟加速發展。一方面促進產業與金融機構互聯互通，推動金融資本服務實體經濟，降低全產業鏈整體融資成本。另一方面推動產業鏈資源配置方式，依賴產能競爭和價格機制帶來的資源配置，推動建立即時生產型資源配置方式，以平台生態再分配產業鏈收益。最終，為中國內地製造業實現規模平台經濟打下基礎，推動製造業高質量發展。

3.3　融資業務

3.3.1　大宗商品產業客戶融資難的問題

以中小微企業為代表的實體經濟「融資難、融資貴」是困擾中國內地宏觀經濟發展的一大難題。作為實體經濟的基礎，大宗商品行業長期以來也面臨相同的問題。受分業經營限制，內地商業銀行可經營的商品實物僅限於貴金屬。對於其餘大宗商品品種，內地商業銀行尚未大規模開展相關的金融服務和自營交易。與境外同業相比，內地商業銀行參與商品市場的廣度與深度都有待進一步發展。

由於存在主體信用不足、底層資產不標準、底層設施缺失、操作環節複雜等實際原因，以銀行為代表的主流金融機構從未真正進入大宗商品行業，導致了幾十萬億元規模的商品融資市場無法從正規的金融機構獲取融資服務，行業融資成本始終居高不下。

3.3.2　QME 提供的解決方案

大宗商品行業需要徹底重塑思維，以「去用戶群體」的邏輯，實行「認貨不認人」，讓大量安全的、基於實體經濟活動和真實貿易背景產生的優質底層資產實現盤活融通，最終為中小企業提供有效的資金流動性支持。以此為目標，QME 能提供以下的融資方式及相關平台：

（1）廠庫倉單融資

廠庫倉單帶有信用倉單性質，是由指定交收廠庫簽發的提貨憑證。QME 與合作銀行對交易系統及銀行系統等多個功能板塊進行對接並實現信息同步交換，從而實現以 QME 電子倉單為可信資產標的的線上融資申請、線上質押、線上放款、線上管理等多項功能。首筆廠庫倉單融資業務已於 2019 年 9 月推出。

（2）倉庫倉單融資

區別於傳統銀行信貸業務對於授信主體的資質要求，倉庫倉單融資的業務邏輯主要圍繞交易標的，即 QME 的倉庫標準倉單。開展包括市場風險、操作風險和流動性風險等各類風險管理手段，客觀上極大地降低了融資的准入門檻。首筆倉庫倉單融資業務於 2020 年 1 月落地。

（3）供應鏈融資

　　基於融資客戶與賣方企業的採購意向，通過供應鏈企業為融資客戶提供全流程線上融資服務。金融機構及供應鏈企業共同形成風險控制整體閉環，以控制倉單資產為風控手段。

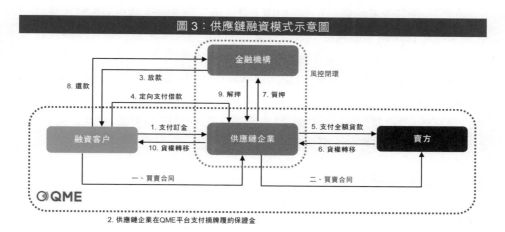

圖 3：供應鏈融資模式示意圖

（4）建設可批量生產標準化資產的金融基礎設施

　　本着「立足現貨、服務實體」的初心，QME 始終致力於金融基礎設施建設，以交易所的身份，利用物聯網等科技手段，將原本場外非標準化的現貨轉換成標準化電子倉單資產，為金融機構開展基於「控貨」邏輯的供應鏈融資提供重要的業務前提和風控的核心基礎。

　　下一步，QME 會繼續協同科技公司、銀行、保險、實體企業、倉儲機構等行業參與者，依託區塊鏈、智能識別和物聯網等科技手段，進一步打造標準化商品數位資產生態，打通「資金與資產」聯通的最後一道屏障。

3.4　境內外聯通 ──「商品通」

2019 年 11 月 26 日，阿里巴巴回歸香港上市，為此，香港交易所對其上市制度做了多項顛覆性的改革：允許同股不同權公司上市、允許已在境外上市的大中華公司選擇香港作為第二上市地等。「立足中國、連接世界」，香港交易所致力於成為中國內地客戶走向世界以及國際客戶走進中國內地的全球性交易所，進而配合內地市場的對外開放戰略。

如今，股票市場的「互聯互通」已平穩運行了超過五年。為了更進一步對接「中國的貨」與「世界的錢」，發揮中國全球工廠、供應鏈生產中心的巨大優勢，香港交易所也在多資產策略三大核心支柱（股本證券、定息與貨幣產品及大宗商品）之一的大宗商品領域尋求互聯互通，因此也就有了「BBC」發展戰略，即「Buy one ── 買一個」：收購 LME；「Build One ── 建一個」：設立 QME；及「Connect ── 連接中國與世界」。

得益於《粵港澳大灣區規劃綱要》的政策支援，QME 有望探索「商品通」，進而成為服務境內外客戶的大宗商品現貨交易平台。

3.4.1　QME 的獨有優勢

（1）地域優勢

QME 地處新時代改革開放最前沿 ── 深圳前海。背靠經濟特區、先行示範區、粵港澳大灣區，集三區政策之利，前海可在重大改革上先行先試，充分發揮深圳與香港具有的比較優勢，增強粵港澳三地的國際競爭力，進而為中國在實現強國夢的道路上踏出穩健、扎實的一步。

制度激發創新，創新注入市場活力。前海擁有內地優秀的制度突破與創新的環境及條件，在前海，QME 可以以最快速度、最佳方式探索創新商品交易所業態。

（2）香港交易所為其股東，具備較強國際化屬性

大宗商品定價權長期被西方發達國家所壟斷，在這當中大宗商品交易市場起了至關重要的作用，例如 NYMEX[3] 之於原油、LME 之於有色金屬、LBMA[4] 之於黃金等。由於資本項目的限制，大部份中國內地企業無法直接參與境外交易所的交易，是導致定價權旁落的重要因素。同時，受制於政治、文化等原因，內地官方交易所的市場組織、參與者的構成和形成的具體價格始終得不到國際市場的完全認可。鑑於此，建立一個同時能夠吸引境內外大宗商品市場參與者的交易市場，形成境內外共同認可的成交價格，是中國獲取大宗商品國際定價權必不可少的基礎設施和先決條件。而由於股東背景等特殊條件，QME 先天具備了較強的國際化屬性和基因，在打造國際市場認同度上具備較強的潛力。

（3）可與 LME 東西呼應，打造國際級大宗商品集散中心

經過近幾年的發展，中國內地的自由貿易區和傳統保稅區建設已取得了較大的進步，但距離新加坡、迪拜等傳統大宗商品貿易和集散中心仍存在較大差距。除地理位置、稅收等因素以外，很重要的一點是內地缺乏類似於新加坡交易所（簡稱「新交所」）、迪拜商品交易所等全球化的商品交易所，而由交易所通過場內基礎交易衍生的貨權交割和場外交易比較欠缺，對境內外機構將實物商品運輸和存放在內地保稅區的驅動力較為缺乏。支持 QME 開展「商品通」跨境業務，與同屬香港交易所的 LME 聯動，可以吸引更多的境內外機構、滙集更多跨境資金和實物商品，提升整體的進出口貿易活躍度及貿易體量，有利於打造全球區域性的大宗商品貿易集散中心。同時，QME 的存在也為境內企業參與大宗商品跨境套期保值交易、規避國際大宗商品價格波動、促進實物交割等提供了物理位置的便利，實實在在幫助企業降低離岸公司的管理成本以及實物資產的物流相關成本。

3.4.2　「商品通」方案簡介

交易所國際化道路不僅可增加中國內地對大宗商品市場的影響力，更是為爭取定價權提供了先決條件。為了使內地更積極地參與並逐步融入到國際大宗商品市場當中，QME 計劃在政策支持前提下比照「股票通」、「債券通」等實施模式，開展「商品通」業務。

3　New York Mercantile Exchange，紐約商業交易所。
4　London Bullion Market Association，倫敦金銀市場協會。

（1）交易設計

「商品通」交易採用雙向交易設計，包含「請進來」及「走出去」兩種方案，提供境內外互聯互通機制。

- **「請進來」**：香港交易所及 LME 的境外交易客戶依託境外既有的交易路徑，參與 QME 境內交易品種的交易。
- **「走出去」**：QME 的境內交易客戶通過互聯互通的機制安排，在限定額度內參與香港交易所和 LME 的指定品種的交易，滿足境內客戶跨境套期保值的需求。

圖 4：雙向交易機制：「請進來」與「走出去」

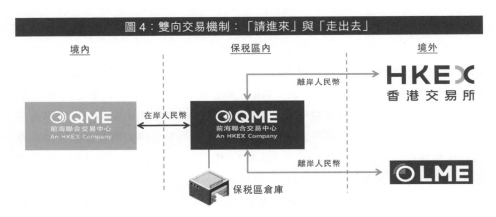

（2）資金結算方案

跨境資金採用「閉環限額」原則管理，保證資金封閉安全運行，降低資金風險。

- **閉環**：參照「股票通」的實施經驗，以交易所為跨境資金的清算主體。賬戶體系方面，均參照中國人民銀行既有賬戶進行設置，保證資金封閉運行。
- **限額**：對每日跨境資金雙邊的流動設置雙重額度，即設置境外投資者每日資金入境淨頭寸及境內投資者每日資金出境淨頭寸。

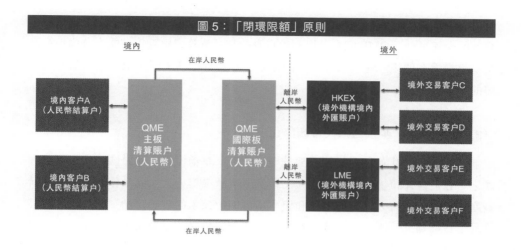

圖 5：「閉環限額」原則

3.4.3　「商品通」方案的意義

在「股票通」順利起步、「債券通」一級市場訊息平台上線後，中國內地商品市場的開放就更有其特殊意義。在 QME 率先開展「商品通」業務，可以真正探索服務實體經濟的新模式，助推未來人民幣國際化和製造業強國建設的國家戰略。

（1）有利於深化大灣區全方位金融創新前沿的地位

深圳市目前還沒有一家於全國具有影響力的大宗商品交易平台，支援 QME 開展「商品通」業務，有利於進一步深化大灣區全方位金融創新前沿的地位。一個交易活躍的大宗商品交易平台不僅可以直接為前海與深圳帶來持續的經濟貢獻和就業機會，更能全面驅動大灣區的貿易、物流、金融、商業服務等多個產業的發展和繁榮。

（2）有利於提高中國內地大宗商品交易市場的整體水平

QME 作為香港交易所集團旗下的大宗商品交易平台，擁有成熟的交易所運作經驗和完整的交易所體系支持，具備能夠被各行業廣泛接受的交易所品牌和市場公信力，同時又是真正市場化、國際化的商業主體。通過搭建並運作公開、透明、高效的交易平台，QME 完全可以利用自身的交易清算與風險管理能力為內地商品交易市場體系的規範建設進行有益的探索，有利於提高中國內地大宗商品交易市場的整體水平。

（3）有利於進一步推進人民幣國際化進程

人民幣國際化始終是中國重要的戰略部署，目前困擾人民幣國際化主要的問題之一在於離岸市場缺乏穩定的人民幣資產投資渠道。大宗商品作為重要的傳統資產配置，是進行人民幣國際化和資本項目開放探索的理想標的。跨境大宗商品交易平台的建立，不但可以成為離岸人民幣配置資產的重要渠道，同時產生的以人民幣計價的交易價格可以成為商品線下長單定價的重要參考依據，有利於人民幣國際化進程。

3.5　衍生品與價格輸出

目前，大宗商品衍生品市場中，除了通過實物交易和交割直接產生相關價格以外，還有其他一些形式，例如新交所的鐵礦石掉期及期貨、上海清算所的鐵礦石掉期、芝加哥商品交易所（CME）的布蘭特（Brent）現金結算原油期貨等。這些品種所使用的結算價格都是參考了其他價格基準，這些價格基準大致可以分為如下三類：資訊諮詢公司通過詢價方式採集形成的價格（簡稱「詢價價格」）、其他交易所的大宗商品交易產生的價格（簡稱「外採價格」），以及自家其他商品產生的價格（簡稱「自有價格」）。

2008 年鐵礦石市場的長期協商價格機制被打破以後，普氏能源（Platts）於當年 4 月推出了普氏鐵礦石指數（Platts Iron Ore Index，簡稱 IODEX 或 IODBZ00），並開始在全球範圍內推廣。2009 年 4 月，新交所率先推出了基於鋼鐵指數（TSI）的鐵礦石掉期合約。2009 年 5 月倫敦結算所（LCH）開始鐵礦石掉期結算服務。2010 年 6 月，CME 也加入到鐵礦石掉期的交易和清算服務行業中。但是從目前的交易情況來看，新交所的鐵礦石掉期和期貨產品是最成功的。這與新加坡的國際商品貿易以及風險管理中心地位有重要的關係，佔據先發優勢的新交所鐵礦石掉期業務逐漸吸引了越來越多的鋼廠和貿易商、礦企到新加坡設立分支機構。根據 2014 年新加坡公司註冊局統計，其中約有 200 多家是來自中國內地金屬和礦業的公司。

　　新加坡鐵礦石市場交易量的增長出現在 2012 年左右，當時鐵礦石價格一直在不斷走跌，從每手 180 美金跌到 80 美金，許多企業認識到運用衍生品管理風險的重要性，紛紛開展了鐵礦石衍生品業務，這也是為甚麼鐵礦石交易會在 2012 年左右開始活躍起來的原因。

3.5.1　構建中國內地商品價格指數

　　從中國內地對全球多種大宗商品的需求佔全球總需求的比例來看，中國內地需求在全球大宗商品市場佔主導地位。而與這一地位極為不符的是，中國內地長期缺乏在國際大宗商品市場的定價權，使其在全球大宗商品價格波動中常常付出巨大的代價。

　　有別於國內現有的期貨交易所，QME 本着「立足現貨、服務實體」的初心，致力於打造創新型交易平台及生態系統，持續為客戶提供現貨基準價格，建成服務境內外客戶的大宗商品現貨交易平台。通過服務實體經濟和產業客戶，重構國內商品市場格局，形成有公信力的現貨商品價格基準，從而構建起大宗商品的「中國價格」。

3.5.2　境外上市發行衍生品

　　基於內地現貨商品實際成交所形成的中國價格，QME 可以充分利用自身具備的天然優勢，借助於香港交易所以及同為集團內的 LME，推出 QME 現貨價格為基準的衍生品，以方便境外的投資者直接在香港及倫敦參與內地大宗商品的投資。

　　借鑒國際已有的成功經驗，QME 可以通過直接授權的方式，以自己平台上交易形成的現貨價格為基準，在 LME 或者香港交易所推出包括期權、期貨、掉期等多種以包括人民幣在內的現金結算產品；也可以通過和資訊諮詢機構合作的方式，把 QME 的價格以一定比例的權重納入到境外現金結算衍生品的基準價格中去。

3.5.3 推動香港、倫敦大宗商品的離岸人民幣結算價格

雖然中國經濟的總量在迅速增長，但是人民幣融入全球金融體系還處於起步階段。以香港、倫敦、新加坡為代表的各大國際金融中心，均看好未來人民幣資產加速融入國際金融市場所帶來的機遇，爭相打造離岸人民幣中心。與股票及債券市場聯通一樣，以 QME 現貨價格為基準的「中國價格」在香港、倫敦的推出，以及境內外大宗商品互聯互通的實現將拓寬離岸人民幣的投資渠道，將會吸引境外投資者通過「商品通」投資內地市場，推動香港、倫敦大宗商品離岸人民幣結算價格的形成，同時也為離岸人民幣資金提供更多的投資工具。

4 結語

作為香港交易所與前海金控合作投資的現貨大宗商品交易平台，QME 旨在能夠於前海 ——「特區中的特區」—— 這一改革高地，打破行政化、歷史原因造成的限制，真正貫徹落實「先行先試」政策指引，試點做制度性創新。緊緊抓住粵港澳大灣區、先行示範區「雙區驅動」的重大歷史機遇，在深港合作上步子邁大一些、做深做實，加速實現在前海建成重要金融基礎設施的目標，打造深港合作標杆性項目。通過現貨價格基準的形成、標準化資產體系的打造和境內外市場的聯通，推動解決供給側、融資難和定價權的痛點，真正探索服務實體經濟的新模式。

第12章

LME 與中國內地大宗商品市場加強聯繫可帶來的機遇

倫敦金屬交易所

摘 要

本章探討讓中國內地大宗商品市場與倫敦金屬交易所加強聯繫，加上與倫敦金屬交易所的母公司香港交易及結算所有限公司和其姊妹公司前海聯合交易中心的協同效應，得以創造更大機遇。

1 背景

　　香港交易所集團於 2012 年收購倫敦金屬交易所（London Metal Exchange，簡稱 LME）後，LME 與集團內其他子公司緊密合作，一同探索如何加強中國境內外大宗商品市場參與者之間的雙向聯繫。2015 年 10 月，香港期貨交易所（簡稱「期交所」）、香港期貨結算有限公司（簡稱「期貨結算公司」）、LME 及 LME Clear 簽署合作備忘錄，準備在期交所與 LME 之間建立交易聯繫（稱「交易通」），以及在期貨結算公司與 LME Clear 之間建立結算聯繫（稱「結算通」）。有關建議措施統一稱為「倫港通」，為實現有關措施，相關工作已隨即啟動。

2 中國在全球金屬市場的地位

　　隨着中國經濟持續增長，外資參與日多，中國在海外市場的影響力不斷提升。內地資本市場允許越來越多國際投資者直接參與其中，加快向國際市場開放的步伐。中國的大宗商品交易所亦逐步向更多海外投資者開放，以提升其在海外市場的地位、提高其於大宗商品的定價能力，以及在人民幣作為國際貨幣影響力越來越大的情況下促進全球貿易。

　　人民幣近年在國際上的地位越來越舉足輕重，不僅推動全球貿易，更獲國際貨幣基金組織認可為「世界主要貨幣」之一。LME Clear 的結算會員於 2015 年 7 月起可使用離岸人民幣作為合資格現金抵押品，以符合其按金要求。有關服務是 LME Clear 抵押品服務的重要一環，尤其是在越來越多中國公司於 LME 進行交易的情況下更顯重要。中資的中銀國際環球商品（LME 首家中資公司會員）率先以人民幣作為抵押品。

　　眾所周知，中國基本金屬的生產量及消費額約佔全球總數的一半[1]，而更重要

1　資料來源：彭博有限合夥企業、World Bureau of Metal Statistics、國際貨幣基金組織。

的是，其全球佔比一直在增加。中國的增長需耗用極大量資源，需要的原材料（尤其是工業金屬）的數量亦越來越多。

市場對金屬的需求源自高度工業化及廣泛城市化項目，其中建築工程、交通基礎設施及通訊網絡帶動了各種基本金屬的消費。

中國對電池材料的需求亦見大幅增長，尤其是用於電動車的製造。越來越多中國消費者偏好最先進及較潔淨的電動車技術，加上政府推出減少污染及提升技術以降低電動車價格的政策，至 2025 年，中國擁有電動車的人口在全球的佔比或可達48%[2]。有關行業帶動着市場對鈷、鎳和鋰等電池材料以及鋁和銅等其他金屬的需求，這行業勢必達到幾何級數的增長。

3 中國與全球市場的聯繫

3.1　境內企業與投資者於境外市場的參與

近年，中國內地透過一系列重點計劃協助境內企業與投資者參與海外市場，為大宗商品市場帶來影響。有關計劃及影響包括：

- 容許若干**中央企業及其他國有企業**可為套期保值目的於海外衍生產品市場進行交易，毋須再另行取得監管批准。由於有關國企的實物大宗商品交易量龐大，它們很可能需要額外的對沖渠道來滿足其需求。

- 計劃推出的**合格境內個人投資者（QDII2）計劃**[3]，以較早前推出的合格境內機構投資者（QDII）計劃為基礎，QDII 計劃允許內地合資格的機構投資者投資於獲中國證券監督管理委員會（簡稱「中國證監會」）認可的海外證券市場。QDII2 計劃可讓內地個人投資者直接投資於海外資本市場，包括衍生產品市場。因此，QDII2 計劃會在所設定的門檻範圍內為內地投資者

2　資料來源：《電動車的前景 2009》（*Electric Vehicle Outlook 2019*），BloombergNEF。

3　可見如 2018 年 11 月 23 日發佈的《國務院關於支持自由貿易試驗區深化改革創新若干措施的通知》。當局尚未就 QDII2 計劃而言，發佈任何特定規則。

提供另一參與海外市場的途徑，讓投資者能更輕易投資於海外證券及衍生產品。

- **「一帶一路」**倡議的實施，旨在建設連接亞洲中部、西部及南部與歐洲及北非一帶的鐵路、高速公路、油氣管道、電網等的經濟帶。這些基礎設施項目必定會增加對建築材料，尤其是基本金屬的需求。此外，內地企業積極參與「一帶一路」項目，會面對更多源自大宗商品供求升跌所產生的價格波動風險。為支持「一帶一路」倡議，LME 於 2015 年 10 月與七家中國及英國金融機構簽署合作備忘錄，以期通過互相合作提升市場參與便利、提供風險管理服務，以及讓更多中國企業與投資者進入全球大宗商品市場。

3.2　境外企業與投資者於內地市場的參與

現時，國際企業與投資者進入中國內地金融市場（包括大宗商品交易所）的限制相對較多。

內地的大宗商品期貨交易現主要集中於三家交易所 —— 上海期貨交易所（簡稱「上期所」）、大連商品交易所（簡稱「大商所」）及鄭州商品交易所（簡稱「鄭商所」）。這些交易所為境內參與者提供一系列的大宗商品期貨產品，但海外參與者仍只能買賣特定的政府批准的人民幣計價的期貨產品，包括由上述三家交易所提供的純對苯二甲酸（PTA）、橡膠、石油及鐵礦石期貨產品，並且只能透過特定的交易商進行買賣，有關交易商須為本地交易所的會員或獲其認可的其他交易商。

中國作為領先的大宗商品大規模生產及消費國，有巨大的潛力進一步發展及向國際參與者開放自己的期貨市場。現在全球大宗商品市場波動日益加劇，市場參與者對可以進一步參與能提供工具以管理價格波動風險的大宗商品交易所，必然會有更大需求。

在增加境外參與者於內地市場的參與度這方面，現時的最大障礙之一是中國的貨幣仍未能完全自由兌換（儘管中國確實有意於未來達到完全自由兌換）。人民幣若可於國際市場完全自由兌換及買賣，將可吸引更多外部流動資金及投資資金的流入，從而促進內地金融市場的國際化，並讓其大宗商品交易所與國際交易所更緊密結合。然而，雖然中國尋求以可控方式放寬資本管制並以此吸引更多外資的參與，但在實行上亦可能需要一段時間。

在人民幣完全自由兌換之前，也許我們可以先開闢一道「橋樑」，讓境外參與者進入境內大宗商品市場，以及讓境內參與者走進境外大宗商品市場，就有如滬深港三地證券交易所之間透過本地經紀及結算所買賣證券的「滬港通」與「深港通」，以及由中國外匯交易中心與香港交易所共同設立、促進中港兩地債券市場互動的「債券通」等機制。在大宗商品互聯互通的機制下，香港交易所及 LME 希望可開通與內地交易所之間的大宗商品期貨交易網絡。

透過建立香港與倫敦市場之間的聯繫，可在國際監管及交易標準的規範下，為內地參與者提供更多參與開放透明市場的渠道。同時，為吸引更多境外參與者走進來，內地市場該設法應對海外參與者對監管及市場政策透明度的要求。進一步開放內地市場的推動因素已然存在，全球相關企業與投資者莫不希望能參與其中。

本章以下部份會細說 LME 為全球市場參與者提供的服務特色，並概述 LME 與香港交易所如何協作提供解決方案，以提升內地與國際大宗商品市場的聯通。

4 LME 可為全球參與者提供甚麼市場服務？

LME 是全球工業金屬的主要衍生產品交易市場。金屬製造商、消費者及交易商都重視 LME 源於以下原因：

- **套期保值（即對沖）**—— 製造商和消費者可透過 LME 對沖價格波動的風險。
- **價格發現**—— LME 每天為全球提供基本金屬參考價格，定價過程公開透明。
- **參考價的定價**—— LME 交易平台上的定價，成為全球實物合約估值和交收的參考價格。
- **價格趨於一致**—— LME 合約可透過其分佈全球的倉庫網絡作實物交收，確保 LME 合約的價格與實物金屬的價格掛鈎。

- **實物交收** —— 獲得 LME 註冊實物市場實際用到的品牌才能作為實物交收。
- **交割日架構** —— 只有 LME 才有種類如此多的遠期合約選擇（按日、按週、三個月及月度），市場用家管理持倉無比靈活。

有關 LME 市場的各項特點詳見本書第六章。

4.1　中國內地客戶參與 LME 的現況

上述 LME 市場的特點，吸引了許多中國客戶透過多種不同方式與 LME 互動。尤其是自 21 世紀初起，內地政府開始批准越來越多的國有企業可以於海外市場進行對沖交易，不少內地大型基本金屬公司活躍於 LME 市場，與 LME 的業務關係趨於密切。許多內地公司亦在香港、新加坡及倫敦等城市設立金屬交易業務，為其參與國際貿易市場。

至 2020 年 5 月，有六家中資公司獲認可為 LME 結算會員，另有近 80 個內地金屬品牌符合 LME 的品質、形狀和重量規格，獲核准為適合在 LME 作實物交割的品牌。

中國與倫敦金屬市場相隔萬里，但交易流量卻將二者聯繫起來：兩個市場的價格差異帶動金屬的進出口業務，套戥活動隨之出現，其本身已經超越了實物參與者的範圍，而包括更多的金融投資活動。這從近年 LME 各個金屬合約在倫敦時間上午 7 時前（上海時間下午 3 時前）的所謂「亞洲時段」內交易量的顯著增長中可見一斑 —— 過去十年，當亞洲市場處於交易日時（即非假日時），LME 市場平均每日成交量一般都較於亞洲市場假期的日子高約 10%[4]。有見亞洲時段交易量的增長，LME 於 2011 年為三個月 LME 鋁、LME 銅及 LME 鋅推出了「LME 亞洲參考價」。這些金屬價格都以成交量加權平均價計算，定價和公佈時間特意配合亞洲交易日的結束時間，好儘早給區內用家使用、反映亞洲時區內市場活動的指引，在當日其中一個最重要及最高流動性的期間進行買賣。兩邊市場已形成一個在電子平台進行交易的網絡，相互連結並因應兩邊市場的價格變動而進行交易。

4　資料來源：LME 研究。

4.2　進一步聯通的需求

市場需要中國內地與 LME 之間有更緊密聯繫，主要受多項因素所驅動。

現時內地的基本金屬交易主要是在場外 (OTC) 市場進行，但市場對場內合約的需求正與日俱增，部份原因是區內金屬的消費急劇上升。尤其是，亞洲市場（包括中國內地）的機構投資者及專業個人投資者都渴望透過較小型、非實物交收的金屬合約，增加參與全球大宗商品市場的機會。

5　透過 LME 進入全球業界網絡

5.1　全球倉庫網絡

為便利進行實物交收和切合國際用戶的需求，LME 設有核准登記倉庫網絡，主要分佈於政治環境穩定、法律制度健全，稅務及商業框架合規的金屬消費地區。LME 核准倉庫遍及英國、歐洲大陸、中東、亞洲和美國。每年進出 LME 這逾 550 個全球核准倉庫作實物交收的金屬約有 500 萬噸。表 1 列出亞洲的 LME 倉庫地點。

表 1：亞洲的 LME 倉庫地點（2020 年 4 月）		
城市/ 國家	地點數目	核准倉庫數目
日本	2	6
馬來西亞	2	117
新加坡	1	17
南韓	3	111
中國台灣	1	22
總計	9	273

資料來源：LME。

亞洲有多個 LME 核准倉庫，但在中國內地暫時還沒有。將 LME 倉庫體系帶入中國是香港交易所集團的長遠戰略目標，LME 與香港交易所現正就此跟內地決策者緊密接觸。

儲存於 LME 核准倉庫的金屬均有「倉單」作紀錄。倉單是倉庫公司對每批存於 LME 核准設施的 LME 核准金屬發出的所有權文件，用於實物交收 LME 合約中的金屬。LME 的倉庫網絡亦廣泛用於促進大宗商品的貿易融資。

LME 設有安全的電子倉單轉移系統 LMEsword，便利 LME 倉單所有權的轉移及庫存報告等流程，亦便利全球各地的金屬進行高效的倉單互換交易。

5.2　全球金屬貿易利用 LME 參考價定價及 LME 的合約

LME 市場對基本金屬的定價是全球通用的價格。金屬製造商與消費者之間磋商的實物供應合約，大都以這些價格為基礎，再因應其他變數（例如地點及金屬純度）而協定溢價。這樣，某個洲的製造商可與其他國家或地區的冶煉廠、加工廠及消費者訂立實物合約。

5.3　倫敦的黃金市場及「LME 貴金屬」

中國是全球黃金消費和製造大國，過去 20 年來已成為全球最大黃金市場。中國人民銀行是全球最活躍央行之一，過去 15 年來一直在穩步增加其黃金儲備[5]。

合併來看，中國內地黃金交易場所的流通量的票期相對較短：上海黃金交易所和上海期貨交易所均少於一年，內地製造商難以透過現金流對沖來支持其作任何境內債務融資或股本投資。沒有較長票期的流動性，意味着銀行對沖風險就要轉向西方市場，例如倫敦的場外市場，又或交易所場內市場，例如透過「LME 貴金屬」平台（LME 的貴金屬買賣及對沖方案）。根據世界黃金協會數據所估計，場內交易可節省的資金成本約 50% 至約 90%，主要是因為資本費用較低[6]。

黃金市場在日趨全球化之下，亦為有意管理基礎風險或對區內供求動態有其看法的市場參與者提供不少交易機會。在此方面，「LME 貴金屬」提供公開透明的場內交易渠道，讓市場人士可用之與全球其他交易所市場配合作交易。自 2017 年 8 月起，「LME 貴金屬」已提供即日 LME 黃金及 LME 白銀現貨參考價，支援貴金屬市場管理整個交易日的價格風險，與流通量高峰期一致。

5　資料來源：世界黃金協會（https://www.gold.org/goldhub/data/monthly-central-bank-statistics）。
6　資料來源：世界黃金協會、LME 及奧緯（Oliver Wyman）的分析。

5.4 與亞洲有密切關聯的 LME 鋼材合約

LME 在 2015 年 11 月推出現金結算的黑色金屬合約系列，首兩隻合約為廢鋼及螺紋鋼合約，自推出以來得到了亞洲參與者的高度參與，尤其是 LME 廢鋼，甫推出即看到亞洲市場的支持和參與。

目前 LME 所提供的鋼材合約種類已擴大至熱軋卷板期貨，其中 LME 熱軋鋼捲中國離岸價（Argus）這產品應對了東亞市場的核心需求。這合約屬意為中國鋼材出口商以及主要出口市場的鋼材進口商和消費者提供有效的風險管理工具 —— 越南、泰國及新加坡等東南亞進口國家的公司早已採用該合約。

6 LME 及香港交易所加強聯通的最新發展

LME 及香港交易所一直嘗試運用自身優勢和專業知識，致力開拓有效途徑，加強香港、中國內地與國際市場之間的聯通。

6.1 香港交易所推出倫敦金屬期貨小型合約

香港交易所倫敦金屬期貨小型合約旨在滿足亞洲參與者的需要，讓他們可以使用離岸人民幣或美元計價的期貨緩解金屬價格風險或作相關的風險投資。小型合約屬月度合約，合約期最長 12 個月，按相應的 LME「母」合約的 LME 官方現貨結算價進行結算。對區內參與者而言，此類合約的額外好處是可以在亞洲時段交易、能提供跨市場套利機會、合約單位較小以及收費相宜。

此類單位較小的合約在香港交易所的衍生產品平台上交易，用於買賣六種基本金屬：鋁、鋅、銅、鎳、錫及鉛；並有兩種交易貨幣可選擇。

表 2：香港交易所倫敦金屬期貨小型合約 —— 重點一覽	
項目	特徵
相關資產	鋁、鋅、銅、鎳、錫及鉛
貨幣	以離岸人民幣或美元交易及定價
合約單位及類型	單位小，月度合約
結算	按 LME「母」合約的官方結算價格以現金結算
交易場所	香港交易所衍生產品平台

資料來源：香港交易所。

香港交易所離岸人民幣倫敦金屬期貨小型合約的設計旨在幫助中國現貨市場持份者管理其以人民幣定價的商品合約的風險、協助建立亞洲時區內的金屬人民幣定價機制，並給市場提供期交所、LME 與上期所之間的套利空間。鋁、銅及鋅期貨於 2014 年率先推出，其後 2017 年進一步推出鉛、鎳及錫期貨。小型合約為月度合約，合約結構標準化，對亞洲投資者的吸引力會較大，加上有期交所龐大的參與者及經紀網路做依託，機構與個人投資者會更容易地買賣這些合約。

為配合現有離岸人民幣產品系列，香港交易所於 2019 年 8 月 5 日推出六隻以美元計價的倫敦金屬期貨小型合約，為亞洲時區投資美元計價相關基本金屬的投資者提供更多選擇，並作為其既有以離岸人民幣計價的期貨合約產品的配套。

表 3：LME 基本金屬合約和香港交易所倫敦小型合約的比較		
	LME 基本金屬合約	香港交易所倫敦小型合約
結算方式	實物結算	按 LME「母」合約的官方現貨結算價以現金結算
合約單位 （以公噸計）	單位較大： • 鋁 — 25 公噸 • 銅 — 25 公噸 • 鉛 — 25 公噸 • 鎳 — 6 公噸 • 錫 — 5 公噸 • 鋅 — 25 公噸	單位較小： • 鋁 — 5 公噸 • 銅 — 5 公噸 • 鉛 — 5 公噸 • 鎳 — 1 公噸 • 錫 — 1 公噸 • 鋅 — 5 公噸
合約類型	• 日度 • 週度 • 月度（直至第 63 至第 123 個月）	• 月度（直至第 12 個月）
交易時段	（倫敦時間） • 交易圈：11:40-17:00 • 電子交易平台 LMEselect： 　01:00-19:00 • 場外辦公室：24 小時	（香港時間，最後交易日除外） • T 時段：09:00-16:30 • T+1 時段：17:15-03:00

(續)

表 3：LME 基本金屬合約和香港交易所倫敦小型合約的比較		
	LME 基本金屬合約	香港交易所倫敦小型合約
交易途徑	透過 LME 會員	透過期交所參與者
主要參與者	• 現貨市場參與者 — 生產商與消費者 • LME 會員與其客戶 • 金融界 — 對沖基金、自營公司、投資公司 • 場外市場參與者	• 熟悉期貨合約的金融業界 • 私人投資者 • 企業客戶 • 套利者 • 亞洲投機者

資料來源：LME。

6.2　LME 與期交所之間的會籍互惠安排

為了擴大倫敦與香港之間的協作機會，LME 和期交所推出會籍互惠安排（RMA），方便 LME 會員或期交所參與者申請成為對方交易所的參與者或會員。RMA 為 LME 和期交所的產品擴大了市場准入，並為新產品提供額外的流動性。根據 RMA，LME 與期交所豁免對方交易所會員或參與者申請成為期交所參與者或 LME 會員的首年年費及手續費[7]。

6.3　與前海聯合交易中心（QME）的協作

香港交易所在 2018 年 10 月，於中國廣東省深圳前海建立大宗商品現貨交易平台 QME，作為發展香港交易所集團為中國內地提供大宗商品服務的整體計劃其中一環。目前 QME 提供多種金屬，包括氧化鋁、鋁和銅杆，並計劃進一步擴展業務。

LME 持續與 QME 合作，憑藉兩家交易所在倉儲、交易及融資三大範疇的優勢，致力實現加強內地與海外大宗商品市場聯繫的願景。

LME 與 QME 正探討如何可將 LME 歷史悠久而穩健的全球倉儲系統與 QME 的本地倉庫網絡連接起來，初步目標是提供兩個網絡之間可供買賣的倉單掉期合約。同時，LME 繼續與內地監管機構討論設立 LME 認可倉庫的可能性。這些措施加起來，會有助減低將金屬由境外 LME 倉庫運送至內地客戶所產生的較長貨運時間、交通與清關等額外成本。LME 倉庫網絡若可擴展至中國內地，會有助大宗商品交易真正全球化，從而促進內地金融市場國際化及便利中國境內金屬存貨透

7　詳情見本書第 14 章〈香港交易所大宗商品市場 —— 連接內地與全球的互聯互通平台〉。

過 LME 融資。

　　另一目標是將 LME 的交易拓展至亞洲時區，同時提升 QME 的大宗商品現貨價格發現的能力，吸引國際投資者參與。現貨「基準」價格是大宗商品期貨交易的基礎，因為期貨合約的價格都是根據商品即時交付的成本而釐定。QME 與 LME 正為此緊密合作，利用現有的 LMEbullion 及 QME 現貨交易平台，亦與其他內地交易所合作，希望可加強這方面的能力。LME 在 QME 的工作基礎上再接再厲，力求為各類金屬產品穩健地提供現貨價格，這會有助建立與國際接軌的內地大宗商品價格基準，亦可供 LME 未來用作推出新產品的基礎 [8]。

7　未來發展方向

　　LME 銳意與香港交易所努力讓內地市場參與者更能獲得優質的產品及服務。

　　按照 LME 的技術路線圖，其交易基礎設施將進行全面的更新與升級，計劃包括利用香港交易所的技術建立全新的交易平台。新平台的其中一項主要優點是：這全新的以網絡為基礎的交易商電子系統（「圖形用戶界面（GUI）」）會開放給亞洲客戶讓其直接進行交易，為亞洲區參與者（包括內地參與者）參與 LME 全球金屬市場提供更具效率及成本效益的路徑。

7.1　聯通內地與國際大宗商品市場

　　LME 致力走在大宗商品定價機制發展的最前線。LME 與香港交易所緊密協作，希望善用各自於內地市場及大宗商品方面的相關經驗為市場提供新的解決方案，能同時服務內地想透過 LME 涉足國際金屬價格投資的投資者，以及海外希望投資中國內地市場的投資者。

8　有關 QME 的詳情以及 LME 與 QME 的關係，見本書第 11 章〈前海聯合交易中心在中國內地大宗商品市場扮演的獨特角色〉。

未來數年當陸續見到 LME 為提升內地與國際大宗商品市場聯通而作出的努力（見上文第 6 節的相關近期發展）。

7.2 消除 LME 與中國內地之間建立更緊密聯繫的障礙

如要在 LME 與中國內地之間建立更緊密的聯繫，首先要克服阻礙准入的一些市場因素，包括：

- **LME 會費**：會籍年費以及獲得各類別會員資格必須持有 LME B 股的這項要求 [9]，可能令中國內地參與者不願直接成為 LME 會員。期交所和 LME 推出的 RMA 為兩所成員提供了另一道較高成本效益的途徑，讓其在對方交易所的市場進行買賣。
- **間接進入市場所涉的成本高昂**：現時，亞洲客戶可以直接參與 LME 市場交易的途徑受到一定限制，間接買賣所涉的經紀費用及連接市場方面的成本會大增。建立與 LME 市場更直接聯通的平台可助降低相關成本。
- **網絡的信息延緩、成本及穩定性**：亞洲市場參與者傾向使用 LME 的電子市場，但經紀或供應商所提供的洲際網絡連結可能會有更長時間的信息延緩、成本更高和穩定性偏低等問題。與 LME 之間建立更直接的交易連結有助提升進入市場的速度及穩定性。

7.3 展望未來

倫敦金屬期貨小型合約的設計與推出，讓倫敦和香港市場的價格得以互動，使 LME 的價格可在期交所用作結算價格，充分利用期交所在亞洲的廣闊客戶羣體。作為建立香港交易所與 LME 互聯互通機制「倫港通」的第一步，這批合約讓期交所參與者可以直接運用美元計價的 LME 價格。

香港交易所與 LME 建立「倫港通」的進一步措施尚有待確定，但預見 LME 將實行「頭寸交接」（pass the book）模式，讓 LME 與期交所各自的結算所能轉移對方的未平倉合約倉位，以盡量提高清算及成本效益。最後一步則包括發展全面的「互

9　LME 的第 1 類和第 2 類會員必須持有至少 25,000 股 LME B 股；第 3 類和第 4 類會員必須分別持有至少 5,000 股和 2,500 股 LME B 股。

聯互通」機制，讓香港交易所與 LME 的買賣盤紀錄「互通」。兩所之間的聯繫更緊密之後，將有助促進兩邊資金匯聚流動，並受惠於可兼享對方交易所的客戶覆蓋網絡。

8　總結

在中國經濟的持續發展及逐步國際化的大環境下，實現更大的雙向投資以及資本流動將是有力的催化劑，包括可促進人民幣的進一步國際化。同時，為市場參與者提供更多參與全球大宗商品市場的渠道，可提高中國在全球大宗商品定價方面的影響力，以更真實地反映中國作為多種大宗商品（包括金屬）的全球最大生產及消費國的地位。

LME 全力支持這一願景，為中國企業和投資者創造更多場內交易的機會，為內地金屬製造商及消費者提供更多管理金屬價格風險的途徑。

香港交易所、QME 與 LME 三者之間會持續協作求進，冀為市場帶來解決方案，切合市場對大宗商品市場須公平、開放、透明及受妥善監管等需要和訴求。香港交易所的市場網絡遍佈全球，具備廣泛的資本市場專業知識，更在與內地政府部門、監管機構及市場參與者合作方面有豐富經驗。LME 在工業金屬交易的全球領導地位源遠流長，向來是全球有色金屬參考價格的來源，亦坐擁遍佈全球的倉庫網絡，便利金屬的倉儲及實物交收，創造貿易融資機會。另一方面，QME 提供一個內地大宗商品現貨交易平台，結合國內倉儲專業，與期貨市場相輔相成。三家交易所當通力合作，尋求更多聯繫內地與全球市場的方法，以創造更多機會，尤其是尋求建立中國基準金屬價格、進一步擴大 LME 在亞洲時區的交易，並探討在互聯互通計劃中加入金屬衍生產品跨境及國際交易以及跨境上市等各種可能性。

註：所有在文中提到在計劃中或發展中的 LME 產品與服務均有待監管批准。

第13章

市場基礎設施
在「基本金屬」市場發展中的角色

香港交易及結算所有限公司
首席中國經濟學家辦公室

摘 要

　　基本金屬大宗商品交易市場不僅僅是提供基本金屬交易的場所，也是實體企業進行套期保值和風險管理的場所，健全完善的市場基礎設施體系，對服務產業客戶、服務實體經濟的功能日益凸顯。

　　西方的基本金屬大宗商品市場都經歷了從初期孕育到逐步成熟的發展過程。從美國的經驗來看，市場在發展初期的秩序存在不夠規範和標準化的問題，當中可體會到支援基本金屬市場交易體系的主要基礎設施和交易支援機制的完善健全，對基本金屬市場的發展意義重大。基礎設施和交易支援機制的標準化、現代化、資訊化程度的提高可以增強市場參與者的經營效率和經濟效益，同時也可以顯著提升實體企業的內部管理效率，節約成本。

　　其中，完善的倉儲物流體系被認為是最重要的大宗商品現貨市場基礎設施。倉儲安全是大宗商品現貨市場交易的基石，是開展各類相關業務的保證。能夠為基本金屬交易市場參與者提供可信的全球參考價格和終端市場的倉庫網路，是現貨金屬市場最重要和最基礎的組成部份。由於基本金屬現貨交易的資金回流存在滯後性，整個生產、物流周轉過程往往需要大量的融資支援，特別是在經濟處於下行週期時，融資往往成為基本金屬生產商和貿易商面臨的一個很大的問題，不合理的倉單質押融資方式存在倉單可信度無法保證的問題，從而導致融資效率低下。由於基本金屬自身具有高價值、易運輸、易儲存、易變現和品質等級明確等特點，具有很強的金融屬性，其倉單質押融資成為現貨交易市場中的一項重要業務環節。2008 年全球金融危機的爆發，從一定程度上反映了市場參與者承受和抵禦金融及經濟動盪的靈活性和市場的透明度嚴重不足。以此為背景，全球各個層面的金融市場陸續開始採納中央清算系統，以取代某些環節的雙邊結算體系，基本金屬大宗商品的金融工具市場也不例外。

　　對於如何衡量大宗商品市場的基礎設施和交易支援機制是否有效建全，最佳標準應在於其是否有利於資源的有效合理配置，從而有利於市場和行業有效降低交易成本。任何一個交易平台（包括期貨交易所）存在的根本意義也在於此，其地位和利益應從屬於這一標準。對於市場參與者來說，哪個定價中心更規範、更透明、參與者更多、更國際化及更公平有效地發揮價格形成和指導機制，就更願意在哪個市場交易。這些考慮對發展中的、並趨於國際化的中國內地基本金屬市場尤其重要。市場的發展和進步需要時間，最終市場會決定甚麼最符合行業需求，這些都值得我們密切關注。

1　全球基本金屬市場的主要基礎設施和交易支援機制

　　全球基本金屬市場主要由較為分散的場外交易（OTC）市場和一些集中的交易所市場組成，當中包括倫敦金屬交易所（London Metal Exchange，簡稱 LME）。自 1877 年 LME 成立以來，基本金屬（或稱「有色」金屬）一直在 LME 交易，隨着這些交易的報價開始在金融報刊上公佈，金屬行業開始將這些價格作為其現貨合約的可靠參考。這一情況延續至今，大部份國際基本金屬仍採用 LME 的價格定價。2019 年，全球 75% 的交易所場內金屬交易均於 LME 進行，總交易價值為 13.5 萬億美元[1]。美國在 20 世紀 70 年代後期停止採用生產商定價體系，自此紐約商品交易所（COMEX）主導美國市場；1990 年成立的上海期貨交易所（簡稱「上期所」）逐步建立了中國有色金屬期貨市場，慢慢形成 LME、COMEX 和上期所的三角競爭關係[2]。

　　西方的基本金屬大宗商品市場都經歷了從初期孕育到逐步成熟的發展過程。從美國的經驗來看，市場在發展初期的秩序存在不夠規範和標準化的問題，倉儲、運輸等基礎設施缺乏，信用程度較差，規範的市場秩序是在經歷了一個漫長的發展過程後，最終逐步建立完善起來的。

　　由此可見支援基本金屬市場交易體系的倉儲物流及結算系統等主要基礎設施和倉單融資及其他第三方機構的專業服務等交易支援機制的完善健全（見圖 1），對基本金屬市場的發展意義重大。基礎設施和交易支援機制的標準化、現代化、資訊化程度的提高可以增強市場參與者的經營效率和經濟效益，同時也可以顯著提升實體企業的內部管理效率，節約成本。

1　資料來源：LME。
2　見魏佳與徐小雅（2019）〈LME 有色金屬市場定價權形成機制研究〉，載於北京金融衍生品研究院《期貨與金融衍生品》，第 105 期，2019 年 1 月。

圖 1：基本金屬市場交易平台中的主要基礎設施和交易支援機制

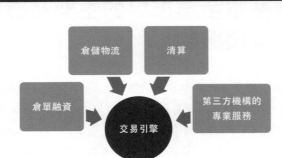

資料來源：香港交易所整理。

1.1　倉儲物流

　　完善的倉儲物流體系被認為是最重要的大宗商品現貨市場基礎設施。倉儲安全是大宗商品現貨市場交易的基石，是開展各類相關業務的保證。基本金屬市場的發展完善也同樣離不開倉庫物流體系的逐步建立、健全和完善。

　　首先，由於基本金屬大宗商品行業的貿易企業眾多，貨物周轉次數較多，物流環節冗長且分散，缺乏規模效應，且面臨貨價在途風險和運輸風險，實體企業的物流成本與市場倉儲物流體系的標準化程度有密切關係。如果倉儲物流缺少了安全保證，貨物的數量、品質以及所有權將無法得到有效保障，也進而限制了現貨業務規模的擴大。倉儲貨物安全，對於產業鏈企業、金融機構和投資機構，特別是廣大的基本金屬貿易商，都是非常重要的。一個專業高效的註冊倉庫網路，能夠為基本金屬市場行業帶來諸多益處，支持市場的高效標準化運轉（見圖 2）。

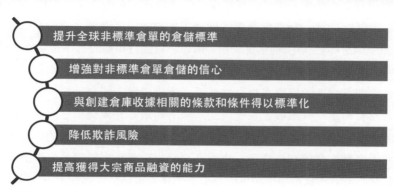

圖 2：專業的倉庫網路對基本金屬市場行業的益處

- 提升全球非標準倉單的倉儲標準
- 增強對非標準倉單倉儲的信心
- 與創建倉庫收據相關的條款和條件得以標準化
- 降低欺詐風險
- 提高獲得大宗商品融資的能力

資料來源：香港交易所整理。

其次，完善的倉儲物流體系使得「期現結合」成為可能，即現貨交割機制能在期貨交易中發揮重要作用，從而確保了大宗商品交易平台向全球基本金屬消費者和生產商提供套期保值和風險管理的功能得以充份發揮。

在大宗商品交易中，儘管實際發生現貨交割的數量在期貨交易總量中的比重很小，現貨交割機制在期貨價格和實體經濟中的現貨交易之間起着重要的紐帶作用。海外市場上的商品交易所都在商品的集中消費地或集中供應地或物流中轉中心，廣泛的設有供交割使用的標準倉庫，作為現貨貿易的最終手段，或輔助手段，在供應過剩時吸納過剩供應，在供應短缺時提供緊缺的供應，即時反映現貨體系裏的邊際供求變化，客觀上起到一個蓄水池的作用。因為有了現貨交割機制的保障，確保了期貨價格與現貨價格的變化是趨同的，不會脫節，也同時使得交易所庫存資料的變化成為市場供求基本面變化的「晴雨表」。一個註冊倉庫網路廣泛，和現貨交割制度完善的交易所所形成的期貨價格，更能凸顯出交易所期貨價格形成的「價格發現機制」，也使得形成的價格更具有價格指導意義。套用於基本金屬市場，覆蓋面廣泛的註冊倉庫網路是將金屬期貨價格與現貨價格聯繫在一起的關鍵一環。當期貨合約越接近到期日之時，期貨合約價格就越趨向現貨價格。儘管最終只有小部份的期貨合約以實物交割來結算，但正是這個進行實物交割的可能性，確保了金屬期貨價格不致過分偏離現貨價格。期貨價格緊貼現貨價格十分重要，因為這是生產商與消費者有效對沖金屬價格波動的基礎。正是完善的倉庫網路將大宗商品的期貨交易及風險對沖，與金屬業實體經濟緊緊地捆綁在一起。

　　在實物合約中產生一個被廣泛接受的參考價格，在大宗商品市場 —— 尤其是基本金屬市場 —— 是一種非常普遍的做法。生產商和消費者之間的合約通常參考全球公認的價格，但也會根據購買或銷售的原材料進行相關的折扣和溢價談判[3]。根據有信譽的參考價格（不包括成本溢價）對材料進行定價的做法，由於其對公司透明度、效率和可選性的好處而越來越普遍。現貨市場上的交易如涉及於未來交割金屬，自然會面臨一些風險，在達成交易合約和最終完成交割之間的時間可以跨越幾天、幾週、幾個月甚至幾年 —— 在這段時間裏，金屬價格可能會發生很大變化。因此大多數生產商和消費者，也就是金屬生產商和金屬製品生產商，會利用有現貨交割基礎的期貨市場中產生的可信的全球參考價格來對沖價格風險。

　　能夠為基本金屬交易市場參與者提供可信的全球參考價格和終端市場的倉庫網路，是現貨金屬市場最重要和最基礎的組成部份，因為它使得大宗商品交易平台如下兩個功能的實現成為可能：

(1) **價格發現：**產生及時、透明、可信和真實的參考價格，這些價格是用風險資本發現的，真正反映了全球的供求關係。市場的對沖能力取決於這些價格的發現。

(2) **價格趨同：**交易合約通過安全可靠的全球倉庫網路進行實物結算交割。這一點很關鍵，因為這意味着在市場上發現的期貨價格與實物金屬趨於一致（見圖 3）。

3　當然也有例外，鋼鐵市場歷來在合約中使用固定價格，包括所有生產成本、費用、保險費等，或直接採用現貨市場價格，面臨市場環境波動對價格影響的風險。

圖3：大宗商品市場現貨實物價格與期貨價格的趨同

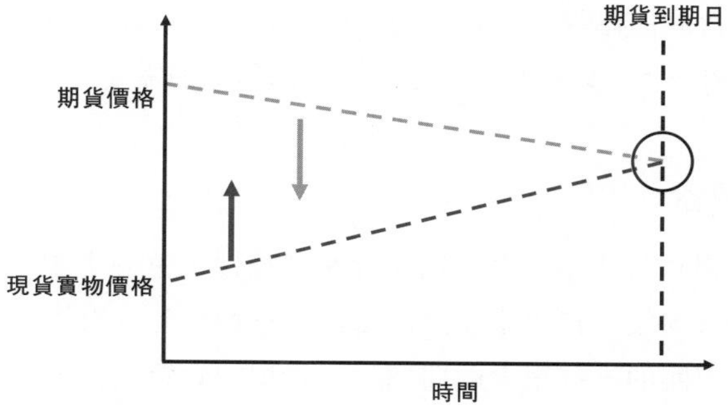

註：當處於期貨價格高於現貨價格的情境。

資料來源：香港交易所整理。

將實物合約與參考價格掛鈎的主要好處可以從以下幾方面來探討：

- 在全球經濟的碎片化和複雜的價值鏈中，生產者和消費者越來越難以持續擊敗市場。通過同意以市場價格進行交易，企業可以從這些價格發現組織和機制提供的更高透明度中獲益。因此，企業可以更好地將精力集中在基本金屬與特定產品之間的溢價或折扣的談判上。這些溢價或折扣可以基於許多因素，包括一些最常提到的因素如地理位置、材料等級、雜質和交貨條件等。

- 通過為價格發現提供一個健全的、受監管的交易場所，允許參考其價格的公司在任何時候都能有效地了解市場的現況。這就消除了企業需要投入大量資源來收集資訊，以便持續自主地發現金屬的市場價格。

- 那些參考全球公認價格的公司，可保留對沖其對標的金屬價格風險敞口的選擇權，而無需承擔該風險敞口的任何基礎風險。

在此值得指出的是，倉庫作為交割地點，必須毗鄰金屬消費方，即利用金屬製造下游產品的地點。過去，北美和北歐是全球主要基本金屬產業鏈的製造中心；今天，越來越多的製造業已遷往亞洲。以 LME 的倉庫體系為例，LME 在亞洲的核准地點漸多，比如高雄、仁川、橫濱等地。中國經過幾十年的經濟騰飛，如今成為全球第二大經濟體[4]，已經是名副其實的「世界工廠」，LME 在亞洲的核准倉庫要比世界其他地方的倉庫更能為亞洲、特別是中國的金屬消費者提供便捷的服務。覆蓋全球的交割倉庫能確保滿足實物交割的需要，即有能力通過全球認可的倉庫網路進行實物金屬交收，以滿足現貨企業和實體經濟的需要。

1.2　倉單融資

由於基本金屬現貨交易的資金回流存在滯後性，整個生產、物流周轉過程往往需要大量的融資支援，特別是在經濟處於下行週期時，融資往往成為基本金屬生產商和貿易商面臨的一個很大的問題，不合理的倉單質押融資方式存在倉單可信度無法保證的問題，從而導致融資效率低下。由於基本金屬自身具有高價值、易運輸、易儲存、易變現和品質等級明確等特點，具有很強的金融屬性，倉單質押融資成為其現貨交易市場中的一項重要業務環節。從實體使用者的情況來看，部份企業面臨着資金周轉壓力大、成本高、融資渠道有限的問題，具體表現在：

- **交易環節** —— 傳統銷售層級包括生產商、大型貿易商和多級代理商等，資訊成本高，不同層級加價導致交易成本上升；
- **生產環節** —— 原材料採購、固定資產投資到最終生產，面對先投入後產出帶來的巨大現金流壓力；
- **貿易環節** —— 賒銷為主的交易模式導致貿易商面臨巨額墊付帶來的周轉資金不足和應收賬款回籠的困難和時滯。

縱觀全球大宗商品市場，因為諸多鮮明的結構性特徵，比如大量的初始資本投資、漫長的全球航運路線和漫長的生產週期，實體使用者利用大宗商品融資來支援其交易及運營管理方面已經較為廣泛並形成一定規模。大宗商品融資在基本金屬行業同樣被廣泛採用，許多量身定制的融資安排已經被基本金屬市場的參與者使用了幾十年，甚至幾個世紀，其中包括礦山、貿易和庫存融資[5]。這些融資業務的一個共同特點是利用公司資產的未來經濟價值，無論這些資產已經作為精煉材

4　2010 年中國經濟總量超過日本，成為世界第二大經濟體，2010 年日本名義國內生產總值為 54,742 億美元，比中國少 4,044 億美元，排名全球第三。資料來源：《人民網》(http://politics.people.com.cn/GB/1026/13594169.html)。

5　資料來源：《倉單融資：借款人和貸款人如何從場內市場商品對沖活動中獲益》("Commodity financing: how hedging on-exchange can benefit both borrowers and lenders")，載於 LME 網站的 *LME Insight*，2018 年 8 月。

料存在，還是正在開發中，還是尚需要從地下開採。下文從貸款人和借款人的角度討論大宗商品融資帶來的益處。

從貸款人角度來說，總體上，貸款人可以要求借款人對其用於抵押的金屬進行套期保值，由此幫助貸款人減少自身面臨的多種風險（如下述），從而獲得更好的經風險調整的資本回報。

首先，套期保值降低了貸款本身的風險，因為抵押品的價值在貸款期間是有保障的。在發生違約和隨後喪失抵押品贖回權的情況下，資產的價值不會受到當前市場價格的影響，因為貸款人可以以當前市場價格出售資產，並通過對沖操作來彌補差額。這是放貸機構對抵押品以較低估值折扣獎勵那些進行對沖的借款人的主要原因。

其次，套期保值可以降低借貸交易中的對手方風險，因為做了套期保值安排的借款人往往承擔較少的價格風險。這使得貸款機構可以根據其自身情況增加對某些公司的風險敞口。

從借款人角度來說，套期保值（或稱對沖）在融資交易中，也會給借款人帶來很多好處。

首先，對抵押品予以較低的估值折扣意味着借款人在同樣情況下可以借到更多的錢，從而減少了對更昂貴融資形式（如無擔保債務或股權融資）的需求，從而提高其營運資金的使用效率，例如借款人可以利用更多的營運資金向客戶和供應商提供更具競爭力的付款條件，或將其再投資於企業或發展項目等。

其次，對沖通常會降低價格風險敞口，降低金屬價格波動對利潤的影響。對沖安排可以幫助借款企業有餘力更多地關注其核心業務，而不是花很多精力猜測其資產的未來價格走勢。

在融資交易中使用抵押品的套期保值有兩種主要方式，即套期保值操作可分別在場內市場（即交易所市場）或場外市場（即 OTC 市場）中進行。場內市場提供集中的交易場所，為交易對手提供共同的流動性和透明的價格。場外市場則主要是雙邊交易，通常僅限於兩個交易對手。表 1 列出在通過場內市場或場外市場構建融資交易對沖時需要考慮的一些關鍵問題。

表1：場內市場商品融資或場外市場商品融資的比較			
考慮因素	影響	場內市場商品融資	場外市場商品融資
管理對沖的保證金要求	由於必須管理初始保證金和變動保證金，公司需要考慮這對增加其營運資本的影響。	初始保證金和變動保證金可以由貸款人自己或第三方專業機構通過三方協議融資。	場外交易通常不要求保證金，但面臨較高的交易對手風險，這可能導致更廣泛的利差，以包括面對信用風險所增加的成本。
為匹配融資的對沖需要（包括任何攤銷）	套期保值的不匹配（過多或不足）會給交易雙方帶來風險。	場內市場提供流動性充足的交易環境，允許交易對手方對其對沖安排隨時進行調整，以配合融資安排上的任何變化。	場外交易的條款是按雙方要求制訂的，任何進一步的調整都需要獲得交易對方的同意。
在違約的情況下，對沖和貸款應該同時退出	這兩種頭寸在平倉過程中的不協調可能會造成不平衡和未能對沖頭寸。	交易所交易頭寸可以與新的交易對手在市場上平倉。	由於場外交易是雙邊交易，在交易開始時雙方必須就違約對沖的解除過程商定適當的條款。

資料來源：香港交易所整理。

通過上述討論和比較可以發現，在商品融資中作適當的風險管理安排（如套期保值）能讓資金更有效地分配，並為交易各方帶來利益。借款人可以以較低的成本獲得更多的金融資源，從而改善其資本結構。貸款機構則一方面可增加其在某些公司和行業的風險敞口，而另一方面亦能減低其希望規避的風險（例如金屬價格風險）。另一個值得再次強調的關鍵點是，貿易融資的有效操作，同樣需要大範圍的倉庫網絡。

1.3　清算及交收

基本金屬大宗商品現貨交易場所往往集合了交易、清算、交收、存管等在內的全部各項職能。而交易場所往往缺乏對清算與交收（合稱結算）環節所涉及資金進行有效管理。由於貿易鏈冗長，且缺乏專業的風險管理機制，整個貿易鏈面臨交易違約、價格波動、貨權歸屬和融資信用等風險。在達成價格協議後，貿易合約的交收履約往往由於市場價格的變化引發違約風險。商品貿易以點對點交易為主，缺乏統一的支付結算體系，此外還可能存在現貨市場交易資金的安全性問題，以及因信用體系脆弱，導致缺乏交易完成後各環節履約行為的約束力。

2008年全球金融危機的爆發，從一定程度上反映了市場參與者承受和抵禦金融及經濟動盪的靈活性和市場的透明度嚴重不足。具體來說，由於部份衍生品市場缺乏透明度、產品越來越複雜、並且滲透到金融市場內的各個領域，被認為是導致全球性金融危機和系統性風險的重要因素。特別是部份場外衍生產品的交易缺乏監管，加上本身顯著的雙邊交易的特點，國際主要監管機構在反思危機之後均認為這是導致市場缺乏透明度和明顯動盪的重要原因之一。以此為背景，中央結算系統得以在全球各個場外金融市場陸續開始被採納，基本金屬大宗商品市場也不例外。

清算的作用是讓交易合約雙方確知其結算後所要承擔的交付責任。在中央結算系統下，結算所充當中央交易對手方（Central Counterparty，簡稱 CCP）—— 即對每一個買家作為賣方，對每一個賣家作為買方 —— 從而保障交易各方不受對方違約的影響。一旦交易進入中央結算，CCP 和每個結算成員（買方和賣方）之間就會建立一個合約作交收依據。

交易雙方都被要求提供擔保以覆蓋與交收相關的風險。在清算成員違約的情況下，CCP 能夠在不使其非違約結算成員承擔任何損失的情況下完成合約執行。在某些情況下，抵押品可以隨客戶頭寸轉移到另一個結算成員 —— 這一過程稱為移植（「porting」）。因此，CCP 作為系統風險管理者，可以顯著降低結算成員的交易對手信用風險。這有助於限制金融危機（如 2008 年金融危機）造成的連鎖效應，並防止單一違約向整個市場蔓延。

是甚麼讓中央結算如此具有系統重要性？對市場參與者而言，當中的直通式交易處理和即時風險管理是其中兩項具吸引力的特點。此外，中央結算系統還通過簡化貿易管理和合約執行，在降低參與者的業務成本方面發揮了重要作用（見圖 4）。最重要的是，使用 CCP 可以簡化和分離場外交易市場中可能存在的複雜交易網路，實行多邊淨額結算簡化了交易對手之間的關係，降低了可能在整個金融領域引發衝擊波的傳染性風險，同時提高了整體市場的營運效率。

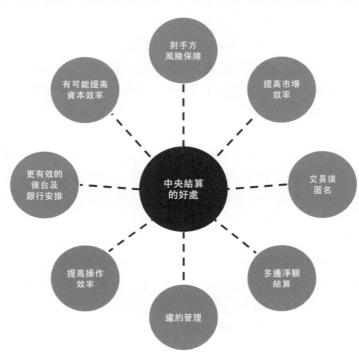

圖 4：中央結算在基本金屬大宗商品市場中的優勢

資料來源：香港交易所整理。

　　正是在中央結算下信用風險的顯著降低，以及在違約發生時 CCP 採取的有效
風險控制，使結算環節在這方面的改進成為監管機構關注的焦點，用以防止 2008
年那樣的金融危機再次發生。通過將自己置於買方和賣方之間，CCP 對於金融市
場非常重要，因為它們能夠理清複雜的交易關係，實現交易的淨額結算和壓縮，
並在違約情況下提供有效的風險管理。另外，它們的存在對於向市場灌輸信心也
非常重要，使它們能夠在市場極端波動和交易對手違約的情況下保證市場的公平
有序運轉。

2 市場基礎設施建設是支援中國基本金屬市場未來發展的關鍵環節

2.1 針對市場的需要出發、尋找對市場長遠發展的最有利方案

對於衡量大宗商品市場的基礎設施和交易支援機制是否有效建全，最佳標準應在於是否有利於資源的有效合理配置，從而有利於市場和行業有效降低交易成本。任何一個交易平台（包括期貨交易所）存在的根本意義也在於此，其地位和利益應從屬於這一標準。對於市場參與者來說，哪個定價中心更規範、更透明、參與者更多、更國際化及更公平有效地發揮價格形成和指導機制，就更願意在哪個市場交易。

站在中國內地的基本金屬大宗商品消費者和生產商的角度，面對內地與國際市場兩個不同的定價體系，如果無法有效地進行價格的順暢對沖，可能會承受經濟上的損失並面對經營上的不確定性。市場的發展和進步需要時間，最終市場會決定甚麼最符合行業需求，這些都值得我們密切關注。

展望未來，建立一個良性循環的生態系統將在長期有利於市場的健全發展，而這個生態系統應至少包括以下四方面的功能或特質（見圖5）：

(1)　服務實體經濟和現貨市場

這應當是一個良性循環的生態系統最關鍵的功能，即確保這個生態系統能夠提供價格發現、風險管理及終端市場服務。

(2)　確保市場公平運作

市場的公平有效在一個良性循環的生態系統中處於中心位置，公平有效不僅是指市場按照監管規定公正無差別地對待市場參與者，更應該將其原則拓展並深深植根於市場機制的設計和運轉方式當中。這其中可以包括並不限於：

- 市場接入，使盡可能多的市場參與者可以平等地進入市場中作投資和風險

管理；

- 相比 OTC 市場，場內市場應盡可能大的發揮其在產品和流程標準化方面的優勢，創造比 OTC 市場更加公平的交易環境。

(3) 增加市場參與者的選擇

從市場結構的角度來看，場內市場的一大特點就是所有市場參與者都應遵循同樣的交易規則。然而，在保證不影響其他市場參與者的前提下，可以對市場結構作多方面的改進以向部份市場參與者提供更靈活的操作選擇。此外，一個良性循環的生態系統還應在產品種類和策略方面不斷創新，以滿足投資者多元化的投資和風險管理需要。

(4) 交易效率和資本使用效率的最大化

交易效率和資本使用效率的提高，符合市場參與者、交易所和整個市場的共同利益。如果一個市場參與者因為交易的「摩擦成本」而選擇不執行一項具備經濟收益的交易（不論作套期保值或純投資），那麼該市場的交易效率及資本使用效率則會被視為不夠水平。

圖 5：尋找對市場長遠發展的最有利方案 —— 建立一個良性生態圈

資料來源：香港交易所整理。

2.2　香港交易所和倫敦金屬交易所支援中國內地市場參與者參與國際基本金屬市場的戰略定位

　　中國是全世界第二大經濟體及最大的大宗商品進口國和主要消費國[6]，香港作為位處中國門戶的全球金融中心，一直是中國內地與全球其他地區之間的超級聯繫人，有很好的條件服務大宗商品市場參與者，為中資企業、區域大宗商品貿易公司以至它們的全球商業夥伴在風險管理需求方面提供更佳的服務。

　　在基本金屬這一大宗商品市場方面，LME 是香港交易及結算所有限公司（簡稱「香港交易所」）的全資子公司，LME 的結算價是全球基本金屬生產及其原材料現貨貿易的指導性定價基礎。LME Clear 是專門為在 LME 交易的金屬遠期、期貨和期權而設立的中央結算所，該公司在風險管理方面採用了最新技術，例如即時

6　資料來源：〈從歷史看大宗商品定價中心的形成及建議〉，《中國期貨》，2018 年第 5 期（總第 65 期）。

清算（使其能夠即時監控和管理風險敞口），使市場更加穩健和安全。在抵押品的多樣化方面，LME Clear 接納包括 LME 倉單在內的各種類別的抵押品。使用倉單作為抵押品可以幫助企業釋放其他類別的抵押品，以提高企業的資本效率[7]。

LME 過去 140 多年來服務實體經濟的成功經驗表明，遍佈世界的核准倉庫網路和完善的每天交割實物交收制度，是實現大宗商品「定價權」的重要基礎和根本保障。截至 2020 年 3 月，LME 在 33 個獲認可的交割地點共設有 550 多個核准倉庫（見圖 6），覆蓋了全球絕大部份的金屬消費地、供應集中地和流轉中心，可以很方便地讓市場參與者在供應過剩時通過交易所進行交割變現，在供不應求時從交易所倉庫裏提取庫存。因此，LME 的庫存資料是全球基本金屬基本面變化的「晴雨表」。

中國企業參與 LME 交易活動由來已久，最早可以追溯到上世紀 90 年代[8]。

LME 的倉庫體系有着以下特點：

- 第一，倉庫所有權不歸屬 LME，具體的經營活動由不同的倉儲公司負責。LME 負責前期對倉庫的位置、倉儲公司及具體倉庫的審核與批准，倉庫在獲核准之後，日常的管理與運作包括倉庫的盈虧完全由各自的倉儲公司承擔。之後，LME 對其批准的倉庫進行持續審計，以確保它們繼續符合其規定的標準。此外，倉庫公司有義務僱用經批准的獨立第三方審計師進行年度百分百的庫存盤點。

- 第二，LME 對倉儲公司的批准要求嚴苛，除了對倉儲公司的資本實力的要求外，還對倉儲公司的管理能力和經驗有嚴格的要求，只有具備相當資本與質素的倉儲公司，才能滿足 LME 嚴苛的要求，成為其倉儲運營商。目前 LME 的倉儲公司基本都是一些從事金屬倉儲多年、具有豐富經驗、信譽良好的專業機構[9]。

- 第三，只有獲得 LME 批准通過的倉儲公司才能申請在交收點設立核准倉庫。LME 還對交收點倉庫的物流設施、管理人員經驗、出入庫及庫存規模都有相應的要求。

---

7 有關 LME 的市場及其運作詳見本書第六章〈倫敦金屬交易所 —— 全球工業金屬交易及定價中心〉。

8 資料來源：LME。

9 資料來源："A detailed guide to the London Metal Exchange", published on the LME's website, 2018.

- 第四，LME 成立了一個倉儲委員會。該委員會由核准倉庫的代表所組成，
  強化了 LME 與倉儲公司之間的關係，滿足各自的要求，實現了雙贏，這
  有助 LME 鞏固其作為全球基本金屬商品交易中心的地位。

  LME 全球倉儲體系的進化歷程對內地大宗商品交易的發展具有很好的啟示意
義。通過完善商品交割倉庫，將現貨和期貨的「距離」拉近，可以更好的支援實體
經濟的發展，對爭取形成大宗商品的人民幣定價機制有積極的意義。

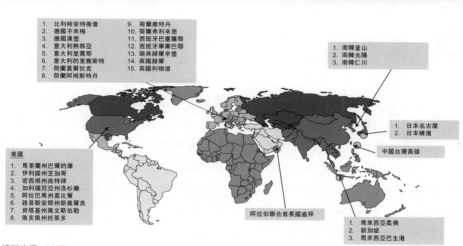

圖 6：LME 的全球倉庫網絡

資料來源：LME。

中國內地在改革開放的新形勢下，內地大宗商品期貨市場的對外開放是一項
十分重要而緊迫的戰略任務。以目前主力「引進來」的對外開放模式過程漫長，在
相當長時間內恐怕難以承擔起增強國際定價話語權的重任。內地商品期貨市場要
在新一輪對外開放中有擔當有作為，就需要雙方向、多路徑積極推動對外開放，
通過「引進來」和「走出去」相結合，將投資者、交割倉庫、價格與國際市場打通，
從而幫助中國企業提升參與國際競爭的能力。

其中之一可以考慮的可行方案是允許 LME 在內地批准倉庫成為其核准交割倉
庫，這將有力推動境內外的基本金屬交易中心相互融通，增強內地與海外市場的
價格互動，協助內地大宗商品期貨市場更好地發揮服務實體經濟的功能，加快提

升中國的國際定價權。如果在中國內地引入國際認可的交割倉庫，還可以積累經
驗，為將來內地交易所的交割倉庫「走出去」做準備。在內地設立 LME 核准倉庫
後，中國企業在平等參與國際定價、降低交割成本、便利實物交割的同時，也能
熟悉和進入了國際交割網路體系；內地的交割倉庫也能了解和掌握按國際標準認
可的倉庫的管理模式，所有這些都為將來中國的企業走出去、交割倉庫走出去乃
至中國的大宗商品期貨市場走出去做好準備。

3　總結

　　基本金屬大宗商品交易市場不僅僅是提供基本金屬交易的場所，其完善的倉
儲物流體系與倉單質押融資機制，以及有效的中央清算系統，既是最重要市場基
礎設施和市場健康有序發展的保證，也是對服務產業客戶、服務實體經濟的重要
基石。有效建全的大宗商品市場的基礎設施和交易支援機制應該有利於資源的有
效合理配置，從而有利於市場和行業有效降低交易成本。這些考慮對發展中的、
並趨於國際化的中國內地基本金屬市場尤其重要。

　　展望未來，中國內地基本金屬行業的平衡發展，提高對資源和環境的利用
效率，需要內地客戶更好地利用國際期貨市場實現風險管理，也需要中國內地期
貨交易所在促進實體經濟發展、推進供給側結構性改革方面發揮更積極的作用。
LME 在國際有色金屬市場中的影響力源於其服務產業經濟的發展戰略，這對中國
內地商品期貨市場有重要的借鑒意義。

第14章

香港交易所大宗商品市場
── 連接內地與全球的互聯互通平台

香港交易及結算所有限公司
大宗商品發展部

摘 要

　　本章載述香港交易及結算所有限公司（簡稱「香港交易所」）怎樣計劃成為全球主要大宗商品市場交易平台。為達到這目標，香港交易所收購倫敦金屬交易所（LME）、設立前海聯合交易中心（QME），並致力開發新產品及聯通基礎設施。

　　近年，香港交易所成功推出黃金期貨、基本金屬期貨及黑色金屬期貨。香港交易所亦擬將「滬港通」及「深港通」（合稱「滬深港通」）的模式套用於大宗商品交易及結算，透過連結 LME 及 QME 來接通內地與國際大宗商品市場的定價。香港交易所推出了會籍互惠安排，以鼓勵 LME 的會員與香港期貨交易所（簡稱「期交所」，香港交易所的附屬公司，為衍生產品交易所）的參與者，一同支持香港交易所衍生產品市場推出大宗商品產品。香港交易所於 2019 年推出 LME 金屬小型期貨，標誌着香港與倫敦互聯互通（「倫港通」）的第一步。此外，香港交易所亦與多家機構（特別是內地機構）簽訂了一系列合作備忘錄，為內地大宗商品市場與國際大宗商品市場無縫接軌作好準備。

1 香港交易所大宗商品市場的特殊地位

1.1　香港交易所如何定位為內地及全球市場的平台

　　香港交易所的大宗商品策略集中於兩方面:「走出去買」和「走進來建」。對外,香港交易所於 2012 年成功收購具有 140 年歷史的倫敦金屬交易所 (LME),踏出收購國際金融基礎設施的第一步。對內,香港交易所實行以中國為中心的戰略,與內地監管者與市場機構緊密合作,並利用香港的特殊地位,務求搭建一個紮根內地、服務實體、守法合規的全新大宗商品現貨交易平台,期望它能打通金融與實體經濟聯繫的渠道。因此,設立前海聯合交易中心 (QME) 成為了香港交易所大宗商品發展戰略中重要的另一步。

　　香港是全球人口最稠密的城市之一,缺乏可促進大宗商品交易的發展環境及傳統背景。我們要發展大宗商品市場必得另闢蹊徑,務求應對香港的現況、善用本地優勢並且滿足本土需求。因此,香港交易所開始探求「兩條腿並行」的「雙贏」大宗商品策略:「期貨」策略 —— 與內地交易所「互聯互通,互掛互惠」;以及「現貨」策略 —— 買入現成而具備所需專業的平台,再建立內部實物交收設施。

　　「走出去買」和「走進來建」戰略的最終目標,是透過香港在亞太區的特殊地位,將從外收購回來的平台與內部自建的平台有效接通,並利用香港的國際金融基礎設施促進內地大宗商品市場國際化,以達到國際大宗商品定價移向東方。這對中國「一帶一路」倡議亦至關重要。「一帶一路」倡議涉及超過 60 個國家,預計十年內中國與這些相關國家的交易量將達 2.5 萬億美元[1],當中大部份會涉及大宗商品資源,發展潛力極其龐大。對內地來説,如何有效管理大宗商品價格波動造成的風險亦將直接影響到「一帶一路」倡議下的許多具體項目的推進。香港及倫敦都是「一帶一路」沿線的兩大國際金融中心。若能成功實行上述「雙贏」策略,香港交易所將可結合倫敦與香港方面的國際經驗,滿足中國實體經濟的需求。

1　資料來源:"China's Xi: Trade between China and Silk Road nations to exceed \$2.5 trillion"(〈習近平:中國與絲綢之路沿線國家交易額將達 2.5 萬億元以上〉),《路透》,2015 年 3 月 29 日。

1.2 香港交易所為成功發展成為大宗商品市場互聯互通平台所作的舉措

香港交易所大宗商品業務近年最重大的發展包括：(1) 於 2012 年收購 LME；及 (2) 於 2018 年設立 QME。兩者均是對應互聯互通機制及「買入及建立」策略所作的重大舉措。

1.2.1 收購 LME

LME 是全球工業金屬的主要定價中心，全球超過 80% 的有色金屬期貨合約均於 LME 平台買賣[2]。金屬定價一直是 LME 的核心功能之一。各大宗商品的主要基準價格（包括 LME 官方價及 LME 收市價）均是於 LME 交易日固定時段在倫敦的「交易圈」（公開喊價交易大堂）進行買賣時所「發現」的價格。交易圈的公開喊價歷史悠久，可追溯至 1877 年，至今仍維持極高流通量。

經慎重評估及廣泛諮詢後，香港交易所於 2012 年成功收購 LME。收購 LME 有兩大原因。其一是 LME 位於歐洲及美國市場交易時區，又是離岸美元融資中心及領先的貨幣市場。其二是香港交易所是領先的離岸人民幣交易中心，又是亞洲市場交易時區的衍生產品交易所。

這次收購是香港交易所建立大宗商品平台的重要舉措，儘管未能解決發展自身大宗商品交易及結算平台時遇到的所有困難，但亦至少踏出了第一步，向全球宣示香港也能成為世界級的大宗商品交易中心，為中國內地大宗商品市場參與者提供邁向國際化的渠道。儘管 LME 位於倫敦，與亞洲有不小的時差，但透過 18 小時運作的 LME 電子交易系統，LME 早市時段與亞洲午市時段重疊，而 LME 涉及亞洲的交易活動每年都有增加。源自亞洲的交易量越大，就越需要於亞洲交易時區內發現價格，以反映亞洲的供需情況。

香港交易所收購 LME 後的第一階段工作主要集中於優化 LME 現有的亞洲業務。在這一階段，金融投資或基礎設施重整不多，但香港交易所進行了不少工作去將 LME 的交易平台變得更簡便及符合亞洲客戶的需求。其後於 2013 年，台灣高雄港成為第九個 LME 認可的亞洲交收地點，其他亞洲交收地點位於新加坡、馬

2　資料來源：LME。

來西亞、南韓及日本。2014 年，香港交易所首次與 LME 合作推出會籍互惠安排。在有關安排下，若干 LME 會員亦成為香港期貨交易所 (簡稱「期交所」，是香港交易所旗下衍生產品市場的營運者) 的合資格參與者，令兩邊相互交易更為簡易。此項計劃將繼續進行，有關會籍互惠安排的詳情於下文另有分節介紹。

　　策略的第二階段是建立香港交易所開展新篇章所需的基礎設施。這一階段所需的時間及成本更多，但回報不限於財政上，亦體現在戰略方面。其中一項主要投資是設立 LME Clear (LME 的結算所)。在 LME Clear 的設立之前，LME 須透過外部結算所進行結算，因此無法完全控制自身發展步伐，尤其是推出新產品的速度及靈活性。在設立 LME Clear 之後，LME 的結算流程完全自主，向市場推出新產品可以加快之餘，亦為 LME 帶來結算收入。此外，在 LME 資訊技術方面的發展由當時的外判模式轉為交回公司內部自行營運發展，這除了提升效率外，還將 LME 的資訊技術轉化為戰略資產。

　　第三階段是吸納更多客戶。這一階段的策略包括實現產品的跨境上市及跨地區授權交易安排，並與其他大宗商品市場主要參與者及機構建立戰略合作關係 (當中基於內地市場的規模及其對國際化的需求，內地大宗商品市場的主要機構將是我們的主要合作夥伴之一)。透過這些合作關係，我們的發展由基本金屬開始，進一步拓展至其他大宗商品。自收購 LME 後，香港交易所前後推出了多隻產品，包括：離岸人民幣計價的 LME 金屬小型合約、雙貨幣 (美元及離岸人民幣) 計價的黃金合約、鐵礦石期貨合約 (香港交易所及 LME 同步上市)，以及於去年 2019 年推出的以美元計價的倫敦金屬期貨小型合約。

1.2.2　設立 QME

　　深圳與香港相鄰，在中國改革開放進程中各有其特殊任務及優勢。中央政府於深圳設立「前海深港現代服務業合作區」，為深圳及香港提供緊密融合的平台。前海亦是中國國家主席習近平於 2012 年中國共產黨第十八次全國代表大會後視察廣東的第一站。習主席特別下了政策指示，指前海要「依託香港、服務內地、面向世界」[3]。在 2019 年全國人民代表大會及中國人民政治協商會議期間，總理李克強提

3　資料來源：前海深港現代服務業合作區管理局網站 (http://qh.sz.gov.cn)。

出須研究及制定「粵港澳大灣區」發展規劃，以進一步促進及深化粵港澳合作關係。

然而，作為國家經濟發展規劃的主要地區之一，華南地區仍缺乏全國性的大宗商品交易市場。經過多年的準備，在深圳市政府的支持下，香港交易所與前海金融控股有限公司合作，充分利用前海的特殊政策優勢，共同創立 QME。

自創立以來，QME 一直與監管機構及行業客戶積極探討政策執行及深度合作方案，希望利用香港交易所的獨特優勢，建立一個紮根內地、連接世界的大宗商品現貨平台。這亦是首次有香港的主要金融基礎設施實體於內地設立金融平台。

QME 於 2018 年 10 月 19 日正式開業，開市首日的交易品種為氧化鋁。首宗現貨交易是國有中國鋁業公司中鋁國貿與廈門象嶼以每噸人民幣 3,030 元的價格成交 3,000 噸氧化鋁，錄得內地市場首個基於實際成交的氧化鋁現貨基準價格。

經過數年間的探索及改進，QME 已有能力應付大宗商品現貨及實體經濟市場。未來透過科技、跨境安排及融資等方式，QME 將建立標準化的資產類別，讓企業可取得資金解決集資方面的困難，並借助現在已屬香港交易所旗下的 LME 所帶來的東西方協同效應，逐步達到將 QME 打造成全球大宗商品人民幣定價中心的戰略目標。

QME 既要借鑒先前 LME 的經驗服務於實體經濟和產業客戶，又絕對不能完全抄襲，必須切合中國國情。QME 就是要創造性地借鑒 LME 服務實體經濟的經驗，服務內地實體經濟，培育以機構客戶（尤其是中小企業）為主的現貨市場。具體而言，QME 準備先建立可靠的倉儲及便利的物流，建立 LME 式的交收倉庫網絡及行業信用，然後圍繞企業需求，為大宗商品用戶、貿易商、物流商和金融中介等各方提供安全、高效的大宗商品現貨交易、融資、倉儲物流及供應鏈管理等一系列綜合服務。另外，QME 將創新服務模式，以盡量降低企業的資金成本及交易成本（特別是降低中小企業套期保值的成本），並為企業提供更個性化的服務。

（有關 QME 的更多詳情，請參閱本書第 11 章。）

2　平台的發展前瞻

2.1　戰略性產品的開發

除了最近推出的黃金、基本金屬及黑色金屬的期貨合約外，香港交易所將繼續引入其他資產的合約，務求涵蓋與亞洲大宗商品市場中各類交投活躍的相關資產，令市場產品組合一應俱全。

除商品期貨外，香港交易所也考慮推出或正積極開發其他可供買賣的商品衍生產品以及各種形式的 delta-1 產品[4]，以期幫助包括生產商和消費者在內的各種商品行業參與者有效率地對沖商品風險。

2.1.1　黃金

香港交易所於 2017 年 7 月 10 日推出實物交收的美元黃金期貨及人民幣（香港）黃金期貨合約（統稱「黃金合約」）。

此黃金合約是世界首對雙幣黃金期貨，在香港以實物交收，備有全球交割機制，並符合由中國內地及全球投資者認可的千克金條標準。黃金合約的對象主要是：(1) 實物市場參與者，例如黃金冶煉廠、製造商及珠寶商等需要對沖金價風險的人士；(2) 金融業參與者，例如銀行及基金利用衍生產品市場與其黃金相關投資產品連繫掛鈎；(3) 套戥者透過在岸與離岸市場之間的價格差異進行買賣，並就匯價及利率差異部署其他交易戰略；及 (4) 其他可能有意涉足黃金交易的投資者及交易商。

憑藉自由市場和轉口港貿易中心的背景，香港是黃金運往中國內地的主要通道。

中國內地擁有極其活躍的現貨金交易市場，是世界主要金市之一，因其是世界上最大的黃金消費國[5] 及進口國 —— 2018 年該金屬的進口量約為 1,500 噸（相等

4　Delta 是用來量度金融衍生品對標的資產價格變化的敏感度。Delta-1 產品就是 Delta 值等於 1 的金融衍生品，反映按百分比計算，衍生品價格的變動幅度是直接追蹤標的資產的價格變化。

5　資料來源：「中國黃金消費量連續 6 年全球第一」，《新華網》(http://www.xinhuanet.com)，2019 年 1 月 31 日。

於全球進口量的三分之一）[6]。雖然至 2019 年 9 月香港在中國黃金進口所佔比例已跌至 40% 左右（主要由於香港政局動盪），但在 2012 年至 2016 年期間，香港所佔的比例平均維持在 60% 左右[7]。對現貨黃金的主要需求來自香港的鄰近城市 —— 深圳佔中國珠寶銷售總額近 70%[8]。香港毗鄰中國內地，與深圳尤近，在服務內地黃金市場方面具有無可比擬的優勢。

再者，香港是全球最大的離岸人民幣中心[9]，在促進人民幣國際化方面有獨特角色。香港推出雙幣黃金合約正是實現這一目標的踏腳石。

香港交易所推出黃金合約的戰略價值如下：

- 推出全球首隻雙幣黃金期貨，使香港黃金市場同時包含活躍的實物市場和衍生產品市場，從而提升香港作為主要黃金交易中心的地位；
- 吸引香港、內地、亞洲其他地區以及西方時區的投資者參與，以期建立香港公斤金條的亞洲基準價格並增強亞洲的商品定價能力；
- 推出香港歷史上首隻實物交收的商品期貨，有助香港交易所建立其實物交收的力量。

香港交易所於 2019 年 6 月 24 日推出六隻以美元及離岸人民幣（香港匯率）計算的黃金期貨指數（簡稱「黃金指數」系列），包括「超額回報指數」、「總回報指數」及「現貨指數」，作為準備推出更多貴金屬衍生產品的關鍵第一步。此系列指數旨在獨立、透明及適時地追蹤香港市場的金價變動情況。指數追蹤美元及人民幣（香港）黃金期貨合約的價格，以 2017 年 7 月 10 日為基準，並根據國際證監會組織（IOSCO）的金融市場基準原則編算及管理。這些指數可作為未來發展相關交易所買賣基金（ETF）及／或 ETF 期權產品的標的指數。

經過大量市場研究，香港交易所準備推出更多新產品，例如白銀期貨和各種形式的黃金衍生產品，以擴大貴金屬產品系列的現有版圖。

6　資料來源：〈消息人士指：中國放寬黃金進口限制〉（"China eases restrictions on gold imports: sources"），《路透》，2019 年 8 月 22 日。

7　資料來源：〈香港黃金市場在政治動盪中黯然失色〉（"Hong Kong gold market losing shine amid political unrest"），《路透》，2019 年 9 月 13 日。

8　資料來源：《香港貿發局經貿研究》（http://china-trade-research.hktdc.com/business-news/article/ 中國消費市場 / 中國珠寶首飾市場概況 /ccm/tc/1/1X000000/1X002MMK.htm）

9　香港於 2019 年 6 月的人民幣總存款達人民幣 6,278 億元，為全球最大離岸人民幣業務樞紐。資料來源：〈財智匯港〉，香港金融發展局單張，2019 年 9 月。

2.1.2　基本金屬

香港交易所於 2019 年 8 月 5 日推出以美元計價的倫敦鋁、鋅、銅、鎳、錫及鉛期貨小型合約 (統稱為「美元倫敦金屬期貨小型合約」)，作為同一批商品的現有人民幣倫敦金屬期貨小型合約 (分兩批於 2014 年 12 月及 2015 年 12 月推出) 的配套產品。

全球對基本金屬的需求持續激增，增幅主要由中國近數十年的經濟擴張所帶動。1983 年至 2018 年期間，中國國內生產總值的年均增長率前所未有地達到 9.7%[10]，相信中國已成為大多數基本金屬的全球最大消費國。需求上升在結構上推動了近幾年實物金屬和相關期貨合約的價格上漲。在芝加哥商品交易所 (CME) 和 LME，基本金屬合約的交易量也有穩定增長[11]。基本金屬市場的交易形態 (原本由傳統實物市場參與者主導) 亦已徹底改變。正如美國商品期貨交易委員會 (CFTC) 官網上發佈的「CFTC 交易人持倉報告」所指出，現時活躍於這類資產交易活動的金融投資者、專業交易商和資金管理人越來越多。

基本金屬期貨在全球場外市場都交投活躍，另外在某些交易所 (例如 LME、CME、上海期貨交易所和印度多種商品交易所 MCX) 亦有掛牌上市。香港交易所於 2012 年收購 LME 後亦初步推出這些基本金屬產品，以利用 LME 的品牌和會員網絡及其受全球實體市場廣泛認可的基本金屬 LME 參考定價機制。美元倫敦金屬期貨小型合約旨在為在亞洲時區投資以美元計價的基本金屬的用戶提供額外的交易機會。

金屬期貨小型合約的每手買賣單位較小 (相對 LME 的標準基本金屬合約而言)，並且是可以現金結算。每手買賣單位較小主要是希望這個傳統上以大型實物市場參與者或機構交易者為主的市場會有多一些散戶參與。為了鼓勵 LME 會員及其客戶參與，期交所與 LME 推出會籍互惠安排，讓 LME 會員或期交所參與者申請成為對方交易所的參與者或會員時可獲豁免大部份費用。

10　資料來源：世界銀行數據 (https://data.worldbank.org)。
11　可參閱美國期貨業協會的統計數字。

2.1.3 黑色金屬

　　黑色金屬是商品市場中的基礎性產品，種類廣泛，可分為鐵礦石、鋼、焦煤和金屬廢料等產品類別，全為非標準化產品。各類別產品又涵蓋多個產品類型。現時，全球衍生產品市場在每個產品類別都只提供幾種主流產品，而市場參與者對期貨市場推出非主流產品的需求卻不斷上升。中國是最大的鐵礦石進口國和鋼材生產國[12]。中國每年的大量黑色金屬進出口，引發了實物和金融市場參與者對使用衍生產品進行對沖、套戥或投機的強烈需求。

　　香港交易所 2017 年推出第一隻黑色金屬產品 —— 鐵礦石期貨（TSI CFR 中國鐵礦石 62% 鐵粉期貨），便是其進軍黑色金屬市場戰略的第一步。透過適當的專設激勵計劃和市場促銷活動，全球專業投資者在此市場的交投日益活躍，有助積累流通量。同時，通過積極夥拍合作夥伴在中國內地和南亞市場進行營銷和業務發展，在 2019 年於該市場進行買賣的交易所參與者和實物市場交易者數量有所增加。在 2019 年，香港交易所與內地的多家報價機構（包括上海鋼聯）簽署了備忘錄，準備進一步涉足商品市場，把握其他黑色金屬產品的潛在機遇。詳情見下文第 2.2 節。

2.2　基建聯通

2.2.1　LME 與 QME 的平台聯通

　　按香港交易所的集團策略，過去的工作主要是通過海外買（LME）與內地建（QME）奠下了全球商品策略的基石，未來十年則要開始加速聯通內地與海外商品市場。未來我們需要努力複製「滬深港通」模式實現商品交易通和清算通，通過產品互掛及建立價格基準等方式讓內地商品市場和國際商品市場的價格接軌，加快內地在岸實物交割的國際化進程。同時，我們也希望利用科技幫助重塑中國內地大宗商品市場的交易和融資生態。

12　2018 年，中國鐵礦石總進口量為 10.644 億噸，粗鋼產量為 9.283 億噸（佔全球粗鋼總產量 18.084 億噸的一半以上）。資料來源：世界鋼鐵協會，2019 年 3 月資料。

2.2.2　會籍互惠安排

會籍互惠安排（RMA）是於 2014 年 11 月首次推出，旨在鼓勵更多 LME 會員成為期交所參與者，以配合支持香港交易所於 2014 年 12 月推出的大宗商品產品（即人民幣（香港）倫敦鋁、銅及鋅期貨小型合約）。RMA 最初為期一年，於 2015 年再延長多一年。在該兩年間，收到數份通過 RMA 成為 LME 會員及期交所參與者的申請。

根據 RMA 的原有條款，LME 與期交所豁免對方交易所會員或參與者申請成為期交所參與者或 LME 會員的首年年費及手續費。RMA 於 2019 年再度推出，基準與之前大致相同（見表 1）。重推 RMA 正正符合香港交易所開發大宗商品業務的策略，包括推出以美元計價的倫敦金屬（鋁、鋅、銅、鎳、錫及鉛）期貨小型合約（已於 2019 年 8 月 5 日推出）等新產品及其他可與 LME 產品產生協同效應的大宗商品產品。

為了鼓勵 LME 會員及其客戶積極參與新推出的美元倫敦金屬小型期貨合約，從而擴大准入、提高流動性並促進國際參與度，申請加入期交所的 LME 會員或其聯屬公司將可獲期交所根據 RMA 條款豁免其參與者費用。另一方面，LME 亦在同一時期推出其 RMA，對申請加入 LME 的期交所參與者或其聯屬公司豁免會員費。

有更多 LME 大宗商品交易商成為期交所參與者，相信會有助聯繫倫敦與香港市場。參與者同時擁有 LME 和期交所的會籍，他們和客戶在產品之間進行套戥以及管理風險等都會更加容易和妥當。可進入期交所市場的 LME 會員亦能夠以莊家或流通量提供者的身份，為美元倫敦金屬期貨小型合約提供合理的基本金屬價格。

RMA 安排僅涵蓋期交所和 LME 的交易所參與者費用，而不包括期交所及 LME 結算參與者費用。就期交所參與者的申請而言，費用豁免將適用於以下申請：期交所視作完備（指已提交所有相關證明文件者），並附有證據（如適用）證明其期交所參與者的申請和其於證券及期貨事務監察委員會（簡稱「香港證監會」）第 2 類牌照的審批均正在處理中。所有其他申請成為參與者的現行標準和費用保持不變。

表 1：RMA 概要			
交易所	推廣期	會員費用豁免	合資格申請人
期交所	2019 年 7 月 29 日 至 2022 年 7 月 29 日 （包括首尾兩日）	• 期交所交易權費用（一次性）：500,000 港元 [13]；及 • 交易所參與者首年年費：6,000 港元	任何 LME 會員或其聯屬公司
LME		• LME 會籍申請人 [14] 申請使用下列服務的首年(年度) 年費（包括每項服務的手續費（如適用））：(i) LME 第 1 至 5 類會員；(ii) LMEprecious 一般清算會員、個人清算會員以及非清算會員；及 (iii) 已註冊的中介經紀人	任何期交所參與者或其聯屬公司

2.2.3 「倫港通」

香港交易所推出倫敦金屬期貨小型合約可說是朝着「倫港通」邁出了第一步。這批小型期貨合約源自 LME 的產品，參照的是 LME 基本金屬合約的細則，是亞洲時區首批同類產品，將豐富和涵蓋亞洲及倫敦時區的基本金屬交易。接下來的第二步，LME 正考慮實行「賬簿交接」(pass the book) 的模式，讓期交所與 LME 兩邊的市場參與者能透過若干協定安排而在兩個時區接續買賣及對沖倉盤。最後一步則包括發展真正的「互聯互通」計劃，讓期交所與 LME 的買賣盤紀錄真正「互通」。

2.2.4 簽署合作備忘錄以發掘更多機遇

承接香港交易所三年策略下的「互聯互通」計劃，進一步延伸大宗商品業務策略，香港交易所前後與四家中國報價機構及業界組織簽署四份合作備忘錄，它們分別是上海有色網信息科技股份有限公司（簡稱「上海有色網」）、北京安泰科信息股份有限公司（簡稱「安泰科」）、上海鋼聯電子商務股份有限公司（簡稱「上海鋼聯」）及無錫市不銹鋼電子交易中心，都是基本金屬或黑色金屬業的信息及指數服務供應商（見表 2）。

13　期交所一次性交易權費用方面，此計劃的合資格申請人將支付 1 港元名義費用，而非 500,000 港元。
14　LME 會員申請資料載於 LME 網站（https://www.lme.com/CN/Access-the-market#tabIndex=0）。

表 2：2019 年香港交易所與專業大宗商品服務供應商簽署的合作備忘錄			
合作備忘錄簽署方	日期	地點	業務範圍
上海鋼聯	2019 年 5 月 7 日	香港	鐵礦石及其他黑色金屬
安泰科	2019 年 5 月 24 日	北京	鋁及基本金屬
上海有色網	2019 年 10 月 30 日	倫敦	基本金屬
無錫市不銹鋼電子交易中心	2019 年 5 月 7 日	香港	不銹鋼及其他鋼材

我們與上海有色網簽署合作備忘錄，是希望建立戰略合作關係，進一步推動雙方在金融和大宗商品領域的發展，最終提升中國內地大宗商品價格的國際影響力。據市場參與者反映，上海有色網的指數廣受內地市場認可，若在香港推出合適的對應衍生產品，全球客戶將有機會接觸到中國的相關資產。

與安泰科簽署合作備忘錄旨在進一步拓展雙方在有色金屬現貨市場領域的廣泛合作，共同推動中國內地有色金屬現貨價格的國際化進程。

與無錫市不銹鋼電子交易中心簽署合作備忘錄是為了加強長效溝通合作機制，推動雙方在金融和大宗商品領域的業務發展。

與上海鋼聯簽署合作備忘錄是希望提高中國內地大宗商品價格的國際影響力。香港交易所一直在研究開發以中國相關資產為標的的產品設計，豐富旗下大宗商品的產品組合，務求令現貨市場參與者獲取真實的市場價格，另一方面亦為金融參與者提供最有效的平台執行其投資策略。

透過與業內的內地夥伴（像簽訂上述合作備忘錄的機構）合作結盟，香港交易所進一步建立其在中國內地的網絡和資源。

我們亦正與內地各交易中心積極探索商機，尋求將互聯互通策略擴展至大宗商品板塊。

3 總結

香港交易所集團開始部署大宗商品方面資產業務的發展策略之前，亞洲區的大宗商品消費者及製造商主要經倫敦、紐約及芝加哥的相應基準合約對沖實物市場的風險，以致亞洲交易時段內都要面對重大的基準風險及流動性風險。中國近數十年來不斷壯大發展，時至今日已成為全球大宗商品的最大消費國，在這情勢下，拉近亞洲現貨與衍生產品市場之間的差距已是香港交易所有必要處理之事。

香港交易所「走出去買、走進來建」的「兩條腿並行」策略（即海外併購及設立直接與內地互聯互通的「商品通」）料可發揮香港自身的國際金融基建優勢，大力推進中國大宗商品市場國際化，繼而促進國際大宗商品轉來東方市場定價。

2012 年對 LME 的收購令香港交易所能直接進入全球公認的工業金屬定價中心。隨後 LME 將交易平台合理化、在台灣設立交收港以及與期交所訂立 RMA 等，令亞洲客戶接觸 LME 的機會增加不少。

及至 2018 年成立 QME，更是香港交易所邁向設立一個立足中國、連接全球的大宗商品現貨交易平台的重要一步。

另一方面，香港交易所平台上一再推出新的大宗商品產品，亦進一步推動中國與其他亞洲區用戶的互聯互通。以美元及離岸人民幣計價的 LME 金屬期貨小型合約有助亞洲貿易商對沖，以及讓亞洲投資者有更多交易機會；實物交收的黃金合約（亦是雙幣計價合約）可迎合中國內地這個全球最大金市的需求，有助推動人民幣國際化的進程；而鐵礦石期貨則可為市場提供對沖中國內地（世界最大鐵礦石入口國兼產鋼國）的鐵礦石現貨市場的高效工具。

此外，香港交易所又與中國報價機構和業界組織簽署合作備忘錄，加強合作，推動各方在金融和大宗商品領域的共同發展，冀最終提升中國內地大宗商品價格的國際影響力。

所有這些（以及未來更多的）舉措，都是希望建立並鞏固香港交易所的互聯互通平台的地位，以有效連接內地與全球大宗商品市場。

後 記

促進大宗商品現貨與期貨交易良性
互動、更好地服務實體經濟

　　在當前全球貿易格局轉變、金融市場動盪加劇、新冠疫情的衝擊等背景下，全球大宗商品市場不斷呈現新的發展趨勢。

　　第一，在全球貨幣寬鬆潮下，地緣政治及貿易爭端引發避險需求攀升，導致全球大宗商品市場波動加大，新的風險管理需求不斷湧現，商品類期貨合約成為國際金融市場新的增長動力。第二，大宗商品衍生品呈現明顯的多元化特徵，新的合約標的不斷推出，特別是與中國、亞太經濟活動緊密相關的新型能源、金屬合約，近年來陸續在全球各主要交易所掛牌，為進一步打通東西方大宗商品市場、滿足實體經濟在全球範圍進行風險管理提供新的金融工具。第三，在新興市場國家崛起的大背景下，中國需求對國際大宗商品價格的影響力不斷提高。中國現已成為鐵礦石、銅、鎳、煤炭、棉花等主要大宗商品的最大消費國，中國經濟增速對國際大宗商品價格走勢已起關鍵性作用。第四，中國內地市場開放的創新舉措持續推進，原油期貨、精對苯二甲酸 (PTA) 期貨、鐵礦石期貨與 TSR20 橡膠期貨被列為境內特定品種，陸續開放給境外參與者交易，使得中國市場對價格的把控能力逐步提升，內地與國際價格之間的互動關係從被動接受國際定價逐步轉而向國際輸出中國定價。因此，在環球金融體系發生巨變的大背景下，大宗商品市場參與者需要對中國境內外的大宗商品體系進行全面審視，不僅要了解現貨市場，還需要了解中遠期市場和相關衍生品市場；不僅要對當前全球大宗商品市場的金融創新進行深入考察，還需要重新審視內地市場會在未來全球大宗商品體系中建立的主導地位。

　　這正是我們着手準備組織編寫這本《全球大宗商品市場：從現貨到期貨》圖書

的初衷。全書從「全球大宗商品市場的格局」、「內地與香港大宗商品市場的演變」和「大宗商品現貨與期貨市場的互聯互通」等三個維度，對中國境內外大宗商品的多個板塊進行了深入分析。在相關題材領域中，相信本書是市場上第一本系統介紹中國境內外大宗商品市場的專著，同時覆蓋了香港、倫敦和內地多個大宗商品市場。在這領域內，倫敦金屬交易所（London Metal Exchange，簡稱 LME）與前海聯合交易中心（Qianhai Mercantile Exchange，簡稱 QME）接受邀請介紹各自的市場與發展。為了向市場分享有關國際大宗商品市場發展的第一手經驗和行業識見，我們亦邀請了於大宗商品市場具有豐富業務經驗的國際專業人士協作完成各章節。

在圖書內容方面，本書覆蓋了從現貨到期貨，從金屬、能源到農產品等不同商品形態，讓內地與海外市場參與者對整個大宗商品市場的宏觀系統和金融生態圈獲得整體的認識。另外，本書還有專門章節探討內地與海外大宗商品市場「互聯互通」的各種金融創新模式，如中國內地可通過與香港、倫敦的合作實現的市場開放，倫敦、香港的商品業務可進入內地市場，以及倫敦和香港之間的業務合作等，為市場參與者了解內地與國際在大宗商品市場的互聯互通模式提供了創新性的觀點。最後，本書特別介紹了香港在大宗商品市場的戰略性佈局和獨特地位。香港交易所通過收購 LME 涉足國際大宗商品市場，又於內地的深圳前海設立 QME，將 LME 的國際標準、發展經驗融入內地的大宗商品現貨市場，並擬利用與內地聯通的獨有優勢開闢內地大宗商品市場的發展新路徑，冀望香港在這一領域的探索創新可以對內地大宗商品市場國際化有所裨益。

本書第一篇「全球大宗商品市場的格局」從國際視野角度出發，為讀者展現了全球大宗商品現貨及衍生產品市場的全景畫面。首章由香港交易所集團總裁李小加主筆，系統介紹了香港交易所在收購 LME 及在內地建立 QME 的總體佈局和發展理念，以及如何支持內地大宗商品市場國際化進程的構思。

大宗商品覆蓋了金屬、農產品、能源等多個領域的現貨和期貨市場，關係國家基礎資源建設，但內地市場參與者及政策制定者對相關的國際市場操作和市場結構還相對陌生。因此，本書第一篇還邀請了上海有色網信息科技股份有限公司、中糧期貨有限公司、花旗環球金融亞洲有限公司、LME 等機構，分別就國際市場的金屬、農產品市場等的發展現狀與實務操作等範疇撰寫章節進行具體闡述，加上香港交易所首席中國經濟學家辦公室關於全球大宗商品衍生產品市場的一章，讓讀者更全面了解國際大宗商品的現貨與衍生產品市場的最新發展和實際操作。

作為全球第二大經濟體，中國已經成為全球最大的商品生產國和消費國之一。如何進一步提高內地對於大宗商品的定價能力，吸引國際機構更為活躍地參與內地市場交易是其中一個重要條件，而讓海外市場參與者更多地了解中國內地的大宗商品市場是引導國際機構參與的關鍵因素。為此，本書的第二篇「內地與香港大宗商品市場的演變」首兩個章節介紹了內地大宗商品市場的整體發展歷程、交易品種、對外開放、現貨與期貨的關聯等方面，相信內地大宗商品期貨市場通過不斷開放，將進一步增加市場流動性，吸引境外機構參與，可為亞洲時區經濟活動提供商品價格指標。同時，本篇另有章節專門介紹了香港的大宗商品市場，特別是期貨市場的產品與具體操作，以及其為香港作為國際金融中心可努力的發展方向。

本書第三篇「現貨與期貨市場的互聯互通」，圍繞大宗商品現貨與期貨市場的聯通，以及內地大宗商品市場與全球互聯互通的創新途徑而展開。本篇首章對全球大宗商品現貨及期貨市場的互動做一概覽，闡述了大宗商品期貨市場對現貨定價等經濟活動的重要性。本篇同時邀請了 LME、QME 和香港交易所大宗商品發展部份別闡述他們在中國內地大宗商品市場的發展路途上可以扮演的獨特角色，介紹了可利用倫敦（LME）、香港和內地平台（QME），將 LME 交易延伸至亞洲時區，拓展亞洲時區大宗商品現貨價格發現能力的願景。此外，由香港交易所首席中國經濟學家辦公室撰寫的一個章節，分析打通市場基礎設施如倉儲網絡對大宗商品期貨與現貨市場聯繫的重要性，有助改善內地市場現有的「現貨弱、遠期強」的行業發展痛點，並為期貨市場夯實基礎，形成真實有效的中國現貨價格基準。在內地大宗商品市場國際化的進程中，香港作為中國接通國際金融市場的大門，大可擔當大宗商品市場「超級連繫人」的角色，以進一步增加內地大宗商品期貨市場與全球市場的互動。

在此，我要特別感謝香港交易所集團總裁李小加先生對本書的鼎力支持，並為本書撰寫了第一章，分享了他對內地大宗商品市場國際化發展的深刻洞察和行動戰略。同時，香港交易所的大宗商品發展部、合規團隊、法務團隊、企業傳訊團隊、翻譯團隊等相關部門在本書的編撰過程中鼎力協助，使本書得以成功出版。我們亦有幸各相關交易所及市場專業機構接受邀請為本書撰寫文章。最後，本書的出版發行得到了商務印書館（香港）有限公司高效率的專業配合，將本書及時推向市場，在此一併表示誠摯的謝意！

　　推進內地大宗商品市場國際化，有許多可供選擇、各具特點的開放路徑。既可通過「引進來」吸引全球相關企業與投資者積極參與，促使中國大宗商品價格得到國際市場的廣泛關注和使用；也可以通過 LME、QME、認證倉庫的建設，提升內地的現貨交易能力，更好地服務內地實體經濟；還可以通過商品市場的互聯互通，打通大宗商品期貨與現貨跨境交易網路，從而多措並舉共同推動內地大宗商品市場的國際化。這些不同的開放方式可以適用於不同的羣體，也各有優勢。在此市場逐步開放的過程中，希望本書的出版能為市場帶來更多有益的專業觀點和思考。

　　基於全球大宗商品市場發展的內在邏輯，本書嘗試將大宗商品的現貨與期貨市場作實務對接，書中缺點錯漏在所難免，敬請廣大讀者批評指正。

巴曙松 教授

香港交易及結算所有限公司　首席中國經濟學家

中國銀行業協會　首席經濟學家

2020 年 5 月

Part 1

The global landscape of the commodities market

Chapter 1

Building a bridge — Connecting China and the global commodities market

Charles LI

Chief Executive

Hong Kong Exchanges and Clearing Limited

Summary

How can we help to build a bridge connecting China and the global commodities market, in order to realise the ultimate goal of becoming a "global commodities trading hub"?

This has been a question lingering in my mind, or actually, in many other fellow practitioners'. We have been pondering this same question, trying to explore and discuss options, to put ideas into practice and to evaluate them afterwards, all in search of a best answer, or the most practical and effective means of achieving our ultimate goal.

This chapter covers a brief introduction and summary of the special features, new development trends, and opportunities for growth within the Mainland commodities market. As the backdrop, there is also a brief account of HKEX's acquisition of the London Metal Exchange and the establishment of the Qianhai Mercantile Exchange. It is hoped that these reflections will enable readers to gain context and better understanding of the development.

Given the sustained and rapid growth and development of China's economy, and hence the increasing efforts towards further opening up its financial market, calls for the internationalisation of the Mainland commodities market are bound to increase and become more pressing.

The discussions in this chapter shall reveal the significance of the close ties between Hong Kong and the Mainland and the role of Hong Kong, which can be leveraged in order to build the bridge to connect China and the global commodities market.

In unity there is strength. Let's hope that our collaborative efforts will bring us ever closer to this goal before long.

1   Introduction

A glance over the chart of the copper price on the London Metal Exchange (LME)[1] spanning over half a century demonstrates the volatility of the metal markets. Yet, with a deeper look, it is not hard to find that somehow each and every turn of the line in the chart appears to be related to China's social and economic developments.

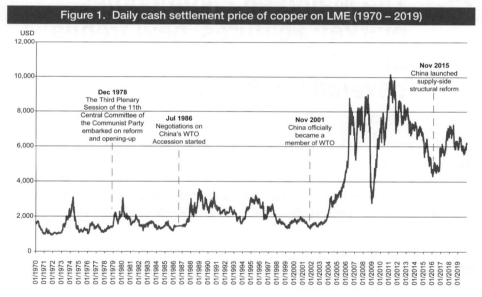

Figure 1. Daily cash settlement price of copper on LME (1970 – 2019)

Note: WTO refers to the World Trade Organisation.
Source: LME.

This is hardly a coincidence.

With China's entry to the World Trade Organisation (WTO) in 2001 and the acceleration of globalisation of the world economy, the Mainland economy has achieved remarkable growth. China's gross domestic product (GDP) reached RMB 91,928.1 billion in 2018[2], surpassing Japan and other developed countries in Europe. The scale of the Chinese

---

1   The Cash Settlement Price of copper on the LME, provided by LME on 23 January 2020.
2   Source: China's National Bureau of Statistics.

economy is expected to exceed RMB 100 trillion in the near future to become the second largest economy and the biggest industrial country in the world.

The truth behind the data is obvious: China's heavy demand for global commodities like energy, metals and agricultural products has never stopped during the past decades.

2 The Mainland commodities market: Features, new trends and great potential for development

Despite being a major consumer of the world's commodities, China has been a price taker in the global markets. However, its economic rise means that a developed, efficient and open commodities market is required to strengthen up China's power in international pricing and this is something we believe that we need to work closely on. Given China's practical needs and international development trends, we believe that the following efforts could be made:

(1) Breaking the geographical boundary of Mainland commodity prices, and gain international influence

Currently speaking, the commodities market within the Mainland are highly regional. And, their prices, both for domestic products and imports, form an ecosystem from within.

As these "local" prices are increasingly a guiding reference in regional markets and with increasing international influence, their interaction with corresponding global commodity prices is strengthening. Given the practical need and demands generated from its economic development, and riding on the continuous momentum of its commodities market, China is well-positioned to have its commodity prices gradually integrated into the pricing and settlement of global commodity trading, and in a number of ways.

(2)   Expanding market presence along the value chain, and facilitate closer interaction between the real economy and the commodities market

As a populous country, China is considered somewhat falling short of resources in the industrial, agricultural and energy sectors, and has been heavily relying on imports of a number of key fundamental resources.

With the globalisation of the world economy, China has been the world's factory over the past decades, serving as a processor in the middle between "resource producers" and "product consumers". It is hard to find enterprises engaged in services towards the two ends of the industry's value chain in the Mainland commodities market.

Judging from the supply chain, the settlement systems in place are yet to cover commodity trading, or major points of circulation, say, covering the major net consumers or net producers, and trade hubs. And in terms of physical settlement, more foreign brands from other countries are yet to gain recognition in the Mainland market.

(3)   Improving market entities' participation, and promote business diversification and internationalisation

A developed commodity market needs to be supported by mature and developed entities. However, futures trading companies on the Mainland are mostly agents in nature and form a key integral part among the participating entities. They provide market access to clients and are the bridge between the exchanges and market participants. According to the China Futures Association, there were 149 futures trading companies in the Mainland as of 2018, with branches and offices across major cities and provinces.

In comparison, commodities-related businesses undertaken by futures trading companies in developed markets are a lot more diversified, and usually include merger and acquisition (M&A) advisory, brokerage, trading and structured financing, infrastructure operations, spot and futures proprietary trading, etc. Apart from achieving economies of scale and scope through vertical integration, this shows a deep and thorough understanding of the sector and reflects a willingness to serve the sector and participating entities along the whole value chain. With the advancement of technology, even brokerages with mainly retail clientele would want to present themselves as digitalised, Internet-based online brokers, through the use of Internet and information dissemination technologies.

Both Mainland futures trading companies and Chinese financial institutions are seen to be on an increasingly fast track to business internationalisation and diversification. Certainly, they benefit from their rich experience in the Mainland market, but if breakthroughs could be achieved in terms of internationalisation, a much more competitive practising community could be formed to support China in further developing its futures market.

In terms of commodity spot markets in the Mainland, settlement is mainly done at the prevailing spot prices. Forward or other more flexible pricing in connection with the futures market, which is relatively popular in global markets, is uncommon. That explains the relatively low institutional participation in the Mainland futures market, as well as the tiny proportion of physical settlement compared to actual turnover and trade volume.

All these features and trends demonstrate the huge potential for development in China's commodities market. Joint efforts from all parties concerned are needed to drive forward the regularisation, diversification and internationalisation of the Mainland commodities market.

3 What is the unique role that Hong Kong could play in linking up the Mainland commodities market with the world?

Hong Kong is well positioned to connect the Mainland market with the rest of the world. Given Hong Kong's market characteristics and comparative advantages, we aspire to work out a blueprint for the development of the Mainland commodities market.

Accordingly, HKEX started to "walk on two legs" in developing its commodities business: "going out to buy while going in to build". In this sense, we are trying to connect with the Mainland exchanges, with the ultimate aim of product cross-listings and in a mutually beneficial manner.

"Going out to buy" means mergers and acquisitions overseas. We successfully acquired the over 140 years' old LME in 2012, our very first step in acquiring international financial infrastructures.

"Going in to build" means returning to our motherland and capitalising on our unique strengths and closely working with the Mainland regulators and related institutions, in order to build a regulated commodities spot trading platform that is rooted on the Mainland and serves the real economy. We hope that it can fill up the market niche by linking up the real economy with financing. In this regard, the establishment of Qianhai Mercantile Exchange (QME) is another key step in our commodities business development strategy.

Both "going out" and "going in" strategies aim to leverage upon Hong Kong's unique advantages in the Asia-Pacific region, so as to effectively link up the platform we have acquired overseas with the platform we have built on the Mainland. We are looking to capitalise on the international financial infrastructures we own to accelerate the internationalisation of China's commodities market and hence helping the shifting of international commodity pricing to the East. This is instrumental to China's "One Belt One Road" (OBOR) initiative. It is expected that China's trade with the over 60 countries along OBOR in the next ten years will reach US$2.5 trillion[3], a considerable portion of which will be in commodities, which depicts a huge potential for development. In addition, to the Mainland, how well commodity price risks are effectively managed will directly impact the progress of many OBOR projects. Both Hong Kong and London are international financial centres along OBOR, and so if our "Walking on Two Legs" strategy works smoothly, we could contribute by applying our international experience in Hong Kong and London to China's real economy via Qianhai.

3.1   Acquisition of LME

We have always acknowledged that Hong Kong, albeit one of the world's three best ports and a vibrant business and trading centre, has never been a centre of any kind in commodities trading or settlement. As a major financial hub in Asia, we could not find many of this type of assets in our markets.

It was a combination of embarrassment and helplessness as well as regret whenever this part of our markets was the talking point. There had been no way out of it despite a number of attempts and efforts of change.

Then one day, finally, we managed to have run into a golden opportunity that might be able to herald a breakthrough.

The HKEX Group made a firm offer to LME in 2012. Representatives of the two parties involved in the negotiation were so confident yet hesitant and excited, as they sensed they were making happen what could be a change in the history and landscape of the global futures market, something they had never imagined before.

---

3   Source: HSBC, "The rise of Asia: The new landscape of the global economy" (〈亞洲崛起：全球經濟新面貌〉), published on the *Hong Kong Economic Journal,* 5 May 2017.

LME is a long-standing establishment that has been in operation for more than a century, its market position and importance comparable to the Queen's crown jewels. It is also a private company with a board comprising representatives of its member shareholders. The list of directors is simply a long list of prominent and veteran global capital market participants that have been in the market for over a century. And it was these institutions who were going to vote on our proposed offer.

And eventually, after so many twists and turns, we beat out all other bidders in the fierce competition and saw our dream coming true.

In the joint statement made on the day our intention to acquire the metal bourse was agreed upon, a few points were particularly noticeable: (1) preserving and enhancing the LME's existing business model; (2) expanding the presence of the LME in Asia and China; and (3) developing the LME over time in accordance with the needs of its members and market participants.

In retrospect, we cannot help feeling grateful about the development of the whole episode. Life is never predictable. We are so thankful for the LME shareholders who had not only wisely voted for us but also for Hong Kong. And more importantly, they had cast a vote of trust and confidence in a rising China.

How shall we reposition LME? How shall we make it a more modernised exchange that stays up-to-date with technological advancements as well as market trends? How shall its unique features and functions be leveraged to better serve the region and the wider global markets? Resolving all of these are of our top priority.

It was against this background that we have taken the following steps progressively over the past few years.

(1) Phase 1: Business expansion in Asia

In 2013, LME approved Kaohsiung in Taiwan of China as a designated delivery point for its metals. This is the ninth among the bourse's other Asian delivery ports in Singapore, Malaysia, Korea and Japan.

In 2014, a Reciprocal Membership Agreement (RMA) was jointly introduced by HKEX and LME, under which certain LME members were given access to the Hong Kong market by becoming participants of the Hong Kong Futures Exchange (HKFE), a subsidiary of HKEX, such that they could serve both markets and facilitate trading across the border.

RMA was reintroduced in 2019, details of which are elaborated in subsequent chapters.

(2)   Phase 2: Establishment of LME Clear, laying a solid foundation for future development

Following more than two years' preparations, in 2014, LME launched LME Clear, its custom-built clearing house of trades on its market.

To HKEX, the launch of LME Clear not only brings autonomy over trade settlement and significant increases in revenues, but also greatly facilitates the development and introduction of new products. A central clearing regime is an integral part of a modern exchange, too.

(3)   Phase 3: Provision of reference and assistance in the development of the commodities market in Hong Kong

Work in this stage includes enabling the cross-listing of products, authorisation arrangements, and strategic partnership with key market participants and institutions. We attempted to start from base metals, drawing reference from LME, before expanding to other types of commodity.

Accordingly, a series of metal futures contracts covering non-ferrous, ferrous and precious metals were introduced in Hong Kong.

3.2   The establishment of QME

The successful acquisition of LME has given us an opportunity to get a closer look at it.

What are the factors that have helped LME stand the test of time and carried it through major historical events like the two world wars and the dissolution of the International Tin Association, making it strong and intact, and able to thrive through all the challenges?

The answer is obvious: the pivotal role that LME plays in the market today might have everything to do with its "genetic" connection with the spot market, and its inseparable long-term connection with the metal trading market. With these factors at work, it is not hard to notice that every critical decision the metal bourse has made in the course of its evolutions and development was inevitable.

With these in mind, it was just natural for our team to make reference to this more than a century old metal exchange when we learnt we might be allowed to establish a commodity trading platform in Mainland China, hoping that it can take root and serve the economy and society at large.

This seed of hope finally fell on the good soil in Qianhai, Shenzhen and thrived to become the Qianhai Mercantile Exchange (QME), a spot trading platform for commodities.

If Shenzhen is considered a pioneer city for reforms and opening up, then Qianhai is like a future centre of this city or even of the entire Pearl River Delta region, the next "Manhattan" that breeds modern services and innovative industries. It is in this sense that the growth of QME against such a background is actually a result of going with the time.

With this inspiration and hoping to pass down the heritage, we have some preliminary thoughts for QME under construction. As a tangible manifestation of our profound understanding of the commodity industry, it was determined that QME will have three essential features: (1) daily settlement; (2) serving the industry chain; and (3) establishing a warehousing network.

(1)　Feature 1: Daily settlement

Most of the world's major futures exchanges provide trading on the basis of monthly quotations and delivery; few offer daily settlement and physical delivery. Nevertheless, there is no doubt that only when daily settlement and delivery is available can the liquidity of the commodities be maximised, substantially saving the time for buyers and sellers on waiting for settlement and delivery.

This may sound like trivial in daily life: it is just the most common mode of sale or exchange of goods. In a convenience store, for example, you take the goods you want from the shelf and go pay for it at the cashier, and then the whole thing is done.

However, in a trading market where settlement is centralised through a central counterparty, daily settlement requires extremely strong settlement and margin management capabilities. This is definitely not simple, and "easier said than done".

At LME, despite the difficulties, they managed to offer daily settlement and delivery within a rolling three-month period. It shall be for this reason and by adhering to its original principles that it stands out and plays a unique role in the market.

So from the very beginning, we have determined to take this as one of the essential features QME shall provide to the market, i.e. always reflect the operations of the spot market.

(2)　Feature 2: Service the industry chain

Most of the major futures exchanges in the world today can be traced back to the 19th century, when they were founded in cities that were distribution centres of commodities. This indicates that futures exchanges have served to help agricultural farmers or metal producers solve their worries about price fluctuations during the production-delivery cycle.

This also illustrates that the spot market is always the cornerstone of the futures market, which is dependent on a whole industry chain comprising producers, processors, traders, consumers, and recyclers. And these businessmen are susceptible to commodity price fluctuations and need tools to avoid or manage risks. It is therefore a permanent interdependent relation between the two.

With this understanding, QME will work closely with the commodity industry chains and look to gradually and naturally develop an inseparable relation with spot traders.

(3)   Feature 3: Establishing a warehousing network

Salt, a common household condiment, has over 5,000 years of history and used to be an important commodity that represented a large share of the government's major fiscal revenue throughout the dynasties. As revealed in his travels note, the Italian merchant Marco Polo was amazed at how developed the salt industry was in ancient China when he travelled through Asia in the 13th century.

Back then, salt sellers even engaged armed escorts to ensure smooth and secure delivery of their goods, making it the pioneer of the escort business today. This reflects the importance of the security of goods and properties in commodity trading.

When people are amazed at LME's delivery warehouse network that covers countries around the world, they often forget one thing: this is actually a combination of multiple independent warehouse operators. Some of them were established in the same era as LME, having gone through good times and bad with it for a century and a half.

History teaches us lessons we shall not forget. So again, right from the start we have made the building of a warehousing network an integral part of QME.

Will this embryonic form of QME look reminiscent of LME? Perhaps one day, this small seedling in Qianhai can grow into a lofty tree and work hand in hand with LME as its partner and complement LME in a mutually beneficial manner, the realisation of which will be the very last step of our vision.

Everything starts with a small step. Our team will spare no effort in implementing our plan step by step to make our vision come true. Time will tell whether it works.

4 Hong Kong in support of the internationalisation of the Mainland commodities market

Finance is the lifeblood of an economy. The opening-up of the Mainland financial market is speeding up and has become the main diver of modernisation of China's economy and comprehensive market opening. As a critical part of the financial market, the futures market is endowed with the historic mission of internationalisation under this new market environment.

Presently, there are four possible pathways through which the Mainland futures market could go for internationalisation, each with its own advantages and challenges. Yet Hong Kong is well positioned to take part in any of them by providing various professional support and collaboration.

4.1 Pathway 1: Direct overseas expansion

Multiple attempts of the Mainland commodities market to "go out" and related initiatives are seen in recent years.

Some chose to set up offices in overseas markets, in a bid to enhance international presence and influence, and hence the appeal to global investors. Others chose to apply for Automated Trading Service (ATS) registration with the Hong Kong Securities and Futures Commission (SFC) to undertake ATS business in Hong Kong.

The benefit of this direct approach is that the whole process is under the control of the Mainland institutions. The challenges would be the deeper and more difficult issues of infrastructure building, e.g. the expansion of overseas delivery warehouse network, the increase in global delivery points, the recruitment and administration of international members, etc. And these processes involve quite a number of areas that Mainland institutions might not have much experience in before their internationalisation, especially in respect of the development of legal and regulatory frameworks as well as industry norms in line with international practices. These are all the areas where Hong Kong, being the connector and transformer between the Mainland and the rest of the world, could contribute in a number of ways.

4.2   Pathway 2: "Drawing in" — Drawing overseas investors to the Mainland market

In the light of the internationalisation of the Mainland futures market, a series of provisional measures and guiding notices on such issues as the administration of trading, foreign exchange, contract laws and futures-related disputes, etc. have been issued by the State Council, the China Securities Regulatory Commission, the State Administration of Foreign Exchange and the Supreme People's Court. Under these special arrangements, overseas investors could trade Mainland futures either through domestic futures trading companies, or by entrusting Mainland futures trading companies through overseas brokerages. These transactions are allowed to be settled by commodities in bonded warehouses, and while they are traded and settled in Renminbi, US dollars are accepted for margin purposes. Moreover, a special clearing account can be used for the settlement, remittance and transfer of funds.

This arrangement has been extremely successful. A number of brokerages have signed up for the business and the number of overseas institutional investors is on the rise.

Looking forward, there are still a lot to do. For instance, how shall the entry barriers for overseas investors and brokerages be lowered further? How shall the relationship between overseas brokerages and domestic futures trading companies be extended from a one-way principal-agent one to where direct participation in trading and capital management are possible? And, how can the related laws and regulations and the legal regime be enhanced? Again, Hong Kong could play a part in many of these areas before the comprehensive opening-up of the Mainland market.

4.3   Pathway 3: "Limited connectivity" — "Exporting" China prices

There has long been a market expectation that one day, investors would be able to find listed exchange-traded funds (ETFs) on a particular Chinese commodity or a commodity index on a basket of Chinese commodities in Hong Kong or other overseas markets, which will give foreign investors access to China prices in overseas markets. This would enable international investors to indirectly take part in China's futures market without modifying their investment mandates regarding the scope of markets to invest and under the original terms. This certainly will offer maximum convenience to overseas investors, but more importantly, it will provide a platform on which China prices are visible to the world, and over time improve their coverages and influence in the global markets.

For hedging purposes, ETF issuers will need to buy the underlying assets from the Mainland futures market. So for Mainland exchanges, a popular ETF with substantial subscriptions is going to bring in significant investment demand from overseas, increasing foreign investors' participation in, as well as enhancing the vitality of, the Mainland market.

In such "exports" of China prices, both the Hong Kong platform and the LME of the HKEX Group are able to provide professional support.

4.4 Pathway 4: "Commodities Connect" —— Full-scale connection in commodities

How to help accelerate the internationalisation of the Mainland futures exchanges?

HKEX has joined hands with the Shanghai Stock Exchange and the Shenzhen Stock Exchange to launch Shanghai Connect and Shenzhen Connect (collectively called Stock Connect) respectively in 2014 and 2016. The two programmes have been running smoothly for a number of years, demonstrating to the world a new model of two-way capital market opening. Subsequently in 2017, in collaboration with the China Foreign Exchange Trading System (CFETS), HKEX introduced Bond Connect to link up with the China Interbank Bond Market (CIBM). This is much welcomed by overseas investors.

The implementation of the Mutual Market Access ("MMA") concept is a successful showcase of a win-win collaboration model in both the securities and bond markets. It demonstrates international investors' recognition of Hong Kong as an international financial centre in Asia, and reflects the immense interests of overseas institutions in accessing the Mainland capital market and holding the related financial assets. The collaboration model successfully links up the two capital markets in the Mainland and Hong Kong that have very different institutional setups. While accelerating the opening-up and internationalisation of the Mainland capital market, it highlights Hong Kong's competitive edge of "One Country, Two Systems".

Let's take metal futures as an example. In London, LME connects all the participants along the whole value chain of the industry, right from mining, smelting, trading and processing to recycling, and hence institutional clients from both the physical side and the financial side. On the other hand, there is an extremely large customer base, predominantly retail investors, in the markets of the Mainland futures exchanges. So far there is no interaction between the two. It's simply exciting just to imagine what it will look like if they are brought together in any way.

Should such MMA model be implemented in the commodities futures market segment, we might be able to see a blueprint for a world-class commodities market that goes far beyond the "Mainland-Hong Kong-London" model. With consideration of the current development landscape of the global commodities market and the objective development needs of the Mainland commodities market, this idea of Commodities Connect shall bring a tremendous impetus and have far-reaching implications in respect of the new developments and internationalisation of the Mainland futures market and the enhancement of Hong Kong's status as an international financial centre.

I therefore look forward to exploring opportunities for our futures exchange and commodities trading platform to integrate with the Mainland counterparties, so that on a win-win basis we can all play a part in contributing to the country by improving and enhancing the pricing, the industries and the wider market.

Chapter 2

The global metals market — The rise of China and the current update

LIU Xiaolei

Analyst

SMM Information & Technology Co. Ltd.

Summary

The metals market in China is expanding, as the outputs of steel, aluminium and other metal products account for more than half of the global total supply. The industry participants in the Chinese metals market have increased their reliance on financial instruments such as futures. The number of types of metal being traded on the futures market has increased. In the future, metals such as alumina, magnesium, titanium and manganese may enter futures trading. The trading volume and frequency of related enterprises in the futures market are constantly increasing.

Trading modes of enterprises in the metals industry, such as time and cash arbitrage and internal and external arbitrage, have emerged on the futures exchanges in the Mainland and between the Mainland market and international markets. These have become a prominent force that cannot be ignored in the global commodity trading sector.

Special policies of Mainland characteristics, such as "supply-side reform" and "environmental protection policy", have become important factors influencing the Mainland metals market in addition to supply and demand factors.

As the Chinese market rises, opportunities and challenges coexist, but more importantly, we should be able to see the vitality of the Chinese market in the future. From the perspective of development, the transformation of the Chinese market will produce more means for financial transactions.

1   Overview

1.1   Global market share of China's Ferrous metals

Ferrous metals traditionally refer to the type of metals that are primarily composed of iron, manganese and chromium. Steel is the most widely used ferrous metal, which is a binary alloy with iron-carbon as the main elements. Based on the carbon content, steel can be divided into low carbon steel, medium carbon steel and high carbon steel. Ferrous metals that are actively traded in the market include steel, manganese steel and chromium steel. Ferrous metals that are currently available for futures transactions in Mainland China include rebar, hot-rolled coil, stainless steel, iron ore, ferrosilicon and silicomanganese. According to data from the World Steel Association (WSA), in 2019, there were 62 countries that produced crude steel, and China produced 993 million tonnes (i.e. metric tons, or "mt") in the year, accounting for 53.8% of the global total production.

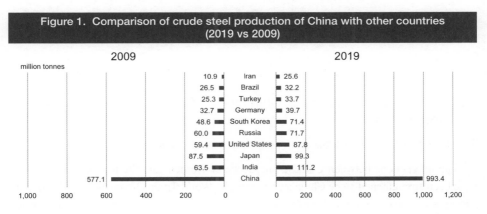

Figure 1. Comparison of crude steel production of China with other countries (2019 vs 2009)

Source: WSA.

1.2   Global market share of China's Non-ferrous metals

Non-ferrous metals are the types of metals other than ferrous metals. Based on unit prices, non-ferrous metals can be divided into base metals and precious metals, which include gold, silver, platinum and palladium. Non-ferrous metals referred to in this paper are the most common base metals including copper, aluminium, lead, zinc, tin and nickel.

Taking aluminium as an example, the world primary aluminium production in 2019 totalled 63.69 million mt, and aluminium production in China accounted for 56.2% or 35.8 million mt, according to data from the International Aluminium Institute (IAI).

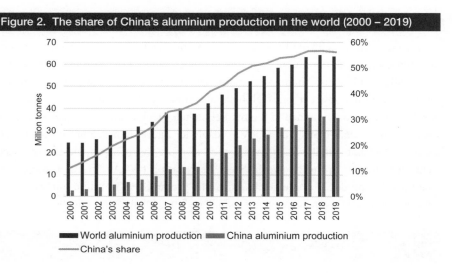

Figure 2. The share of China's aluminium production in the world (2000 – 2019)

Source: International Aluminium Institute (IAI).

1.3 Overseas expansion of China's non-ferrous and ferrous metal industries

1.3.1 Accelerated expansion of overseas market

The interactions between Chinese producers, consumers and the international markets have been strengthened since China's entry into the World Trade Organization (WTO), with strong development in the fields of investment, technology and finance. China has opened up to the world and transformed itself from a self-sufficient market to the world's largest supplier and consumer. The connection between the Mainland and overseas markets has become closer, which in turns reinforces the interdependence of the two sides.

In recent years, Mainland companies have increased their overseas investments, with an increasing number of overseas projects, as reflected in the statistics showing Mainland investment in overseas copper mines (see Table 1).

Table 1. Mainland companies investing in overseas copper mine projects					
Company	Mine project	Location	Shareholding ratio (%)	Year of acquisition	Acquired amount (US$ million)
China Molybdenum	Tenke	D. R. Congo	56	2017	2,650
China Nonferrous Metal Mining	Gecamines	D. R. Congo	—	2017	2,000
China Minmetals	Las Bambas	Peru	63	2015	7,005
Zijin Mining	Kamoa	D. R. Congo	47	2015	412
Zijin Mining	Kolwezi	D. R. Congo	51	2014	480
China Molybdenum	Northparkes	Australia	80	2013	820
China Minmetals	Kinsevere	D. R. Congo	100	2012	1,300
Jinchuan Group	Ruashi	D. R. Congo	75	2012	1,360
Jinchuan Group	Kinsenda	D. R. Congo	85	2012	
Jinchuan Group	Musonoi	D. R. Congo	77	2012	
Jinchuan Group	Lubembe	D. R. Congo	75	2012	
Jinchuan Group	Chibuluma South	Zambia	77	2012	
Tongling Nonferrous Metals Group	Mirador	Ecuador	70	2011	4,411
China Minmetals	Sepon	Laos	90	2010	1,386
China Minmetals	Golden Grove	Australia	100	2010	
China Minmetals	Rosebery	Australia	100	2010	
China Nonferrous Metal Mining	Baluba copper mine, Muliashi copper mine	Zambia	80	2010	50
China Minmetals	EL Galeno	Peru	60	2008	450
China Metallurgical Group (MCC)	Aynak copper mine	Afghanistan	75	2008	3,700
Chinalco	Toromocho	Peru	100	2008	860
Pengxin International Mining	Shituru copper mine	D. R. Congo	80	2008	—
China Railway & Sinohydro Group & MCC	Cuvette Dima mining area	D. R. Congo	Infrastructure construction in exchange for resources	2008	—
Zijin Mining	Rio Blanco copper-molybdenum mine	Peru	80	2007	160

(continued)

Company	Mine project	Location	Shareholding ratio (%)	Year of acquisition	Acquired amount (US$ million)
MCC	Saindak copper-gold mine	Pakistan	Business operations under lease	2001	-
China Nonferrous Metal Mining	Chamishi copper mine	Zambia	85	1999	20

Source: Compiled from publicly available information.

1.3.2 Challenges and opportunities for Chinese metals enterprises' investment overseas

When it comes to investment overseas including mergers and acquisitions, Mainland metals enterprises are faced with challenges. These include: (1) Unfamiliarity with the legal environment of the targeted region of investment may lead to a lack of corresponding legal support when there are changes in tariffs and policies; (2) There is the possibility that the region which is planned for investment may be hit by political instability and turmoil such as war; (3) If the company is not well informed about the culture of the region that it wishes to invest in, it may lead to cultural conflicts and eventually increase the company's operating costs; (4) Mainland enterprises may also face problems such as high indirect investment cost, insufficient infrastructure, workers of low-level literacy and backward technology in the destined region of investment.

In addition to the above-mentioned problems encountered in planning for overseas investment, Mainland enterprises are also facing various challenges in the export of their products. Increasing cases of anti-dumping investigations on Mainland products in recent years have brought considerable operational risks to Mainland companies. (See Figure 3 and Table 2 for an example on aluminium products.)

Figure 3. Number of global anti-dumping cases on China's aluminium products (1995 – 2019)

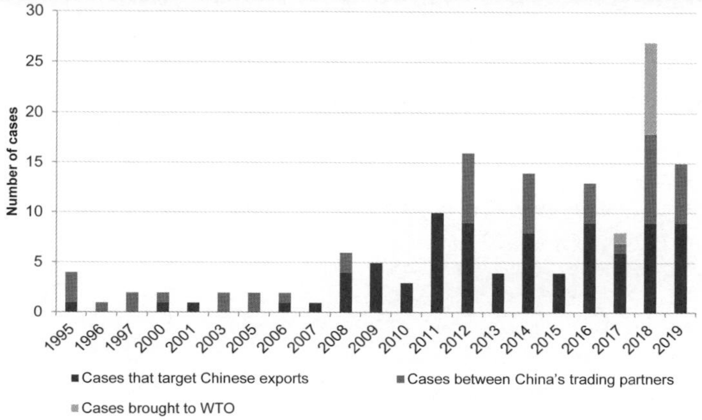

- Cases that target Chinese exports
- Cases between China's trading partners
- Cases brought to WTO

Source: China Trade Remedies Information (CTRI)

Table 2. Anti-dumping cases on China's aluminium products (1995 – Feb 2020)

Anti-dumping case	Type	Date
Anti-dumping case launched by South Africa against Chinese aluminium tableware	Actions against exports from China	15/09/1995
Anti-dumping case launched by South Africa against aluminium tableware produced in Hong Kong, China	Cases among trade members	15/09/1995
Anti-dumping case launched by South Africa against Zimbabwean aluminium tableware	Cases among trade members	15/09/1995
Anti-dumping case launched by South Africa against Egyptian aluminium tableware	Cases among trade members	27/10/1995
Anti-dumping case launched by Argentina against US aluminium chloride	Cases among trade members	23/05/1996
Anti-dumping case launched by EU against Thailand's high-power aluminium electrolytic capacitors	Cases among trade members	29/11/1997
Anti-dumping case launched by EU against US high-power aluminium electrolytic capacitors	Cases among trade members	29/11/1997
Anti-dumping case launched by EU against Chinese aluminium foil	Actions against exports from China	18/02/2000
Anti-dumping case launched by EU against Russian aluminium foil	Cases among trade members	18/02/2000
Anti-dumping case launched by Argentina against Chinese aluminium phosphide pesticide	Actions against exports from China	22/08/2001
Anti-dumping case launched by South Africa against India's overhead aluminium core cables	Cases among trade members	10/10/2003

(continued)

Anti-dumping case	Type	Date
Anti-dumping case launched by US against South African aluminium plate	Cases among trade members	12/11/2003
Anti-dumping case launched by Argentina against India's solid aluminium phosphide	Cases among trade members	15/04/2005
Anti-dumping case launched by Mexico against Venezuelan aluminium hose containers	Cases among trade members	25/11/2005
Anti-dumping case launched by Brazil against Chinese PS plates (pre-coated photosensitive aluminium plates)	Actions against exports from China	18/04/2006
Anti-dumping case launched by Brazil against US PS plates (pre-coated photosensitive aluminium plates)	Cases among trade members	18/04/2006
Anti-dumping case launched by South Africa against Chinese aluminium extrusion	Actions against exports from China	10/08/2007
Anti-dumping case launched by Turkey against Chinese aluminium plate molds	Actions against exports from China	20/03/2008
Anti-dumping case launched by EU against Chinese aluminium foil	Actions against exports from China	12/07/2008
Anti-dumping case launched by EU against Armenian aluminium foil	Cases among trade members	12/07/2008
Anti-dumping case launched by EU against Brazilian aluminium foil	Cases among trade members	12/07/2008
Anti-dumping case launched by Canada against Chinese aluminium extrusion	Actions against exports from China	18/08/2008
Anti-subsidy case launched by Canada against Chinese aluminium extrusion	Actions against exports from China	18/08/2008
Special safeguard measures imposed by India on Chinese aluminium sheet and foil	Actions against exports from China	27/01/2009
Special safeguard measures imposed by India on imported unwrought aluminium and aluminium scrap	Actions against exports from China	22/05/2009
Anti-dumping case launched by Australia against Chinese aluminium extrusion	Actions against exports from China	24/06/2009
Anti-subsidy case launched by Australia against Chinese aluminium extrusion	Actions against exports from China	24/06/2009
Anti-dumping case launched by EU against Chinese aluminium alloy wheels	Actions against exports from China	13/08/2009
Special safeguard measures imposed by Indonesia on imported aluminium foil food containers	Actions against exports from China	19/01/2010
Anti-dumping case launched by US against Chinese aluminium extrusion	Actions against exports from China	27/04/2010
Anti-subsidy case launched by US against Chinese aluminium extrusion	Actions against exports from China	27/04/2010
Anti-dumping case launched by Thailand against Chinese hot-dip galvanised cold-rolled steel, hot-dip plate or aluminium-zinc alloy cold-rolled steel	Actions against exports from China	08/07/2011
Anti-dumping case launched by Thailand against Chinese aluminium-zinc alloy coated plates	Actions against exports from China	08/07/2011

(continued)

Anti-dumping case	Type	Date
Anti-dumping case launched by Colombia against Chinese aluminium laminates	Actions against exports from China	03/08/2011
Anti-dumping case launched by EU against Chinese aluminium radiators	Actions against exports from China	12/08/2011
Australia's anti-dumping case against Chinese aluminium wheels	Actions against exports from China	07/11/2011
Australia's anti-subsidy case against Chinese aluminium wheels	Actions against exports from China	07/11/2011
Australia's anti-dumping case against Chinese aluminium wheels	Actions against exports from China	07/11/2011
Australia's anti-subsidy case against Chinese aluminium wheels	Actions against exports from China	07/11/2011
EU's anti-dumping case against Chinese rolled aluminium foil	Actions against exports from China	20/12/2011
EU's anti-dumping case against Chinese rolled aluminium foil	Actions against exports from China	20/12/2011
Canada's anti-dumping case against Chinese aluminium unitised curtain wall	Actions against exports from China	16/07/2012
Canada's anti-subsidy case against Chinese aluminium unitised curtain wall	Actions against exports from China	16/07/2012
Canada's anti-dumping case against Chinese aluminium unitised curtain wall	Actions against exports from China	16/07/2012
Canada's anti-subsidy case against Chinese aluminium unitised curtain wall	Actions against exports from China	16/07/2012
Australia's anti-dumping case against Taiwanese aluminium-plated zinc plate	Cases among trade members	05/09/2012
Australia's anti-dumping case against Chinese aluminium-plated zinc plate	Actions against exports from China	05/09/2012
Australia's anti-dumping case against South Korean aluminium-plated zinc plate	Cases among trade members	05/09/2012
Australia's anti-dumping case against Taiwanese aluminium-plated zinc plate	Cases among trade members	05/09/2012
Australia's anti-dumping case against Chinese aluminium-plated zinc plate	Actions against exports from China	05/09/2012
Australia's anti-dumping case against South Korean aluminium-plated zinc plate	Cases among trade members	05/09/2012
Australia's anti-subsidy case against Chinese aluminium-plated zinc plate	Actions against exports from China	26/11/2012
Australia's anti-subsidy case against Chinese aluminium-plated zinc plate	Actions against exports from China	26/11/2012
India's anti-dumping case against Chinese casting aluminium alloy wheels or alloy wheels	Actions against exports from China	10/12/2012
India's anti-dumping case against Thailand casting aluminium alloy wheels or alloy wheels	Cases among trade members	10/12/2012

(continued)

Anti-dumping case	Type	Date
India's anti-dumping case against South Korean casting aluminium alloy wheels or alloy wheels	Cases among trade members	10/12/2012
India's anti-dumping case against South Korean casting aluminium alloy wheels or alloy wheels	Cases among trade members	10/12/2012
Colombia's anti-dumping case against Chinese aluminium extrusions	Actions against exports from China	27/02/2013
Canada's anti-dumping case against Chinese aluminium unitised curtain wall	Actions against exports from China	04/03/2013
Canada's anti-subsidy case against Chinese aluminium unitised curtain wall	Actions against exports from China	04/03/2013
Turkey's anti-dumping case against Chinese aluminium foil	Actions against exports from China	21/12/2013
Brazil's anti-dumping case against Chinese aluminium pre-coated photosensitive plate	Actions against exports from China	25/02/2014
Brazil's anti-dumping case against Chinese aluminium pre-coated photosensitive plate	Actions against exports from China	25/02/2014
Brazil's anti-dumping case against aluminium pre-coated photosensitive plate from Hong Kong	Cases among trade members	25/02/2014
Brazil's anti-dumping case against aluminium pre-coated photosensitive plate from Taiwan	Cases among trade members	25/02/2014
Brazil's anti-dumping case against aluminium pre-coated photosensitive plate from the EU	Cases among trade members	25/02/2014
Brazil's anti-dumping case against US aluminium pre-coated photosensitive plate	Cases among trade members	25/02/2014
India's safeguard measures case against imported non-alloy unwrought aluminium ingots	Actions against exports from China	07/04/2014
India's safeguard measures case against imported non-alloy unwrought aluminium ingots	Actions against exports from China	07/04/2014
Trinidad and Tobago's anti-dumping case against Chinese aluminium extrusions	Actions against exports from China	22/08/2014
Trinidad and Tobago's anti-dumping case against Chinese aluminium extrusions	Actions against exports from China	22/08/2014
EU's anti-dumping case against Russian aluminium foil	Cases among trade members	08/10/2014
EU's anti-dumping case against Russian aluminium foil	Cases among trade members	08/10/2014
EU's anti-dumping case against Chinese aluminium foil	Actions against exports from China	12/12/2014
EU's anti-dumping case against Chinese aluminium foil	Actions against exports from China	12/12/2014
Mexico's anti-dumping case against Chinese aluminium cookware	Actions against exports from China	15/04/2015
Mexico's anti-dumping case against Chinese aluminium cookware	Actions against exports from China	15/04/2015

(continued)

Anti-dumping case	Type	Date
India's anti-dumping case against Chinese aluminium foil	Actions against exports from China	15/12/2015
India's anti-dumping case against Chinese aluminium foil	Actions against exports from China	15/12/2015
India's anti-dumping case against China's aluminium radiator, radiator components and radiator core	Actions against exports from China	01/01/2016
India's anti-dumping case against China's aluminium radiator, radiator components and radiator core	Actions against exports from China	01/01/2016
India's safeguard measures case against on imported unforged aluminium	Actions against exports from China	19/04/2016
India's safeguard measures case against on imported unforged aluminium	Actions against exports from China	19/04/2016
Argentina's anti-dumping case against Chinese aluminium alloy wheels	Actions against exports from China	07/07/2016
Argentina's anti-dumping case against Chinese aluminium alloy wheels	Actions against exports from China	07/07/2016
Jordan's safeguard measures case against imported aluminium bars, aluminium rods and aluminium extrusions	Actions against exports from China	24/07/2016
Australia's anti-dumping case against Vietnamese aluminium extrusions	Cases among trade members	16/08/2016
Australia's anti-subsidy case against Vietnamese aluminium extrusions	Cases among trade members	16/08/2016
Australia's anti-dumping case against Malaysian aluminium extrusions	Cases among trade members	16/08/2016
Australia's anti-subsidy case against Malaysian aluminium extrusions	Cases among trade members	16/08/2016
South Korea's anti-dumping case against Chinese aluminium pre-coated photosensitive plates	Actions against exports from China	08/09/2016
Paraguay's anti-dumping case against Chinese aluminium extrusion products	Actions against exports from China	28/09/2016
WTO dispute case on China's primary aluminium subsidy measures	WTO dispute case	12/01/2017
US anti-dumping case against Chinese aluminium foil	Actions against exports from China	28/03/2017
US anti-subsidy case against Chinese aluminium foil	Actions against exports from China	28/03/2017
Mexico's anti-dumping case against Chinese aluminium foil balloon	Actions against exports from China	26/06/2017
Australia's anti-dumping case against Chinese aluminium profiles	Actions against exports from China	19/10/2017
Australia's anti-dumping case against Thailand aluminium profiles	Cases among trade members	19/10/2017
US anti-dumping case against Chinese aluminium alloy thin sheet	Actions against exports from China	28/11/2017

(continued)

Anti-dumping case	Type	Date
US anti-subsidy case against Chinese aluminium alloy thin sheet	Actions against exports from China	28/11/2017
Eurasian Economic Commission (formerly Russia-Belarus Customs Union)'s anti-dumping case against Chinese aluminium wheels	Actions against exports from China	26/02/2018
Eurasian Economic Commission (formerly Russia-Belarus Customs Union)'s anti-dumping case against Chinese casting aluminium turntable	Actions against exports from China	02/03/2018
TWO dispute case on US measures against Chinese steel and aluminium products	WTO dispute case	05/04/2018
Lebanon's anti-dumping case against Chinese special aluminium extrusion	Actions against exports from China	11/05/2018
Lebanon's anti-dumping case against Egyptian special aluminium extrusion	Cases among trade members	11/05/2018
Lebanon's anti-dumping case against Saudi Arabian special aluminium extrusion	Cases among trade members	11/05/2018
Lebanon's anti-dumping case against UAE special aluminium extrusion	Cases among trade members	11/05/2018
WTO dispute case on India's appeal against US tariffs and quotas on steel and aluminium products	WTO dispute case	18/05/2018
WTO dispute case on the EU's appeal against US tariffs measures on steel and aluminium products	WTO dispute case	01/06/2018
WTO dispute case on Japan's appeal against US tariffs measures on steel and aluminium products	WTO dispute case	05/06/2018
WTO dispute case on Canada's appeal against US tariffs measures on steel and aluminium products	WTO dispute case	06/06/2018
WTO dispute case on Norway's appeal against US tariffs measures on steel and aluminium products	WTO dispute case	14/06/2018
Argentina's anti-dumping case against Chinese household aluminium radiators	Actions against exports from China	28/06/2018
Argentina's anti-dumping case against Italian household aluminium radiators	Cases among trade members	28/06/2018
Argentina's anti-dumping case against Spanish household aluminium radiators	Cases among trade members	28/06/2018
WTO dispute case on Switzerland's appeal against US tariffs measures on steel and aluminium products	WTO dispute case	09/07/2018
WTO dispute case on Russia's appeal against US tariffs measures on steel and aluminium products	WTO dispute case	27/07/2018
WTO dispute case on Turkey's appeal against US tariffs measures on steel and aluminium products	WTO dispute case	20/08/2018
Mexico's anti-dumping case against Chinese foil coils	Actions against exports from China	28/08/2018
Indonesia's safeguard measures case on imported aluminium foil coils	Actions against exports from China	09/10/2018
US anti-dumping case against Chinese aluminium wire and cable	Actions against exports from China	12/10/2018

(continued)

Anti-dumping case	Type	Date
US anti-subsidy case against Chinese aluminium wire and cable	Actions against exports from China	12/10/2018
Pakistan anti-dumping case against Turkish aluminium beverage bottles	Cases among trade members	01/11/2018
Pakistan anti-dumping case against Sri Lanka aluminium beverage bottle	Cases among trade members	01/11/2018
Pakistan anti-dumping case against Jordan aluminium beverage bottle	Cases among trade members	01/11/2018
Pakistan's anti-dumping case against UAE aluminium beverage bottles	Cases among trade members	01/11/2018
Mexico's anti-dumping case against Chinese aluminium high-pressure cooker	Actions against exports from China	20/12/2018
Vietnam's anti-dumping case against Chinese aluminium profiles	Actions against exports from China	11/01/2019
Argentina's anti-dumping case against Chinese aluminium plate	Actions against exports from China	25/02/2019
Argentina's anti-dumping case against Chinese aluminium foil	Actions against exports from China	08/03/2019
India's anti-dumping case against Chinese aluminium-zinc plated alloy flat rolled steel products	Actions against exports from China	02/04/2019
India's anti-dumping case against Vietnamese aluminium-zinc plated alloy flat rolled steel products	Cases among trade members	02/04/2019
India's anti-dumping case against South Korean aluminium-zinc plated alloy flat rolled steel products	Cases among trade members	02/04/2019
Eurasian Economic Commission (formerly Russia-Belarus Customs Union) anti-dumping case against Chinese aluminium strip	Actions against exports from China	07/05/2019
Eurasian Economic Commission (formerly Russia-Belarus Customs Union) anti-dumping case against Azerbaijan aluminium strip	Cases among trade members	07/05/2019
Argentina's anti-dumping case against Chinese aluminium tubes	Actions against exports from China	07/05/2019
Argentina's anti-dumping case against Brazilian aluminium tubes	Cases among trade members	07/05/2019
Ukrainian anti-dumping case against Chinese aluminium wheels	Actions against exports from China	19/07/2019
Ukrainian anti-dumping case against Russian aluminium wheels	Cases among trade members	19/07/2019
Mexico's anti-dumping case against Chinese aluminium discs	Actions against exports from China	09/08/2019
Indonesia's anti-dumping case against Chinese aluminium-zinc coated steel	Actions against exports from China	26/08/2019
Indonesia's anti-dumping case against Vietnam's aluminium-zinc coated steel	Cases among trade members	26/08/2019
Brazil's anti-dumping case against Chinese seamless steel and seamless aluminium-alloy gas cylinders	Actions against exports from China	31/01/2020

(continued)

Anti-dumping case	Type	Date
EU's anti-dumping case against Chinese aluminium extrusions	Actions against exports from China	14/02/2020
Australia's anti-dumping case against Chinese aluminium extrusions	Actions against exports from China	17/02/2020

Source: CTRI.

Following the rise of protectionism, the United States (US) has raised tariffs and other barriers to trade with other nations including China since 2018, in order to spur the reshoring of US manufacturing. This has hit Mainland metals companies and is also a fresh challenge faced by Mainland metals companies since China joined the WTO in 2001.

Mainland non-ferrous and ferrous metals enterprises are gaining maturity in dealing with these challenges. Mainland companies are venturing overseas as they have accumulated knowledge on the overseas markets and seen success stories. Meanwhile, Mainland China is also changing its development mode from resource and energy consuming, labour intensive to technological, environmentally-friendly and sustainable. This trend brings not only challenges but also more opportunities. With years of manufacturing experience, Mainland China is shifting towards a market-oriented economy.

2 Importance of China's metals market

2.1 Intrinsic pricing demand in China's metals market

New exchanges and trading products in the metals market have emerged after the establishment of the London Metal Exchange (LME) which has over 140 years of experience in metals trading. Nowadays, commodity pricing may not rest only with physical demand and supply ever since the launch of financial derivatives such as futures and options, with increased speculation, arbitrage and hedging activities.

Financial concepts are emerging and receding in this market. Pricing remains the basic function of commodity futures demanded by global commodities market participants ever since the products first came into existence. Futures contracts are harnessed as an important financial tool in price discovery and hedging of commodities in the global market today.

2.2   Increasing financial penetration of China's metals market

The Shanghai Futures Exchange (SHFE) and the Dalian Commodity Exchange (DCE) have been playing an increasingly important role in China's metal futures market. They have together launched over 10 metal contracts. The Mainland steel industry and investing institutions rely heavily on the SHFE and the LME. Metal producers that are engaged in foreign trade and investment would rely much on the LME, while smelters and traders that focus on the Mainland market rely more heavily on the SHFE.

As the Chinese economy continues to develop, the pricing power of China has strengthened as its market share in the global metals market increases. Mainland metal producers and investors have gained knowledge from overseas markets, and helped forming independent and evolving metal futures and spot markets in Mainland China.

2.3   Opportunities and challenges to overseas markets imposed by the metals spot and futures markets in China

There is a shift of focus of the Mainland market opening-up from the physical sectors to the financial sectors. Chinese capital has been among the most dynamic ones in the global commodities space, the Chinese metals market has also become one of the key focuses of the world. As the Mainland market continues to open up, the interactions between Mainland and foreign capitals in the metals market is becoming more apparent.

China's metals market has significant impacts on the international metals market. For instance, aluminium capacity in China has been expanding due to the advantage of low costs. This resulted in an oversupply of global primary aluminium, forcing existing high-cost capacity out of the market and changing the aluminium industry landscape. China's aluminium products have accounted for an increasing share in overseas market after joining the WTO. China's production of primary aluminium accounted for about 11.3% of the global total production in 2000, and the ratio increased by about 44.9 percentage points to 56.2% over the past two decades. China provides low-cost raw materials for the overseas markets and also exerted a profound impact on the existing modes of trade and pricing.

In terms of trading mode, for instance, Mainland metal smelting enterprises can import raw materials such as bauxite, alumina and coal, to process them into electrolytic aluminium, and then export to overseas markets. Advantages in scale and technology and relatively low energy costs helped Mainland exporters drive high-cost competitors from other countries out of the market. In addition, technology and scale improvement in China's aluminium processing sector prompted some aluminium companies from countries such as Japan and Russia to carry out processing trade in China to reduce the production cost of intermediate products.

In terms of trade mode, there has been an increasing number of Mainland smelters, traders, and downstream processors that have engaged in futures hedging and regular spot trade. The relevant metal market participants can either choose to hedge with futures contracts traded on the SHFE to lock in smelting profits and avoid price risks, or hedge with futures on the LME to lock in forward prices. Those actions have improved the overall trading volume and activity of the exchanges.

In terms of pricing mechanism, with the expansion of production and trade scale, Mainland companies have actively engaged in the metal pricing function that relies on LME metals trades. But the original raw material pricing mechanism started to change, following the increase in the number and variety of metals and processed products exports from China. For example, Mainland aluminium processing companies recommend metals spot prices or indices published by independent third-party agencies such as Shanghai Metals Market (SMM) to overseas consumers to be used as a settlement for their benchmarks. This shows that Mainland companies are aware of the importance to commodities pricing, especially the pricing power of metal-related products.

In addition to being the key global supplier of raw materials, China is also the most dynamic consumption market in the world. China's metals and related futures markets have broadened the spot metals trading market and futures investment market with their endogenous power. Overseas investors can trade on existing overseas exchanges, such as the LME, as well as on exchanges in Mainland China, the largest commodities supply and consumer market, and increasingly able to sustain investment capital.

The price spreads on metal commodities between Mainland and overseas markets often create new arbitrage models. This is evidenced from the observation on the long-term relationship between the aluminium price ratio between the products on SHFE and the LME. China's aluminium exports help achieve demand and supply balances in the domestic and overseas markets. The response time to reach a balance via the import and export of physical goods between the Mainland and overseas markets was longer than that for SHFE's and LME's futures price movements, which are usually gauged by the ratio of SHFE prices to LME prices. This creates arbitrage opportunities between the Mainland and overseas markets. If LME aluminium prices rise on primary aluminium shortages overseas and do so faster than SHFE prices, the SHFE/LME aluminium price ratio will fall. When the SHFE/LME aluminium price ratio falls below 6.5, market participants could consider selling LME aluminium and buying SHFE aluminium for arbitrage. LME aluminium prices will drop after an increase in China's aluminium exports, which helps fill the supply gap overseas, while SHFE aluminium prices will receive support. (See Figures 4 and 5.)

Figure 4. Aluminium price ratio of SHFE to LME (3-M) (2 Jan 2014 – 19 Mar 2020)

Note: "3-M" refers to 3-month futures contract.

Source: LME, SHFE.

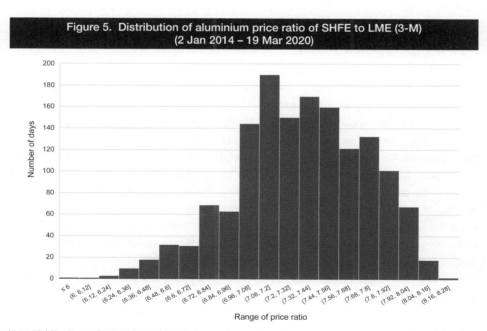

**Figure 5. Distribution of aluminium price ratio of SHFE to LME (3-M)
(2 Jan 2014 – 19 Mar 2020)**

Note: "3-M" refers to 3-month futures contract.

Source: LME, SHFE.

3 The Mainland spot and futures metals markets

3.1 Current status

Metals futures and spot markets were gradually formed during the boom in the Chinese metal industry since 1980s when China began its economic reform and market opening. Since then, China is in great need for raw materials for the economic development and Chinese enterprises grasp the opportunity to expand supply. The two markets, however, are subject to deliverable brands on the SHFE and LME. Many on-exchange tradable metals which are not the deliverable brands cannot be delivered. Other metals which cannot be traded on exchanges are traded off-exchange. Spot markets are tremendous in size compared to the on-exchange futures market, providing a huge space of development for the futures market.

3.2 Hedging and arbitrage operations

Metals producers can efficiently hedge their risks using the futures market. Here is an illustration. In March, a primary aluminium smelter produces at a cost of RMB 13,000 per mt, with the spot price of primary aluminium standing at RMB 14,000 per mt and the price of the futures contract for May delivery at RMB 14,300 per mt. To lock in spot profits in May, the producer sells May contracts of aluminium futures. In May, in the event that futures aluminium price increases to RMB 14,500 per mt and spot price rises to RMB 14,200 per mt, the producer loses RMB 200 per mt on futures and gains profits of RMB 200 per mt in the spot market, keeping its overall profits flat at RMB 1,000 per mt. In the event that futures price declines to RMB 14,000 per mt with spot price falling to RMB 13,700 per mt, the producer makes a profit of RMB 300 per mt on futures, which is offset by a loss of RMB 300 per mt in spot trading. Therefore, the aluminium producer is able to mitigate risk from price fluctuations through hedging practices on the futures market.

Besides, different price formation mechanisms in the spot and futures markets of metals would generate room for arbitrage between the two markets. Spot market participants, such as domestic smelters, miners, processing companies and traders, settle their metal transactions with reference to the daily price quotes in the spot market by a third party, such as SMM. The quotes by the third party for the transaction objects, mostly non-deliverable metal products, are generated based on spot trades with reference to inventories, sales and purchases. Futures prices are derived from trading parties including smelters, traders and downstream processing companies, and the objects of transaction are standard deliverable warrants.

Taking primary aluminium as an example, the daily quotes of SMM A00 spot aluminium ingots are taken as benchmark prices in the spot market, and a fixed price premium/discount is generated on a daily basis for SMM A00 spot aluminium ingots relative to the SHFE front-month contract. The premium/discount is assessed during the trading hours where transactions are most concentrated during the day (see Figure 6). When the spot price of SMM A00 primary aluminium is lower than the futures price, traders can buy spot cargoes and sell futures at the same time; when the discount narrows as the futures contract is approaching maturity, traders can sell spot cargoes and buy futures to make a profit.

Figure 6. Price spread between SMM A00 aluminium spot and futures (premium/discount) (4 Jan 2010 – 21 Feb 2020)

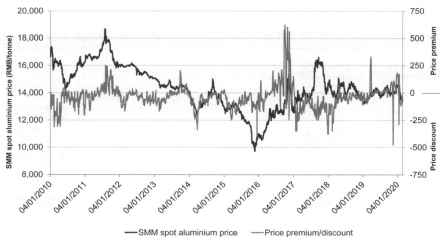

Source: SMM.

This arbitrage operation based on price spread is also applied in copper, zinc, nickel, tin and lead futures markets.

3.3 Different demand for financial derivatives throughout the production cycle in the Mainland metals market

Market participants at different stages of the industry chain have needs for different products in the futures market. Relatively speaking, due to the limited varieties of related futures products, there are still a significant number of metals that have no futures trading, e.g. silicon, magnesium and titanium, which thus lack the corresponding tools to hedge against risks from price fluctuation.

In addition, products at the different stages of the industry chain for a single type of metal also lack the corresponding tools to hedge against risks from price fluctuation due to their different pricing methods. An example is the series of product including bauxite, alumina and others in the aluminium industry chain. While price risks of raw material cost (the cost of primary aluminium) can be hedged against through aluminium futures, there are no related futures to hedge with against price risks of processed aluminium products in the downstream of the aluminium industry chain (see Figure 7).

All in all, there is general aversion among market participants to the risk of price fluctuations and a very strong need for risk hedging for products at different stages of the industry chain.

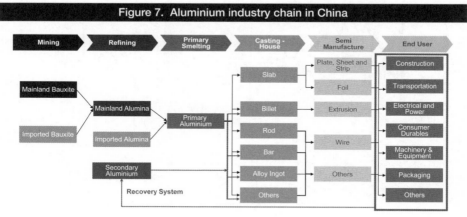

Figure 7. Aluminium industry chain in China

Source: Shanghai Metals Market (SMM).

In general, downstream companies that directly consume primary aluminium as raw materials have a stronger need to use futures as a hedging tool, as compared with upstream miners and alumina companies. Similarly, in the iron and steel market, the upstream raw material iron ore has been traded as a futures product and an independent alumina futures product on the SHFE is in the pipeline. Along with the development of the Mainland metals commodity market, more metals are expected to become futures trading products in the future, which will in turn provide related enterprise with price risk hedging instruments for these products.

Due to the big difference in the pricing models for products at different production stages, there are demand for different futures products at different stages.

For raw material producers, such as aluminium smelters, their main dependence on futures comes from seeking pricing basis for the product and the need for hedging transactions. For downstream consumer enterprises, their dependence on futures mainly comes from futures pricing and hedging functions of futures. Aluminium producers and consumers differ from each other in their use of futures in that aluminium producers are mainly sellers of futures whereas aluminium consumers are mainly buyers of futures. At the same time, with the spot market gradually expanding, the participation of traders as intermediaries has also boosted the need for hedging, and their hedging models are also different. Traders in the spot aluminium market could either sell or buy futures for hedging purpose, depending on the spread between spot and futures prices.

4 Development outlook of China's metals market

4.1 Mid-term to long-term view of the Mainland metal futures market

The trading volumes and value of non-ferrous and ferrous metal futures in the Mainland market increased steadily over time. Taking the SHFE for example, there were only copper and aluminium available for trading on the exchange in 2000. The number of metals listed on the exchange increased to 6 in 2010, comprising copper, aluminium, zinc, gold, rebar and wire rod. The number increased further to 12 by 2019, with the addition of lead, tin, nickel, silver, hot-rolled coil and stainless steel.

The trading value of metal-related futures contracts on the SHFE rose to RMB 81.15 trillion in 2019, with a compound annual growth rate of 6.4% between 2000 and 2019. The corresponding trading volume climbed to 1,037.12 million lots in 2019, with a compound annual growth rate of 7.7% during the same period (see Figures 8 and 9).

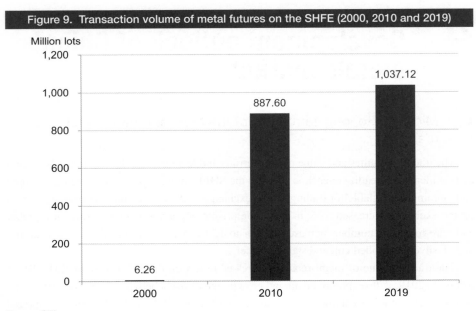

Figure 8. Transaction value of metal futures on the SHFE (2000, 2010 and 2019)

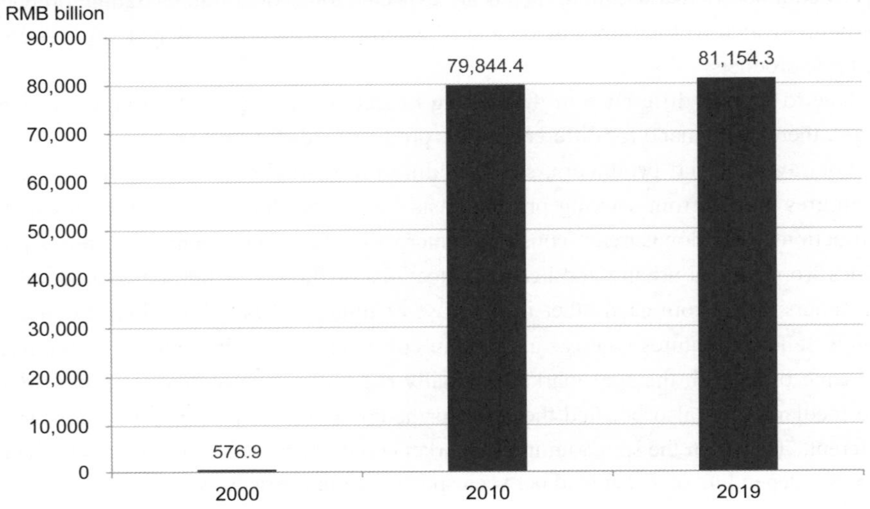

Source: China Futures Association (CFA).

Figure 9. Transaction volume of metal futures on the SHFE (2000, 2010 and 2019)

Source: CFA.

With the further opening-up of the Mainland financial market, we are expecting more overseas investors, smelters, trading firms and downstream processing companies entering the Mainland commodity trading market. In addition, as the Mainland export and import trading business continues to expand, trading volumes of overseas metal commodities by Mainland companies would also have an enormous growth potential.

It is expected that more varieties of metals are likely to be traded in the Mainland futures market, such as alumina, titanium, magnesium and electrolytic manganese. At the same time, the global demand for non-ferrous and ferrous metals remain buoyant, which would sustain an upward trend of the world metal production and an increasing demand for safe-haven financial instruments such as futures.

4.2   Impact of government policies on the Mainland metals market

In the future, China is expected to remain as the world's largest supplier and consumer of metals. As China's traditional heavy industry that had high energy consumption and pollutant emissions is being transformed from volume-driven mode of development to assume sustainable, intelligent and technological development, its demand for financial instruments such as futures has gradually increased across Mainland metal enterprises. For studying metals market movements from the aspects of demand and supply, we need to consider the impact of the environment, tariffs and industry policies on spot and futures prices.

4.2.1   Long-term impact of the supply-side reform policies

During 2016 to 2017, the Chinese government announced supply-side reform policies for coal, steel and aluminium sectors, which strengthened the supervision and administration of market entry into these industries and contained illegal capacities. The policies will have a long-term impact on the growth of China's metals market. The supply-side reform has been expanded from coal, steel and aluminium sectors to electricity, chemical and other commodity sectors. There will be a short-term impact on copper, zinc, nickel and other metals that are in short supply. The reform is likely to further expand to other industries that have excess capacities or unbalanced development.

The supply-side reform has curbed the original mode of "construct first, apply later" for capacity growth, and has established a replacement mechanism for redundant capacities that have high exit costs. This will not only satisfy the current market demand, but will also offer effective support for capacity growth over a period of time in the future. Rigorous regulation is therefore imposed on the operation and development of the entire industry, especially for addressing issues such as resources inequality and disorderly growth.

4.2.2 Impact of stringent environmental policies

Over the 40 years of economic reform, Mainland China's economic development mode has been gradually transformed from the initial mode of "pollute first, treat later" to the mode of "access mechanism".

Along with the improvement of living standards, increasing emphasis has been put on green environment. The ferrous and non-ferrous metals sectors have also increased their investments in environmental protection. Environmental policies will, in the long run, have an impact on the Mainland metals market. For upstream miners and smelters, the additional environmental costs will bolster their mining and production costs. This will translate into higher input costs for downstream sectors which have already been subject to stricter environmental policies. From an economic perspective, the tightening of environmental protection policies will increase the capital investment of enterprises and increase production costs. This will also have a great impact on the current process of the Mainland's transition from an export-oriented economy to an inward-oriented economy. After all, Mainland metal companies still face competition from overseas enterprises. The corresponding increase in production costs will weaken the competitiveness of Mainland metal products against overseas rivals.

5 Conclusion

The metals market in China has evolved over the past 30 years to not only meet the needs of domestic economic development, but has also supported the expansion of the global economy. Market participants in the Chinese metals markets have gained more knowledge on the financial tools and leveraged on financial instruments such as futures. In addition to futures pricing and hedging practices, market participants continue to explore new trading models and arbitrage opportunities in both the Mainland and foreign markets. We have good reasons to believe that, along with the further opening-up of the Mainland economy and the deepening of exchanges between Mainland and overseas markets, more trading varieties and models will emerge to unleash greater market vitality.

Chapter 3

The global agricultural market and the international development strategy of China's agricultural futures market

JIAO Jian

Vice President, COFCO Futures Co., Ltd
President of Futures Research Institute, COFCO Futures Co., Ltd

Summary

The agricultural product futures market is a major component of the agricultural product market. Since the establishment of the first futures exchange, Chicago Board of Trade (CBOT), in 1848, the international agricultural futures market has made great progress. Nowadays, major agricultural countries have established agricultural futures exchanges, covering major categories of agricultural products. CBOT and ICE have become the pricing centres for major agricultural products. Since 1988, Mainland China's futures market has experienced four stages of development: initial exploration, rectification, standardisation and comprehensive development. Since 2000, Mainland China's agricultural futures market turns to the real economy, and the functioning of the futures market has been increasingly improved. Price discovery and hedging functions have been deeply applied, "futures + insurance" and hedging by means of options combined with futures and other innovative applications have also made great progress. The internationalisation process has been increasingly accelerated too. On the current backdrop of the globalisation of agricultural markets, opportunities and challenges coexist in the Mainland agricultural product futures market. Reforms should be deepened in respect of new products development and product delisting, modification of mechanisms, legislation and supervision, innovations, internationalisation and other aspects.

1   Trends of the global agricultural market

1.1   The basic landscape of the global agricultural market

1.1.1   Plantation, trade and consumption of agricultural products

The main farming products in the world can be divided into 4 classes: cereals, oilseeds, sugar and cotton. The diverse climate and agricultural means of production (quality of soil and seeds, and agricultural techniques) across the world lead to the uneven distribution of main products, but each kind has a relatively stable contribution to crop production. The main crop production in 2019 was concentrated in North America (19%), Eastern Asia (19%), Southern Asia (13%), South America (13%) and Europe (11%) (see Figure 2). Cereals (grains as the representative kind) are mainly planted in Asia, North America, South America and the European Union (EU); oilseeds (soybean and rapeseeds as the representative kinds) in North America, South America and Eastern Asia; sugar crops in South America, European Union and Southern Asia; and cotton in North America and Asia.

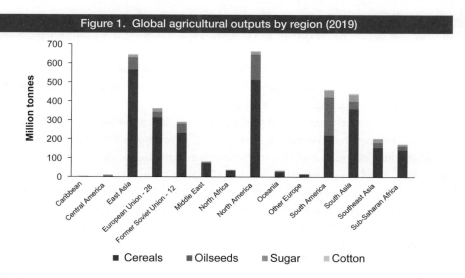

Figure 1. Global agricultural outputs by region (2019)

Source: United States Department of Agriculture (USDA), Wind, COFCO Futures.

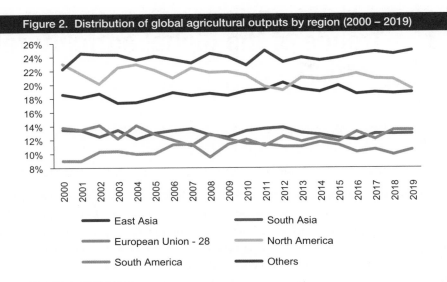

Figure 2. Distribution of global agricultural outputs by region (2000 – 2019)

Source: USDA, Wind, COFCO Futures.

The comparative advantages in agricultural resources and productivity are not only the reason of diversity in agricultural production, but also the internal driving force of the global trades in agricultural products, with which a country can balance its agricultural supply and demand and achieve different goals on agricultural development. After years of trade and development, current global agricultural trades show a trend of trade shifting from North America and Oceania to the Eurasian Continent, with five main flows below:

(1) Trade flows from North America to Eastern Asia, with China as the main destination;

(2) Trade flows from South America to Eastern Asia, with China as the main destination;

(3) Trade flows between EU member countries;

(4) Trade flows between North America, Central America and South America; and

(5) Trade flows from Australia to Asia, with China as a major destination.

After a long period of evolution in intercontinental trades, the global agricultural market shows the following characteristics: (1) Asia (China as the core) is the important region for the production, consumption and import of agricultural products; (2) North America (the United States (US) as the core) and South America are important regions for the production and export of agricultural products; and (3) the EU region is basically self-sufficient in agricultural production and consumption.

In parallel with trade flows, there are three main consumption regions of world agricultural products: (1) the densely, populated Asian region (China as the core consumer);

(2) the North America region (the US as the core consumer) which has massive per-capita consumption of agricultural resources; and (3) the densely populated and developed European region.

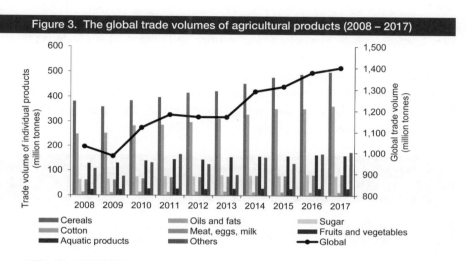

Figure 3. The global trade volumes of agricultural products (2008 – 2017)

Source: USDA, Wind, COFCO Futures.

Cereals and oilseeds have the largest global trade volumes among all agricultural products. The most significant export destinations of these products are North and South America, while the main exporters are the US, Brazil and Argentina. Production and processing of these products are often separately conducted in different parts of the world — primary farming products are sold to consumer countries where they are further processed. One exception is Argentina in oilseed trades, which mainly exports extracted oil rather than oilseeds, for gaining more profit margin on its processed agricultural products in the light of its comparative advantage in the industry.

1.1.2 Overview of the international agricultural futures market

The agricultural product futures market is a major component of the agricultural product market. Since the establishment of the first futures exchange, Chicago Board of Trade (CBOT), in 1848, the international agricultural futures market has made great progress based on the huge agricultural spot market. Nowadays major agricultural countries have established agricultural futures exchanges, covering major categories of agricultural products, as shown in Table 1. Among the major agricultural futures exchanges, the CBOT now under the CME Group and the Intercontinental Exchange (ICE) are the most influential ones. At present, the spot trading of grain, oil, sugar, and cotton in the international market uses the corresponding commodity futures prices at CBOT and ICE as the benchmark prices.

The agricultural futures listed on the CBOT are mainly classified as cereals and oilseeds. Cereal futures include corn, wheat, oats and rice, and oilseed futures include soybeans, soybean meal and soybean oil. The agricultural futures listed on the ICE are mainly soft commodity futures, including cotton, sugar, cocoa and coffee. A slowly rising trend is observed in the open interests of agricultural commodity futures listed on the CBOT and ICE; and the market is very liquid, with the trading volume far exceeding the production volumes of the commodities.

Table 1. Major agricultural futures exchanges in the world			
Futures exchange	Country	Agricultural product types	Number of futures product classes
CBOT	USA	Cereals, oilseeds	7
ICE	USA	Soft commodities, juice	5
Chicago Mercantile Exchange (CME)	USA	Animal products, forest products	4
Dalian Commodity Exchange (DCE)	China	Cereals, oilseeds, egg	9
Zhengzhou Commodity Exchange (ZCE)	China	Cereals, oilseeds, soft commodities	13
Bursa Malaysia Derivatives Exchange (BMD)	Malaysia	Palm oil	1

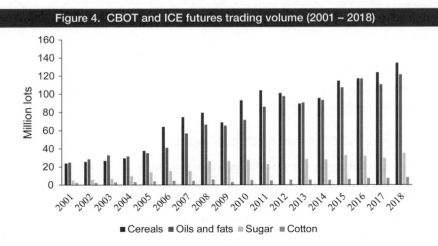

Figure 4. CBOT and ICE futures trading volume (2001 – 2018)

■ Cereals ■ Oils and fats ■ Sugar ■ Cotton

Source: Bloomberg, Wind, COFCO Futures.

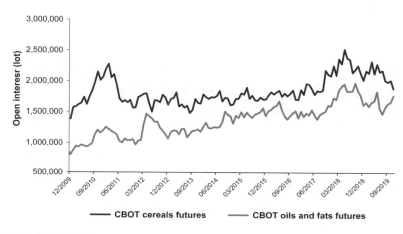

Figure 5. Month-end open interest of cereals and oils and fats futures on CBOT
(Dec 2009 – Nov 2019)

Source: USDA, Wind, COFCO Futures.

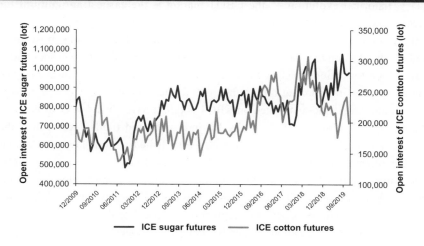

Figure 6. Month-end open interest of cotton and sugar futures on ICE
(Dec 2009 – Nov 2019)

Source: USDA, Wind, COFCO Futures.

Figure 7. Month-end open interest of cocoa and coffee futures on ICE (Dec 2009 – Nov2019)

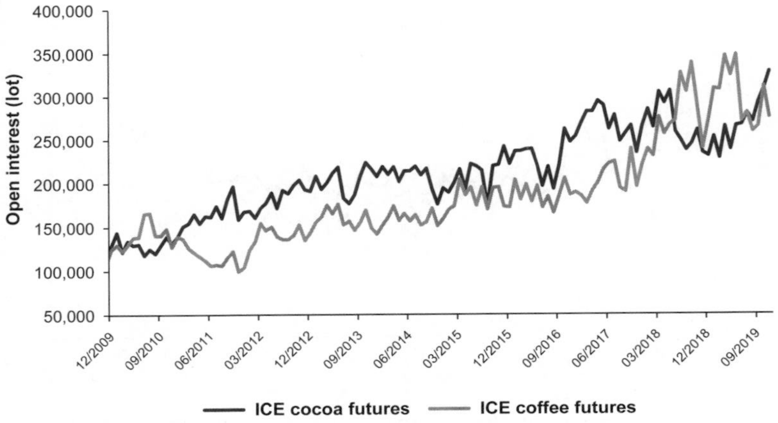

Source: USDA, Wind, COFCO Futures.

There are three main reasons why CBOT and ICE have become the pricing centres for agricultural products:

(1) Historical evolution — the CBOT market is the earliest agricultural futures market, and is currently the world's largest agricultural futures trading market;

(2) Regional advantages — the US is currently one of the world's most important agricultural production regions, and has a natural geographical advantage in spot trade;

(3) Price formation efficiency and institutional governance — transaction volume and liquidity play an important role in the price formation process. The trading volumes of agricultural futures products listed on CBOT and ICE have always been at the forefront of the world, providing ample liquidity for industries and funds. Alongside, the US government and related institutions have also established various laws and policies to ensure the efficiency of the futures market. The US government provides legal protection for the futures market through the introduction of futures administration law, restricted speculation law and commodity trading law[1]. The US Commodity Futures Administration Commission also launched a series of regulations to regulate the futures market, timely analyse the data and information of member companies, together with the large position

---

1   See YANG Xia. (2014) "Comparison of the agricultural futures market between China and America" (〈中美農產品期貨市場比較研究〉), Dalian Maritime University.

reporting system, the system for hedging transactions, holding limits and other means to ensure an open and fair market. Though heavily regulated, the trading environment is relatively less stringent and more flexible in terms of price volatility, the delivery system and futures-spot transformation, so as to reduce restrictions on investors and to facilitate smooth trading.

1.2   Globalised food corporate groups

Global food corporate groups play an extremely important role in the global agricultural trade. Multinational food corporate groups ship food and raw materials from the production regions to sales regions. They are represented by ABCCDE (ADM, Bunge, Cargill, COFCO, Louis Dreyfus and Yihai Kerry) which in aggregate control more than 80% of the global food trade, forming a "dumbbell-shaped" pattern of global food trade[2]. At the two ends of the dumbbell are respectively the large groups of producers and consumers of agricultural products, and in the middle of the dumbbell are the multinational food corporate groups with ABCCDE as the core[3].

In the long-term competition of international food merchants, the entire industrial chain landscape of the international agricultural market has been formed, and major multinational food corporate groups have gradually evolved from food warehousing trade to diversified multinational groups. They have established the entire agricultural industry chains centred on their core businesses. Take the long-established four major food producers "ABCD" as an example, ADM focuses its business on biofuels, Bunge on the construction of the industrial chain in South America, Cargill on its the well-developed logistics system, while Louis Dreyfus focuses more on risk management. However, they have all made great efforts in the vertical development of the entire agricultural industrial chain, being involved in the different stages of production, storage, transportation, processing and sales[4].

Large international grain producers act as the producers of agricultural products and the suppliers of agricultural resources at the upstream, play the role of agricultural product processors at midstream, and at downstream use their respective comparative advantages in logistics to control product circulation and sales, allocate resources rationally, and reduce

2   Source: YANG Chuanli. (2015) "Insights of the development mode of large-scale multinational grain enterprises to Chinese grain enterprises" (〈大型跨國糧食企業發展模式對中國糧食企業發展的啟示與借鑒〉), Yunnan University.

3   See ZHANG Xiuqing. (2014) "Research on the operation mode of the four international grain companies" (〈國際四大糧商運作模式研究〉), *International Economic Cooperation*,(《國際經濟合作》), Vol. 2014(9), pp.40-44.

4   See LIANG Jingli. (2015) "Comparative analysis of grain futures market at home and abroad" (〈國內外糧食期貨市場對比分析〉), Henan Normal University.

intermediary costs[5]. In addition, in order to cope with the risks of agricultural product price fluctuations, international grain merchants use their comparative advantages and experience in the agricultural sector to do risk hedging and capital management for themselves and for their customers, such that they can continue stable operation under high-risk business environment[6].

Although large international grain merchants have comparative advantages in their development in the industry, their models are not unique. In recent years, many multinational companies in other industries have also started to actively arrange global agricultural trade. Examples are Glencore, Marubeni, Sumitomo, Bayer, which have developed into a new type of food trader. Facing the competition of new strong comers, the long-established international grain merchants will further explore their advantages in the landscape of the entire industrial chain while refocusing their businesses, and use their accumulated experience in their long-term development to meet the challenges[7].

2 Development of China's agricultural futures market

2.1 Four stages of development

The futures market in the Mainland began to develop in 1988. After more than 30 years, it has made significant achievements. It not only plays an important role in mitigating the risks of price fluctuations for enterprises in the real economy, but has also gradually become an important component of China's contemporary emerging capital market for asset allocation by investors. The history of the Mainland futures market can be divided into four stages — initial exploration, rectification, standardisation and comprehensive development.

---

5   See LI Xuezhu. (2014) "Research on global agricultural trade and international competitiveness of Chinese agricultural products" (〈全球農產品貿易與中國農產品國際競爭力研究〉), *Agricultural Economy*, (《農業經濟》), Vol. 2014(8), pp.108-109.

6   See YANG Xiaodong. (2018) "The new development of world food trade and its impact on China's food security" (〈世界糧食貿易的新發展及其對中國糧食安全的影響〉), Jilin University.

7   See ZHANG Liyang and ZHANG Xicai. (2011) "The impact of external shocks on the price fluctuation of agricultural products in China: A perspective of agricultural industrial chain" (〈外部衝擊對我國農產品價格波動的影響研究 —— 基於農業產業鏈視角〉), *Management World*, (《管理世界》), Vol. 2011(01), pp.79-89.

Table 2. Four stages of commodity futures market development in the Mainland		
Stage	Period	Significant event
Initial exploration	1988 - 1994	October 1990, China's first commodity futures market commenced in Zhangzhou
		October 1992, the first futures brokerage company was set up
Rectification	1994 - 2000	Two rounds of rectification of the futures market in 1993 and 1998 respectively, retaining only three futures exchanges
		1999, a series of futures rules, including the *Provisional Regulations on the Administration of Futures Trading*, were introduced
		December 2000, China Futures Association was established to be the first self-regulatory organisation in the industry
Standardisation	2000 - 2010	May 2006, China Futures Margin Monitoring Centre was established
		March 2007, the State Council promulgated the *Regulations on the Administration of Futures Trading*
Comprehensive development	2010 to present	April 2010, CSI 300 Index futures were launched
		March 2017, the first commodity option were launched
		March 2018, the first internationalised product — crude oil futures — was launched
		The number of futures derivatives in the Mainland reached 70 before October 2019

Source: COFCO Futures.

During the development of the Mainland futures market in more than three decades, the agricultural futures market has also gone through four stages of development. The agricultural futures market emerged and has developed into a regularised mode of operation and innovation, with continuous improvement[8].

(1)   Initial exploration stage (1988 – 1994)

In June 1988, the State Council began a pilot programme on the futures market, approving pilot trading of futures on the Zhengzhou Grain Wholesale Market (ZGWM) at the end of 1990, forming the Mainland's China's first commodity futures market. The introduction of standardised futures contracts on the ZGWM in June 1993 marked the formal completion of the transition to the futures market. After ZGWM, a number of exchanges began to emerge, which were engaged in agricultural futures business. As of the end of 1993, the number of domestic futures exchanges reached 38. At this stage, the rapidly developing futures market resulted in various market incidents of over-speculation

---

8   See CHANG Qing, "Key choices in the history of Chinese futures" (〈中國期貨史上的關鍵抉擇〉), *Financial Services Development* (《金融業發展》), 8 August 2016.

and cornering the market. For example, some exchanges had even listed coffee futures even though China produces little coffee and its domestic consumption and trade in coffee are extremely low. In addition, in order to attract customers, exchanges competed with each other fiercely, leading to the listing of the same grain and oil futures on different exchanges. In May 1993, the Shanghai Grain and Oil Commodity Exchange launched Japonica futures. In August the same year, natural disasters occurred in China as a result of which grain prices rose higher and higher and bull market prevailed, deteriorating people's livelihood. At that time, the State Council promulgated the *Notice of the State Council on Effectively Resolving the Unregulated Development of the Futures Market on* 12 October 1993, and the Notice effectively restricted the unregulated development of the market.

(2)   The rectification stage (1994 – 2000)

The early days of unregulated development of the futures market led to a series of problems, such as the "9609 futures contract" incident on rice and coffee in 1994, the C513 corn futures' price surge in 1995, and the Tianjin Red Bean Futures incident in 1996. In March 1994, overseas futures trading was suspended in the Mainland. At the same time, the State Council suspended futures trading of rice, rapeseed oil, and sugar. The "327 government bond futures turmoil" in 1995 further prompted the State Council to conduct a second round of rectification of the futures market in 1996. The rectification during this stage significantly reduced the number of agricultural futures products, their trading volume and value. By 1999, futures exchanges in the Mainland were streamlined into three — the Shanghai Futures Exchange (SHFE), the Zhengzhou Commodity Exchange (ZCE) and the Dalian Commodity Exchange (DCE). In November 2000, the China Futures Association was established, and this has much impact on the entire futures industry regulatory system.

(3)   Standardisation stage (2000 – 2010)

In 2001, there were only four agricultural futures products nationwide — mung beans and wheat on the ZCE and soybean meal and soybeans on the DCE. Along with the orderly development of the market, the varieties of agricultural futures have been increasing every year. After ten years of regulated development, the agricultural futures market has been growing rapidly, both in terms of trading volume and trading value. With the establishment of the China Securities Regulatory Commission (CSRC) in 1992, a three-tier regulatory system has been implemented in the Mainland futures market. On 24 June 2006, the establishment of the China Futures Margin Monitoring Centre was approved, which has far-reaching significance in ensuring the safety of funds and safeguarding the interests of investment entities.

(4)   All-round development stage (2010 to present)

As the Mainland futures trading market system has been gradually formed, the types of futures product introduced in the Mainland futures market have gradually diversified and the structure has become increasingly rationalised. Since 2010, the types of agricultural product futures in the Mainland have also increased — as of the end of 2019, there were a total of 22 agricultural futures products, of which 13 were listed on the ZCE and 9 on the DCE. In addition, in 2017, the CSRC approved the ZCE and the DCE to launch option products on white sugar and soybean meal, which became the first domestic on-exchange agricultural options, and marking the formal opening of an options era in the Mainland derivatives market. In January 2019, corn and cotton options were launched.

With the foundation built on futures products, the further development of the market in agricultural options trading can better meet the needs of agricultural enterprises for sophisticated and diversified risk management, improve the price formation mechanism of agricultural products, improve the level of agricultural industrialisation, and accelerate the transformation of the agricultural development model in the Mainland. The innovation of listed products has laid a solid foundation for managing risks in the futures market while developing the domestic market and for gaining the international pricing power of agricultural products[9]. The degree of regularisation and legalisation of the futures market has also increased year by year, with various regulatory systems and legal systems being further enhanced. In May 2014, the State Council promulgated a new "Nine Articles" [10] document, which has far-reaching significance as a high-level policy document for deepening reforms of the Mainland financial market. In 2016, the CSRC issued the *Administrative Measures on the Suitability of Securities and Futures Investors,* which was the first document issued by China for protecting the interests of investors in the securities and futures market.

---

9   See CHANG Qing, "Innovating the way of futures trading and serving the real industry accurately" (〈創新期貨交易方式　精準服務實體產業〉), *China Securities Journal* (《中國證券報》), 8 August 2016.

10   *Opinions of the State Council on Further Promoting the Healthy Development of the Capital Market* (《國務院關於進一步促進資本市場健康發展的若干意見》), 8 May 2014.

Table 3. Changes of agricultural futures products in the Mainland (2001 – 2019)				
Year	Newly launched agricultural futures products on Mainland exchanges			
	ZCE	DCE	Number	Remark
2001	Wheat PM, green gram	Soybean, soybean meal	4	The initial products
2002		No.1 Soybean	4	Name changed
2003	Wheat WH		5	
2004	Cotton	No.2 Soybean, corn	8	
2006	Sugar	Soybean oil	10	
2007	Rapeseed oil	Palm oil	12	
2009	Early indica rice		12	Green gram delisted from ZCE
2012	Rapeseed meal, rapeseed		14	
2013	Japonica rice	Egg	16	
2014	Late indica rice	Corn starch	18	
2017	Cotton yarn, apple		20	
2019	Jujube	Polished round-grained rice	22	

Source: COFCO Futures.

2.2 Agricultural futures market turns to the real economy

Since the Mainland futures market resumed development in 2001, futures exchanges and futures brokerage companies are constantly exploring how to better fulfil the functions of the futures market and serve the real economy. Based on its hedging function, the Mainland futures market has steered towards introducing new structured products based on practical consideration[11]:

(1)   In the early stage of the futures market, the price discovery function was used to solve the problem of the dual-track price system, achieving the goal of unified price formation for commodities and completing the historical mission of commodity price reform.

(2)   Along with the enhancement of the functioning of the futures market and the in-depth application of futures instruments by business enterprises, market participants have become increasingly mature, the market system has been further enhanced, and the futures market's role and function for risk mitigation have been further exerted. This expands the room for innovation.

(3)   As business enterprises have gained benefits from the hedging function, the futures industry begins to explore and study on how to improve services to the real

---

11 See SHEN Panpan, HU Yibo and LI Yanrong. (2019) "Development of agricultural product futures market in China" (〈我國農產品期貨市場現狀及發展路徑〉), *Agricultural Engineering* (《農業工程》), Vol. 9(8), pp.150-152.

economy. Study areas include the application and development of futures pricing method in oilseeds, cotton, and corn. In the field of agricultural products, the 2016-2019 No. 1 Central Document[12] clearly stated the steady expansion of the "futures + insurance" pilot programme. *In the Guiding Opinions on Financial services for Rural Revitalisation* issued jointly by multiple government departments in 2019, it was also proposed to steadily expand the pilot of "insurance + futures" and explore the pilot of "order agriculture + insurance + futures (rights)". During 2016 to 2018, the futures market launched 249 "futures + insurance" pilot projects, including 53 on the SHFE, 66 on the CZCE and 130 on the DCE, involving corn, soybeans, cotton, sugar, apples, and natural rubber, covering 3.95 million tons of spot products, a plantation area of 10.72 million mu, providing price and income security for 390,000 farmers[13].

(4)   Options combined with futures hedging can optimise the efficiency of funds utilisation. Trades embedded with options enable the adoption of different strategies to cope with different trading risks for optimising the trade model. Over-the-counter (OTC) options are reflected in terms of trade terms. Embedding options into ordinary trades to form "trade with options" has formed a new model and new popular practice of determining base spread for soybean meal. More and more risk management companies are combining futures and OTC options businesses in hope of achieving business breakthroughs. Currently, guaranteed floor prices, cap prices and secondary point prices are widely used.

2.3   Internationalisation process of the Mainland agricultural futures market

The internationalisation process of the Mainland agricultural futures market is a process of "bringing in" and "going out". In the initial stage of exploration, Mainland futures companies and investors "went out" to carry out futures trades in foreign markets, such the overseas agency futures trading became increasingly active. However, due to the multiple layers of overseas agency transaction chains and the high costs, conflicts and risk events occurred frequently. In March 1994, the State Council issued an order to ban

---

12 Document No. 1 of the Central Committee of the CPC, 2016-2019: *Certain Opinions on the Implementation of the New Concept of Development to Accelerate the Modernisation of Agriculture to realise the Goal of Achieving an All-round Well-Off Society* (《關於落實發展新理念加快農業現代化實現全面小康目標的若干意見》), *Certain Opinions on Deepening the Supply-Side Structural Reform of Agriculture and Accelerating the Cultivation of New Drivers for Agricultural and Rural Development* (《關於深入推進農業供給側結構性改革加快培育農業農村發展新動能的若干意見》), *Certain Opinions on the Implementation of the Strategy for Rural Revitalisation* (《關於實施鄉村振興戰略的意見》), *Certain Opinions on Giving Priority to Agricultural and Rural Development and Doing a Good Job in the Work Related to Agriculture, Rural Areas and Farmers* (《關於堅持農業農村優先發展做好「三農」工作的若干意見》).
13 Source: China Futures Association.

overseas futures agency business. During the rectification stage, the internationalisation of the Mainland futures market basically halted. With China's accession to the World Trade Organisation (WTO), the internationalisation of the Mainland futures market resumed. Domestic investors "went out" again to obtain the rights to participate in overseas futures trading for hedging. Futures companies were increasingly "going out" to establish branches in Hong Kong and overseas. At the same time, futures exchanges were also stepping up their internationalisation process and seeking breakthroughs.

Product internationalisation is the core part of the internationalisation of the entire futures market. The internationalisation of the Mainland's futures products began in 2018. In that year, crude oil futures were listed and foreign participation has been allowed since its listing, trading of iron ore futures and PTA futures is also opened to foreign investors. These marked the first step in the internationalisation of the Mainland futures market. TSR 20 rubber futures was listed in 2019, becoming the fourth internationalised product in the Mainland. However, in the agricultural product segment, the pace of opening up to foreign investors still needs to be further accelerated[14].

In parallel with China's increasingly important economic status in the world, the Mainland agricultural futures market should shift from simply building up a domestic commodity pricing centre to becoming an internationalised futures market with international pricing power, so that "Chinese price" could also become an important component in the world's agricultural market pricing. The development of the Mainland agricultural futures market should integrate with the current pace of the Mainland's capital market opening to the outside world, explore the ideas and strategies for opening up to the world by actively launching agricultural futures products for foreign participation on agricultural products that have a huge share in international trade. At the same time, the market should continue to improve the relevant policies and regulations on market opening to reduce the unnecessary restrictions on market entry of foreign investors, so as to proactively attract foreign participation.

In addition, the opening-up of the Mainland agricultural futures market should also be accelerated, with expansion in the scope of qualified foreign institutional investors so as to enable more foreign investors to participate in the domestic agricultural futures market, and strengthen the mobility of investing communities between the domestic and foreign futures markets. Besides, the number and types of market investment entities should be increased, and the interaction and cooperation between domestic and foreign investment entities should be enhanced, so as to promote the development of the domestic investor base.

---

14 See HU Yuyue, "The choice for the Internationalisation path of China's futures market" (〈我國期貨市場國際化的路徑選擇〉), *Futures Daily* (《期貨日報》), 9 September 2016.

3 Prospects of the global agricultural spot and derivatives markets

3.1   Changes in the globalisation landscape of agricultural markets

The global integration of agricultural markets has caused a huge flow of agricultural production factors and capital. As the scale of trade continues to expand, the degree of interdependence between countries has become higher and higher. However, with the emergence of trade tensions between China and the US in recent years, the global integration of the agricultural industry will inevitably change.

Agricultural trade is a kind of fundamental trade. Trade competition in different agricultural products is mainly realised through price setting, geographical advantages and added value. Besides, agricultural trade competition also arises from the substitutability in terms of product and geography. There has been a long-term game between market-based activities and government's administrative intervention, and agricultural trade barriers emerged as a result.

The trade tensions between China and the US in recent years helped to break the old barriers to global agricultural trade, prompting governments to review national food security, to actively reduce agricultural trade barriers, to reduce unilateral dependence on international agricultural trade, and to build diversified agricultural trade channels and modes.

The establishment of diversified agricultural trade channels and modes will lead to changes in agricultural development policies and directions between countries. The comparative advantages in industrial layout and industrial chain of established international grain merchants may be weakened, and new competitive companies may gain opportunities of development or expansion. They may use their comparative advantages in certain niches to participate in international agricultural trade. This was exactly the development path of the established international grain merchants represented by ABCD. In the development process of more than a century, the established international grain merchants experienced several times of impact from era changes and war, but each time they saw the impacts as development opportunities. By deepening their industrial layout or exploiting trade routes, they continuously enhance their vitality and competitiveness. The trade tensions between China and the US has disrupted global agricultural integration, which is both a challenge and an opportunity for enterprises engaged in the different stages of the agricultural industry chain.

3.2 Opportunities and challenges to the Mainland agricultural market

At present, the development of the Mainland agricultural futures market has become more and more important in the world. However, there are only a small number of products in the Mainland market which also lacks pricing power. In the context of the "new-normal" development mode of the Mainland economy, the marketisation of agricultural products has accelerated and the prices of agricultural products have fluctuated frequently. Besides, the economic and trade friction between China and the US since 2018 has further aggravated the volatility and risks of domestic agricultural futures. The price discovery and hedging functions of agricultural futures are yet to be enhanced. After more than 30 years of development, the international competitiveness of the DCE and the ZCE has been continuously improving. However, they are still unable to achieve futures pricing power as developed markets in the US and Europe such as CME or ICE. There is still much room for improvement in their core competitiveness[15].

In the current new era of changes, the Mainland futures industry needs to change and its agricultural futures market is facing unprecedented opportunities and challenges:

(1) Expanding new product range of agricultural futures

Currently, the types of agricultural futures in the Mainland are just a few and the futures product structure is not quite rational. It is suggested that qualified new agricultural futures products should be developed as soon as possible, such as hog futures and garlic futures.

(2) Improving the product range structure, the delisting and modification mechanisms

Among listed agricultural futures products in the Mainland, only soybean meal, cotton, sugar, soybean oil, palm oil and corn have relatively high percentage shares in terms of

---

15 See ZHANG Guosheng and WANG Wenju. (2019) "The stage-wise characteristics and future prospects of China's futures market" (〈中國期貨業發展的階段性特徵及未來展望〉), *Economics and Management Studies* (《經濟管理研究》), Vol. 40(11), pp.41-55.

open interest. Other product types have relatively small shares, resulting in unreasonable structure and imbalance. Due to reasons such as contract design, capital flow, market knowledge of the underlying asset and the design of the delivery system, certain products have few participants and are very inactive in trading volume and value terms. It is difficult for these products to play the functions of price discovery, hedging and resource allocation. In most cases, the correlation between futures and spot prices is not significant. These products therefore could not provide guidance on pricing to the industry.

(3)   Improving the legislation and establishing a multi-layer market supervision system

A sound legislative and regulatory system is needed in order to ensure the orderly operation of the futures market to realise the "open, fair and just" trading principles. The "Futures Law" should be introduced as soon as possible. Governance by legislation and regulations is the cornerstone for the healthy and stable development of the futures market.

(4)   Exploring and developing options and innovative index tool

By the end of 2019, there were only four agricultural options in the Mainland. New option classes should be explored and introduced in order to provide investors with more price hedging tools and to serve the hedging demand of business enterprises. Agricultural index futures can reflect the price trend of the whole agricultural product market. They have many advantages that futures on a single agricultural product would not offer. They can not only meet the demand of the hedgers, but can also provide a new kind of investment tool for investors.

(5)   Accelerate the pace of "going global" and strengthen cooperation between the Mainland and Hong Kong

On the backdrop of the "Belt and Road" initiative and the development strategy of Guangdong-Hong Kong-Macao Greater Bay Area, domestic futures companies should accelerate the pace of "going global" to promote their international business and to seek breakthroughs. The cooperation between Mainland and Hong Kong institutions should be strengthened and Mainland futures companies should be actively encouraged to set up an international futures business platform in Hong Kong, in order to promote the internationalisation of the Mainland futures market and to provide diversified investment channels for Mainland and foreign investors.

Chapter 4

Commodities trading and hedging in practice

Anthony Yan Chi YUEN, Ph.D.

Managing Director, Head of Commodities Pan-Asia
Citi Research and Global Insights
Citigroup Global Markets Asia Limited

Edward L. MORSE, Ph.D.

Managing Director, Global Head of Commodities
Citi Research and Global Insights
Citigroup Global Markets Limited

Tracy Xian LIAO

Vice President, Citi Research and Global Insights
Citigroup Global Markets Asia Limited

Judy Xiaolin SU

Assistant Vice President, Citi Research and Global Insights
Citigroup Global Markets Asia Limited

Summary

This chapter discusses various aspects of (1) commodities pricing, (2) hedging by producers and consumers of commodities, (3) investing and trading by financial market participants, and (4) facilitation by intermediaries such as banks and trading houses. It then highlights the importance of choosing the right price benchmarks, what makes them successful, and how they may apply to China.

1 Practicalities and pricing of commodities

1.1 Basic concepts

For commodities, either supply or demand or both, are lumpy, and often seasonal, which impacts consumption patterns. Given the asymmetries between the timing of supply and demand, commodities need to be stored in anticipation of consumption at later points in time. These patterns can be regular and seasonal, and are especially distinctive in agricultural and energy commodities. For millennia, it has also been understood that storage has a value, and a cost. Storing for potential future use, when markets perceive such future use has a higher value than current use, can be a powerful incentive for investment in storage. Today, forward price curves, based on futures contracts, can signal when the net present value (NPV) of storage is greater than the NPV of use. We can see these in "contango" markets, where futures prices can be higher than the combination of the costs of buying material and of storing it. When available storage gets "tight" or used up, investors often bid up the price of storage to enable them to benefit from their evaluation of the NPV of stored commodity, such as oil.

Commodities are usually highly politicised as well. More than 50% of commodities fall into two categories: agricultural and energy goods, or in common parlance, food and fuel. Populations feel entitled to lower-cost goods, but producers of these primary products not only want higher prices but also want to push the burdens of adjustment to price changes onto other parties — hence the creation of organisations such as the Organisation of the Petroleum Exporting Countries (OPEC), designed in a zero-sum world to push the burden of price adjustments onto others.

1.2 Pricing of commodities

In the short run, **supply versus demand versus inventories** count most. It is obvious that a predominance of one versus the others will determine whether prices are likely to fall or rise. But it may well be that seasonality can play a role in outright balances. Inventories are important. They can rise or fall in absolute terms, but they can, counter-intuitively, reflect a different value of forward demand cover. Hence, just because supply might be greater than demand does not mean the market is weaker. What counts is whether the days of forward cover of demand rises or falls with absolute inventory changes. In a fast-growing demand environment, inventories might grow, but days of forward demand might fall, providing a bullish rather than a bearish tone to markets. Incremental demand might reach a level such that all of the cheapest oil or other commodities available to the market at that price has already been tapped. In such an environment, the incremental demand for an incremental ton of copper, for example, might require tapping into more expensive copper, thus triggering a price increase for all copper.

In the longer run, how **commodity investment cycles** work affects pricing as well. Each commodity is subject to the same cyclical tendency whereby companies move alternatively in patterns to respond to high prices by marshalling too much capital. The result is over-investment in new supply, followed by abrupt drops in prices and a period of companies being reluctant to invest in new capacity, which, in turn, results in a new period of underinvestment. Investment cycles tend to be short-run for agricultural commodities — today's price signals can induce farmers to increase next year's plantings to favour the best-performing commodities and to reduce plantings in crops that underperformed in the present cycle. Such changes in plantings can impact yields fairly substantially from one year to the next. Cycles are longer for bulks, and even longer for base and precious metals, and especially longer for energy.

Super cycles occur, but are largely unpredictable. There are long periods of cost stability, which give rise to periods of mean-reverting prices and fairly stable forward curves. And there are also periods of cost inflation and cost deflation. Generally speaking, longer-term costs go down through technology. Even so, cycles rarely coincide, but all commodities are energy intensive, providing a link that frequently leads them to correlate strongly with one another.

Over the years, there have been multiple efforts to **financialise commodities** through the creation of auctions and the development of exchanges on which they could be traded. But these were, by and large, small markets for a limited group of producers and consumers of commodities.

Commodity derivatives and other financial instruments, both on exchanges and over the counter, do have a clear advantage for investors — they allow and facilitate investors to buy commodities at arm's length without worrying about the costs and risks of storage in the course of taking delivery, including, for agricultural commodities, infestation from disease, vermin and rats; or deterioration of quality of liquids; or rust and other problems in the case of metals. Producers and consumers actively participate because markets provide hedging tools, allowing for balancing. These are generally on a medium- to longer-term part of the forward cure, though shorter-term is possible as well. In addition, the rapid growth of investments in new financial instruments coincided with the so-called Commodities

Super Cycle during 2003 to 2007[1]. If we look at the key players in these markets, there is a structural bias for managed money to be naturally long commodities, so we see pension funds seeking investable assets, and a base of asset under management (AUM). These are on the prompt part of the forward curve. We also see "fast money" (e.g. hedge funds) because the market allows for short-term speculation. These are concentrated on prompt or short-term contracts. And finally, we see Commodity Trading Advisors (CTAs) and algorithmic traders who are also concentrated on prompt or short-term contracts.

2 Hedging by producers and consumers of commodities

Hedging by producers to secure revenue of future production and hedging by consumers to lock in costs of future commodities consumption are common risk management strategies. This section discusses how hedging can be done by national oil companies, exploration and production companies, other energy consumers, metals producers and consumers, as well as agricultural producers.

The main objective of **price protection is** to manage market risks that can jeopardise cash flow and impact long-term capital programmes. Protecting the revenue of a defined share of output is typically appropriate when: (i) developing new output that has been financed through debt that needs to be repaid at a defined future date; (ii) the revenue from the output has been earmarked for special projects; (iii) overall production levels are at risk, especially if prices were to fall; and (iv) when multi-year capital programs need to be protected, etc. For producers, downside price risk management is generally appropriate when the costs of insuring against the risks are clearly known and quantified in advance, and the execution of the hedging programme is done so as to minimise market impacts. The same applies to consumers of commodities on upside price risk management. However, from time to time, some have abandoned strategic hedging. On the one hand,

---

1   The "Commodities Super Cycle" during 2003-2007 refers to the rise in prices of commodities, as demand for energy and metals, especially from China, climbed, while supply either disappointed despite strong growth expected years ago, or were still being planned but would take years to come online. The tightness in the supply-demand fundamentals led to higher prices.

some producers stop hedging as spot prices and deferred prices are rising and insurance is not thought to be necessary. On the other hand, some consumers stop hedging as prices are falling, and they think prices could stay low for a long time. But both scenarios — prices higher for longer and prices lower for longer — cannot be right at the same time. Further, some might have applied strategies that are not necessarily the most suitable. For example, "costless" collars[2] are not always the best options, as they cap prices and are very costly in a volatile or rising price environment for a producer. At times, "put protection"[3] might be a better mechanism. While buying put options is the simplest form of risk management and price protection, it can be done in different ways. Price protection can be sought either via a calendar-year swap with one annual settlement, or with a monthly strip and monthly settlements. More complex variations are also available. Further, "internal politics" can also intrude, as there could be criticism about losses incurred in hedging.

Some state-owned firms conduct **strategic hedging,** and some government entities in oil-producing countries engage in strategic hedging. For example, the finance ministry of an oil-producing country enters the market to protect cash flows from oil sales. It conducts an annual programme, buying put options to provide a price floor to its oil production. The year 2020 is particularly instructive in that, while many other oil-producing countries suffered severe losses in revenue after the oil price collapse, Mexico's well-publicised hedging programme, conducted annually for years, protected its cash flow and contribution to government revenue.

Producer hedging by independent exploration and production companies in the United States (US) is also well-documented, with volumes implied from weekly positioning data released by the US Commodities Futures Trading Commission and eventually reported in the Swap Data Repository (SDR). An example of this was the increase in merchant gross shorts on ICE Brent in the week of 29th November 2016 to 6th December 2016, in anticipation of OPEC's output agreement triggering an increase in activity in late 2016. The increase was 119 thousand lots (119 million barrels) week-on-week and was the second-largest weekly increase seen for the category since records started in 2011[4]. At the time, ex-US producer activity was also on the rise.

---

2   Costless collars (or zero-cost collars) is a protective options strategy, with offsetting premia on a put option and a call option. An investor/trader buys an out-of-the-money put option and simultaneously sells an out-of-the-money call option with the same expiration dates and at the same premia, so that the call and put options positions cancel each other out. This strategy can hedge price volatility in the underlying asset through purchases of call and put options that place a cap and floor on the profits and losses.

3   A "put" option is a financial instrument that allows a holder of the option to sell the underlying financial asset at a predetermined price and a predetermined time. The option is profitable to exercise when the price of the underlying financial asset falls below the predetermined price.

4   Source: US Commodity Futures Trading Commission.

Other than absolute price levels, **the shape of futures curves** could also encourage hedging by either producers or consumers. On the one hand, for consumers, as term structure strengthens (i.e. near-term prices rise more than long-dated prices along the futures curve) and perhaps even inverts (i.e. near-term prices are higher than long-dated prices), locking in prices further out the futures curve at below near-dated prices, whether storage cost is adjusted or not, could be attractive. On the other hand, for producers, if longer-dated prices further out the futures curve are higher than near-term prices, especially if this time spread looks to widen further, and if prices are higher than production costs, then it could be attractive for producers to hedge. Storage cost, as explained in the previous section, is key to the structure of the futures curve and hedging behaviour.

Chinese commodity market participants have also been increasingly using financial products to reduce price risks. For example, a major copper producer in China started using the futures market for hedging in 1992, and it also established a futures brokerage for internal trading for the company. Its hedging strategies successfully helped the company endure difficult times during the 2008 great recession, when copper prices crashed. Further development of China's financial markets, including futures markets, has expanded the set of available financial tools and raise Chinese companies' awareness of the importance of risk management. From December 2016 to 26 April 2017, for example, more than 20 non-ferrous metals companies in China disclosed their commodity futures hedging plans for 2017[5]. The types of commodity hedged included gold, aluminum, copper, zinc, tin and nickel.

In agriculture, producer hedging is similarly influenced by time spreads and storage costs. Akin to hedging done for other commodities, agricultural goods suppliers have to manage and secure their cash flows, subject to storage economics. However, there are time-lags going from plantings, harvests, loadings and delivery, all the while producers need to manage the cost and need of storage. For example, suppose the front of the futures curve (i.e. near-term price) is depressed by investor flows and speculative trading activity so that the time spread is wider than what storage or carrying cost would imply (i.e. the front of the futures curve is much lower than the back, in other words, near-term price is much lower than longer-term price). In this case, a producer should sell contracts at the back of the futures curve to lock in a profit. Agriculture also confronts issues related to a reasonable timeframe, otherwise agricultural products would become spoiled.

5　Source: Press reports.

3 Investing and trading by financial market participants

As natural buyers and sellers of physical commodities often do not exactly match each other's position sizes and tenors, investors and speculators often enter the market to invest, trade or harvest risk premia, thus insuring physical hedgers. Physical producers and consumers of commodities usually do not have perfect offsetting positions to each other, which can give rise to risk premium and open an opportunity for financial participants to become counterparties of the traders. The simple fact is that more producers hedge than do consumers on some contracts. The offset may be imperfect not just in total long/short contracts, but also across locations and calendar positions. For example, producers may hedge with (sell) both short and long-dated contracts, while consumers may hedge with (buy) short-term ones. Thus, financial investors could take advantage of these mismatches, besides trading on a fundamental view of where prices could go. Storage economics, and in particular, the limitations of storage arbitrage when capacity is nearly empty or full, can drive convexity, which can be extracted by calendar alpha investors[6]. Many commodities also feature strong seasonality in their demand (e.g. energy) or their supply (e.g. agriculture), which may drive seasonality in hedging demand and risk premia.

The sub-sections below discuss active management that often involves taking fundamental views, and passive management that takes advantage of various risk premia.

3.1 Active management

The classic case of active management is taking a directional view of prices. Traders could go long a commodity if their fundamental analysis points to a greater likelihood of further price appreciation, and vice versa.

Due to different locations, timing and quality of products, prices of the same commodity could be different at certain points, thus giving rise to arbitrage opportunities. Traders

---

6   "Calendar Alpha Strategies" take advantage of the shape of the futures curve and general tendencies of contract prices when they roll from one month to another, such as going from being the second month to the front month contract. For example, an investor would earn a positive roll yield when the futures curve is backward-sloping, or in a backwardation. As the nearby contract expires, an investor sells at a higher price and buys a farther-dated contract at a lower price, since the futures curve is downward-sloping. If the curve shape is preserved and market conditions remain similar, then the price of this far-dated contract but soon-to-be nearby contract would rise. Thus a positive roll-yield is generated.

could exploit these arbitrage opportunities to maximise returns, which could also enhance market efficiencies. Some investors may be able to foresee the infrastructure build-out schedule better than some producers and consumers of commodities, so that these investors could estimate how time spreads and regional price differentials could evolve better than others. For example, in US oil and gas, some investors could gain better insight by paying attention to multiple sectors, including exploration and production, midstream, refining, and utilities, so they could have a better understanding of, say, the production schedule and online dates of new pipelines. The ability to analyse a vast amount of information, in depth within a sector and in breadth across sectors, and making sense of it through robust integration of these data and modelling, could give some investors advantages over other market participants.

One example is the case of Waha natural gas. In the years up to early 2018, forward basis differentials of Waha natural gas to Henry Hub, the benchmark natural gas price in the US, in the oil-rich Permian basin in the US, was not much different from historical Waha spot basis differentials. Individual producers in the Permian basin knew their own individual companies' expected outputs well, but not outputs from others. An investor who was able to forecast a massive growth of oil and associated natural gas production, who also knew that the natural gas pipeline capacity was not remotely sufficient to take all the gas out of the region, and who had a good understanding of the price dynamics and formation, could forecast a crash in Waha natural gas prices, perhaps even to negative prices. An investor could trade on this view. This example illustrates that even producers and consumers, who supposedly know their corners of physical markets very well, may lack a sufficiently broad and/or deep understanding of multiple subsectors within the energy sector, such that investors can outperform with superior information and understanding of sectors beyond the physical market.

3.2   Passive investments

Some relatively passive investors might simply look to gain exposure to commodities as an asset class as a part of the asset-allocation process, as prior literature suggests that investing in commodities could improve risk-adjusted returns. Long-only indices such as the Bloomberg Commodity Index (BCOM) and the S&P GSCI, which have allocations to energy, metals and agricultural products, are common tools for investors to gain exposure to commodities more passively. However, as simple long-only strategies lose attractiveness after the end of the commodity super-cycle, investors have shifted to more enhanced-beta or alpha-focused commodity strategies, such as calendar spread or seasonality premia strategies.

(1)   Total returns of commodity rolling strategies

Beyond long-only indices such as BCOM and GSCI, some enhanced passive commodity indices attempt to mimic theoretical returns of commodities by investing in the nearest-month futures contract with a fixed rolling schedule. For example, an investor could earn a negative roll yield when the futures curve is upward-sloping, or in a contango. As the nearby contract "t" expires, an investor sells this nearby contract at a lower price and buys a farther-dated "t+1" contract at a higher price, since the futures curve is upward-sloping. If the curve shape is preserved (i.e. similarly upward-sloping) and market conditions remain similar, then the price of this far-dated contract but soon-to-be nearby contract should fall. Thus a negative roll-yield is generated. An investor could seek to profit from this general quality by shorting this negative roll yield and vice versa.

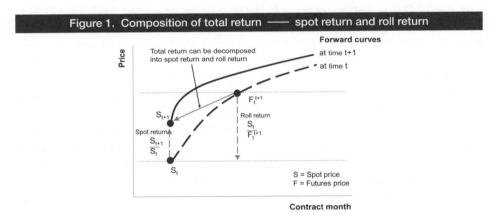

Figure 1. Composition of total return —— spot return and roll return

(2)   Seasonality in risk premia

Seasonality is one of the primary sources of risk premia in commodity markets. Unlike many financial markets, commodity futures markets can feature strong seasonality in the physical spot market and supply and demand balances. For example, demand for various energy commodities can show strong seasonal variation. Colder weather in winter months can stimulate demand for heating fuels. Regular refinery maintenance periods and restarts cause refinery demand for crude oil to rise and fall systematically over the year. Summers typically see peak load demand for electricity to run air conditioners and refrigerators. Similarly, the supply of agricultural commodities can show seasonal variation due to different crop cycles, with harvest season generally bringing peak physical supply for grains and soft commodities in the autumn months in the Northern Hemisphere.

Furthermore, tail risks to the demand and supply outlook can also peak around specific periods of the year. For example, the risk driven by an unusually cold winter can heighten demand for natural gas. Other risks include the annual hurricane seasons that fall upon the US Gulf Coast, or summer droughts that could afflicted the US Corn Belt. With these seasonal variations in risk, it is only natural that hedging demand and therefore risk premia, both positive and negative, can concentrate during specific months of the year and around specific delivery dates along the futures curve.

An investor seeking to reap seasonality-driven outperformance must concern himself with seasonality in risk premia, which can be different from seasonality in spot prices. It is important to differentiate between the two. Risk premia are defined as the difference between futures prices and expected future spot prices. If futures prices are below the expected spot price in the future, then there are positive risk premia. In this case, an investor purchasing that futures contract and waiting until maturity could gain positive outperformance. If futures prices are above expected spot prices in the future, then there are negative risk premia. In this case, an investor taking a long position in the futures contract is expected to lose money. If seasonality in spot prices is already priced into futures curves, then there is no further seasonal risk premia to extract and an investor cannot gain alpha. However, measuring seasonal risk premia is challenging because expected spot prices, and therefore risk premia, cannot be observed directly. Nevertheless, from the passive investment perspective, consistent hedging behaviour by producers and consumers could leave open such seasonal risk premia that investors could capture. From a more active investment perspective, an investor could additionally capture these seasonal risk premia by developing an in-depth understanding of supply/demand fundamentals and their influence on prices.

Figure 2. Negative risk premia at the point of seasonal high in spot prices

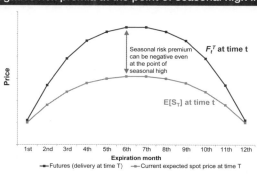

(3) Inflation hedging

Investors often look to commodities and other real asset classes to provide protection against negative consequences of unexpected inflation on portfolio real returns. Yet their efficacy can vary across asset classes and investment time horizons. When inflation is controlled, the average consumer pays little attention to day-to-day purchasing decisions. With higher inflation or time horizons of multiple years, the purchasing power of nominal assets such as equities and bonds can be severely eroded. Commodities, mainly energy and food, directly or indirectly form nearly half of the US consumer basket and affect inflation.

However, it is important to distinguish between expected inflation and unexpected inflation. Expected or anticipated inflation should already be reflected in asset prices, while unexpected inflation is not. Surveys and other imperfect measures of inflation expectations suggest they tend to be myopic and backward-looking[7]. Given an investment time horizon and risk tolerance level, one can structure an optimal inflation-hedging basket.

Proper inflation hedging is a complex process that requires a holistic grasp of the relationship and vulnerability of one's investment portfolio to inflation. The following steps are key:

- Assess one's investment objectives and its vulnerability to unexpected inflation;
- Decide whether to shift to inflation-defensive equity/bond positioning or proceed with direct inflation hedging;
- Determine the asset classes that may serve as potential inflation hedges, such as Treasury Inflation-Protected Security (TIPS), real estate investment trusts (REITS), or commodities;
- Determine one's investment horizon and level of risk tolerance in one's direct inflation hedge; and
- Optimise a basket according to the various risk and inflation hedging characteristics of each potential inflation hedge over the investment horizon.

---

7 See, for example, Axelrod, Sandor et. al. (2018) "Perceptions and expectations of inflation by U.S. households", *Finance and Economics Discussion Series 2018-073*, Board of Governors of the Federal Reserve System, USA.

4 Facilitation by intermediaries, including banks and trading houses

As commodity producers and consumers are generally located in different places and have different hedging horizons, intermediaries can help match up producers and consumers of commodities to reach the best combination of a deal, taking into account transportation and freight costs. Banks and trading houses perform similar functions in that they share some similarities in risk management, such as hedging for clients, and sometimes in trade finance. However, banks have traditionally been more active in paper trading, derivatives and customised financial products that could also involve participation by investors and speculators. Physical commodity delivery is more in the domain of trading houses, since they have much more extensive logistical networks, as well as upstream and downstream facilities.

Banks help to provide market liquidity as market makers, facilitate efficient price formation, provide risk management solutions, and engage in project finance and trade finance. As market makers, banks help to bring buyers and sellers together in the market and bear some price risk. Some banks also participate in the physical commodities markets, but generally only to the extent of facilitating hedging by producers and consumers. As the shipping of commodities also ties up a sizable amount of working capital of corporates, banks therefore often step in to provide working-capital solutions. However, regulations have made banks' holdings of physical assets and participation in physical markets much more restricted, especially since the Global Financial Crisis in 2008. One of the goals of the regulations that were developed at that time was to reduce unnecessary risks a bank can be exposed to, when banking is integral in modern global finance and in bridging finance with the real economy. Banks engage not only in trade finance, but also in project finance, where they help finance infrastructure projects through credit extensions.

For example, an air conditioner producer in China may want to hedge copper price risk one year forward for planning or budgeting purposes, while a copper miner in Chile may also want to hedge copper prices but in a five-year timeframe for capital investment. The different time, tenor, and location of the underlying product (finished copper products versus copper ores) create demand for intermediaries. Other corporate consumers with longer hedging horizons, along with investors who may have a positive outlook on copper, could all be matched up in this example. Through this process, banks help to facilitate transactions that serve the needs of different market participants.

Banks are intimately involved in trade finance and commodities trading, as the transport of commodities from seller A to buyer B often involves the participation of many other parties involved in shipping, warehousing, etc. For example, the bank of an importer (or the buyer) would issue a letter of credit (LC) to the bank of the exporter (the seller), which is a validation of the buyer's capability of paying for the goods once the terms of agreement from the exporter have been met. The exporter would need to present the document, usually called the bill of lading (BL), to prove that the shipment has occurred.

Banks also engage in various other types of financing. These include reserve-based lending (RBL) common in US shale oil and gas projects, construction financing, debt financing such as bank term loans and bond market private placements, mezzanine financing (mezzanine debt, leasing), pool financing (inverted leases, asset-backed securities (ABS)), and master limited partnerships (MLP), etc. The overall financing transaction may also include derivative hedging (interest rate, foreign exchange (FX), commodities, power) in securing cash flows from commodity production or locking in the cost of commodity consumption. For example, a foreign buyer (from country X) of a renewable energy project (in country Y) might want both debt financing and derivatives hedging to finance the purchase of the project and secure future cash flows. Since it is a cross-border purchase, with future revenues potentially repatriated from country Y back to country X, then the types of derivatives hedging could include the interest rate of the debt financed, FX of future cash flows of the project, power prices received by the renewable energy project, and perhaps even using natural gas as a proxy hedge for long-dated power prices in country X.

Besides the types of transaction discussed above, transactions could also originate from the investment banking side through mergers and acquisitions and corporate banking side through lending, etc. For example, a bank that helps company A buy company B might also lend to or help issue securities for company A to conduct this purchase. But to secure the lending, a bank might require company A to hedge company B's domestic and overseas production to secure the cash flow, which could involve the hedging of interest rates, FX and commodity production.

Due to regulatory requirements stipulated after the Global Financial Crisis in 2008, banks are generally no longer in the proprietary trading business, which involves the use of a company's own balance sheet and capital to trade. Banks now operate to facilitate client transactions. Trading houses, which are lightly regulated (to be discussed below), do conduct proprietary trading as a main line of business.

Unlike banks that are more active on the financial side of commodities, commodity trading houses generally serve as intermediaries in the physical commodities world, connecting producers (sellers) and consumers (buyers). This usually involves transactions across different locations, in different time zones (or length of periods) and with varied demands for products from buyers and sellers. For trading houses, scale often matters, due to their ability to source counterparties, their advantage of gathering market intelligence, and their need to drive revenue as margins have shrunk. Some of the largest commodities trading houses individually could trade 5 to 10 million barrels a day of crude oil and petroleum products, in a crude oil market that is about 100 million barrels per day in size. Trading arms of some supermajor energy companies, including Royal Dutch Shell and BP, operate like trading houses as well. The growth of trading volumes by trading houses is also closely tied to the growth of markets. In addition, trading houses continue to explore new trading opportunities. For example, with margins narrowing in the crude oil business, liquefied natural gas (LNG) trading has seen rapid expansion since 2018, given the relatively large price differentials across different regions. Understanding market fundamentals of historically segregated regional gas markets requires the kind of in-depth knowledge of regional supply/demand fundamentals of multiple fuels that play to the forte of physical trading houses. The ability to move tankers or ships of other commodities globally is now readily applied to moving LNG cargos worldwide.

In physical commodity markets, a trading house also matches market supply and demand across locations, time spans and quality of the products. A trading house could provide sourcing service (the trading house's direct relationships and offtake agreements with raw material producers). It is also likely to have storage capability (e.g. storing iron ore for six months before shipping it so as to match the time demand for the steel mill). It can offer blending services (e.g. mix grades of Brazilian ore to match the grade requirement for the buyer) and logistical networks (e.g. the use of railcars, trucks, barges and dry-bulk carriers to ship the iron ore from the trading house's warehouse to the customer). Trading houses are much more lightly regulated than banks, so that proprietary trading is often a core business that leverages off physical market transactions and information.

Below is an example to illustrate how a trading house could facilitate transactions between producers and consumers. A Chinese steel mill might want to purchase iron ore at a specific grade for its steel production in its peak production time in eight months from now, while a Brazilian iron ore producer would want to sell its mined ore now to the market. The consumer of iron ore in China and the producer in Brazil do not necessarily know each other and they are located in different countries, with slightly different time periods for their purchase/sale and different demand for ore grades. Trading houses as market intermediaries tend to be in a good position to go through the whole supply chain to connect the buyer and the seller and deliver the required product to the buyer. To do so, in this example, they essentially need to transport the commodity (iron ore) from Brazil to

China (location match), guarantee delivery time by storing iron ore at their own or their partly-owned warehouses (synchronised in time), and mixing and blending the ore grade so as to meet the demand from the Chinese steel mill.

In another example, if an automaker needs aluminium in six months and is willing to pay a premium for future delivery, a market participant with physical trading capability (such as a trading house) can profit from using the spot and futures price differentials. The market participant could buy the aluminium at today's price (say US$1,500 per tonne) while selling in the futures market at a premium (as the automaker agrees to, say at US$1,600 per tonne) with an expiry date in six months. During the six months, the intermediary, in this case a trading house, could store aluminium at a relatively low cost in its own warehouse, assuming only US$50 per tonne of storage cost.

5   Choosing the right price benchmark

5.1   Qualities of successful benchmarks

Prices are what link all market participants in financial and physical markets together, such that choosing the right price benchmark is key. The corollary is that there are certain qualities that make some price benchmarks successful.

This is a particularly relevant question in Asia, because a number of Asian countries have expressed frustration at the alleged "Asian premium" in commodity prices, especially in energy. In the crude oil market, some governments and market participants believe that establishing a local or regional commodity contract could eliminate the so-called "Asian premium" and could serve as a key step towards a more transparent price discovery process, especially given the significant shares of commodity consumption in the region out of total global demand. Such governments and market participants argue that no contract is available to reflect what is happening in Asia. Energy pricing is dominated by exchanges in North America and Europe, even as demand and flow activities are surging in Asia, but without price indices to reflect the fundamentals in Asia. Even Oman and Dubai crudes, based in the Middle East, do not form a fair benchmark in the view of some market participants, given the way exporters from the Middle East impose complicated formulae that appear to impose a premium to fair market value.

However, it is very important to distinguish the difference between having pricing power and having prices more accurately reflect regional fundamentals. Having a futures exchange and energy contracts, ideally if they become very liquid, does not mean that the country that hosts the exchange has outsized weight on energy price determination, as prices should be reflective of market supply and demand. Futures contracts that have good liquidity should more accurately reflect regional fundamentals, but this does not give the host country the additional pricing power over the benchmark.

Indeed, successful price benchmarks share the following characteristics, at least at the beginning, before establishing themselves as global benchmarks. Overall, to integrate a commodity contract, such as oil, into the global market, a contract would have to prove why it is worthwhile and how it delivers a better alternative than, say, Dubai as a benchmark for medium sour crude. In the case of oil, the following characteristics of a futures contract generally assure liquidity, consistency, and competitiveness of the underlying crude oil, so that market participants can have confidence in the delivered product and that pricing is not manipulated:

- **High volume:** A sufficient amount is available for trading to take place, and there is a multiplicity of both sellers and buyers that already support spot sales and an informal forward market.

- **Consistent quality:** Buyers would be certain that they can use and price the oil, with the quality being consistent over time. If the quality changes, the mix of products refined would be different, as would the gross product worth of crude streams used. The dumb-belling of crude is not desirable, as the average crude quality may look the same but the products refined would again be different, where one blend can yield more middle distillate but another has more light-ends and heavier products but not the middle.

- **Security of supply:** The market wants to be certain that a sufficient amount of oil would be available on a consistent basis over time.

- **Diversity of market participants:** The pricing of the crude would have to be competitive, so that no one participant has outsized market power to distort pricing, including both active buyers and sellers.

- **Broad acceptance:** Market participants would have to feel confident that the crude is widely traded and widely accepted to be representative of the grade and location of the crude.

- **Contract sanctity and rule of law:** Ultimately, it is important for market participants to be able to get their money back and believe that they would not be unfairly disadvantaged. After all, market participants are in the market to make money, not to lose it.

- **Confidence in the clearing mechanism:** In a related manner, the ease of and confidence over the trading process are important to entice market participants to join. The entire process involves the ability to clear trades, collect and maintain margin, the security of the capital, and a smooth and trusted storage and delivery process.
- **Full currency convertibility:** In a similar vein as above, capital controls or a lack of full currency convertibility could reduce the appetite for market participants to join the market, if in the end profits made cannot be repatriated.

In the crude oil market, Brent in the early 1980s exhibited all these qualities. When volume started declining, other crude streams were added. These were initially two crude streams of similar quality, Forties and Oseberg, that created the Brent-Forties-Oseberg (BFO) construct to bolster the overall volume, with the Ekofisk grade also added later to form the Brent-Forties-Oseberg-Ekofisk (BFOE). When crude from the Buzzard field was first commingled with Forties, the blended crude became sourer, making Forties the lowest-priced grade of the four crudes.

West Texas Intermediate (WTI) also exhibits these qualities but, at first glance, it would not have been a good global benchmark because of its land-locked nature and the initial inability to export the crude, especially after the shale boom starting in 2012 caused production gluts and infrastructure issues. The tremendous liquidity, with huge futures trading volume behind it, helped to overcome these challenges. New York Mercantile Exchange (NYMEX) chose WTI as the primary crude for the futures contract mainly due to operational reasons. The extensive pipeline network ensured a diverse supply domestically. The huge volume and liquidity allowed the market price to quickly react to changes in fundamentals, thereby creating greater price transparency. But since the shale oil boom, WTI prices, despite their prominence globally, can depart significantly from other global crude grades from time to time because of pipeline and export constraints. The Brent/WTI spread widened to nearly US$30 per barrel in late 2012[8] because of such constraints. The relaxation of export restrictions has significantly helped remove these dislocations. Yet, WTI is not as much a global benchmark as Brent, even as US exports grow significantly.

5.2   The case for Asia

Asia does not have a good benchmark for a variety of reasons. In oil trading, Brent, WTI and Dubai are all based near production areas, so that producers and consumers

---

8   Source: Bloomberg.

can both hedge. Dubai comes close, though trading is still much lighter than Brent and WTI. Dubai is now used more as a proxy for sour versus sweet crude in the form of the Brent/Dubai spread. Malaysian Tapis and Indonesian Minas are geographically within the Asian market, but the small volume of production and spot sales, with a few companies controlling production, has limited the effectiveness of both as price benchmarks. Basing the contract in a consuming country is a possibility. Some other established commodity exchanges, such as the London Metal Exchange (LME), are based in consuming countries or where active trading is located. However, whether it would work in oil trading is a question.

An interesting case in Asia is the Dalian iron ore contract. It was set up in the world's largest importing and consuming country (China), attracted substantial domestic liquidity following its launch in 2013, particularly in the first half of 2016, when the contract became one of the top 10 most traded commodity futures contracts in the world by trading volume[9]. Similar to the mix of crude within the Shanghai oil contract, the iron ore contract on the Dalian Commodity Exchange (DCE) also allows physical delivery of a wide range of iron ore products from the 65% Carajas fines to the 61% Roy Hill fines, with premiums and discounts assigned to most of the deliverable products. The DCE has opened the iron ore contract for foreign participation following the crude contract.

But a few characteristics of the DCE iron ore contract are worth noting. It has substantial speculative retail flows and dislocations between prices of contracts upon settlement and actively traded contracts. Similar to other Chinese industrial metal futures contracts and in contrast to other globally traded contracts, daily trading volumes of DCE iron ore have been consistently higher than open interest due to substantial speculative flows and high-frequency trading activities.

Whether DCE's actively traded iron ore contract has helped China gain pricing power in the physical iron ore market is subject to debate. On the one hand, we believe that the DCE contract has been leading its offshore counterpart, the iron ore swap contract on the Singapore Exchange (SGX), in price discovery over the past few years. The night trading session that DCE offers also allows price discovery beyond daytime trading hours. On the other hand, we attribute China's increasing pricing power in iron ore primarily to its predominance in the physical market as the world's largest consumer and 70% of the seaborne imports[10]. This would have even happened without the DCE contract. Nonetheless, the DCE iron ore contract has benefitted from a lack of established contracts elsewhere globally. In iron ore, there is a wide range of market participants and balanced

---

9   Source: Bloomberg.

10 Source: Based on countries' import and export data via Global Trade Information Services (GTIS).

hedging flows that help boost liquidity, even when this flow still pales in comparison to speculative flows. Major market makers include large steel mills and physical trading houses. Physical liquidity in iron ore is also fairly deep, usually with ample ores sitting at Chinese ports, a decent proportion of which are qualified for delivery into the DCE contract. Finally, the iron ore contract attracts liquidity, particularly speculative flows, from similarly actively traded steel and coking coal contracts, which enable market participants to perform relative-value trades including those related to steel mills' margins.

Participation from global investors and physical players are crucial to the ultimate success of a futures contract. To establish itself as a reliable price benchmark, prices should not sharply deviate from other price benchmarks globally, unless there are fundamental supply or demand constraints. These could include such factors as the takeaway congestion issues that blew out the Brent/WTI spread to nearly US$30 per barrel (see Section 5.1 above). Simply having plenty of domestic speculators trading a contract does not necessarily make it a successful, viable contract that reflects market fundamentals. Indeed, domestic speculators could either add tremendous liquidity or destabilise it.

In general, traders and hedgers opt to trade the most liquid contracts. For example, NYMEX has a Brent contract, but with very little trading because Brent trading is dominated on ICE. Looking back, traders also predominantly used the leaded regular gasoline contract — started in the 1980s for trading and hedging gasoline — even after leaded gasoline was phased out. Despite the availability of an unleaded gasoline contract, liquidity was low until the exchange ceased trading of the leaded gasoline contract.

For exchanges in Mainland China, the right kind of liquidity and market participation could help bolster their development. The Mainland commodity exchanges have very high volume, but mostly from local and even day traders (speculators) who have limited connection to the real, physical markets. Actual buyers and sellers in the Mainland physical market would need to do hedging or transaction via a local exchange to help with their risk management. The types of commodity with a reason to trade would be the most common types that are supplied and consumed, such as oil. These highlight the importance of quality consistency, supply security and broad acceptance as mentioned above. As China is largely a commodity importing country, international suppliers would have to participate. This is where the diversity of market participants, contract sanctity, rule of law, confidence in the clearing and settlement mechanism and full currency convertibility come into play. Commodity consumers trading on the local market are generally local businesses, but sellers, many of whom are international, would have to feel very comfortable about transacting, getting their money back and pursuing any recourse within a fair legal system before they will participate in the market. Therefore, strong policy support to these factors is critical to allow international participants to at least consider trading on exchanges in the Mainland. The system will be tested at some point, as circumstances arise. How the system handles these in times of stress would help demonstrate the soundness and appeal of the Mainland exchanges.

6   Conclusion

Commodities are foundational to any economy throughout history, as producers make and consumers use things. Although physical commodity producers and consumers, in theory, are natural counterparties to each other, differences in their timing of hedges, planning horizon, locations, qualities of commodity produced or consumed, and volumes, open up opportunities for investors and intermediaries, such as banks and trading houses, to link them together and complete the market. Storage is supposed to bridge their divides but most producers and consumers are not well-positioned to organise sellers and buyers together to find the right mix of commodities at the right place and the right time. For example, producers, whose whole business is to produce a certain kind of commodity, could require or may feel comfortable hedging over a long horizon. But for commodity consumers, the costs of commodities might only form a part of their total costs of operation, and they might only be interested in short-term hedges. Thus, these mismatches in timing, location, grade and volume leave open an opportunity for investors and intermediaries to arbitrage. While trading houses generally offer services to bridge differences on the physical side, banks typically serve to bridge differences on the financial side, while helping financial investors capture risk premia generated by hedges of producers or consumers.

For all market participants, using the right prices and price benchmarks of underlying commodities is critical to the price discovery, trading and hedging processes, with exchanges facilitating these transactions. Successful price benchmarks established on an exchange share certain characteristics, at least at the beginning, before establishing themselves as global benchmarks. These characteristics include the exchange having a high volume of transactions, consistent quality of the commodity, security of supply, diversity of market participants, broad acceptance, contract sanctity, rule of law, confidence in the clearing and settlement mechanism and full currency convertibility. These qualities would also be fundamental for exchanges in Mainland China to succeed in the future.

Chapter 5

An overview of the global commodity derivatives market

Chief China Economist's Office
Hong Kong Exchanges and Clearing Limited

Summary

Commodities are physical assets that are tradable and supplied without substantial differentiation by the general public. Major categories are precious metals, base metals (or non-precious metals), agriculture and energy products. Commodity trading refers to the trading of commodities in the physical (spot) market as well as the trading of commodity derivatives, which include the standardised products of futures and options on exchange markets and unstandardised products like swaps in the over-the-counter market.

A growing trend is observed over the past decade in the trading of on-exchange commodity derivatives, along with the growing market share of Asian exchanges. This can be attributed to: (1) the global economic growth which has increased the demand for hedging for commodity trades; (2) the increased use of commodity derivatives in portfolio investment for hedging against risks of investment in financial products like equities and bonds or for pure investment purposes; and (3) the rise of the Mainland economy which further boosted global trading in commodities and related hedging demand and of the Mainland commodity exchanges which have an increased significance in the world.

More than half of the derivatives exchanges in the world offer commodity derivatives in their product suites, the majority of which are futures. While the developed markets in the US and Europe may have taken the lead in terms of number of commodity products offered, the Mainland commodity derivatives exchanges have assumed a leading role in terms of trading volume. At least one of the three Mainland exchanges were among the top three in terms of trading volume in 2019 for three of the four commodity categories — precious metals, non-precious metals and agriculture. They fell behind only for energy products, these products however constituted the majority of global commodity derivatives trading volume (mainly from crude oil futures). Moreover, foreign participation in the Mainland commodity derivatives market is highly restricted — only a few designated products have been opened to foreign participants. In other words, the high trading volume on the Mainland exchanges are basically contributed by domestic participants only. Commodity contracts on the Mainland exchanges are typically of a smaller contract size and are traded in relatively high turnover ratios than their counterparts in the western developed markets.

With the further development and opening-up of the Mainland exchanges, the global landscape of commodity derivatives market will continue to evolve

1 What are commodities and commodity derivatives?

A basic economic definition of a commodity is that it is a physical good attributable to a natural resource that is tradable and supplied without substantial differentiation by the general public[1]. Commodities comprise a diverse set of asset classes, covering various sectors including precious metals, industrial or base metals, energy, livestock and grains and other agricultural products (often known as "soft commodities" which are grown rather than extracted or mined from nature).

Commodities are physical assets as opposed to the financial assets of equities and bonds. While the valuation of a financial asset is based on the discounted value of expected future cash flows from the asset, the valuation of a commodity is based on the discounted forecast of future possible prices of the physical asset based on such factors as the supply and demand of the physical asset[2].

A derivative is a security which has the value derived from an underlying asset or a group of assets (a benchmark). The common forms of derivatives include futures, forwards, options and swaps[3]. A commodity derivative is a derivative with a commodity or a commodity benchmark as the underlying asset. Commodity derivatives are often used by commodity producers and consumers to hedge against future price changes in the underlying commodities. Other traders of commodity derivatives include speculators who speculate on price changes in the underlying commodity and arbitrageurs who seek profits from market inefficiencies such as price inefficiencies between markets.

Commodity trading refers to the trading of commodities in the physical (spot) market as well as the trading of commodity derivatives on exchange markets or over-the-counter (OTC). Derivatives exchanges offer standardised futures and options contracts

---

1   Source: The CFA Institute's website (https://www.cfainstitute.org).
2   Source: Ditto.
3   A futures contract is an agreement between two parties for the purchase and delivery of the underlying asset at an agreed price at a future date. Futures contract have standardised terms and are traded on exchanges. A forward contract is similar to a futures contract but has customised terms negotiated between the buyer and the seller and are traded over-the-counter instead of on exchanges. An option contract is an agreement between two parties to buy or to sell an asset at a predetermined future date for a specific price but the option buyer is not obliged to exercise its right to buy or sell the asset at that future date. A swap contract is an agreement to exchange one kind of cash flows with another. A commodity swap is a swap where the cash flows are dependent on the price of an underlying commodity. Swaps are often traded over-the-counter.

on commodities while unstandardised forwards, options and swaps are traded in the OTC market. Investors in commodities may also choose to invest in structured products on commodities available on securities exchanges. These include exchange-traded commodities (ETCs) which are exchange-traded funds (ETFs) that track the performance of an underlying commodity index based on a single commodity or a group of commodities, and commodity contracts for difference (CFDs) which mirror the price movements of the underlying commodity or commodity index.

OTC trading of commodity derivatives had been very active. However, in contrast to the steady growth in the trading of commodity derivatives on exchanges, OTC trading in commodity derivatives has declined significantly since mid-2008 upon the outbreak of the Global Financial Crisis which revealed the severe problems in the unregulated, non-transparent OTC market in derivatives. The trend of global trading of commodity derivatives are discussed in the following sub-sections.

1.1   OTC commodity derivatives trading

Figures 1 and 2 show the total notional amount and the total gross market value[4] of outstanding OTC commodity derivatives over the 21-year period from the end of June 1998 to the end of June 2019, based on the semi-annual OTC derivatives statistics compiled by the Bank for International Settlements (BIS). The notional amount and the gross market value of OTC commodity derivatives rose rapidly after the end of 2004 and reached their peaks by June 2008. They then dropped significantly in a couple of years following the 2008 Global Financial Crisis.

---

4   According to the definition in BIS statistics, the gross market value of outstanding contracts represent the maximum loss that market participants would incur if all counterparties failed to meet their contractual payments and the contracts were replaced at market prices on the reporting date.

Figure 1. Total notional amount of OTC commodity derivatives (Jun 1998 – Jun 2019)

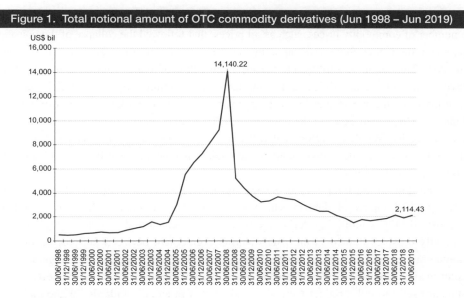

Source: BIS OTC derivatives statistics on the BIS website.

Figure 2. Total gross market value of OTC commodity derivatives (Jun 1998 – Jun 2019)

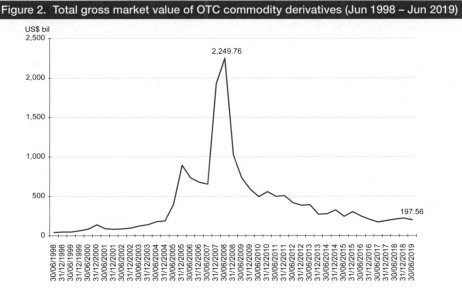

Source: BIS OTC derivatives statistics on the BIS website.

The surge in OTC commodity derivatives activities came along with rapid increases in a number of commodity prices, such as oil prices, that followed the collapse of the housing bubble in the United States (US) upon the outbreak of its subprime mortgage market crisis in 2007. This might be attributed to the speculative flow of money from housing and other investments into commodities, and/or the increasing sentiment of raw materials scarcity in a fast-growing world that led to long positions in those markets. The 2008 Global Financial Crisis then exposed the flaws in the OTC market due to its non-transparency. In the aftermath of regulatory reforms after the crisis, there has been further standardisation in the OTC commodity derivatives market and greater inclination towards central clearing of OTC commodity contracts[5].

According to the International Swaps and Derivatives Association (ISDA), there is already a high degree of standardisation within the OTC commodity derivatives market. Almost all OTC commodity derivative trades are executed under standard legal terms, typically those contained in the ISDA Master Agreement between the parties, or in a limited number of cases in the national equivalent. The vast majority of all contracts are confirmed electronically via confirmation matching platforms. Transactions are effectively standardised through product templates and market practice standards for the majority of non-economic fields. The industry framework enables customisation of transactions without foregoing the benefits delivered by a standardised infrastructure.

The OTC commodity derivatives market has developed a very high level of straight-through processing (STP), from the use of electronic trade booking and trade confirmation through confirmation matching platforms, to central clearing counterparty (CCP) processing. For non-centrally cleared transactions, there is widespread use of bilateral collateral arrangements. A significant percentage of commodity futures, options and forwards are executed on exchanges and settled via CCPs. A number of exchanges provide CCP service for non-exchange-traded transactions. Exchange clearing houses that offer such OTC clearing services for commodity derivatives transactions include ICE Clear (gas and oil products, crude oil, coal, emissions, etc.), CME ClearPort (gas, base metals, precious metals, oil products, crude oil, agriculture, etc.) and LCH.Clearnet (base metals, precious metals, plastics products, freight, iron ore, etc.). A relatively high degree of pre-trade and post-trade transparency is provided by market agencies like brokers, price reporting agencies, electronic trading platforms or confirmation services as well as clearing venues.

---

5   Source: *OTC Commodity Derivatives Trade Processing Lifecycle Events*, an ISDA Whitepaper, April 2012. This paper
    is also the source of information on OTC commodity derivatives market operations presented in this section.

1.2   On-exchange commodity derivatives trading

Commodities traded on global exchanges are in the form of derivatives, typically futures and options. According to classification by the Futures Industry Association (FIA), commodity asset classes underlying exchange-traded futures and options are divided into four categories — precious metals, non-precious metals (i.e. base metals), agriculture and energy. These are derivatives with physical goods as the underlying assets, in contrast to asset categories underlying financial derivatives which include equities (indices and individual equities), interest rates and currencies.

Figures 3 and 4 show the growing trends in the annual trading volume and year-end open interest of exchange-traded derivatives in the world by asset class during the period from 2009 to 2019. In terms of both trading volume and open interest, equity derivatives have been the majority contributor. Nevertheless, the percentage share of commodity derivatives rose from 12% in 2009 to 18% in 2019 in terms of trading volume and from 8% to 11% in terms of open interest (see Figure 5). Notably, as a result of such differential percentage shares in turnover volume and open interest, the turnover ratio (ratio of turnover volume in a period to period-end open interest) of commodity derivatives had been higher than that of financial derivatives and had been rising from 38% in 2009 to 66% in 2019 (see Figure 6).

Figure 3. Annual trading volume of all derivatives on global exchanges by asset class (2009 – 2019)

Source: FIA monthly statistics (December report of each year).

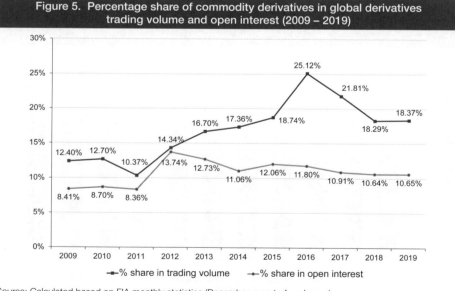

Figure 4. Year-end open interest of all derivatives on global exchanges by asset class (2009 – 2019)

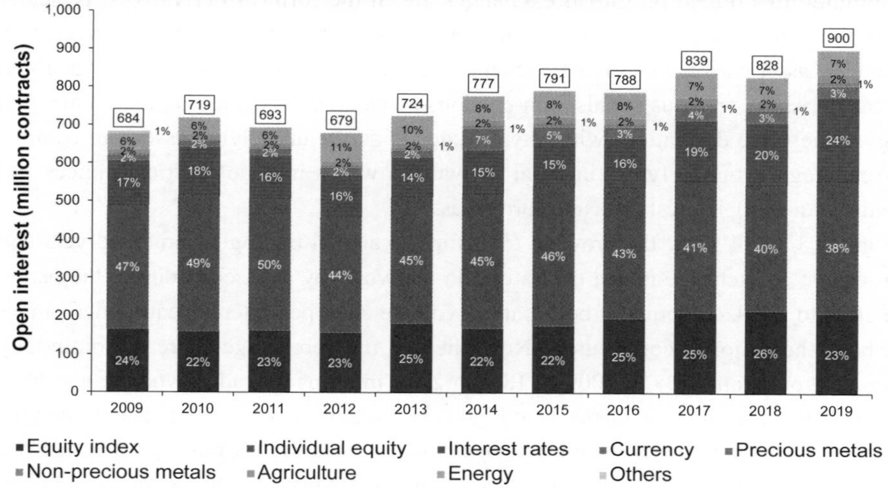

Source: FIA monthly statistics (December report of each year).

Figure 5. Percentage share of commodity derivatives in global derivatives trading volume and open interest (2009 – 2019)

Source: Calculated based on FIA monthly statistics (December report of each year).

Figure 6. Turnover ratios of commodity and financial derivatives (2009 – 2019)

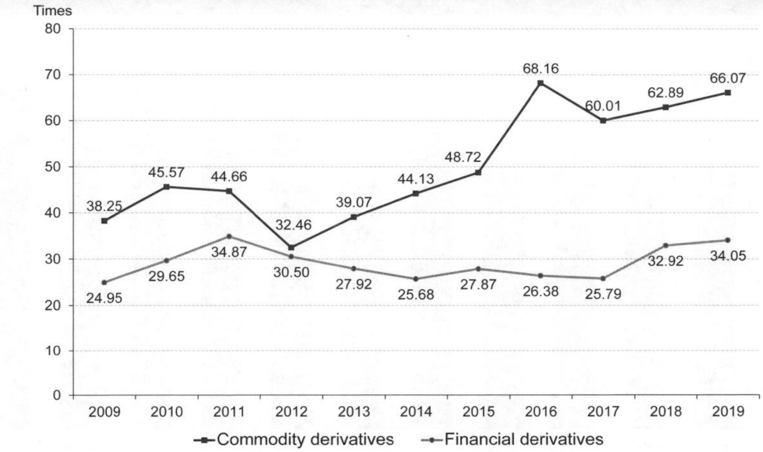

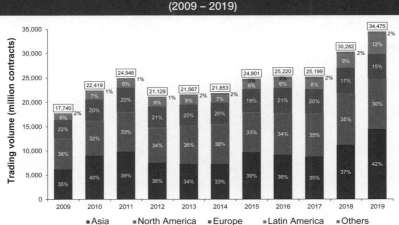

Source: Calculated based on FIA monthly statistics (December report of each year).

Along with the growing percentage share and turnover ratio of commodity derivatives was the growing contribution of Asian exchanges to the trading volume and open interest of global derivatives — from 35% in 2009 to 42% in 2019 in terms of trading volume; and from 4% in 2009 to 9% in 2019 in terms of open interest (see Figures 7 and 8).

Figure 7. Annual trading volume of all derivatives on global exchanges by region (2009 – 2019)

Source: FIA monthly statistics (December report of each year).

Figure 8. Year-end open interest of all derivatives on global exchanges by region (2009 – 2019)

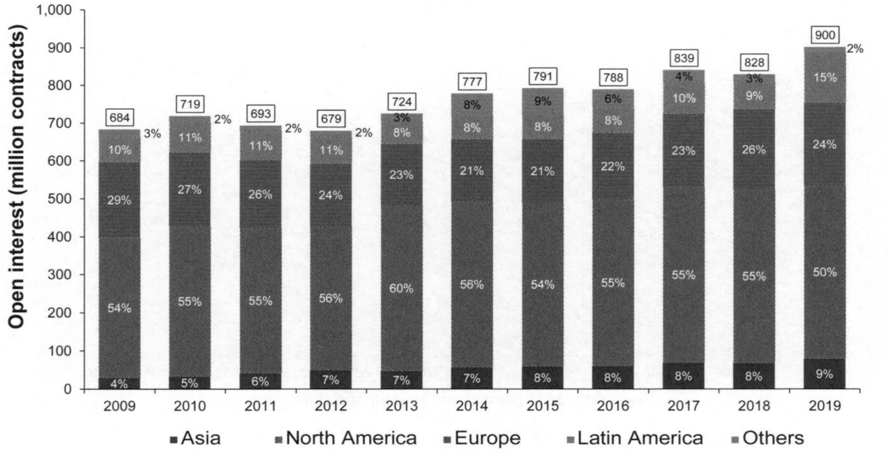

Source: FIA monthly statistics (December report of each year).

Further analysis of activities by region revealed that the percentage contribution of Asian exchanges in global commodity derivatives fluctuated somewhat around 55% in terms of trading volume during the period from 2009 to 2019 (with the highest of 61% reached in 2016) but increased significantly from 9% to 20% in terms of open interest (see Figures 9 and 10). During the period, commodity derivatives on Asian exchanges achieved a compound annual growth rate (CAGR) of 111% in trading volume and 114% in open interest, surpassing those of exchanges in America and more or less in par as European exchanges[6].

---

6   The corresponding CAGR in trading volume and open interest during the period were 108% and 101% respectively for exchanges in North America, 104% and 103% respectively for exchanges in Latin America, and 116% and 115% respectively for exchanges in Europe. Source: Calculations based on FIA statistics.

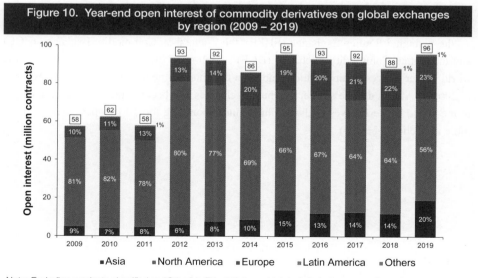

Figure 9. Annual trading volume of commodity derivatives on global exchanges by region (2009 – 2019)

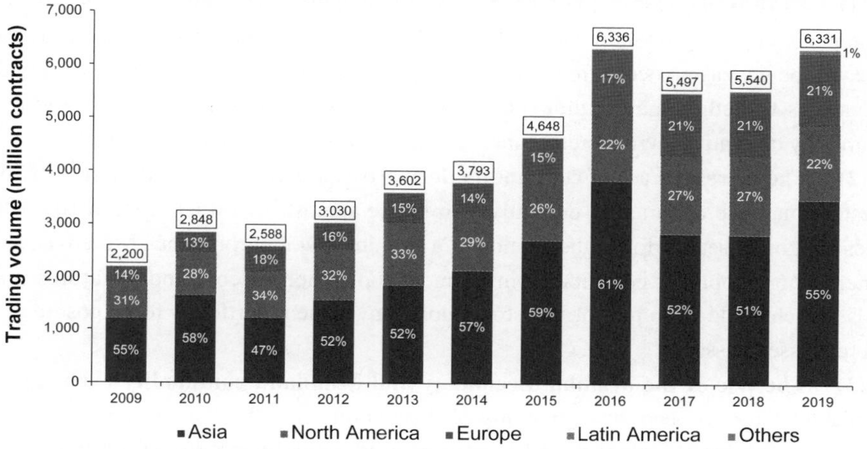

Note: Excluding products classified as "Other" in FIA statistics, which include both commodity and non-commodity asset classes.

Source: FIA monthly statistics (December report of each year).

Figure 10. Year-end open interest of commodity derivatives on global exchanges by region (2009 – 2019)

Note: Excluding products classified as "Other" in FIA statistics, which include both commodity and non-commodity asset classes.

Source: FIA monthly statistics (December report of each year).

The growing trading activities in commodity derivatives and the growing share of Asian exchanges in these can be attributed to three main factors:

(1)   Global economic growth — The growth in global economy is naturally accompanied by the growth in commodity production, consumption and trade. As a result, there will be increasing needs from commodity producers and consumers to use commodity derivatives to hedge against their positions in the physical commodities. Trading in commodity derivatives will therefore increase due to increased hedging activities.

(2)   The increased use of commodity derivatives in portfolio investment[7] — Global investors may use commodity derivatives to hedge against investment risk in equities or bonds risk or in search for higher yields in a low interest environment. Moreover, there is increasing supply of commodity investment tools such as commodity futures index funds, which could form part of investors' global investment portfolios for exposure to the different asset classes.

(3)   The rise of the Mainland economy and Mainland commodity exchanges — Mainland China has been the engine of global economic growth. It achieved a remarkable average annual real growth rates of 12.7% in its gross domestic products (GDP) during the decade up to 2018, compared to the 3.5% for the world's economy[8], and surpassed Japan in 2010 to become the second largest economy in the world[9]. Along with the economic growth is the rising significance of the commodity derivatives exchanges in the Mainland to serve the increasing hedging needs of the Mainland commodity sectors.

The three futures exchanges in the Mainland that offer trading in commodity derivatives — the Shanghai Futures Exchange (SHFE), the Zhengzhou Commodity Exchange (ZCE) and the Dalian Commodity Exchange (DCE) — fell short of the top ten exchanges in the world by derivatives trading volume and even fell short of the top 20 by open interest back in 2009[10]. After a decade's time, the three exchanges had become the top three exchanges in the world by derivatives trading volume and among the top 10 by open interest. (See more in Section 3 below.)

---

7   See Parantap Basu and William T. Gavin (2011), "What explains the growth in commodity derivatives?", *Federal Reserve Bank of St. Louis Review*, January/February 2011.

8   Source: Wind.

9   Source: "China overtakes Japan as world's second-biggest economy", *BBC News* on the BBC website, 14 February 2011.

10   Source: The rankings were produced based on FIA monthly statistics (December 2009).

2 Global exchanges offering commodity derivatives

Out of the 83 exchanges in the world that reported derivatives statistics to the FIA as of end-2019, 45 offered a total number of 1,463 commodity derivative products[11] (see Table 1). Most of these products were futures (1,162 in number or 79% of the total), with options being the minority. Among the four commodity asset classes, energy products constituted the most in number — 876 in number or 60% of the total (63% of futures and 46% of options). Agricultural products ranked the second — 308 in number or 21% of the total (18% of futures and 34% of options). More exchanges (44 in number) offered commodity futures than commodity options (28 in number). Non-precious metals had the least number of products (24 futures and options) and offered by the least number of exchanges (17 exchanges).

Table 1. Commodity product offerings by global exchanges (end-2019)				
Product type	Asset class	No. of exchanges offering products	No. of products	% share in no. of products by asset class
Futures	Precious metals	22	106	9.1%
	Non-precious metals	16	85	7.3%
	Agriculture	33	206	17.7%
	Energy	27	737	63.4%
	Others	6	28	2.4%
Total		44	1,162	100%
Options	Precious metals	11	28	9.3%
	Non-precious metals	8	29	9.6%
	Agriculture	19	102	33.9%
	Energy	11	139	46.2%
	Others	2	3	1.0%
Total		28	301	100%

---

11 In the detailed analysis of commodity products and trading activities in 2019 in this paper, unless otherwise specified, products classified as "Other" in FIA statistics are judgementally re-classified into commodity products and non-commodity products according to their underlying assets. Those classified as commodity products are included as a commodity class in the analysis as "Others". The underlying assets of these include chemical products and commodity indices.

(continued)

Product type	Asset class	No. of exchanges offering products	No. of products	% share in no. of products by asset class
Futures and/or options	Precious metals	24	134	9.2%
	Non-precious metals	17	114	7.8%
	Agriculture	34	308	21.1%
	Energy	28	876	59.9%
	Others	6	31	2.1%
Total		45	1,463	100%

Table 1. Commodity product offerings by global exchanges (end-2019)

Note: Percentages may not add up to 100% due to rounding.

Source: FIA monthly statistics (December 2019 report).

(See Appendix for the full list of exchanges offering commodity derivatives as of end-2019.)

Among the exchanges, the New York Mercantile Exchange (NYMEX) in the US offered the most number of commodity products (576, 39% of the global total as of end-2019), the vast majority of which are energy products (561 in number, 64% of the global energy products total). Nasdaq NFX, also in the US, took the second place, but its number of commodity products (118 or 8% of the global total) fell much short of NYMEX. In fact, six out of the top 10 exchanges by number of commodity products are in the US. Viewing futures and options separately, five out of the top ten exchanges by number of products as of end-2019 are in the US for both futures and options and notably, US exchanges assumed the top 4 places for commodity options products. (See Figure 11.)

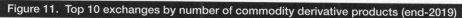

Figure 11. Top 10 exchanges by number of commodity derivative products (end-2019)

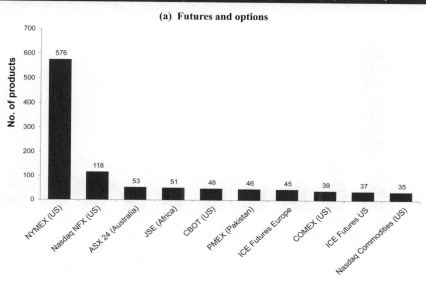

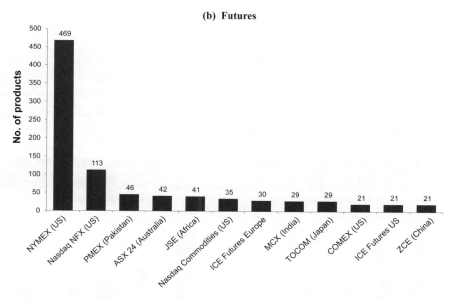

(continued)

Figure 11. Top 10 exchanges by number of commodity derivative products (end-2019)

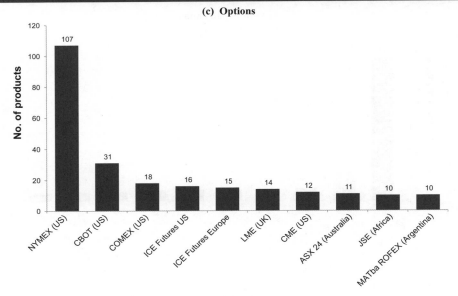

(c) Options

Source: FIA monthly statistics (December 2019 report).

The top 5 exchanges offering the most number of products by commodity asset class as of end of 2019 are given in Figure 12. Pakistan Mercantile Exchange (PMEX) took the lead in precious metal products; the London Metal Exchange (LME) took the lead in non-precious metal products; the Chicago Board of Trade (CBOT) took the lead in agricultural products; and NYMEX took the lead in energy products.

Figure 12. Top 5 exchanges by number of commodity derivative products for each asset class (end-2019)

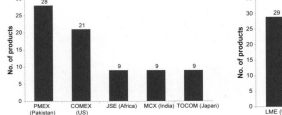

(a) Precious metals   **(b) Non-precious metals**

(continued)

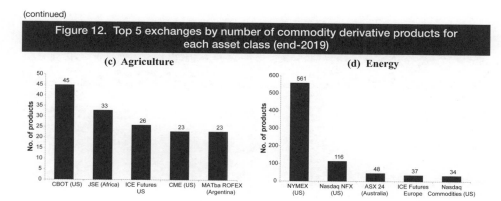

Figure 12.   Top 5 exchanges by number of commodity derivative products for each asset class (end-2019)

Source: FIA monthly statistics (December 2019 report).

In terms of trading volume, futures constituted over 90% for each of the commodity asset classes, while options constituted only a minority in 2019 (see Table 2). Futures products also dominated in terms of open interest of commodity derivatives as of end-2019, though to a lesser extent than that in terms of trading volume (see Table 3). This reflects the genuine characteristic of commodity futures being the natural hedging tool for the commodity industry. (See Section 3 for more detailed analysis of the trading activities.)

Table 2.   Global commodity derivatives trading volume on exchanges by product type (2019)

Asset class	Trading volume (mil contracts)		% share	
	Futures	Options	Futures	Options
Precious metals	562.53	19.77	96.60%	3.40%
Non-precious metals	1,423.91	15.85	98.90%	1.10%
Agriculture	1,650.58	117.14	93.37%	6.63%
Energy	2,403.36	138.23	94.56%	5.44%
Others	886.48	0.39	99.96%	0.04%
Overall	6,926.87	291.38	95.96%	4.04%

Source: FIA monthly statistics (December 2019 report).

Table 3. Global commodity derivatives open interest on exchanges by product type (end-2019)				
Asset class	Open interest (mil contracts)		% share	
	Futures	Options	Futures	Options
Precious metals	3.44	1.46	70.16%	29.84%
Non-precious metals	7.50	1.22	86.03%	13.97%
Agriculture	17.04	5.36	76.08%	23.92%
Energy	45.39	14.43	75.88%	24.12%
Others	3.53	0.08	97.85%	2.15%
Overall	76.89	22.54	77.33%	22.67%

Source: FIA monthly statistics (December 2019 report).

3 Global on-exchange commodity derivatives trading activities

3.1 The growing trend in commodity derivatives trading

Over the past decade, commodity derivatives trading on global exchanges has had a remarkable growth, achieving an overall CAGR of 111% in trading volume and 105% in open interest. The CAGRs in both trading volume and open interest reached over 100% for each asset class. Energy products have become the major contributing asset class in terms of trading volume for four consecutive years since 2016, superseding agricultural products; which had been the majority asset class by open interest during 2009 to 2019. (See Figures 13 and 14.)

Figure 13. Annual trading volume of commodity derivatives by asset class (2009 – 2019)

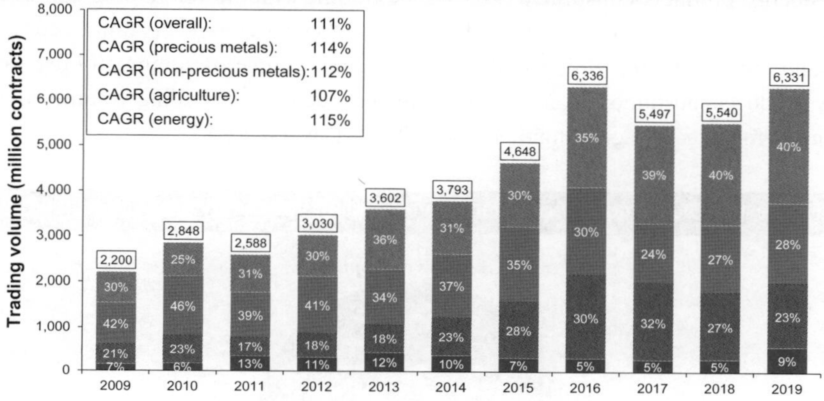

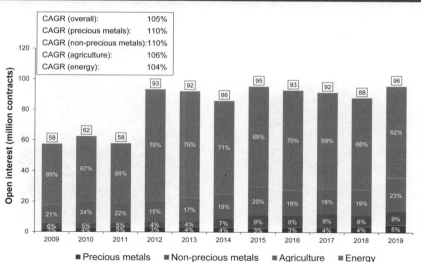

CAGR (overall): 111%
CAGR (precious metals): 114%
CAGR (non-precious metals): 112%
CAGR (agriculture): 107%
CAGR (energy): 115%
Trading volume (million contracts)
2,200
2,848
2,588
3,030
3,602
3,793
4,648
6,336
5,497
5,540
6,331
2009 2010 2011 2012 2013 2014 2015 2016 2017 2018 2019
Precious metals
Non-precious metals
Agriculture
Energy

Note: Excluding products classified as "Other" in FIA statistics, which include both commodity and non-commodity asset classes.

Source: FIA monthly statistics (December report of each year).

Figure 14. Year-end open interest of commodity derivatives by asset class (2009 – 2019)

CAGR (overall): 105%
CAGR (precious metals): 110%
CAGR (non-precious metals): 110%
CAGR (agriculture): 106%
CAGR (energy): 104%
Open interest (million contracts)
58
62
58
93
92
86
95
93
92
88
96
2009 2010 2011 2012 2013 2014 2015 2016 2017 2018 2019
Precious metals
Non-precious metals
Agriculture
Energy

Note: Excluding products classified as "Other" in FIA statistics, which include both commodity and non-commodity asset classes.

Source: FIA monthly statistics (December report of each year).

Taking a closer look into the composition of on-exchange commodity activities in 2019, energy products constituted 35% of the trading volume for futures and 47% for options; agricultural products constituted 24% and 40% respectively. As futures constituted 96% (and options the remaining 4%) of total trading volume of commodity derivatives, energy products constituted 35% of total commodity derivatives trading volume on global exchanges, followed by agricultural products (24%). (See Figure 15.)

Figure 15. Global commodity derivatives trading volume by asset class (2019)

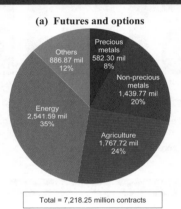

(a) **Futures and options**

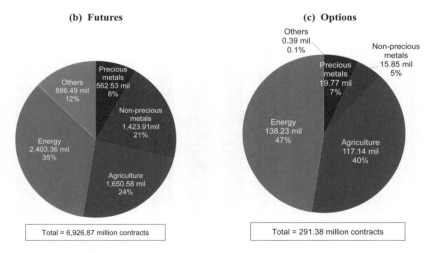

(b) **Futures**   (c) **Options**

Note: Percentage may not add up to 100% due to rounding.

Source: FIA monthly statistics (December 2019 report).

In respect of geographical distribution of commodity trading activities, most of the commodity futures trading took place on Asia-Pacific exchanges — 63% of the total commodity futures volume in 2019; and the majority of the commodity options trading took place in North American exchanges — 64% of the total commodity options volume in 2019. As commodity futures dominated the total commodity derivatives trading, Asia-Pacific exchanges constituted the majority (61%) of total commodity derivatives trading volume in the world in 2019. (See Figure 16.)

Figure 16. Global commodity derivatives trading volume by region (2019)

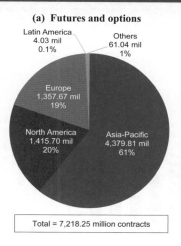

(a) Futures and options

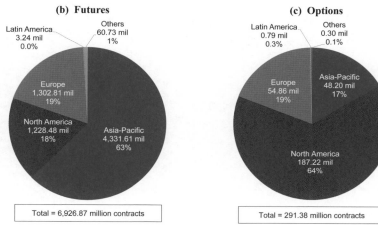

Note: Percentage may not add up to 100% due to rounding.

Source: FIA monthly statistics (December 2019 report).

3.2 Key commodity exchanges

Figures 17 and 18 show the top 20 exchanges by commodity derivatives trading volume and year-end open interest in 2019. The three Mainland exchanges — SHFE, DCE and ZCE — ranked top three by trading volume but ranked below the exchanges in the US and Europe by open interest. It has to be noted that in contrast to free market entry in the western developed markets, foreign participation in the Mainland derivatives market is currently highly restricted[12]. In other words, the high trading volume on their exchanges are basically contributed by domestic participants only.

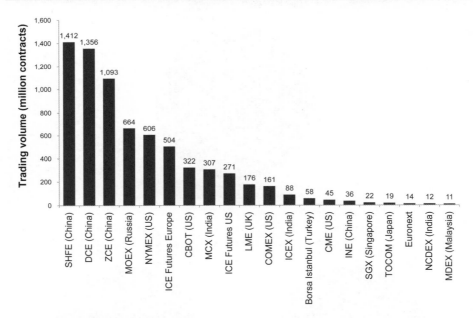

Figure 17. Top 20 exchanges by commodity derivatives trading volume (2019)

Source: FIA monthly statistics (December 2019 report).

---

12 Foreign participation is only allowed for a few designated products (see the speech of the Chairman of the China Securities Regulatory Commission at the 11th Lujiazui Forum on 13 June 2019, on the Lujiazui Forum website).

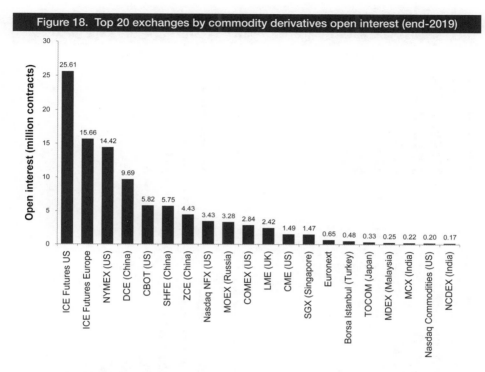

Figure 18. Top 20 exchanges by commodity derivatives open interest (end-2019)

Source: FIA monthly statistics (December 2019 report).

When looking at different asset classes, in 2019, the SHFE took the lead in the trading of precious metals and non-precious metals, followed by COMEX in the US and the Indian Commodity Exchange (ICEX) for precious metals and the DCE and the LME for non-precious metals; the DCE took the lead in the trading of agricultural products, followed by ZCE and CBOT; and Moscow Exchange (MOEX) in Russia took the lead in the trading of energy products, followed by NYMEX and ICE Futures Europe. (See Figure 19.)

Figure 19. Top 10 exchanges by trading volume of commodity derivative products for each asset class (2019)

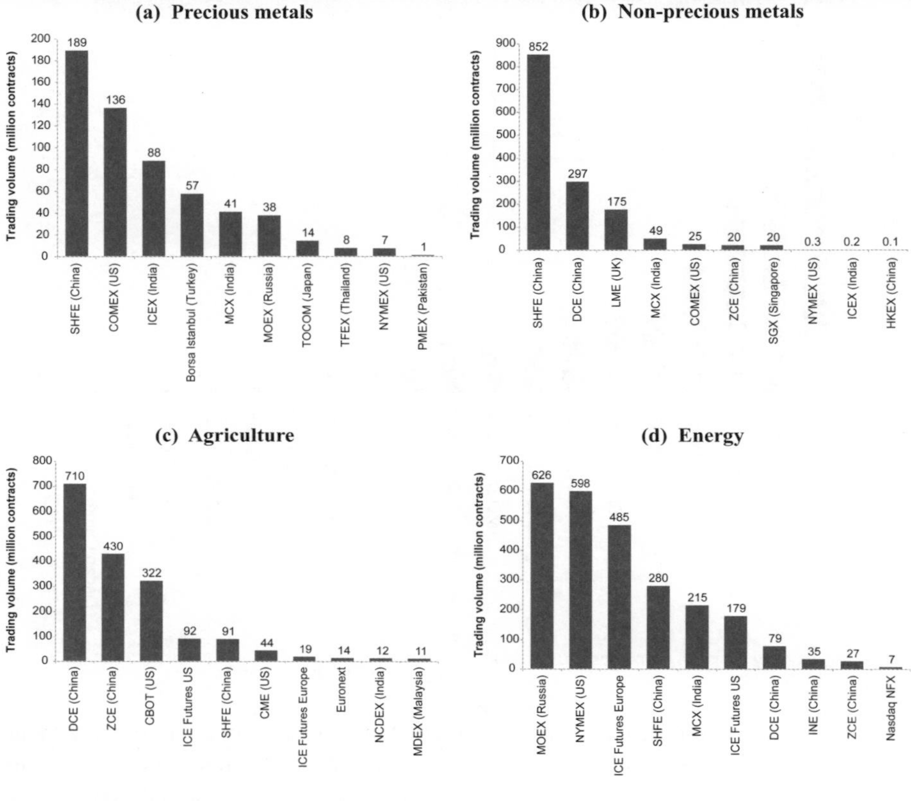

(a) Precious metals

(b) Non-precious metals

(c) Agriculture

(d) Energy

Source: FIA monthly statistics (December 2019 report).

In terms of open interest, COMEX attracted the largest open positions as at the end of 2019 for precious metals, followed by the SHFE and Borsa Istanbul in Turkey; the SHFE took the first place for non-precious metals, followed by the LME and the Singapore Exchange (SGX); the DCE ranked top for agricultural products, followed by CBOT and ICE Futures US; ICE Futures US ranked top for energy products, followed by ICE Futures Europe and NYMEX. (See Figure 20.)

Figure 20. Top 10 exchanges by open interest of commodity derivative products for each asset class (end-2019)

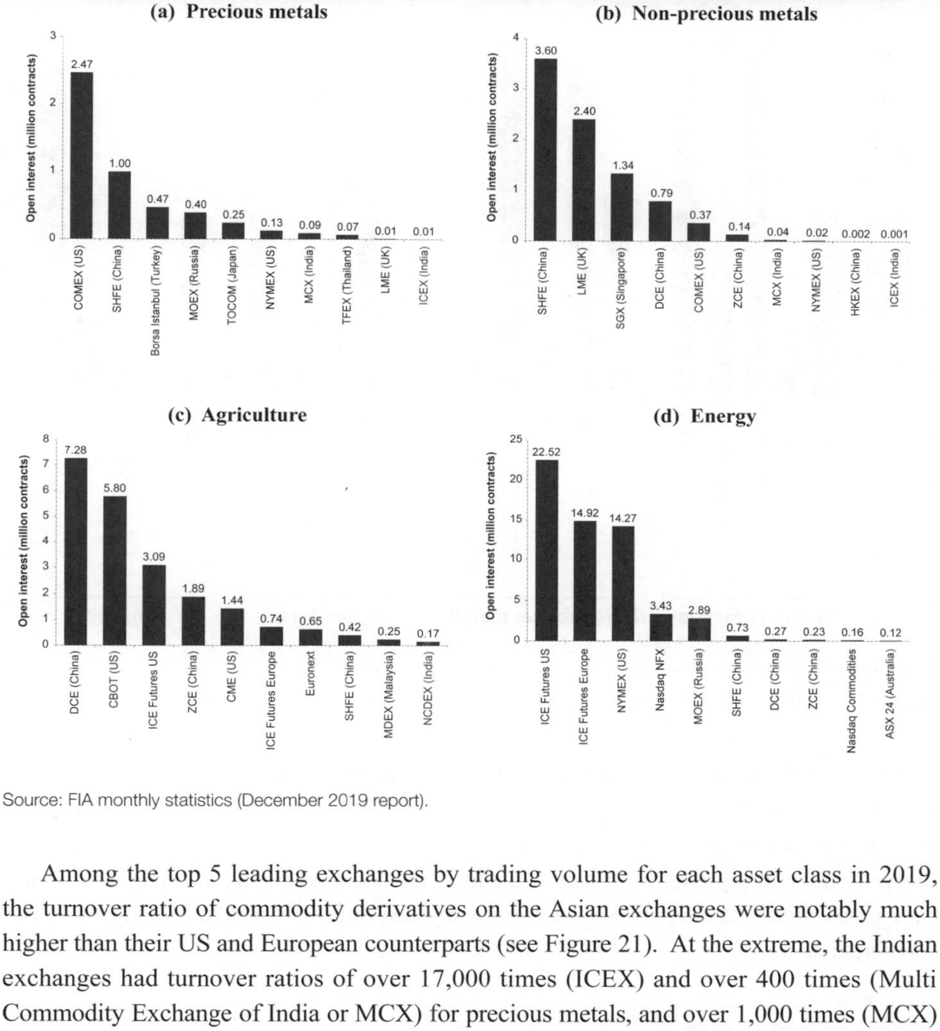

(a) **Precious metals**

(b) **Non-precious metals**

(c) **Agriculture**

(d) **Energy**

Source: FIA monthly statistics (December 2019 report).

Among the top 5 leading exchanges by trading volume for each asset class in 2019, the turnover ratio of commodity derivatives on the Asian exchanges were notably much higher than their US and European counterparts (see Figure 21). At the extreme, the Indian exchanges had turnover ratios of over 17,000 times (ICEX) and over 400 times (Multi Commodity Exchange of India or MCX) for precious metals, and over 1,000 times (MCX) for non-precious metals and over 2,000 times (MCX) for energy products. The Mainland exchanges had turnover ratios of 190 times (SHFE) compared to the 55 times of COMEX for precious metals; 237 times (SHFE) and 374 times (DCE) compared to 73 times of the LME for non-precious metals; 98 times (DCE) and 227 times (ZCE) compared to 55 times (CBOT) and 30 times (ICE Futures US) for Agriculture; and 382 times (SHFE) compared to 42 times (NYMEX) and 33 times (ICE Futures Europe) for energy products.

Figure 21. Turnover ratio of top 5 exchanges by commodity derivatives trading volume (2019)

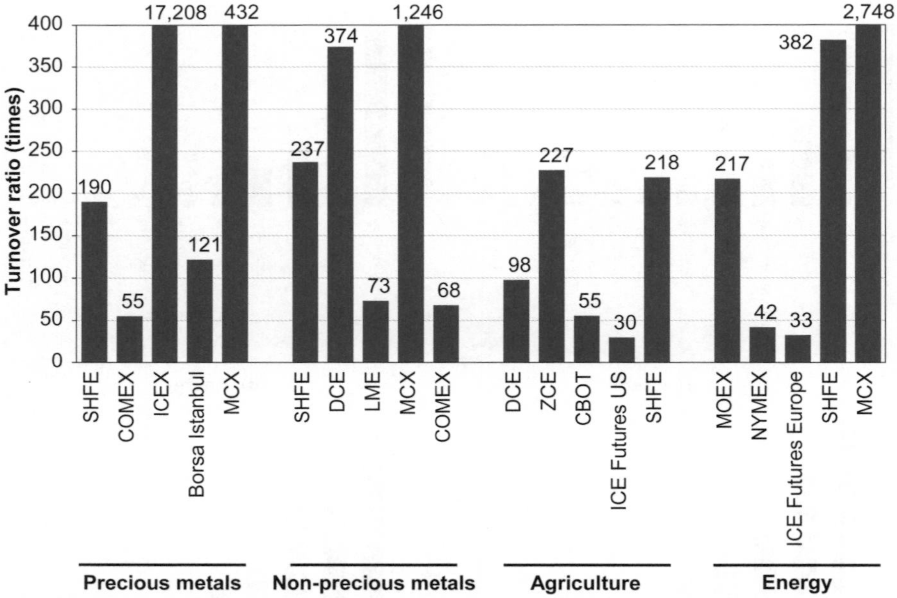

Note: Bars with turnover ratio exceeding 300 times are not shown in full.

Source: FIA monthly statistics (December 2019 report).

In summary, the Mainland futures exchanges are among global leading exchanges in the trading of commodity derivatives for three out of the four major commodity asset classes, namely precious metals, non-precious metals and agricultural products, but relatively not as strong in energy products. Asian exchanges, including Mainland exchanges, typically have much higher turnover ratios for commodity derivatives than their US and European counterparts.

3.3   Key products

3.3.1   Precious metals

The most heavily traded precious metal products on exchanges have been silver and gold. The leading exchange in this asset class by trading volume in 2019, the SHFE, offered only three products — silver futures and gold futures and options. The second ranking exchange, COMEX, offered 21 futures and options in precious metals. Nevertheless, the trading on COMEX was dominated by only a few products on gold and silver as well — gold futures (64% of its precious metal products' total trading volume), silver futures (18%) and gold options (11%). Comparably, the gold contracts of the SHFE have a smaller contract size than those of COMEX. The third ranking exchange, ICEX, offered diamond futures. (See Table 4.)

Table 4. Top 3 products on the top 3 exchanges by trading volume (2019) — Precious metals						
Exchange	% share of exchange in global volume of the asset class	Product	Contract size	2019 Trading volume (contracts)	% share in all precious metal products on the exchange[1]	Cumulative % share in global volume[2]
SHFE	32.5%	Silver futures	15 kg	142,823,743	75.5%	32.5%
		Gold futures	1 kg	46,208,567	24.4%	
		Gold options on futures	1 kg	40,926	0.0%	
COMEX	23.4%	Gold futures	100 troy ounces (~3.11 kg)	86,508,741	63.6%	21.6%
		Silver futures	5,000 troy ounces (~155.68 kg)	24,149,148	17.7%	
		Gold options	100 troy ounces (~3.11 kg)	15,043,949	11.1%	
ICEX	15.1%	Diamond 1CT futures	1 carat	86,164,857	98.2%	15.1%
		Diamond 0.5CT futures	0.5 carat	1,544,910	1.8%	
		Diamond 0.3CT futures	0.3 carat	463	0.0%	

Notes:
(1)   Trading volume of the product as percentage of all precious metal products' trading volume on the exchange.
(2)   Total trading volume of the top 3 products as percentage of all precious metal products' global trading volume.
Source: FIA monthly statistics (December 2019 report).

3.3.2 Non-precious metals

In 2019, the top three non-precious metal products by trading volume on the top-ranked exchange, the SHFE, were steel rebar futures, nickel futures and zinc futures. The second-ranked exchange, the DCE, offered only iron ore products. Products on this single metal asset of DCE already constituted 21% of the global trading volume in non-precious metals. The third-ranked exchange, the LME, had the highest volumes in aluminium, copper and zinc products. In respect of zinc futures, the SHFE product again has a much smaller contract size than the LME product. (See Table 5.)

Table 5. Top 3 products on the top 3 exchanges by trading volume (2019) —— Non-precious metals						
Exchange	% share of exchange in global volume of the asset class	Product	Contract size	2019 Trading volume (contracts)	% share in all non-precious metal products on the exchange[1]	Cumulative % share in global volume[2]
SHFE	59.2%	Steel rebar futures	10 tons	465,171,782	54.6%	48.4%
		Nickel futures	1 ton	160,444,120	18.8%	
		Zinc futures	5 tons	71,066,468	8.3%	
DCE	20.6%	Iron ore futures	100 metric tonnes	296,538,011	99.9%	20.6%
		Iron ore options on futures	100 metric tonnes	363,865	0.1%	
LME	12.2%	Aluminium futures	25 metric tonnnes	66,046,920	37.6%	9.2%
		LME copper futures (Grade A copper)	25 metric tonnnes	37,047,230	21.1%	
		LME zinc futures (special high-grade zinc)	25 metric tonnnes	29,648,051	16.9%	

Notes:

(1) Trading volume of the product as percentage of all non-precious metal products' trading volume on the exchange.

(2) Total trading volume of the top 3 products as percentage of all non-precious metal products' global trading volume.

Source: FIA monthly statistics (December 2019 report).

3.3.3 Agriculture

Agricultural products have a great variety traded on global exchanges. Key products include soybean meal futures, RBD palm olein futures and corn futures on the DCE;

rapeseed meal futures, white sugar futures and cotton futures on the ZCE; and corn futures, soybean futures and wheat futures on the CBOT (see Table 6).

Table 6. Top 3 products on the top 3 exchanges by trading volume (2019) —— Agriculture						
Exchange	% share of exchange in global volume of the asset class	Product	Contract size	2019 Trading volume (contracts)	% share in all agricultural products on the exchange[1]	Cumulative % share in global volume[2]
DCE	40.2%	Soybean meal futures	10 metric tonnes	272,869,691	38.4%	28.7%
		RBD palm olein futures	10 metric tonnes	135,504,196	19.1%	
		Corn futures	10 metric tonnes	99,119,054	14.0%	
ZCE	24.3%	Rapeseed meal futures	10 metric tonnes	138,085,360	32.1%	18.2%
		White sugar futures	10 metric tonnes	119,288,327	27.8%	
		Cotton no.1 futures	5 metric tonnes	63,971,129	14.9%	
CBOT	18.2%	Corn futures	5,000 bushels (~136 metric tonnes)	134,508,582	41.8%	13.5%
		Soybean futures	5,000 bushels (~136 metric tonnes)	66,841,024	20.8%	
		Chicago soft red winter wheat futures	5,000 bushels (~136 metric tonnes)	37,753,766	11.7%	

Notes:

(1)   Trading volume of the product as percentage of all agricultural products' trading volume on the exchange.

(2)   Total trading volume of the top 3 products as percentage of all agricultural products' global trading volume.

Source: FIA monthly statistics (December 2019 report).

3.3.4 Energy

Among the different asset classes, energy products have the largest number on exchanges (see Section 2 above). Of the 876 energy products as at the end of 2019,

NYMEX alone offered a total number of 561 (64%). However, the top ten most traded energy products on NYMEX already constituted 96% of total energy product volume on the exchange[13].

Crude oil products were the dominant type by trading volume. The most actively traded energy product on the top three exchanges (MOEX, NYMEX and ICE Futures Europe) by trading volume in 2019 were on crude oil. (See Table 7.)

Table 7. Top 3 products on the top 3 exchanges by trading volume (2019) — Energy						
Exchange	% share of exchange in global volume of the asset class	Product	Contract size	2019 Trading volume (contracts)	% share in all energy products on the exchange[1]	Cumulative % share in global volume[2]
MOEX	24.6%	Brent oil futures	10 barrels	625,284,893	99.9%	24.6%
		Light sweet crude oil futures	10 barrels	769,032	0.1%	
NYMEX	23.5%	WTI light sweet crude oil futures	1,000 barrels	291,465,320	48.7%	17.5%
		Henry hub natural gas futures	10,000m British thermal units (MMBtu)	103,394,504	17.3%	
		RBOB gasoline physical futures	42,000 gallons	49,851,807	8.3%	
ICE Future Europe	19.1%	Brent crude oil futures	1,000 barrels	246,921,939	50.9%	15.1%
		Low sulphur gas oil futures	100 metric tonnes	80,210,173	16.5%	
		WTI light sweet crude oil futures	1,000 barrels	57,292,213	11.8%	

Notes:
(1) Trading volume of the product as percentage of all energy products' trading volume on the exchange.
(2) Total trading volume of the top 3 products as percentage of all energy products' global trading volume.

Source: FIA monthly statistics (December 2019 report).

---

13 Source: FIA monthly statistics (December 2019 report).

4   Conclusion

Commodity derivatives are traded both on-exchange and in the OTC market. While OTC trading had declined after the 2008 Global Financial Crisis, a growing trend is observed in the trading of on-exchange commodity derivatives, mainly futures, along with the growing market share of Asian exchanges. This can be attributed to the global economic growth, the increased use of commodity derivatives in portfolio investment and the rise of the Mainland economy and Mainland commodity exchanges in the world.

While the developed markets in the US and Europe may have taken the lead in terms of number of commodity products offered, the Mainland commodity derivatives exchanges have assumed a leading role in terms of trading volume. At least one of the three Mainland exchanges were among the top three in terms of trading volume in 2019 for three of the four commodity categories — precious metals, non-precious metals and agriculture. They fell behind only for energy products, which however constituted the majority of global commodity derivatives trading volume (mainly from crude oil futures).

Commodity contracts on the Mainland exchanges are typically of a smaller contract size and are traded in relatively high turnover ratios compared with their counterparts in the western developed markets. Compared to overseas counterparts, the Mainland commodity derivatives exchanges are currently highly restricted to foreign participation. With the further development and opening-up of the Mainland exchanges, the landscape of the global commodity derivatives market will continue to evolve.

Abbreviations of exchanges

Note: Country/Region is put in brackets.

ASX 24	ASX Trade24 (Australia)
CBOT	Chicago Board of Trade (US)
CME	Chicago Mercantile Exchange (US)
DCE	Dalian Commodity Exchange (China)
Euronext	Euronext Derivatives Market (Europe)
HKEX	Hong Kong Exchanges and Clearing Limited (China)
ICEX	Indian Commodity Exchange (India)
JSE	Johannesburg Stock Exchange (South Africa)
LME	London Metal Exchange (UK)
MDEX	Malaysia Derivatives Exchange (Malaysia)
MOEX	Moscow Exchange (Russia)
MCX	Multi Commodity Exchange of India (India)
Nasdaq Commodities	The commodities platform of Nasdaq Inc. (US)
Nasdaq NFX	Nasdaq Futures, Inc. (US)
NCDEX	National Commodity & Derivatives Exchange Limited (India)
NYMEX	New York Mercantile Exchange (US)
PMEX	Pakistan Mercantile Exchange (Pakistan)
SHFE	Shanghai Futures Exchange (China)
INE	Shanghai International Energy Exchange (China)
SGX	Singapore Exchange (Singapore)
TFEX	Thailand Futures Exchange (Thailand)
TOCOM	Tokyo Commodity Exchange (Japan)
ZCE	Zhengzhou Commodity Exchange (China)

Appendix

List of exchanges offering commodity derivative products (end-2019)

No.	Exchange name	No. of commodity derivative products
1	Asia Pacific Exchange	5
2	ASX 24	53
3	B3	17
4	Borsa Istanbul	5
5	Borsa Italiana — IDEM	1
6	Budapest Stock Exchange	1
7	Chicago Board of Trade	48
8	Chicago Mercantile Exchange	28
9	Commodity Exchange (COMEX)	39
10	Dalian Commodity Exchange	22
11	Dubai Gold & Commodities Exchange	11
12	Dubai Mercantile Exchange	3
13	Eurex	12
14	Euronext Derivatives Market	7
15	Hong Kong Exchanges and Clearing	13
16	ICE Futures Canada	3
17	ICE Futures Europe	45
18	ICE Futures Singapore	3
19	ICE Futures U.S.	37
20	India International Exchange	3
21	Indian Commodity Exchange	12
22	Indonesia Commodity & Derivatives Exchange	6
23	JSE Securities Exchange	51
24	Korea Exchange	2
25	London Metal Exchange	31

(continued)

No.	Exchange name	No. of commodity derivative products
26	Malaysia Derivatives Exchange	4
27	MATba ROFEX	27
28	Minneapolis Grain Exchange	2
29	Moscow Exchange	16
30	Multi Commodity Exchange of India	34
31	Nasdaq Commodities	35
32	Nasdaq NFX	118
33	National Commodity & Derivatives Exchange in India	22
34	New York Mercantile Exchange	576
35	New Zealand Futures Exchange	8
36	North American Derivative Exchange	7
37	Osaka Dojima Commodity Exchange	10
38	Pakistan Mercantile Exchange	46
39	Shanghai Futures Exchange	19
40	Shanghai International Energy Exchange	2
41	Singapore Exchange	16
42	Taiwan Futures Exchange	4
43	Thailand Futures Exchange	5
44	Tokyo Commodity Exchange	29
45	Zhengzhou Commodity Exchange	25
Total number of derivative products		1,463

Note: The names of the exchanges follow those given in the source.

Source: FIA monthly statistics (December 2019 report).

Chapter 6

The London Metal Exchange —
The world's industrial metals
trading and pricing venue

The London Metal Exchange

Summary

This chapter gives an introduction to the London Metal Exchange, a brief history, an overview of market structure, contracts traded, operations and services.

Introduction to the London Metal Exchange

The London Metal Exchange (LME) is the world centre for industrial metals price discovery, hedging and trading. The physical metals industry — those who mine metal, produce metal and make things out of metal, together with financial participants who trade metal — use the LME to transfer or to take on price risk.

A wholly-owned subsidiary of HKEX Group, the LME provides a forum bringing together participants from the metals and financial communities to create a robust and regulated market where there is always a buyer and a seller, where there is always a price and where there is always the opportunity to transfer or take on risk — 24 hours a day.

The majority of all non-ferrous (also known as "base metals") futures business is transacted on its three trading venues: LMEselect (electronic), the Ring (open outcry) and the 24-hour telephone market. In 2019, 176 million lots were traded at the LME equating to US$13.5 trillion and 3.9 billion tonnes of metal.

Market participants can trade a variety of contracts on the LME including physical futures, options and cash-settled futures as well as average-price and premium contracts. Metals currently available to trade are alumina, aluminium, aluminium alloy, cobalt, copper, gold, NASAAC (North American Special Aluminium Alloy Contract), lead, molybdenum, nickel, silver, steel, tin and zinc.

Investors value the LME not only as a vibrant futures exchange but also for its close links to industry. The possibility of physical delivery via the world-wide network of LME-approved warehouses and deep liquidity makes it an attractive hedging venue for industry and provides a trusted and robust reference price. The prices "discovered" on the LME's platforms are used as the global reference and as a basis for physical trading as well as in the valuation of portfolios, in commodity indices and for metal exchange traded funds (ETFs).

Since being formally established in 1877, the LME has sought to innovate whilst maintaining its traditional strengths and relationships. The LME remains close to its traditional users by ensuring its contracts continue to be relevant to the physical metals industry. With the recent introduction of a suite of cash-settled contracts; the expansion of the LME's ferrous suite; the introduction of gold and silver futures; greater engagement with battery materials and electric vehicle industries; and a commitment to develop a transparent lithium pricing solution, more and more participants have the opportunity to benefit from LME risk-management tools and liquidity.

Counterparty risk is mitigated by LME Clear, the LME's own clearing house which was purpose-built for the metals market. All LME registered trades made on the Ring, the electronic market and by telephone are cleared and settled by LME Clear.

The LME is a Recognised Investment Exchange (RIE), regulated directly by the UK's Financial Conduct Authority (FCA). The FCA also regulates those LME members that conduct investment business. As an RIE, the LME maintains orderly markets in all its contracts, providing proper protection to investors. LME Clear is regulated by the Bank of England.

1   History of the LME

The origins of the LME can be traced back as far as the opening of the Royal Exchange in London in 1571 during the reign of Queen Elizabeth l. It was there that traders in metals and a range of other commodities began to meet on a regular basis.

Table 1 gives an account of the significant events in the history of the LME.

Table 1. Significant events in the history of the LME	
Date	Event
Early 1800s	The Jerusalem Coffee House, off Cornhill in the City of London, became the favourite of the metal trading community and it was here that the tradition of the Ring was born.
1869	The opening of the Suez Canal reduced the delivery time of tin from Malaya to match the three-month delivery time for copper from Chile. This gave rise to the LME's unique system of daily prompt dates for up to three months forward, which still exists to this day.
1877	The traders formed the London Metals and Mining Company and moved into their first premises over a hat shop in Lombard Court in the City of London. Copper and tin have traded on the LME since the Exchange was established.
1881	Membership increased rapidly and, after surpassing the three hundred mark, a move was made to a purpose-built exchange in Whittington Avenue in the City of London, where it remained for 98 years.
1903	The trading of lead began.
1914	Market closed for several months with the advent of World War I.
1915	Zinc began trading on the LME.
1939	Trading came to a virtual standstill as World War II broke out.
1963	The first European LME warehouse was authorised in Rotterdam.

(continued)

Table 1. Significant events in the history of the LME	
Date	Event
1978	Primary aluminium was introduced in December of this year. The contract has since become the LME's most "liquid" (most heavily traded) contract.
1979	Nickel commenced trading on the LME.
1987	The LME became a centrally cleared and regulated exchange.
1987	The first non-European LME warehouse was authorised in Singapore.
1988	The LME becomes a Recognised Investment Exchange (RIE).
1989	The Vendor Feed System (VFS) — the first electronic price feed from the LME — was launched. In the same year, the first Japanese LME warehouse was authorised.
1991	The LME authorised its first US warehouse in Baltimore.
1992	Aluminium alloy began trading on the LME.
1994	After a period of 14 years at Plantation House in Fenchurch Street, the LME moved to Leadenhall Street in the City of London.
2000	The LME demutualised.
2006	LMEminis — small-sized, cash-settled monthly futures — were introduced for copper, aluminium and zinc.
2008	The LME made a move into ferrous metals with the introduction of two regional contracts for steel billet. In July 2010, these contracts merged into a single global contract.
2010	Two minor metals futures contracts for cobalt and molybdenum were introduced.
2012	The LME was acquired by Hong Kong Exchanges and Clearing Limited (HKEX).
2014	LME Clear, a customised clearing house was built from scratch to specifically meet the needs of the metals community.
2015	The LME launched LME Steel Scrap and LME Steel Rebar, together with a suite of physically settled aluminium premium contracts.
2015	The LME moved to its current home in Finsbury Square.
2017	LMEprecious, the service offering LME Gold and LME Silver contracts for the precious metals market, was launched.
2019	The LME set out responsible sourcing requirements for its approved metal brands. HKEX London Minis were launched for aluminium, copper, lead, nickel, tin and zinc on the HKEX derivatives market. Seven new cash-settled contracts were introduced for alumina, aluminium premiums, cobalt, molybdenum and steel hot-rolled coil.

2　Who uses the LME?

The LME connects physical and financial market participants to create a global pool of liquidity. These participants buy and sell LME futures and options to transfer (hedge) and take on (invest in) price risk and in that process discover globally relevant prices.

Participants on the LME include:

- Metal producers such as miners, smelters and refiners;
- Metal consumers such as industrial manufacturers;
- Merchants and physical traders;
- Banks, financial funds and commodity trading advisers (CTAs);
- Proprietary traders, algorithmic / high-frequency traders; and
- Brokers and clearing institutions.

2.1 Physical market participants

The LME has been helping metal producers and consumers manage their price risks since 1877. It performs this task in several ways:

- **Hedging** — Producers and consumers use the LME to hedge their price risk. The time between a physical contract being agreed and the time it is settled can span days, weeks, months and years — and in that time a lot can happen to the price of a metal. It is this risk that the physical market seeks to mitigate. Benefits of hedging include:
  - protection against price movements;
  - the ability to lock in margins and offer long-term fixed prices to customers;
  - improving budget forecasts;
  - the opportunity to turn inventory into cash or security for finance;
  - protection of physical inventory against price falls; and
  - hedging physical purchases in time of production challenges.
- **Price discovery** — The LME provides the world with daily, transparent and real reference prices. The prices are discovered using risk capital and are truly reflective of global supply and demand. The ability to hedge is dependent on these prices.
- **Price convergence** — LME physical futures contracts are settled via its global warehouse network. This is key because it means that futures prices discovered on its markets converge with (and are reflective of) the prices of physical metal.
- **Physical settlement** — Only LME-registered brands of metal that are actually used by the physical market are accepted for good delivery. This, coupled with ongoing testing and reference to numerous global standards, means its contracts are always relevant.
- **Prompt-date structure** — No other market offers such a range of prompt dates and no other market provides the metals community with such flexibility in matching and hedging their real-world needs.
- **Reference pricing** — The prices discovered on LME trading platforms are global reference prices used for valuing and settling physical contracts.

3   The physical market

In times of extreme shortage or over-supply, the LME also provides producers and consumers with a physical market of last resort. This is achieved via the LME's global warehouse network.

All metals stored on warrant in LME-approved warehouses are LME-approved brands from LME-approved producers, which ensures that the LME's strict rules on commodity grade, quality and shape are met consistently. The LME warehouse network complements the physical market. The possibility of physical delivery — supported by storage facilities around the world and numerous LME listed brands — results in price convergence ensuring its prices remain in line with the physical industry.

The combination of price convergence, the global reach of over 550 LME storage facilities and almost 500 listed metal brands, the fact that physical deals are negotiated using LME prices, and its high levels of liquidity, mean that the world gains reference prices it trusts.

3.1   Prompt-date structure

A key feature of the LME is the unique settlement-date structure of its physical contracts and its focus on the physical market. Designed to reflect the nature and timing of bilaterally negotiated metal trades, market participants can use the LME's contracts to transfer or take on risk against metal prices every business day out to 3 months, weekly out to 6 months and monthly out to anything up to 123 months (depending on the underlying metal) — that is over 10 years in the future. The prompt-date structure from cash to 123 months is illustrated below.

Figure 1. Prompt-date structure of contracts on the LME

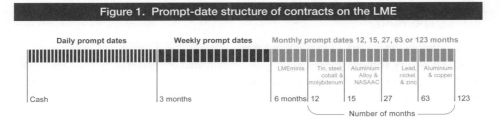

The cash date is the nearest delivery date and is two working days from the date of executing the contract. LME contracts for 3-month delivery (that is, the furthest away daily prompt) are typically the most actively traded contract on any business day. The 3-month contract is most commonly traded on the LME's electronic platform, LMEselect.

3rd Wednesday contracts are monthly futures that exist within the current prompt-date structure for all major LME contracts. These contracts only expire on the 3rd Wednesday of each month. Therefore, they are monthly futures. 3rd Wednesdays are also the underlying contracts for LME options. Up to 65% of open interest (open positions) sits on LME 3rd Wednesday expiry dates.

The 3-month contract and the uniform 3rd Wednesday contracts interact as pivotal points of concentrated liquidity within the LME prompt-date structure.

3.2   Calendar spread trading

Calendar spread trading, or "carry trading" is the act of buying a contract with a particular prompt date and simultaneously selling another contract with a different date. It allows market participants to adjust dates and roll positions that are due to expire. It can also be a way to hedge physical inventory or to finance stock. Financial traders, meanwhile, can buy and sell spreads in the LME's liquid carry market to profit from changes in the shape of the forward curve.

4   Trading venues and pricing

4.1   LME trading venues

4.1.1   The Ring

Trading hours: 11:40 – 17:00 London time

Open-outcry trading floor: Liquidity is concentrated in short trading sessions known as "Rings". There are up to 200 tradable dates per LME metal and open-outcry is the most efficient way of trading multiple dates. LME Official, Unofficial and Closing Prices are all, or in part, derived from trading activity on the Ring.

- The LME Official Price is used by the industry when entering into physical contracts.
- The LME Unofficial Price is the last bid and offer quoted during the third Ring and

is a good indicator of afternoon trading. It is particularly used as a reference price in markets in different time zones.

- LME Closing Prices, also known as the Evening Evaluations, are used by LME Clear and LME members to calculate margins and mark positions to market.

4.1.2   LMEselect

Trading hours: 01:00 – 19:00 London time

Electronic trading platform: It offers a range of advanced features for the trading of all LME contracts, all tailored to the LME's unique prompt-date structure. LMEprecious trading hours on LMEselect are 01:00 – 20:00.

The LME is working on developing a new electronic trading platform to replace LMEselect as at time of print. The existing LMEsource data platform will also be enhanced to include data from all LME venues: LMEselect, inter-office telephone market and the Ring. The new trading platform will have an entirely new architecture, leveraging HKEX technology, and will bring higher performance capability, more stability, and will be even more dynamic to facilitate future development.

4.1.3   Inter-office (telephone) market

Trading hours: 24 hours

Member's indicative quotes are distributed via the vendor network and can be executed by telephone.

Real-time bid and offer prices are available 24 hours a day via the LME's market data services, LMElive, and from approved data vendors. LMElive provides a comprehensive view of futures and options trading with digital access to prices. The LME also aggregates and publishes a set of reference prices that are based on highly liquid periods of the trading day.

5   LME contracts

The LME is a meeting place of buyers and sellers of metal futures and options. The owner of a long futures contract has the right and the obligation to buy an underlying metal at a predetermined time in the future, while the owner of a short futures contract has an obligation to sell in the future, unless they "close out" their positions before that date.

The owner of an option has the right but not the obligation to buy or sell an underlying metal at a specified price on or before a predetermined date in the future.

The LME provides producers and consumers of metal around the world with the means to manage their exposure to the risk created by metal price volatility.

Producers (those who sell the metal they mine and refine) are at risk of prices falling, and consumers (those who buy and make things from metal) are at risk of prices rising. Hedging against these price movements using the LME's futures and options contracts enables the metals industry to focus on their core business.

LME base metal contracts are, strictly speaking, forward contracts. This means that, unlike standard futures, profits and losses are realised at expiry, not before.

All LME contracts are traded in lots which vary in size depending on the contract type and the underlying metal.

Broadly speaking, there are two main types of LME contract — physically settled and cash settled.

Table 2 below shows the list of LME contracts as of February 2020 including how each is settled, the types of contract available for each metal and the prompt dates. (Section 5.1 below describes the different contract types.)

Table 2. LME contracts (as of May 2020)					
Contract name	Settlement type	Lot size	Contract type	Prompt dates	First traded
LME Alumina (CRU/ Fastmarkets MB)	Cash	50 metric tonnes	Futures	Monthly prompts out to 15 months	2019
LME Aluminium	Physical	25 metric tonnes	• Futures • Monthly Average Futures • LMEminis • HKEX London Minis • Traded options • Traded Average Price Options (TAPOs)	• Daily: out to 25 days • Weekly: 3 out to 6 months • Monthly: 7 out to 123 months (63 months for traded options and TAPOs)	1978
LME Aluminium Alloy	Physical	20 metric tonnes	• Futures • Monthly Average Futures • Traded options • TAPOs	• Daily: out to 3 months • Weekly: 3 out to 6 months • Monthly: 7 out to 27 months	1992
LME Aluminium Premiums US Premium/ West-Europe Premium/ East-Asia Premium/ South-East Asia Premium	Physical	25 metric tonnes	Futures	3rd Wednesday of each maturity month, subject to trading regulations	2017

(continued)

Table 2. LME contracts (as of May 2020)					
Contract name	Settlement type	Lot size	Contract type	Prompt dates	First traded
LME Aluminium Premiums Duty Paid US Midwest (Platts) / Duty Unpaid European (Fastmarkets MB)	Cash	25 metric tonnes	Futures	Monthly prompts out to 15 months	2019
LME Cobalt	Physical	1 metric tonne	Futures	• Daily: out to 3 months • Weekly: 3 out to 6 months • Monthly: 7 out to 15 months	2010
LME Cobalt (Fastmarkets MB)	Cash	1 metric tonne	Futures	Monthly prompts out to 15 months	2019
LME Copper	Physical	25 metric tonnes	• Futures • Monthly Average Futures • LMEminis • HKEX London Minis • Traded options • TAPOs	• Daily: out to 25 days • Weekly: 3 out to 6 months • Monthly: 7 out to 123 months (63 months for traded options and TAPOs)	1877
LME Gold	Physical	100 fine troy ounces	Futures	• Daily: out to 25 days • Monthly: out to 24 months • Quarterly: out to 5 years	2017
LME Lead	Physical	25 metric tonnes	• Futures • Monthly Average Futures • LMEminis • HKEX London Minis • Traded options • TAPOs	• Daily: out to 25 days • Weekly: 3 out to 6 months • Monthly: 7 out to 63 months	1920
LME Molybdenum (Platts)	Cash	2,205 lbs	Futures	Monthly prompts out to 15 months	2019
LME NASAAC	Physical	20 metric tonnes	• Futures • Monthly Average Futures • Traded options • TAPOs	• Daily: out to 3 months • Weekly: 3 out to 6 months • Monthly: 7 out to 27 months	2002
LME Nickel	Physical	6 metric tonnes	• Futures • Monthly Average Futures • LMEminis • HKEX London Minis • Traded options • TAPOs	• Daily: out to 3 months • Weekly: 3 out to 6 months • Monthly: 7 out to 63 months	1979

(continued)

Table 2. LME contracts (as of May 2020)					
Contract name	Settlement type	Lot size	Contract type	Prompt dates	First traded
LME Silver	Physical	5,000 fine troy ounces	Futures	• Daily: out to 25 days • Monthly: out to 24 months • Quarterly: out to 5 years	2017
LME Steel HRC FOB China (Argus)	Cash	10 metric tonnes	Futures	Monthly prompts out to 15 months	2019
LME Steel HRC N. America (Platts)	Cash	10 short tons	Futures	Monthly prompts out to 15 months	2019
LME Steel Rebar	Cash	10 metric tonnes	Futures	Monthly prompts out to 15 months	2015
LME Steel Scrap	Cash	10 metric tonnes	Futures	Monthly prompts out to 15 months	2015
LME Zinc	Physical	25 metric tonnes	• Futures • Monthly Average Futures • LMEminis • HKEX London Minis • Traded options • TAPOs	• Daily: out to 3 months • Weekly: 3 out to 6 months • Monthly: 7 out to 63 months	1920

5.1   Contract types

(1)   Physically settled contracts

LME physical futures contracts are unique and designed to mirror physical trading. Futures that are not closed out by an opposite sale or purchase are physically settled. All LME futures are settled on the prompt date with initial and variation margins called during the term of a contract. LME contracts can be settled using physical stock stored in LME-approved warehouses. Since most participants use LME contracts to hedge or gain exposure to the price curve, less than 1% result in actual delivery of metal. The vast majority of LME contracts are "closed out" before settlement.

More flexible than futures, LME options provide the metal and financial communities with alternative opportunities to reduce price risk (through hedging trades) or take on price risk (on expected price moves). Tradeable out up to 63 months (depending on metal), LME options can be exercised any time up to and including the expiry date (these are American-style options). The underlying is the equivalent 3rd Wednesday LME future, which is itself physically settled. LME options are currently available on eight underlying metals.

(2)   Cash-settled contracts

Alongside its physically settled futures, the LME offers a suite of cash-settled futures contracts. These contracts are not physically tied to an underlying metal, but instead settle against an average price. Settlement prices are most often provided by a Price Reporting Agency (PRA). The PRA's role is to survey the market to assess a fair value (based on bids, offers and trades, combined with market intelligence) to generate a price assessment for the underlying asset. The LME then uses this price assessment to calculate the final settlement price for its cash-settled contracts.

(3)   TAPOs

Traded Average Price Options (TAPOs) give the metal community a flexible way of hedging exposures to average metal prices in their business contracts. This is particularly useful because a large proportion of physical contracts are negotiated based on the average prices over particular time periods. TAPOs are financially settled Asian options, whose payoff depends on the Monthly Average Settlement Price (MASP) for the contract month. TAPOs can be traded on aluminium, aluminium alloy, NASAAC, copper, lead, nickel, tin and zinc.

(4)   Monthly Average Futures

Monthly Average Futures are designed specifically for members of the metal community who need to hedge against the monthly average price. They were the first of their type in the world to be traded on-exchange and available for all LME non-ferrous metals.

(5)   LMEminis

LMEminis are five-tonne cash-settled monthly futures contracts which settle against the LME "parent" contract's Official Settlement Price. They are available for copper, aluminium and zinc.

(6)   HKEX's London Metal Mini Futures

HKEX's London Metal Mini Futures are contracts designed to meet the needs of Asian participants who want to mitigate or take on metal price risk using futures denominated in offshore Renminbi (CNH) or US dollar (USD). Traded on the HKEX derivatives platform in Hong Kong, the small-lot contracts are available in six base metals — aluminium, zinc, copper, nickel, tin and lead. Like LMEminis, these contracts are cash settled against the LME "parent" contract's Official Settlement Price.

5.2   LMEprecious

LMEprecious is the initiative created by the LME, the World Gold Council and a group of leading industry participants to introduce exchange-traded, loco London precious metals products. LME Gold and LME Silver futures provide new opportunities for trading, price discovery and risk management, creating an enhanced market structure for the precious metals community.

LMEprecious was developed in response to market demand and in close consultation with key precious metals stakeholders. Offering daily and monthly futures for both gold and silver, LMEprecious delivers greater choice for market participants, modernising the gold and silver markets to better reflect the needs of global players in precious metals markets.

The LME currently works with the London Platinum and Palladium Market (LPPM) to administer and distribute LBMA Platinum and LBMA Palladium prices. This solution is delivered via LME's custom-built electronic auction platform, LMEbullion.

5.3   Electric vehicle battery materials

The LME is in the process of delivering new risk-management tools for battery materials and electric vehicle (EV) industries. It is working with global market participants along the value chain to identify and serve the evolving risk management requirements of these industries. Some key battery metals such as nickel, lead, copper, cobalt and aluminium are already well established on the LME. The LME aims to launch new futures contracts to provide further hedging and trading opportunities for battery materials, starting with a cash-settled LME Cobalt (Fastmarkets MB) contract launched in 2019, and is working in partnership with Fastmarkets MB to develop a transparent and robust pricing solution for lithium.

6   LME warehousing

LME warehouses are used to store LME-approved brands of metal, which themselves are used as the underlying assets for physically settled contracts traded on the LME. To support the mechanism of physical delivery, the LME approves and licenses a network of warehouses and storage facilities around the world. There are over 550 LME-approved storage facilities in many locations across the United States, Europe and Asia.

The possibility of physical delivery via the worldwide network of LME-approved warehouses makes it an appealing hedging venue for industry. The LME delivery system relies on a user being guaranteed a specified quality and quantity of metal. To ensure consistency in quality, all metal delivered into LME-approved storage facilities must be of an LME-approved brand and conform to specifications on quality, shape and weight. Producers looking to register their production for LME delivery must meet certain criteria for each brand before gaining LME approval.

The LME does not own or operate warehouses, nor does it own the material they contain. It authorises warehouse companies and the warehouses they operate to store LME-registered brands of metal, on behalf of warrant holders, and issue LME warrants (documents giving title to metal in warehouses) through their London agent for material delivered into LME-approved warehouses. Warrants are allocated from the seller of metal to the buyer of metal via LMEsword, the LME's secure electronic system. LMEsword facilitates the transfer of ownership of LME warrants and stock reporting. Warrants are held in a central depository and produced to a standard format and include a unique barcode. Owners of warrants can also use LMEsword to transfer title to metal held on warrant to facilitate stock financing and other commercial arrangements. Detailed stock level reports are produced and distributed each day by LME market data vendors. Daily stock reports are produced by LMEsword and are a key part of operating an orderly and transparent market.

LME warehouse companies must meet strict criteria before they are approved for the handling of metals and are typically located in high-consumption areas or logistical trading hubs for the shipment of material.

All metals stored in LME-approved storage facilities on warrant are LME-approved brands from LME-approved producers ensuring conformance to the LME's strict rules on commodity grade, quality and shape.

The LME regularly reviews possible reforms to its global physical network of warehouses to ensure it represents best practice for physical market infrastructure storage and logistics.

6.1   Location premiums and discounts

When an LME contract is physically settled, the buyer could receive the warrant for metal in an LME-approved warehouse in any approved LME location and in any of the approved LME brands or shapes. Warrants are randomly allocated from seller to buyer through LMEsword.

The metal price traded on the LME is a global price. However, as certain regions have tighter supply-demand balances than others, and transportation from one region to another incurs costs, metal from a specified delivery destination might come at a premium or discount to the LME price. The same is true if the buyer requires a specific metal brand.

Furthermore, if the buyer wishes to cancel the warrant for their metal and take physical delivery of it, the price will need to accommodate an extra premium to reflect the cost of loading out the metal, and whether a queue exists to withdraw metal from the relevant LME location.

6.2   LME responsible sourcing requirements

On 25 October 2019, the LME published its requirements for the responsible sourcing of LME-listed brands. These requirements are underpinned by the Organisation for Economic Co-operation and Development (OECD) *Due Diligence Guidance for Responsible Supply Chains of Minerals from Conflict-Affected and High-Risk Areas.*

7   LME Clear

LME Clear is the clearing house custom-built specifically for users of the LME. Launched in 2014, it was designed in consultation with the market to provide cost-efficient clearing services which are compliant with the European Market Infrastructure Regulation (EMIR), using cutting-edge technology. It delivers innovative clearing and settlement services for traded transactions.

LME Clear is the central counterparty (CCP) for all LME clearing members and their trading activities. It provides a financial guarantee to every traded contract, acting as "the seller to every buyer and the buyer to every seller". In the event of a clearing member's default, LME Clear will step in and manage the defaulting clearing member's outstanding risk positions swiftly and efficiently.

LMEmercury, LME Clear's clearing system, allows members to monitor and assess the risk they are taking on in real time. This in turn means that clearing members have more control over their business in key areas such as portfolio management, option expiry handling and reporting.

LME Clear regularly introduces new services to meet customer needs. Recently added services include a position-transfer service, inter-prompt spread methodology, trade compression, accepting warrants and CNH as collateral, new averaging solutions and a new gross aggregated account.

7.1   Warrants as collateral

LME warrants entitle the holder to metals stored in LME-approved warehouses and are bearer documents. In other words, an LME warrant is the bearer document for one lot of metal held in an LME-approved warehouse. As a terminal market for the metals that are traded on the LME, the amount of metal held on warrant in LME warehouses is often used as an indicator of the underlying global supply and demand situation for a metal.

LME Clear has expanded its collateral service for members to pledge LME warrants against their margin requirements. Metal warrants are accepted as an alternative to cash and high-quality government bonds.

Warrants of a metal can only be accepted as collateral for the underlying metal, e.g. aluminium warrants will be acceptable as collateral to cover aluminium positions only. Copper, aluminium, zinc, nickel, lead and tin can currently be used to cover margin requirements on a metal-for-metal basis.

7.2   VaR margin methodology

As part of the LME's larger technology roadmap, the LME is currently working on a custom-designed Value at Risk (VaR) methodology to calculate initial margin for the LME market that best suits its members and their clients. VaR is a widely adopted risk valuation methodology, used in many asset classes by various central counterparties and other financial institutions. There are many different mathematical approaches for calculating VaR. In general, VaR is a portfolio-based calculation which looks to estimate the potential level of loss of the portfolio based on a set of simulations applied.

The key advantages of VaR are that it looks at how the whole portfolio would perform together, reflecting current market conditions, and takes into account portfolio risk composition. The new solution will also be custom-designed specifically for LME markets.

In comparison, the current methodology adopted by the LME looks at combinations of positions and the potential loss of each combination individually before these are aggregated. This can be less efficient, particularly for portfolios with many spread positions.

8   Conclusion

Throughout its history, the LME has provided metals and financial industries with the means to trade and manage metals price risk. Innovative new products and services developed in conjunction with the market have allowed the LME to continue to stay at the forefront of commodities markets around the world. As the company looks ahead, new initiatives such as major technology developments and enhancements, requirements for responsibly sourced metals and environmental considerations will help to shape the future of metals markets. The LME and HKEX Group have worked closely together to develop products and plans for markets in Mainland China and this will be discussed further in Chapter 12 of this book.

Appendix

Special terminology of products and services at the LME

LME Clear	The LME's clearing house for all trading
LMEbullion	The LME's custom-built electronic auction platform for administering the LMBA Platinum and LBMA Palladium prices
LMElive	The LME's market data application, providing customers with LME pricing, information and tools for metals traded on its markets
LMEmercury	The core clearing system used by LME Clear, which allows trading member firms to monitor risk in real time
LMEminis	Five-tonne cash-settled contracts for aluminium, copper and zinc which settle against the LME Official Settlement Price for the "parent" contract
LMEprecious	The initiative which provides the market with exchange-traded, loco London precious metals risk-management products, including LME Gold and LME Silver
LMEselect	The LME's electronic trading platform
LMEsource	The LME's real-time multicast market data dissemination platform
LMEsword	The LME's system which facilitates the transfer of ownership of LME warrants, and stock reporting
Ring	The LME's open-outcry trading venue, where Category 1 member firms trade key industrial metals face-to-face

Part 2
The Mainland and Hong Kong commodities markets

Chapter 7

The spot commodities market in Mainland China — Brief history, current status and connection with the futures market

Qianhai Mercantile Exchange Co., Ltd.

Summary

This paper aims to give a brief introduction on the definition and classification of commodities in Mainland China, as well as the history and current status of its commodity exchanges. With reference to the development of international spot commodities and commodity futures markets, a multi-tiered market framework is proposed to help build a world-class commodities trading hub in Mainland China.

1   Mainland commodities: Concepts and features

As defined by the *Standards for Electronic Trading in Commodities* (GB/T 18769-2003), commodities refer to material goods that could be circulated (but not in the retail sector) and traded in bulk for industrial and agricultural production and consumption.

Commodities are vital to a country's economy and its people's livelihood. For example, price rises of crude oil as a result of a cut in oil production by the Organisation of the Petroleum Exporting Countries (OPEC) will directly impact on the ways of commuting to work, a drop in soybeans supply because of droughts will affect what a family will have on their dining table.

For instance, in 2019, pork prices in the Mainland surged significantly due to a number of factors, including the downside "pork cycle", the African swine fever and the trade war between the United States (US) and China. Apart from being a major agricultural product, pork is also a staple of daily meat consumption. Mainland residents consumed an average of 22.83kg of pork per person in 2018[1] or, based on a population of 1,395 million[2], an aggregate annual consumption of 31.85 million tonnes.

Alongside the pork price rise in the first quarter of 2019 was the hog futures prices in the US. The prices of lean hogs futures on the Chicago Mercantile Exchange (CME) reached their all-time highs across the board. Settlement prices of actively traded contracts almost touched 100 US cents per pound at one point. Afterwards, with the aggravated trade tensions and factors such as funding and demand and supply, the two prices were seen "crossing" each other (see Figure 1).

---

1   Source: National Bureau of Statistics of China.
2   Source: National Bureau of Statistics of China.

Figure 1. Pork price in Mainland China and pork futures price in the US

Source: Wind (data from *www.agri.gov.cn* and CME).

There is no doubt that commodities are critical ingredients and end products in industrial and agricultural production, which are the foundation of the real economy. In the long run, commodities are also a key component in a diversified portfolio. As reported[3], non-commercial long positions accounted for 25% to 35% of the total long positions of the major agricultural futures products in the US, with asset management products (including commodity index funds) being a major participant in commodity futures market.

Characterised by huge trading volumes and price volatility, commodities are highly financial by nature and have become something not to be neglected in the operation of the real economy and financial markets.

---

3 "Institutions 'knock the door', value of commodities in asset allocation is highlighted", *China Securities Journal*, 28 August 2019.

2 Commodities in the Mainland: Classification

In terms of trading nature, commodities can be divided into two broad categories: goods and entitlements. Alternatively, they can be classified as commodity futures and spot commodities depending on whether they are listed and traded on a futures exchange.

Table 1. Classification of commodities		
Category	Sub-category	Type
Goods	Energy	Crude oil, gasoline, natural gas, steam coal, etc.
	Basic metals	Iron, copper, aluminum, lead, zinc, nickel, tungsten, rubber, iron ore, etc.
	Precious metals	Gold, platinum, silver, etc.
	Agricultural products	Corn, soybean, wheat, rice, oat, barley, rye, pork belly, live pig, live cattle, calf, soybean meal, soybean oil, cocoa, coffee, cotton, wool, sugar, orange juice, rapeseed oil, etc.
Entitlements	Shipping rights, forest rights, carbon emission rights, etc.	

2.1 Goods

Traditionally, commodities refer to basic goods only and are widely traded on different types of futures and spot exchanges. Table 2 lists out the major commodity futures available for trading in the Mainland:

Table 2. Types of commodity futures						
	2017		2018		2019	
Type	Trading Volume (in 10,000 lots)	Turnover (in RMB 100 million)	Trading Volume (in 10,000 lots)	Turnover (in RMB 100 million)	Trading Volume (in 10,000 lots)	Turnover (in RMB 100 million)
Soybean No. 1	2,632	10,246	2,211	8,079	1,845	6,422
Linear low-density polyethylene (LLDPE)	6,142	29,148	3,674	17,105	6,344	24,492
Soybean meal	16,288	45,854	23,816	73,500	27,287	76,030
Soybean oil	5,716	35,473	5,414	31,020	8,754	52,512
Soybean No. 2	4	14	2,448	8,337	1,779	5,499

(continued)

Table 2. Types of commodity futures					
	2017		2018		2019	
Type	Trading Volume (in 10,000 lots)	Turnover (in RMB 100 million)	Trading Volume (in 10,000 lots)	Turnover (in RMB 100 million)	Trading Volume (in 10,000 lots)	Turnover (in RMB 100 million)
Corn	12,732	21,071	6,681	12,323	9,912	18,841
Corn starch	5,043	9,927	2,261	5,103	1,656	3,808
Palm oil	6,805	37,804	4,434	21,635	13,550	71,298
Polyvinyl chloride (PVC)	3,900	12,783	3,636	12,192	3,379	11,246
Coking coal	4,219	31,144	4,647	35,478	2,287	17,763
Coke	4,012	77,295	6,907	149,675	5,568	111,372
Iron ore	32,874	170,795	23,649	115,281	29,654	198,731
Egg	3,726	14,228	1,992	7,847	3,713	15,673
Plywood	0	1	0	0	0	0
Polypropylene	5,669	24,264	4,935	23,009	9,371	38,902
Fiberboard	—	—	3	13	117	235
Round-grained non-glutinous rice	—	—	—	—	41	150
Styrene	—	—	—	—	396	1,442
Aluminum	6,542	49,265	4,662	33,557	3,276	22,746
Fuel oil	0	3	3,927	12,048	17,672	42,710
Natural rubber	8,934	137,511	6,185	73,625	5,385	64,483
Copper	5,410	133,874	5,125	129,768	3,652	87,251
Zinc	9,145	107,026	9,235	104,117	7,107	72,001
Rebar	70,202	242,706	53,098	201,710	46,517	169,470
Wire	0	0	16	58	17	68
Gold	1,948	54,193	1,612	44,248	4,621	149,962
Silver	5,311	32,028	4,225	23,232	14,282	89,385
Lead	1,251	11,555	1,020	9,605	771	6,359
Tin	208	3,014	274	4,044	325	4,541
Nickel	7,415	65,030	11,482	119,696	16,044	183,879
Asphalt	9,744	25,327	6,980	21,964	10,291	32,733
Hot rolled coil	10,313	37,779	8,682	33,056	7,041	25,440
Crude oil	—	—	2,651	127,383	3,464	154,760
Plastic No. 20	—	—	—	—	94	997
Purified terephthalic acid (PTA)	14,039	36,964	17,085	55,862	31,247	88,820
White sugar	6,106	39,561	6,397	33,194	11,250	59,494

(continued)

Table 2. Types of commodity futures						
	2017		2018		2019	
Type	Trading Volume (in 10,000 lots)	Turnover (in RMB 100 million)	Trading Volume (in 10,000 lots)	Turnover (in RMB 100 million)	Trading Volume (in 10,000 lots)	Turnover (in RMB 100 million)
Rapeseed oil	2,599	17,374	3,508	23,262	3,779	26,958
Cotton	2,606	20,124	5,847	49,272	6,381	43,616
Strong gluten wheat	38	218	11	55	1	6
Early long-grain non-glutinous rice	0	1	4	20	0	1
Late long-grain non-glutinous rice	0	0	54	308	2	10
Glass	4,109	11,072	2,514	7,069	3,092	8,830
Methanol	13,701	36,574	16,390	46,842	26,509	61,002
Rapeseed	0	1	0	1	6	25
Rapeseed meal	7,974	18,510	10,436	25,419	13,809	32,013
Triticum	0	0	0	0	0	0
Steam coal	3,071	18,353	4,887	30,198	2,749	15,957
Japonica rice	0	0	1	8	0	2
Manganese silicon	2,492	8,513	1,885	7,537	1,117	3,941
Ferrosilicon	1,628	5,604	2,156	7,094	931	2,768
Apple	79	637	9,996	94,013	3,746	33,655
Urea	—	—	—	—	469	1,630

Source: China Futures Association and Wind.

2.2   Entitlements

Entitlement-type commodities cover a wide varieties. These include navigation rights, shipping rights, rights to mine, rights to forest and rights to emit carbon dioxide, etc. Up to the end of 2019, there were still no futures on this category of commodities in the Mainland. A brief on shipping and carbon emission trades is given below.

2.2.1   Shipping trades

Shipping trades include ship trading and leases, cruise trading, shipping finance and insurance.

In November 1996, the Shanghai Shipping Exchange was established upon the approval by the State Council. It was the first state-level shipping exchange in Mainland China.

Thereafter, Chongqing, Guangzhou, Wuhan, Ningbo and Xiamen followed suit and set up their own shipping exchanges. However, given the significant differentiation in the subjects of shipping and ship trading, potential participants in a transaction are rather limited.

Table 3. Ship trading on the Shanghai Shipping Exchange						
Transaction date	Type of ship	Deadweight tonnage (tonne)	Date of construction	Port of registry	Navigation area	Transaction price (in RMB 10,000)
2019-12-24	Bulk carrier	626	2009-06-18	Huzhou	Inland water	62
2019-12-24	Bulk carrier	430	2006-04-29	Huzhou	Inland water	29.58
2019-12-23	Miscellaneous	3,490	2016-05-25	Yiyang	Inland water	300
2019-12-23	Bulk carrier	3,000	2005-04-22	Wuhu	Inland water	180
2019-12-23	Multi-purpose ship	1,825	2012-11-07	Guigang	Inland water	206.8
2019-12-23	Product tanker	980	2012-08-16	Changde	Inland water	26

Source: Shanghai Shipping Exchange.

2.2.2 Rights of carbon emissions

Emissions trading is a market-based mechanism set out in the *Kyoto Protocol*, aiming at reducing global greenhouse gas emissions, with reference to the *United Nations Framework Convention on Climate Change* (UNFCCC). It allows countries that have emission units to spare to sell their excess capacity to countries that have emissions in excess of their targets. The economic rationale behind is: the costs of reducing greenhouse gas emissions vary, depending on which country, industry or sector a company is in, and the differences in technology and the style of management. So an emission rights trading market encourages enterprises with lower cost of reducing emissions to cut emissions beyond their quota, and sell their excess capacity to companies with higher cost of reducing emissions, helping the latter to meet their emission reduction targets, and thereby effectively reducing the overall cost of cutting emissions.

In October 2011, the National Development and Reform Commission (NDRC) of China issued a notice on launching a carbon trading pilot scheme, allowing pilot carbon emissions trading in Beijing, Tianjin, Shanghai, Chongqing, Shenzhen, Hubei and Guangdong. By the end of 2019, there were already eight major carbon emissions exchanges in different regions of the country:

- Guangdong: China Emissions Exchange in Guangzhou (CEEX)
- Shenzhen: China Emissions Exchange (CERX)
- Beijing: China Beijing Environment Exchange (CBEEX)

- Shanghai: Shanghai Environment and Energy Exchange (CNEEEX)
- Hubei: China Hubei Emission Exchange (CHEEX)
- Tianjin: Tianjin Climate Exchange (China TCX)
- Chongqing: Chongqing Carbon Emissions Trading Centre (CCETC[4])
- Fujian: Haixia Equity Exchange (HXEE)

CERX was the first to start trading on 18 June 2013. By 31 December 2019, the accumulated turnover of the eight carbon emissions exchanges reached 273 million tonnes, or RMB 5.76 billion.

Figure 2. Distribution of cumulative trading volume on major carbon emissions trading venues in Mainland China

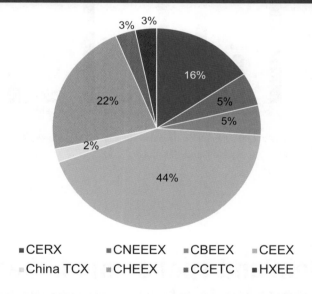

Note: The respective cumulative trading volumes are from inception date to 31 December 2019.
Source: CERX, CNEEEX, CBEEX, CEEX, China TCX, CHEEX, CCETC, HXEE.

---

4   Not the official English name but a translated English name of the Chinese name for indication purpose.

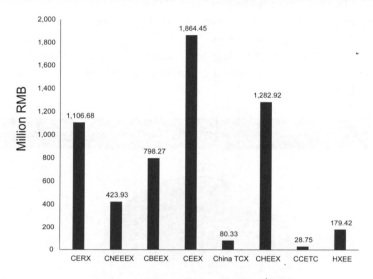

Figure 3. Cumulative turnover value on major carbon emission trading venues in Mainland China

Note: The respective cumulative trading values are from inception date to 31 December 2019.

Source: CERX, CNEEEX, CBEEX, CEEX, China TCX, CHEEX, CCETC, HXEE.

3 Mainland spot commodities markets: History and current status

3.1 History

The spot commodities market in Mainland China refers to the commodities trading market other than those operated by national futures exchanges. Its origin dated back to the 1980s, when allocation of resources in Mainland China was still handled by administrative means under a planned economy model. The quantities, prices and modes of production and circulation of commodities were all directed and determined by government departments.

In 1985, Chongqing proposed to build itself into a trading centre of industrial and agricultural products. Commodities trading was seen at wholesale level, and started shifting from administrative allocation to a free trade model. In 1989, the Ministry of Commerce decided to officially establish wholesale markets and introduced systems for forwards, which were similar to futures. With the rapid development of computers and Internet technologies, network-based e-commerce platforms emerged in the Mainland in 1997, providing spot and forward trading. Since then, the Mainland commodities market started to grow rapidly. The government, medium-sized to large enterprises and industry associations were all seen setting up their own commodities trading platforms, and offering more and more trading services in terms of products and modes of trading.

However, due to regulatory deficiencies, compliance issues and risks were getting serious on these trading platforms. To prevent financial risks and establish market order, the State Council issued a number of documents, including the *Decision of the State Council on Rectifying Various Trading Venues to Effectively Prevent Financial Risks* (State Council Document [2011] No. 38), the *Opinions of the General Office of the State Council on Implementing Efforts to Rectify Various Trading Venues* (State Council General Office Document [2012] No. 37). Led by the China Securities Regulatory Commission, an inter-ministerial joint convention (IMJC) system was established involving the relevant ministries and departments on rectifying various trading venues.

Under the basic principles of "total quantity control, prudent approvals and sensible planning", IMJC held four meetings in February and July 2012, January 2017 and July 2019, at which the progress to rectify various trading venues was reported. According to the statistics given at these meetings, there were a total of 596 commodities trading venues across 36 provinces, municipalities, autonomous regions and special administrative regions. Of these, 89 offered trading in precious metals, 59 offered trading in crude oil (23 of which also offered trading in precious metals and crude oil), and 113 offered trading in relation to cultural and art pieces (37 offered trading in relation to stamps, coins and cards). Over one-third of them were demanded a halt of trading due to regulatory breaches. Those that have not yet launched new product types or developed profitable business models are in a "wait-and-see" state, and have become "zombie" trading venues.

Commodity exchanges have economies of scale. Their merits do not lie in quantitative terms, but in terms of quality, branding and influence. Major exchanges shall capitalise on local resources and industry demands and work to develop product suites that serve the real economy and promote the healthy development of the commodities sector.

3.2   Current status

Compared to futures trading, the spot commodities market is more diversified, flexible and customised in nature, and could provide professional instruments for investors with specific investment or hedging needs. They complement commodity futures in terms of geographical and clientele coverage, and help address the relative lack of customisation in the highly standardised futures market, greatly facilitating participation in the commodities market by investors with hedging and investment needs.

Spot trading in the Mainland commodities market mainly involve physical goods. Spot commodities trading is more flexible and at lower costs than futures trading. In terms of product types, the spot market covers agricultural products, metals, energy and chemicals, etc. In other words, it covers basically all the commodities actively traded in the Mainland.

Table 4. An overview of major spot commodities exchanges in Mainland China		
Year of establishment	Name	Basic information and main products
2002	Shanghai Gold Exchange	It provides the venue, facilities and related services for trading precious metals such as gold, silver, and platinum. Orders are matched in price and time priority. Traders can trade non-standard products through inquiry and by quoting prices and negotiating the transactions on their own. Members can choose to conduct transactions either on the venue or remotely.
2008	Tianjin Precious Metals Exchange	It is an exchange initiated and established by the Tianjin Property Rights Exchange with the approval of the Tianjin Municipal Government. There are six types of precious metals listed on the Exchange: spot platinum, spot palladium, spot nickel, spot silver, spot copper and spot aluminum. The shareholders of the Exchange include CITIC Group Corporation, Tianjin Property Rights Exchange and China Gold Group Corporation. The business scope of the Exchange is "spot wholesale and retail as well as delayed delivery of precious metals (including gold and silver) and non-ferrous metals, and providing an electronic platform for such transactions as well as consultation services in relation to the aforementioned and other approved businesses".
2011	Zhejiang Zhoushan Bulk Commodity Exchange	It was initiated by the People's Government of Zhoushan City and is directly supervised by the Management Committee of China (Zhoushan) Bulk Commodity Trading Center. It mainly trades Zheshang oil* and tungsten concentrates and its third-party custodian banks are the Construction Bank and Industrial and Commercial Bank of China.

(continued)

Table 4. An overview of major spot commodities exchanges in Mainland China		
Year of establishment	Name	Basic information and main products
2012	Hainan Commodity Trading Centre*	It was initiated and set up with a registered capital of RMB 100 million by Hainan State Farms Group*, which holds 51% of its shares, and four other shareholders including Shanghai Daxin Huayi Logistics Network Co., Ltd.*, Hainan Runde Investment Co., Ltd.*, Xinhu Holding Co., Ltd. and Grand Agriseeds Technology Inc. The major products traded are betel nut, platinum, palladium and silver.
2013	Nanning Bulk Commodities Exchange	Nanning Bulk Commodities Exchange, also known as Nanning (China-ASEAN) Commodity Exchange, mainly provides spot trading of commodities such as chemicals, agricultural products, forestry products, iron and steel products, non-ferrous metals, and refined oil products.
2013	Bohai Commodity Exchange	In accordance with the positioning and requirements of the Tianjin Municipal People's Government and in response to market demand, Bohai Commodity Exchange has been continuously providing up-to-standard products for spot trading and such products include petroleum and chemicals, metal commodities, coal and other energy commodities as well as agricultural and forestry commodities.
2014	Fujian Jinya Commodity Trading Centre*	A subsidiary of Huazhao Investment (Beijing) Co., Ltd.*, the Trading Centre mainly provides B2B (Business-to-Business), B2C (Business-to-Consumer) and other electronic trading services for the spot trading market. Commodities traded include silver, asphalt, copper, and nickel.
2014	Guangdong International Commodity Trading Centre*	The Guangdong International Commodity Trading Centre* was approved by the Guangdong Provincial People's Government and set up with a registered capital of RMB 100 million by Guangdong Provincial Commercial Enterprise Group with the assistance of Guangzhou Xiangneng Investment Co., Ltd.. It is the first professional international commodity trading platform in Mainland China. The main commodities traded are fuel oil, Guangdong silver* and Guangdong copper*.

* For identification purpose only and should not be regarded as the official English translation of the Chinese names. In the event of any inconsistency, the Chinese names prevail.

Source: Official websites of the respective exchanges, news reports.

At present, the spot commodities marketplaces in the Mainland are mostly electronic trading markets, which fall short of international peers in the developed over-the-counter (OTC) spot markets, in terms of contract types, market entities, operating models and risk management, etc. Their roles in strengthening the futures markets and optimising resources allocation are also limited.

4   Connection between spot and futures markets

4.1   Development history of international commodities markets

The development of international commodities markets can be divided into three phases: (1) traditional spot trading; (2) OTC derivatives markets; and (3) exchange-traded futures markets. The international commodities trading regime is therefore mature and well developed, serving its market functions effectively.

On the international front, commodities trading markets started growing rapidly after the 1970s. Different countries were competing rigorously for gaining pricing power in global commodities. Many international exchanges have built robust and dynamic trading systems, sound physical delivery systems, as well as various financial and logistics services.

Currently, leading commodity trading markets include London Metal Exchange (LME), Singapore Commodity Exchange (SICOM), Intercontinental Exchange (ICE) and CME, which are mostly in economically developed regions with the backing of strong commercial and financial systems.

Table 5. Selected major commodity trading markets in the world		
Region	Year of establishment	Name
Europe	1877	London Metal Exchange
	1988	Eurex Exchange
North America	1856	Kansas City Board of Trade
	1874	Chicago Mercantile Exchange
	1874	Montreal Exchange
	1998	Intercontinental Exchange
Asia	1951	The Tokyo Commodity Exchange
	1952	The Tokyo Grain Exchange
	1990	Zhengzhou Commodity Exchange
	1990	Shanghai Futures Exchange
	1993	Dalian Commodity Exchange
	2007	Dubai Mercantile Exchange
	2010	Singapore Commodity Exchange

In our view, the development models of these global commodity exchanges could be divided into two main types: "organic" and "inorganic".

"Organic" model of development refers to the gradual development of a commodity trading market into a regional and then global commodity trading venue, by initially providing spot trading and then shifting to futures trading. CME is a good example. Futures trading in the modern sense dated back to Chicago in the 19th century when the city was a major hub of food distribution in the US. Through launching standardised forward contracts, it gradually became a trading hub of commodity futures. Similarly, LME was established and gradually developed at the time when London was turning into an international financial centre.

Under this model, commodities trading markets were developed along a "physical/ spot — forwards — futures — OTC" route, with more active physical (spot) trading seen in the early stages of development. Trading is of physical nature and distributed. As the spot market developed, market participants needed to avoid or manage risks, creating demand for forward trading for commodities — a forward contract has the price, product type, terms, margin, quantity, etc. all specified. As the forward market further developed, participants had greater demand for managing default risks and for the liquidity of forwards. This, together with technological advancement and the development of financial credit systems, made futures contracts increasingly standardised, facilitating the formation of exchange-traded futures markets. Nevertheless, a standard contract would not fully meet every trader's specific needs. Therefore, with the development of financial derivatives, OTC commodities markets have been expanding.

Under an "inorganic" development model, it is a government initiative to build an international commodities trading venue in response to financial market development trends and the need to build a regional financial centre, capitalising on the strengths and geographical advantages of a market. Futures exchanges in the Mainland are a typical example. With clearly defined positioning and policy support, exchanges of this type develop rather fast. As they are not gradually evolved from spot trading, market support is often less than adequate under this model.

4.2   Connection between spot and futures trading in the Mainland commodities market

Commodities trading usually comprises three tiers: Tier 1 are participants in the real economy, like producers, consumers and physical logistics companies; Tier 2 are trade and financial services providers or intermediaries serving the real-economy participants; and Tier 3 are purely financial investors.

Comparing the Mainland and overseas commodities markets, one can find that trading in the overseas markets is structured as a classical pyramid covering all three tiers of users, with Tier 1 and Tier 2 participants as the major ones. On the contrary, the trading structure in the Mainland commodities market is an inverted pyramid — trading from Tier 1 (real-economy participants), and Tier 2 (trade and financial services providers and intermediaries) are not very developed nor significant in size, with weak credibility support in warehousing certification. Financing for commodity circulation is difficult. The operations of the entire spot market system are costly and inefficient with very high risks. In contrast, futures trading is extremely active at Tier 3 (financial investors), where the participants are predominantly retail investors and physical delivery is not common. Hence in the Mainland, the connection between the spot and futures commodities markets is still not high enough and financial services for commodities fall way short of what are needed in the real economy.

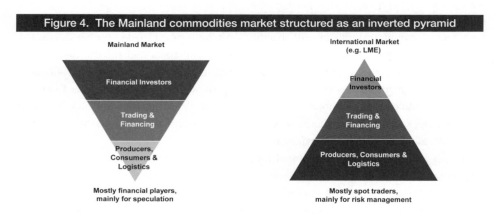

Figure 4. The Mainland commodities market structured as an inverted pyramid

4.3   Proposed enhancements for the Mainland commodities market

4.3.1   To build a multi-tiered market regime

Development of a multi-tiered commodities market could link up effectively the various types of participant in the market economy, and meet the needs for the circulation of goods and for risk management needs of the real economy.

Firstly, a trading mechanism connecting the spot and futures markets should be established. There should be a market system covering commodities and their derivatives, connecting the national futures markets and the local spot markets. It shall be able to fully exhibit the roles of the national commodity exchanges, local futures intermediaries and local commodity trading platforms, providing diversified and customised trading and risk management services for commodity market participants.

Secondly, the existing market features, functions and mechanisms should be well utilised. In particular, the centralised pricing and clearing functions of the futures market should be enhanced. There shall be a good connection between the national futures markets and local spot commodities markets, so that the overall commodities market could better serve the real economy.

4.3.2   To build an international commodities trading hub

An international commodities trading hub is a focal point in global commodities trading, an indicator of the region's degree of competitiveness in global goods trade.

While China is the largest producer, importer and consumer of commodities and its goods trade is ever expanding, there is not any commodities trading hub in the country that has global influence. This somehow constrains China's competitiveness in world trade.

Going forward, commodities exchanges in the Mainland are bound to make innovative changes to their trading, delivery and settlement models and, by building on spot markets and trade chains, work to transform themselves into world-class international commodities trading markets.

5   Conclusion

Commodities are an integral part of our daily lives, and in recent years have become an important investment subject in asset management. As the Mainland economy continues its rapid growth and accelerates its market opening, its commodities market is also increasingly internationalised. Notwithstanding these and despite the fact that China is the largest importer and consumer of a number of commodities, the Mainland commodities market, being a late comer, has certain issues to address, including the limited degree of market opening-up, and the lack of a proportionate say in international pricing. In addition, there are in general imbalanced market development, overlapping businesses and inadequate regulation.

An overview of the development of selected major commodities trading markets with international influence reveals that the Mainland futures exchanges have been developed in an "inorganic" way — fast development with clearly defined positioning and policy support, but market support is less than adequate. As a result, the connection between commodities futures exchanges and the spot market is not high, with financial services falling way short of the real economy's needs. To better regularise the Mainland spot commodities market, it is proposed that the authorities shall offer full support to the development of the spot commodities market, and take the initiative to build a multi-tiered market system and establish an international commodities trading hub, in an attempt to further raise China's competitiveness in world trade.

Chapter 8

Commodities market in Mainland China — International status and opening-up

Qianhai Mercantile Exchange Co., Ltd.

Summary

This article examines the international status of the commodities market in Mainland China, noting the mismatch between the market's needs and its pricing power in the industry chain. Policy suggestions are proposed to further open up the Mainland commodities market, including enhancing the synergies between domestic exchanges, reforming the financial regulatory system, and capitalising on Hong Kong's edge as a financial centre.

1   The international status of the Mainland commodities market

1.1   A country with large consumption

China is the world's second largest economy behind the United States (US) and has become the largest consumer of major commodities such as iron ore, copper, nickel, coal and cotton, importing nearly 70% of the world's iron ore[1] and 40% of its copper concentrate[2]. Despite the slackening growth in the world economy and the increasingly complex global environment, coupled with escalating downside pressure faced by the Mainland economy, China maintains a relatively high import growth rate in most commodities, especially in oil products. Mainland China imported 462 million tonnes of crude oil and 33.48 million tonnes of refined oil products in 2018, up 10.09% and 12.96% respectively from 2017. Given that its crude oil imports accounted for 37.61% of the total global exports of the Organisation of the Petroleum Exporting Countries (OPEC) in 2018, China has overtaken the US (accounted for 18.60% of the total) to become the world's largest crude oil importer[3].

Type	Value of imports in 2018		Volume of imports in 2018	
	(US$ million)	% change from 2017	(million tonnes)	% change from 2017
Soybean	38,087	-3.91%	88.04	-7.84%
Coal	24,761	9.39%	281.89	4.06%
Crude oil	**240,380**	**48.08%**	**461.89**	**10.09%**
Steel	16,435	8.34%	13.17	-0.98%

Table 1. Imports of selected commodities

Source: National Bureau of Statistics of China.

---

1   Data from the World Steel Association shows that the world's volume of iron ore imports in 2017 was 1,577 million tonnes, of which China accounted for 1,075 million tonnes, equivalent to 68% of the total. (Source: Wind.)
2   Source: Observatory of Economic Complexity (OEC)'s website (https://oec.world/en/profile/hs92/260300/), viewed on 17 January 2020.
3   Source: Calculations based on data from National Bureau of Statistics of China, General Administration of Customs of China and OPEC.

1.2 Lack of pricing power

As shown in the supply and demand structure of the international commodities markets, Mainland China is undoubtedly the largest consumer of many types of commodity. However, China's increasing demand has become an important factor causing the rise in commodity prices in the world's commodities markets. Mainland China's dependence on the outside world for crude oil exceeds 70%, so when the crude oil import price rose by 34.51% from an average of US$386.89 per tonne in 2017 to US$520.43 per tonne[4], China bore the brunt. Lacking international pricing power, China has become the largest victim of the fluctuations in global commodity prices.

Traders in the Mainland commodities market are voluminous and fragmented, and there are no unified and effective industry associations. In addition, key companies have weak overall control over the upstream and downstream activities in the industry chain. These factors have given rise to the strange phenomenon that in spot trading of international commodities, the Chinese importers always buy goods at the international price, but the Chinese exporters compete with each other by lowering their prices. Despite being the most important commodities trading country in the world, China's large demand has not given it a pricing advantage in the industry chain and its influence on the pricing of major commodities remains very limited. Assuming such a passive role, China has no alternative but to take the international market prices.

2 The opening-up of the Mainland commodities market

2.1 Admission of foreign investors

Allowing foreign investors to participate in the Mainland commodities market is an important measure taken at the current stage to open up the market. Formulating policies to attract global investors to widely participate in domestic commodities trading will help draw the international markets' attention to Chinese commodities market prices and

---

4   Source: Calculations based on data from National Bureau of Statistics of China, General Administration of Customs of China and OPEC.

encourage them to adopt these prices, thereby the futures market can fully exhibit its risk control and hedging functions. By lowering the admission requirements on the product type and allowing more overseas participants into the market, the free circulation of goods, capital, transportation and information, etc. between the Mainland and the neighbouring countries and regions will be facilitated. Through this, the economic cooperation and partnership between the Mainland and the neighbouring countries can be developed, the "Belt and Road" initiatives can be promoted, and mutual economic and social development can be enhanced, and in the end the market can move towards building a community of shared interests with mutual trust in politics, economic integration and cultural harmony.

Major current foreign investor admission policies are shown in Table 2 below.

Table 2. Policies and regulations on the admission of foreign investors into the Mainland commodities market			
Year of issuance	Policy / Regulation	Issued by	Details
2015	*Provisional Measures for the Administration of Trading in Designated Domestic Futures Products by Foreign Traders and Foreign Brokerage Agencies*	China Securities Regulatory Commission (CSRC)	The Measures stipulate that foreign traders can choose to engage in the trading of designated Mainland futures products through domestic futures companies or foreign brokerage agencies in consideration of their own situations and business needs; qualified foreign traders could also trade designated futures products on futures exchanges directly. Foreign brokerage agencies entrusted by foreign traders may, where appropriate, entrust a domestic futures company to trade designated Mainland futures products. These Measures provide a way for foreign investors to directly trade futures on futures exchanges and facilitate the internationalisation of futures trading in Mainland China, addressing the problems faced by foreign institutions engaged in world trade in the course of their trading of designated types of product such as crude oil futures in the Mainland.
2017	*Regulation on the Administration of Futures Trading (2017 Revision)*	State Council of the People's Republic of China	Article 8 of the Regulation stipulates that, *"The members of a futures exchange shall be enterprises with legal person status or other economic organisations established and registered within the territory of the People's Republic of China."* Article 17 explicitly states that, *"A futures company shall be subject to the licensing system. The futures regulatory institution of the State Council shall grant it a permit according to the business type such as commodity futures and financial futures. Apart from a domestic futures brokerage licence, a futures company may apply for engaging in overseas futures brokerage, futures investment consultation and other futures businesses as prescribed by the futures regulatory institution of the State Council."* The 2017 revision of the Regulation materially expands the scope of business that foreign commodities trading institutions can conduct in Mainland China, increasing the appeal of the Mainland commodities market to foreign institutions and enabling foreign institutions to compete in the Mainland commodities market under fairer conditions, thereby promoting the connectivity between the Mainland commodities market and the international markets.

(continued)

Year of issuance	Policy / Regulation	Issued by	Details
Table 2. Policies and regulations on the admission of foreign investors into the Mainland commodities market			
2017	*Measures for the Administration of Foreign-Funded Futures Companies*	CSRC	From the market opening-up experience of the financial industries of banking, securities and insurance, the admission of foreign strategic investors can help domestic futures companies learn sophisticated concepts and enhance their equity structure and institutional systems, bringing in branding advantages and core technologies while facilitating their access to overseas markets whereby they can tap into global customer resources. The companies' presence in the global markets can also be enhanced, paving the way for their internationalisation.

Source: Summarised from news reports.

Since 2005, international investment banks such as JP Morgan Chase, Goldman Sachs, Royal Bank of Scotland, Société Générale, and UBS have invested in futures companies in Mainland China in a bid to introduce international elements in their mode of operation. However, according to the regulations in force in the Mainland at that time, futures company located in Mainland China could not be majority-owned by foreign investors and foreign capital could not be involved in the establishment of domestic futures exchanges. Thus, there is a long way to go for the Mainland commodities market to open up. In order to address these issues and to further open up the market, the State Council released the *Opinions of the State Council on Further Utilising Foreign Investment Effectively* on 23 October 2019 in which it proposed that the foreign stake ceiling of 51% for securities companies, securities investment fund management companies, futures companies, and life insurance companies would be lifted in 2020 and that the process of opening-up the financial industry would be accelerated. This may speed up the opening-up of the Mainland commodities market.

Name	Foreign financial institution	Shareholding ratio	Operation
Table 3. Selected foreign financial institutions participating in futures trading in the Mainland			
Galaxy Futures	Royal Bank of Scotland	16.68%	The first joint-venture futures company in the Mainland, ranking fourth in the 2019 China Futures Association list, with a credit rating of AA
JPMorgan Chase Futures	JPMorgan Chase	49%	Ranks 30th in the 2019 China Futures Association list, with a credit rating of A
CITIC Newedge Futures Co., Ltd.	Newedge Group	42%	Merged into CITIC Futures in 2014, foreign capital had been withdrawn.

Source: Summarised from news reports.

2.2   Progress of internationalisation of Mainland commodities exchanges and product types

2.2.1   Opening-up of the commodity futures exchanges

The three commodities futures exchanges in Shanghai, Dalian and Zhengzhou accounted for nearly 60% of the world's total commodity futures and options trading volume[5]. The number of futures and option products has reached 70, basically covering all major areas of national economic development. As the Mainland exchanges are getting more professional and regularised, these three commodities futures exchanges are also exploring ways of internationalisation. Starting from 4 May 2018, as part of a pilot scheme, foreign investors have been allowed to trade iron ore futures, the very first time foreign participation is permitted for an already listed commodity futures contract in the Mainland. Subsequently, Shanghai International Energy Exchange (INE), a subsidiary of Shanghai Futures Exchange, launched crude oil and No. 20 rubber futures, both of which allow foreign participation in trading starting from the time of listing.

Table 4. Progress of internationalisation of Mainland commodity futures exchanges	
Name of exchange	Internationalised products and details
Dalian Commodity Exchange (DCE)	Starting from 4 May 2018, DCE allows foreign traders to trade its iron ore futures. After more than a year of stable operation, the internationalisation of iron ore futures has basically taken root in the sense that the markets saw active participation by foreign traders and an improving market structure. In 2018, China ranked the first among the world's iron ore derivatives markets, with a trading volume that was 22 times of the iron ore swaps and futures volume on the world's second largest iron ore derivative market, SGX, providing sufficient liquidity for corporate hedging. In recent years, basis trading based on iron ore futures prices has also being gradually developed. In 2017, the spot basis trading volume of iron ore was less than 5 million tonnes; but in 2018, it climbed to 10 million tonnes, and in the first half of 2019, the trading volume was already equal to the total volume in 2018.
Zhengzhou Commodity Exchange (ZCE)	On 30 November 2018, as part of a pilot scheme, purified terephthalic acid (PTA) futures were officially opened up to trading by foreign traders. This will further promote China's role as a global pricing centre for polyester products.

---

5   Source: "China's commodity futures trading volume has ranked first in the world for 7 years in a row", China Network Television's website, 18 June 2017.

(continued)

Table 4. Progress of internationalisation of Mainland commodity futures exchanges	
Name of exchange	Internationalised products and details
Shanghai Futures Exchange (SHFE) and its subsidiary, Shanghai International Energy Exchange (INE)	Crude oil futures, the first internationalised futures product in the Mainland, was listed on INE on 26 March 2019, marking the first milestone of internationalisation of the Mainland's crude oil futures market. Trading in the product was good, with the daily trading volume reaching the level of 150,000 lots per side by the end of 2018, making China the world's third largest crude oil trading market with product prices gradually gaining market recognition.
	On 12 August 2019, No. 20 rubber futures was officially listed on SHFE, making it the second RMB-denominated internationalised commodity futures in the Mainland available for trading by foreign traders.

Source: Summarised from news reports.

To connect with the international markets, Mainland China has offered foreign investors four types of futures products for trading on the exchanges, including crude oil, iron ore, PTA, and No. 20 rubber. By the end of 2019, the cumulative trading volume of INE crude oil futures was 122 million lots, with a cumulative turnover value of RMB 56.4 trillion[6]. The number of overseas trader accounts opened also increased by several folds since the initial listing stage. With the internationalisation of more futures products, more foreign investors will engage in trading in the Mainland futures markets. As a result, more foreign institutions will participate in the Mainland futures industry, thus facilitating the improvement of the professional service capabilities of Mainland institutions in the industry.

Table 5. Trading status of certain internationalised futures products in the Mainland			
Type	Average daily trading volume in 2019	Foreign participation	Percentage share of foreign traders
Iron ore futures	~2.431 million lots	By the end of October 2019, more than 170 overseas clients from 15 countries and regions have opened accounts, of whom 20% came from Singapore.	Up to April 2019, foreign traders accounted for 19% of the iron ore trading volume.
PTA futures	~2.561 million lots	By the end of September 2019, a total of 115 overseas clients have opened accounts and 29 overseas intermediaries have completed filing. Open interests held by overseas clients exceeded 10,000 lots, and the market has been operating well.	Up to the end of 2019, foreign traders accounted for 7.6% of the PTA trading volume.

---

6   Source: Wind (data from SHFE).

(continued)

Table 5. Trading status of certain internationalised futures products in the Mainland			
Type	Average daily trading volume in 2019	Foreign participation	Percentage share of foreign traders
Crude oil futures	~284,000 lots	By the end of October 2019, the number of overseas clients who have opened accounts exceeded 100 and they were from nine countries including the United Kingdom, Australia and Singapore as well as cities such as Hong Kong, Taiwan and Macau. Fifty-three overseas intermediaries from Hong Kong and countries including Singapore, the United Kingdom, South Korea, Japan and the Netherlands have also completed filings.	Up to October 2019, foreign traders accounted for 17.5% of the total trading volume and 23.7% of the average daily open interest.

Source: Summarised from news reports and Wind data.

From iron ore and PTA to crude oil and No. 20 rubber, the Mainland futures market is steadily expanding the range of products available to foreign traders. It is highly important to firstly open up the trading of products of a higher degree of maturity and with Mainland characteristics for attracting foreign participation because this can enhance the international influence of Mainland commodity prices and provide price reference and risk management tools to Mainland enterprises for their cross-border operations.

2.2.2   Opening-up of commodity spot trading exchanges

The opening-up of commodity spot trading exchanges in Mainland China started relatively late. Shanghai Gold Exchange and Bohai Commodity Exchange are notable ones which have made attempts to explore ways of internationalisation.

Table 6. Progress of internationalisation of commodity spot trading exchanges in the Mainland	
Name of Exchange	Internationalised products and details
Shanghai Gold Exchange (SGE)	SGE's International Board is the first internationalised trading platform in Shanghai which allows foreign investors to invest in the Mainland gold market. The product is called "Shanghai gold". On 31 July 2019, the designated warehouse of the SGE International Board was set up in Shenzhen.

(continued)

| Table 6. Progress of internationalisation of commodity spot trading exchanges in the Mainland ||
Name of Exchange	Internationalised products and details
Bohai Commodity Exchange (BOCE)	Tianjin-based BOCE currently offers more than 80 types of products in seven major categories, including consumer goods, agricultural and forestry products, petrochemicals, mineral resources, and non-ferrous metals. It has created the "BEST" spot trading system[7] where the e-commerce platform operated by the exchange provides global fund settlement, market services, information publicity as well as warehousing and logistics functions. In April 2013, with the approval of the People's Bank of China, BOCE became the first RMB settlement platform for cross-border transactions in China.

Source: Summarised from news reports.

3 Suggestions for the opening-up of the Mainland commodities market

Promoting the opening-up of the Mainland commodities market is an important means to accelerate the circulation of international capital and commodities and thereby form an information network for international commodities trades. This is strategically critical in helping Mainland traders as commodity buyers to acquire the bargaining power and the RMB pricing power in the global commodities market.

Firstly, the Mainland commodity exchanges should capitalise on their respective geographical advantages and strengthen the synergy of trading while preventing vicious competition, so as to achieve a win-win situation and a well-defined and rich positioning along their respective development paths in the commodities market.

Secondly, deepened reforms of the financial regulatory system at the institutional level could be considered to build and enhance a regulatory system which combines macro-prudential management with micro-level supervision, so as to facilitate the orderly and healthy progress in the internationalisation of the Mainland commodities market.

---

7   Specifically, the BEST system includes systems such as delayed settlement compensation, intermediate warehouse compensation and spot transactions.

Thirdly, Hong Kong's comparative advantages in respect of its geographical position and market strengths could be fully utilised and relevant advanced supportive institutional system designs could be reasonably introduced, so as to enhance the overall degree of internationalisation of the Mainland commodities market.

Chapter 9

The Hong Kong commodities market

Commodities Development
Hong Kong Exchanges and Clearing Limited

Summary

As a global financial centre, Hong Kong has achieved remarkable performances in many areas of the financial sector. However, the development in the commodities market in Hong Kong is relatively weak and currently sits behind other commodity trading hubs such as New York and London. One of the key elements of a successful commodity trading hub is the easy access to commodity exchanges and a wide range of price discovery and hedging solutions.

The only self-regulated spot commodities market in Hong Kong is operated by the Chinese Gold & Silver Exchange Society (CGSE). It provides platforms, facilities and related services for its members to trade gold and silver. Alongside, the only regulated commodity derivatives market is operated by the Hong Kong Futures Exchange (HKFE) which has been actively enriching its product offerings to support and facilitate Hong Kong's commodities market development in recent years.

During 2014 to 2019, HKFE launched futures contracts on precious metals, base metals and ferrous metals to foster commodities' hedging and arbitrage activities in the Asian time zone. In respect of precious metals, while liquidity steadily improves in the Gold Futures, six gold futures indices denominated in both US dollar (USD) and offshore Renminbi were launched in June 2019. This paved the way for introduction of more precious metal derivative products in the future.

As for HKFE's base metal products, six USD London Metal Mini Futures contracts, namely Aluminium, Copper, Lead, Nickel, Tin and Zinc were introduced to the market in August 2019. These mini futures simplified the base metal trading mechanism of the traditional base metal contracts on the London Metal Exchange (LME). In the meantime, HKEX and LME have been engaged in constructive discussions for various collaboration schemes towards a "Hong Kong-London Connect".

HKEX is also making inroads into the ferrous sector. The HKFE's cash-settled TSI Iron Ore Fines 62% Fe CFR China Futures (Iron Ore Futures) commenced trading in November 2017 and saw respectable trading activity in 2019.

As HKEX rolled out its commodity strategies, market participants reflected a lot of feedback and useful suggestions for future development which would require integrated efforts. Suggestions include having warehousing in Hong Kong to enable physical delivery of base metals, reducing the current contract size of Gold Futures and recognizing gold bars manufactured by qualified local refineries. There is still much room for further cooperation between the CGSE, HKFE and the over-the-counter commodity market to elevate Hong Kong's international status as a global commodity trading centre.

1 The commodities market in Hong Kong — Low base but high potential

Hong Kong is well regarded by the world as a preeminent international financial centre, with remarkable performance in many areas of the financial sector, including the possession of the highest concentration of insurers and the highest insurance density in Asia[1], the largest offshore liquidity pool for Renminbi ("RMB") in the world[2], and a stock exchange which ranked among the top five globally every year in the past decade in terms of funds raised from initial public offerings ("IPO")[3]. Nonetheless, heavy focus on equities has resulted in the relative under-development in other areas, such as fixed income and commodities. Developing a broader and deeper array of asset classes is of paramount importance as this will lessen the dependence of the Hong Kong financial market on a particular type of financial instruments (i.e. a particular market segment), thereby strengthening up the overall Hong Kong financial sector to be more resilient, especially when a particular market segment underperforms.

Compared to the fixed-income sector, the commodities sector might even be a weaker link. Commodity trading has a unique economic model and distinctive risks that need to be managed. It requires special skills to master it well. Many companies, therefore, set up standalone units for their commodity trading activities. This forms a centre of excellence that pools skills across trading, marketing, logistics and risk management. Further, centres of such excellence are often located in the commodity trading hubs.

There are a number of commodity trading hubs around the world. Examples are Chicago — a major hub for agricultural products, London — a hub for metals and Houston — a hub for energy trading. At the centre of Asian commodity trade routes, Singapore acts as the commodity trading hub for rubber, iron ore and precious metals. Many of these hubs have existed for decades as assembly points for commodity trading. Proximity to physical

---

1　With 162 authorised firms operating in 2019 and insurance premiums per capita of US$8,863 in 2018. Source: "Think Finance Think Hong Kong", Financial Services Development Council's leaflet, September 2019.

2　With total deposits of RMB 627.8 billion as of June 2019. Source: "Think Finance Think Hong Kong", Financial Services Development Council's leaflet, September 2019.

3　Based on market statistics on the website of World Federation of Exchanges (WFE).

flows and infrastructure for commodity transport is often the historical reason of why many of the largest global commodity hubs are located where they are today and why different hubs have become specialised in different commodity products.

One of the key elements of a successful commodity trading hub is the easy access to commodity exchanges and a wide range of price discovery and hedging solutions, such as soybean futures on the Chicago Board of Trade (CBOT), West Texas Intermediate (WTI) light sweet crude oil futures on the Intercontinental Exchange (ICE) and rubber futures on the Singapore Commodity Exchange (SICOM).

In Hong Kong, the only regulated spot commodities market is operated by the Chinese Gold & Silver Exchange Society (CGSE), while the Hong Kong Futures Exchange (HKFE), a wholly-owned subsidiary of Hong Kong Exchanges and Clearing Limited (HKEX), operates the only regulated commodity derivatives market. The CGSE, by its name, offers spot trading only for gold and silver. On the other hand, in the light of the weak commodity segment in Hong Kong, the HKFE has been actively enriching its product offerings of commodity derivatives in recent years. See Figure 1 for an illustration of gold trading in Hong Kong and sub-sections below on a briefing of CGSE and HKFE.

Figure 1. Gold trading in Hong Kong

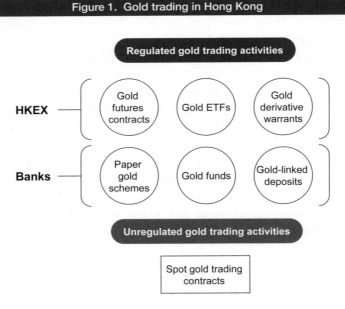

Source: The Investor and Financial Education Council's website.

1.1   The Chinese Gold & Silver Exchange (CGSE)[4]

Founded in 1910, the CGSE is a self-regulating organisation. Its functions include providing a platform, facilities and related services for precious metals trading, as well as establishing and implementing rules and regulations, and normalising transactions for the industry.

The CGSE operates under a membership system. Its members must be registered as companies. CGSE members can use the trading platform of the CGSE for precious metals trading. London Gold is traded via an e-trading platform of the CGSE, where the recognised e-trading members can process clients' transactions (with the option to trade clients' transactions on the e-trading platform with other members, or to directly trade with clients and then declare to the CGSE). Transactions processed through the recognised e-trading member of the CGSE come with a transaction number, which can be used by investors to retrieve information about the transaction.

However, there is no legal requirement that gold dealers must join the CGSE to participate in spot gold trading, which means that current gold dealers who carry out spot gold trading are not limited to the CGSE members. As a result, there is unregulated over-the-counter (OTC) trading in gold.

1.2   Hong Kong Futures Exchange (HKFE)

HKFE is a futures exchange regulated by the Securities and Futures Commission (SFC) in Hong Kong. It was established in 1976 and has become a wholly-owned subsidiary of HKEX in 2000 under a merger scheme with the Stock Exchange of Hong Kong (SEHK) and their affiliated clearing houses. HKFE offers a variety of options and futures contracts linked to stock market indices, stocks, short-term interest rates, foreign exchange and commodities. In parallel with the physical gold market operated by CGSE in Hong Kong, the current commodities product suite of HKFE include gold futures contracts. (See Section 2 for more details of the on-exchange commodity market on HKFE.)

As a centralised financial exchange where people can trade standardised derivative contracts trustworthily, there is a lot HKFE could do to support and facilitate Hong Kong's commodities market development.

---

4   Source: The webpage, "Understanding the current protections when trading gold and its related products", on the Investor and Financial Education Council's website, dated 14 February 2018, viewed on 16 December 2019.

2   The current on-exchange commodity derivatives market

Hong Kong, whose name in Chinese means "Fragrant Harbour", is renowned for its ideal location as a port in Southern China. Attributed to the financial hub's free market and tradition of entrepôt trade, Hong Kong enjoys the status as one of the major bullion markets in the world with bustling physical gold trading. In addition, being the largest offshore RMB centre, Hong Kong has a unique position in facilitating the implementation of China's plan for RMB internationalisation. With these innate advantages, HKEX is determined to serve better the commodities market by building a commodities platform in the Asian time zone that offers globally competitive products in Hong Kong.

HKEX laid out in its *2016-2018 Strategic Plan* its objective to establish new price-discovery capabilities, benchmarks and risk management tools in fixed income, currency and commodities. Towards this objective, in the second half of 2017, HKEX launched a pair of gold futures contracts denominated in US dollar (USD) and offshore RMB (i.e. CNH) with settlement by physical delivery in Hong Kong **(USD and CNH Gold Futures)** and a USD-denominated cash-settled TSI Iron Ore Fines 62% Fe CFR China Futures contract **(Iron Ore Futures)**.

With further vision drawn in its *2019-2021 Strategic Plan* in respect of the continued expansion of the commodities product suite, the evolution of commodity pricing and commodity "Connects", HKEX introduced the USD-denominated cash-settled London Metal Mini Futures contracts **(USD London Metal Mini Futures)** in the second half of 2019, which complement the CNH-denominated London Metal Mini Futures contracts **(CNH London Metal Mini Futures)** already introduced in two batches in December 2014 and December 2015 respectively.

With the offering of futures contracts on precious metals, base metals and ferrous metals (see sub-sections below), the on-exchange market facilitates commodities' hedging and arbitrage activities in the Asian time zone. Hong Kong's on-exchange commodities platform is constituted of a network of HKFE participants with Mainland Chinese backgrounds and the liquidity from global financial market participants which connects Chinese trade in commodities with the world.

2.1   Precious metal derivatives

One of the key features of the USD and CNH Gold Futures is physical delivery which enables the convergence of futures prices and spot prices to take place in a transparent and regulated venue.

In spite of the many challenges faced in the development of a "new commodities market" in Hong Kong, concrete liquidities in the Gold Futures has been gradually building up. The average daily trading volume (ADV) increased by over 50% from about 1,300 contracts at the beginning of 2019 to more than 2,000 contracts by end of 2019 (see Figure 2). Open Interest also reached a record high of 1,272 contracts on 27 December 2019. In order to concentrate incentives provided to Liquidity Providers (LPs) and Proprietary Traders (PTs) with higher efficiency, the respective total numbers of LPs and PTs were reduced from about 30 to 20 in 2019. Bid-ask spread of USD Gold Futures has also tightened to one to two ticks for 40%-60% of the trading hours in 2019[5].

Figure 2. Monthly ADV and month-end open interest of Gold Futures in Hong Kong (2019)

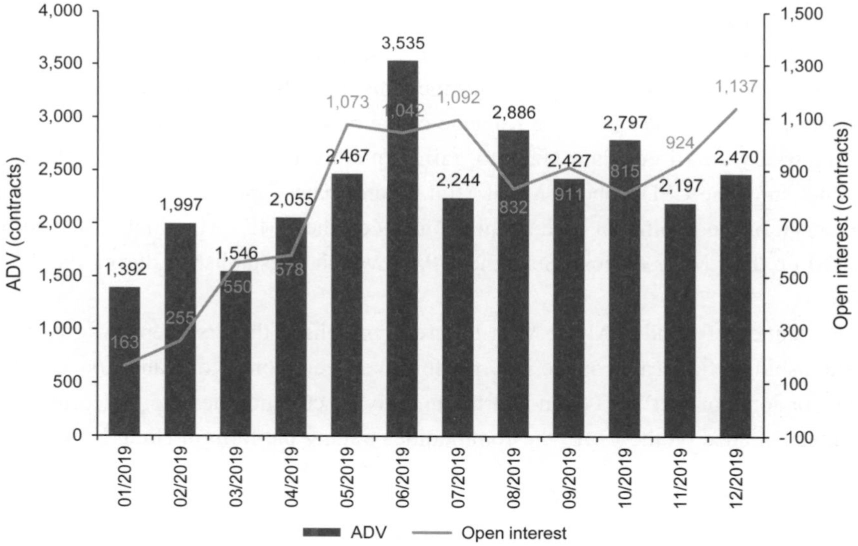

Source: HKEX.

---

5   Source: HKEX for all related market statistics and information.

2.2   Base metal derivatives

CNH London Aluminium/Zinc/Copper Mini Futures were launched on 1 December 2014 as the first batch of RMB-traded commodity contracts in Hong Kong. They were designed to meet the hedging needs of Mainland physical market participants for their exposure to commodities priced in RMB, to ease margin financing needs for entities holding RMB and to establish RMB pricing of metals in Asian trading hours. The second batch of RMB-traded London Metal Mini Futures contracts on nickel, tin and lead were launched on 14 December 2015 to complement the first batch. These metals, along with aluminium, zinc and copper, are among the most liquid futures contracts on the London Metal Exchange (LME), a wholly-owned subsidiary of HKEX. As each of the six metals has distinctive characteristics, uses and supply-and-demand dynamics, HKEX's CNH London Metal Mini Futures can meet the various needs of base metal users, producers and investors, particularly those who are based in Asia and want to be able to buy and sell futures contracts during their business day.

Further to the RMB products, the USD London Metal Mini Futures contracts were launched on 5 August 2019. This product series consist of futures contracts on the same six base metals as the RMB products. The USD products provide additional trading opportunities for users who have exposure in the underlying USD-denominated base metals in the Asian time zone and offer new investment instruments for both retail and institutional investors who would like to take advantage of the products' monthly cash-settled features and relatively small contract sizes to gain exposure to the underlying metals. The introduction of the USD London Metal Mini Futures has simplified the base metal trading mechanism of the traditional base metal contracts on the LME. The final settlement price is based on the LME's Official Settlement Price which is established during the 2nd Ring Close[6].

The launch of London Metal Mini Futures symbolised the first step towards the goal of establishing a full-scale connectivity platform between Hong Kong and London ("Hong Kong-London Connect")[7]. Given that the underlying commodities are the corresponding base metals traded on the LME, the commodities trading platform in Hong Kong could be

---

6   On the LME, trading activities take place in designated five-minute periods known as "rings" during which traders and floor brokers are engaged in open outcry trading that takes place in a six-metre ring-shaped trading pit. Ring sessions are different for trading different instruments. 2nd Ring trading at the LME occurs during 12:30 p.m. to 1:15 p.m.. LME Official Prices, used as a reference in physical contracts, are established during the 2nd Ring. The LME Official Price is the last bid and offer price quoted during the 2nd Ring session and the LME Official Settlement Price is the last cash offer price.

7   See more in Chapter 17, "The connectivity platform offered by the HKEX commodities market for the Mainland and the world", in this book.

developed in cooperation with the LME, bringing together both the physical and financial communities in the commodities market.

2.3   Ferrous metal derivatives

The cash-settled TSI Iron Ore Fines 62% Fe CFR China Futures (Iron Ore Futures) was the first ferrous metal product launched by HKEX on 13 November 2017. The product aims to provide maximum price transparency and equal access to all market participants. By improving the price discovery process in the iron ore derivatives market, the contract has the potential to lower the cost of trading. The final settlement price for a contract is based on the arithmetic average of all TSI 62% Fe CFR China index values published in that contract month. The last trading day is the last Hong Kong business day of a calendar month that is not a Singapore public holiday. Both monthly and quarterly contracts are available to enhance exposure.

2019 was a refreshing year for the Iron Ore Futures. With an incentive program in place, coupled with marketing efforts, market participation in the product improved. Both daily trading volume and open interest reached record high levels in the same year (see Figure 3).

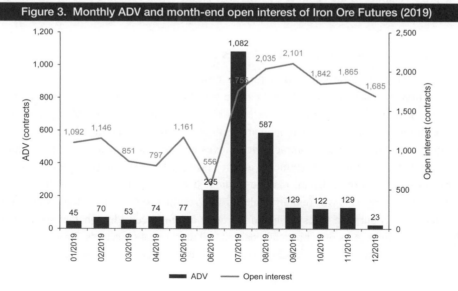

Figure 3. Monthly ADV and month-end open interest of Iron Ore Futures (2019)

Source: HKEX.

2.4   Market operations

It is relatively easy to get started trading commodity products on HKFE.

(1)   Open a futures account

An investor has to firstly open an account with a futures broker who is a Participant of HKFE ("Exchange Participant" or "EP") that supports trading in HKFE products. The futures broker will determine the amount of risk it allows the investor to take on, in terms of margin and positions, based on the investor's experience, income and net worth. Different brokers may offer different channels for investors to place orders for futures contracts, e.g. online trading systems or futures trading hotline.

(2)   Deposit initial margin

Prior to placing an order, the investor must have enough funds deposited into its account to cover the initial margin — a small percentage of the contract value. HKFE determines and sets futures margin rates based on the risk of market volatility. An additional initial margin on top of such minimum requirement may be required by the broker depending on the price volatility of the contract type. In general, the initial margin varies by product and is subject to change from time to time.

(3)   Investor eligibility and related risks

The risk of loss in commodity futures trading can be substantial, as financing a transaction by a deposit of collateral can be significant. Investors may sustain losses in excess of the initial margin funds, cash and other assets deposited as collateral with the futures broker and may be called upon at short notice to deposit additional margin deposits or interest payments if the contract price moves against one's position. If the required margin deposits or interest payments are not provided within the prescribed time, the investor's position or collateral may be liquidated without prior consent of the investor. Moreover, the investor will remain liable for any resulting deficit and interest charged on the futures account. An investor should therefore carefully consider whether such trading is suitable in light of its own financial position and investment objectives. There are several risk factors to bear in mind, including geopolitical risks, speculative risks, delivery risk and corporate governance risks.

(4)   Place an order with a futures broker

When placing an order with a futures broker, the investor should specify the following information:

- Side — The buy or sell indication;
- Quantity — The number of contracts;
- Contract information — Which product and maturity;
- Order type — Instruction to the broker on how to handle the order (common order types are "Market"[8], "Limit"[9], and "Stop"[10];
- Price — The price at which the order should be executed;
- Time in force — How long the order stays open (common times in force include "Day"[11] and "Good Till Cancelled"[12])
- Account number — The investor's account identification number in the broker's tracking system.

The order will be passed to the Order Management System (OMS) controlled by the broker and connected to HKFE. Before the order is submitted to HKFE, the broker will perform pre-trade risk check to ensure the order meets approved sizing controls. If the order passes these checks, it is then sent on to HKFE's trading system; orders that fail the checks will be rejected by the OMS.

(5)   Trading process

HKATS, the trading system for HKEX's derivatives market, is an electronic system that automatically matches orders in real-time based on price and time priority. This means that the best price is used to match orders and that an order entered earlier into the open order book has a higher priority than orders entered later at the same price. This can easily be thought of as "First-In, First Out" at each price level. Orders are placed in the Central Orderbook. As soon as a trade is executed, the trade information will be reported to the EP via OMS. At the same time, the trade information is transmitted to the HKFE Clearing Corporation Limited "HKCC" for registration and clearing.

---

8   Market order is an order type to buy/sell a contract at the current market price.
9   Limit order is an order type to buy/sell a contract at a specified or a better price.
10 Stop order is an order type to buy a contract at a price above or sell at a price below a specified price.
11 A Day order is valid until the close of the trading day the order is entered — the order is automatically purged from the system at the end of the current trading day.
12 A Good Till Canceled (GTC) order is valid until the order is cancelled, and is not automatically cancelled by the system. The trader must cancel their outstanding GTC orders if they are not filled in order to remove them from the system.

(6)   Mark to market

Marking to market is a procedure conducted by the clearing house on a daily basis, which determines the value for the asset covered by each futures contract, and profit and loss is then settled between the long and the short positions. The clearing house uses margin as the main tool to mitigate its future credit exposure to its counterparty. Margin requirement is calculated based on the assessment of the maximum potential losses of a futures or an option contract or a portfolio of futures and option contracts over a one-day period under 16 simulated scenarios and a defined confidence level. The clearing houses monitor the margin levels on a daily basis in order to ensure that they are at adequate levels.

At HKCC, Portfolio Risk Margining System (PRiME) is the margining methodology adopted in Derivatives Clearing And Settlement System (DCASS) to calculate the margin requirements of futures and option products. EPs can make use of the clearing house's Risk Parameter File (RPF) distributed by HKEX for calculation of clearing house margins. If funds in the margin account drops below the required level, the broker will ask the investor to replenish the funds back to the initial margin level. This process is known as "Margin Call".

(7)   Position limits

Any EP holding positions in excess of a given Reporting Level for its own account or for any client shall file a report (i.e. the Large Open Position or "LOP" report) with HKFE no later than 12:00 noon of the next business day after the positions are opened or accumulated, and continue to file a LOP report for as long as the EP holds positions in excess of the Reporting Level. The SFC's "Guidance Note on Position Limits and Large Open Position Reporting Requirements" specifies the requirements on the aggregation of positions held or controlled by different persons, the positions held or controlled at multiple firms, and the reporting for omnibus accounts.

(8)   Cash settlement of futures contracts

When a contract is cash-settled, settlement takes place in the form of a credit or debit made for the value of the contract at the time of contract expiration. The HKFE cash-settled commodity products include USD and CNH London Metal Mini Futures and the monthly and quarterly USD TSI Iron Ore Futures. Buyers and sellers of these futures contracts who hold their positions up to final settlement time will have their accounts credited the difference, in cash, between the initial price and the final settlement price if there is a profit; if there is a loss, their accounts will be debited the difference in cash. Clearing house and the broker will ensure trader accounts are debited or credited accordingly and that cash settlements are made in a timely and accurate fashion.

(9)   Physical settlement of futures contracts

HKFE USD and CNH Gold Futures are physically-settled contracts which involve, upon settlement, the change-hands of gold bars from the seller to the buyer who then makes full payment. Brokers who plan to physically settle the Gold Futures contracts are required to maintain accounts with all Approved Depositories designated by HKCC for gold delivery, or have in place the necessary arrangement with another HKCC Participant who maintains accounts with all Approved Depositories for the delivery of the underlying gold in the final settlement of the Gold Futures contracts ("Physical Delivery Participants"). Upon final settlement, the underlying gold will be earmarked on the business day after the Last Trading Day, and will then be transferred from the selling HKCC Participant's account to the buying HKCC Participant's account with the Approved Depository on the Final Settlement Day. Detailed arrangements on final settlement are given in the HKFE's documents for related market operations — "Derivatives Settlement Services", "List of Recognised Depositories, Refiners, Forwarders and Assayers" and "List of HKFE EPs Offering Physical Delivery Services for Gold Futures".

(10) Risk management process

HKCC has certain powers which it uses to assist in the risk management process and to ensure smooth settlement and delivery. Where necessary, HKCC may require its participants to provide additional deposits or replenish the depleted funds; HKCC may request a participant to provide evidence of its holding of such amount of the underlying commodity or instrument as may be required to satisfy its settlement obligations. It has also the power to require a Non-delivery HKCC Participant to close out and/or transfer any open positions by such time as shall be specified by HKCC from time to time. The risk management process is governed by the "Rules and Procedures of HKFE Clearing Corporation Limited".

(11) Liquidity Provider / Proprietary Trader system

HKFE commodity futures operate under a market-making system. Registered traders supply market liquidity by providing continuous quotes onto the trading system upon request. Such traders are known as Liquidity Providers (LP). Proprietary Trader (PT) is an EP trading through its House Account. It can also be a client represented by an EP trading through an Individual Client Account who commits to meeting the minimum monthly clearing volume in the Eligible Products assigned. HKFE offers LP/PT Program for its commodity products. LP/PT Program is a commercial arrangement for HKFE to appoint LPs to provide liquidity for new products that require more flexibility in terms of LP obligations and LP incentives which are not stipulated in the exchange rules and procedures. LPs/PTs receive both financial and non-financial benefits for fulfilling certain market making obligations and providing market liquidity in commodity derivatives.

3 Possible integrated efforts for future development

The low participation in commodities trading and limited development in related financial products in Hong Kong are often ascribed to its insufficient commodity trading infrastructure. Hong Kong lacks the logistics and warehousing arrangements to facilitate the physical trading of commodities. As a matter of fact, commodity futures contracts were originally invented to help users of the underlying physical assets to hedge against price fluctuations.

Take base metals as an example, opinions have been revealed by brokers in Hong Kong that Mainland metal users want to have physical delivery as they need the metals for their production. Market participants also commented on the need for warehousing in Hong Kong to enable physical delivery[13]. In other words, the metal derivatives traded in Hong Kong need an associated physical delivery mechanism in order to attract users in Mainland China to trade in Hong Kong. However, physical delivery means setting up warehouses for the metals and this could be challenging. In a sense, a commodity through-train scheme would be helpful, yet hard to achieve. An alternative might be to list Mainland commodity products in Hong Kong under licence agreements from the Mainland exchanges or to jointly develop new products with the Mainland exchanges which could be offered in Hong Kong to international market participants and approved Mainland entities. HKEX could also plan for greater market integration of its HKFE market with the LME market, and

---

13 "Hong Kong 'not ready to be a commodities trading centre'", *South China Morning Post*, 26 June 2013.

further leverage on the LME platform to collaborate with Mainland commodity exchanges, as well as to develop the essential logistics and warehousing infrastructure to facilitate the physical trading of commodities.

As for the Hong Kong gold market, with much of the physical gold being transported into Mainland China from Europe and elsewhere routed via Hong Kong, it is one of the most active physical gold trading markets in the world[14]. Hong Kong is strategically positioned as a gateway to China, the world's biggest importer of gold. With local operations of international bullion banks, refineries, vaults and transport providers, Hong Kong as a gold trade entrepôt has the intrinsic potential to become the gold price setter in Asia, at par with the developed markets of New York and London in the west, helping China and Asia not to be just a price taker. Further cooperation between the CGSE, HKFE and the OTC gold market could be explored to make the best of Hong Kong's existing precious metals network.

Feedback from some participants reflected that they appreciated the physical delivery feature of HKFE's gold futures but the current minimum delivery size of 1 kilogram could be too much for retail clients. They advised HKFE to consider smaller contract size and minimum delivery size.

The CGSE has accredited a list of refineries in Hong Kong as approved refineries for its various deliverable gold contracts. Most of these refineries are locally owned and are accredited to produce the 999.9 kilobars. The CGSE also fully owns and operates the "Hong Kong Precious Metals Assay Centre". Some EPs and CGSE members suggested to HKFE that HKFE could consider recognising gold bars manufactured by some of these local refineries as acceptable delivery bars for its gold futures contracts, and approving the "Hong Kong Precious Metals Assay Centre" as its recognised assayer. This could help home-grown commodity firms go abroad, and bring in regional commodity counterparts as they internationalise. To the on-exchange market, this could mean improved liquidity and more diversified participants in its gold contracts. To participants in the physical market, trading cost would be reduced and supply security would be increased if better risk-hedging instruments are made available. Such a win-win situation would add value for every party in the market.

Similar to the foreign exchange market, the gold market trades around the clock. Gold price responds instantly to important political events and other breaking news such as a hike in the US interest rates. HKFE could look into extending its gold futures' trading hours as Mainland China and international investors are likely to need 24-hour servicing

---

14　In 2018, Hong Kong has the highest consumer demand per capita of 7.0 grams in the world. Source: "Gold Demand Trends Q3 2019 Statistics", World Gold Council, 5 November 2019.

which is also the most often heard comment from the market participants. HKFE could also consider expanding the current metal product offerings to further develop and include products which are highly differentiated and based on regional and China pricing to build up a commodities platform with a more comprehensive product range.

Asia's share of global commodity production and consumption has been rising and more commodities are being traded in the Asian time zone[15]. Key financial centres in the region like Singapore and Shanghai, have conducted strategic reviews and come up with initiatives aiming at remaining competitive and ahead of the game. Hong Kong should leverage on its current strengths, including world-class business infrastructure, sound regulatory environment, and its unique mutual access platform between Mainland China and the world for grasping market opportunities and develop itself into a commodity trading hub in Asia. It is critical for Hong Kong to define a holistic strategy in commodity market development in order to maintain and preserve its status as one of the most important international financial centres in the world.

To realise the vision and benefit from the market opportunities described above, it is crucial for the government, the industry, the regulators, and the community to work together for the long-term interests of Hong Kong. It is also important to enhance efforts at the government-to-government level.

4 Conclusion

Hong Kong is well recognised by the world as a leading financial centre for capital raising, offshore RMB pricing and risk management. Notwithstanding this, it is still relatively weak in the commodities sector compared to other global financial venues.

To build Hong Kong into a global commodity trading centre, active initiatives have been taken by HKEX, the parent company of the only local futures exchange, HKFE. Sixteen exchange-traded commodity futures contracts under the umbrella of precious, ferrous and base metals and six non-tradeable gold indices have been rolled out to the market in the past decade, together with the acquisition of LME and the establishment of QME by

---

15 In 2018, consumer demand for gold in Asia countries was 2,176.3 tonnes, which was over 65% of world total demand, compared to 1,942.9 tonnes in 2010 which was less than 60% of world total demand. Source: "Gold Demand Trends Q3 2019 Statistics", World Gold Council, 5 November 2019.

HKEX. Consequently, Hong Kong's commodity derivatives market is steadily gaining momentum. However, its potential is yet to be fully realised. Hong Kong's commodities sector is mainly faced with two key challenges: to provide highly differentiated products based on regional and China pricing, and to develop a matching trading mechanism with high efficiency.

Given Hong Kong's weakness in physical delivery capacity, prospective product development can focus on the construction of cross-border product listings and licensing arrangements with domestic exchanges in the Mainland. This can be followed by building a trading mechanism that expands the through-train between Hong Kong and the Mainland to include commodities and allows cross-border commodity trading. Such initiatives would require close collaboration between HKEX and the Mainland and Hong Kong regulatory bodies to explore possible areas of new policy enforcement and compliance, as well as wide consultation with market participants to determine suitable products and trading routes that can bring deep liquidity.

The feedback from HKFE Participants also revealed that the market desires further enhancements on existing products including the reduction of the tick size for gold contracts and more flexible contracts duration. Likewise, trading mechanism reforms such as extended trading hours, expedited physical delivery process, recognition of local refineries and assayers would enhance the appeal and competitiveness of Hong Kong's commodity derivatives market. HKEX would also continue its active research on new underlying assets and contract types to address the rapidly changing industrial development and the growing demand of the Hong Kong market.

Despite the fact that the Hong Kong commodities market sits relatively behind other global trading centres in terms of liquidity and comprehensive product and service offerings, Hong Kong still has the right ingredients to become Asia's commodities pricing centre, backed by its unique position as a gateway to one of the world's largest commodities consumers — Mainland China. The product development and market infrastructure enhancement initiatives would not only help transform Hong Kong into an all-round financial centre with multi-asset class capabilities, but also give investors a unique access to liquidity in both China and global markets.

Appendix

Contract specifications of commodity products on the HKEX derivatives market

(a) USD Gold Futures

Feature	Details
Underlying	1 kilogram gold of not less than 0.9999 fineness bearing a serial number and identifying stamp of a Recognised Refiner
HKATS Code	GDU
Contract Size	1 kilogram
Trading Currency	USD
Contract Months	Spot Month and the next eleven calendar months
Minimum Fluctuation	USD 0.01 per gram
Last Trading Day (LTD)	The third Monday of the Contract Month Postponed to the next business day if it is a Hong Kong public holiday
Trading Hours[1] (Hong Kong Time) (other than on LTD)	Day trading session: 8:30 a.m. to 4:30 p.m. After-hours trading (AHT) session: 5:15 p.m. to 3:00 a.m. the next morning
Trading Hours[2] on LTD (Hong Kong Time)	8:30 a.m. to 4:30 p.m.
Final Settlement Day	The second Hong Kong Business Day after the LTD
Settlement Method	Physical settlement
Settlement Currency	USD
Final Settlement Price	Volume weighted average price of all trades[3] in the expiring Contract Month during the last thirty minutes of trading on the LTD
Delivery Site	An Approved Depository
Minimum Delivery Size	1 kilogram
Holiday Schedule	Follow HKFE holiday schedule
Trading Fee[4] (per contract per side)	USD 1.00
Settlement Fee[4] (per contract per side)	USD 2.00
SFC Levy[5] (per contract per side)	USD 0.07
Commission Rate	Negotiable

Notes:

(1)   There is no trading after 12:30 p.m. on the eves of Christmas, New Year and Lunar New Year. The trading hours on those three days shall be 8:30 a.m. – 12:30 p.m.. There is no AHT session if it is a bank holiday in the United Kingdom, the United States and the People's Republic of China.

(2)   There shall be no trading after 12:30 p.m. on the eves of Christmas, New Year and Lunar New Year. The trading hours on those three days shall be 8:30 a.m. – 12:30 p.m..

(3)   All trades other than Block Trades in the expiring Contract Month that result from the matching on the trading system of (i) two orders in the individual market series; or (ii) a standard combination order and an order in the individual market series, and executed during the last thirty minutes of trading on the LTD.

(4)   The amount indicated is subject to change by the HKFE from time to time.

(5)   The USD equivalent of HKD0.54 per contract at the exchange rate determined by the HKFE from time to time.

(b)   CNH Gold Futures

Feature	Details
Underlying	1 kilogram gold of not less than 0.9999 fineness bearing a serial number and identifying stamp of a Recognised Refiner
HKATS Code	GDR
Contract Size	1 kilogram
Trading Currency	RMB
Contract Months	Spot Month and the next eleven calendar months
Minimum Fluctuation	RMB 0.05 per gram
Last Trading Day (LTD)	The third Monday of the Contract Month Postponed to the next business day if it is a Hong Kong public holiday
Trading Hours[1] (Hong Kong Time) (other than on LTD)	Day trading session: 8:30 a.m. to 4:30 p.m. After-hours trading (AHT) session: 5:15 p.m. to 3:00 a.m. the next morning
Trading Hours[2] on LTD (Hong Kong Time)	8:30 a.m. to 4:30 p.m.
Final Settlement Day	The second Hong Kong Business Day after the LTD
Settlement Method	Physical settlement
Settlement Currency	RMB
Final Settlement Price	Volume weighted average price of all trades[3] in the expiring Contract Month during the last thirty minutes of trading on the LTD
Delivery Site	An Approved Depository
Minimum Delivery Size	1 kilogram
Holiday Schedule	Follow HKFE holiday schedule
Trading Fee[4] (per contract per side)	RMB 6.00
Settlement Fee[4] (per contract per side)	RMB 12.00

(continued)

Feature	Details
SFC Levy[5] (per contract per side)	RMB 0.50
Commission Rate	Negotiable

Notes:

(1)　There is no trading after 12:30 p.m. on the eves of Christmas, New Year and Lunar New Year. The trading hours on those three days shall be 8:30 a.m. – 12:30 p.m.. There is no AHT session if it is a bank holiday in the United Kingdom, the United States and the People's Republic of China.

(2)　There shall be no trading after 12:30 p.m. on the eves of Christmas, New Year and Lunar New Year. The trading hours on those three days shall be 8:30 a.m. – 12:30 p.m..

(3)　All trades other than Block Trades in the expiring Contract Month that result from the matching on the trading system of (i) two orders in the individual market series; or (ii) a standard combination order and an order in the individual market series, and executed during the last thirty minutes of trading on the LTD.

(4)　The amount indicated is subject to change by the HKFE from time to time.

(5)　The RMB equivalent of HKD0.54 per contract at the exchange rate determined by the HKFE from time to time.

(c)　USD London Aluminium/Zinc/Copper/Lead/Nickel/Tin Mini Futures

Feature	Details					
	USD London Aluminium Mini	USD London Zinc Mini	USD London Copper Mini	USD London Lead Mini	USD London Nickel Mini	USD London Tin Mini
Underlying Commodity	High Grade Primary Aluminium as defined in the rules and regulations of the LME from time to time	Special High Grade Zinc as defined in the rules and regulations of the LME from time to time	Copper – Grade A as defined in the rules and regulations of the LME from time to time	Standard Lead as defined in the rules and regulations of the LME from time to time	Primary Nickel as defined in the rules and regulations of the LME from time to time	Tin as defined in the rules and regulations of the LME from time to time
Trading Symbol	LUA	LUZ	LUC	LUP	LUN	LUS
Contract Size	5 tonnes / contract			1 tonne / contract		
Trading Currency	USD					
Settlement Currency	USD					
Contract Months	Spot month and the next eleven calendar months					
Trading Fee[1]	USD 0.50 per contract per side					
Settlement Fee[1]	USD 0.20 per lot					
SFC Levy[2]	USD 0.07 per contract per side					

(continued)

Feature	Details					
	USD London Aluminium Mini	USD London Zinc Mini	USD London Copper Mini	USD London Lead Mini	USD London Nickel Mini	USD London Tin Mini
Last Trading Day (LTD)	The LTD determined by the LME for the Aluminium/Zin/Copper/Lead/Nickel/Tin Futures Contract, which is two London business days before the third Wednesday of the Spot Month. If it is not a HK Business Day, the LTD shall be the immediately preceding HK Business Day.					
Trading Hours (Hong Kong Time) (other than on LTD)	Day trading session: 9:00 a.m. to 4:30 p.m. After-hours trading (AHT) session: 5:15 p.m. to 3:00 a.m. the next morning There is no trading after 12:30 p.m. on the eves of Christmas, New Year and Lunar New Year. The trading hours on those three days shall be 9:00 a.m. – 12:30 p.m. There is no after-hours trading session if it is a bank holiday in the United Kingdom, the United States and the People's Republic of China.					
Trading hours on LTD	Day trading session: 9:00 a.m. – 4:30 p.m.; AHT session: 5:15 p.m. – 8:00 p.m. (British Summer Time) / 9:00 p.m. (outside British Summer Time)	Day trading session: 9:00 a.m. – 4:30 p.m.; AHT session: 5:15 p.m. – 7:55 p.m. (British Summer Time) / 8:55 p.m. (outside British Summer Time)	Day trading session: 9:00 a.m. – 4:30 p.m.; AHT session: 5:15 p.m. – 7:35 p.m. (British Summer Time) / 8:35 p.m. (outside British Summer Time)	Day trading session: 9:00 a.m. – 4:30 p.m.; AHT session: 5:15 p.m. – 7:50 p.m. (British Summer Time) / 8:50 p.m. (outside British Summer Time)	Day trading session: 9:00 a.m. – 4:30 p.m.; AHT session: 5:15 p.m. – 8:05 p.m. (British Summer Time) / 9:05 p.m. (outside British Summer Time)	Day trading session: 9:00 a.m. – 4:30 p.m.; AHT session: 5:15 p.m. – 7:45 p.m. (British Summer Time) / 8:45 p.m. (outside British Summer Time)
Minimum Fluctuation	USD 0.5 / tonne				USD 1 / tonne	
Final Settlement Date (FSD)	The second HK Business Day after the LTD					
Final Settlement Price (FSP)	Shall be determined by the Clearing House, and shall be the Official Settlement Price determined and published by the LME two London Business Days before the third Wednesday of the Spot Month					
Settlement Method	Cash-settled					
Holiday Schedule	Follow HKFE holiday schedule					
Combined Position Limits (USD and CNH contracts)	25,000	25,000	50,000	25,000	50,000	15,000

Notes:
(1)   The amount indicated is subject to change by the HKFE from time to time.
(2)   The USD equivalent of HKD0.54 per contract at the exchange rate determined by the HKFE from time to time.

(d) CNH London Aluminium/Zinc/Copper/Lead/Nickel/Tin Mini Futures

Feature	Details					
	CNH London Aluminium Mini	CNH London Zinc Mini	CNH London Copper Mini	CNH London Lead Mini	CNH London Nickel Mini	CNH London Tin Mini
Underlying Commodity	High Grade Primary Aluminium as defined in the rules and regulations of the LME from time to time	Special High Grade Zinc as defined in the rules and regulations of the LME from time to time	Copper – Grade A as defined in the rules and regulations of the LME from time to time	Standard Lead as defined in the rules and regulations of the LME from time to time	Primary Nickel as defined in the rules and regulations of the LME from time to time	Tin as defined in the rules and regulations of the LME from time to time
Trading Symbol	LRA	LRZ	LRC	LRP	LRN	LRS
Contract Size	5 tonnes / contract				1 tonne / contract	
Trading Currency	RMB					
Settlement Currency	RMB					
Contract Months	Spot month and the next eleven calendar months					
Trading Fee[1]	RMB 3.00 per contract per side					
Settlement Fee[1]	RMB 1.20 per lot					
SFC Levy[2]	RMB 0.44 per contract per side					
Last Trading Day (LTD)	The LTD determined by the LME for the Aluminium/Zin/Copper/Lead/Nickel/Tin Futures Contract, which is two London business days before the third Wednesday of the Spot Month. If it is not a HK Business Day, the LTD shall be the immediately preceding HK Business Day.					
Trading Hours (Hong Kong Time) (other than on LTD)	Day trading session: 9:00 a.m. to 4:30 p.m. After-hours trading (AHT) session: 5:15 p.m. to 3:00 a.m. the next morning There is no trading after 12:30 p.m. on the eves of Christmas, New Year and Lunar New Year. The trading hours on those three days shall be 9:00 a.m. – 12:30 p.m. There is no after-hours trading session if it is a bank holiday in the United Kingdom, the United States and the People's Republic of China.					

(continued)

Feature	Details					
	CNH London Aluminium Mini	CNH London Zinc Mini	CNH London Copper Mini	CNH London Lead Mini	CNH London Nickel Mini	CNH London Tin Mini
Trading hours on LTD	Day trading session: 9:00 a.m. – 4:30 p.m.; AHT session: 5:15 p.m. – 8:00 p.m. (British Summer Time) / 9:00 p.m. (outside British Summer Time)	Day trading session: 9:00 a.m. – 4:30 p.m.; AHT session: 5:15 p.m. – 7:55 p.m. (British Summer Time) / 8:55 p.m. (outside British Summer Time)	Day trading session: 9:00 a.m. – 4:30 p.m.; AHT session: 5:15 p.m. – 7:35 p.m. (British Summer Time) / 8:35 p.m. (outside British Summer Time)	Day trading session: 9:00 a.m. – 4:30 p.m.; AHT session: 5:15 p.m. – 7:50 p.m. (British Summer Time) / 8:50 p.m. (outside British Summer Time)	Day trading session: 9:00 a.m. – 4:30 p.m.; AHT session: 5:15 p.m. – 8:05 p.m. (British Summer Time) / 9:05 p.m. (outside British Summer Time)	Day trading session: 9:00 a.m. – 4:30 p.m.; AHT session: 5:15 p.m. – 7:45 p.m. (British Summer Time) / 8:45 p.m. (outside British Summer Time)
Minimum Fluctuation	RMB 5 / tonne		RMB 10 / tonne	RMB 5 / tonne	RMB 10 / tonne	
Final Settlement Date (FSD)	The second HK Business Day after the LTD					
Final Settlement Price (FSP)	Shall be a whole number, determined by the Clearing House, and shall be the Official Settlement Price determined and published by the LME for its Aluminium/Zinc/Copper/Lead/Nickel/Tin Futures, and converted to RMB equivalent using the USD/CNY(HK) Spot Rate published by the Treasury Markets Association in Hong Kong at or around 11:30 a.m. Hong Kong time on the LTD. It is rounded up if the figure in the first decimal place is 5 or above and rounded down if it is below 5.					
Settlement Method	Cash-settled					
Holiday Schedule	Follow HKFE holiday schedule					
Combined Position Limits (USD and CNH contracts)	25,000	25,000	50,000	25,000	50,000	15,000

Notes:

(1)   The amount indicated is subject to change by the HKFE from time to time.

(2)   The RMB equivalent of HKD0.54 per contract at the exchange rate determined by the HKFE from time to time.

(e)   Iron Ore Monthly Futures

Features	Details
HKATS Code	FEM
Underlying	TSI Iron Ore Fines 62% Fe CFR China Index
Contract Size	100 tonnes
Trading Currency	USD
Price Quotation	USD and cents per tonne
Contract Months	Spot Month and the next 23 calendar months
Minimum Fluctuation	USD 0.01 per tonne
Maximum Fluctuation	Nil
Last Trading Day (LTD)	The last Hong Kong Business Day of a calendar month that is not a Singapore public holiday
Trading Hours[1] (Hong Kong Time) (other than on LTD)	Day trading session: 9:00 a.m. to 4:30 p.m. After-hours trading (AHT) session: 5:15 p.m. to 3:00 a.m.
Trading Hours on LTD[2] (Hong Kong Time)	Day trading session: 9:00 a.m. – 4:30 p.m. AHT session: 5:15 p.m. – 6:30 p.m.
Final Settlement Day	The second Hong Kong Business Day after the LTD, provided that if (i) the LTD is on the last Hong Kong Business Day before New Year's Day or the Lunar New Year, (ii) the Trading Hours of the Spot Month Contract and the Spot Quarter Contract end at 12:30 p.m., and (iii) the day trading session of other Contract Months ends at 4:30 p.m., the Final Settlement Day shall be the first Hong Kong Business Day after the LTD.
Final Settlement Price	Arithmetic average of all TSI Iron Ore Fines 62% Fe CFR China Index values published in that Contract Month, rounded to 2 decimal places
Settlement Method	Cash settled
Holiday Schedule	Follow HKFE holiday schedule
Trading Fee[3] (per contract per side)	USD 1.00
Settlement Fee[3] (per contract per side)	USD 1.00
Levies[4] (per contract per side)	USD 0.07
Commission Rate	Negotiable

Notes:

(1)   There is no trading after 12:30 p.m. on the eves of Christmas, New Year and Lunar New Year. The trading hours on those three days shall be 9:00 a.m. – 12:30 p.m..

(2)   There is no trading after 12:30 p.m. on the LTD that is the last Hong Kong Business Day before New Year's Day or the Lunar New Year, and which is also the last day before New Year's Day or the Lunar New Year on which the TSI Iron Ore Fines 62% Fe CFR China Index is published. The trading hours on those two days shall be 9:00 a.m. – 12: 30 p.m..

(3)   The amount indicated is subject to change by the HKFE from time to time.

(4)   The current rate is set at HK$ 0.54 per contract, for which the USD equivalent will be determined by the HKFE from time to time.

(f)   Iron Ore Quarterly Futures

Features	Details
HKATS Code	FEQ
Underlying	TSI Iron Ore Fines 62% Fe CFR China Index
Contract Size	100 tonnes
Trading Currency	USD
Price Quotation	USD and cents per tonne
Contract Months	Spot Quarter and the next seven calendar quarters (i.e. calendar quarters are January to March, April to June, July to September and October to December)
Minimum Fluctuation	USD 0.01 per tonne
Maximum Fluctuation	Nil
Last Trading Day (LTD)	The LTD of the last Monthly Contract in the calendar quarter
Trading Hours[1] (Hong Kong Time) (other than on LTD)	Day trading session: 9:00 a.m. to 4:30 p.m. After-hours trading (AHT) session: 5:15 p.m. to 3:00 a.m.
Trading Hours on LDT[2] (Hong Kong Time)	Day trading session: 9:00 a.m. – 4:30 p.m. AHT session: 5:15 p.m. – 6:30 p.m.
Final Settlement Day	The second Hong Kong Business Day after the LTD, provided that if (i) the LTD is on the last Hong Kong Business Day before New Year's Day or the Lunar New Year, (ii) the Trading Hours of the Spot Month Contract and the Spot Quarter Contract end at 12:30 p.m., and (iii) the day trading session of other Contract Months ends at 4:30 p.m., the Final Settlement Day shall be the first Hong Kong Business Day after the LTD.
Final Settlement Price	Arithmetic average of the Final Settlement Prices of the three corresponding Monthly Contracts in that Contract Quarter, rounded to 2 decimal places
Settlement Method	Cash settled
Holiday Schedule	Follow HKFE holiday schedule
Trading Fee[3] (per contract per side)	USD 1.00
Settlement Fee[3] (per contract per side)	USD 1.00
Levies[4] (per contract per side)	USD 0.07
Commission Rate	Negotiable

Notes:

(1)   There is no trading after 12:30 p.m. on the eves of Christmas, New Year and Lunar New Year. The trading hours on those three days shall be 9:00 a.m. – 12:30 p.m..

(2)   There is no trading after 12:30 p.m. on the LTD that is the last Hong Kong Business Day before New Year's Day or the Lunar New Year, and which is also the last day before New Year's Day or the Lunar New Year on which the TSI Iron Ore Fines 62% Fe CFR China Index is published. The trading hours on those two days shall be 9:00 a.m. – 12: 30 p.m..

(3)   The amount indicated is subject to change by the HKFE from time to time.

(4)   The current rate is set at HK$ 0.54 per contract, for which the USD equivalent will be determined by the HKFE from time to time.

Part 3

Commodities spot and futures market connectivity

Chapter 10

Global experience of commodity futures serving the real economy

Chief China Economist's Office
Hong Kong Exchanges and Clearing Limited

Summary

A commodity futures contract is a standardised agreement traded on the exchange to buy or sell a predetermined amount of a commodity at a specific price on a specific date in the future. The global commodity futures market has demonstrated a close linkage with the spot market. In the US and the UK, major producers and consumers gathered for spot transactions and the futures market was then established to address the uncertainties on prices and timing of physical delivery. The prices of commodity futures, therefore, have become benchmark prices for spot transactions of commodities. Theoretically, commodity futures prices can be affected by spot market elements, including spot prices, interest rate, storage costs, contract tenor and potential benefits to use inventories for production. Empirical evidence showed that the global commodity futures market has a close linkage with the spot market and that linkage reflects economic fundamentals and market structure.

The commodity futures market serves different needs of hedgers and financial investors. Hedgers are key players in global commodity futures markets. They include commodity producers, consumers and trading firms who use commodity futures to hedge against adverse movements of commodity spot prices. The physical settlement of commodity futures through the global network of warehouses is key to the strong linkage between the spot and futures market as it provides a cost-effective way to obtain commodities for commercial uses. Financial investors treat commodity futures as an asset class for passive investment or active returns. Empirical evidences show that commodity futures could diversify investment portfolios by potentially giving higher returns and lower volatilities.

Mainland China's commodity futures market serves the real economy not as effectively as its developed counterparts in the world. The spot commodity market in Mainland China is fragmented such that the transaction prices usually vary across regions without reference to the corresponding commodity futures prices. The price volatility in the Mainland commodity futures market may be high due to speculative trading activities, which would affect the effectiveness of hedging. Besides, the limited choices of warehouses for physical delivery of commodities may increase the costs of storage, transportation and import taxes and the narrow range of product and currency denomination may not meet the various business needs in the Mainland. These affect the effective linkage between the Mainland commodity spot and futures markets. China is the second largest economy and one of the largest producers and consumers of a number of key global commodities. However, the Mainland commodity futures market has limited global interaction such that onshore and offshore hedgers cannot sufficiently reflect their price views on the global and Mainland commodity futures markets respectively. This contributes to the price difference between the two markets.

For the Mainland commodity futures market to better serve the real economy, the linkage between the Mainland spot and futures markets should be strengthened, and the Mainland futures market should have a greater pricing influence in the global market. To achieve this end, a number of initiatives could be considered. The use of commodity futures prices as benchmark prices in the spot market could be facilitated by consolidating trading and enhancing trade transparency in the Mainland spot market. The deviation of futures prices from the underlying fundamentals due to excessive speculation and transportation costs could be reduced by enhancing market regulation and expanding the warehouse network. The business needs of various sectors could be met by widening the product range and currency denomination. Moreover, the Hong Kong market, being an international financial centre at the front-door of China, could take the role as a super-connector in the commodities sector to further increase the global interaction of the Mainland commodity futures market, thereby helping strengthen the Mainland commodity futures market to better serve the real economy.

1 Commodity futures in connection with the real economy

A commodity futures contract is a standardised agreement traded on the exchange to buy or sell a predetermined amount of a commodity at a specific price on a specific date in the future. The underlying commodity can be base metals, precious metals, agricultural products, energy products, chemicals and others. The futures contracts can either be physically settled (delivery of the physical underlying assets from the seller to the buyer) or cash settled (delivery of the settlement value in cash between the buyer and the seller).

The traders of commodity futures include producers, consumers, trading firms and financial investors, which overlap those in the commodity spot market in the real economy. Therefore, the price of commodity futures usually serve as the benchmark price of the underlying commodity. The trading of commodity futures in value terms has been dominated by exchanges in the United States (US) and Europe (see Figure 1). These partly reflect their key roles in the global commodity markets, particularly in terms of pricing power. Nevertheless, the Mainland commodity futures exchanges were also among the top ones ranked by nominal trading value in 2019.

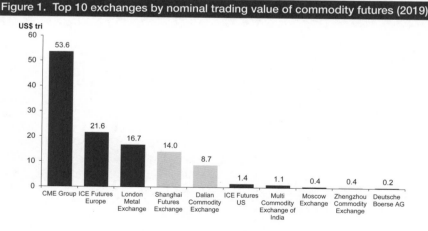

Figure 1. Top 10 exchanges by nominal trading value of commodity futures (2019)

Note: The data of ICE Futures Europe and ICE Futures US were up to October 2019 and August 2019 respectively.

Source: Statistics published on the website of World Federation of Exchanges (WFE).

The global and Mainland commodity futures exchanges have different development paths, given the differences in the structure of the respective commodity markets. The experience in the global market has demonstrated a close linkage between commodity spot and futures markets, which is important for the price discovery of commodities. This shed light on the next steps of development for China's commodity futures exchanges.

1.1   Brief history of the global commodity futures market

The history of commodities futures in global markets has demonstrated its function to serve the real economy. In the US and the United Kingdom (UK), the spot markets of commodities have been developed for a long time and already gathered a critical mass of commodity users before the emergence of commodity futures exchanges. Commodity futures exchanges in these markets were established to centralise market trading in order to meet the demand for better price discovery and risk management.

In the US[1], Chicago became a regional hub of agricultural commerce in the early 19th century after the completion of canal and railroad infrastructure centered around the city. It facilitated spot commodity transactions at a centralised place to address chaotic price fluctuations and unpredictable supply and other challenges faced by US agricultural producers and consumers. The Chicago Board of Trade (CBOT), which was the world's first futures exchange, was formed in 1848 for spot transactions of grains between agricultural producers and consumers initially. Then the CBOT offered the earliest "forward" contracts[2] in 1851. In 1865, the CBOT launched the world's first commodity futures for grain trading, which were standardised agreements with physical delivery, clearing operations and "margin" (or "performance bonds") to be posted by buyers and sellers of grains. Subsequently, the New York Mercantile Exchange (NYMEX) and the Chicago Mercantile Exchange (CME) were formed in 1872 and 1919 respectively for initially spot trading of other agricultural products and launched commodity futures subsequently. Since late 1960s, these commodity exchanges expanded their product coverage to non-agricultural products, including metals, currencies, crude oil, interest rates and financial indices, etc. The NYMEX merged with Commodity Exchange (COMEX) in 1994 and were acquired by the CME Group in 2008, which was formed by the merger of the CME and the CBOT in 2007. The CME has then become a leading pricing centre of agricultural products and crude oil.

---

1   Source: "Midwest Grain Trade: History of Futures Exchanges", published on the website of the CME Group, viewed on 8 November 2019; "美國六大期貨交易所 —— CBOT、CME、NYMEX……", published on *kknews.cc*, 8 August 2017.

2   Forward contracts are different from futures contracts in that the contract specifications (e.g. contract size and settlement date) are not standardised and the contracts are often traded over-the-counter but not on-exchange.

The UK[3] has a long history of copper and tin trading for production of bronze and alloys. At first, metal trading was only for the domestic market. Since the UK had become a major exporter of metals more than a hundred years ago, London then became a centre for European traders of physical metals. The London Metal Exchange (LME) was established in 1877 to facilitate business activities on metals for commodity traders, ship charterers and financiers, with metal trading through the Ring (the early form of open-outcry trading). Back in early 19th century, the UK had been self-sufficient in copper and tin with quoted prices that remained fixed for long periods. Upon the Industrial Revolution, metal traders expanded trading and faced uncertainty on the arrival date for their imports of metal ores and concentrates from as far as Chile and Malaya. Technological advancement upon the invention of the telegraph led to more predictable arrival dates and facilitated the physical transactions with delivery on a fixed date. Further, the opening of the Suez Canal reduced the delivery time of tin and copper to London to three months. These led to the establishment of the LME's unique system of daily prompt dates for up to three months forward, which still exists to this day. Physical trading then expanded to a wider range of metals, including copper, tin, lead, zinc, aluminium and nickel as well as ferrous metals, precious metals and other metals. Now, the LME has become a leading price centre of metals and accounted for more than 70% of all metals traded on global exchanges in 2016[4].

As seen from the development paths of commodity markets in the US and Europe, the demand for commodities has mainly come from commodity users, including producers, consumers, physical logistics and trading firms, which support the upstream sectors (the suppliers of raw materials in the production chain) and downstream sectors (the customers of raw material and the producers of finished goods) as well as business activities in the real economy. As the commodity spot market grew, an increasing range of commodities were traded and the commodity users faced uncertainties in prices and physical delivery. These resulted in the demand for a commodity futures market to serve the different needs of commodity users.

1.2 Why the commodity futures market is needed for price discovery?

The spot market has played a key role in the real economy and dominated trading in the commodities market. As an illustration, the traditional spot market (price negotiated at the time of goods sale just before delivery) accounted for about 60% of agricultural

---

3 Source: "History", published on the website of the London Metal Exchange, viewed on 8 November 2019; "Basic knowledge of futures 6: The development process of futures market" (〈期貨基礎知識六：期貨市場的發展過程〉), published on *xueqiu.com*, viewed on 7 November 2019.
4 Source: "LME pauses fund charm offensive to calm traditional members", *Reuters,* 1 November 2016.

commodities in the US in early 2001[5]. For transactions in the commodity spot market, the price can be set through the following pricing mechanisms[6]:

- **Bilateral contract:** It is the predominant form of transaction mechanism in the spot market. A bilateral contract is customised between a buyer and a seller that specifies the commodity specification, price, quantity, time and location of physical delivery.

- **Transfer price:** It is the price set for internal transactions between two entities (e.g. an upstream subsidiary and a downstream subsidiary) of a vertically integrated corporation. The transparency is low as the trade can only be found in financial statements of these firms. In the case of cross-border transfer transactions, the import prices tend to be underpriced to reduce the burden of tariff.

- **Posted price:** It is the price instituted by the government to avoid tariff evasion. It can be set with reference to the production cost or the prevailing transaction prices between independent parties.

- **Producer-dictated price:** It is the price set by a few number of the largest producers given their high concentration of market power.

- **Consumer-driven price:** It is the price set by a few number of the largest consumers given their high concentration of market power.

- **Private auction:** The price is set either through ordinary auction (priced at the highest bid price of buyers) or Dutch auction (priced at the lowest offer price of sellers). Private auction accommodates many buyers and sellers in the market and the commodity specification is not standardised. Private auctions are not continuously conducted.

The prices in the spot market are highly decentralised and vary significantly across the types of pricing mechanisms mentioned above. The user's choice among these mechanisms depends on tariffs, government policy, commodity specification, timing of transaction and the relative market power of producers and consumers. While certain commodity users can take advantage of the customised contracts at favourable prices, these transaction prices may not be good reference prices for all market transactions. Take bilateral contract as an example. The contract price of major producers can be a reference price for certain commodities. However, the price information is private and may not be transparent to the market. Another concern is the reliability of such reference price. For metals and energy

---

5   Source: MacDonald, J. M. et. al. (2004) "Contracts, markets, and prices: Organising the production and use of agricultural commodities", *Agricultural Economic Report* No. 837, published on the website of the US Department of Agriculture (USDA).

6   See Radetzki, M. (2013) "The relentless progress of commodity exchanges in the establishment of primary commodity prices", *Resources Policy*, Vol. 38, pp.266-277.

products, a study[7] reported that the share of total world production of the top four or five leading producers declined significantly for aluminium, nickel and crude oil during 1955 to 1990. The transaction prices of these producers therefore became less representative. Besides, as the terms on bilateral contracts are customised, the commodity specification or contract tenor may not be comparable across contracts. As a result, the actual prices of transactions in the spot market can deviate to different extents from the prevailing reference price and less systematic for certain commodities.

In the light of this, the commodity futures market is complementary to the spot market for price discovery. Commodity futures are highly standardised in respect of commodity specification, contract size and settlement date. Commodity futures exchanges allow continuous price auctions between buyers and sellers without entry barriers. Besides, the pricing information in the futures market is much more transparent than those in the spot market, and this facilitates the price discovery of commodity prices. Furthermore, commodity futures exchanges act as the central counterparty to mitigate the counterparty risk and facilitate the clearing and settlement of commodity transactions. The demand for commodity futures has been evidenced by the growing transaction volume of commodity futures for metals, agricultural and energy products in the global commodity market (see Figure 2). Active trading increases the reliability of futures prices as the reference prices of the underlying commodities.

Figure 2. Annual turnover of commodity futures in global markets by type of commodity (2009 – 2019)

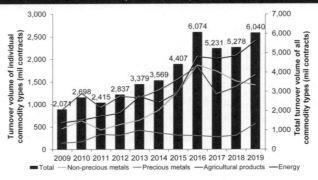

Note: The contract size of commodity futures varies across exchanges. The same turnover volume of different futures products may not represent the same nominal trading value.

Source: Futures Industry Association (FIA).

---

7   Radetzki, M. (2013) "The relentless progress of commodity exchanges in the establishment of primary commodity prices", *Resources Policy*, Vol. 38, pp.266-277.

1.3   Empirical evidences on commodity futures as a key for price discovery in the spot market

Commodity futures in global markets are usually physically settled and this involves commodity storage costs (e.g. warehousing, insurance). Besides, commodity users have the choice between consumption today and holding the physical inventory of a commodity as a consumption good rather than as a financial asset. The pricing of commodity futures is therefore different from that of financial futures, which only take into account the interest rate for the expected value.

To price commodity futures, we can consider that a commodity user has two ways to obtain the commodity in a future time. First, the user can borrow money at interest rate "r" to buy the commodity now at spot price "S" and hold the commodity with storage costs "k" and enjoy the benefit of holding the physical commodity as inventory with a convenience yield[8] "ψ" for "T" years. The second way is to long a commodity futures contract that commits to buy the commodity at a strike price "F" after T years and then invest the present value of F into a risk-free asset to ensure the sum for future purchase. The two ways should have the same cash flows and costs in an efficient market. Otherwise, an investor can go for the cheaper way to get the commodity and sell it at a higher price through the other way to make arbitrage profits without any risks. As a result, the logical relationships are that the commodity futures price (F) is positively associated with the spot price (S), the interest rate (r), the storage cost (k) and tenor of contract (T), but negatively associated with convenience yield (ψ)[9].

Besides, the level of inventories can affect the futures price in different scenarios of demand and supply of commodity in the real economy. A study[10] looked into the spot price, futures price and inventory data of base metals traded on the LME during July 1997 to June 2009. The study discussed the price and inventory adjustments in backwardation[11] and contango[12] situations. The study found that:

- In a backwardated futures market, the level of inventories is likely to be too low to meet the demand in the real economy, such that the inventories become more

---

8   Convenience yields apply to storable commodities that the demand can be met out of current production or inventory. The potential benefits include the ability to profit from temporary shortages and the ability to keep a production process running.

9   See Pindyck, R. (2001) "The dynamics of commodity spot and futures markets: A primer", *Energy Journal*, Vol. 22, pp.1-29.

10   Roache, S. and N. Erbil. (2010) "How commodities price curves and inventories react to a short-run scarcity shock", *International Monetary Fund (IMF) Working Paper*, WP/10/222.

11   Backwardation is the situation where the futures price of an underlying asset is lower than the spot price.

12   Contango is the situation where the futures price of an underlying asset is higher than the spot price.

valuable to commodity users (e.g. to keep production process running) and the convenience yield will be higher (see Figure 3). This could push up the spot price and drag the futures price below the spot price[13].

- In a contangoed market, the level of inventories is likely to be abundant to meet the demand in the real economy, the convenience yield will be diminished and lead to a lower spot price than the futures price.

Figure 3. Illustrative diagram on the relationship between convenience yield and inventories

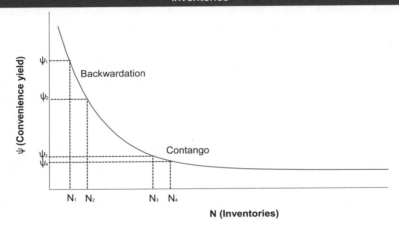

Source: Roache, S. and N. Erbil. (2010) "How commodities price curves and inventories react to a short-run scarcity shock", *IMF Working Paper*, WP/10/222.

A number of studies gave empirical findings on the relationship between the commodity futures market and the real economy:

- Empirical evidence showed that the prices and open interests of commodity futures have a close linkage with the real economy. A study[14] examined the characteristics of price performance of commodity futures by constructing an equal-weighted commodity futures index covering all commodity futures using the data of the Commodity Research Bureau (CRB) in the US and of the LME during July 1959 to March 2004. It found that the price return of commodity futures was positively

---

13 This is the case of "strongly backwardated" market. If the spot price is only higher than the discounted value of the futures price, then the market is "weakly backwardated".

14 Gorton, G. and K.G. Rouwenhorst. (2006) "Facts and fantasies about commodity futures", *Financial Analysts Journal*, Vol. 62, pp.47-68.

correlated with inflation, unexpected inflation and changes in expected inflation. Another study[15] found that the open interests of commodity futures in the US during December 1964 to December 2008 were highly procyclical and positively correlated with macroeconomic activities. The study findings showed the predictive power of open interests of commodity futures in commodity returns, bond returns and short-term interest rates. This may be attributable to the hedging activities of commodity producers and consumers in the futures market (see Section 2.1).

- The linkages among commodity futures prices revealed the linkages in different sectors of the real economy. Commodity futures are heterogeneous that the pricing in different markets of commodity futures have different levels of efficiency[16]. This is in line with the fact that the prices of goods in upstream industries usually respond more quickly than the prices of goods in downstream industries. The prices of finished goods in downstream industries will adjust with a time lag if the price change of raw material is persistent. An example[17] is demonstrated in the economic linkages of commodity futures of palladium, natural rubber and gasoline in the automobile industry in Japan (which accounted for more than 50% of world consumption) that the shocks of volatility (or volume) in palladium futures affected the volume (or volatility) of natural rubber and gasoline futures.

- Commodity futures prices serve as reference prices for the logistics sector. A research[18] studied the daily price data of the forward agreements on dry bulk freights at Baltic Exchange as well as the futures available in the US and Europe and the over-the-counter (OTC) derivatives on commodities transported in the freight during May 2006 to October 2009. The paper found that the shocks on price return and volatility appeared in the commodity futures first and then spilled over to the freight derivatives.

- The economic fundamentals and structural differences of major commodity markets contribute to the price discovery of commodity futures. An example is soybean. The exports of soybeans from the US and Brazil are the largest in the world (about 83% of total exports during 2016-2017[19]). The direct trading access (or order routing) of

---

15　Hong, H. and M. Yogo. (2012) "What does futures market interest tell us about the macroeconomy and asset prices?", *Journal of Financial Economics*, Vol. 105, pp.473-490.

16　See Kristoufek, I. and M. Vosvrda. (2014) "Commodity futures and market efficiency", *Energy Economics*, Vol. 42, pp.50-57.

17　See Chng, M.T. (2009) "Economic linkages across commodity futures: Hedging and trading implications", *Journal of Banking and Finance*, Vol. 33, pp.958-970.

18　Kavussanos, M. G., I. D. Visvikis and D. N. Dimitrakopoulos. (2014) "Economic spillovers between related derivatives markets: The case of commodity and freight markets", *Transportation Research Part E*, Vol. 68, pp.79-102.

19　Source: Gale, F., C. Valdes and M. Ash, "Interdependence of China, United States, and Brazil in soybean trade", published on the USDA Economic Research Service's website, June 2019.

futures by qualified investors between the CME and Brazil's BM&F Bovespa (referred to as "BM&F") began in September 2008 for the access to the CME and in February 2009 for the access to BM&F. A study[20] found that the qualified investors contributed to the transmission of information flows and helped the price discovery of soybean futures in the two markets during the partly overlapped trading hours.

- The structural differences between commodity futures markets in respect of their connection with the physical market contributed to futures price differentials. In the case of copper futures, the CME copper futures traded at a premium over the LME contracts between 2014 to March 2017 because of the difference in the coverage of the exchanges' warehouse networks (34 global locations for the LME but limited to US locations for the CME) and the expectation of tariffs imposed by the US[21].
- Another study[22] found that the US futures market had a larger driving force in price discovery in soybean and copper than the Chinese market and the effect of information flows from the US market to the Chinese market was stronger than the other way round. This illustrates the difference in the pricing power of commodities in the global commodity futures market.

The global commodity futures exchanges are crucial in the price discovery of commodities. The pricing power is attributable to the close linkage between commodity spot and futures markets in serving the different needs of commodity users.

---

20 Plato, G. and L. Hoffman. (2011) "Price Discovery in U.S. and Foreign Commodity Futures Markets: The Brazilian Soybean Example." *Proceedings of the NCCC-134 Conference on Applied Commodity Price Analysis, Forecasting, and Risk Management*, St. Louis, Missouri.

21 See "LME and CME copper arbitrage: When global and regional prices meet", *LME Insight*, March 2017.

22 See Liu, Q. and Y. An. (2011) "Information transmission in informationally linked markets: Evidence from US and Chinese commodity futures markets", *Journal of International Money and Finance*, Vol. 30, pp.778-795.

2   Commodity futures to meet user needs in the real economy

2.1   Different user needs in the real economy

Key participants in the global commodity futures market include hedgers and financial investors. A hedger can be a producer, consumer or trading firm and starts with a price exposure in the commodity, buys or sells futures contracts, and therefore offsets the price exposure. A financial investor starts without price exposure, buys or sells futures contracts, and therefore takes on price exposure. As they play different roles in the real economy, the products and services of the commodity futures market fit their needs in different ways.

(1)   Producers

Producers in the upstream industries produce commodities as raw materials for further processing. The production usually operates throughout the year, unless it is interrupted by policy guidance on the supply or adverse climate conditions. It is quite costly and timely to restart production facilities, for example steel smelters, and it is therefore not flexible to adjust the quantities of a commodity in the production process. In other words, producers have fixed schedules of output supply. Sharp declines of the output price will turn out to be losses.

For commodity producers to hedge against the downside risk of declines in output prices, one possible way is to take short positions of physically settled futures or long put options to sell a given amount of commodity outputs at a pre-determined price at the date of output. Taking the LME market as an example, the metal contracts have prompt date structures out to 123 months to meet the production schedules that can be physically settled on a daily basis up to 3 months, on a weekly basis on Wednesdays between 3 to 6 months and on a monthly basis on the third Wednesdays between 7 months to 123 months. As producers usually want to sell their outputs evenly throughout the year at a relatively stable price, the LME's contracts that average the pricing meet their needs. Producers can also hedge through option strategies to enhance returns[23]. Certain producers may hold

---

23 See Taušer, J. and R. Čajka. (2014) "Hedging techniques in commodity risk management", *Agricultural Economics*, Vol. 60, pp.174-182.

long or short positions more than their commercial needs, in order to generate extra profits from predictions of price fluctuation (referred to as "selective hedging"). They tend to take relatively more long (more short) positions in commodity futures for hedging with positively (negatively) skewed returns distribution.

Producers may still bear basis risk after hedging, which arise from the difference in the price between the commodity being hedged and the hedging instrument (e.g. due to the characteristics and quantities specified in the commodity futures contract). Nevertheless, the commodity futures price is usually a reference price for a similar type of commodity in the spot market. For example, a research paper[24] noted that the prices of LME contracts have become reference prices for several industrial metals in bilateral transactions.

As commodity futures meet the hedging needs of producers, producers are usually key participants in the global commodity futures market. Although producers and consumers mainly rely on the spot market to trade commodities, the efficient settlement of commodity futures transactions through physical delivery at warehouses also facilitate the transactions of commodities for commercial uses. This would strengthen the linkage between commodity spot and futures markets. The futures prices in the global market are therefore indicative of commodity market prices and global hedgers can use futures prices as benchmarks for commodity spot transactions. For example, the LME is able to gather key producers in the base metals market for price discovery — the largest global base metal hedgers gather for trading through the Ring (open-outcry) on the LME, which is assisted by other trading mechanisms. To facilitate trading, the LME has a global network of more than 550 approved warehouses in 33 locations[25] to provide physical delivery with minimised transportation costs.

(2) Consumers

Commodity consumers include second-tier producers using commodities as raw materials in the downstream industries or end users of commodity products. Their purchase of commodities is part of their cost of inputs. To avoid disruption of production or consumption due to shortage of inputs, they may keep certain levels of inventory. As end-products for consumption usually do not have a centralised secondary market, the changes of price tend to be less frequent. In the light of this, an unexpected increase of input prices

---

24 Valiante, D., "Price formation in commodity markets: Financialisation and beyond", published on the Centre for European Policy Studies (CEPS)'s website, July 2013.

25 The LME does not own or operate warehouses, nor does it own the material they contain. It simply authorises warehouse companies and the warehouses they operate to store LME-registered brands of metal. See "Presentation by HKEX Chief Operating Officer at a media workshop about London Metal Exchange update", the HKEX's news release, 7 June 2016.

will put pressure on their costs and hence the profits.

For commodity consumers to hedge against the upside risk of input prices, one possible way is to take long positions of physically settled futures or call options to purchase a given amount of commodity inputs at a pre-determined date. Consumers may also undergo selective hedging as in the case of producers and face basis risk for hedging as the characteristics and quantities of futures contracts may not perfectly meet their needs. In contrast to commodity producers, the schedule of commodity usage or consumption is usually different from that of commodity production. Major commodity futures markets usually provide average pricing for futures contracts (e.g. Monthly Average Futures and Traded Average Price Options (TAPOs) on the LME) to address the issue of timing mismatch. Besides, the geographical distribution of producers and consumers may be different. Major commodity futures exchanges approved a global network of warehouses of their own for physical delivery at settlement of their commodity futures. Proper management of inventories at warehouses also helps. An example is the LME's warehouse reforms during 2013 to 2016, which included linked load-in/load-out rule (LILO) and per-warehouse queue length report[26]. These effectively reduce the chance of long queues of consumers to take out commodities from certain warehouses.

(3)   Trading firms

Commodity trading firms are intermediaries between commodity producers and consumers to address their mismatches with the use of products and services in the commodity futures market. In the global markets, there are a few dominant commodity trading firms. Each of the biggest four had a revenue of more than US$100 billion in 2018 (versus about US$30-40 billion for the fifth one) from their businesses covering a wide range of commodities (e.g. metals, energy products, agricultural products and carbon emission)[27]. Commodity trading firms may own upstream or downstream businesses themselves. Besides, commodity producers and consumers may ask for their help to manage the market risk of price fluctuations for their commodity holdings or transactions. To meet different needs of producers and consumers, a trading firm gather a number of different orders to take long and short positions in commodity futures at different maturities.

Commodity trading firms also play a role in financing the commodity trade[28]. Major global commodity trading firms usually own midstream facilities (e.g. warehouses and

---

26 See "Warehouse reform 2013 - 2016", webpage on the LME's website, viewed on 30 January 2020.

27 Source: "Another battlefield of competition between major economies: Value chain of commodities" (〈大國競爭的另一個戰場：大宗商品供應鏈〉), published on *Huexiu.com*, 25 September 2019.

28 Ditto.

shipping terminals) to smoothen out demand and supply shocks through holding inventories and capture some short-term arbitrage opportunities. They rely extensively on banks to finance short-term arbitrage activities and generally finance each transaction at 100% of the value of collaterals and are marked to market periodically (e.g. weekly). They also provide different forms of financing to their customers, including traditional trade credit (as receivables on the trading firm's balance sheet) and structured transactions through an "off-take agreement" among the producer, the trading firm and the bank to get prepayment for contract sales. An analysis[29] showed the linkages of commodity prices with bank lending and the real economy — an unexpected increase of one percentage point in China's bank lending could result in price increases of 10%-12% for some base metals, including copper, and one percentage point change in industrial production could lead to price changes of 7%-9% of aluminium, copper and crude oil. Such commodity financing activities require reliable records and proper management of inventories at warehouses.

(4)   Financial investors

Financial investors include index traders and money managers (e.g. hedge funds) who treat commodity futures as an asset class. They may adopt active strategies (e.g. long-short strategy of futures) or passive strategies (e.g. through index futures or exchange-traded funds (ETFs) tracking commodity futures indices) in order to generate trading profits from arbitrage opportunities or speculation or for the diversification of equity portfolios[30]. A study showed that adding commodity futures indices or gold futures to an equity portfolio had increased both annualised returns and risk-adjusted returns (Sharpe ratio) during bull and bear markets in the period around the Global Financial Crisis in 2008 (see Figure 4). As financial investors focus more on the short-term returns, they may prefer highly standardised futures contracts with high liquidity or cash-settled contracts to avoid physical settlement.

---

29 Roache, S. and M. Rousset. (2015) "China: Credit, collateral and commodity prices", *Hong Kong Institute for Monetary and Financial Research (HKIMR) Working Paper*, No. 27/2015.
30 See Mayer, J. (2009) "The growing interdependence between financial and commodity markets", United Nations Conference on Trade and Development (UNCTAD)'s Discussion Paper, No.195.

Figure 4. Annualised returns and Sharpe ratios of portfolios with commodity futures versus equity portfolio

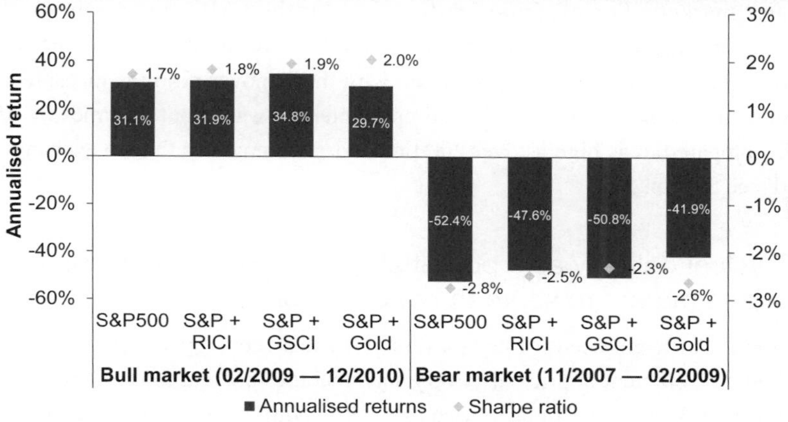

Note: GSCI refers to S&P Goldman Sachs Commodity Index tracking the performance of 24 commodity futures on the CME and RICI refers to Rogers International Commodity Index tracking the performance of 38 commodity futures on nine exchanges in four countries.

S&P 500 — S&P 500 Index

S&P + RICI — A portfolio comprising 85% of S&P 500 Index and 15% of RICI

S&P + GSCI — A portfolio comprising 85% of S&P 500 Index and 15% of GSCI

S&P + Gold — A portfolio comprising 85% of S&P 500 Index and 15% of the spot gold price in the US

Source: Batavia, B., N. Parameswar and C. Wague. (2012) "Portfolio diversification in extreme environments: Are there benefits from adding commodity futures indices?", *European Research Studies*, Vol. 15, pp.33-48.

Financial investors are an important source of liquidity in the global commodity futures market. They may apply strategies with different combinations of commodity futures, options or swaps. Empirical evidence in the US on 26 commodity futures during 2 January 1994 to 1 November 2014[31] showed that short-term position changes are mainly driven by financial investors (speculators) while long-term position changes are mainly driven by the hedging demand from hedgers[32]. In other words, financial investors trade more frequently than hedgers. It is suspected that speculative trading increases price volatility. However, a study[33] found that the long-short strategies of speculators in five agricultural commodity

---

31 Kang, W., K.G. Rouwenhorst, K. Tang. (2020) "A tale of two premiums: The role of hedgers and speculators in commodity futures markets", *Journal of Finance*, Vol. 75, pp.377-417.

32 Hedgers refer to commercial traders, including producers, processors, manufacturers or merchants handling the commodity or its products or byproducts while speculators refer to non-commercial traders. "Commercial traders", "non-commercial traders" are classified in the US Commodity Futures Trading Commission (CFTC)'s Commitment of Traders (COT) dataset.

33 Bohl, M.T. and C. Sulewski. (2019) "The impact of long-short speculators on the volatility of agricultural commodity futures prices", *Journal of Commodity Markets*, Vol. 16, pp.1-30.

futures in the US market during 2006 to 2017 reduced market volatilities instead.

Nevertheless, financial players are the minority participant group in the global commodity market. For example, participants on the LME are mostly producers, consumers and traders, which accounted for about 75% of the trading volume of global non-ferrous metals in 2016[34]. This explained why the turnover ratio (as measured by the ratio of annual trading volume to year-end open interest) was about 73 times in 2019 for the LME, compared to as high as over 200 times for a commodity futures exchange in the Mainland (see Section 3.2).

2.2 Physical delivery as a potential challenge of global commodity futures market to serve the real economy

To serve the different needs of key players in the real economy, the commodity futures market should be efficient in price discovery such that the spot and futures prices converge at the settlement date. If the futures price of a commodity deviates significantly from the spot price at settlement, it may be translated to (1) lower revenue for producers or higher cost for consumers compared to their unhedged positions, and (2) more uncertainties of investment returns for financial investors. The efficiency of physical delivery of commodities at settlement of futures contracts may be one key contributing factor to the spot and futures price convergence.

In the US, the prices of certain major agricultural futures (e.g. corn, soybean and wheat) were found to be persistently higher than the respective spot prices at settlement during 2005 to 2010 in a study[35]. The study examined the factors contributing such non-convergence between commodity spot and futures prices. Although many thought that the cause was the excessive speculative investments of financial investors (see Section 2.1), empirical evidence showed that the costs involved in physical delivery of commodities to settle futures played a key role. One of the key factors was the difference of storage costs between the spot and futures markets[36] — the storage cost rate for physically settled wheat futures on the CBOT was lower than the spot market price of storage by 4.5 US cents per unit per month in 2008, which was expanded by 2.6 US cents from 2004 to 2008. In this

---

34 Source: "Presentation by HKEX Co-head of Market Development Li Gang at a media workshop about the overview of the Mainland China's commodities market" (Media workshop: China's commodities market — The past and present), news release on HKEX's website, 7 June 2016.

35 Adjemian, M. K. et. al. (2013) "Non-convergence in domestic commodity futures markets: Causes, consequences, and remedies", the USDA ERS's *Economic Information Bulletin*, No.115.

36 At settlement of physically-settled commodity futures on the CME Group, warehouse receipts will be delivered to long position holders who can choose to store the commodities at exchange-approved warehouses and the exchange will collect the associated storage costs.

relation, the changes of production patterns and transportation logistics affect the costs of physical delivery of commodities to settle futures. For example, the production and marketing channels of Chicago's grain market had shifted away from the Great Lakes region which was the original delivery market when the CBOT was established in the mid-19th century and became less commercially important. However, the CBOT did not revise the delivery points for corn and soybeans until 2000 and for wheat until 2009. These contributed to the expensive costs to obtain commodities for arbitrage activities during the sample period, which affected the price discovery at the futures market.

The efficiency of the commodity futures market to serve the real economy relies on the infrastructure to facilitate physical delivery of commodities to settle commodity futures, particularly the network of warehouses. Although the CME has a wide range of products, the network of warehouses may not fit global commodity users' needs. For example, copper futures can be settled physically for delivery through US warehouses only for contracts on the CME, compared to 24 global locations in the US, Europe, the Middle East and Asia for contracts on the LME[37]. If the commodity users are closer to the network of warehouses, the transportation costs will be lower. This may facilitate the arbitrage activities for their inventories, which help price discovery of commodities.

3   Comparison of the Mainland commodities market with the world's

In serving the real economy, the Mainland commodity futures market is considered not effective enough to meet the needs of users[38]. With reference to the experience of global commodity futures markets, there are two main underlying reasons: first, the linkage between the Mainland commodity spot and futures markets has been relatively weak such

---

37 The information of the CME copper futures is as of 26 March 2020 (source: "Metal warehouse stocks statistics", published on the CME Group's website, viewed on 30 March 2020) and that of the LME copper futures is as of 30 March 2020 (source: Daily data on "Stocks breakdown" webpage on the LME's website).

38 See Hu, Y. and H. Zhang. (2017) "Assessment on China's commodity futures market serving real economy", *Futures and Financial Derivatives* (《期貨與金融衍生品》), Issue no. 98, pp.16-29.

that the futures price may not be able to serve as reference price for the spot price; second, the pricing in the Mainland commodity futures market could not exert sufficient influence on global commodity futures prices. Although China has become the largest producer and consumer of major commodities[39] (see Figure 5), Mainland commodity users (producers and consumers) are very often price takers of global commodity futures prices.

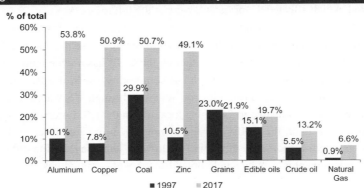

Figure 5. China's share of global commodity consumption (1997 and 2017)

Source: "The implications of tariff for commodity markets", *Commodity Markets Outlook*, published on the World
Bank's website, October 2018 issue.

The factors contributing to above weaknesses of the Mainland commodities market vis-à-vis global developed counterparts are discussed in the following sub-sections.

3.1 A fragmented commodity spot market

Large producers who dominate the different commodity sectors in the global economy[40] would actively hedge their positions on well-established global commodity futures markets. The commodity futures prices so generated through their transactions are typically used as benchmark prices for spot transactions.

However, such a pricing mechanism is weak in the Mainland. For example, the market share of the top four companies in the steel sector accounted for about 80% of

---

39 Source: "Charts show China's explosive consumption of four critical commodities", published on *cnbc.com*, 24
    September 2019.
40 Global spot trading of a number of commodities, including aluminium, cocoa and coffee, is dominated by a few large
    producers. Source: Cinquegrana, P. "The need for transparency in commodity and commodity derivatives markets",
    published on the website of the Centre for European Policy Studies (CEPS), 15 December 2018.

steel production in the US and Japan in 2017, compared to about 20% in the Mainland[41]. The Mainland spot commodities market has relied heavily on a large number of localised commodity trading firms to intermediate the trading of commodities, including agency trading and proprietary trading[42]. Traditionally, the spot price is set at the average processing costs in the production region plus a premium as profit margin. Further, the specification of the commodities can vary significantly across spot transactions such that there are a number of spot prices for the same type of commodities. These spot transactions may be conducted through electronic trading platforms operated by local governments, state-owned enterprises or market participants[43]. The key participants include securities companies, futures companies and their risk management subsidiaries, and private funds. These electronic trading platforms also offer OTC derivatives trading on commodities, which may not have sound risk management framework[44]. In the light of market irregularities, a policy document was issued by the State Council in 2011[45] to rectify the commodity spot market to facilitate the healthy development of the sector. The number of spot trading platforms, once rose to more than 3,000 in 2017, had been consolidated to about 30 platforms in 2019[46].

As a result of such spot trading practices, the price of a commodity in the Mainland spot market may vary across regions. These prices do not necessarily make reference to futures prices or converge to form a benchmark price and the prices discovered may not be timely to reflect current market fundamentals.

3.2 Relative dominance of speculative activities in the commodity futures market

There are currently three futures exchanges in Mainland China that offer trading in commodity futures — the Shanghai Futures Exchange (SHFE), the Zhengzhou Commodity

---

41 Source: "The production chain of steel sector and the transformation in major countries — Series on steel rebar (1)" (〈鋼鐵產業鏈及其背後的大國變遷——螺紋鋼系列（一）〉), CIB Research, 27 February 2019.

42 See "The research report on commodity trading sector in China 2017" (〈2017 年中國大宗商品貿易行業研究報告〉), published on the United Credit Ratings' website, 2017.

43 See "The analysis and legal risk mitigation on the trading modes of commodity spot trading platforms" (〈大宗商品現貨平台交易模式分析與法律風險防範〉), published on *zhihu.com,* 7 December 2017.

44 See examples given in "How do the huge losses from positions of PTA OTC options of many futures companies happen?" (〈讓多家期貨公司集體穿倉的 PTA 場外期權爆倉事件是怎麼發生的？〉), published on *yocajr.com,* 31 July 2019.

45 *State Council's Decisions about Rectifying Various Types of Trading Venues to Mitigate Financial Risks Prudently* (《國務院關於清理整頓各類交易場所切實防範金融風險的決定》), issued by the State Council, 24 November 2011.

46 Source: "Assessment on spot trading in 2019" (〈2019 年現貨貿易良心測評〉), published on *yaobang-metal.com,* 20 October 2019.

Exchange (ZCE) and the Dalian Commodity Exchange (DCE). The trading volume of commodity futures on these exchanges are among the largest in the world. In terms of number of contracts, at least one of the Mainland exchanges was among the top five exchanges with the highest derivatives (including futures and options) trading volume for each major category of commodity in 2019 (see Figure 6).

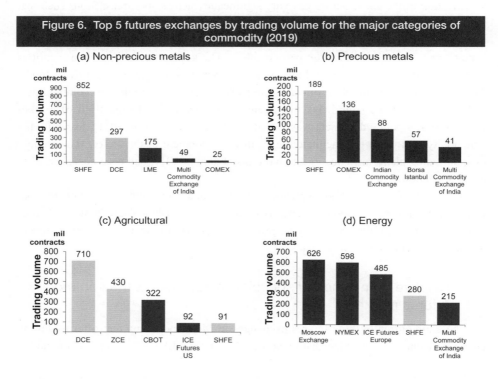

Figure 6. Top 5 futures exchanges by trading volume for the major categories of commodity (2019)

Note: There is a large variation in contract sizes across markets. For instance, the contract size varies from 10 metric tonnes (MT) to 100 MT for metal contracts, from 10MT to 127MT for agricultural contracts and from 10 barrels to 1,000 barrels for crude oil contracts.

Source: FIA monthly statistics (December 2019).

Behind such high turnover volumes on the Mainland commodity futures exchanges are high turnover ratios — the annual trading volume to year-end open interest. In 2019, the ratio was 249 times for the SHFE, 247 times for the ZCE and 140 times for the DCE, compared to 73 times for the LME and 46 times for the CME Group[47] (see Figure 7). This

---

47 Calculated from the year-to-month statistics in FIA monthly statistics (December 2019).

can be interpreted as ultra-short holding time for commodities in the Mainland, implying a high degree of speculative trading. It was estimated that the average holding period of a position of steel rebar on the SHFE or iron ore on the DCE was just 4 hours in 2016 (the turnover ratios in 2016 were about 440 times and 290 times for the respective commodity derivatives on the SHFE and the DCE[48]), compared to about 40 hours and about 70 hours for copper and natural gas respectively on the CME[49]. In this relation, the contract sizes of futures on the Mainland commodity exchanges are usually smaller — for example, the contract size of copper futures was 5 tonnes on the SHFE compared to 25 tonnes on the LME[50].

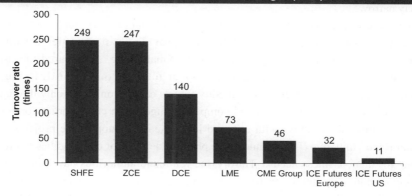

Figure 7. Ratio of annual trading volume to year-end open interest of commodity futures and options on selected exchanges (2019)

Note: The figure for SHFE includes products on the Shanghai International Energy Exchange (INE). The figure for CME Group covers products on CBOT, CME, COMEX and NYMEX.

Source: FIA monthly statistics (December 2019).

The speculative activities may be attributable to the high proportion of retail investor participation. A study[51] reported that the open interests held by individual investors' accounts was over 86% in 2016 in the Mainland, compared to less than 15% in the US. The same study suggested that individual investors are likely to have less information and more herding behaviour, which contribute to highly speculative behaviour.

48 Calculated from the year-to-month statistics in FIA monthly statistics (December 2016).

49 Source: "A life expectancy under 4 hours shows China commodity frenzy", *Bloomberg*, 26 April 2016.

50 See the contract specifications at the SHFE's and the LME's website, viewed on 16 December 2019.

51 Fan, J. H. and T. Zhang. (2020) "The untold story of commodity futures in China", *Journal of Futures Markets*, Vol. 40, pp.671-706.

The relative dominance of speculative activities and retail trading may increase price volatility of commodity futures and discourage hedging activities. Nevertheless, there are some signs of growing participation of hedgers in the Mainland futures market in recent years to counteract the dominance of retail speculative trading. Taking the DCE as an example, the share of institutional investors rose from 44% of total open interests as of end-October 2016 to 54% of total open interests as of end-July 2018[52].

3.3 Relatively narrow warehouse network

Compared to developed commodity futures market in the world which have established extensive global warehouse networks (see Sections 2.1 and 2.2 above), the warehouse network of the Mainland commodity futures exchanges for physical settlement are relatively narrow.

Firstly, the warehouse network for the Mainland market may not be nationwide. For example, copper futures on the SHFE only provide physical settlement through 17 warehouses in Shanghai, Jiangsu, Jiangxi and Guangdong[53], compared to a global network of warehouses in 24 locations of copper futures[54] on the LME in the UK. Secondly, the physical settlement of commodity futures can be conducted only through the warehouses in the Mainland. Mainland companies engaged in cross-border commodity exports and imports and those with outward investments to support the projects of the "Belt and Road" Initiative (BRI) cannot have physical delivery of commodities at offshore locations for their business needs. Thirdly, the Mainland authorities have not approved any foreign commodity futures exchanges to have warehouses in the Mainland to provide physical delivery of commodities for companies trading on their markets that have the business needs in the Mainland. An onshore hedger may trade commodity futures in the offshore markets through its subsidiary because of attractive prices, but the commodity futures can only be settled through an offshore warehouse and then imported to the Mainland. This will incur extra costs for storage and transportation (see Section 2.2) and taxes on cross-border trades (e.g. tariff and value-added tax for imports[55]).

Such narrow coverage of the warehouse network for Mainland commodity futures

---

52　Source: "The gradual change of investor composition in the futures market"(〈期貨市場投資者結構悄然變化〉), published on *jrj.com.cn*, 9 September 2018.

53　See the contract specification of copper futures, published on the SHFE's website, viewed on 30 January 2020.

54　"Warehouse company stocks and queue date January 2020", published on the LME's website, viewed on 20 February 2020.

55　See "Announcement No. 5 [2018] of the Customs Tariff Commission of the State Council" (《國務院關稅稅則委員會公告 2018 年第 5 號》), issued by the Ministry of Finance, 24 July 2018, market is costly and inadequate to meet business needs of hedgers in different locations and would disincentivise hedging through Mainland commodity futures.

3.4   Narrow product range and currency denomination

In the global commodity futures market, the underlying commodities cover the main categories of metals, energy, chemicals and agricultural products. As of January 2020, there were over 160 commodity derivatives on the CME and over 1,660 commodity derivatives on the Intercontinental Exchange (ICE), covering a wide range of asset types (see Table 1). The wide range of global commodity derivatives would fulfill the needs of different types of commodity users for different purposes, including hedging and portfolio investment. In comparison, the product range on the Mainland commodity futures exchanges is relatively narrow — just over 70 commodity derivatives, which are mostly futures (60 in number as of end-January 2020) and a few commodity options (11 in number as of end-January 2020) (see Table 1). These may not be able to serve the different industrial sectors in the Mainland.

Table 1. The number of commodity futures and options of selected exchanges by commodity category (2020)						
Commodity category	ICE	CME	Mainland exchanges			
			SHFE (incl. INE)	ZCE	DCE	All
Agriculture	46	46	—	16	13	29
Energy	1,546	80	3	—	2	5
Metals	15	40	14	2	2	18
Others	58	—	6	8	5	19
Total	1,665	166	23	26	22	71

Note: Data as of 22 January 2020.

Source: Websites of ICE, CME, SHFE, DCE and ZCE.

Commodity futures on the Mainland exchanges are priced in Renminbi (RMB) only. This can meet the needs of onshore hedgers for uses in Mainland China, but not for offshore uses (e.g. in BRI projects). It is reported that a large amount of BRI-related projects were funded in USD[56]. The lack of choices of foreign currency denomination may

---

56 See "Dollar constraints may lead to more multilateral approach for China's Belt and Road", published on *chathamhouse.org*, 23 October 2018.

drive Mainland hedgers to use global commodity futures markets. In respect of portfolio diversification, onshore financial investors have limited choice of currency denomination for commodity exposure.

3.5 Limited market opening for global interaction

While major commodity futures markets in the world are open to free access by international investors, foreign investors' access to the Mainland commodities market is still very restricted and the access to overseas commodity futures markets by Mainland users is highly regulated too:

- For foreign participation in the Mainland market, only designated commodity futures are opened directly to foreign investors. As of the end of February 2020, the designated futures products are crude oil and rubber on the Shanghai International Energy Exchange (INE, an SHFE's subsidiary), PTA on the ZCE and iron ore on the DCE. For other products, trading is limited to onshore participants only, which may include certain Sino-foreign joint ventures.

- For overseas market participation by Mainland users, only a limited number of state-owned enterprises (SOEs) got official approval to participate in cross-border hedging in the global commodity futures markets[57]. Alternatively, onshore commodity users can hedge in the global market through their offshore subsidiaries. However, the imports of commodities settled as a result of offshore hedging are subject to taxes and the money flows of offshore cash-settled commodity futures are restricted.

As a result, global and Mainland hedgers and financial investors are not free to participate in each other's market such that the global and Mainland commodity futures markets remain separate from each other without adequate price interactions.

An imbalance of investor participation can be illustrated by the big difference in the open interests of agricultural futures in the US and Mainland markets, given that agricultural futures in the Mainland market are currently not open to foreign participation. Despite the growing global significance of the Mainland economy, the agricultural commodity open positions through futures in the US market was significantly higher than those in the Mainland market (see Table 2). Figure 8 shows an example of the non-convergence of futures prices on the Mainland and US commodities markets in the case of soybean — the

---

57 Thirty-one SOEs were approved in 2016 for cross-border hedging activities. Source: "Guantao insights: SASAC cancelled the approval of offshore commodity derivative business of central SOEs"(〈觀韜解讀：國資委取消央企境外商品衍生業務核准事項〉), published on *guantao.com*, 30 August 2016.

soybean futures prices in the US persistently stayed below those in the Mainland during 2008 to 2019.

Table 2. Agricultural commodity open positions through futures in the US and Mainland China (2018)			
Type of commodity	US (mil tonnes) (A)	China (mil tonnes) (B)	Ratio of (A)/(B) (times)
Wheat	114.78	0.02	5,001
Soybean meal	41.26	18.42	2
Corn	252.98	9.08	28
Soybean	116.40	1.63	71
Soybean oil	13.34	4.91	3
Grain	0.73	0.00	—
Cotton	6.17	1.05	6
Sugar	46.13	3.37	14
Total	591.80	38.69	15

Note: Data as of 13 March 2018. The summation of individual figures of open positions may not equal the total due to rounding.

Source: Xie, X. (2018) "The formation and recommendation of commodity pricing centre from historical perspective" (〈從歷史看大宗商品定價中心的形成及建議〉), *China Futures* (《中國期貨》), Vol. 65 (2018 Issue no.5), pp.51-56.

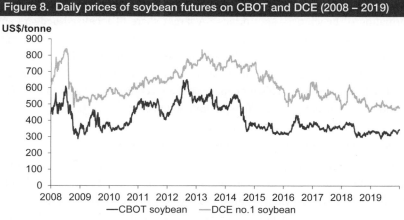

Figure 8. Daily prices of soybean futures on CBOT and DCE (2008 – 2019)

Note: The price of no.1 soybean futures on the DCE is converted into US dollars based on Bloomberg's USD/RMB daily exchange rate.

Source: Bloomberg.

4 How can the Mainland commodity futures market better serve the real economy?

For the Mainland commodity futures market to better serve the real economy in the same way as the global commodity futures market, firstly the linkage between the Mainland commodity spot and futures markets should be strengthened. This could facilitate the price discovery of commodities in the futures market such that the futures prices can in turn be the benchmark prices of spot transactions and commodity futures could effectively support hedging activities. Secondly, given China's dominance of global consumption and production of commodities, global interaction of the Mainland commodity futures market should be promoted such that China's pricing power in global commodities could be enhanced, which would enable Mainland commodity producers and consumers to play a part in global commodity price setting, rather than price-taking only. Possible ways to achieve these two objectives include the following:

(1) Consolidating trading and enhancing trade transparency in the spot market

The consolidation of spot trading platforms, possibly driven by policy, could enable the formation of benchmark spot prices. A larger share of localised hedgers and other market users may conduct customised transactions of commodities on these platforms. In this relation, trade transparency should be enhanced to let market users observe the price dynamics in the commodity spot market, including the price difference from the centralised commodity futures market. This may increase the incentive of hedgers to use commodity futures prices as benchmark prices for spot transactions.

(2) Enhancing regulation to combat excessive speculation

Excessive speculation leads to excessive price volatility such that the futures prices would deviate from the underlying fundamentals and the deviation would erode the effectiveness of futures as hedging tools. To curb excessive speculation, the experience of the US in implementing regulatory measures[58] suggested the possible way of banning high-

---

58 Berg, A. (2011) "Chapter 10. The rise of commodity speculation: from villainous to venerable", *Safeguarding Food Security in Volatile Global Markets,* Food and Agriculture Organisation of the United Nations (FAO).

frequency trading in the futures market. In a volatile market, limiting the order size and timely adjustments to lower position limit and/or to increase margin requirements could help combat excessive speculation.

(3)   Expanding and strengthening the network of warehouses for physical delivery

The geographical distribution of warehouse network of commodity futures exchanges could be expanded in the Mainland in order to minimise the time and transportation cost for the delivery of commodities for onshore usage. To meet the business needs, inventories at warehouses should be managed more efficiently and effectively (e.g. through efficient load-in and load-out processes) to make the logistics schedule more predictable. To support hedging for cross-border trades, the authorities could approve more warehouses in "bonded zones" for physical delivery of commodities to settle Mainland and global commodity futures, to take the advantage of tax-free cross-border delivery[59].

(4)   Widening the product range and currency denomination

To better serve the various needs of hedgers and financial investors in different sectors, the commodity futures market should have a wider range of derivative products, in terms of product type (e.g. options or swaps), underlying commodities (e.g. with more variation in specifications) and currency denomination.

(5)   Further opening up the Mainland commodity futures market

Authorities may consider widening the two-way market access for more global interaction. Greater foreign participation in the Mainland market would help Mainland commodity futures prices incorporate the views of global users. Possible ways include designating more product types for direct access by foreign users, the cross-listing of Mainland products on offshore markets, expanding the scope of eligible investors to include Qualified Foreign Institutional Investors (QFIIs), RMB QFIIs (RQFIIs)[60] and other foreign users. Similarly, greater overseas participation by Mainland users can increase pricing influence of Mainland users in the global market. Possible ways include enlarging the

---

59 See "What's the bonded zone?", published on *ftz-shanghai.com*, viewed on 17 December 2019.
60 Proposed rules amendment for opening up the access to Mainland commodity futures and options by QFIIs and RQFIIs was issued in January 2019. See *Explanation about the Administrative Measures for Domestic Securities Futures Investment of QFIIs and RQFIIs (Draft for Consultation) and Related Rules* (《關於〈合格境外機構投資者及人民幣合格境外機構投資者境內證券期貨投資管理辦法（徵求意見稿）〉及其配套規則的說明》), issued by the China Securities Regulatory Commission, 31 January 2019.

scope of eligible Mainland users for cross-border hedging in offshore markets and the cross-listing of offshore products on the Mainland market. In addition to these, a commodities connectivity platform similar to Stock Connect and Bond Connect would be an efficient and convenient channel for opening up the two-way market access.

In respect of product varieties and market opening discussed above, the Mainland commodities market can leverage on the comparative advantage of the Hong Kong market. Complementary to Mainland commodity futures market, the Hong Kong market offers users with easy access to LME metal products in the Asian time zone. Hong Kong market could also help to gather commodity users and investors by serving as a financing centre for BRI projects of both Mainland and global enterprises. In fact, a number of Mainland and global commodity trading firms have already established offices in Hong Kong. The Mainland-Hong Kong Mutual Market Access programme may also be extended to the commodities sector to facilitate greater foreign participation in the Mainland market and vice versa. All these would facilitate the formation of an ecosystem of Mainland and global commodity users in the Hong Kong market to support the development of the commodity futures market and the further opening-up of the Mainland market.

5   Conclusion

Drawing on experiences of the evolution of global commodity futures exchanges, the strong linkage between commodity spot and futures markets is fundamental in that commodity futures need to provide benchmark prices for commodities in the spot market such that they can be efficiently used to meet the hedging needs of producers, consumers and intermediaries in the real economy. Through the global network of warehouses, the commodity futures market helps reduce uncertainties on timing and provide a cost-effective alternative, in complement to the spot market, for physical delivery of the underlying commodities for commercial uses.

The Mainland commodity futures market have not been able to serve the real economy effectively in this way. In the Mainland, the price setting in the fragmented spot market, which may not come up with a standard price for a commodity, does not very often make reference to commodity futures prices. The reference value of commodity futures prices to spot prices in the Mainland may be undermined by the excessive price volatility from speculative trading activities, extra transportation costs for physical delivery through a relatively narrow warehouse network and the limited choices of product and currency denomination. These may also disincentivise hedging activities through commodity futures in the Mainland. Besides, limited market opening has led to the difference in futures prices between Mainland and global commodity markets. The Hong Kong market, being an international financial market at the front-door of China, could take the role as a super-connector in the commodities sector to further increase the global interaction of the Mainland commodity futures market, thereby help strengthening up the Mainland commodity futures market to better serve the real economy.

Remark: This chapter has made reference to views and feedback on commodities market developments sought from futures companies in the Mainland and Hong Kong markets.

Chapter 11

QME's unique role in the commodities market in Mainland China

Qianhai Mercantile Exchange Co., Ltd.

Summary

Currently, the international commodities markets show a marked trend of globalisation. In Mainland China, many of the commodity raw materials and industrial products that are closely linked to industries in the real economy involve significant volumes of imports and exports. This has given rise to an urgent need for a truly market-oriented and internationalised commodity trading platform. Qianhai Mercantile Exchange (QME) strives to establish a regulated and transparent nation-wide spot trading platform for commodities in a systematic and organised manner, so as to facilitate the orderly development of the spot market. QME will also innovate and explore new business models to solve the financing problems faced by commodity enterprises, and attempt to progressively set up a Renminbi (RMB) pricing centre for global commodities in phases through connecting Mainland China with the world.

1 Background of establishing QME

China's status as the world's leading trader and consumer of commodities is not matched by a proportionate pricing power and influence in the global market. One of the important reasons is that the development of the commodities market in Mainland China has inclined towards commodity futures and other derivatives which have a speculative nature, neglecting the spot commodities market which truly serves the real economy, resulting in the latter's severe underdevelopment and apparent shortcomings. Lacking an exchange which is supposed to perform the major functions of spot trading, delivery, physical settlement, supply-chain finance and other market functions closely related to the real economy, the Mainland is unable to capitalise on its industry demand and large consumption such that the pricing power for major commodities currently rests mainly in established western exchanges such as those in London, New York and Chicago. Furthermore, without a reliable nation-wide spot commodity exchange, infrastructure services that meet financial risk control requirements and industry standards and specifications are not available. The lack of such services coupled with the high financing and logistics costs in the manufacturing industry and spot market results in a large number of enterprises, especially small and medium-sized enterprises (SMEs) and traders, facing the problem of not being able to obtain effective financial support. In light of these issues, there is an urgent need to speed up the construction of a regularised and transparent national commodity spot trading market in Mainland China, whether for the purpose of competing for pricing power or serving the enterprises, to provide participants in the upstream, mid-stream and downstream of the industry chain and institutional participants with benchmark prices that reflect the fundamental supply and demand of physical goods. Henceforth, a complete, multi-level and mature modern commodities market system can be formed jointly with the futures market and other derivatives markets.

Currently, the international commodities markets show a marked trend of globalisation. In Mainland China, many of the commodity raw materials and industrial products that are closely linked to industries in the real economy involve significant volumes of imports and exports. This has given rise to an urgent need for a truly market-oriented and internationalised commodity trading platform in Mainland China. After its acquisition of the London Metal Exchange (LME) in 2012, Hong Kong Exchanges and Clearing Limited (HKEX) started in April 2016 the preparation work for the project of setting up Qianhai Mercantile Exchange (QME) in Qianhai Cooperation Zone in Shenzhen. This initiative was taken as an integral part of the HKEX Group's global commodities market plan and in response to the actual needs of the Mainland market and real industries for a nation-wide spot commodities platform. On 11 October 2016, the Office of the Shenzhen Municipal People's Government for Financial Development Services issued the "Letter on Approval of the Establishment of QME in Shenzhen" to the project initiator and the major shareholder, HKEX Group (with HKEX Investment (China) Limited being the investor), and Shenzhen Qianhai Financial Holdings Company Limited ("Qianhai Financial Holdings") which provided funds on behalf of the Shenzhen Municipal Government, stating its agreement to the establishment of QME jointly by these two companies.

After more than four years of exploration and planning, QME has confirmed its development plan of starting from spot commodities and proceeding onto serving the real economy. Setting a foothold in the Qianhai Economic Zone which is designated as the first to run pilot programmes, QME will be engaged in innovations and explorations of its business to remedy the shortcomings of the Mainland spot commodities market, so as to provide enterprises in the real industry chain with modern supply-chain infrastructure and public services across the border such as commodity storage, delivery and settlement services. Leveraging on cutting-edge technologies such as Internet of Things (IoT), intelligent recognition and blockchain, it is hoped that a standardised asset system connecting the financial system and the real entities can be built. In collaboration with LME, a subsidiary of the HKEX Group that has been a crucial USD pricing centre in the global commodities market, QME would develop itself in phases into an important RMB pricing centre in the global commodities market, thereby supporting the implementation of the national strategies of RMB internationalisation and developing China into a major manufacturing power.

2 Positioning and goals of QME

2.1 Restructuring the Mainland commodities market and establishing a spot price benchmark

Since the development of the spot market lags far behind the futures market, currently most of the spot prices of commodities in the Mainland that are related to real industry chains are inevitably needed to be set with reference to the futures prices. However, the price generation mechanism in the futures market is different from that in the spot market since the Mainland commodity futures market is often dominated by speculative funds, with a lot of retail investors jumping on the bandwagon, resulting in price fluctuations that deviate from the fundamentals of the market and fail to truly reflect the market equilibrium in the real economy. They also fail to meet the demands of enterprises in the upstream, mid-stream and downstream of the industry chain for spot commodity pricing in the actual production and operation processes. For this reason, there is an urgent need for a mechanism to generate benchmark prices founded on real spot trading activities. Through price discovery in the spot market, the supply and demand of entities in the upstream and downstream can be effectively modulated, and at the same time the derivatives markets such as commodity futures and options can be provided with an anchor price based on the fundamentals of the real economy. Following this logic and the regular path of commodities market development, QME, as a spot commodity exchange serving enterprises in the real economy and institutional customers, will start from serving the industries by setting benchmark spot prices based on real economic and actual trade activities, so as to offer effective support to enterprises in the industry chain by meeting their needs for open and transparent trading prices. This will provide more efficient and market-oriented management and modulating tools for the supply-side reform of specific industries (such as non-ferrous metals, iron and steel, coal, etc.) in the Mainland.

2.2   Creating a standardised asset system to solve the financing difficulties faced by enterprises

The Mainland market has long been facing the issue of a disconnection between the financial sector and enterprises in the real economy. On the one hand, a large number of enterprises, especially SMEs, face difficulties and high costs in obtaining financing. On the other hand, banks and other financial institutions cannot find good-quality and safe targets for their investments, resulting in a substantial shortage of investment assets. The Mainland's real industry base guarantees a large circulation volume of underlying spot assets in the market, which is supposed to be a favorable condition for the development of trade finance and supply-chain finance based on movable assets and cargo rights. However, such an advantage has not been leveraged on. One of the main reasons is the lack of spot price benchmarks for commodities, which prevents banks and financial institutions from effectively assessing the value of assets in the process of conducting trade finance and supply-chain finance businesses. Another reason is the lack of protection for spot commodity assets in terms of their authenticity, security and liquidity. As most of the underlying assets are traded over the counter (OTC) and exist in non-standardised forms, they fail to meet the risk control requirements of banks and financial institutions in relation to their circulation including trading, storage and settlement. This situation from time to time gives rise to incidents like the "Qingdao Port" incident [1] and "steel trade crisis"[2].

In addition to supporting the formation of spot price benchmarks for commodities based on actual transactions, QME will also strive to create an innovative warehousing technology system, applying the latest technologies such as IoT, intelligent recognition, and blockchain to various aspects of physical transactions such as trading, settlement, storage and logistics. Through technology empowerment and system integration, the entire life cycle of spot commodities will become transparent and traceable, and the essential platform functions will be better utilised, so that the infrastructure and public services that are urgently needed for building a standardised asset system can be provided to the industry in a truly market-oriented way. The important advantage of a spot exchange in the market is that it can serve as an impartial party, acceptable to all stakeholders, to help build technology-empowered systems in collaboration with factories and leading producers, processors, traders, and end-consumer enterprises as well as warehouses, logistic companies, insurance companies, banks and financial institutions. By creating a highly credible asset system that meets unified management standards and technical standards and that has "blockchain warehouse warrants" as the carrier, spot commodities traditionally traded in the market can be turned into good-quality, safe and liquid short-term assets that can directly penetrate to the bottom layer. This will open up important channels for banks and financial institutions to provide funding support under reliable risk-controlled conditions to enterprises, especially SMEs and traders who have difficulties in obtaining financing in the traditional credit system. This will enable enterprises to focus on technology research and development as well as product upgrades, and thereby enhancing the overall competitiveness of the manufacturing industry in Mainland China. On the other hand, enterprises will be able to take advantage of the warehouse warrant system developed and endorsed by a credible spot exchange to significantly increase their production turnover and capital utilisation efficiency, and to ensure a continuous supply to banks and financial institutions of the underlying assets that can be securitised based on real economic and actual trade activities. This is especially vital

---

1   In early June 2014, a large-scale commodity financing fraud case that took place in Qingdao Port was unveiled. The company, Dezheng Resources, was investigated for pledging the same batch of metals as collateral for multiple bank loans. The case involved many banks. Source: "Qingdao Port Financing Fraud" (〈青島港融資詐騙案〉), Baidu Encyclopedia (https://baike.baidu.com), viewed on 9 February 2020.

2   Since 2012 when the capital chain of the steel trading industry in East China suddenly broke apart, large-scale credit defaults and trade defaults have occurred among steel trading companies. Many steel trading companies went bankrupt due to poor management while many others were sued, dealing a heavy blow to the entire steel trade industry. This incident is called the "steel trade crisis" by the industry. Source: "Supreme Judge: Looking at the loopholes in collateral management from the steel trade crisis" (〈最高法官：從鋼貿危機看擔保品管理的漏洞〉), published on Caixin's website (http://opinion.caixin.com/2015-06-15/100819271.html), 15 June 2015.

in the context of the current financial deleveraging campaign and the newly promulgated asset management rules.

2.3   Establishing a RMB pricing centre for global commodities by connecting Mainland China with the world

As far as commodities are concerned, the biggest strength of the Mainland market is the volume of spot trading and consumption generated by the physical industry base, rather than the over-speculative commodity futures market with a short development history. Therefore, in order to maximise the Mainland's influence on pricing in the global commodities market, the best strategy will be to emphasise the strengths and evade the weaknesses. This means that the Mainland shall truly manifest its power and influence on pricing in the global commodities market and on strategic resources through exporting its benchmark spot prices, which are formed on an internationally-recognised spot exchange and essentially based on real transactions conducted by Mainland enterprises in the upstream and downstream of the industry chain. Through such power and influence on pricing, Mainland enterprises can gain bargaining advantages and tangible benefits in the process of obtaining upstream spot raw materials in key sectors from overseas.

As the sole legal-entity exchange of the HKEX Group operating in Mainland China and a spot trading platform for commodities, QME is well qualified and uniquely positioned to connect the Mainland and overseas commodities markets. It can leverage on the well-established institutional systems, rules and successful operational experience of LME under the Group, take advantage of Hong Kong's unique status as an international financial centre and draw on the technological innovation capabilities of the Guangdong-Hong Kong-Macao Greater Bay Area ("Greater Bay Area"), especially Shenzhen. In this way, it can better serve the physical industry hinterland in Mainland China while connecting the resource markets along the "Belt and Road", so that an RMB pricing centre for global commodities can gradually be set up in phases to magnify the integrated effect of QME and LME. (See Figure 1.)

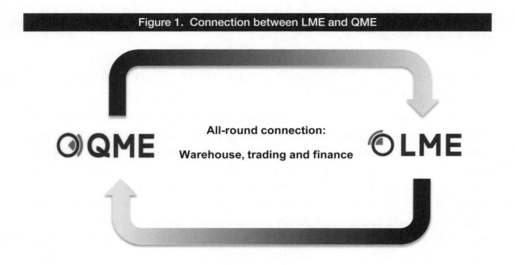

Figure 1. Connection between LME and QME

(1) Connection of warehouses

This serves to create a warehouse warrant system mutually recognised by LME and QME based on the QME warehouse warrant system, and through which to engage in interactions with LME in matters concerning warehousing, brand certification and warehouse management systems, etc. This will solve the long-standing difficulty resulting from the failure of having LME-authorised warehouses in the Mainland to effectively meet enterprises' needs.

(2) Connection of trading

This serves to facilitate customers' cross-market trading and delivery based on the warehouse warrants mutual-recognition system, so as to reduce the hedging costs and market hedging risks of Mainland enterprises, and enhance the status of the RMB as an international settlement currency.

(3) Financial connection

Leveraged on the advantages of the exchange trading platform, two-way capital flows can be opened up on the pre-conditions of a closed-loop and quota system. Limited opening of China's capital account will be explored, so as to facilitate the provision of comprehensive financial support by financial institutions in the entire process of cross-border trade.

Based on cross-border factor market trade and by fully relying on the comprehensive financial licensing system and industrial and institutional customer resources possessed by the HKEX Group in overseas markets, QME will create a new highland for the opening-up of the Mainland market. It will strive to provide the world with benchmark prices for spot commodities denominated and settled in RMB, where the prices are formed in the Mainland based on the demand and supply of Mainland enterprises and real transactions. It will work towards making these benchmark prices become the actual benchmark settlement prices for commodities traded on developed derivatives markets such as those in Hong Kong and London. Through the transmission of spot market prices, the pace of gaining RMB pricing power for commodities in global markets could be effectively accelerated.

3   Business development of QME

3.1   Trading business

3.1.1   Spot listing

QME commenced business on 19 October 2018 with spot commodity listing and trading. Under the spot trading mode, participants publish supply and demand information, including the type, specification, quality, quantity and price of the products to be traded, in accordance with the relevant business rules of QME and enter into transactions with participants who accept their listed information and conditions. Once the transaction is concluded, a delivery contract will be generated, followed by the delivery process. The spot commodity listings are divided into sale listings and purchase listings according to the trading direction, and into warehouse warrant listings and margin deposit listings according to the form of performance deposit. Margin deposit listings are further divided into two types — fixed-deposit listings and floating-deposit listings.

Trading by spot listing is a complete spot transaction process which is characterised by the participants' publication of sales or purchase information and selection of counterparties for transactions according to their own wishes. It is a process not involving any centralised matching. Secondly, each transaction involves physical delivery and the issuance of an invoice, the absence of either one will constitute a default in delivery. Lastly, only corporate entities on the real economy are allowed to participate in the spot trading of listed products and natural persons are excluded.

3.1.2 Warehouse warrants and commodities traded

Trading by spot listing covers commodities with standard warehouse warrants and those without.

A standard warehouse warrant is a warehouse warrant issued by a designated delivery institution in accordance with the procedures prescribed by QME, involving goods of a quality that conforms to the QME regulations. Standard warehouse warrants exist in the warehouse warrant management system in electronic form but not paper form. The electronic warehouse warrant issued by the designated delivery institution through the QME warehouse warrant management system is the only legal proof of the right to take delivery of the goods stated thereon. Standard warehouse warrants are divided into warehouse standard warrants and producer standard warrants, the former referring to the delivery certificates issued in accordance with QME's requirements and procedures by the designated delivery warehouses and the latter, by the designated producer warehouses.

Products without warehouse warrants refer to products that do not possess standard warehouse warrants as mentioned above nor the electronic warehouse warrants issued by the designated delivery institutions of QME.

3.1.3 Settlement and delivery

Settlement refers to the transfer of payment and the relevant bills after the conclusion of a transaction agreement between participants. Settlement can be done online or offline. In the case of online settlement, payment and receipt of the settlement amount shall be done through transfer of funds in the participants' settlement accounts. The purchaser shall ensure that there are sufficient funds in its corresponding settlement account at the time of settlement, failing to do so will constitute a default of delivery which will be dealt with according to the relevant rules. In the case of offline settlement, the participants will handle the transfer of settlement payments through their respective bank accounts using various settlement tools, and complete the offline transfer of legitimate invoices according to the contract terms. For offline settlement, the purchaser needs to upload a picture of the payment receipt, and the seller needs to upload a picture of the legitimate invoice that complies with the contract terms, onto the QME system within the time specified by QME. QME reserves the right to inquire with relevant institutions about such settlement.

Commodity delivery can be done online or offline. Under online delivery mode, both parties to a transaction complete the transfer of the rights to the goods at a specified time or within a specified period by the transfer of standard warehouse warrants through the QME system. Under offline delivery mode, both parties to the transaction arrange for the delivery of commodities without warehouse warrants to complete the transfer of the rights to the goods at a specified time or within a specified period.

After a spot trading transaction is concluded, the purchaser and the seller will enter the stage of settlement and delivery. Both parties shall discharge their settlement and delivery obligations within a prescribed period, including submitting warehouse warrants or arranging delivery, making payments, delivering and inspecting warehouse warrants or commodities, issuing or checking invoices, etc.; otherwise it will constitute a default of delivery.

3.2   Warehouse technology

3.2.1   Arrangement of certified warehouses

QME strives to make an overall arrangement of certified warehouses nationwide. With the actual needs of the industry in mind, QME provides qualitied services to the industry through standardised certified warehouses and works on enhancing the logistics efficiency of the warehouses. As of December 2019, the number of QME certified warehouses nationwide has reached 13, covering a variety of industry chains, including alumina, aluminium billets, aluminium ingots, copper rods and copper cathode, providing industrial customers with comprehensive warehouse and trading services.

3.2.2   Digital upgrade in warehouses

Warehousing institutions are carriers of commodity storage rights. So, in order to provide a guarantee on the authenticity and exclusivity of the storage right of the goods, IoT sensor device can be deployed in warehouses. The IoT sensor device shall be managed by the unified management platform on cloud, so as to ensure that its identification information is reliable, its testing data is normal and the collected data is not tampered with. These devices can then form a trusted sensor network. With such a trustworthy IoT solution, commodities can be continuously monitored with the use of technology so as to reduce uncertainties caused by manual supervision and to boost confidence in the credit status of the warehouses.

With the use of a secure industry gateway connecting the sensors of the storage institutions with the cloud IoT management platform, the confidentiality and reliability of the data link can be ensured. The underlying encryption mechanism will also ensure the security of the sensor data transmitted on the Internet, effectively lowering the cost and entry threshold of the deployment of sensors by the storage institutions while guaranteeing the stable operation of the system.

The IoT management platform uses an assembled device registration method whereby the fingerprint information will be recorded when the device is registered for the first time and at every subsequent operation including stoppage of supervision, replacement, upgrade, etc. to ensure secure access of the device. At the same time, the IoT platform provides a well-established user management and access authorization management system and arranges different sensors for different batches of commodities. It only allows stakeholders to access the relevant sensor data and provides a more complete data analysis algorithm to ensure the effectiveness and credibility of the sensors in continuously monitoring the commodities.

To cater for internal management needs, the management platform will store historical sensor data or forward real-time videos at the request of the stakeholders. The IoT platform guarantees the performance and capacity of the system and allows many devices to be shared on the network at a lower cost. The management platform, on the other hand, enables customers to customise the sensor alarm thresholds and risk control standards. With the use of machines to implement monitoring rules, human intervention is minimised, thereby reducing the risks incurred by manual operation and enhancing the credibility of the storage ecology.

3.2.3   Warehouse warrants 2.0 open ecosystem

QME promotes the creation of an open ecosystem of warehouse warrants 2.0, under which the warehousing and logistics systems can firstly be upgraded with the aid of technology, and secondly be connected with the banking and insurance systems to provide the basis for a closed-loop business model. With the help of blockchain technology, this ecosystem can solve two problems. The first problem concerns the recognition of QME's own data. The second relates to the validity of IoT device information and its own security. At the same time, the construction of a common platform will allow cross-validation of multi-party data.

The main purpose of the setup of the intelligent IoT for warehouses is to enhance information accuracy and the assurance of the authenticity and security of goods, so that by way of technology empowerment, the need for recognising the credibility of individual warehouses can be gradually reduced. The setup of the blockchain warehouse warrant platform could promote the transparency of the information concerning the generation and transfer of assets that go with warehouse warrants as well as the circulation of the production factors, thereby reducing the barriers and costs arising in the factors' circulation. On top of the above technology empowerment measures, QME has also undertaken insurance on warehouse warrants to offer further protection in respect of information accuracy and the authenticity and security of goods. These efforts are helpful for participants with higher risk requirements, such as financial institutions, in containing tail risk.

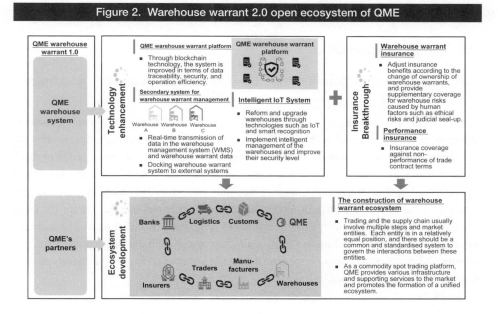

Figure 2. Warehouse warrant 2.0 open ecosystem of QME

IoT and blockchain technologies provide a solid foundation for the construction of the platform and offer technical support for hundreds of thousands of real enterprise nodes and trading enterprise nodes. The IoT platform needs to be open and able to work with and be compatible with various sensor networks, so as to generate structured data output results. It also needs to make available the efficient provision of sensor data such as videos as well as a storage system with a large capacity. The blockchain platform, on the other hand, supports large-capacity node coverage with a view to ensure the security and privacy protection of digital assets.

The warehouse warrant 2.0 open ecosystem will reform the traditional way of factors circulation and accelerate the development of a digital platform economy. On the one hand, it promotes the connection between industry and financial institutions while facilitating the use of financial capital in serving the real economy and reducing the overall financing costs of the entire industry chain. On the other hand, it promotes resources allocation in the industry chain that relies on the competition in respect of production capacity and the pricing mechanism, and fosters the establishment of a real-time production resources allocation model while redistributing the revenue from the industry chain based on the platform ecology. The ultimate goal is to lay the foundation for the operation of sizable platform economics for China's manufacturing industry, thereby to foster the high-quality development of the industry.

3.3   Financing services

3.3.1   Financing difficulties faced by customers in the commodities industry

The difficulty for the real economy, represented by SMEs and micro enterprises, in obtaining financing coupled with high financing costs is a major problem that hinders the macroeconomic development of Mainland China. This is also a long-term problem faced by the commodities industry which is the basis of the real economy. Due to the regulatory restriction of separate business operation, Mainland commercial banks can only be engaged in the business of a single physical commodity type — precious metals. As for the other types of commodity, Mainland commercial banks have not yet started providing financial services and proprietary trading in a large scale. Compared with overseas counterparts, the breadth and depth of Mainland commercial banks' participation in the commodity market needs to be further developed.

In the face of practical issues such as insufficient credit of the commodity entities, non-standardised underlying assets, lack of infrastructural facilities and complicated operations, mainstream financial institutions represented by banks have never really appeared at the scene of the commodities industry. As a result, the commodities market with a scale of tens of trillions of RMB is unable to obtain sufficient financing services from conventional financial institutions, and suffers from the persistently high financing costs.

3.3.2   Solutions provided by QME

The commodities industry needs to transform its mindset to get rid of the concept of "user community" and to focus on the commodities themselves rather than on the parties involved. In this way, a large number of high-quality and secure underlying assets generated from real economic activities and with an actual trade background can be pledged to obtain financing, ultimately providing effective liquidity support for SMEs. To this end,

QME could provide the following modes of financing and the related platform:

(1)   Producer warrant financing

Producer warrants contain credit elements and are delivery certificates issued by designated delivery warehouses. QME and banks cooperating with it have docked the various functional sections of the trading system with the banking system and realised simultaneous exchange of information. This enables the use of QME's electronic warehouse warrants as the trusted target assets to perform various functions such as online application for financing, online pledging, online drawdown of loan and online management. The first producer warrant financing business was launched in September 2019.

(2)   Warehouse warrant financing

As opposed to traditional bank financing business which usually imposes qualification requirements on the borrower, warehouse warrant financing is more concerned about the underlying asset of the transaction, i.e. QME's standard warehouse warrants. With warehouse warrant financing, the threshold for access to financing is substantially lowered through various means to manage different types of risk including market risk, operational risk and liquidity risk. The first warehouse warrant financing business was launched in January 2020.

(3)   Supply-chain financing

This is a way of providing a series of online financing services to clients through supply-chain enterprises based on the procurement intentions of clients and corporate sellers. Financial institutions and supply-chain enterprises jointly form a closed loop for risk control, and use warehouse warrant assets to contain risks.

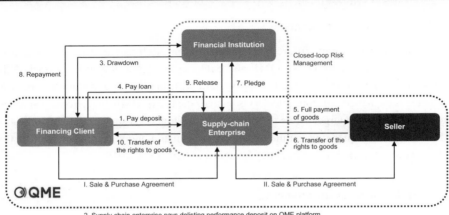

Figure 3. Schematic view of the supply-chain financing model

(4) Construction of financial infrastructures capable of mass production of standardised assets

With the original intention of "setting a foothold in spot market while serving the real economy", QME has always been dedicated to the construction of financial infrastructures. In the capacity of an exchange and by employing technologies such as IoT, QME managed to convert the initially non-standardised OTC goods into standardised electronic warehouse warrant assets, laying the groundwork for financial institutions' supply-chain financing business based on the logic of "controlling goods" while providing a core foundation for risk control.

In the next step, QME will continue to cooperate with industry participants such as technology companies, banks, insurance companies, real-economy entities, and warehousing institutions, to further develop a standardised commodity digital asset ecosystem with the aid of technologies like blockchain, intelligent recognition and IoT, and dismantle the last barrier for the interconnection of "capital and assets".

3.4 Connecting Mainland China with the world — Commodity Connect

On 26 November 2019, Alibaba returned to Hong Kong for listing. To this end, HKEX has made groundbreaking reforms of its listing regime. These include allowing the listing of companies with a weighted voting rights structure and permitting Chinese companies that have already listed overseas to choose Hong Kong as the place for secondary listing. With the focuses of "China Anchored and Globally Connected", HKEX is committed to becoming a global exchange for Mainland Chinese customers to explore the global market and international customers to access the Chinese market, thereby supporting the strategy of internationalisation of the Mainland market.

Stock Connect has been running smoothly for over five years. In order to further connect "Chinese goods" with "global capital" and to leverage on China's advantageous position as the world's factory and a supply-chain production centre, HKEX has also sought to achieve mutual market access in the area of commodities which is one of the three core pillars (equity securities, fixed-income and currency products, and commodities) of its multi-asset strategy. This gives rise to the "BBC" development strategy, namely "Buy one" (i.e. acquiring LME), "Build one" (i.e. building QME), and "Connect" (i.e. connecting China with the world).

Thanks to the policy support offered by the *Outline Development Plan for the Guangdong-Hong Kong-Macao Greater Bay Area,* QME is expected to be able to explore the development of a Commodity Connect, and become a commodity spot trading platform serving domestic and overseas customers.

3.4.1 Unique competitiveness of QME

(1) Geographical advantages

QME is situated in Qianhai, Shenzhen, the forefront region of reforms and liberalisation in the new era. With the backing of the special economic zone, the pilot demonstration zone and the Greater Bay Area, Qianhai enjoys the combined policy benefits of all three and of being the first to undertake trial runs of major reforms. It is able to magnify the comparative advantages of Shenzhen and Hong Kong and strengthen the international competitiveness of Guangdong, Hong Kong and Macau, paving the way for China's steady development into a strong country in the world.

Institutional setups stimulate innovations which inject vitality into the market. Qianhai has an excellent environment and conditions favorable for institutional breakthroughs and innovations. Situated in Qianhai, QME can explore innovative business models for a commodity exchange in the best and fastest way.

(2) HKEX as its shareholder provides relatively strong international attributes

The pricing power on commodities has long been monopolised by western developed countries, in which the commodity trading markets have played a vital role. Examples are

NYMEX[3] for crude oil, LME for non-ferrous metals, and LBMA[4] for gold. Due to China's controls over its capital account, most enterprises in Mainland China cannot directly participate in transactions on overseas exchanges. This is an important factor leading to its giving away of the pricing power. Besides, due to political and cultural reasons, the official Mainland exchanges, the composition of their participants and the prices so formed have all failed to gain full recognition from the international market. In view of this, a commodity trading market that is attractive to both Mainland and overseas participants and is able to form a mutually recognised trading price, is an essential infrastructure and a prerequisite for China to obtain international commodity pricing power. In this regard, QME has relatively strong potential in obtaining such recognition from the international market, given its uniqueness in respect of its HKEX genes which imbues QME with stronger international attributes and elements.

(3)   Echoing with LME to build an international commodity distribution centre

After several years of development, great progress has been made to the construction of free trade zones and traditional bonded zones in Mainland China. However, they still lag far behind the traditional commodity trading and distribution centres in countries such as Singapore and Dubai. One major reason, aside from geographic location and taxation, is that the Mainland lacks an internationalised commodity exchange like Singapore Exchange ("SGX") or the Dubai Mercantile Exchange. There is also a lack of delivery of the rights to goods derived from transactions concluded on spot exchanges and OTC transactions, and hence a lack of incentive for Mainland and overseas institutions to transport and store physical goods in bonded zones in the Mainland. If QME conducts cross-border business through Commodity Connect by linking with LME which is also a subsidiary of HKEX, it will be able to appeal to more Mainland and overseas institutions and draw in more cross-border funds and physical goods, driving up the vibrancy of overall import and export trade and the volume of trade. This would facilitate the establishment of a global and regional commodity trade distribution centre. In addition, QME also provides geographical convenience for Mainland enterprises to engage in cross-border commodity hedging transactions without being subject to fluctuations in international commodity prices and facilitates physical delivery, thereby effectively helping companies reduce the management costs of offshore companies and physical asset logistics costs.

---

3   New York Mercantile Exchange.
4   London Bullion Market Association.

3.4.2   Introduction of Commodity Connect

The internationalisation of exchanges will not only increase the influence of Mainland China on the commodities market, but will also provide a prerequisite for seizing the pricing power. In order to encourage the Mainland to actively participate in and gradually integrate into the international commodities market, QME plans to proceed with the Commodity Connect initiative with reference to Stock Connect and Bond Connect, subject to approval by the authorities.

(1)   Trading model

Under Commodity Connect, transactions will be conducted in a two-way manner — "Coming-In" and "Going-Out", to provide mutual market access between the Mainland and overseas.

- **"Coming-In"** — Overseas customers at HKEX and LME trading Mainland products on QME through existing overseas trading channels.
- **"Going-Out"** — QME's Mainland customers trading designated products on HKEX and LME through the mutual market access mechanism, subject to quota imposed, thereby satisfying their needs for cross-border hedging.

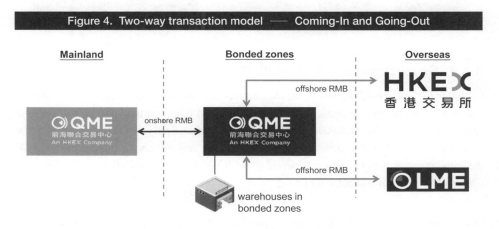

Figure 4. Two-way transaction model ── Coming-In and Going-Out

(2)   Fund settlement plan

Cross-border funds are managed in accordance with the "closed-loop and quota" principle to ensure closed and safe operation of funds and to reduce capital risks.

- **Closed-loop:** Drawing reference from the implementation of Stock Connect, the exchange will be the party responsible for settlement of cross-border funds. The account system will be set up in accordance with the system applicable to existing accounts in the People's Bank of China to ensure closed operation of funds.
- **Quota:** Separate quotas are set for daily bilateral cross-border capital flows to limit daily net inflow of funds from overseas investors and daily net outflow of funds by domestic investors.

Figure 5. The "closed-loop and quota" principle

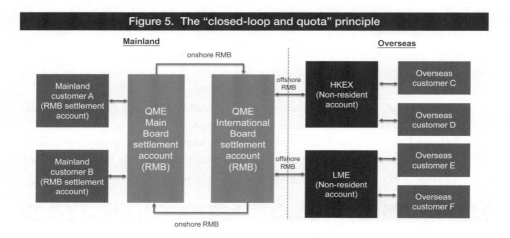

3.4.3 Significance of Commodity Connect

After the successful launch of Stock Connect and the Bond Connect primary market information platform, the opening-up of the Mainland commodities market will become especially meaningful. Launching Commodity Connect firstly at QME will enable the practical exploration of a new model for serving the real economy, paving the way for the implementation of the national strategies of RMB internationalisation and developing China into a major manufacturing power.

(1) Solidify the Greater Bay Area's position at the forefront of all-round financial innovations in Mainland China

Shenzhen currently does not have a nation-wide influential commodity trading platform. The development of Commodity Connect will therefore be conducive to further solidifying the Greater Bay Area's position at the forefront of all-round financial innovations. An active commodity trading platform will not only bring continuous economic benefits and employment opportunities to Qianhai and Shenzhen, but also comprehensively drive the development and prosperity of multiple industries in the Greater Bay Area including trade, logistics, finance and business services.

(2)   Enhance the overall standard of the Mainland commodity trading market

As a commodity trading platform under HKEX Group, QME has rich experience in operating an exchange and the support of a complete exchange system. It has the exchange brand name and market credibility that would be widely accepted by various industries. It is also a truly market-oriented and internationalised business entity. By establishing and operating an open, transparent and efficient trading platform, QME can leverage fully on its own trading, settlement and risk management capabilities to explore the setup of a regularised Mainland commodity trading market system, so as to elevate the overall standard of the commodity trading market in Mainland China.

(3)   Further accelerate the internationalisation of RMB

The internationalisation of the RMB has always been an important strategic objective of Mainland China. One of the main problems hindering the internationalisation of the RMB is the lack of stable RMB asset investment channels in offshore markets. Being an important component of traditional asset allocation, commodities are ideal target assets for RMB internationalisation and for exploring the opening-up of China's capital account. A cross-border commodity trading platform, once established, will not only become an important channel for offshore RMB asset allocation, but also provide RMB-denominated transaction price which can serve as an important benchmark for the offline pricing of long-term orders, thereby being conducive to RMB internationalisation.

3.5   Derivatives and export of prices

In the commodity derivatives market, apart from directly generating relevant prices through trading and delivery of physical goods, there are other forms of price formation, such as iron ore swaps and futures on SGX, iron ore swaps on the Shanghai Clearing House, cash-settled Brent crude oil futures on Chicago Mercantile Exchange (CME), etc. The settlement prices used for these products are determined with reference to other benchmark prices which can be roughly divided into the following three categories: prices collected by information consulting companies through enquiries ("Enquiry Price"), prices generated by commodity transactions on other exchanges ("Adopted Price") and prices derived from other commodities on the same exchange ("Exchange Price").

After the long-term negotiated price mechanism of the iron ore market lost its effect in 2008, Platts launched the Platts Iron Ore Index (IODEX or IODBZ00) in April 2008 and began to promote it to countries around the world. In April 2009, SGX was the first exchange to launch iron ore swap contract based on the Steel Index (TSI). In May 2009, the London Clearing House (LCH) started providing settlement for iron ore swaps. Around a year later in June 2010, CME also followed suit by joining the iron ore swap trading and clearing services industry. So far, current trading information reflects that SGX's iron ore swaps and futures products are the most successful. This is mainly due to Singapore's status as an international commodity trade and risk management centre. Enjoying pioneer advantages, SGX's iron ore swap business gradually attracted more and more steel mills, traders and mining companies to set up branches in Singapore. According to the statistics of the Singapore's Accounting and Corporate Regulatory Authority for the year 2014, around 200 of the said branches were set up by metals and mining companies from Mainland China.

The growth in the trading volume of the Singapore iron ore market occurred around 2012. At that time, the price of iron ore kept falling from US$180 to US$80 per lot, alerting many enterprises of the importance of using derivatives to manage risks, prompting them to launch their iron ore derivatives business. This explains why iron ore trade has turned active since around 2012.

3.5.1 Establishing commodity price indices in Mainland China

Evidenced by the high percentage share of Mainland China's demand in the total global demand for various commodities, Mainland China's demand has dominated the global commodities market. Yet, all along, this dominant position has not turned into a proportionate pricing power in the international commodities market, leaving the Mainland stricken by huge cost burden amid global commodity price fluctuations.

As opposed to existing futures exchanges in the Mainland, QME holds on to the initial intention of "setting a foothold in spot market while serving the real economy" and dedicated to creating an innovative trading platform and ecosystem to continuously provide customers with benchmark spot prices and to setting up a commodity spot trading platform serving both Mainland and overseas customers. By serving the real economy and industrial customers and restructuring the Mainland commodities market, credible spot commodity benchmark prices can be formed and "China prices" for commodities can then be realised.

3.5.2   Derivatives issued and listed overseas

Based on the "China prices" formed by the actual spot commodity transactions in the Mainland, QME can make full use of its natural advantages and launch derivatives based on the QME spot prices with the help of HKEX and LME under the same corporate group. In this way, foreign investors can conveniently invest in Mainland commodities directly in Hong Kong and London.

Drawing on successful international experience, QME may launch a variety of RMB-denominated cash-settled products including options, futures and swaps on LME or HKEX based on the spot prices formed on its platform as benchmarks through direct authorisation. Through cooperation with information consulting agencies, QME may also enable the incorporation of its prices, with a certain weighting, into the benchmark prices of overseas cash-settled derivatives.

3.5.3   Promote offshore RMB settlement prices for Hong Kong and London commodities

Despite the rapidly growing total economic value of Mainland China, the integration of the RMB into the global financial system is still at an initial stage. Major international financial centres including Hong Kong, London and Singapore are optimistic about the opportunities brought about by the accelerated integration of RMB assets into international financial markets in the future, and are competing to build an offshore RMB centre. As in the case of Stock Connect and Bond Connect, an introduction of "China prices" in Hong Kong and London based on QME spot prices, together with the realisation of Commodity Connect between the Mainland and overseas markets, will provide more offshore RMB investment channels to attract overseas investors to invest in the Mainland market through Commodity Connect. This will promote the formation of offshore RMB settlement prices for commodities in Hong Kong and London while providing more investment tools for offshore RMB funds.

4   Conclusion

As a spot commodity trading platform jointly invested by HKEX and Qianhai Financial Holdings, QME aims at breaking the restrictions imposed by administrative and historical reasons in Qianhai, the most special zone and innovation hub, and truly implementing the policy guidelines on "being the first to run pilot programs" and trying out institutional innovations. It is hoped that by seizing the major unprecedented opportunity offered by developing the Greater Bay Area and pilot demonstration zone, the scope and depth of Shenzhen-Hong Kong cooperation would be expanded and the setup of important financial infrastructure in Qianhai could be accelerated, contributing to the building-up of a key Shenzhen-Hong Kong cooperation project. Through the formation of spot price benchmarks, the establishment of standardised asset systems, and the connection of the Mainland and overseas markets, the supply-side problems, financing difficulties and the lack of pricing power could be addressed and the vision of a new model serving the real economy may become a reality.

Chapter 12

The opportunities offered by greater connectivity between the LME and the Mainland commodities market

The London Metal Exchange

Summary

In this chapter we will look at the opportunities for building greater connections between Mainland China commodities markets and the London Metal Exchange, working with its parent company, Hong Kong Exchanges and Clearing Limited (HKEX), and its sister company, the Qianhai Mercantile Exchange (QME).

1   Background

HKEX Group acquired the London Metal Exchange (LME) in 2012. Since then, LME and other companies within the corporate group have worked closely together to look at ways to offer greater two-way access to commodity markets for participants both inside and outside Mainland China. In October 2015, the Hong Kong Futures Exchange (HKFE), HKFE Clearing Corporation Limited (HKCC), the LME and LME Clear signed a memorandum of understanding (MOU) for the proposed development of a trading link between HKFE and the LME and a clearing link between HKCC and LME Clear, called "Hong Kong-London Connect" and work has continued since then to build this vision.

2   China's position in global metal markets

As the Chinese economy continues to expand, greater foreign involvement is contributing to China's increasing overseas influence. The Mainland's capital markets are progressively becoming more accessible with increasing direct international participation permitted in the Mainland markets. Its commodity exchanges are gradually allowing more foreign participation to increase China's overseas footprint, gain commodity pricing power, and to facilitate global trade driven in part by the increasing significance of the Renminbi (RMB) as an international currency.

The RMB has become more internationally significant in recent years, facilitating global trade and gaining recognition as one of the International Monetary Fund's "main world currencies". From an LME Clear perspective, since July 2015 clearing members have been able to use offshore RMB as eligible cash collateral to cover their margin requirements. This service is an important part of the LME Clear collateral offering, particularly as increasing numbers of Chinese companies trade on the LME. Chinese-owned BOCI Global Commodities — the first Chinese firm to become an LME member — was the first to submit RMB as collateral.

It is widely acknowledged that China's production and consumption of base metals is around 50% of the global total[1], and that this share of the global total continues to grow. China's growth is heavily resource intensive, requiring increasing quantities of raw materials, particularly industrial metals.

Metals demand has been powered by intensive industrialisation and widespread urbanisation projects, with construction, transport infrastructure and communications networks driving the consumption of a wide variety of base metals.

China has also seen sizeable growth in demand for battery materials, particularly for the production of electric vehicles (EVs). An increasing proportion of Chinese consumers prefer the state-of-the-art and cleaner technology of EVs. This, combined with government policy to reduce pollution and improvements in technology making EVs more affordable, mean that it is likely that China will account for 48% of global ownership of passenger EVs by 2025[2]. Driving increased demand for battery materials such as cobalt, nickel and lithium alongside other metals such as aluminium and copper, this sector is set to grow exponentially.

3 China's connection with the global market

3.1 Overseas market access

Mainland China has facilitated more access to overseas markets in recent years via a number of key programmes which have implications for the commodities market. These include:

- A number of **Central Government-Owned Enterprises (CGOEs) and other state-owned enterprises (SOEs)** have been granted permission to trade overseas derivatives markets for hedging purposes without the need to obtain further regulatory approval. Given the large quantity of physical commodities they trade, these Chinese SOEs are likely to have significant demand for additional hedging routes.

---

1   Sources: Bloomberg L.P.; World Bureau of Metal Statistics; International Monetary Fund.
2   Source: *Electric Vehicle Outlook 2019*, BloombergNEF.

- The planned introduction of the **Qualified Domestic Individual Investor 2 (QDll2) programme**[3], to build on the Qualified Domestic Institutional Investor (QDII) programme introduced earlier which allows Mainland qualified institutional investors to invest in foreign securities markets approved by the China Securities Regulatory Commission (CSRC). QDII2 plans to offer direct access for Mainland individuals to some specific areas of foreign capital markets including derivatives. QDll2 therefore will introduce another route for Mainland investment into overseas markets within set thresholds, providing greater access to overseas securities and derivatives.
- The launch of **the "Belt and Road"** initiative (BRI), which seeks to create an economic belt of railways, highways, oil and gas pipelines, power grids and other links across Central, West and South Asia to Europe and North Africa. The infrastructure projects under the BRI would inevitably drive up the demand for construction materials, and in particular base metals. In addition, Mainland enterprises are actively involved in these BRI projects, with the resulting increase in exposure to price changes driven by fluctuations in the supply and demand of commodities. In support of the BRI, the LME signed an MOU with seven Chinese and UK financial institutions in October 2015, with the intention of working together to increase market access, offer risk management services and widen China's access to global commodities markets.

3.2   Foreign participation in the Mainland market

Currently, there is relatively limited international access to Mainland China's financial markets, including for its commodity exchanges.

At present, Mainland commodity futures trading centres on three exchanges — the Shanghai Futures Exchange (SHFE), the Dalian Commodity Exchange (DCD) and the Zhengzhou Commodity Exchange (ZCE). These exchanges offer a range of commodity futures for domestic participants. However, access for foreign participants is still restricted to certain special RMB-denominated government-approved futures including pure terephthalic acid (PTA), rubber, oil and iron ore offered by these exchanges. In addition, trading by foreign participants can only take place via specific trading entities which are either members of, or are approved by, the domestic exchange.

Given China's leading role as a large-scale producer and consumer of commodities, it

---

3   See, for example, the *State Council Notification About Certain Measures for Supporting the Deepening Reform and Innovations in the Pilot Free Trade Zones* (《國務院關於支持自由貿易試驗區深化改革創新若干措施的通知》), released on 23 November 2018. No specific rules for the implementation of the QDII2 programme have been released.

has huge potential for developing and opening up its futures markets to wider international participation. With increasing volatility in global commodity markets, there is certainly a growing need for greater access to commodity exchanges which offer the means to manage the risk of fluctuating prices.

A key obstacle for increased foreign participation at present is that China's currency is not fully convertible, although it is clear that there is an aspiration for this to be achieved in the future. Full convertibility and free trading of the RMB on the international market would attract more external liquidity and investment flows, helping to facilitate the internationalisation of the Mainland financial markets and allowing its commodity exchanges to become more closely integrated with international exchanges. However, while China seeks to ease capital controls in a controlled manner to increase foreign participation, it is likely that this will take some time to implement.

In the meantime, one potential route could be to open up a "bridge" for both inward foreign and outward domestic investment in commodities. This would echo the Stock Connect collaboration between stock exchanges in Hong Kong, Shanghai and Shenzhen for the trading of securities using local brokers and clearing houses; and Bond Connect, a joint venture established by China Foreign Exchange Trade System and HKEX, which facilitates greater interaction between the bond markets of Hong Kong and the Mainland. In a commodities connectivity model, HKEX and the LME would seek to enable trading links for commodity futures with Mainland exchanges.

Building more connections between the Hong Kong and London markets could offer Mainland participants greater access to open and transparent markets with international regulatory and trading standards in place. At the same time, for attracting greater foreign participation, the Mainland market should address the needs of overseas participants, who will expect greater transparency of regulation and market policies. The drivers for granting more open access to the Mainland market exist, with global enterprises and investors keen to participate.

The following sections of this chapter will examine the LME's offering for global market participants in more detail, together with an overview of how the LME and HKEX are working together to provide solutions for greater connectivity between the Mainland and international commodities markets.

4 What does the LME offer global participants?

The LME is the key global derivatives market for the trading of industrial metals. Producers, consumers and traders of metal across the globe already value the LME for a number of reasons. These include:

- **Hedging** — producers and consumers can use the LME to hedge their exposure to volatile prices.
- **Price discovery** — the LME provides the world with transparently generated, daily reference prices for metals.
- **Reference pricing** — the prices discovered on LME trading platforms are global reference prices used for valuing and settling physical contracts.
- **Price convergence** — LME contracts can be physically settled via the global LME warehouse network which ensures pricing is anchored to the physical metal.
- **Physical settlement** — only brands of metal that are actually used by the physical market are accepted for good delivery.
- **Prompt-date structure** — no other market offers such a range of forward dates (daily, weekly, 3-month and monthly) offering market users unparalleled flexibility in managing their positions.

These attributes and features of the LME's markets are detailed extensively in Chapter 6 of this book.

4.1   Current Mainland China participation on the LME

Thanks to the attributes detailed above, the LME already has numerous Chinese clients who interact in many different ways with the Exchange. Strong working relationships also exist with a number of large Chinese base metals companies who are active on the LME, particularly since the early 2000s when the Chinese government began to grant an increasing number of trading licences to SOEs to hedge on overseas markets. Many Chinese companies have also set up trading arms in cities such as Hong Kong, Singapore and London where their metals trading desks can access international markets.

As of May 2020, there were six Chinese companies authorised as LME clearing members. In addition, almost 80 Chinese metals brands were listed as good for LME delivery, meeting the LME's specifications for quality, shape and weight.

Chinese and London metals markets might be thousands of miles apart, but they are connected by trade flows as the difference in prices on both markets can incentivise imports and exports of metal. This leads to arbitrage activity between the two markets, which itself is evolving beyond physical participants to include more financial investment activity. This is illustrated by London volumes before 7 a.m. London time (before 3 p.m. Shanghai time), or "Asian hours", which have seen increased engagement across LME metals contracts — over the past ten years, average daily volumes have generally been around 10% higher when Asian markets are not on holiday[4]. This increase in Asian hours volumes led the LME to launch the LME Asian Reference Price for 3-month LME Aluminium, LME Copper and LME Zinc in 2011. These prices are calculated using a volume-weighted average price, and are discovered and published to coincide with the end of the Asian trading day. This gives users in the region a useful early-day guide to trading in one of the most significant and liquid periods of the day, reflecting market activity in the Asian time zone. A network of on-screen traders has developed to connect and react to the price moves in both markets.

4.2   The demand for greater connectivity

There are a number of key drivers which contribute to the demand for greater links between Mainland China and the LME.

Base metals are currently actively traded in over-the-counter ("OTC") markets in the Mainland, but the demand for exchange-traded contracts is growing, driven in part by the rapid increase in the consumption of metals in the region. In particular, institutional investors and individual professional investors in Asian markets, including Mainland China, have expressed a desire for increased opportunities to access the wider global commodities markets via smaller, financially settled metals contracts.

---

4   Source: LME Research.

5 Accessing a global industry network via the LME

5.1   A global warehouse network

To facilitate physical delivery and to meet the needs of its international users the LME
has an approved network of registered warehouses. These are predominantly in metal-
consuming regions which are politically stable and have effective legal, tax and commercial
frameworks in place. LME-approved warehouses are located throughout the UK,
Continental Europe, the Middle East, Asia and the USA. Each year, around five million
tonnes of metal is physically delivered in and out of over 550 LME-approved warehouses
around the world. Table 1 shows LME's current warehouse presence in Asia.

Table 1. The LME's warehouse presence in Asia (as at April 2020)		
City/Country	No. of locations	No. of listed warehouses
Japan	2	6
Malaysia	2	117
Singapore	1	17
South Korea	3	111
Taiwan, China	1	22
Total	9	273

Source: LME.

There are a number of LME-approved warehouses across Asia, but as yet, none are
located in Mainland China. Bringing LME warehousing to China is a long-term strategic
aim of HKEX Group, and the LME and HKEX are working closely with Chinese policy
makers to advance this aspiration.

Metal is stored in LME-approved warehouses on warrant. Warrants are documents
of possession, issued by the warehouse company, for each lot of LME-approved metal
held within an LME-approved facility. They are used as the means of delivering physical
metal under LME contracts. The LME's network of warehouses is also used extensively in
facilitating commodity trade financing.

LMEsword is the secure electronic transfer system for LME warrants, facilitating the
transfer of ownership of LME warrants and stock reporting. This system also facilitates
efficient warrant swap trading for material in different global locations.

5.2   The global use of LME reference pricing and LME contracts

Base metal prices discovered on the LME represent the global price. These prices are used in the majority of bilaterally negotiated physical supply contracts between producers and consumers of metal. The parties to these contracts then agree premiums based on variables (such as location and purity of metal) referencing this global price. This allows producers in one continent to agree physical contracts with smelters, fabricators and consumers in other countries or regions.

5.3   London's gold market and LMEprecious

China is the biggest global consumer and producer of gold, and over the past two decades has become the largest gold market in the world. The People's Bank of China is one of the most active central banks in the world, and has steadily increased its gold reserves over the past fifteen years[5].

Liquidity on domestic gold trading venues in the Mainland coalesces at relatively short tenors: less than a year on both the Shanghai Gold Exchange (SGE) and Shanghai Futures Exchange (SHFE). This makes it difficult for domestic producers to hedge cash flow to support debt financing or equity capital investment in the domestic market. The absence of liquidity over longer tenors means banks must turn to Western markets to hedge risk, such as London's OTC market, or on-exchange (via LMEprecious, the LME's precious metals trading and hedging solution, for example). The World Gold Council commissioned analysis which estimates that all-in cost savings from on-exchange trading could range from ~50% to ~90%, due primarily to lower capital charges[6].

The increasing globalisation of the gold market also provides trading opportunities for market participants looking to manage basis risk or take a view on regional supply and demand dynamics. To this end, LMEprecious provides a transparent on-exchange solution to trade in combination with other exchanges across the globe. Since August 2017, LMEprecious has provided intra-day LME Gold and LME Silver spot reference prices aligned with periods of peak liquidity, to support the precious metals market in managing their price risk throughout the trading day.

5.4   LME steel contracts with strong Asian links

The LME's cash-settled ferrous suite, which saw its first two contracts for steel scrap

---

5   Source: World Gold Council (WGC) (https://www.gold.org/goldhub/data/monthly-central-bank-statistics).
6   Source: WGC, LME and Oliver Wyman analysis.

and rebar launched in November 2015, has seen significant involvement from Asian participants from inception. LME Steel Scrap in particular saw early engagement and support from Asian markets.

The LME's steel contract offering has expanded to include hot-rolled coil futures, with LME Steel HRC FOB China (Argus) catering for the epicentre of the East Asian market. This contract is designed to provide an effective risk management tool for both Chinese exporters and steel importers and consumers in key export markets. This has been demonstrated with the early adoption by companies located in importing countries in South-East Asia including Vietnam, Thailand and Singapore.

6 Recent developments at the LME and HKEX facilitating greater connectivity

The LME and HKEX have been working to leverage their respective strengths and expertise to develop effective routes for greater connectivity between Hong Kong, Mainland China and international markets.

6.1 The launch of HKEX London Metal Minis

HKEX London Metal Minis are contracts designed to meet the needs of Asian participants who want to mitigate or take on metal price risk using offshore RMB (CNH) or US dollar-denominated futures. The minis contracts offer market participants the opportunity to trade straightforward monthly contracts out to 12 months, settling against the Official Price of the corresponding LME "parent" contract. The additional benefits for participants in the region are that the minis are available to trade during Asian hours; they provide arbitrage opportunities with other markets; and are small-lot sized contracts with a competitive fee structure.

Traded on the HKEX derivatives platform, these small-lot contracts are available for six base metals: aluminium, zinc, copper, nickel, tin and lead; and in two currencies.

Table 2. HKEX London Metal Minis —— Key highlights	
Feature	Characteristics
Underlying assets	Aluminium, zinc, copper, nickel, tin and lead
Currency	Traded and priced in CNH or US dollars
Contract size and type	Small lot size, monthly contracts
Settlement	Cash settled against LME parent contract Official Settlement Price
Trading venue	HKEX derivatives platform

Source: HKEX.

HKEX CNH London Metal Mini contracts are designed to match Chinese physical market stakeholders' exposure to commodities contracts priced in RMB, establishing RMB pricing of metals during Asian trading hours and offering arbitrage opportunities between HKFE, the LME and SHFE. Aluminium, copper and zinc were launched in 2014, with lead, nickel and tin joining the suite in 2017. The more standardised monthly contract structure offered by the minis contracts, is more attractive to Asian investors, while HKFE's extensive network of exchange participants and brokers would offer institutional and private investors a more accessible route to trade these contracts.

To complement the existing CNH suite, on 5 August 2019 HKEX introduced six US dollar-denominated HKEX London Metal Minis. These contracts provide additional options for investors with exposure to base metals denominated in US dollars in the Asian time zone and complement HKEX's existing futures products in CNH.

Table 3. Comparison of LME base metals contracts and HKEX London Metal Minis		
	LME base metal contracts	HKEX London Metal Minis
Type of settlement	Physically settled	Cash settled against the Official Price of the LME "parent" contract
Contract size — in metric tonnes (mt)	Large lot sizes: • Aluminium – 25mt • Copper – 25mt • Lead – 25mt • Nickel – 6mt • Tin – 5mt • Zinc – 25mt	Small lot sizes: • Aluminium – 5mt • Copper – 5mt • Lead – 5mt • Nickel – 1mt • Tin – 1mt • Zinc – 5mt
Contract type	• Daily • Weekly • Monthly (out to 63 or 123 months)	• Monthly (out to 12 months)
Trading hours	(London time) • Ring: 11:40 – 17:00 • LMEselect: 01:00 – 19:00 • Inter-office: 24 hours	(Hong Kong time, other than Last Trading Day) • T session: 09:00 – 16:30 • T+1 session: 17:15 – 03:00
Access to the market	Via LME members	Via HKFE participants

(continued)

Table 3. Comparison of LME base metals contracts and HKEX London Metal Minis		
	LME base metal contracts	HKEX London Metal Minis
Key participants	• The physical community — producers and consumers • LME members and their clients • Financial community — hedge funds, proprietary firms, investment firms • OTC market participants	• Financial community, familiar with futures contracts • Private investors • Corporate clients • Arbitragers • Asian speculators

Source: LME.

6.2   LME and HKFE reciprocal membership

To broaden the opportunities for greater collaboration between London and Hong Kong, the LME and HKFE offer reciprocal membership (the "RMA") for applicants who already hold a membership or participantship at either one of the exchanges. Reciprocal membership of LME and HKFE allows broader access to products on each exchange, and provides additional liquidity for new products. Under the RMA, the LME and HKFE waive their respective first year's annual subscription and application processing fees for new applicants who already hold a membership or participantship at the other exchange[7].

6.3   Collaboration with Qianhai Mercantile Exchange (QME)

In October 2018, HKEX launched the QME, a spot-trading commodities platform based in Qianhai, Shenzhen in China's Guangdong province, as part of wider plans to develop HKEX Group's commodities offering for Mainland China. QME currently offers spot trading in a number of metals, including alumina, aluminium and copper rods, with plans for further expansion.

The LME continues to work in partnership with QME to develop the vision to provide increased connectivity between the Mainland and overseas commodities markets, building on the strengths of both exchanges in three key areas: warehousing, trading and finance.

The LME and QME are exploring the creation of links between the LME's longstanding and robust global warehousing system and QME's local warehouse network, with the initial aim of offering tradeable warrant swaps between the two networks. At the same time, the LME continues to discuss the possibility of establishing LME-approved onshore warehouses with Mainland regulators. Together, these measures would help to alleviate the additional costs including increased delivery time, transport and customs clearance which

---

7   See more details in Chapter 14 of this book. "The connectivity platform offered by the HKEX commodities market for the Mainland and the world".

are a consequence of metal being delivered from LME warehouses outside the Mainland to onshore customers. The expansion of the warehouse network into Mainland China would help to truly globalise commodity trading, aiding in the internationalisation of the Mainland financial market and facilitating the financing of onshore Chinese metal inventories on the LME.

Another goal is to extend LME trading into the Asian time zone, alongside the expansion of commodity spot price discovery capabilities at QME, enabling greater access for international investors. The spot "benchmark" price forms the basis of commodity futures trading, as contracts are priced based on the cost of a commodity for immediate delivery. QME and the LME are working together to build out this capability, leveraging both the existing LMEbullion and QME spot trading platforms and partnerships with other Mainland exchanges. Building on QME's work to date to deliver robust spot prices for a range of metals would support the development of internationally accepted Mainland commodity price benchmarks, which the LME will seek to use as the basis for launching new products in the future[8].

7   The way forward

The LME has the determination to more effectively serve Mainland market participants with an enhanced product and service offering, in collaboration with HKEX.

The LME's technology roadmap will deliver a comprehensive refresh and upgrade to the exchange's trading infrastructure. As part of this programme, a new LME trading platform is currently being built, leveraging HKEX technology. One of the key advantages of this new platform is that the new web-based electronic system for traders (the "Graphical User Interface" or "GUI") will offer direct trading access for Asian clients. This will deliver a more efficient and cost-effective route to connect Asian participants, including Mainland participants, with the LME's global metals market.

---

8 For more detail on QME, and the LME's relationship with QME, please see Chapter 11 of this book, "QME's unique role in the commodities market in Mainland China".

7.1   Connecting the Mainland and international commodities markets

As the mechanisms of commodities pricing advance, the LME aims to be at the forefront of this evolution. Working closely together with HKEX, the two exchanges will leverage their relative experience in Mainland markets and commodities to offer new solutions — both for Mainland investors wishing to gain international metals price exposure via the LME, and for foreign investors wishing to access Mainland Chinese markets.

The coming years will see the LME's efforts to accelerate the connection between the Mainland and international commodities markets (see related recent progress of developments in Section 6 above).

7.2   Eliminating barriers to greater links between the LME and Mainland China

There are several market-based barriers to entry which need to be overcome in creating further links between the LME and Mainland China. These include:

- **The cost of LME membership:** the annual membership fee, and requirement to purchase LME B-shares for some categories of membership[9], can be seen as an obstacle to encouraging more direct Chinese membership of the LME. HKFE and the LME's RMA provides an alternative cost-effective route for members of either exchange to trade on the other.

- **The cost of indirect access:** At present, there are still a lot of restrictions and limitations for Asian clients to have direct trading access to the LME's markets. This can significantly increase brokerage and access costs. Providing a more direct link to the LME's market could reduce these costs.

- **Network latency, cost and stability:** Asian market participants have a preference to access the LME's electronic market, but intercontinental network links provided by brokers or vendors can result in higher latency, higher costs and a less reliable service. A more direct trading link with the LME would increase the speed and stability of access to its markets.

---

9   Category 1 and 2 member firms of the LME are required to hold a minimum of 25,000 LME B-shares. Each Category 3 member is required to hold a minimum of 5,000 LME B-shares and each Category 4 member is required to hold a minimum of 2,500 LME B-shares.

7.3   What does the future hold?

The development and introduction of the London Metal Mini Futures has provided valuable price connectivity between the London and Hong Kong markets, allowing LME prices to be used for settlement on HKFE, leveraging its broad distribution network in Asia. This first step in HKEX and LME's "Hong Kong-London Connect" initiative provides HKFE participants with direct access to US dollar-denominated LME prices.

Further phases of the Connect initiative are being identified, and could see the LME implement a "pass the book" model that will allow transfer of open interest across the LME and HKFE clearing houses to maximise clearing and cost efficiencies. The final step would include the development of a full connect scheme, where both HKEX and LME's order books are connected. This improved connectivity between both exchanges would pool liquidity across both venues while benefiting from the distribution and reach of both respective markets.

8   Conclusion

As China's economy continues to grow and internationalise, enabling greater inward and outward investment and capital flows would assist with this growth, including the further internationalisation of the RMB. At the same time, offering greater access to the global commodities markets will give China a larger influence in global commodities pricing, more accurately reflecting its position as the world's largest producer and consumer of a number of commodities, including metals.

The LME is committed to supporting this ambition, creating more opportunities for Mainland enterprises and investors to trade on-exchange, and providing additional routes for Mainland metal producers and consumers to manage their exposure to metals price risk.

HKEX, QME and the LME will continue to collaborate and deliver solutions which meet the need for fair, open, transparent and well-regulated commodity markets. Together with global reach and extensive capital markets expertise, HKEX brings deep experience in working with Mainland authorities, regulators and market participants. The LME, with its rich heritage as the global leader in industrial metals trading, is home to the global reference price for non-ferrous metals and a global warehouse network facilitating the storage and physical delivery of metals and trade financing opportunities. In parallel,

QME provides a Mainland spot-trading commodities venue which supplements the futures market, in combination with domestic warehousing expertise. Working together, the three exchanges will look at more ways to bring Mainland and global markets together to create even more opportunities, with the added possibility of establishing benchmark metal prices for China, further expanding LME trading in Asian time zones, exploring cross-border and international trading and the cross-listing of metal derivatives as part of the wider Connect programme.

Note: All LME products and services mentioned in this paper that are planned or being developed are subject to regulatory approval.

Chapter 13

The role of market infrastructure in the development of the base metals market

Chief China Economist's Office
Hong Kong Exchanges and Clearing Limited

Summary

The commodities market for base metals is not only a venue for trading base metals, but also a place where industrial enterprises engage in hedging and exercise risk management. In light of this, a sound infrastructure system underpinning the market has become increasingly important in serving the needs of industrial customers and the real economy.

The base metals markets in the West have all gone through the gradual evolution from their embryonic forms to where they are as mature markets today. This market in the United States, for example, also faced the problem of insufficient regulation to maintain market order and insufficient standardisation at its early stage of development. Their experience accentuated the importance of sound major infrastructure and trade-support mechanisms in supporting the base metals trading system and thereby driving the growth of the base metals market. Further, the standardisation, modernisation and informatisation of such infrastructure and trade-support mechanisms could enhance the operational efficiency and economic benefits of market participants, while remarkably improving the internal management efficiency of industrial enterprises and reducing costs.

Among all the infrastructures underpinning the spot commodities market, a well-developed warehouse logistics system is considered the most important. Safety of the warehouse system is a cornerstone of spot trading in commodities in that it gives participants the assurance to conduct various types of related business. Thus, a warehouse network which can provide reliable global reference prices and "markets of last resort" for base metals market participants is an indispensable and fundamental part of the physical metals market. Spot trading of base metals often requires huge financing support in the entire production and logistics process because of the time lag in capital recycling. Given such a large demand for financing support, base metals manufacturers and traders often get operationally constrained during economic downturn when such financing support is insufficient. This kind of financing support efficiency is also lowered in case of irrational warehouse receipt financing practices whereby the credibility of the warehouse receipts cannot be guaranteed. Since base metals by nature are of high value, easy to transport and store, readily liquid and subject to a clearly defined quality grading system, they are actually very good financing tools. Therefore, warehouse receipt financing has become a crucial integral part of the spot market in base metals. The outbreak of the global financial crisis in 2008 reflected to a certain extent the serious lack of flexibility of market participants in withstanding financial and economic turmoil as well as the deficiency in market transparency. Against this backdrop, global financial markets at all levels have begun shifting to adopt central clearing and settlement in place of a bilateral system in certain sectors. The commodity financial derivatives market for base metals is hardly an exception.

The soundness and effectiveness of the infrastructure and trade-support mechanisms of a commodities market is best judged by whether they are conducive to effective and efficient resource allocation, thereby helping the market and the industry to lower transaction costs. This is also one of the most fundamental purposes for which any trading platforms (including futures exchanges) exist, and their position and interests shall all be in accordance with such purpose. As for market participants, they will naturally go for whichever pricing centre that is more regularised, more transparent, with abundant participants, more internationalised and more capable of manifesting the price formation and guidance mechanism fairly and effectively. These considerations are particularly important for Mainland China's base metals market which is in the process of development and internationalisation. Market development and improvement do take time, and ultimately the market itself will decide what best meets the needs of the industry. All these are worth our continuous attention.

1 Global base metals markets: Major infrastructure and trade-support mechanisms

The global base metals market is largely comprised of a decentralised over-the-counter (OTC) market and a number of centralised exchange markets, including the market of the London Metal Exchange (LME) amongst others. Base (or "non-ferrous") metals have been traded on the LME since its inception in 1877, and as the prices being quoted for those trades began to be published in the financial press, the metal industry started to use those prices as a dependable reference for their physical contracts. This continues to this day, with the majority of international base metals still priced using the LME price. In 2019, 75% of global on-exchange metal trading took place on the LME, with a total trading value of US$13.5 trillion[1]. In the late 1970s, the United States (US) stopped using the manufacturer pricing system. Since then the New York Mercantile Exchange (now COMEX) has dominated the US market. Meanwhile, the Shanghai Futures Exchange (SHFE) established in 1990 has built up the non-ferrous metal futures market in China, forming gradually a triangular competitive relationship between the LME, COMEX and SHFE[2].

The commodities markets for base metals in the West have all gone through the gradual evolution from their embryonic forms to where they are as mature markets today. This market in the US, for example, also faced the problem of insufficient regulation to maintain market order and insufficient standardisation, coupled with the lack of infrastructure such as warehousing and transportation facilities and poor creditworthiness, at its early stage of development. It has taken a long development process before regularised market order has ultimately come into play.

The US' experience accentuated the importance of sound major infrastructure such as warehousing and logistics as well as clearing and settlement, and trade-support mechanisms such as warehouse receipt financing and third-party professional services in supporting

---

1   Source: LME.
2   See Wei Jia and Xu Xiaoya, "Research on the Pricing Power Formation Mechanism for the Nonferrous Metals Market on the LME" (〈LME 有色金屬市場定價權形成機制研究〉), *Futures and Financial Derivatives* (《期貨與金融衍生品》) (Institution of Financial Derivatives of Beijing), Vol. 105, January 2019.

the base metals trading system (see Figure 1), which have driven the growth of the base metals market. Further, the standardisation, modernisation and informatisation of such infrastructure and trade-support mechanisms could enhance the operational efficiency and economic benefits to market participants, while remarkably improving the internal management efficiency of industrial enterprises and reducing costs.

Figure 1. Major infrastructure and trade-support mechanisms underpinning a base metals market trading platform

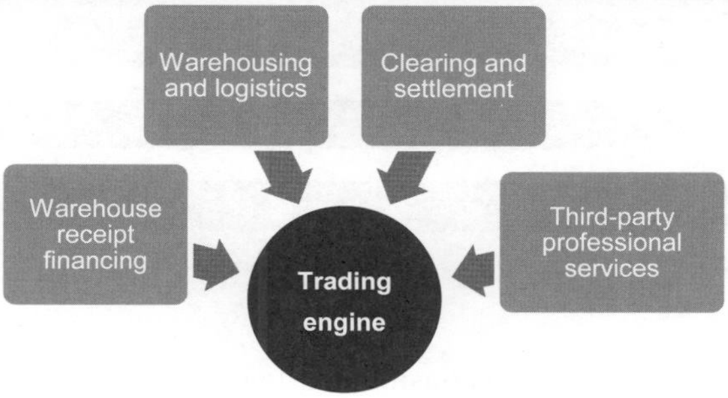

Source: HKEX analysis.

1.1   Warehousing and logistics

Among all the infrastructures underpinning the spot commodities market, a well-developed warehouse logistics system is considered the most important. Safety of the warehouse system is a cornerstone of spot trading in commodities in that it gives participants the assurance to conduct various types of related businesses. The development of a spot base metals market also entails the gradual development and enhancement of a robust warehouse logistics system.

First of all, the logistics costs in commodities incurred by industrial enterprises are closely tied with the degree of standardisation of the warehouse logistics system in the market due to the large number of enterprises participating in the trading of base metals, the high turnover rate of goods, the lengthy and distributed logistic process, the lack of economies of scale, and the risk of price fluctuation and damage to goods in transit. Without an assurance of the security of warehousing and logistics, the quantity, quality and ownership of goods could not be effectively guaranteed, which in turn will constrain the business expansion in spot commodities. Therefore, the security of goods in warehouses is crucial for enterprises along the industrial chain, as well as the financial institutions and investment institutions involved, especially the numerous base metals traders. A professional and efficient network of registered warehouses can thus bring many benefits to the base metals industry, and support the market to function more efficiently (see Figure 2).

Figure 2. Benefits of a professional warehouse network to the base metals industry

- Enhance global warehouse storage standards for non-standard warehouse receipts
- Boost confidence in the safe storage of goods under non-standard warehouse receipts
- Standardise terms and conditions related to creating warehouse receipts
- Reduce risk of fraud
- Enhance ability to secure commodities financing

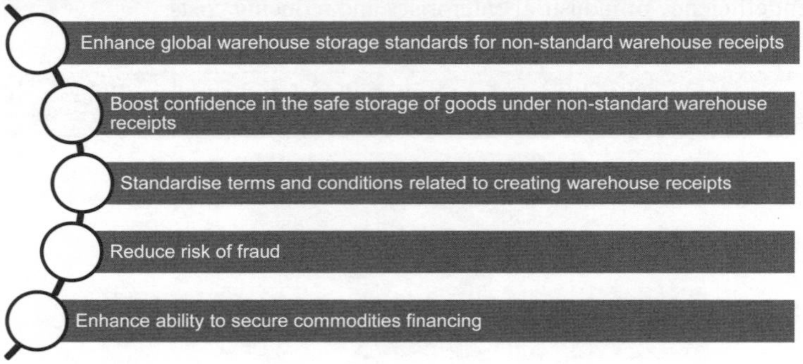

Source: HKEX analysis.

Secondly, a fully-fledged warehousing and logistics system makes it possible to integrate futures trading with spot trading, i.e. the physical delivery mechanism can play an important role in futures trading, thereby ensuring that the commodities trading platform can fully deliver its functions to global base metal consumers and producers for hedging and risk management.

In commodities trading, although contracts involving ultimate physical settlement account for only a very small proportion of the total futures contracts traded, the physical delivery mechanism plays a pivotal role in linking futures prices with spot transactions in the real economy. Overseas commodities markets have invariably set up extensive standard warehouses at logistics transit centres or places where commodities consumers and suppliers cluster, as the final, or auxiliary, means of physical trading. These warehouses will store the excess supply and provide the goods when there is a shortage, so they can instantly reflect the marginal changes in supply and demand in the physical goods system, and serve practically as a reservoir of goods. Thanks to the protection offered by the physical delivery mechanism supported by the warehouse system, changes in futures prices and spot prices can be in line and do not substantially deviate from each other, thus enabling the inventory information of the exchanges to serve as a "barometer" of the fundamentals underlying the changes in market supply and demand. Futures prices formed on an exchange that is equipped with a wide network of registered warehouses and a well-established physical delivery system can also bear testimony to the effectiveness of the "price discovery mechanism" of on-exchange futures prices. Applying the same to the base metals market, an extensive network of registered warehouses is crucial in linking the futures prices with the spot market prices. As the expiration date is approaching, the futures contract price will move closer to the spot price, because despite only a small proportion of futures contracts will be settled by physical delivery at the expiration date, the possibility of physical delivery has ensured that the metal futures price does not deviate far from the spot price. The convergence of the futures price and the spot price is of utmost importance because it forms the basis on which producers and consumers effectively hedge against movements in base metal prices. So it's the robust warehouse network that tightly binds trading and risk management via the commodities futures market with the base metals industry in the real economy.

It is a common practice in the commodities market, especially the base metals market, to generate widely accepted reference prices in physical goods contracts. Usually, the prices in the contracts between basic metal producers and consumers are determined with reference to globally accepted prices. They will also negotiate price discounts and premiums relevant to the raw material that is being bought or sold[3]. The practice of pricing materials based on reputable reference prices (excluding costs and premiums) is becoming increasingly popular given the benefits to the companies in terms of transparency, efficiency and the availability of choices. Transactions in the spot market that involve delivering metals in the future inevitably carry risks because metal prices may fluctuate significantly during the period from the signing of the contract to the final delivery, which could last for days or weeks, if not months or years. Most producers and consumers, i.e. metal producers and metal product manufacturers, will therefore adopt reliable global reference prices generated in the futures markets with physical delivery mechanisms to hedge against price risks.

A warehouse network which can provide reliable global reference prices and terminal markets for base metals market participants constitute an indispensable and fundamental part of the spot market in metals. This is because it enables the commodities trading platform to perform the following two functions:

(1) **Price discovery:** Generate timely, transparent, credible and real reference prices. The prices are discovered using risk capital and are truly reflective of global supply and demand. The market's ability to hedge is predicated on its ability to discover these reference prices.

(2) **Price convergence:** Products underlying the contracts are settled and delivered

---

3   There are nonetheless exceptions, such as the steel market where contract prices are always fixed and include all production costs, expenses, insurance premiums, etc., or spot prices are directly adopted, thereby exposing contract holders to the risk of market price fluctuations.

through a secure and reliable global warehouse network. This is critical because it means that the futures price discovered in the market will tend to converge with the spot price of the metal (see Figure 3).

Figure 3. Convergence of spot price and futures price in the commodities market

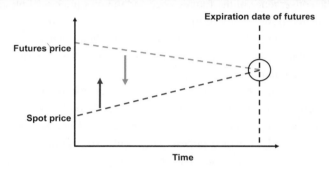

Note: The scenario is where the futures price is higher than the spot price.
Source: HKEX analysis.

The major benefits of linking physical contracts to a reference price are discussed below:

- Against the backdrop of a fragmented global economy and a complex value chain, it is increasingly difficult for producers and consumers to beat the market on an ongoing basis. Instead, by agreeing to trade at market prices, market participants could benefit from the greater transparency provided by these price discovery entities and mechanisms. Therefore, companies could turn their focus to negotiating the price premiums or discounts between base metals and specific products. Such premiums and discounts are based on many factors, including some of the most frequently mentioned factors like geographic location, material grade, impurities, and delivery conditions.
- Through the provision of a robust and regulated trading venue for price discovery, market participants that refer to the prices discovered on the venue will be able to keep fully abreast of the latest market conditions. This will enable them to continuously and autonomously discover the market prices of metals without the need of investing a lot of resources to collect information.
- Companies that refer to globally recognised prices could retain the option to hedge their risk exposure to the benchmark metal price without bearing the underlying risks of such risk exposure.

It is worth noting that as a delivery point, the warehouse must be near the metal consumers who use the metals to produce downstream products. North America and Northern Europe used to be the world's major manufacturing centres in the base metals industry chains. Nowadays, more and more manufacturing industries have moved to Asia. Taking the warehouse system of LME as an example, it has approved an increasing number of warehouse locations in Asia over the years, such as Kaohsiung, Incheon, and Yokohama. As for China, after decades of rapid economic growth, it has emerged as the second largest economy in the world[4], and has effectively become a "world factory". Given China's economic power, the approved warehouses of LME in Asia are more capable than those in other regions in providing convenient services for metal consumers in Asia, particularly those in China. A warehouse network that covers the whole world can ensure that the need for physical delivery is sufficiently met. In other words, through a globally recognised warehouse network for physical delivery of metals could fulfil the needs of industrial enterprises and the real economy at large.

1.2   Warehouse receipt financing

Spot trading of base metals often requires huge financing support in the entire production and logistics process because of the lag in capital recycling. Given such a large demand for financing support, base metals manufacturers and traders often get operationally constrained during an economic downturn when such financing support is insufficient. This kind of financing support efficiency is also lowered in case of irrational warehouse receipt financing practices whereby the credibility of the warehouse receipts cannot be guaranteed. Since base metals by nature are of high value, easy to transport and store, readily liquid and subject to a clearly defined quality grading system, they are actually very good financing tools. Therefore, warehouse receipt financing has become a crucial integral part of the spot market in base metals. As observed from the situation of corporate users, some industrial enterprises are struggling with the problems of capital liquidity, high costs and limited means of financing, manifested in the following areas:

- **Transaction** — The multi-layer traditional sales chain that consists of producers, large-scale traders and multi-level agents, etc., pushes up the cost of information and the increase in price at various levels results in higher transaction costs;
- **Production** — The process from the purchase of raw materials to the investment

---

4   China overtook Japan in 2010 to become the world's second largest economy. Japan ranked third, with its nominal gross domestic product being US$5,474.2 billion, which was US$404.4 million less than that of China. Source: *People.cn* (http://politics.people.com.cn/GB/1026/13594169.html).

in fixed assets to final production creates huge cash flow pressure during the period between input and output;

- **Trade** — The trading model based on credit sales leads to huge prepayments as well as difficulties and time lags in recovery of accounts receivables, which in turn brings the problem of insufficient working capital.

Due to the various distinctive structural features of the global commodities market, such as large initial capital investments, long global shipping routes and protracted production cycles, it has become common for market participants to secure commodity financing to support their trading and operational management, and such financing has achieved a considerable scale. Commodity financing is also widely used in the base metals industry, with many tailor-made financing arrangements, including mining, trade, and inventory financing. These have been adopted by participants for decades, or even centuries[5]. A common feature of these financing businesses is that they are taking advantage of the future economic value of the companies' assets, whether they already exist in the form of refined materials or are still under development or pending mining from underground. The benefits of commodity financing from the respective perspectives of lenders and borrowers are discussed below.

For lenders, in general, they could ask the borrowers to hedge the metals which they use as collateral for their loans, thereby helping reduce the lenders' exposure to various risks (as described below) and achieve a better risk-adjusted return on their capital.

Firstly, hedging reduces the risk of the loan itself, because the value of the collateral is protected during the loan period. In the event of default of contract and subsequent foreclosure, the value of the asset will not be affected by the prevailing market price because the lender can sell the asset at the prevailing market price and make up any shortfall through the hedging. This is the main reason why lenders reward borrowers who hedge with a smaller haircut on the collateral.

Secondly, hedging can reduce the counterparty risk in this kind of financing transactions, because borrowers who have made hedging arrangements often bear less price risk. This will allow lenders to increase their risk exposure in relation to certain companies based on their own preferences.

From the borrowers' perspective, hedging will also bring many benefits to them in financing transactions.

Firstly, a smaller haircut on the collateral, given other conditions are the same, implies a larger sum of loan to be lent to the borrower and thus saves it from more expensive forms

---

5   Source: "Commodity financing: how hedging on-exchange can benefit both borrowers and lenders", *LME Insight* on LME's website, August 2018.

of financing (such as unsecured debt or equity financing), thereby enhancing the operational efficiency of the borrower's working capital. For example, the borrower can then use the extra capital to offer more competitive payment terms to its customers and suppliers or to reinvest the same amount of capital in the enterprise or development projects.

Secondly, hedging usually reduces price risk exposure and so the impact of metal price fluctuations on profits. By making hedging arrangements, corporate borrowers will be able to focus more on their core businesses rather than devoting considerable efforts on predicting future price movements of their assets.

There are two major ways to hedge risks using collaterals in financing transactions: via the on-exchange market or the OTC market. Exchanges provide counterparties with a centralised trading venue with two-way liquidity and transparent prices. The OTC market, on the other hand, is characterised by bilateral transactions which are usually limited to two counterparties. Table 1 sets out some key issues that need to be considered when engaging in hedging in financing transactions conducted on-exchange or in the OTC market.

Table 1. Commodity financing on-exchange vs OTC			
Consideration	Impact	On-exchange commodity financing	OTC commodity financing
Managing margin requirements in hedging	The company has to consider the additional working capital required for managing initial margin and variation margin	Initial and variation margins can be financed by the lender itself or by a third-party professional institution via a tripartite agreement for margin funding	OTC transactions often do not require margins, but are exposed to higher counterparty risk, which can result in much wider spreads in order to include credit value adjustment charges
The hedge needed to match the financing (including any amortisation)	Excessive or inadequate hedging would create risks for both counterparties	Adequate liquidity offered by on-exchange markets allow for adjustments of the hedge to match any changes in the financing schedule	OTC transactions are bespoke according to specific requirements of both parties. Any subsequent adjustments would require the agreement of both parties
In case of a default, the hedge and the loan should be exited simultaneously	Uncoordinated unwinding of the two could create unbalanced and unhedged positions	On-exchange positions can be closed out in the market with new counterparties	As the OTC transaction is bilateral, appropriate clauses must be agreed upon at the beginning of the deal with regard to the unwinding process of the hedge in case of default

Source: HKEX analysis.

The above discussion and comparison reveal that proper risk management arrangements (such as hedging) in commodity financing can facilitate more effective capital allocation, benefiting all parties to the transaction. The borrower will have access to broader financial resources at a lower cost, thereby improving its capital structure. The lender can increase its risk exposure in certain companies and industries while circumventing specific risks (such as metal price risks). Another key point that should be re-emphasised is that the effective operation of trade finance also requires an extensive warehouse network.

1.3 Clearing and settlement

Spot trading venues for base metal commodities usually integrate all functions including trading, clearing and settlement, and depository. These trading venues often lack effective management of funds or capital involved in the clearing and settlement processes. Due to the long transaction chain and the absence of professional risk management mechanisms, the entire transaction chain is exposed to risks associated with transaction defaults, price fluctuations, ownership of rights to goods, and financing credit. Among the said risks, default risk is often triggered as a result of market price movements after a contact is agreed. Bilateral commodity trades lack a unified payment settlement system. The market also faces the problems concerning the safety of funds in spot market trading as well as the fragile credit system. These problems usually weigh on the execution efficiency and effectiveness of the post-trade phases of such contracts.

The outbreak of the global financial crisis in 2008 reflected to a certain extent the serious lack of flexibility of market participants in withstanding financial and economic turmoil as well as the deficiency in market transparency. Specifically, the lack of transparency and the increasingly complex products spectrum in certain derivatives markets which have impacted various segments of the financial market were considered to be the major factors causing the global financial crisis and triggering systemic risks. Such lack of market transparency and large-scale market disorder were, according to major international regulatory bodies which studied the causes of the crisis, attributable to, inter alia, the absence of supervision of certain OTC derivatives trading as well as their distinctive nature as bilateral transactions. Against this backdrop, global financial markets at all levels have begun shifting to adopt central clearing and settlement in place of bilateral clearing system in certain sectors. The commodity financial derivatives market for base metals is hardly an exception.

The purpose of clearing is to let both parties to a contract know clearly their respective delivery responsibilities upon settlement. Under a central clearing and settlement system, the clearing house acts as the Central Counterparty (CCP) which serves as the seller to every buyer, and the buyer to every seller, with the aim of protecting the parties to a transaction from the other party's default. Once the transaction enters the central clearing and settlement system, a contract will be established between the CCP and each clearing member (the buyer and the seller), i.e. both members now have a contract for clearing and settlement with the CCP directly.

Both parties in the transaction are required to provide guarantees to cover the risks associated with settlement. In case of a clearing member's default, the contract will still be executed via the CCP without making non-default clearing members bear any losses. In some cases, the collateral together with the client's position may be transferred to another clearing member in a process known as "porting". In this way, as a systemic risk manager, the CCP can significantly reduce the counterparty credit risk faced by clearing members, thereby minimising the cascading effects of a financial crisis (such as the 2008 global financial crisis) and preventing a single default from jeopardising the entire market.

What makes central clearing and settlement so systemically important? For market participants, the straight-through-processing of transactions and real-time risk management are two of its attractive features. On top of that, central clearing and settlement can effectively reduce the operational costs of participants by streamlining trade management and contract execution (see Figure 4). Moreover, the CCP can untangle and simplify the complex trading network that may exist in the OTC market. Multilateral netting simplifies the relationship between counterparties, which reduces any contagious risk that might deal a blow to the entire financial market and heightens the overall operational efficiency of the market.

Figure 4. Advantages of central clearing and settlement in the base metals market

Source: HKEX analysis.

In view of the advantages of the central clearing and settlement process in respect of the significant reduction of credit risk and effective risk controls that CCPs have in place in the event of default, market regulators consider such a process in place of bilateral clearing and settlement a way to prevent financial crisis like the one which happened in 2008 from recurring. By assuming the role of an intermediary between buyers and sellers, CCPs are very important to the financial market in that they can streamline complex transaction relationships, achieve netting and compression of transactions and provide effective risk management in the event of default. Apart from this, the presence of CCPs is also crucial in boosting market confidence and enabling the fair and orderly operation of the market during times of extreme volatility and in the event of counterparty default.

2 Market infrastructure construction is key to supporting the future development of the Mainland base metals market

2.1 Taking a market-oriented approach to explore the best solution for the long-term development of the market

The soundness and effectiveness of the infrastructure and trade-support mechanisms of a commodities market are best judged by whether they are conducive to effective and efficient resource allocation, thereby helping the market and the industry to lower transaction costs. This is also one of the most fundamental purposes for which any trading platforms (including futures exchanges) exist, and their position and interests shall all be in accordance with such purpose. As for market participants, they will naturally go for whichever pricing centre that is more regularised, more transparent, with abundant participants, more internationalised and more capable of manifesting the price formation and guidance mechanism fairly and effectively.

From the perspective of consumers and producers of base metals in the Mainland, given the distinct pricing systems of the Mainland and the international markets, they may suffer certain economic losses and face operational uncertainty if the prices cannot be hedged effectively and smoothly. Market development and improvement do take time, and ultimately the market itself will decide what best meets the needs of the industry. All these are worth our continuous attention.

Looking ahead, the establishment of a sound ecosystem will be conducive to the healthy and complete development of the market in the long run. In particular, this ecosystem shall embody at least the following four functions or characteristics (see Figure 5):

(1)   Serving the real economy and the physical market

This should be the core mission of a sound ecosystem, and such ecosystem shall provide price discovery, risk management and terminal market services.

(2)   Ensuring fairness in market operation

Market fairness is the core feature of a sound ecosystem, which means that the market operates in a fair and non-discriminatory manner to all market participants. The principle of fairness shall extend beyond pure regulatory obligations and supervision, and shall be implanted more deeply in the design and implementation of the market mechanisms. This includes but is not limited to:

- allowing the broadest possible range of participants to fairly access the market for investment and risk management;
- the on-exchange market shall leverage to the fullest extent its advantages of the standardisation of product offerings and the transaction process, to deliver a trading environment that is fairer than the OTC market.

(3)   Providing more user choices

With regard to the market structure, it is a natural feature of the exchange market that all market participants must comply with the same set of trading rules. That said, it is also possible to improve the various aspects of the market structure to offer certain segments of market participants with more flexible operational options provided that it does not affect other market participants. A sound ecosystem shall also continue to innovate in product offerings and strategies to accommodate investors' needs for diversified investment and risk management.

(4)   Maximising the efficiency in trading and in the use of capital

Enhancement of the efficiency in trading and in the use of capital is in the common interest of market participants, exchanges and the entire market. If a market participant chooses not to execute an otherwise economically-rational hedging or investment trade due to the friction cost of that trade, the market will be considered deficient in trading efficiency and capital use efficiency.

Figure 5. Exploring the best solution for the long-term development of the market —
Establishing a sound ecosystem

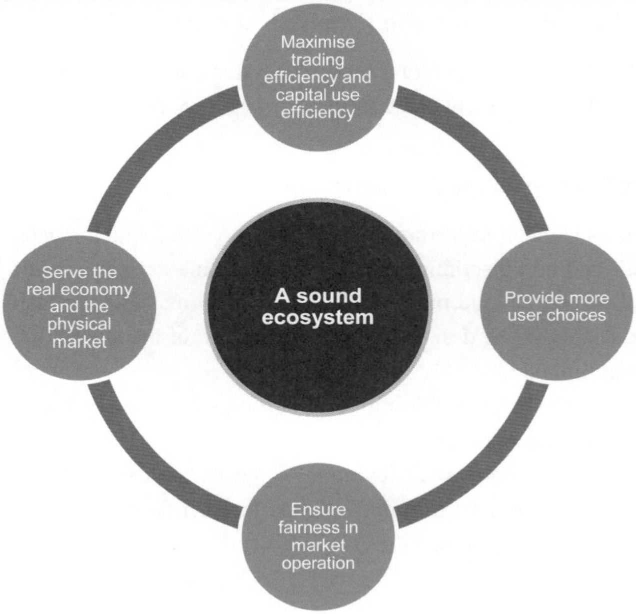

Source: HKEX analysis.

2.2 Strategic roles of HKEX and the LME in facilitating Mainland market participants' participation in the international base metals market

China is the world's second largest economy as well as the largest commodities importer and a major commodities consumer[6]. As a global financial centre and a gateway to

---

6   Source: "The history of the formation of commodity pricing centres and recommendations" (〈從歷史看大宗商品定價中心的形成及建議〉), *China Futures*, Vol.5 of 65 (2018).

the Mainland, Hong Kong has always been serving as a super-connector between Mainland China and the rest of the world. It is well positioned to serve commodities market participants and provide efficient and effective risk management services for Chinese enterprises, regional commodities trading companies and their global business partners.

As regards the base metals market, the settlement prices discovered on the markets of the LME, a wholly-owned subsidiary of Hong Kong Exchanges and Clearing Limited ("HKEX"), are universally recognised as the global standards for base metals pricing in the physical market, either for the metals' production or the raw materials. LME Clear is a central clearing house set up specifically for metal forwards, futures and options traded on LME. By adopting the latest technology for risk management, such as real-time clearing (which enables real-time supervision and management of risk exposure), LME Clear helps maintain a more stable and robust market. In terms of eligible collaterals, the LME allows clearing members to use a variety of cash and non-cash collateral, including LME warrants, to cover their liabilities. The acceptance of LME warrants as collateral can help companies release other types of collateral and improve their capital efficiency[7].

The LME's successful experience in supporting and serving the real economy in the use of base metals over the past 140 years shows that a global warehouse network and sound settlement mechanisms with daily physical delivery are of paramount importance for commodity pricing. As of March 2020, the LME has licensed a network of more than 550 approved warehouses in 33 locations across the globe (see Figure 6), covering the vast majority of metals consumption, supply and logistics centres. With this warehouse network, market participants could sell the excess supply in return for cash through trading on LME and withdraw inventory from LME-approved warehouses when demand exceeds supply. Therefore, the LME's inventory data serves as a "barometer" of changes in the fundamentals of global base metals.

Chinese companies' participation in the trading activities on the LME can be traced back to the 1990s[8].

The LME's warehouse system has the following characteristics:
- Firstly, the LME does not own warehouses or the metals stored in them, and the specific business activities are handled by different warehousing companies. The LME is responsible for the initial review and approval of the locations of the warehouses, the warehousing companies and the specific warehouses. After the approval is granted, the daily management and operation of the warehouses,

---

7   See Chapter 6 of this book, "The London Metal Exchange — The world's industrial metals trading and pricing venue", for details of the LME market and its operation.
8   Source: LME.

including their profit and loss management, will be fully undertaken by the respective warehousing companies. The LME then manages an ongoing audit programme for LME-approved warehouses to ensure that they continue to meet the LME's prescribed standards. In addition, warehouse companies are obligated to have an annual 100% stock count undertaken by an approved Independent Third Party Auditor.

- Secondly, the LME has imposed strict requirements on the warehousing companies in terms of their capital adequacy, management capabilities and industrial experience. In other words, only warehousing companies that have ample capital and a high standard are able to meet the LME's stringent prerequisites to become approved warehouse operators. The existing LME warehousing companies are mostly professional institutions with rich experience and good reputation, having been engaged in metal storage for many years[9].

- Thirdly, only warehousing companies approved by the LME can apply for the establishment of approved warehouses at the delivery points. Such warehouses are also the subject to the LME's requirements with respect to their logistics facilities, management capabilities, deposit and withdrawal, as well as storage capacities.

- Fourthly, the LME has established a Warehousing Committee. This committee, which is made up of representatives from approved warehouses, strengthens the relationship between the LME and the warehousing companies, meeting their respective requests and achieving a win-win situation, which has contributed to the LME's position as a global base metals commodities trading centre.

The evolution of the LME's global warehousing system could provide a strong demonstration effect for the development of the Mainland commodities market. The improvement in the warehousing system could narrow the "gap" between the spot and futures markets. It could also support the growth of the real economy, thereby facilitating the formation of a sound RMB pricing mechanism for commodities.

---

9   Source: "A detailed guide to the London Metal Exchange", published on the LME's website, 2018.

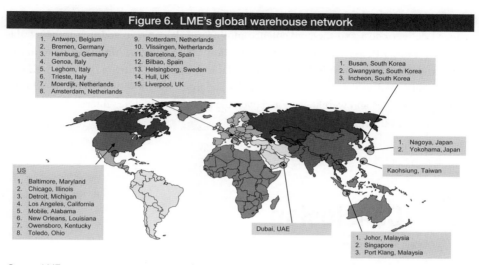

Figure 6. LME's global warehouse network

1. Antwerp, Belgium
2. Bremen, Germany
3. Hamburg, Germany
4. Genoa, Italy
5. Leghorn, Italy
6. Trieste, Italy
7. Moerdijk, Netherlands
8. Amsterdam, Netherlands
9. Rotterdam, Netherlands
10. Vlissingen, Netherlands
11. Barcelona, Spain
12. Bilbao, Spain
13. Helsingborg, Sweden
14. Hull, UK
15. Liverpool, UK

1. Busan, South Korea
2. Gwangyang, South Korea
3. Incheon, South Korea

US
1. Baltimore, Maryland
2. Chicago, Illinois
3. Detroit, Michigan
4. Los Angeles, California
5. Mobile, Alabama
6. New Orleans, Louisiana
7. Owensboro, Kentucky
8. Toledo, Ohio

1. Nagoya, Japan
2. Yokohama, Japan

Kaohsiung, Taiwan

Dubai, UAE

1. Johor, Malaysia
2. Singapore
3. Port Klang, Malaysia

Source: LME.

Against the new backdrop of Mainland China's reform and opening-up, the internationalisation of the Mainland's commodities futures markets has become a very important and imminent strategic mission. Yet, the opening-up of the Mainland market in the existing mode that focuses mainly on "inward opening" is in fact a lengthy process, which to some extent might make it difficult for Mainland market participants to exert substantial influence in international pricing in the near future. In order for the Mainland commodities futures market to take a more active role with remarkable achievements during the new round of opening-up, a two-way multiple-route approach of opening-up shall be adopted, that is to combine "inward opening" with "outward opening" and to open the gateway for investors, warehouses and prices to connect with the international market, thereby enhancing Chinese enterprises' competitive edges in the international marketplaces.

One of the feasible ways that can be considered to support achieving the said goal is to allow the LME to approve warehouses in the Mainland, so as to promote the mutual connectivity and strengthening the price interaction between the Mainland and overseas base metals markets. Through this process, the Mainland commodities futures market will be able to perform its function of serving the real economy in a more effective way, thereby accelerating the rise in China's influence over global pricing in this industry. If internationally recognised warehouses can be introduced into the Mainland, the Mainland can accumulate experience and set the global stage for warehouses run by its exchanges in the future. If LME-approved warehouses are allowed in the Mainland, Chinese enterprises will be able to participate in international pricing on equal footing while enjoying a reduced delivery cost and the convenience in physical delivery, in addition to being able to utilise and participate in the international delivery network. Mainland warehouses could also benefit from this by gaining understanding and knowledge in warehouse management models that meet international standards. All these will pave the way for Chinese enterprises and warehouses, and even the entire commodities futures market in the Mainland, to go international in the future.

3 Conclusion

The commodities market for base metals is not only a venue for trading base metals. A well-developed warehouse logistics system and a warehouse receipt financing mechanism, together with an effective central clearing and settlement system, are crucial market infrastructure guaranteeing the sound and orderly operation of the market and important cornerstones for serving industry customers and the real economy at large. Mature and sound infrastructure and trade-support mechanisms underpinning the commodities market should be conducive to the efficient and effective allocation of resources, thereby helping the market and the industry to reduce transaction costs. These considerations are particularly important for the base metals market in the Mainland which is undergoing the process of development and internationalisation.

Looking ahead, the balanced development of the base metals industry in Mainland China and enhancement in its efficiency in utilising resources and the environment require Mainland customers to make better use of the international futures market for risk management, and entail a more proactive role played by the Mainland futures exchanges in supporting the real economy while steering structural reform to the supply side. The LME's influence in the international base metals market stems from its development strategy of serving the real economy. Its successful experience could provide an important reference for the Mainland commodities futures market.

Chapter 14

The connectivity platform offered by the HKEX commodities market for the Mainland and the world

Commodities Development
Hong Kong Exchanges and Clearing Limited

Summary

This chapter describes how the Hong Kong Exchanges and Clearing Limited (HKEX) aims to position itself as a major commodities market trading platform in the world. In its endeavour to do so, it has acquired the London Metal Exchange (LME), established the Qianhai Mercantile Exchange (QME) and is currently focusing on developing new products as well as its infrastructure connectivity.

In recent years, HKEX successfully launched gold futures, base metals futures and ferrous metal futures. It also aims to replicate the Stock Connect model for commodities trading and clearing, connecting the prices formed in the Mainland and international commodities markets by linking LME and QME. Reciprocal Membership Arrangement has been introduced in order to encourage LME members to join the Hong Kong Futures Exchange (HKFE, the derivatives exchange subsidiary of HKEX) in support of the launch of commodity products on the HKEX derivatives market. The launch of LME Metal Mini Futures in 2019 symbolised the first step of "Hong Kong – London Connect". In addition, various Memoranda of Understanding have been signed, in particular with Mainland organisations, in order to seamlessly connect the Mainland commodities market with the international commodities market.

1 The unique positioning of the HKEX commodities market

1.1 How HKEX position itself as a platform for the Mainland and the world

HKEX's commodity strategy is set to focus on two aspects: buy and build. Externally, in 2012, HKEX successfully acquired the 140-year-old London Metal Exchange (LME), which was its first step in the acquisition of international financial infrastructure. Internally, HKEX deploys a China-centric strategy, cooperates closely with Mainland regulatory authorities and institutions, and leverages Hong Kong's unique position. These efforts are focussed on building a new commodity spot market in the Mainland, serving industry entities as well as complying with laws and regulations, and serves to open up channels for linking finance with the physical economy. Qianhai Mercantile Exchange (QME) was then established as a leap towards HKEX's commodities vision.

Hong Kong is one of the most densely populated cities in the world which lacks a development environment and traditional background conducive for trading commodities. A unique approach is required to develop the commodities market that addresses Hong Kong's current situation, leverages its advantages and fulfils domestic demand. As a result, HKEX began to explore a "Win-Win" commodities strategy: a "futures" strategy — achieving mutual benefits via mutual connection with the Mainland exchanges; and a "spot" strategy — by buying existing platforms with desired expertise and building in-house physical delivery facilities.

The ultimate goal of the buy-and-build strategy is to effectively connect the externally acquired platform with the internally built platform by utilising Hong Kong's unique position in Asia-Pacific, and to accelerate the internationalisation of the Mainland commodities market by taking advantage of Hong Kong's international financial infrastructure, achieving the eastward shift in the pricing of international commodities. This is also essential to the "Belt and Road" initiative (BRI) of China. The BRI involves more than 60 countries and it is estimated that within a decade, the trade volume between China and the involved countries will reach US$2.5 trillion[1], a remarkable proportion of which would be commodity resources that embody huge development potential. For the

---

1   Source: "China's Xi: Trade between China and Silk Road nations to exceed $2.5 trillion", *Reuters*, 29 March 2015.

Mainland, how to effectively manage the risks caused by commodity price fluctuations will also directly affect the progress of many projects under the BRI. Hong Kong and London are two international financial centres along the Belt and Road. If the "Win-Win" strategy is successfully implemented, HKEX will be able to link the international experience of London and Hong Kong to the needs of China's physical economy.

1.2　What has HKEX done to develop itself into a successful connectivity platform for the commodities market

The most important development of HKEX's commodity business in recent years has been: (1) the acquisition of LME in 2012; and (2) the establishment of QME in 2018. These two major moves correspond to the Mutual Market Access (MMA) programme and the buy-and-build strategy.

1.2.1　LME acquisition

LME is the major pricing centre of global industrial metals, with over 80% of global non-ferrous metals futures contracts traded on its platform[2]. Pricing metals has always been one of the core functions of LME. The main benchmark prices, including the LME Official Price and the LME Closing Price for each commodity product, are "discovered" by trading through the open outcry trading hall, the Ring in London, during fixed time slots on LME trading days. The open outcry in the Ring has a long history, which can be traced back to 1877 and still has a very high circulation volume today.

HKEX successfully acquired LME in 2012 after prudent evaluation and extensive consultation. There are two main reasons for acquiring LME. Firstly, LME is in the European and US market trading time zone and is an offshore US dollar (USD) financial centre as well as a leading currency market. Secondly, HKEX is a leading offshore Renminbi (RMB) trading hub and a derivatives exchange located in the Asian market trading time zone.

This acquisition is an important step in building HKEX's commodities platform. Although it cannot solve all challenges in developing its own commodity trading and settlement platform, it is the first attempt which announces to the world that Hong Kong can become a world-class commodity centre and provide a means towards internationalisation for Mainland China's commodity market participants. Although LME is located in London and has a big time difference with Asia, through the 18-hour LME electronic trading

---

2　Source: LME.

system, the morning trading session of LME overlaps with the afternoon trading session of Asia, and the Asia-focused trading activities at LME are increasing year by year. The higher the trading volume originated from Asia, the greater the need for the price to be discovered in the Asian trading zone to reflect Asia's supply and demand.

The first phase after the acquisition of LME focused on improving LME's existing Asian business. In this phase, there was not much financial investment or infrastructure restructuring, but most efforts were devoted to make LME's trading platform simpler, easier to access, and better to meet the demand of Asian clients. Consequently in 2013, Kaohsiung port in Taiwan, became the 9th LME-recognised delivery location in Asia, with the others in Singapore, Malaysia, South Korea and Japan. In 2014, HKEX launched a reciprocal membership arrangement (RMA) in conjunction with LME for the first time. Under this arrangement, a number of LME members also became qualified for membership of the Hong Kong Futures Exchange (HKFE), the derivative arm of HKEX, making bilateral transactions easier. This plan continues to go forward and the details of RMA are discussed in sections below.

The second phase of the strategy is to build the infrastructure of HKEX's new chapter. This phase takes longer and costs more, yet the returns are not only financial, but also strategic. One major investment is the establishment of LME Clear. Prior to this, LME had to settle through an external clearing house. As a result, LME could not take full control of its own development pace, especially the speed and flexibility of new product launches. After the establishment of LME Clear, LME has thereby gained autonomy in settlement, thus can accelerate the launch of new products to the market and generate its own revenue therefrom. In addition, LME's information technology development has been shifted from the then outsourcing mode to in-house development. While improving efficiency, this shift has also turned the information technology of LME into a strategic asset.

The third phase is to capture more clients. The strategy of this phase includes accomplishing cross listings and licensing arrangements of cross-regional products, and establishing strategic partnerships with key players as well as institutions from other commodity markets. In particular, principal institutions in the Mainland commodity market will be among our main partners given the scale of the Mainland market and its need to go international. Driven by these partnerships, our development began with base metals and further expanded into other commodities. Since the acquisition of LME, HKEX has successively listed LME metal mini contracts denominated in offshore RMB (CNH), dual-currency-denominated gold contracts (in USD and CNH) and iron ore contracts listed concurrently with LME, and the most recent USD-denominated LME metal mini contracts listed in 2019.

1.2.2 QME establishment

Shenzhen and Hong Kong are adjacent to each other, and each bear special missions and unique advantages in China's reform and opening-up process. The central Chinese government set up the Qianhai Shenzhen-Hong Kong Modern Service Industry Cooperation Zone in Shenzhen, providing a platform that closely integrates Shenzhen and Hong Kong. Qianhai was also the first stop of the Chinese President, Xi Jinping, in his visit to Guangdong in 2012 after the 18th National Congress of the Communist Party of China. He specifically gave policy-directions that Qianhai should "rely on Hong Kong, serve the Mainland and face the world"[3]. At the time of the National People's Congress and the Chinese People's Political Consultation Conference in 2019, Premier Li Keqiang put forward the need to study and formulate a development plan of the Guangdong-Hong Kong-Macao Greater Bay Area urban agglomeration to further promote and deepen Guangdong-Hong Kong-Macao cooperation.

However, as one of the key geographical regions in the national economic development plan, southern China still lacks a national commodities trading market. After years of preparation, under the support of the Shenzhen Municipal Government, HKEX teamed up with Qianhai Financial Holdings Co., Limited to fully exploit Qianhai's special policy advantages and jointly founded QME.

Since its inception, QME has been actively exploring policy implementation and in-depth cooperation programs with regulatory bodies and industry clients, in the hope of establishing a China-anchored, globally connected commodities spot platform by leveraging HKEX's unique advantages. This is also the first time that a major Hong Kong financial infrastructural entity set up a financial platform in the Mainland.

QME officially made debut on 19 October 2018 with trading in alumina. The first spot transaction saw 3,000 tonnes of alumina changed hands between Chalco Trade and Xiamen Xiangyu at a price of 3,030 yuan a tonne, recording the first benchmark pricing of spot alumina based on actual transactions in the Mainland market.

In the past few years of exploration and evolution, QME has been geared towards spot commodities and the physical economy. In the future, by means of technology, cross-border arrangements and finance, QME will build standardised asset classes that connect entities with finance to resolve the fund-raising difficulties of business enterprises, and leverage the East-West coordination effect derived from LME, now a subsidiary of HKEX, to gradually achieve the strategic goal of building QME into a global commodity RMB

---

3   Source: The website of the Authority of Qianhai Shenzhen-Hongkong Modern Service Industry Cooperation Zone (http://qh.sz.gov.cn).

pricing centre.

While absorbing LME's prior experience in serving the physical economy and industrial clients, QME cannot completely replicate the LME model and must fit China's national conditions. LME's experience of serving the physical economy should be creatively used for QME's reference to serve the Mainland and cultivate a spot market focused on institutional clients, in particular small and medium-sized industrial enterprises (SMEs). Specifically, QME will begin with building reliable warehouses and convenient logistics to establish LME-style delivery warehouse network and industry credibility. To follow up, it will focus on serving the needs of enterprises and provide commodity users, traders, logistics service providers, financial intermediaries, etc. with a series of comprehensive services such as secure and efficient commodity spot trading, financing, warehousing and logistics as well as supply chain management. Thirdly, QME will innovate its service model to minimise the capital and trading costs of enterprises, especially to reduce the cost of hedging for SMEs, and to provide them with more customised services.

(See Chapter 14 in this book for more details about QME.)

2   Prospective platform developments

2.1 Strategic product developments

Apart from the recent launch of futures contracts on gold, base metals and ferrous metals, HKEX will continue to introduce contracts on other assets in order to capture the full spectrum of actively traded underlying assets pertinent to Asian commodities experience.

Apart from commodity futures, other tradable commodity derivatives as well as various forms of delta-1 products[4] are also under consideration or in active development, in order to serve various types of commodity industry participants, including producers and consumers, to efficiently hedge their commodities exposure.

---

4   "Delta" is the measurement of the sensitivity of a financial derivative to movements in the price of the underlying asset class. "Delta-1 product" is a financial derivative with delta equals to 1, which means that it directly tracks the price of its corresponding underlying asset, in terms of its percentage change.

2.1.1 Gold

On 10 July 2017, HKEX launched USD and CNH gold futures contracts with physical settlement ("the Gold Contracts").

The Gold Contracts are the world's first pair of dual-currency futures that are settled with physical delivery in Hong Kong, with global delivery mechanism and kilo-bar standards recognised both by Mainland China as well as global investors. They are designed primarily to serve (1) physical market participants such as gold refiners, fabricators and jewellers who need to hedge gold price risks; (2) financial participants such as banks and funds which utilise the derivatives market to link their gold-related investment products; (3) arbitrageurs who trade on price disparity between onshore and offshore markets and adopt other trading strategies involving foreign exchange and interest rate differentials; and (4) other investors and traders who may have potential appetite to gain exposure in gold.

Attributed to the free market and tradition of being an entrepot trading hub, Hong Kong serves as the main physical gateway of gold channelled to Mainland China.

The Mainland has an extremely active physical gold trading market and enjoys the status as one of the major bullion markets in the world — it has been the world's largest consumer of gold[5] as well as the largest gold importer, with around 1,500 tonnes of metal (equivalent to one-third of world's supply) imported in 2018[6]. Although Hong Kong's share of China's gold imports has recently dropped to around 40% by September 2019 (primarily because of political unrest in Hong Kong), it was consistently at an average of 60% during 2012 to 2016 [7]. The primary demand for physical gold comes from Hong Kong's adjacent city, Shenzhen, which accounts for almost 70% of the total Chinese jewellery sales[8]. Hong Kong's geographical proximity with Mainland China, and in particular Shenzhen, thereby puts it at an unparalleled advantage to serve the Mainland bullion market.

In addition, as the largest offshore RMB centre, Hong Kong has a unique position in facilitating RMB internationalisation. The launch of the dual-currency Gold Contracts in Hong Kong is a stepping stone to achieve this objective.

The strategic values of introducing the Gold Contracts on HKEX are seen as follows:

- To enhance Hong Kong's status as a key gold trading centre with both active physical market as well as derivatives market by introducing the first dual-currency gold

---

5   Source: "China tops world's gold consumers for 6th year", *XINHUANET* (http://www.xinhuanet.com), 31 January 2019.

6   Source: "China eases restrictions on gold imports: sources", *Reuters*, 22 August 2019.

7   Source: "Hong Kong gold market losing shine amid political unrest", *Reuters*, 13 September 2019.

8   Source: *HKTDC Research* (http://china-trade-research.hktdc.com/business-news/article/China-Consumer-Market/China-s-Jewellery-Market/ccm/en/1/1X000000/1X002MMK.htm]

futures in the world;

- To attract the participation of investors from Hong Kong, the Mainland, the rest of Asia as well as the western time zones, with the aim to build an Asian benchmark price for gold kilo bar in Hong Kong and to enhance the pricing power of commodities in Asia;

- To help HKEX obtain physical delivery capability by introducing the very first physical-delivered commodity futures in the history of Hong Kong

As the first key step to prepare for introducing more precious metal derivative products, six gold futures indices, namely Excess Return Index, Total Return Index and Spot Index (the "Gold Indices") in both USD and CNH were launched on 24 June 2019. The Gold Indices offer independent, transparent and timely benchmarks for tracking gold price changes in the Hong Kong market. The indices are based on prices of the USD and CNH Gold Futures contracts with 10 July 2017 as the base date. They are calculated and administered in accordance with the Principles for Financial Benchmarks as published by the International Organisation of Securities Commissions (IOSCO). These indices provide the basis as underlying indices for future development of relevant exchange-traded funds (ETFs) and/or ETF option products.

After considerable market research, HKEX is prepared to launch more new products such as silver futures and various forms of gold derivatives to contribute to an expanded landscape of the precious metal product suite.

2.1.2   Base metals

On 5 August 2019, HKEX launched the USD-denominated London Aluminium, Zinc, Copper, Nickel, Tin and Lead Mini Futures Contracts (collectively called the "USD London Metal Mini Futures"). These contracts were designed to complement the existing set of London Metal Mini Futures on the same commodities that are denominated in CNH (launched in two batches in December 2014 and December 2015).

The global demand for base metal consumption has been growing rapidly. It is primarily led by China's multi-decade long economic expansion. During 1983 to 2018, China enjoyed an unprecedented average annual growth rate of 9.7% in its gross domestic products (GDP)[9] and it is believed that it has become the biggest consumer in the world for a majority of the base metals. This growing demand has structurally driven up the prices of physical metals and related futures contracts in recent years. Trading volumes of base metal contracts on both the Chicago Mercantile Exchange (CME) and LME have also increased

---

9   World Bank Data (https://data.worldbank.org)

steadily[10]. The trading landscape in base metals, which used to be dominated by traditional physical market participants, has also changed dramatically. A larger number of financial investors, professional traders and money managers are now actively engaged in this asset class, as indicated from the Commitments of Traders Reports of the US Commodity Futures Trading Commission (CFTC) published at the CFTC official website.

Base metal futures are actively traded in over-the-counter ("OTC") markets globally and are also listed on a number of exchanges such as LME, CME, the Shanghai Futures Exchange ("SHFE") and the Multi Commodity Exchange of India ("MCX"). After HKEX's acquisition of LME in 2012, these base metal products on HKEX were primarily launched in order to leverage on the branding and membership network of LME, as well as on LME's reference pricing in base metals which is widely adopted by physical markets worldwide. The USD London Metal Mini Futures aim to provide trading opportunities for investors that have exposure in USD denominated base metals in the Asian time zone.

The metal mini futures contracts are designed with much smaller lot-size (as compared to LME's standard base metal contracts) and are cash settled. Smaller lot-size is primarily aimed to encourage retail participation in a market which has been traditionally dominated by large physical market participants or institutional traders. In order to encourage the participation from LME members and their clients, HKFE has set up RMA with LME, which allows significant fee waivers for new applicants who already hold a membership or participantship at either one of the exchanges.

2.1.3 Ferrous metals

Ferrous metals are fundamental products in the commodities market and cover a broad range of products. They can be classified into product classes like iron ore, steel, coking coal and scrap, all of them are non-standardised products. Each product class is very diverse in product types. Currently, global derivatives markets only offer a few mainstream products in each product class. Market participants have increasing demand for the non-mainstream products to be launched in the futures market. China is the biggest importer of iron ore and producer of steel[11]. A significant volume of Chinese imports and exports in ferrous metals every year has triggered a strong demand from both physical and financial market participants for hedging, arbitrage or speculation using derivative products.

Launching the Iron Ore Futures (the TSI Iron Ore Fines 62 per cent Fe CFR China

---

10 Reference can be made to the statistics of the Futures Industry Association (FIA).

11 In 2018, China's total import of iron ore was 1,064.4 million tonnes, crude steel production was 928.3 million tonnes (more than half of the world's total crude steel production of 1,808.4 million tonnes). Source: World Steel Association, as of March 2019.

Futures) in 2017 as the first product in the ferrous sector is HKEX's strategy to set a foothold into the ferrous market. With a suitably designed incentive programme and marketing efforts, there has been increasing participation from global professional investors in this market segment to help build up the liquidity pool. Meanwhile, with the effort and cooperation with our partners on marketing and business development in Mainland China and south Asia, we saw an increase in the number of Exchange Participants and physical market traders engaged in the market in 2019. In 2019, HKEX signed several Memoranda of Understanding (MoUs) with Chinese Price Release Agencies (PRAs) including Mysteel to further extend its reach into the commodity market and exploit potential opportunities in other ferrous products. More details will be elaborated in Section 2.2 below.

2.2   Infrastructure connectivity

2.2.1   Platform linkage with LME and QME

In line with HKEX's group strategy, the focal work has been to lay the foundation for our global commodities strategy with the acquisition of LME and the establishment of QME. The next ten years will see our efforts to accelerate the connection between the Chinese and international commodities markets. We will work to replicate the Stock Connect model for commodities trading and clearing, connect the prices of the Chinese and international commodities markets through product cross-listings and developing price benchmarks, and to accelerate the internationalisation of onshore physical deliveries in China. We will also attempt to use technology to help reshape the trading and financing ecosystem of China's commodities market.

2.2.2   RMA (Reciprocal Membership Arrangement)

The RMA was first introduced in November 2014 to encourage LME members to join HKFE in support of the launch of commodity products on HKEX in December 2014, namely the CNH London Aluminium, Copper and Zinc Mini Futures contracts. The RMA had an initial duration of one year and an extension was granted in 2015 for a further year. A few LME membership and HKFE participantship applications under the scheme were received during the two years.

Under the original terms of the RMA, LME and HKFE waived their respective first year's annual subscription and application processing fees for new applicants who already held a membership at either HKFE or LME. The RMA was re-introduced in 2019 on broadly the same basis as previously (see Table 1). The re-introduction of the RMA is considered in alignment with HKEX's strategy for developing its commodities business, including the launch of new products such as the USD-denominated London Metal (Aluminium, Zinc, Copper, Nickel, Tin and Lead) Mini Futures contracts (launched on 5 August 2019) and other commodity products that may have synergies with LME products.

In order to encourage participation from LME members and their clients with the launch of the new USD London Metal Mini Futures, thus broadening access, providing liquidity, and growing international participation, HKFE will waive its membership fees for LME members or affiliates of LME members wishing to join HKFE under RMA. In conjunction with this initiative, LME has also introduced a RMA during the same period as HKFE's RMA and will waive the membership fees for HKFE or affiliates of HKFE Participants wishing to join LME.

It is believed that additional commodities traders from LME who become HKFE Participants will help connect the London and Hong Kong markets. The cross-exchange membership should allow brokers and clients to more easily arbitrage between products and to better manage their risks. LME members who have access to HKFE will also be able to provide reasonable base metal prices by acting as market makers or liquidity providers for the USD-denominated London Metal Mini Futures contracts.

The RMA will cover HKFE and LME Exchange Participant fees only, not HKFE and LME Clearing Participant fees. With respect to HKFE membership applications, the fee waiver will be applied to applications received that are deemed complete by the HKFE (i.e. submitted with all relevant supporting documentation) and accompanied by evidence, where applicable, that an application for HKFE membership and the approval of the Hong Kong Securities and Futures Commission (SFC) for Type 2 licence are in progress. All other current membership criteria and costs remain unchanged.

Table 1. Summary of RMA			
Exchange	Effective period	Membership fee waiver	Eligible applicants
HKFE	29 July 2019 – 29 July 2022 (both dates inclusive)	• Futures Exchange Trading Right fee (one-off): HK$500,000[12]; and • 1st year's Exchange Participantship subscription fee (annual): HK$6,000	Any LME member or affiliate of an LME member
LME		• 1st year's (annual) service subscription fee (inclusive of the application processing fee, as applicable for each service) for LME membership applicants[13] for the following services: (i) LME Categories 1 – 5; (ii) LMEprecious General Clearing Members, Individual Clearing Members and Non-Clearing Members; and (iii) Registered Intermediating Brokers	Any HKFE Participant or affiliate of an HKFE Participant

---

12 For the HKFE one-off trading rights fee, eligible applicants will pay a nominal fee of HK$1 instead of HK$500,000.

13 LME membership information is available on the LME website (http://www.lme.com/en-gb/trading/membership/).

2.2.3   Hong Kong-London Connect

The launch of London Metal Mini Futures symbolised the first step of "Hong Kong-London Connect". The mini futures were derived from LME products, based on LME base metals' contract specifications, and first offered in the Asian time zone. It will supplement and cover both Asian hour and London hour time zone for base metals trading. As a second step, LME is considering implementing a "pass the book" model that allows market participants of each of HKFE and LME to trade and hedge positions in both time zones by means of certain agreed arrangements. The final step would include the development of a true "Connect" scheme where both HKFE and LME's order books are literally "connected".

2.2.4   MoU signed to explore more opportunities

Continuing with the "Connect" scheme under HKEX's three-year strategy to further extend the commodities business strategy, HKEX signed four MoUs with Chinese PRAs and industrial organisations respectively, namely SMM information & Technology Co., Ltd (SMM), Beijing Antaike Information Co Ltd (Antaike), Shanghai Ganglian E-Commerce Holdings Co., Ltd. (Mysteel) and Wuxi Stainless Steel Exchange. Each of them is an information and index service provider in base metals or ferrous metals industry (see Table 2).

Table 2. MoUs signed by HKEX with professional commodity service providers in 2019			
External party in MoU	Date	Location	Business scope
Mysteel	7 May 2019	Hong Kong	Iron ore and other ferrous metals
Antaike	24 May 2019	Beijing	Aluminium and base metals
SMM	30 October 2019	London	Base metals
Wuxi Stainless Steel Exchange	7 May 2019	Hong Kong	Stainless steel and other steel products

The MoU with SMM was signed to establish strategic partnership in commodities business and promote mutual business development in the financial and commodities markets, with the ultimate aim of raising the international influence of Mainland China's commodity prices. In light of the market recognition of the SMM Indices in the Mainland as reflected by market users, suitable corresponding derivative products based on the SMM indices, if launched in Hong Kong, would be able to provide global clients with exposure to Chinese underlying assets.

The MoU signed with Antaike aims at further expanding cooperation in the spot market of non-ferrous metals, and jointly promoting the internationalisation of spot prices of Mainland China's non-ferrous metals.

The MoU signed with the Wuxi Stainless Steel Exchange works towards strengthening communications and cooperation, as well as stimulating mutual business development in financial and commodities markets.

The MoU signed with Mysteel seeks to raise the international influence of Mainland China's commodity prices. HKEX has been continuously working on the potential product design with Chinese underlyings to enrich its commodity product suite, in the hope of effectively helping physical market participants discover the true market price and offering financial participants with the most efficient platform to execute their investment strategies.

By aligning Chinese partners in the industry like the above MoU partners, HKEX is further building up its network and resources in Mainland China.

HKEX is also in active discussions with domestic Chinese exchanges to exploit potential business opportunities and extend the connectivity strategy into the commodities sector.

3   Conclusion

Before the HKEX Group initiated its strategic focus on commodity asset classes, consumers and producers of commodities in Asia would primarily hedge their risk in the physical market through corresponding benchmark contracts in London, New York and Chicago, thereby exposing themselves to significant basis risk and liquidity risk during Asian trading hours. China's decades-long expansion which has eventuated in it becoming the biggest consumer of global commodities has necessitated the Hong Kong bourse to close this gap between the physical and derivatives markets in Asia.

HKEX's dual strategy of "buy and build" (i.e. overseas mergers/acquisition and the establishment of a direct Commodities Connect with the Mainland) is expected to be a significant impetus to accelerate the internationalisation of China's commodities market by taking advantage of Hong Kong's own international financial infrastructure, thereby helping achieve the eastward shift in the pricing of international commodities.

The acquisition of LME in 2012 gave HKEX the direct access to a globally recognised pricing centre of industrial metals. The subsequent rationalisation of LME's trading platform, the set up of a delivery port in Taiwan and the RMA between HKFE and LME has improved access to LME by Asian clients.

The establishment of QME in 2018 is a key step towards establishing a China-anchored, globally-connected commodity physical trading platform.

A series of commodity product developments on the HKEX platform further progress the connectivity strategy for users in China and other Asian regions. The LME metal mini futures contracts denominated in both USD and CNH support Asian traders for hedging and provide Asian investors with trading opportunities. The physically delivered Gold Contracts, also in dual currency, serve Mainland China's gold market, the biggest bullion market in the world, and to facilitate RMB internationalisation. The Iron Ore Futures provide efficient hedge to the underlying physical market in Mainland China, the biggest importer of iron ore and producer of steel.

Furthermore, enhanced cooperation between HKEX and Chinese PRAs and industrial organisations through signing MoUs seek to promote mutual business development in the financial and commodities markets. The ultimate aim is to strengthen the international influence of Mainland China's commodity prices.

All these initiatives (and more to come) are undertaken to build and solidify the HKEX connectivity platform for effective connection between the Mainland and the world's commodity markets.

Afterword

Better serve the real economy by facilitating healthy interaction between the spot and futures trading of commodities

New development trends have emerged in the global commodities market against the backdrop of the changing global trade environment, the increasing turmoil of the financial market and the impact of the coronavirus pandemic.

The first trend is that, due to global quantitative easing measures, geopolitical and trade disputes have triggered stronger risk aversion, resulting in increased volatility in the global commodities market. The market sees soaring demand for risk management using commodity futures contracts, which have now become a new growth driver in the international financial markets. The second trend is that, commodity derivatives have apparently become more diversified with new types of contract launched one after another. Among these are notably contracts on new types of energy and metal closely related to economic activities in Mainland China and the Asia-Pacific region. These have been listed on major exchanges in the world in recent years, providing new financial instruments for further connecting the commodities markets in the East and the West while satisfying the real economy's needs for global risk management. The third trend is that, with the rise of emerging market countries, China is seen to have more and more influence on international commodity prices. Given that China is the largest consumer of major commodities including iron ore, copper, nickel, coal and cotton, its rapid economic growth plays a crucial role in shaping the international price trends of these commodities. The fourth trend is that, thanks to the Mainland's incessant efforts in promoting innovative measures for opening up the Mainland market, a series of domestic designated products including crude oil futures, pure terephthalic acid (PTA) futures, iron ore futures and TSR20 rubber futures have been opened to foreign participation. Mainland China is exercising greater control over commodity prices and gradually changing from a passive taker of international prices to an exporter of Chinese prices to the global markets. Given the dramatic changes in the global financial system, commodities market participants would have to conduct a comprehensive review of the commodities systems inside and outside Mainland China to understand not only the spot market, but also the forward markets and the related derivatives market. Apart from in-depth study of the financial innovations in the global commodities markets, they will also need to rethink about the dominant role that the Mainland market is going to play in the future global commodities system.

This is exactly the original intent of our preparation and compilation of this book entitled *Global Commodities Market: From Spot to Futures.* This book provides an in-depth analysis of the various aspects of commodities inside and outside Mainland China from three dimensions, namely "the global landscape of the commodities market", "the Mainland and Hong Kong commodities markets" and "commodities spot and futures market connectivity". Among the publications on similar topics, this book is believed to be the first monograph to systematically introduce the commodities markets inside and outside Mainland China, covering markets in Hong Kong, London and the Mainland. In this respect, the London Metal Exchange (LME) and Qianhai Mercantile Exchange (QME) have kindly consented to provide us with an introduction to their markets and developments. We have also invited international professionals with extensive business experience in the commodities market to contribute the various chapters, so as to provide the market with first-hand experience and industry insights regarding the development of the international commodities market.

The book covers different commodity forms from spot to futures and from metals, energy to agricultural products, depicting to market participants both in the Mainland and abroad the big picture of the macro system and financial ecosystem of the entire commodities market. In addition, there are chapters dedicated to exploring the various financial innovative models of "connectivity" between the Mainland and foreign commodities markets, including the possibility for Mainland China to open up its market through cooperation with Hong Kong and London, the opportunity for London and Hong Kong's commodities business to enter the Mainland market, and the business cooperation between London and Hong Kong. This provides market participants with an innovative perspective to understand the connectivity models between the Mainland and the international commodities markets. Last but not least, the book describes Hong Kong's strategic perspective and unique position in the commodities market. Hong Kong Exchanges and Clearing Limited (HKEX) set foot in the international commodities market through its acquisition of the LME, and established QME in Qianhai, Shenzhen in the Mainland, bringing the LME's international standards and development experience into the Mainland commodities spot market. Leveraging the unique advantages of its connectivity with the Mainland, it seeks to open up new paths for the development of the Mainland commodities market, in the hope that Hong Kong's exploration and innovation in this area could give impetus to the internationalisation of the Mainland commodities market.

Part 1 of the book, "The global landscape of the commodities market", gives the reader a panoramic view of the global commodities spot and derivatives markets from an international perspective. Written by Charles Li, the Chief Executive of HKEX, the first chapter systematically lays out the overall concept and philosophy behind HKEX's acquisition of the LME and its establishment of QME in the Mainland, and also shares his thoughts on the ways to support the internationalisation of the Mainland commodities market.

Commodities cover various product categories including metals, agricultural and energy products traded in the spot and futures markets. They are fundamental to a nation's resources development. However, Mainland market participants and policy makers remain relatively unfamiliar with the operation and structure of the international commodities markets. In light of this, SMM Information & Technology Co. Ltd., COFCO Futures Co., Ltd., Citigroup Global Markets Asia Limited and the LME were invited to each contribute an article in Part 1 to give specific accounts of the current status and practical operations of the international markets, including metals and agricultural products markets. These chapters, together with the Chapter on the global commodity derivatives market written by the Chief China Economist's Office of HKEX, give readers a more comprehensive understanding of the latest developments and practical operations of the international commodities spot and derivatives markets.

As the world's second largest economy, Mainland China has become one of the world's largest producer and consumer of commodities. To raise the Mainland's pricing power in commodities, active foreign participation in the Mainland market is a crucial factor. For attracting greater foreign participation, enabling foreign participants to have a better understanding of the Mainland commodities market is the key. To this end, the first two chapters of Part 2 of the book, "The Mainland and Hong Kong commodities markets", describe the overall evolution of the Mainland commodities market, the types of product, the opening up of the market to the world and the relationship between the spot and futures markets. It is believed that through the continuous opening-up of the Mainland commodity futures market, market liquidity will further increase to attract more foreign institutional participation in the market, thereby helping to set up commodity price benchmarks for economic activities in the Asian time zone. Another chapter in Part 2 introduces the Hong Kong commodities market, in particular the specific products and operations of its futures market as well as the development direction that it may take to strengthen Hong Kong's role as an international financial centre.

Part 3 of this book, "Commodities spot and futures market connectivity", focuses on the connectivity between the commodities spot and futures markets as well as the innovative ways to link up the Mainland and global commodities markets. The first chapter in this part outlines the interaction between the global commodities spot and futures markets and explains the importance of the commodity futures market for economic activities, especially in spot pricing. The LME, QME and the Commodities Development Department of HKEX were invited to describe the unique roles they play in the development of the Mainland commodities market, laying out their visions of leveraging the LME platform and the platforms in Hong Kong and the Mainland (QME) to extend LME trading to the Asian time zone, so as to strengthen price discovery capabilities in commodity spot trading in the Asian time zone. Furthermore, a chapter written by the Chief China Economist's Office of HKEX discusses the importance of connectivity of market infrastructure, such as warehouse networks, in linking up commodity futures and spot markets, in helping resolve the existing problem of "weak spot market and strong forward market" in the Mainland which hinders industrial growth, and in laying down a solid foundation for the futures market to facilitate the formation of genuine and effective price benchmarks for China's spot market. In the internationlisation of the Mainland commodities market, Hong Kong which serves as a gateway to connect China with the international financial market, can certainly function as a "super-connector" in reinforcing the interaction between the Mainland and global commodity futures markets.

I would like to extend my gratitude to Mr. Charles Li, Chief Executive of HKEX, for his valuable support to this book and for writing up the first chapter to share his deep insights into the internationlisation of the Mainland commodities market and actionable strategies. My thanks also go to HKEX colleagues in Commodities Development, Regulatory Compliance, Legal Services, Corporate Communications, Translation and other business teams for their generous assistance, without which this book would not have been published. We are also indebted to the various exchanges and professional market institutions for their contributions to the content of the book. Last but not least, thanks to the efficiency and professionalism of our publisher, the Commercial Press (H.K.) Ltd., we have been able to release the book onto the market at the right time. To all these parties, we sincerely express our gratitude.

To advance the internationalisation of the Mainland commodities market, a number of alternative ways, each with their unique features, may be considered. One way is to attract the active participation of related business enterprises and investors from the world, thereby facilitating the widespread recognition and use of Chinese commodities prices by the international markets. Another way could be the improvement of the Mainland's spot trading capabilities through LME, QME and the establishment of approved warehouses for the sake of better serving Mainland China's real economy. Possible connectivity in the commodities market may also be considered to provide for cross-border trading network in commodity futures and spot markets. The internationalisation of the Mainland commodities market can be expedited through these multiple measures. These various modes for opening up the market, each has its own advantages, are suitable for different types of participant. In this gradual market opening-up process, we hope the publication of this book would provide the market with useful and professional perspectives and ideas in this regard.

Based on the intrinsic logics in the development of the global commodities market, this book attempts to practically link up the commodity spot and futures markets. It may have imperfections and any feedback you may have are most welcome.

Professor BA Shusong
Chief China Economist, Hong Kong Exchanges and Clearing Limited
Chief Economist, China Banking Association
May 2020